Thomas Aquinas's
Summa Contra Gentiles

D1454017

Thomas Aquinas's *Summa Contra Gentiles*

A Guide and Commentary

BRIAN DAVIES

OXFORD
UNIVERSITY PRESS

OXFORD
UNIVERSITY PRESS

Oxford University Press is a department of the University of Oxford.
It furthers the University's objective of excellence in research, scholarship,
and education by publishing worldwide. Oxford is a registered trade mark of
Oxford University Press in the UK and in certain other countries.

Published in the United States of America by Oxford University Press
198 Madison Avenue, New York, NY 10016, United States of America

© Oxford University Press 2016

Library of Congress Cataloging-in-Publication Data
Names: Davies, Brian, 1952–
Title: Thomas Aquinas's Summa contra gentiles:
a guide and commentary / Brian Davies.
Description: New York, NY : Oxford University Press, 2016. |
Includes bibliographical references and index.
Identifiers: LCCN 2015044427|
ISBN 978-0-19-045654-2 (pbk. : alk. paper) |
ISBN 978-0-19-045653-5 (cloth : alk. paper)
Subjects: LCSH: Thomas, Aquinas, Saint, 1225?–1274.
Summa contra gentiles. | Thomas, Aquinas, Saint, 1225?–1274. |
Apologetics—Early works to 1800.
Classification: LCC BX1749.T45 D38 2016 |
DDC 239—dc23 LC record available at http://lccn.loc.gov/2015044427

For Christopher Arroyo
and Paul Kucharski—once again.

Contents

Preface

THOMAS AQUINAS'S *Summa Contra Gentiles* stands out among his many writings. It is not a report of a disputed question over which he presided; nor is it a commentary on a text. It is not a short treatise on a single topic; and it does not range over Christian beliefs in the manner of the more famous *Summa Theologiae*. Its main conclusions cohere with what we find in Aquinas's commentary on the *Sentences* of Peter Lombard (1100–1160) and with much that he argues for in his *Summa Theologiae*. However, even a glance at these two works will leave readers recognizing that the *Summa Contra Gentiles* is seriously different from either of them. It does not come with "questions" and "articles." Indeed, it resembles a contemporary book since it consists of chapters and flows along in a way that the *Sentences* commentary and the *Summa Theologiae* do not. And it reads as produced by someone keen to argue for a number of theses while ignoring certain medieval conventions for discussing them. It comes across as a text in which Aquinas is trying to explain his views on what people can know about God and divine revelation. You might even say that it comes across as a work in which he contributes to philosophy of religion and theology in ways that contemporary philosophers and theologians can appreciate.

In this book I present an overview of the *Summa Contra Gentiles* for students and teachers of theology and philosophy, and anyone with an interest in Aquinas. This volume can therefore be regarded as a sequel to my *Thomas Aquinas's "Summa Theologiae": A Guide and Commentary* (Oxford: Oxford University Press, 2014).[1] Like that book, this one aims to be introductory, if also comprehensive, and it does not presume that its reader is already familiar with medieval thinking.

I begin by trying to situate the *Summa Contra Gentiles* historically; so I present a brief account of Aquinas's life and writings. I also consider the questions "When did he draft the *Summa Contra Gentiles*?" "Why did he do so?" and "What kind of work is it?" I then move systematically through its four books while following their arguments in detail. In doing so, my primary aim is expository. I strive chiefly to explain what Aquinas is saying. But I also spend a lot of time commenting on what he has to say.

The *Summa Contra Gentiles* has been far less studied and written about than the *Summa Theologiae*. But it is a remarkable work, and it provides us with access to Aquinas's mind on certain topics in a way that the *Summa Theologiae* does not. That is largely because it discusses the question "What can people deduce philosophically concerning God?" in more detail than does the *Summa Theologiae*. I might add that, as is not the case with the *Summa Theologiae*, a considerable amount of the *Summa Contra Gentiles* comes to us in Aquinas's own handwriting and with signs of much editing by him. It is a work that we know him to have significantly brooded on and revised before letting go.

I am assuming that most readers of this book will need to rely on translations of Aquinas's writings. The best available English edition of the *Summa Contra Gentiles* is the five-volume one published by the University of Notre Dame Press in 1975.[2] So I quote from this, though often with many emendations.[3] When referencing my quotations, I employ the abbreviation "ND" followed by the volume number, page reference, and paragraph number.[4] I sometimes cite works of Aquinas other than the *Summa Contra Gentiles*. When doing so, I refer to easily accessible and reliable translations.[5]

In what follows I abbreviate "*Summa Contra Gentiles*" as SCG. Translations from the Bible come from the New Revised Standard Version. I should add that I have tried to avoid gender-specific reference to God. In some instances, however, I have used "he"/"his" simply to avoid awkwardness in wording. Aquinas himself did not have to strive to write with an eye on inclusive language since Latin is inclusive in a way English is not.

For advice on earlier versions of what follows, or on parts of it, I am, with the usual disclaimer, much indebted to Christopher Arroyo, James Claffey, Samuel Kampa, David Kovacs, Paul Kucharski, Turner Nevitt, Michael Torre, and Zita Toth, who created the appendix. For her work as in-house editor, I am also grateful to Cynthia Read at Oxford University Press. I am also grateful to Gwen Colvin of Oxford University Press.

Thomas Aquinas's
Summa Contra Gentiles

I

The *Summa Contra Gentiles* and Its Context

IT IS POSSIBLE to make some sense of texts without knowing much about their authors. It is also possible to benefit from reading them without knowing when and why they were written. Yet properly to appreciate what texts have to offer requires that one does know something about their authors, when they wrote, and their intentions in writing. In this chapter, therefore, I turn to the *Summa Contra Gentiles* (SCG) by first offering a short account of the life and works of Aquinas. I then briefly characterize his thinking in general while going on to discuss when the SCG was written and why Aquinas embarked on it.

1.1 Aquinas's Life

Thomas Aquinas entered the world as a member of a wealthy and aristocratic family.[1] But he died as one among a group of people committed to poverty.[2] He was born around 1224–1226. He was dead by the end of 1274.[3] His birthplace was the castle of Roccasecca in southern Italy, which was his family's home. His death occurred at the Cistercian Abbey of Fossanova, not far from Rome. His remains are now in the church of the Jacobins in Toulouse, France. He was canonized as a saint by Pope John XXII in 1325; his feast day is celebrated by the Catholic Church on January 28, though before the Second Vatican Council (1962–1965) it was celebrated on March 4.[4]

At the age of five or six, Aquinas was sent to study at the Benedictine Abbey of Monte Cassino, whose abbot was one of his relatives. Here he was instructed in grammar and writing. He was also introduced to biblical texts and to the works of Christian theologians such as St. Augustine of Hippo (354–430). But military conflict between the Emperor Frederick II (1194–1250) and Pope Gregory IX (d. 1241) led to Aquinas leaving Monte Cassino so as to continue his education at the University of Naples, founded by Frederick II in 1224 as a training place for potentially useful civil servants. This university, however, had a wide-ranging curriculum that included philosophy and theology.[5]

While studying in Naples, Aquinas became acquainted with the Order of Preachers, better known as the Dominicans, founded by St. Dominic Guzman (1170–1221). The Dominicans were an order of friars, and they had only a few men working in Naples when Aquinas got to know them. But he took the Dominican habit in 1242 or 1243. His family was not happy with this decision and detained him under house arrest for some time, though they eventually released him to go his own way.

To begin with, Aquinas lived among Dominicans in Paris, which at that time, along with Bologna and Oxford, was home to one of the major medieval universities. Here, he might have had some connection with the university's Faculty of Arts, and he was almost certainly working under the direction of St. Albert the Great (Albertus Magnus), at that time one of the most prominent and influential of Dominican scholars.[6] Aquinas continued to work under Albert's direction when Albert moved to Cologne in 1248 so as to establish a house of studies there. While at Cologne, Aquinas acted as Albert's secretary. He may also have started commenting on the Bible. Also in Cologne, Aquinas probably wrote his *De Principiis Naturae* (*On the Principles of Nature*), a short text that discusses themes developed early in Aristotle's *Physics*.[7]

In 1251 or 1252 Aquinas returned to the University of Paris to begin work as a teacher. Initially, he delivered lectures commenting on biblical books. He then lectured and commented on the *Sentences* of Peter Lombard (c. 1096–1160).[8] In 1256 he became a Master of Theology, a post he relinquished around 1259. Writings of Aquinas that derive from this period of his life include a commentary on Lombard's *Sentences* (*Commentum in Libros Sententiarum Petri Lombardi*), a commentary on the *De Trinitate* (*On the Trinity*) by Boethius (c. 480–524) (*Super Boethium De Trinitate*), and *On Being and Essence* (*De Ente et Essentia*). At this stage in his career Aquinas also began to write his *Summa Contra Gentiles*.

Aquinas's function as a Master of Theology was to lecture on the Bible, to preach, and to preside over academic debates referred to as "Disputed Questions."[9] Around the time when he became a Master of Theology, however, Aquinas was also drawn into an acrimonious argument that had arisen between teachers at the University of Paris who were members of the Dominican and Franciscan orders of friars and those who, though clerics, were not Dominicans or Franciscans. In 1256 Aquinas defended the friars in *Contra Impugnantes Dei Cultum et Religionem* (*Against Opponents of the Worship of God and Religion*). In later years he followed up this defense in two other works.

In 1261 or thereabouts, Aquinas moved to Orvieto in Italy in order to teach Dominican friars in their priory there.[10] Dominican legislation of the day required that Dominican priories had in residence a "conventual lector" whose job was to ensure that friars continued with studies regardless of their age or experience; and it was as the Orvieto priory's conventual lector that Aquinas became a member of that house. In 1265, however, he was assigned to set up a Dominican institute of studies at the priory of Santa Sabina in Rome. It was at this time that he began to write his monumental *Summa Theologiae*, on which he was still working at the time of his death.[11]

In 1268 Aquinas returned to Paris as a Master of Theology, and his duties were the same as they had previously been. In 1272, however, he was directed to found a Dominican study house in Naples and to teach at the university there. But his health was evidently failing around this time. He stopped writing from the end of September 1273, and he died in 1274. His death occurred while he was making his way to France in order to attend the Second Council of Lyons so as to advise concerning disagreements between Greek and Latin Christians. He was already fairly ill by the time he set out for the council. On his way to it he became increasingly sick and was taken to the Abbey of Fossanova, where he died on March 7.

1.2 Aquinas's Writings

I have mentioned some of Aquinas's writings while sketching his biography. At this point, however, I should say something about them as a whole and something about Aquinas's thinking in general.[12]

An important point to note is that Aquinas wrote voluminously and in works with different structures and purposes.

We have from him short philosophical treatises, like *De Principiis Naturae* and *De Ente et Essentia*. But Aquinas liked to write commentaries on various texts. So we derive a number of biblical commentaries from him: on Isaiah, Jeremiah, Job, Psalms, Matthew, John, and several letters of St. Paul.[13]

Then, there are a number of commentaries on works by Aristotle, such as the *Sententia Libri De Anima* (on Aristotle's *De Anima* [*On the Soul*]), the *Sententia Super Physicam* (on Aristotle's *Physics*), the *Expositio Libri Perihermeneias* (on Aristotle's *On Interpretation*), the *Expositio Libri Posteriorum* (on Aristotle's *Posterior Analytics*), the *Sententia Libri Ethicorum* (on the *Nicomachean Ethics*), and the *Sententia Super Metaphysicam* (on Aristotle's *Metaphysics*).

Aquinas also wrote more than one commentary on Boethius and a commentary on Pseudo-Dionysius's *The Divine Names*.[14] He also commented on the *Liber de Causis* (*The Book of Causes*).[15] And he produced a number of

Disputed Questions. He wrote his *De Veritate* during his first teaching period in Paris, but he went on to edit a number of other Disputed Questions, including *De Potentia* (*On the Power of God*), *De Anima*, and *De Malo* (*On Evil*).

In addition to all of this we have what Jean-Pierre Torrell calls "theological syntheses."[16] These include Aquinas's commentary on the *Sentences* of Peter Lombard, the *Summa Theologiae*, and (so I would say, though Torrell does not), the *Compendium Theologiae* (*Compendium of Theology*).[17] Aquinas's theological syntheses also include the *Summa Contra Gentiles*.

Aquinas produced more than the foregoing works, but you will get a sense of the range of his writing interests from what I have been saying.[18] They are those of someone concerned to engage in both philosophy and theology.

Some have argued that Aquinas was not really a philosopher since his thinking is always theological, and this position is defensible for a number of reasons. Aquinas never formally taught philosophy and never describes himself as a philosopher. He would have understood the word "philosopher" to signify a pagan thinker, not a Christian, and certainly not someone functioning as a Master of Theology or a teacher of Dominicans. Again, almost all of Aquinas's writings are heavily influenced by the Bible, from which he frequently quotes while also making numerous respectful allusions to classical Christian theologians such as Augustine of Hippo, St. Gregory the Great (540–604), and St. Jerome (347–420). Aquinas often refers to "the articles of faith," which he takes to derive from biblical teaching and to amount to the content of Christian documents such as the Apostles' Creed and the Nicene Creed.[19] And it is the articles of faith that Aquinas is constantly trying to clarify and reflect on in many of his writings, including the SCG. So there can be no doubt that Aquinas was primarily a theologian. He takes himself to be chiefly concerned with Christian faith. In this connection, I should emphasize that Aquinas does not believe that Christian faith can be derived from purely philosophical reasoning or that it has to be. He consistently denies that the articles of faith can be philosophically proved to be true. Again, in his study of Boethius's *De Trinitate* he roundly declares: "Someone may err by making reason precede faith when it comes to matters of faith rather than making faith precede reason, as when someone is willing to believe only what that person is able to discover by reason. It should in fact be just the other way around."[20]

On the other hand, though, Aquinas writes a lot of what most contemporary philosophers would recognize as philosophy, even if they disagree with it. In his commentaries on Aristotle, he aims to elucidate and reflect on the work of a highly influential philosopher. Again, he spends a lot of time dealing with traditional philosophical questions such as "What are human beings?" "Can reason unaided by revelation demonstrate that God exists?" "Can we take language used to talk about God as making sense?" "What are the basic constituents of things in the spatiotemporal world?" and "Can we give people reasons for acting virtuously?" Aquinas evidently believes that he has true answers to some of these questions even before he proceeds to discuss them, answers to be found in the teachings of some distinguished Christian thinkers. Yet Aquinas also believes that he can go a long way to defending these answers without invoking the articles of faith as premises in his arguments. As I will show, Aquinas maintains that "there is a twofold mode of truth in what we profess about God." Some of this "exceeds all the ability of the human reason," but "there are some truths which the natural reason also is able to reach."[21] So, Aquinas holds that reason without revelation can arrive at truth about God, and he thinks the same when it comes to certain truths concerning what is not divine.[22] In this sense, Aquinas is perfectly prepared to engage in philosophy, considered as a matter of rational evaluation and argument not presupposing the truth of any theological doctrine. And never more so than in the SCG.

This is obviously the work of a Christian theologian. But it is the work of one anxious to think philosophically about some key religious beliefs, especially ones about the existence and nature of God. Aquinas begins the SCG by quoting Proverbs 8:7, and biblical quotations are plentiful as the SCG proceeds, though their number increases in book 4. Yet three of the SCG's four books consist of arguments that Aquinas offers for conclusions concerning God that he takes to be defensible without invoking the authority of the Bible, great as he takes this to be. So, three of the SCG's four books amount to an extended essay in what is often called "natural theology."

I take natural theology to be any attempt to reason about the existence and nature of God without dependence on purportedly divine revelation.[23] Natural theology is a philosophical enterprise. Without employing theological premises, it seeks to show that we have good reason to believe that God exists and that something can truly be said when it comes to what God is. And much of the SCG offers natural theology on this understanding of it. So, as Norman Kretzmann nicely puts it, in books 1–3 of the SCG Aquinas presents "theology from the bottom up."[24] Book 4 finds Aquinas explicitly drawing on "the articles of faith" as he adds to the contents of SCG 1–3. Be that as it may, however, the bulk of the SCG is a sustained essay in natural theology.

I am told that the great twentieth-century theologian Karl Barth (1886–1968) was asked in 1962 to summarize what he said in his many writings. He is said to have replied: "Jesus loves me, that I know, for the Bible tells me so." This story might be apocryphal, though it fits in with the drift of Barth's theology. The point I want to stress now, however, is that, though Aquinas is in agreement with Barth when it comes to the importance of revelation, he thinks, as Barth did not, that philosophy can be quite a useful aid to theologians.[25] This fact is very evident from the text of the SCG.

1.3 When and Why Did Aquinas Write the Summa Contra Gentiles?

There has been much scholarly debate concerning the dating and purpose of many of Aquinas's writings, or writings attributed to him.[26] And such debate continues when it comes to the SCG. But we do have a critical edition of this work produced by the Leonine Commission, so we at least know that Aquinas wrote it.[27]

The Leonine Commission consists of a group of scholars deputed to produce the best possible editions of Aquinas's writings, ones that most accurately reflect what he actually wrote. It was founded in 1879 under the influence of Pope Leo XIII. When thinking of the work of the Leonine Commission, we have to remember that Aquinas did not write using a computer. Indeed, he lived before the invention of the printing press, at a time when literary works still had to be copied by hand and circulated in manuscript form. And manuscripts of Aquinas's writings that survive sometimes differ from each other even when it comes to a single work such as the SCG. Indeed, some of his "writings" survive in reports of what he said rather than in texts drafted by him and subsequently copied. In short, there are serious problems when it comes to getting as close as we can to what Aquinas wrote in what is authentically attributable to him.[28] Hence the need for the Leonine Commission.

Textual matters aside, however, there remains the question "When did Aquinas write the SCG?" Largely due to the labors of René-Antoine Gauthier, we can be fairly sure as to how to answer this question.[29] We can reasonably conclude that Aquinas began the SCG when he first taught in Paris, that he continued work on it in Italy, having moved there from Paris, and that he had finished writing it around 1265–1267.

Gauthier notes that much of SCG 1, in manuscripts of it that come from Aquinas's hand, are written on the same parchment and with the same ink as Aquinas's commentary on Boethius's *De Trinitate*. This fact allows us to date the beginning of the SCG to some time prior to June 1259, when Aquinas, together with St. Albert, was present at a Dominican General Chapter at Valenciennes. However, the parchment and ink change at a certain point, suggesting that Aquinas had then left Paris for Italy. Also worth noting is that quotations from Aristotle at a certain stage in the SCG rely on translations that were not available in Paris in the 1250s but were available in Italy around 1260–1265, suggesting that SCG 3,85 was not written before 1263–1264.[30] Yet also worth noting is that Aquinas refers to the SCG in works that can be dated to soon after 1265. Bearing in mind such facts, Gauthier, with whom I would not dream of trying to quarrel, concludes that Aquinas had completed and revised the SCG by the autumn of 1265, just before, or around, the time that, he started to write the *Summa Theologiae*.

But why did Aquinas embark on his first *summa*, the *Summa Contra Gentiles*?[31] When it comes to this question, answers are harder to provide than ones we might offer when it comes to the dating of the SCG.

It has often been said that Aquinas wrote the SCG as a manual or textbook to be used by Dominican missionaries working in Spain, in which Islam was then a force to be reckoned with by Christians. It has also been claimed that he did so at the request of Raymund of Peñafort, who was Master General of the Dominican Order from 1238 to 1240. This tradition of thinking concerning the SCG derives from the *Chronicle of the King of Aragon, James I* written by a Dominican called Peter Marsilio, who finished his work around 1314. Peter says that Raymund was anxious to convert infidels and that he asked Aquinas, considered as a scholar of great renown, to write what turned out to be the SCG. There are, however, reasons for doubting the historical accuracy of this account.

It is not that nothing can be said in its favor. For one thing, the SCG is evidently an apologetic work since it defends a series of Christian beliefs from criticism, or potential criticism, and since its earliest and best attested title is *Liber de Veritate Catholicae Fidei contra Errores Infidelium (A Book on the Truth of the Catholic Faith against the Errors of Unbelievers)*.[32] Again, Raymund of Peñafort worked in Spain, where the influence of Islam was considerable, and from the middle of the thirteenth century Dominicans had a definite interest in missionary work among Muslims. In 1255, for example, the Dominican Master General, Humbert of Romans (c. 1194–1277), called, with considerable success, for Dominicans to volunteer for foreign missions. In some of his writings he stressed the need for there always to be Dominican treatises against the errors of unbelievers. So we might suppose that Aquinas could have written the SCG with some kind of missionary aim in mind, or as a work to aid Dominican missionaries in some way.

Yet the SCG does not seem to be especially targeting Islam. Insofar as it criticizes various ideas, these are ones coming from many people, including ancient philosophers, Jewish thinkers, and Christians whom Aquinas took to have fallen into heresy. I doubt that anyone reading the SCG today with no prompting as to its purpose would speedily say "This is obviously a treatise against Islam." It just does not read like such a work. It refers to Islamic teaching from time to time. But we have reason to believe that Aquinas was not very well informed about Islamic thinking, though he was familiar with the writings of some famous Islamic philosophers such as Avicenna (Ibn Sīnā, c. 980–1037) and Averroes (Ibn Rushd, 1126–1198).[33] We should also note that Peter Marsilio does not specify that the SCG was written as a tract against Islam. Peter speaks only of "pagans" or "unbelievers" (*infidelium*), which is highly ambiguous since he could here be thinking of any people who are not orthodox Christians.

Also to be noted is the fact that Aquinas did not dedicate the SCG to Raymund of Peñafort. Had he written the work at Raymund's request, one would expect him to have done so given the custom of the time, one to which he conformed in a number of his writings.[34] Even more significant than this fact, however, is one concerning chronology. Aquinas had completed the first fifty chapters of SCG 1 by autumn of 1259, which suggests that he had begun to work on them possibly as early as 1257. By this time in his career, however, Aquinas was not the renowned scholar he is said to be by Peter Marsilio. He had barely finished his commentary on the *Sentences* and had not yet published his *De Veritate*. As Gauthier observes, far from having been struck by the reputation of Aquinas, Raymund of Peñafort had probably never even heard of him when he started to work on the SCG.[35]

Again, therefore, what was Aquinas trying to do in writing the SCG? Perhaps the best way to discern a correct answer to this question is to read what he says in SCG 1,1–9, in which he provides what reads like an extended preface to the work, one that makes little reference to Muslims or to missionary matters.

1.4 Aquinas Explains Himself

Aquinas begins the SCG by talking about "the office of the wise man." "They are to be called wise," he says, "who order things rightly and govern them well" (SCG 1,1).[36] He adds that "the rule of government and order for all things directed to an end must be taken from the end." So, he argues, "a thing is best disposed when it is fittingly ordered to its end." But what if there is a universal end for all things? In that case, the "absolutely wise person," as opposed to someone wise in some particular art or skill, will be concerned with "the end of the universe, which is also the origin of the universe."[37] Here Aquinas is thinking of God as "the first principle whereby all things are." Yet, Aquinas quickly adds, thinking about God not only involves the truly wise person meditating on God. It also "belongs to that person to refute the opposing falsehood."

Hence, in SCG 1,2 Aquinas observes that "in the name of divine Mercy, I have the confidence to embark on the work of a wise person," which is "the task of making known, as far as my limited powers will allow, the truth that the Catholic faith professes, and of setting aside the errors that are opposed to it."[38] Aquinas's focus in the SCG, therefore, is on truth and error concerning God in general. Indeed, as he continues with SCG 1,2 he makes this quite clear by referring to different kinds of people subscribing to what he takes to be error concerning divine things. More specifically, he mentions those censored by "ancient doctors of the Church" in their criticisms of "Gentiles"—by which Aquinas means people who are neither Jewish nor Christian. He also refers to (1) heretics (by which he means people who claim to be Christian but do not adhere to orthodox Christian belief), and (2) Muslims and Jews (whom he takes to be religious but non-Christian in their beliefs). He also mentions "pagans," presumably referring to anyone who is not a Christian, a heretical Christian, a Muslim, or a Jew. But how does Aquinas think that he is able to refute all of these classes of people?

When it comes to Jewish people and Christian heretics, Aquinas notes that "the wise person" can at least appeal to biblical texts. So, "against the Jews we are able to argue by means of the Old Testament, while against heretics we are able to argue by means of the New Testament."[39] Yet Aquinas adds that Muslims and pagans "accept neither the one nor the other," which leaves him concluding with three sentences that effectively indicate the basic line of thought behind the SCG:

> We must, therefore, have recourse to the natural reason, to which all people are forced to give their assent. However, it is true, in divine matters, that the natural reason has its failings. Now while we are investigating some given truth, we shall also show what errors are set aside by it; and we shall likewise show how the truth that we come to know by demonstration is in accord with the Christian religion.[40]

By "natural reason" here Aquinas means what we might call "philosophical insight" or "philosophy" or just "reason." He is referring to what we can figure out on our own by trying to think well and clearly and without recourse to anything that we might take to be divine revelation. More specifically, however, he is thinking of reason as able to demonstrate certain truths. As I will show, Aquinas distinguishes between different kinds of demonstration. Following Aristotle, however, he always takes a demonstration to be an argument that proceeds from evidently true premises while entailing a conclusion that cannot be denied given that the premises are accepted. In the passage just quoted, therefore, Aquinas is saying that he is going to try to demonstrate certain things about God, while adding that he will also be arguing that what he has demonstrated accords with orthodox Christian teaching, this, in turn, being what Aquinas takes to be found in the Bible, in creeds such as the Apostles' Creed or the Nicene Creed, and in the teachings of church councils prior to his time. In that case, however, what does Aquinas have in mind when he says that "in divine matters the natural reason has its failings"?

Here Aquinas is anticipating a conclusion for which he argues later in the SCG and elsewhere in his writings. We can express the conclusion as "Articles of Christian faith cannot be demonstrated." At this point I should again note that Aquinas frequently refers to what he calls "the articles of faith." He takes these to be the *uniquely* Christian teachings: that God is Trinity (Father, Son, and Holy Spirit), that Christ was divine, and that people shall be raised from the dead. Aquinas does not take "God exists" to be an article of faith since he knows very well that there are Jews and Muslims who accept much that he does when it comes to the existence and nature of God. Aquinas thinks that the truth of "God exists" is what the articles of faith *take for granted* or *presuppose*, and he holds that one can demonstrate that God exists. Yet he consistently denies that one can demonstrate the truth of the articles of faith. Why? Because he does not think that we have premises known by us to be evidently true that guarantee their truth.

Take, for example, the doctrine of the Trinity. As I will show, Aquinas's view is that this doctrine cannot be philosophically demonstrated since, while reason can prove that there is something that is divine, it cannot prove this something is a trinity of persons all of whom, according to orthodox Christian teaching, are equally divine. Again, consider the claim that Christ was divine. Aquinas typically denies that this can be philosophically demonstrated since nothing that we can know about the life of Christ can be used so as to construct an argument along the lines (1) Christ was evidently A,B,C; (2) anything A,B,C is divine (3); therefore Christ was divine. Aquinas's view is that what we can know about Christ based on empirically based testimony is only going to give us knowledge of what a particular human being said and did. You might suppose that the miracles of Jesus establish his divinity without question. To this supposition, however, Aquinas usually says something like "The miracles of Jesus might show us that Jesus was graced by God, but they do not demonstrate that Jesus was God incarnate."

Aquinas clearly has high standards when it comes to demonstration. As I have said, he thinks that we have a demonstration when we have evidently true premises leading inevitably to a certain conclusion. So where does this leave him as playing the part of the wise person in the SCG? It leads him to recognize that, while the articles of faith do not admit of demonstration, reason, without presupposing the truth of Christian revelation, can lead us to demonstrate much about the existence and nature of God. So we find that the first three books of the SCG are entirely devoted to a defense of this thesis. Then, in the fourth book, Aquinas argues that the articles of Christian faith do not present us with what is unreasonable to believe even though these articles cannot themselves be demonstrated to be true.

I take all of this to mean that Aquinas must have written the SCG so as (1) to reflect at length concerning what reason can tell us about God, (2) to note ways in which what reason tells us about God harmonizes with what revelation teaches, and (3) to defend the articles of faith against charges of irrationality. Whether or not he had missionaries and their aims in mind, this seems to have been what he was most intent on when drafting and correcting the SCG.[41] As I have said, in *The Metaphysics of Theism*, Norman Kretzmann refers to "theology from the bottom up." Correspondingly, he also talks about "theology from the top down."[42] By "theology from the top down" Kretzmann means "reflecting on God in the light of divine revelation." By "theology from the bottom up" he means "reflecting on God without recourse to revelation." And, although Aquinas is clearly writing as a Christian from the start of SCG, he might, I think, have been willing to accept Kretzmann's distinction. I suspect that he might have been happy to describe SCG 1–3 as "theology from the bottom up" and SCG 4 as "theology from the top down." Be that as it may, however, SCG 1–3 certainly amounts to a long treatise on natural theology, albeit that it comes from someone who clearly believes in God and is happy to cite biblical texts and various Christian authorities as he continues about his business.

Natural theology has been seriously criticized both by philosophers and by a number of theologians. Philosophers who attack it, or examples of it, tend to do so because they do not find certain philosophical arguments concerning the existence and nature of God to be plausible. Theologians hostile to natural theology are usually against it because they think it impious to hold God against the bar of human reasoning or because they think that to do so is somehow to act in opposition to the teaching of the Bible.[43] Be that as it may, however, Aquinas is very much in favor of natural theology and thinks that he can provide a good and substantial amount of it. And the SCG is, perhaps, the work in which he most displays his interest in and talents for natural theology. It is a presiding thesis of Aquinas that truth cannot contradict truth. In the SCG he shows himself to uphold this thesis in the way in which he tries to apply reason even while accepting that there is such a thing as divine revelation.

Before he gets seriously down to business in his efforts on this front, however, Aquinas has some more things to say in SCG 1,1–9. In fact, he argues for three theses while going on to explain the SCG's order and manner of proceeding.

The first thesis is that even though reason cannot demonstrate the articles of faith, it does not follow that those who assent to them are being foolish (SCG 1,6). The second is that truths that reason can discern do not conflict with any articles of faith (SCG 1,7). The third is that reason can seek to get a grip on some truths about God even though God exceeds the range of human reasoning in a serious way (SCG 1,8).

As I have noted, Aquinas does not take the articles of Christian faith to be demonstrable. Yet he does not think that those who accept them are being unreasonable or foolish. For one thing, he argues, the articles of faith are revealed by God, who knows everything. Then again, he observes, while the articles of faith may not be strictly demonstrable, there are "fitting arguments" for their truth.[44] In this connection, for example, Aquinas notes that even uneducated people can be filled with great wisdom concerning divine things and, in being so, appear to fulfill Old Testament prophecy. Such wisdom, Aquinas holds, is not to be found among the adherents of non-Christian religions.[45]

When it comes to the claim that truths established by reason do not conflict with the articles of faith, Aquinas argues that "only the false is opposed to the true,"[46] and that what reason demonstrates to be true cannot conflict with truths divinely revealed by God. He also maintains (1) that our ability to know things by reason comes from God and cannot, therefore, be at odds with what God has revealed, and (2) that revelation cannot conflict with what we can know by reason since this would entail that God is hindering us from knowing truth, which is an impossible supposition. So, Aquinas concludes SCG 1,7 by writing:

> Whatever arguments are brought forward against the doctrines of faith are conclusions incorrectly derived from the first and self-evident principles imbedded in nature. Such conclusions do not have the force of demonstration; they are arguments that are either probable or sophistical. And so, there exists the possibility to answer them.[47]

The main point that Aquinas is making here is that what reason can demonstrate cannot conflict with truths that God has revealed and cannot be proved to do so. One might, of course, wonder what might be said against claims to the effect that this or that article of faith can be shown to be false. Yet, as I will show, Aquinas goes on in the SCG to indicate how he thinks about this matter with respect to specific arguments against particular articles of faith. At this point in the SCG, however, he is basically laying down some general principles to which he will adhere as he continues. He is, so to speak, showing his hand, but not his full hand. And that is what he is doing again in SCG 1,8, in which he briefly says that we can profitably reason about God even though we cannot demonstrate the truths of the articles of faith so as to arrive at a comprehensive understanding of God. How we can profitably reason about God while not attempting to demonstrate the truth of the articles of faith will turn out to be the major topic of SCG 1–3, which brings us to SCG 1,9 in which Aquinas talks about his order and manner of procedure in the SCG.

As we might expect, he repeats some of what he has already said in SCG 1,1–8. Specifically he makes the following points: (1) The wise person should be concerned with what can be known of God by reason and by revelation; (2) The wise person should consider what can be known of God by reason unaided by revelation and should also be concerned to refute objections to truths about God known by reason and objections to truths about God revealed by God.

When it comes to what can be known of God by reason, Aquinas is thinking of what can be demonstrated concerning God. When it comes to what is true of God insofar as God has revealed it, Aquinas says that, since this cannot be demonstrated to be true, "our intention should not be to convince our adversaries by arguments; it should be to answer their arguments against the truth; for, as we have shown, natural reason cannot be contrary to the truths of faith."[48] So:

> This, then, is the manner of procedure we intend to follow. We shall first seek to make known that truth which faith professes and reason investigates. This we shall do by bringing forth both demonstrative and probable arguments.... Then, in order to follow a development from the more manifest to the less manifest, we shall proceed to make known that truth which surpasses reason, answering the objections of its adversaries and setting forth the truth of faith by probable arguments and by authorities, to the best of our ability.[49]

In short, Aquinas tells us that his intention in writing the SCG is to provide an extended essay in natural theology (which will occupy him through books 1–3) and then to offer defenses of the articles of faith (which will occupy him in book 4). And that, I think, is all that we can confidently refer to when it comes to the question "Why did Aquinas write the SCG?"

I have tried to indicate why the "missionary manual" account of the SCG is to be distrusted. But Aquinas's own account of his purposes seems fairly clear and indicates that he thought of the SCG as a technical and somewhat apologetic work designed to offer a series of demonstrations concerning the existence and nature of God while concluding with reflections on reason and the articles of faith. The bulk of the SCG is an extended essay on natural theology and is, in Kretzmann's phrase, concerned with "theology from the bottom up." Its concluding book is much concerned with objections to articles of faith based on various grounds to which Aquinas responds with no intention of demonstrating that these articles are true.

Yet what kind of approach does Aquinas take to demonstration when it comes to the existence and nature of God? He starts to explain himself on this matter in SCG 1,10–14, to which I now turn.

2

Approaching the Question of God's Existence (SCG 1,10–12)

AS I HAVE said, Aquinas thinks that there can be knowledge about God that does not depend on divine revelation. In this sense, he is an advocate or friend of natural theology. Yet what kind of natural theology does Aquinas favor, and from what kind does he distance himself? Also, should he be bothering with natural theology at all? For might not natural theology be dismissed or ignored on the basis of faith in God's existence? To put this question another way, might it not be that it is only on the basis of faith, not reason, that we are entitled to claim to know that God exists? In SCG 1,10–12 we find Aquinas trying to deal with all of these questions.[1]

2.1 Kinds of Natural Theology (SCG 1,10–11)

Aquinas was certainly aware that defenses of natural theology can vary in nature. The natural theology that he favors in the SCG and elsewhere consists of demonstrative arguments grounded on what God might be thought of as producing or bringing about. His basic line is that certain things of which we have knowledge can, on reflection, be thought of as effects of God, who stands to them as a cause.

The word "cause" has a long philosophical history, and Aquinas himself distinguished, as did Aristotle, between causes of four kinds. So, what sense of "cause" (*causa*) is he working with for the purposes of his discussions of natural theology in the SCG? The answer is "the sense of cause in which a cause is an *agent* or *efficient* cause." But that answer needs some explanation.

Here we might start by noting our familiar word "because." We say that this or that happened or is happening *because* of something or other, and in doing so we seem to be seeking to offer explanations of some kind. The word "cause" can be related to the word "explanation." But there are explanations of different kinds just as there are reasons of different kinds.

I might, for example, wonder why my cat seems to love eating meat while horses seem uninterested in it. The answer, of course, lies in the fact that cats are by nature carnivorous while horses are naturally herbivores.

Again, I might wonder why married friends of mine are getting divorced while other married couples stay together, or why I can slice an apple with a knife but cannot slice a diamond with one. Here the answers might lie (1) in different intentions or aims on the part of my friends who are divorcing and on the part of people who remain married, and (2) on ways in which apples and diamonds differ from each other physically or materially.

So we can distinguish between what Aquinas would have called "formal," "final," and "material" causes or explanations. For Aquinas, we appeal to a formal cause when we try to explain how it is that cats like meat and horses do not because of what they are by *nature*, because of what Aquinas would call their "substantial form."[2] And Aquinas holds that we can appeal to "final" and "material" causes as we (1) note goals that influence people or ends to which even nonhuman things can be drawn, and (2) draw attention to how the physical structure of things can account for what happens to them or what can be done to them. Again, we can make sense of Aquinas's thinking here by reflecting about contexts in which we use the word "because." We can make sense of statements like "My cat loves meat because it is a carnivorous animal," "Jane and Bill split up because Bill's cheating on Jane led her to want him out of her life," and "I can cut an apple with a knife but cannot cut a diamond with one because apples have *this* physical make-up and diamonds have a *quite different* one."

Now, however, consider another use of "because." Suppose that someone stumbles across a human corpse and asks "Why the dead body?" In such a context people could end up settling for an explanation in terms of what are usually referred to as "natural causes." It might be agreed, for example, that the person whose corpse we are thinking about died of a heart attack. But it might be concluded that the person committed suicide. Or it might be decided that neither "natural causes" nor suicide accounts for what is now in question. For what if it looks as though we are dealing with a case of murder? Should the evidence point in that direction, then, there is an obvious question to raise: "Who did it?"—and this question gives us an entry into what Aquinas means when he talks about agent or efficient causes.

Ludwig Wittgenstein (1889–1951) once observed: "Calling something 'the cause' is like pointing and saying: '*He's* to blame!'"[3] We have a sense of "cause" in which a cause is something that acts or operates so as to bring about what we take to be an effect. So one person might be called the cause of another person's death. Or I might be said to be the cause of a wall becoming painted. Or a particular virus might be taken to be the cause of someone developing certain physical symptoms. And this sense of "cause" is what Aquinas has in mind when he speaks of agent or efficient causes. In his *De Principiis Naturae* he writes: "Copper is potentially a statue, but can't make itself into a statue: it needs a workman to draw the statue's form out of potentiality into actuality." He adds:

> For the form won't exist unless the thing is made, whereas the maker exists in the coming to be, that is, while the thing is coming to be. So besides matter and form there must be some active principle or origin, which we call the efficient cause or mover or agent, from which the change originates.[4]

Here, the idea is that something can be thought of as a cause insofar as it brings about an effect in something else, and, according to Aquinas, God is a cause in this sense. In Aquinas's view, thinking about natural theology can lead us to recognize that God exists as one who accounts for things that we observe in the world. He knows that some natural theologians argue that God can be known to exist without reference to effects. But he rejects what he takes to be their line of argument, to which he turns explicitly in SCG 1,10, in which he discusses "the opinion of those who say that the existence of God, being self-evident, cannot be demonstrated."[5]

Aquinas contrasts "being self-evident" with "being able to be causally deduced." So, he writes:

> There are some people to whom the inquiry seeking to demonstrate that God exists may perhaps appear superfluous. These are those who assert that the existence of God is self-evident, in such wise that its contrary cannot be entertained in the mind.[6]

Here Aquinas is thinking of someone claiming that "God exists" follows immediately from an understanding of what God is. That is clear from the arguments he cites in SCG 1,10 as coming from people saying that "God exists" is self-evident. There are five such arguments.

1. If you know what the word "whole" means, then you immediately know that every whole is greater than its parts. But "God" means "something than which a greater cannot be thought." From this it follows that God cannot just be a concept we have in our minds. God must be something that exists in reality, not just as thought about by us. From the very definition of "God" as "something than which a greater cannot be thought," therefore, it follows that God must exist in reality since it is greater to exist in reality rather than only as something in our minds.

2. We can think that there is something that cannot possibly not exist, and such a thing would be greater than something that can be thought not to exist. But God is something than which a greater cannot be thought, in which case God cannot be something that can be thought not to exist. The notion of not being able not to exist is part and parcel of what we mean by the word "God."

3. Propositions like "Human beings are human beings" or "Human beings are rational animals" are evidently true. But God's very nature or essence is to exist (his being is his essence). So "God exists" is like "Human beings are human beings" or "Human beings are rational animals."

4. What we know by nature is self-evident and not based on deduction. But we know by nature that God exists since we naturally desire God as our ultimate end.

5. That by which we know other things is self-evident, not deduced. But by God's light we know all that we know.

Yet Aquinas rejects these arguments in SCG 1,11.[7] But why?

To start with, he indicates that he sympathizes to some extent with people who offer them. It is, he says, understandable that people taught to call on God throughout their lives should just think it obvious that God exists. "What the mind is steeped in from childhood it clings to very firmly, as something known naturally or self-evidently."[8] But he still finds fault with these five arguments. In doing so, he makes one general point and then replies to each of the arguments.

The general point is that while it is true that "God exists" is "self-evident in an absolute sense" (*notum per se simpliciter*), it is not "self-evident to us" (*quoad nos notum*). If we understood what God is as, for example, we understand what wholes and parts are, then, Aquinas agrees, we would immediately see that "God exists" has to be true since "what God is is his own being." Yet, Aquinas adds, "we are not able to conceive in our minds what God is." Here he means that we lack a comprehensive knowledge of God's nature and therefore lack the wherewithal to see that God exists in the same way that we can immediately see, from our knowledge of the nature of wholes and parts, that every whole is greater than its parts.

Why does Aquinas take this line about us not understanding what God is? You will get a fuller sense of why he does so as you continue working through this book and through the SCG. For now, however, let me briefly explain what Aquinas seems only to presume in SCG 1,11 while spelling it out in detail later. The main point to note is that, according to Aquinas, we lack what we might call a "scientific" understanding of God. When it comes to God's nature, thinks Aquinas, we lack *scientia*.

By "scientific" here I mean "thorough and detailed." Aquinas would have said that it is, in principle, possible to have a thorough and detailed understanding of what something is; but only insofar as (1) we can pick it out as existing in the physical world, and (2) we can locate the thing in terms of genus or species, thereby understanding how to classify it against a background of other things. If you like, Aquinas means that we have *scientia* concerning something to the extent that we can define it and thereby capture what is unique about it.

Take cats: the biological family *felidae,* of which there are a number of species. We all know something about these creatures, some of which are domesticated and some of which are not. Yet few of us are able to elaborate on them as certain biologists or zoologists can. The experts on cats know a great deal about them, even if they do not know everything about them. Such experts will be able to pick out cats of different species and explain how they differ from or resemble other kinds of cat. They will also be able to tell us how cats in general may be distinguished from certain other living animals. Experts on cats will, for example, be able to lecture us at length about how it is that cats are carnivorous, how some of them are solitary while others form colonies, how they tend to have bodies of a certain size and shape, how some of them have distinctive markings, how their eyes work, how their teeth work, what noises some of them characteristically make, how eight "lineages" of cat have been genetically identified, and so on. In this sense, some people have developed a scientific understanding of what cats are based on copious empirical investigation. Yet, so Aquinas thinks, nobody has developed a corresponding understanding of what God is, even though many people will be able to give some account of what the word "God" means.

Why not? Aquinas's basic answer to this question is: Because God is not something in the universe that we can examine and compare or contrast with other things in the universe so as to come up with anything like the account of what cats are that some people can offer. As I will show, Aquinas holds that God is not a material object, not part of the universe, and not something in time. Aquinas does not even think that God is one of a kind of which there could be more than one member. And all of these points, though developed by Aquinas as he writes the SCG, are there in embryo, as it were, in what he says in SCG 1,11 about us not knowing what God is as we know what wholes and parts are. Yes, he agrees that, if we had a God's-eye understanding of God, we would understand what God is as some understand what a certain kind of cat is. We would thereby immediately understand that it belongs to God to exist by nature and that there is something amounting to self-contradiction in the claim "God does not exist." However, says Aquinas, we do not have a God's-eye understanding of

God. Such understanding of God's nature as is open to us in the present life is going to have to be derived from what we might infer about God on the basis of what God has produced—as we engage in theology "from the bottom up."

So much for what I am calling Aquinas's "general" point in SCG 1,11. Now for his more particular responses to the five arguments he cites in SCG 1,10. Here is what he says:

1. Not everyone takes the word "God" to mean "something a greater than which cannot be thought." Even if one does take "God" to mean "something than which a greater cannot be thought," it does not follow that God actually exists since a bare understanding of the meaning of the word "God" cannot entail that there is anything in reality to correspond to it.
2. We are not going to be able to show that God cannot be thought not to be unless we have an understanding of what God is, which we lack.
3. In our present life, and unlike the blessed in heaven, who see God, we lack a scientific or adequate understanding of what God is; so our understanding of God is not to be compared to our understanding of what wholes and parts are, and so on. "To those seeing the divine essence in itself [the blessed in heaven] it is supremely self-evident that God exists because his essence is his being. But, because we are not able to see God's essence, we arrive at the knowledge of his being, not through God himself, but through his effects."[9]
4. We naturally desire God by desiring union with God. But the fact that we desire this does not mean that we know, straight off, that God exists. It only means that we yearn for less than what God is.
5. It is true that we know what we know by virtue of God. But to say this is to suppose that God exists and is what somehow helps us to know. It does not imply that we cannot know unless we know what God is as we know the truth of certain self-evident truths.

2.2 *Faith versus Demonstration (SCG 1,12)*

So Aquinas denies that "God exists" is self-evident to us, and this conclusion will lead him in the SCG to consider how God's existence might be demonstrated. Yet now we come to the objection to natural theology grounded on faith. Should we not hold that "God exists" cannot be demonstrated since it is held to be true, or should only be held to be true, on the basis of divine revelation? This is the question that Aquinas is concerned with in SCG 1,12, and his answer to it is no.

As I noted in chapter 1, Aquinas has no problem with the notion of divine revelation. Indeed, to suggest that he does would be grossly to misrepresent him. He firmly believes that God has revealed truths that we cannot demonstrate to be true. He also holds that someone might be warranted in believing that God exists just by reading the Bible and by taking it to contain divine revelation. Yet Aquinas is also aware of arguments suggesting that the project of demonstrating that God exists is doomed on philosophical grounds. As I have said, some theologians have held that natural theology is an abomination to be theologically condemned. But Aquinas does not refer to any such theologians in SCG 1,12. Rather, he starts by vaguely alluding to the claim that purported demonstrations that God exists fail as demonstrations because they amount to weak arguments. He then proceeds to note precise objections to the quest for demonstrations of the truth of "God exists," objections that he clearly takes to be philosophical ones.[10]

They can be presented thus:

1. If God's essence is to be, if God's essence and existence are identical, and if we cannot know what God is, then we can hardly demonstrate that God exists.[11]
2. Aristotle says that in demonstrating whether something exists we must begin with an understanding of what we name by the thing in question.[12] He also says that the meaning signified by a name is its definition.[13] But we cannot rely on an understanding of God when it comes to demonstrating that God exists if we do not have a knowledge of God's essence or "whatness" (*quidditas*).
3. Again, Aristotle says that we know how to provide demonstrations insofar as we are dealing with objects open to sensory investigation.[14] But God is no such object.

Yet Aquinas denies that these arguments show that "God exists" is not demonstrable. Or, rather, he denies that they show that "God exists" is *in no sense* demonstrable since there are two kinds of demonstration. "In arguments proving the existence of God it is not necessary to assume the divine essence or quiddity as the middle term of the demonstration.... In place of quiddity, an effect is taken as the middle term, as in demonstrations *quia*."[15]

Following Aristotle, Aquinas takes a demonstration to be an argument with evidently true premises that entail its conclusion. More precisely, he takes a demonstrative argument basically, though not always exactly, to have the form: (1) "All X is Y" (e.g., "All human beings are mammals"); (2) "All Y is Z" (e.g., "All mammals breath air"); (3) "Therefore, all X is Z" (e.g., "Therefore, all human beings breath air"). With that said, however, I also need to note that

Aquinas recognizes two kinds of *causal* demonstration: (1) from cause to effect, and (2) from effect to cause.

In *Summa Theologiae* 1a,2,2 he writes: "There are two kinds of demonstration. One kind, *propter quid* ('on account of which' or 'of the reason for'), argues from cause to effect and proceeds by means of what is unqualifiedly first. The other, demonstration *quia* ('that'), argues from effect to cause and proceeds by means of what is first so far as we are concerned."[16] What is Aquinas thinking here? His distinction can be grasped by means of examples.

Suppose we reason thus:

1. Hydrogen is the element with atomic number one.
2. The element with atomic number one is the lightest gas.
3. So hydrogen is the lightest gas.
4. Any balloon filled with the lightest gas rises in air.
5. So any balloon filled with hydrogen rises in air.

Here we start from a definition of what something is, and we end up arguing syllogistically for the occurrence of a visible effect. Our procedure here is an example of what Aquinas has in mind by "demonstration *propter quid*," which he thinks of as an argument from cause to effect starting with a grasp of the nature of the cause.

However, suppose we reason:

1. This balloon is rising in the air.
2. Every rising balloon is full of something that makes it rise.
3. So this balloon is full of something that makes it rise.
4. Everything that fills a balloon and makes it rise must be lighter than air.
5. So this balloon is full of something lighter than air.

Here we make no appeal to what it is precisely that fills this balloon rising in the air; we do not claim to know what exactly that is. Is it hydrogen, helium, or just hot air? But we do try to account for what we perceive in terms of a cause of some sort. We reason from effect to cause. Our procedure here is an example of what Aquinas has in mind when he refers to demonstration *quia*, which he thinks of as a syllogistic argument from effect to cause.[17]

Now, according to Aquinas, if we know, and do not just believe, that "God exists" is true, that can only be by virtue of a demonstration *quia*.[18] Demonstration *propter quid* is, he thinks, impossible when it comes to the truth of "God exists." Why? Because, as I have now shown, Aquinas thinks that we do not understand what God is, because we do not know God's nature or essence. The second objection in *Summa Theologiae* 1a,2,2 runs: "The middle term in a demonstration is what something is. But, as Damascene tells us, we do not know what God is, only what he is not."[19] The objection in question here is arguing that one cannot at all demonstrate that God exists, and Aquinas denies that conclusion. However, he does not quarrel with what I have just quoted from the objection. Instead, he draws attention to the fact that there are two kinds of demonstration, one of which does not presume a knowledge of what God is. Then he says that one can demonstrate that God exists by means of an argument from effect to cause. "When we demonstrate a cause from its effect," he observes,

> the effect takes the place of what the cause is in the proof that the cause exists, especially if the cause is God. For, when proving that something exists, the middle term is not what the thing is (we cannot even ask what it is until we know that it exists) but what we are using the name of the thing to mean. But when demonstrating from effects that God exists, we are able to start from what the word "God" means.[20]

This is the line that Aquinas takes in SCG 1,12. In his view, there can be demonstration *quia* for the truth of "God exists," even if we cannot understand what God's essence is. Such demonstration will not offend against the idea that demonstration "takes its origin from sense" since it will amount to concluding to "God exists" on the basis of sensible things. "Although God transcends all sensible things and the sense itself, God's effects, on which the demonstration proving his existence is based, are nevertheless sensible things."[21] Aquinas takes this conclusion to cohere with what St. Paul says in Romans 1:20: "Ever since the creation of the world his [i.e., God's] eternal power and divine nature, invisible though they are, have been understood and seen through the things he has made."[22] Indeed, says Aquinas, even Aristotle thought that there could be demonstration concerning what is not a "sensible substance," something we can know about by means of our senses.[23]

2.3 Comments on the Above

As I have said, my aim in this book is primarily to explain what Aquinas says in the SCG. Yet what I have just reported him as claiming raises questions that you should, perhaps, reflect on as you read SCG 1,10–12. So let me now list and briefly comment on some of them.

2.3.1 Should Natural Theology Not Be Avoided Altogether?

I noted in the previous chapter that, although Aquinas is an advocate of natural theology, some philosophers and theologians have been suspicious of it in general. In the present chapter, I have explained that the natural theology that Aquinas favors consists of deductive causal arguments. Before we even bother to look at how he develops his position on this matter, however, might we not consider rejecting his line of thinking on it at the outset? For are there not reasons for supposing that there never could be any worthwhile natural theology?

Philosophers and theologians hostile to natural theology have defended themselves in a variety of ways, not all of which I can flesh out here. But some of the most discussed among them boil down to the following theses:

1. There could never be any good natural theology since the assertion "God exists" is not even possibly true or since its truth is highly unlikely.
2. It is not the job of philosophy to argue that God exists. All philosophers can do is explain what belief in God amounts to.
3. To engage in natural theology is to offend against God by preferring to rely on human reasoning rather than divine revelation.
4. The whole enterprise of natural theology stands condemned on biblical grounds.

Why suppose that there *could not* be a God? One notable answer to this question holds that God is supposed to be a nonmaterial being, while the notion of a nonmaterial being is nonsensical. Such was the view of A. J. Ayer (1910–1989) and of members of the school of philosophical thinking known as logical positivism. According to them, "God exists" is strictly meaningless since it does not express a truth of logic, does not express a mathematical truth, and is not a statement that can be verified by means of sense experience.[24] Even before the time of Ayer and logical positivism, this was a position embraced by David Hume (1711–1766). "If we take in our hand any volume; of divinity or school metaphysics," says Hume, "let us ask, *Does it contain any abstract reasoning concerning quantity or number?* No. *Does it contain any experimental reasoning concerning matter of fact and existence?* No. Commit it then to the flames: For it can contain nothing but sophistry and illusion."[25]

What Hume says here is surely somewhat beguiling, like the call of the sirens as depicted in Homer's *Odyssey*. Considered as a philosophical movement, logical positivism lost the interest of philosophers some years ago, largely for technical reasons concerning its criteria for meaningfulness.[26] But Hume seems to be saying what tons of people believe: that there is something very fishy in any claim to the effect that there exists something whose existence cannot be empirically confirmed even in principle. One might, of course, reasonably believe in the existence of something that one has not been able to see or touch for oneself. Yet what if someone says that X exists, where X is supposed to be completely beyond the grasp of human sensation? Would we even understand what someone who says this might mean? One might say that someone who lacks understanding at this point is just lacking imagination. But can one *imagine* something existing that is beyond the grasp of human sensation? Surely not, since to imagine there being such and such is to be able concretely to *picture* it somehow.

This line of thinking does not, however, show that there can be nothing nonmaterial. At best, it indicates why such a thing would be something the nature of which would defy our abilities to classify and comprehend as we take ourselves to classify and comprehend things in the material world. And, as I have said, Aquinas positively insists that God is not something to be classified and understood as strictly comparable to such things. Aquinas is well aware that God is not subject to empirical investigation, but he does not therefore conclude that God cannot exist. Instead, he asks if there are any reasons to suppose that God does exist, and one might wonder why he should be forbidden in advance to do so. It might be said that we know that X cannot possibly exist for various reasons. But proof that X exists is, of course, proof that the existence of X is possible. So, perhaps, rather than supposing in advance that Aquinas is deluded as he embarks on his natural theology in the SCG, it might be prudent to let him carry on with this and see what results from it.

What, however, of the supposition that the existence of God is *unlikely* as opposed to impossible? Here again one can hear the sirens calling, and for many people they call because of the evils that we find in the world. For God is supposed to be wholly good, while we know very well that there is much that is bad in the world. There is cancer, from which people often die in much pain. There is AIDS and there is Ebola. There are natural disasters that cause endless amounts of grief, and on top of all of that there are people who inflict great misery on others. Think of the Holocaust, or think about the history of warfare in general. How could a God who is wholly good permit any of this to occur? It obviously has occurred. So, should we not forget about arguments of natural theology while assuming to begin with that what they purport to establish is hugely unlikely to be true given what we know about badness in the world?

Once again, however, proof that such and such exists is proof that it exists and has to be deemed as trumping arguments to the effect that it probably does not exist. So even the occurrence of great evil in the world cannot be thought of as rendering God's existence so unlikely as to force us to conclude that we should just ignore any arguments for the conclusion that God, indeed, exists. As he continues to write the SCG, Aquinas is obviously assuming that this is a reasonable assumption on which to proceed, which it surely is. In SCG 1,10–11 Aquinas does not refer to badness in the world as an objection to considering arguments for God's existence. But he does so in *Summa Theologiae* 1a,2,3. There, while citing an objection to what he wants to go on to say, he writes:

> It seems that there is no God. For if one of two contraries were infinite, the other would be completely destroyed. But by the word "God" we understand a certain infinite good. So, if God existed, nobody would ever encounter evil. But we do encounter evil in the world. So, God does not exist.[27]

In response to this argument, Aquinas replies: "As Augustine says, 'Since God is supremely good, he would not permit any evil at all in his works, unless he were sufficiently powerful and good to bring good even from evil.' So, it belongs to the limitless goodness of God that he permits evils to exist and draws good from them."[28] Considered as a response to the objection just quoted, this remark might seem somewhat lame. Yet Aquinas clearly does not take it to be a final word on how it is that evil and God can both be real. He is pointing forward to things he will go on to say in the *Summa Theologiae* concerning why God can be thought to be both supremely good and all-powerful. Taken in context, therefore, what he is saying presumes that a case can be made for a good and omnipotent God existing. Now it may be that no such case can be made. Yet the issue should surely not be decided in advance of any such case being offered and considered on its merits. The reality of evil might leave one skeptical concerning the existence of God just as the behavior of a husband might leave his wife skeptical concerning his fidelity to her. Such skepticism, however, would be unreasonable if it amounts to a refusal to consider any arguments offered for conclusions that might show it to be misguided.

What, however, of the view that one should not argue that God exists but should confine oneself to giving an account of what belief in God amounts to? This is a view that has been championed by philosophers claiming to be influenced by Wittgenstein, a notable example being D. Z. Phillips (1934–2006). According to Phillips: "It is not the task of the philosopher to decide whether there is a God or not, but to ask what it means to affirm or deny the existence of God."[29] Why so? Because, says Phillips, philosophical arguments for the truth of "God exists" ignore the fact that belief in God is not a hypothesis based on grounds and held to by believers in a tentative way, and it is certainly not an empirical hypothesis. Phillips writes:

> One will never understand what is meant by belief in God if one thinks of God as a being who may or may not exist.... Let us assume, for a moment, that the reality of God is akin to the reality of a physical object. It will then make sense to assume that one day we will be able to check whether our belief is true. Let us assume, further, that such a day comes, and that we find that there is a God and that He is as we had always thought Him to be. What kind of a God would we have discovered? Clearly, a God of whom it would still make sense to say that He might not exist. Such a God may, as a matter of fact, never cease to exist.... A God who is an existent among existents is not the God of religious belief.[30]

Indeed, Phillips adds, "God exists" is not an indicative statement. He says:

> Talk of God's existence or reality cannot be considered as talk about the existence of an object.... To ask whether God exists is not to ask a theoretical question. If it is to mean anything at all, it is to wonder about praising and praying: it is to wonder whether there is anything in all that. This is why philosophy cannot answer the question "Does God exist?" with either an affirmative or a negative reply.... "There is a God," though it appears to be in the indicative mood, is an expression of faith.[31]

If Phillips is right here, then Aquinas's interests in natural theology in the SCG derive from confusion. But is Phillips right?

Phillips was always much concerned to attack natural theology that has as its focus a notion of God that takes God to be part of a collection of things, something whose existence might be confirmed by sensory investigation, something that might be thought of as a "Top Person," a very knowledgeable and powerful, though invisible, human being, or something seriously like a human being.[32] Yet Phillips never paid any serious attention to the natural theology of Aquinas, who would, I suspect, have sympathized with much that Phillips says concerning what it is to believe in God. As I will show, Aquinas holds that God belongs to no species or genus. He also holds that it is God's nature to exist. In this sense, Aquinas would be at one with Phillips when it comes to the statements "God is not an existent among existents" and "God is not an object." And he would certainly deny that God is something in the world accessible by empirical investigation or inference from this. Arguably, therefore, Phillips's attack on natural theology, while possibly undermining some kinds of natural theology, does not undermine that of Aquinas since it does not engage with it.[33]

At this point, though, we are still left with questions 3 and 4 above. Does someone embarking on an essay in natural theology not display unseemly pride before God, whose word is Truth? And is natural theology not condemned by the Bible?

Insofar as the first question here is implying that one should not prefer human reasoning to what God has revealed, Aquinas would obviously approve of it. He takes God to be Truth itself, and he thinks that one would be wrong to deny what he takes to be divine revelation (the articles of faith). But he does not, therefore, jump to the conclusion that reason can lead us nowhere when it comes to God. And he is surely right to do so since "We should believe what God has revealed" does not entail "We should believe only what God has revealed" or "It is an offense against God to argue about the existence of God without relying on revelation."

When it comes to the Bible and natural theology, I take James Barr (1924–2006) to have well demolished the claim that the Bible can be cited as condemning natural theology in some wholesale way. He does so in his book *Biblical Faith and Natural Theology.*[34] As Barr well argues, though the Bible does not contain anything that reads like a sustained essay in natural theology, it seems to leave plenty of room for there being a knowledge of God apart from Christian revelation.[35]

Take, for example, Acts 17. Here we are told that St. Paul spoke at the Areopagus in Athens. He praises the Athenians for being "extremely religious," and he notes their altar inscribed "To an Unknown God." He goes on to say "What therefore you worship as unknown, this I proclaim to you."[36] So Acts 17 clearly has Paul, in a thoroughly Gentile context, appealing to some knowledge of or belief in God not derived from Christian revelation. All human beings, says Paul, come from God, *as even Athenian poets have said.*[37] The most natural reading of Acts 17 is to see it as attempting to place specifically Christian belief in the context of a universal knowledge of God, incomplete as it might be, independent of Christian or Jewish revelation. As Barr observes, "Acts 17 cannot be fully expounded without opening the gate to some sort of natural theology."[38]

Again, consider the first chapter of St. Paul's Letter to the Romans. Defenders of the notion that belief in the existence of God might not be something that has to rely only on revelation have long appealed to this text. Hence, for example, the First Vatican Council teaches that "God, the beginning and end of all things, can be known, from created things, by the light of natural human reason." Having said this, Vatican I goes on immediately to cite

Romans 1:20: "Ever since the creation of the world his eternal power and divine nature, invisible though they are, have been understood and seen through the things he has made."[39]

Paul's argument in Romans 1 (and it clearly is an *argument*) can be represented thus:

1. God's wrath is revealed against all who are ungodly and wicked (vs. 18).
2. These people know something about God since his power and nature have been understood and seen through what he has made (vss. 19–20).
3. These people are, therefore, without excuse for engaging in idolatry and making images of God in the form of people and animals (vss. 19–23).
4. So, as punishment, God "gave them up" to "impurity" and "degrading passions" (vss. 24–27).
5. And, for the same reason, God "gave them up" to all sorts of wrongdoing (vss. 28–32).

Paul seems to suppose that there is some knowledge of God apart from Christian or Jewish revelation. As Barr observes, Romans 1 appears "to imply that there is something 'known of God,' which is accessible to all human beings through their being human."[40] And, as Barr goes on to note, it is not astonishing that St. Paul should think along these lines since he had precedent for doing so in both the Old Testament and the writings of Hellenistic Judaism. In the Old Testament, we might, for example, note Psalm 104, which points to the world as evidence for and as manifestation of God's generosity. We might also note Psalm 19, with its insistence that "the heavens are telling the glory of God and the firmament proclaims his handiwork."[41] When it comes to Hellenistic Judaism, the book of Wisdom comes especially to mind. As Paul seems to do in Romans 1, Wisdom declares that there is a knowledge of God on which people have culpably failed to act, a failure leading to vices of all kinds.[42]

In short, the Bible does not exclude, and even seems to encourage, the belief that God can somehow be known by human reason. If to sympathize with the claim that natural theology is at least worth taking a look at is to suppose that there might be something in the idea that God is knowable through one's perception of the world, and to think that this knowledge might have been available or accessible to people regardless of Christian revelation, then the Bible contains natural theology. So, if it is said that God is beyond reason because of what the Bible asserts, the claim should be rejected. Or, so one might more provocatively say: "If you thoroughly reject natural theology, and if natural theology underlies the Bible in any significant degree, then you must judge that the Bible is inadequate as a theological guide."[43]

2.3.2 "God Exists" as Self-Evident

What now of Aquinas's arguments to the effect that "God exists" is not self-evident but needs to be made evident by causal reasoning? As I have shown, a major refrain running through them is that we do not know what God is, but I shall leave that refrain aside for the moment since it is something that Aquinas develops in some detail later in the SCG than SCG 1,10. I should, though, say something about his first and second argument to the effect that "God exists" is not self-evident to us at present (*per se notum quoad nos*). That is because these arguments seem to be rejecting what many have taken to be true—that there is a valid "ontological argument" for the truth of "God exists."

By "ontological argument" I mean an argument that purports to prove that God exists because of what the word "God" means. Many such arguments have been provided over the centuries.[44] I think it fair to say, however, that, with one notable exception, most distinguished contemporary philosophers find arguments for "God exists" based on what "God" means to be unsound.[45] I also think it fair to say that those who are skeptical when it comes to ontological arguments for belief in God predominantly tend to be so because, to put it bluntly, they think that one cannot define something into existence. From "A wizard, by dictionary definition, is a being with properties X, Y, and Z" it surely does not follow that there are any wizards. So, why should it follow from "God is, by definition, X, Y, and Z" that God exists? As I have noted, Aquinas thinks that to suppose that it does so is wrong. He holds that a bare understanding of the meaning of the word "God" cannot entail that there is anything in reality to correspond to it.

I would suggest that Aquinas is right here. We should distinguish between the "is" in dictionary definitions (as in "A wizard is someone who casts spells") and the "is" we have in mind when saying that something actually exists (as in "There is such a continent as Asia"). If we knew that God exists, and if we knew that God's nature is to exist as something that could not fail to exist, then we would, as Aquinas himself agrees, presumably know that there is no question of God not existing. The question, however, is "Do we know that God exists and do we know that God's nature is to exist as something that could not fail to exist"? In his *Proslogion*, St. Anselm of Canterbury famously holds that it is absurd to say that God, if taken to be "something than which nothing greater can be conceived" can be thought to be nothing but an idea in our heads and not something "out there," as it were. And his arguments for this conclusion are nothing if not sophisticated.[46] But they always seem to be articulating what belief in God entails rather than proving that God exists.[47] So, perhaps Aquinas is reasoning well when it comes to his SCG treatment of the thesis that we can know that God exists because of what "God" means.

Yet some philosophers would say that "God exists" is "self-evident" because we can actually perceive God directly as readily as we can perceive things around us, the existence of which Aquinas would take to be self-evident to us. If I bump into you, it would seem that I could be taken to know of your existence directly and noninferentially. So, what is to stop someone saying that God is something that we can perceive by experience, and that "God exists" is therefore a proposition that can be thought of as "self-evident"?

The thesis that "God exists" can be known on the basis of something like our perception of objects around us has been defended. Many people have claimed to have had a direct experience of God, and the claims of these people have been supported, in principle, at least, by some well-known philosophers. Take, for example, William Alston (1921–2009). He recognizes that some people say that they are *immediately* aware of God, and he argues that we should not assume that they are wrong to do so. Why not? One reason Alston gives is that "any supposition that one perceives something is *prima facie* justified." According to Alston, one is justified in supposing that one perceives something "unless there are strong reasons to the contrary." "Beliefs formed on the basis of experience," Alston suggests, "possess an initial credibility by virtue of their origin. They are innocent until proved guilty." He adds: "Unless we accord a *prima facie* credibility to experiential reports, we can have no sufficient reason to trust *any* experiential source of beliefs. This is the only alternative to a thoroughgoing scepticism about experience."[48]

In other words, Alston thinks that people like Aquinas would be wrong to discard the claim that "God exists" can be known to be true as self-evident because based on experience of God. And some other philosophers would agree with him on this, even if they do not target Aquinas by name, as, indeed, Alston himself does not.[49] Yet should we now conclude that, contrary to what Aquinas says in SCG 1,10 and 11, "God exists" can be known to be true directly and noninferentially on the basis of experience? I think that Aquinas would reply to Alston by arguing that, in the present life and apart from a miracle, there is no direct knowledge of God akin to what we have in the sensory perception of things in the world.

Aquinas never denies that there can be noninferential knowledge of this, that, or the other. In general, he thinks that, for example, I can be justified in thinking that there is a cat in front of me just because I seem to be seeing a cat in front of me. Aquinas also thinks that noninferential knowledge of God's existence is had by the blessed in heaven. The saints, he says, enjoy "the beatific vision," which he sharply distinguishes from what we have on the basis of a deductive argument.[50] Again, in his discussion of ecstasy (*raptus*) in *Summa Theologiae* 2a2ae,175, Aquinas, with reference to 2 Corinthians 12, accepts that, even before he died, St. Paul directly saw the essence of God. So it is not as though Aquinas denies that there can be a direct and noninferential knowledge of or contact with God. On the other hand, however, he thinks that such knowledge cannot come about just as living people employ their natural (albeit God-given) faculty of knowing. He thinks that grace has to be at work if someone directly and noninferentially enjoys anything that might be called "perception of God." And he does so because, as I will show, he thinks that human beings are essentially material individuals whose knowledge of things other than themselves typically arises because of the impact on them of material objects. In other words, Aquinas holds that, abstracting from miracles and considerations to do with life after death, our ability directly to know other things is confined to our knowledge of material things and does not extend to knowledge of God.

In response to this conclusion one might say that it stinks of what Alston calls "epistemic imperialism," which he defines as "subjecting the outputs of one belief-forming practice to the requirements of another."[51] Here I take Alston to be saying that one should not suppose that claims to be directly aware of God must be ruled out because they seem to be suspect by criteria commonly used to validate ordinary claims to have perceived something in the world. Yet, and especially because of what he says about St. Paul and ecstasy, I do not think that Aquinas would disagree with Alston on this point. On the other hand, Aquinas, and, I presume, Alston, would say that direct knowledge of God comparable to perception of things in the world is the exception rather than the rule, which is the thought that lies behind SCG 1,10 and 11. In these chapters Aquinas is concerned with what human beings can rise to as things in the world whose ability to know (where "know" means "know what X is essentially") generally depends on what they can figure out on the basis of sensory experience. He argues that God is not an object of sensory experience and, therefore, cannot be known as such. So, the most damning criticism of SCG 1,10 and 11 based on the claim that God is directly known by people in this life would have to establish that God is indeed something the essence of which all of us have the ability or potential to know or understand just by being human. At this point I leave it to you to consider if such a criticism can be defended, especially in the light of what Aquinas goes on to say in the SCG concerning the nature or essence of God. As I have said, Aquinas has no problem with the suggestion that we might know that something is there because we have encountered, perceived, or stumbled across it. On the other hand, he does have a problem with the suggestion that we can know that it is *God* that we have encountered or perceived or stumbled across in something like the way in which we might perceive a cat and know it to be a cat and not, say, a dog. If I know, even without inference, that there is a cat in front of me, then, thinks Aquinas, I must have already acquired some concept of what a cat is. Yet, Aquinas asks, to what prior understanding of God can we appeal when claiming, on the basis of "perception" or "experience," that God exists?

As you will now realize, in his SCG discussion of God, Aquinas does not take us to have a knowledge of what God is that entitles us to claim that we know that "God exists" is obviously true without argument. But what kind of argument for the truth of "God exists" does Aquinas have in mind as he writes SCG 1,10–12? This is the question he turns to in SCG 1,13.

3

Arguing for God's Existence (SCG 1,13)

AQUINAS BEGINS SCG 1,13 by writing: "We have now shown that the effort to demonstrate the existence of God is not a vain one. We shall therefore proceed to set forth the arguments by which philosophers and Catholic teachers have proved that God exists."[1] These arguments make up the contents of SCG 1,13, most of which is given over to a defense of thinking that Aquinas derives from Aristotle.[2] Aquinas and Aristotle are obviously not of one mind when it comes to the meaning of "God exists" since Aquinas, as a Christian, holds beliefs about God that Aristotle never did. Yet in SCG 1,13 Aquinas is obviously drawing on Aristotle's thinking, or on what he presumes this to be. So let me now explain how he does so.

3.1 Argument One

The first argument in SCG 1,13 is one that Aquinas takes himself to inherit from Aristotle's *Physics* VII.[3] It runs thus:

1. Everything that is moved is moved by another.[4]
2. Some things are obviously in motion (are moved) and are therefore moved by something else.
3. What moves something else is either moved or not moved.
4. If what moves something else is not moved, then there is an unmoved mover, which is what God is supposed to be.
5. If what moves something else is moved, it is moved by another mover.
6. There cannot be an infinite number of things moving other things while themselves being moved by other things.
7. So we must posit "some prime unmoved mover."

This argument appears to be formally valid. But Aquinas immediately goes on to note that two propositions in it themselves need to be proved, namely (1) and (6). Before proceeding to an account of what he says in this connection, however, I should comment on what Aquinas means by "motion" or "movement," for which his Latin word is *motus*.

I presume that most of us understand motion or movement chiefly to amount to local motion: the change that something undergoes as it changes place. So we would naturally say that cars move around when driven or that people move when they walk to work. But, of course, we also speak of being moved emotionally, which does not imply a reference to local motion. Also without thinking of local motion we can make sense of sentences like "Fred moved up in the company." So, even we have a sense or senses of "move" where local motion is not in question, and, I now need to note, *motus*, for Aquinas, though it does sometimes refer to local motion, basically means what we would call "change."

We speak of things changing their position. Yet we also speak of things changing in quality and quantity (as when John acquires a suntan or as when he puts on weight). So we can distinguish between change of place, change of quality, and change of quantity, all of which Aquinas would have taken to be instances of *motus*. We have *motus*, he thinks, as something is in process of changing from one place or state to another. Or, as he would have said, *motus* depends on something first being actually thus and so while able to become different, and the *motus* of something is the movement to the state arrived at. Aquinas analyzes *motus* in terms of what he calls "actuality" and "potentiality." He thinks, for example, that if I am on the way to acquiring a suntan, then (1) I must first be actually nonsuntanned, and (2) I must be able to (have the potentiality to) become suntanned. Aquinas thinks of my ending up suntanned as a matter of my having arrived by a process of change from one state to a different one, and it is change in this sense that he is concerned with in SCG 1,13. He thinks of it as a process that some particular existing thing actually undergoes. If you fall in love with me, then I might be said to have become loved by you, and one might be tempted to think of this as a "real change" in me. But, of course, it is not. I can become loved by you without being modified in any respect and without even knowing about you. If anything is really changed as I become loved by you, it is you, and it is only "real change" in something that Aquinas is concerned with as he talks about *motus*, which he regards as a genuine modification that something undergoes, a genuine movement (i.e., process of change) in something.[5]

In his first SCG 1,13 argument, therefore, Aquinas, taking motion as obviously there to be observed in the world, thinks that it is something that has to be accounted for. He also thinks that it cannot be accounted for in terms of an endless series of movers.[6]

You may think that X's motion is to be entirely attributed to X, that motion in something need not be motion due to something other than X. But proposition (1) in the above argument is stating that this is not so. As I have noted, however, Aquinas clearly thinks that the proposition "Everything moved is moved by another" needs defense, and he seeks to defend it by means of three arguments. You may immediately think that no defense is required here, for, you might say, if something is moved then it has to be moved by something else. "Moved" looks like a verb in the present passive form, unlike the intransitive "moves." Is it not, therefore, obvious that if something is *moved* it is moved by something *else*? But this is not really obvious at all. I will be moved by myself if I punch myself in the face or feed myself. So it is not clear that if something is moved it is moved by something else, as Aquinas is aware.[7]

Let me, therefore, now report on his SCG arguments in defense of (1).

3.1.1 "Everything That Is Moved Is Moved by Another"

The first runs thus:

1. Something that moves itself has "within itself the principle of its own motion."[8] If it does not have the principle, or origin, of its own motion in itself, it is moved by something else.
2. Something moved by itself must also be "primarily moved" by itself. "It must be moved by reason of itself, and not by reason of a part of itself" since, if moved by a part of itself, "a whole would not be moved by itself, but a part, and one part would be moved by another."[9]
3. Something moved by itself must also be divisible and have parts since "whatever is moved is divisible."[10]
4. Nothing primarily moved is moved because of a part of itself moving while another part of itself is "at rest." But "nothing that is at rest because something else is at rest is moved by itself" since "that being whose rest follows upon the rest of another must have its motion follow upon the motion of another" and is, therefore, not moved by itself.[11]

Aquinas immediately notes a possible objection to this argument. For might one not say that when something moves itself no part of it can be at rest? Yet, argues Aquinas, the force of the argument he is now defending lies in the fact that if something moves itself *primarily*, then there is no "other" involved, and certainly no moving part of itself involved, while *the moving of divisible things depends on their parts*. We do not, says Aquinas, have to presume in some "absolute" sense that "a part of a being moving itself is at rest." But we should assume that *if the part were at rest, the whole would be at rest.*[12] Evidently, Aquinas is here thinking that if something can be truly said to be thus and so by virtue of a part of it, then the thing as a whole, considered as an individual, can be said to be thus and so. He is thinking, for example, that if I have no hairs on my chest but a lot of hairs on my head and legs, I can be said to be hairy.

Aquinas's second line of thought in defense of proposition (1), a line of thought that he calls "inductive," amounts to a series of reinterpretations of counter examples that an objector might present as evidence against (1).[13] He observes:

1. Something moved whose movement does not follow from what it is essentially or by nature is not moved by itself but by another.
2. What is moved by violence is not moved by itself.
3. What is moved by its nature, as animals, for example, are, is not moved by itself since all the movement of such things depends on a nature that they have but have not manufactured for themselves.
4. Heavy and light bodies move because of generating causes and causes removing impediments to them moving.[14]

The next argument in defense of (1) draws on the notions of actuality and potentiality. Perhaps it would be best for me to quote the argument in full rather than lay it out in stages. The argument reads:

> The same thing cannot be at once in act and in potency with respect to the same thing. But everything that is moved is, as such, in potency. For motion is *the act of something that is in potency inasmuch as it is in potency.* That which moves, however, is as such in act, for nothing acts except according as it is in act. Therefore, with respect to the same motion, nothing is both mover and moved. Thus, nothing moves itself.[15]

The idea here is that if something is moving so as to become F, it cannot already be F. It is actually not F and is only able to become F. Aquinas is also saying that if something comes to be F, this can only be by virtue of something able to bring this about. It has been claimed that Aquinas is here falsely saying that what is not F can only be made to be F by something that is actually F. Hence, for example, Anthony Kenny, as if contradicting Aquinas, observes that "a kingmaker need not himself be king, and it is not dead men who commit murders."[16] Aquinas, however, is not denying any of this.

His reasoning seems to be (1) that what only potentially exists does not actually exist and cannot account for any actualizing of potentiality, and (2) the nonexisting F-ness of something, which, as nonexisting, does not exist in the thing, cannot be invoked to account for the thing's coming to be F. Aquinas means that what a thing does not have is not something that can account for change that it undergoes and that, in this sense, nothing moves itself. In some places, Aquinas distinguishes between "univocal" and "equivocal" causes, between causes that are just like their effects and causes that produce effects without resembling them exactly.[17] When thinking of efficient or agent causality, Aquinas's view is that, since nothing can give what it does not have, there has to be a sense in which the effects of causes somehow show them forth or, if you like, resemble them. He does not, however, mechanically assume that cause X of effect Y looks like Y or is exactly like what Y is. If he assumed this, he would have to assume, as he does not, that God looks like grass because God accounts for the existence of grass. As John Wippel explains, Aquinas does not mean to suggest that something "must be or have formally that which it communicates to something else through motion. It must either be or have such formally, or else produce the characteristic virtually; this is to say, it must have the power to produce its effect."[18] So, the third SCG 1,13 argument has to be read as concluding that nothing moves itself since it does not have within itself the wherewithal to bring about in itself what it does not have to start with.

So now to proposition (6) in the first SCG 1,13 argument: "There cannot be an infinite number of things moving other things while themselves being moved by other things." Why does Aquinas take this claim to be true?

3.1.2 "There Is No Procession to Infinity among Movers and Things Moved"

In SCG 1,13 Aquinas is arguing that there is a first unmoved mover. He claims that a series of things moved by others must terminate in what is not moved by anything else. But why should he think this? After all, we can keep counting without end. There is, presumably, no number beyond which there is no other number. So why should there be any end when it comes to movers moving? In defense of proposition (6), however, Aquinas offers three arguments.

The first is this:

1. Assuming that what is moved is material (and, therefore, divisible into parts), an infinite series of movers and things moved will be bodily (material).

2. Every body that moves something moved is itself moved while moving it.

3. So an infinite series of movers and things moved will itself have to be moved, considered as a whole, which means that all of the members of the series, considered as a whole, are moved if any of them are moved.

4. If one of the members is finite, however, it is moved in a finite time, which means that all of the infinite series of movers and things moved are moved in a finite time, which is impossible.

5. "It is, therefore, impossible that among movers and things moved one can proceed to infinity."[19]

The second is this:

1. In "an ordered" series of movers and things moved, if the first mover is "removed or ceases to move" no other mover will move or be moved.

2. If movers and things moved went on infinitely, there would be no first mover and none of the others would be able to be moved and there would be nothing moved.

It is important to note that when he speaks of a series of movers and things moved that is "ordered" (*ordinatus*) Aquinas is not thinking of just any collection of movers and things moved. He is not, for example, thinking of a series of things moving and moved going back into the past infinitely: a series such as we would have if, say, I came to be because of movements of my parents, who came to be because of movements of their parents, who came to be because of movements of their parents, and so on without beginning. In SCG 2,35–38, Aquinas holds that one cannot demonstrate the impossibility of such a chronologically backwardly running series. He does the same in *On the Eternity of the World* (*De Aeternitate Mundi*), where he denies that it can be philosophically proved that the world had a beginning.[20]

So the above argument is not asserting that if X is moved by Y, and if Y is moved by Z, there has to be a temporally first mover accounting for this. Rather, Aquinas is saying that if movers X, Y, and Z are all equally dependent for their movement on something distinct from them as each of them moves, then there has to be a mover not dependent in the same way, a mover that accounts for the movement of X, Y, and Z considered as a unity.

Suppose that I kick a ball that hits another ball and pushes it along. Also suppose that the second ball hits another ball and moves that along, and so on, for as many balls as you care to think about. Clearly, I am not directly moving all the balls in the series. In this sense, the movement of all of them need not depend on me. Indeed, I could drop dead having kicked the first ball.

Now, however, consider a different scenario. I hold in the palm of my hand a book, on which rests another book, on which rests another and another. I then move my hand from left to right and back again. In this scenario, I am responsible for the movement of each of the books as it occurs, and it will stop occurring if I stop moving my hand on which the books rest. In this scenario, each book supporting the one above it is, so to speak, only an instrument of me. Remove me, and all the books crash to the ground since all of them depend on me moving my hand while they rest on it and move in space.

When he speaks of an ordered series, Aquinas is thinking of a series of movers like that in the hand/book scenario, not a series like the kicking of the balls one. His argument is that if such a series proceeded to infinity it would impossibly consist only of instrumental movers. Or, as Aquinas himself says: "If there are movers and things moved following an order to infinity, there will be no first mover, but all would be as intermediate movers."[21] As Aquinas goes on to observe, the same point can be made in reverse, starting with a first mover instead of a series of things moved by it. We read: "That which moves as an instrumental cause cannot move unless there be a principal moving cause. But, if we proceed to infinity among movers and things moved, all movers will be as instrumental causes, because they will be moved movers and there will be nothing as a principal mover."[22]

3.2 *Argument Two*

Aquinas's second SCG 1,13 argument for "God exists" is another argument from motion inspired by what he takes Aristotle to maintain. Here is how it goes:

1. If "Every mover is moved" is a true proposition, then it is true "either by itself or by accident."
2. If "by accident," then the proposition is not necessarily true, and it might be true that no mover is moved.[23]
3. Someone might argue that if a mover is not moved, it does not move, thereby concluding that it is possible that nothing is moved since if nothing moves, nothing is moved.
4. But this implies what Aristotle takes to be impossible: that there is no motion at any time.
5. Therefore, if "Every mover is moved" is true, it is not so "by accident" since a proposition that is false and impossible does not follow from a proposition that is possibly true but actually false.[24]

I should note that Aquinas immediately defends the same conclusion as the above argument arrives at in a different way. Here is his alternative argument:

1. Something can have two accidental features without having them of necessity.[25]
2. If something happens to be accidentally (*per accidens*) both a mover and a thing moved, there could probably be an unmoved mover (just as there might probably be something lacking one of any two accidental features).[26]
3. So, if being a mover and being moved is what something is only accidentally, and if something else can be moved without it being a mover, it is probable that there is a mover that is not moved.

This argument is offered by Aquinas not as a demonstration but only as providing some support for the conclusion that "Every mover is accidentally moved by another" is false. The argument is suggesting that if "being a mover" and "being moved" do not both have to be predicated of (ascribed to) something of necessity, then there could be a mover that is unmoved.

Yet Aquinas also thinks that it is not necessarily true (or in his language, true *per se*) that every mover is moved by another, and here is his argument for this conclusion.

1. If "Every mover is moved by another" is necessarily true, the mover must be moved either by "the same kind of motion" as that by which it moves, or "by another."[27]
2. If every mover is moved by the same kind of motion, then, for example, a "cause of alteration must itself be altered" or "a healing cause must itself be healed" or "a teacher must be taught" with respect to the same knowledge.
3. But this is impossible. If it were true, "the same thing would be possessed and not possessed by the same being."
4. If every mover is moved by a different kind of motion, since the kinds of motion are finite in number "it will follow that we cannot proceed to infinity" and there will have to be a first mover that is not moved by another.[28]

But need a first mover that is not moved by something else be absolutely unmoved? Aquinas raises this question and says that the answer to it is no. For something might be moved by itself (a point he has already made in SCG 1,13). If it is, though, Aquinas adds, the thing in question cannot be moved entirely by itself as a whole; it would have to be moved by a part or parts of itself, meaning that a first mover must ultimately be moved by what is absolutely unmoved if there cannot be an infinite regress in things moving and being moved. In this sense, there has to be an unmoved source of movement even when it comes to things, such as people, that move themselves. Indeed, there has to be such a source whether or not the things in question come to be and pass away over time considered as lacking beginning or end. It is "necessary either to arrive immediately at an unmoved separate first mover, or to arrive at a self-moved mover from whom, in turn, an unmoved separate first mover is reached."[29]

3.3 Three More Arguments

As I have said, arguments concerning motion form the bulk of SCG 1,13. Before he concludes this chapter, however, Aquinas adds three more arguments, though he presents them very briefly and with nothing like the detail he engages in when it comes to the arguments I have noted above. Here are the arguments.

3.3.1 The First Argument

The first of the three final arguments is this:

1. "In all ordered efficient causes, the first is the cause of the intermediate cause, whether one or many, and this is the cause of the last cause."
2. "When you suppress a cause, you suppress its effect."
3. "If you suppress the first cause, the intermediate cause cannot be a cause," and "if there were an infinite regress among efficient causes, no cause would be first" and "all the other causes which are intermediate, will be suppressed."
4. So we have to suppose "that there exists a first efficient cause" (i.e., God).

You should notice that Aquinas is here assuming that there are efficient or agent causes, and that some of them are ordered to their effects, not in a chronological or linear way but in the hierarchical way exemplified by my example of moving books resting on my hand. So Aquinas is not now arguing that God exists since we can posit a past series of causes going backward in time to some temporally first efficient cause. If we could posit such a series of causes, then, Aquinas thinks, we would have a quick and powerful argument for the existence of God along the lines "Whatever has a beginning of existence must have a cause; the world had a beginning; so there must have been a cause for the origin of the world."[30] But that is not the present argument, which is claiming that there cannot be an infinite regression in a hierarchically ordered series of efficient causes.

3.3.2 The Second Argument

The second of the three final arguments in SCG 1,13 goes like this:

1. There are degrees of truth in things since some things are more true (and therefore more in being) than others.
2. The existence of such degrees of truth in things implies that there is something supremely true and most in being.

3.3.3 The Third Argument

The final argument in SCG 1,13 runs as follows:

1. "Contrary or discordant things cannot, always or for the most part, be parts of one order except under someone's government, which enables all and each to tend to a definite end."[31]
2. In the world we find that "things of diverse natures come together under one order, and this not rarely or by chance, but always or for the most part."[32]
3. There is therefore some being by whose providence the world is governed.

As you will see by checking the text of SCG 1,13, the argument I have just represented really does say nothing more than I say that it does. So we are not dealing here with a very developed line of thinking. All Aquinas appears to be saying is that, though the world contains different kinds of things, there is an interaction between them that allows us to think of the world as a system implying an orderer, given that regular interaction among things forming a system needs to be accounted for in terms of intelligence.

3.4 What Has Aquinas Achieved in the Natural Theology Offered in SCG 1,13?

3.4.1 Some Initial Problems

Aquinas evidently thinks that his arguments for "God exists" in SCG 1,13 are good demonstrative ones. But has he succeeded in doing this? My view is that this is not an easy question to answer since some of the arguments contain stages that are difficult to understand.

Consider the very last argument. What is Aquinas thinking of when he says what I report as (1) in it? Perhaps he means that parts of machines would not work together were they not set up and maintained by a mechanic of some kind. But it is not obvious that he means this since he does not provide examples to back up what he says in (1). Nor does he give examples to illustrate what he says in (2). Perhaps (2) is just drawing attention to the fact that things that interact with each other in the world are law-governed in some way. But then one wonders why any law-governed process should be thought to imply the existence of intelligent agency. If Aquinas thinks that it does, he does not explain why.

Again, consider the argument concerning degrees of truth. What does Aquinas mean when saying that one thing can be more true than another? In this connection he refers to Aristotle's *Metaphysics* IV, but he does not explain or justify what he takes Aristotle exactly to be driving at. This leaves us somewhat in the dark when it comes to understanding what Aquinas takes himself to be saying in the argument from degrees of truth.[33]

Yet again, what kinds of motion does Aquinas have in mind in the SCG 1,13 arguments based on motion? As I have noted, Aquinas has a general view of *motus* as being a progression from potentiality to actuality, and he sometimes explicitly draws on this general view in SCG 1,13. Sometimes, however, he seems to be focusing only on local motion and taking himself to be able to draw a significant theological conclusion simply from it. So does he think that local motion is especially able to lead us to the conclusion that God exists? If he does, he does not say so, which leaves me, at any rate, wondering how the SCG 1,13 arguments based on motion hang together in Aquinas's mind.

You may think that the arguments should just be considered and evaluated individually. Still, I suspect that Aquinas is of the view that there is something binding them together, and I do not see what he takes this to be unless it is the idea that motion always involves a progression from potentiality to actuality. Perhaps that, indeed, is what is running through all the arguments from motion in SCG 1,13. But then why do we have so many different arguments from motion in SCG 1,13?

It could be that Aquinas wants to pay attention to distinct arguments that he believes to be offered by Aristotle, considered as an especially famous philosopher. Even if that is so, however, the SCG arguments from motion amount to a difficult set of texts to interpret and evaluate considered as a whole, and the difficulty is compounded if one bears in mind that, as I have noted, what Aristotle meant by the word "God" seems to be significantly different from what Aquinas means by "God." I am sure that Aquinas was himself aware of this fact and that he is interested in Aristotle on God only because he thinks that there is some overlap between what he thinks about God and what he took Aristotle to think about what he refers to as God.[34] Yet there is still a general puzzle here, and in SCG 1,13 Aquinas does not go out of his way to explain how it is to be dealt with, which leads us to another question when it comes to understanding the arguments for God in SCG 1,13: why does Aquinas think that this chapter's largely Aristotelian-inspired arguments should be thought to show that it is God that exists?

This question arises because when he goes on to talk about God later in the SCG, and when he talks about God in other works, Aquinas obviously takes God to be much more than what he claims God to be in the arguments of SCG 1,13. Aquinas believes that God is omnipotent and omniscient, but neither omnipotence nor omniscience feature explicitly in SCG 1,13. Again, Aquinas thinks of God as the creator of all things while denying that for God to create something is for God to bring about a change in it. He thinks that for God to make something to be, to create it, is not to modify it since it does not exist unless God makes it to be. Yet the notion of existing by virtue of God does not explicitly feature in SCG 1,13's arguments for "God exists." So why does Aquinas think that they successfully argue that God exists? On the basis of what look like teeth marks, I might reasonably conclude that there is a rodent loose in my home; but I should not conclude there is a mouse around, as opposed, say, to a squirrel or a guinea pig. So what leads Aquinas to identify what he takes himself to be arguing to exist in SCG 1,13 with God? And is he entitled to do so?

When it comes to the second question here, my answer is yes because of what I take to be the correct answer to the first question. If Aquinas thought that in SCG 1,13 he had said all that can be said about God on the basis of reason, he would have stopped writing the SCG having completed 1,13, just as he would have stopped writing his *Summa Theologiae* having written *Summa Theologiae* 1a,2, which contains arguments for God's existence, some of which seem at least superficially similar to what we find in SCG 1,13.

In SCG 1,13 Aquinas purports to have shown that God exists since: (1) there is an unmoved and immovable mover that is not composed of bodily parts; (2) there is an uncaused efficient or agent cause; (3) there is something supremely true and most in being; and (4) something governs the world as a whole. In *Summa Theologiae* 1a,2,3, Aquinas takes himself to have shown that God exists since he takes himself to have shown (1) that there is some "first cause of change not itself changed by anything," (2) that there is a first efficient cause, (3) that there is something intrinsically necessary that accounts for there being anything contingent and anything necessary that is created,[35] (4) that there is something that "causes in all other things their being, their goodness, and whatever other perfection they have," and (5) that there is something "with intelligence who directs all natural things to ends."[36] Following up on SCG 1,13 and *Summa Theologiae* 1a,2, however, Aquinas says a great deal more about God than he does in these texts. The reason why he is happy with them as they stand, considered as containing arguments for the existence of God, is that he is working with certain nominal definitions of "God" that he assumes would be accepted by orthodox Christians.

Aquinas regularly distinguishes between nominal definitions and real ones. He thinks of a nominal definition as capturing what something might be thought to be, whether it exists or not, without reporting all that it is essentially should it happen to exist. Correspondingly, he thinks of a real definition as what we end up with as we examine something that does exist and arrive at a serious grasp of what it is, what makes it tick, how it differs from other existing things, what its origins are, and so on. So Aquinas would say that, for example, I can happily define "cat" nominally as "something with ears and whiskers," and that I can nominally define "wizard" as "someone able to cast spells," even if there are no wizards.[37] He would also say that a real definition of something is what we might, hopefully, end up with having carefully examined the thing in question, this, for Aquinas, having to be something spatio-temporal. As I have noted, however, Aquinas denies that one can construct a demonstration *propter quid* for the truth of "God exists" since he thinks that we cannot know what God is. So the arguments for "God exists" in SCG 1,13 are working from nominal definitions of "God." But are they working from definitions of "God" that allow Aquinas to conclude that he has argued well for "God exists"?

I think that they are since Aquinas has reason for supposing that he and his thirteenth-century readers, not to mention his twenty-first-century readers, could hardly deny that when Christians, Jews, and Muslims speak of God they *at least* mean what Aquinas refers to as God in SCG 1,13. What Christian, Jew, or Muslim would deny that, for example, God accounts for there being movement in the world? Again, do not Christianity, Judaism, and Islam clearly proclaim that God is one who acts providentially in the universe and that God is the first cause lying behind all other causes? Not all Christians, Jews, and Muslims have taken God to be "immovable," as Aquinas puts it. Many people who claim to believe in God would say that God undergoes change. On the other hand, however, there is a long theological tradition according to which God is wholly immutable. That God is this is taught, for example, by the Fourth Council of Constantinople (869–870), the Fourth Lateran Council (1215), and the First Vatican Council (1869–1870). In short, Aquinas's nominal definitions of God in SCG 1,13 make sense in the light of some long-standing beliefs concerning God. It might be said that the nominal definitions now in question can be faulted since God is more than they take God to be and since Aquinas cannot claim to have demonstrated that God exists unless he has successfully shown that God is all that those who believe in him take him to be. But that view erroneously supposes that one cannot demonstrate that X exists unless one has demonstrated that X is all that it actually is. One might, for example, demonstrate that speech heard on a radio channel derives from a human being while also being unable to demonstrate that it derives from someone who is right-handed, an orphan, or a lover of ferrets. That Aquinas recognizes this fact is shown by the way in which he follows up on SCG 1,13 by arguing for the truth of various statements about God that he does not seek to demonstrate in that chapter.

3.4.2 Aquinas on Motion in SCG 1,13

What, though, of the arguments concerning God and motion in SCG 1,13? Are these open to challenge? It has been argued that they are. I cannot here even hope to document and comment on all the criticisms that have been leveled against them, but here are some of the major ones to be found in recent philosophical literature:

1. Aquinas assumes that something in motion has to be moved. But there is no problem in assuming that something in motion is *just moving* with nothing accounting for its movement.[38]
2. In SCG 1,13 Aquinas writes in ignorance of Newton's first law of motion, according to which a body will continue to move in a straight line unless interfered with.[39]
3. We have no good reason to suppose that there cannot be an endless or infinite series of things moving and being moved. Why suppose that there *has to be* an absolutely first mover in a series of things moving and being moved?[40]
4. "If something can be made F by an agent which is merely potentially F, there seems no reason why something should not actualize its own potentiality to F-ness."[41]
5. Even if "Whatever is moved is moved by something else" is a true proposition, it does not follow that God exists since there might be many unmoved movers. Yet those who believe in God insist that there is but one God.

How effective are these objections when it comes to what Aquinas argues in SCG 1,13? Let me say something about each of them in order.

1. The first objection uncritically accepts that the movement of a thing should be taken as a brute fact not calling for explanation. But why should we take the movement of something as brute in this sense? After all, we do not generally presume that instances of movement are self-explicable. We assume, for example, that if my cat is vomiting, then something is causing him to do so. We make assumptions like this continually, and it would be hard to understand someone who did not, someone who, confronted by movement, simply said "Well, there it is; nothing more to be said." You may think that our demand for causal explanations of motion simply reflects an unreasoned prejudice on our part. But if "reasonable" means anything, then it surely describes the raising of causal questions concerning motion. Can we, for example, make sense of someone asserting that airplanes fly just because they do, or that dogs bark just because they do, or that grass grows just because it does? In any case, Aquinas does offer a reason for supposing that what he calls movement or real change has to be something that requires explanation in terms of something other than a thing moved or in motion. This lies in his claim that something undergoing change is acquiring what it does not actually have since change or motion is the movement from being potentially F to becoming actually F. Aquinas thinks that nothing can give itself what it does not have, that the movement of X from being potentially F to becoming actually F is not explicable in terms of X in its state of being potentially F. Aquinas thinks this because he takes it that some new state of X comes about as X proceeds from being actually G to becoming actually F, and he is surely right to think this. In that case, however, what X is while being actually G cannot account for X coming to be actually F. There is a difference coming about here that is just not explicable by merely reporting what is there before the difference comes about. The F-ness of X when acquired by X does not exist when X is actually G and only potentially F. So why should we not ask "How come the existence of the F-ness of X?" If "X is F" were true of logical necessity, this question, which I take to be a causal one, would not arise, any more than it does when it comes to propositions like "All triangles have three sides." But if X's F-ness does not have to exist as a matter of logical truth, then it might never have existed, which seems to raise the question "What accounts for it existing?" This question can hardly be adequately answered by describing X in its non-F state and leaving the matter there. If nothing else, the existence of X's F-ness at one time raises the question "Why does it exist at that time and not at another time?"

2. Newton's first law of motion does seem to tell against what Aquinas argues in SCG 1,13. That is because it conjures up the picture of there being

something unmoved that goes through local motion without acceleration, reduction of speed, or change of direction, something moving along in an idealized frictionless plane, as it were. Aquinas seems to hold that if X moves "primarily" from position A to position B, it must be moved by something else. Newton's first law of motion, however, appears, while invoking the notion of inertia, to countenance exceptions to this rule. Recognizing this fact, some philosophers have suggested that we should take SCG 1,13 as defeated by Newton when it comes to local motion but should note that it can be defended with respect to *motus* considered only as change of quantity and quality.[42] Yet, perhaps, this concession is premature. For one thing, Aquinas did not believe that everything undergoing motion has to be moved by something as it undergoes its motion. As John Wippel notes, Aquinas's account of motion "does not imply that a distinct moving cause must be constantly conjoined with a body which it moves naturally."[43] Again, even Newton never believed that something beginning to move locally lacks a cause of its moving. Nor did he think that variations in a thing's local motion lack a cause, or that there is no cause for there being local motion at all. He argued that, hypothetically speaking, something could remain in a state of unvarying motion without any physical object causing it to do so. But he did not cite examples of things remaining in such a state, which is unsurprising since things undergoing local motion do not actually exist as unaffected by other things in the world. As Edward Feser observes: "At every moment in which an object is moving through space, and not merely at its initial acquisition of momentum, its motion is being affected in a way that requires explanation in terms of something outside it. But in that case, even with respect to the explanation of local motion, the principle of inertia seems practically moot."[44] Along with Feser, I would add that Newtonian inertial motion is commonly taken to be a "state" as opposed to a process, which raises the question "Is it an example of what Aquinas would have taken to be *motus*?" When he talks about motion in SCG 1,13, Aquinas is focusing on genuine alteration of some kind, not an abiding "state," which, I suspect, he would have taken to be a case of *stasis* or lack of motion. On the other hand, Newton's uniform rectilinear motion seems to be a constant state rather than an instance of change.

3. We would, of course, beg the question if we argued that there is a first unmoved mover since there is a series of secondary movers that can be thought of as its agents. That is because any "first" and "secondary" distinction seems to presume that there is a first to be distinguished from a secondary. But there is nothing wrong in arguing that, given a series of secondary (as opposed to unmoved) movers, that series has to depend on

what is not secondary and is unmoved insofar as it accounts for the move-ment of the movers that it moves. Think again about the books held up by my hand. All of them fall to the ground if I take my hand away from them. But book A can be thought of as supported by book B, and book C by book D, and so on. Here we have a series of causes of the kind that Aquinas would have described as *per se*, a series in which something being such and such owes this not just to some temporal predecessor in a causal chain but to something whose causal power runs through the chain in such a way as to make the members of the chain do what they do or be what they are. And it seems hard to see how such a chain can exist if there is not something outside it, if there is no cause that is not part of the chain considered as containing members that equally depend on a cause. A cause whose cau-sality runs through its effects, as I am when holding books in the palm of my hand and moving them from left to right and back, does not, of course, have to be immutable. After all, I am not immutable. But that does not mean that we should doubt that in any causal series *per se*, there has to be a first cause.

4. The fourth of the above arguments against Aquinas is simply not en-gaging with what he says. As I have noted, it is not Aquinas's view that, for example, only what is red can bring it about that something is red. What he thinks is that only something with the ability to bring it about that something is red can account for something becoming red.

5. The virtue of the fifth of the above arguments lies in the fact that in SCG 1,13 Aquinas does not offer a demonstration to the effect that there is but one unmoved mover. Yet that virtue also undermines the argument as an objection to SCG 1,13 since it amounts only to an account of what Aquinas does not argue in that text, and an account of what Aquinas does not argue can hardly be held to be a refutation of him. I mean that if, for example, I argue that my cat is hungry, but do not argue that it is black and white in color, my argument for my cat being hungry is not to be impugned with ref-erence to my not arguing that it is black and white. By the same token, if Aquinas argues for there being an unmoved mover, but does not explain why there is only one such mover, he is not to be impugned for not arguing that there is only one unmoved mover since he is not concerned to argue for this conclusion. As I will show, however, Aquinas proceeds in the SCG to single out the question of God being one (i.e., nonmultipliable) so as to deal with it directly. The fact that he does not do this in SCG 1,13 is nothing against him even though it might provoke impatience in a person who wants Aquinas to start talking about the oneness of God before he is ready to do so.

There is doubtless a great deal more to be said about the arguments of SCG 1,13. But I hope that I have now said enough about them to get you thinking for yourself concerning them. Before I move on to other matters, however, I would like to make two points to round off this chapter. The first concerns Aquinas's conception of efficient causation in general. The second concerns the extent to which SCG 1,13 can be read as concerned not just with motion but with the topics of existence and nonexistence.

3.4.3   Aquinas on Efficient Causation

As I have explained, in SCG 1,13 Aquinas moves to his various conclusions with an eye on what he would have called "efficient" or "agent" causation. Yet I should note that what Aquinas means by "efficient" or "agent" cause is not what some philosophers mean by "cause." More precisely, there have been influential accounts of causality that are at odds with what Aquinas has in mind when talking about efficient or agent causes. To be even more precise, there is David Hume's theory of causation.

Hume argues that causal statements like "X was caused to move by B" are not necessarily true in the way that, say, "Any bachelor is unmarried" is necessarily true. We assume, says Hume, that such and such was the cause of whatever because we are accustomed to associate events of type A with events of type B. But, he thinks, a cause and its effect are distinct, and we can conceive of there being what we are pleased to call an effect without it having any cause at all.[45] According to Hume, therefore, we can even conceive of something beginning to exist without a cause, implying that from what we take to be an effect we cannot demonstrate that it has a cause (an efficient cause, in Aquinas's language). On this view causal reasoning derives its force from habit, from our previous experience of connecting what we call effects to what we call causes. It is not to be grounded in reason.

If Hume is right here, then Aquinas is wrong to argue as he does in SCG 1,13. For Aquinas there claims to be demonstrating the existence of a certain cause. Aquinas thinks that efficient causal agents have powers that produce effects, while Hume separates cause and effect so as to allow for there being no necessity when it comes to what we take to be an effect having a cause. So, if Hume's approach to causation is right, then there is something amiss with SCG 1,13.

The virtues of Aquinas's largely Aristotelian view of efficient causation, and the virtues of Hume's very different approach, have been much discussed by philosophers. This is not the place for me to try to pursue them in detail, but I do think it worth observing that Aquinas, unlike Hume, intimately relates

effects to causes and, therefore, does not end up with some of Hume's skeptical conclusions concerning reasoning from effect to cause. That is because
Aquinas thinks that "what the agent does is what the patient undergoes" and
that "action and passion are not two changes, but one and the same change,
called action in so far as it is caused by an agent, and passion in so far as it
takes place in a patient."[46]

The idea here is that something can only be said to be the cause of some
event *as the event is occurring by virtue of its cause.* Hence, for example, on
Aquinas's account I am the cause of my bed getting made *only as my bed is actually getting made by me,* or I am teaching you *only insofar as you are learning
by virtue of me.* On this account, cause and effect are not separable in the way
that Hume seems to think. Aquinas allows that there can be effects that come
about without causes in the natural world, for he believes that God can work
miracles (a topic Aquinas turns to in SCG 3). Aquinas also believes that there
can be chance events that lack a single cause while also falling under God's
will.[47] In general, though, Aquinas regards efficient causation as always involving both cause and effect, and he does so because he takes an efficient or agent
cause to be something exerting its power in or on something else. Hume
would say that we form the concept of a cause as we note the constant conjunction of various kinds of events. Aquinas, however, would say that we form
the notion of efficient causation as we seek to explain changes in terms of
agents able to bring them about. This approach to causation would seem to be
more at work in the way we typically think about causes and effects than is the
approach associated with Hume, but I leave it to you to consider whether it is
a viable one and superior to what Hume advances. That there is matter for
debate here seems evident, which, perhaps, at least indicates that the causal
reasoning of SCG 1 should not be dismissed as obviously archaic or unsound
in principle.

3.4.4 Existence and Nonexistence in SCG 1,13

As I have emphasized, the bulk of SCG 1,13 is taken up with arguing for the
truth of "God exists" with reference to motion. This, however, might seem
surprising since in many of his writings Aquinas speaks of God as accounting
for things simply existing. It is a presiding view of Aquinas that God brings it
about that everything other than God exists from moment to moment only
because God is causing it to do so, and this is a view that features quite a lot
in the SCG later than SCG 1,13. Yet is the notion of God as a cause of the being
of things entirely absent from SCG 1,13? I do not think that it is, and that is
because of SCG 1,13's use of the principle that something coming to be actu-

ally F having previously been only potentially F has to be accounted for in terms of something actual bringing about actuality from potentiality.

For Aquinas, being actually thus and so involves being in some way. For him, something actually F is something that exists as that which is actually F. Aquinas does not think that there are nonexisting actual things. So, when attributing something's being moved by God to God as first mover, he is implicitly saying that God accounts for things existing in some way. To be sure, Aquinas does not in SCG 1,13 speak of God as, for example, making things to exist from nothing, which is what Aquinas takes God to do given that God is the creator of all things. We have to wait until SCG 3 for Aquinas to tackle the notion of God as creator head on. Yet even in SCG 1,13 we find Aquinas talking about God bringing something about while not being potentially this, that, or the other. The unmoved mover of SCG 1,13 has to be something in which there is no possibility of a transition from potentiality to actuality, meaning that it is something in which no change can occur, and something not lacking what it might have but does not. If one reads through the SCG and through other works by Aquinas, however, one will be left in no doubt that Aquinas takes only God, the creator of all things, to be fully actual in this sense because he thinks that potentiality always requires to be actualized by what lacks potentiality in some way. Yet this thought concerning actuality and potentiality is very much in evidence in SCG 1,13, not only in its arguments from motion but also in its argument for a first efficient cause. So the notion of God as being what accounts for what exists, while potentially nonexistent, is definitely lurking around in SCG 1,13 even if it is not spelled out. As Edward Feser says: "If motion is just the reduction of potency to act, then since the existence of a thing no less than its activity involves (in everything other than that which is pure act) the reduction of potency to act, any explanation of motion must account for the existence of things and not just for their activities."[48] I take it that Feser is suggesting that something that actually exists, but does not have to exist, is potentially nonexistent, and that its sheer existence depends on it being actualized by what cannot not-exist. And, of course, Aquinas thinks of God as not able not to exist.

Yet how does Aquinas develop his thinking about God's nature as he continues with the SCG? In the next chapter I shall begin to note how he does so while he concentrates on what we cannot take God to be. You may wonder why Aquinas should embark on a discussion of God's nature in the SCG by talking about what God is not. As I will show, he has his reasons.

4

God as Eternal and Simple (SCG 1,14–27)

SCG 1,14 OPENS with the words "We have shown that there exists a first being, whom we call God. We must, accordingly, now investigate the nature of this being."[1] Yet Aquinas immediately adds that we are unable to apprehend God by knowing what God is and are best advised to "especially make use of the method of remotion."[2] He means that we should especially aim to consider what God is *not* rather than what God is. As I have noted, Aquinas does not think that we can have *scientia* when it comes to God. He holds that reflection should lead us to see that God is not understandable in the way that things in the world are. In Aquinas's view, we can understand what something is insofar as it is spatiotemporal and can be classified with respect to genus and species. Our ability to classify things in this way is, thinks Aquinas, confined to material things, while God is not material. Aquinas, however, does not conclude that we can make no progress at all when it comes to an account of God's nature. Hence his allusion to "the method of remotion," which, in SCG 1,14, he first employs so as to claim that God is not moved. That God is not moved, he says, seems to have been established by SCG 1,13.

4.1 Divine Eternity (SCG 1,15)

Also on the basis of SCG 1,13, Aquinas declares in SCG 1,15 that God is eternal. Here, and in line with the "way of remotion," Aquinas construes "eternal" in negative terms, in terms of God *not* being something or other. For Aquinas, something eternal does *not* have a beginning or end and does *not* have existence that can be measured by time.

Beginning or ceasing to exist, Aquinas argues, depend on motion or change. If God is immutable, however, then God must lack beginning or end. When it comes to eternity as not involving temporality, Aquinas appeals to something that Aristotle says about time in *Physics* IV. According to Aristotle, we can only "measure" a thing temporally on the basis of changes that it undergoes. We cannot conceive of something having a history if the thing in question is immutable. So there is no "before" and "after" in God, and God must have "his whole being at once" and is, therefore, eternal.[3]

Could it, however, be that God began to exist having formerly not existed? No, replies Aquinas, since that would mean that God derives from a cause while God is the first cause. "That which has been everlastingly," says Aquinas, "has the power to be everlastingly."[4] To this argument Aquinas adds another:[5]

1. The world contains things subject to generation and corruption, things that can equally be or not be.
2. Something that can equally be or not be must have a cause of its being.
3. As we saw in SCG 1,13, there cannot be an infinite series of hierarchical causes.[6]
4. So there must be at least one necessary being.
5. A necessary being must either have the cause of its necessity from something other than itself or it must have its necessity from itself.
6. "One cannot proceed to infinity among necessary beings the cause of whose necessity lies in an outside source."[7]
7. So there is "a first necessary being, which is necessary through itself."[8]

In this argument, "necessary" is contrasted with "being generated" and is not equivalent to "being logically necessary" or "having to exist as a matter of logical necessity." Aquinas is not saying that there has to be something (God) the existence of which it would be self-contradictory to deny. Nor is he saying that there could only be one necessary being. He is saying that something not generated exists and that its existence is either derived from something else or had by nature by the thing in question. Either way, thinks Aquinas, we are led to suppose that there is something that is necessary and owes its being to nothing outside itself. And, says Aquinas, such a being can be thought of as eternal, as the Bible says that God is.

4.2 *God as Lacking Passive Potency and Matter (SCG 1,16 and 17)*

The next two chapters of SCG 1 amount to a drawing out of some implications of what Aquinas has already argued. In SCG 1,16 he claims that there is no passive potency in God. In SCG 1,17 he maintains that there is no matter in God.

By "passive potency" (*potentia passiva*) Aquinas means "an ability or power to be acted on or changed by something else." He would say, for example, that

I have a passive potency to be pushed by you, to be lifted up by someone, or to be injured. Given that he has already argued that God is the first unmoved source of change, Aquinas obviously has to conclude that God cannot be subject to alteration by the agency of something else, which is the drift of SCG 1,16. Indeed, he says, if God is eternal, God cannot even not exist. "God is the first being and the first cause. Hence, he has no admixture of potency in himself."[9] On this account, God is "pure act" (*actus purus*) and not something actually thus and so while potentially different in some way or to some degree.

By "matter" (*materia*) Aquinas means something that is always in potency. We might naturally speak of the matter left in a test tube at the end of an experiment, and we would think of this as stuff of some kind that is able to interact with things causally. In SCG 1,17, however, Aquinas is using the word "matter" in a more technical and restricted sense, one that is not very easy to grasp. On his view, matter is not stuff of some kind. It is the precondition for change or coming to exist in the physical world. For this reason it is not a special member of the world or something to be classified in terms of genus, species, or acquired or acquirable characteristics.

We sometimes say that we live in a material world. When we do this, and unless we assume that everything that exists has to be physical, we are not describing the nature of the world considered as a thing of some kind, as, for example, when we say that such and such is wooden or made of gold. We are basically saying that we live in a world in which things come to be and pass away, a world that contains things subject to change for as long as they exist, a world in which things of various kinds can emerge from things of other kinds.[10] Running through this notion of "material" is the idea of the "material world" being made up of a series of changes within a whole that is, so to speak, able to accommodate or favor them; and it is this idea that Aquinas is working with when he speaks of "matter." Here, "matter" is, so to speak, the playground in which various changes take place. So, of course, Aquinas concludes that God does not contain matter since God is wholly actual and lacks any real potentiality.[11]

4.3   God as Noncomposite (SCG 1,18)

Continuing with his account of what God is not, Aquinas argues that God is not composite, that God lacks *compositio*. Since something composite is somehow made up of parts, one might naturally ask what parts Aquinas is thinking of when he declares in SCG 1,18 that God lacks them, that there is no composition in God. Yet Aquinas would have sympathized with this question since he believed that something can be composite in different ways, ones to which he refers in SCG 1,20–27. For the moment, however, let me note that Aquinas always takes what is composite to be potential in some way. "In every composite," he writes, "there must be act and potency."[12] That is what he is basically saying in SCG 1,18, which can be considered as a kind of overture to the SCG's treatment of what is commonly referred to as Aquinas's doctrine of divine simplicity. That overture, I might add, can be taken to continue into SCG 1,19, in which he denies that there is anything "violent or unnatural" in God.[13] In SCG 1,19 he effectively says that God cannot be acted on or added to by anything interfering with the divine nature.

4.4 God as Simple (SCG 1,20–27)

In SCG 1,18 it becomes clear that, when Aquinas says that God is not composite, he is claiming that God is simple (*simplex*). Hence, as part of his defense of the claim that there is no composition in God, Aquinas holds that something "which is at the peak of nobility among all beings must be at the peak of simplicity."[14] That Aquinas understands the assertion "God is not composite" to mean "God is simple" is, perhaps, clearer from *Summa Theologiae* 1a,3 than it is from SCG 1,20–27.[15] For *Summa Theologiae* 1a,3, though raising some questions that Aquinas addresses in SCG 1,20–27, is explicitly titled *God's Simplicity (De Dei Simplicitate)*, and it breaks down into articles asking "Is God composed of this, that, or the other?" However, what Aquinas means by "divine simplicity" in *Summa Theologiae* 1a,3 is very much what he is also concerned with in SCG 1,20–27.

To start with, he assumes that something might be composite by being a body and having bodily parts. Correspondingly, therefore, he holds that something might be simple inasmuch as it is not a body with bodily parts.

Aquinas also thinks that something might be composite by being distinct from its nature or essence, by being an individual *having* an essence. Correspondingly, therefore, he holds that something might be simple by just *being* an essence, not *having* an essence.

Again, Aquinas holds that something might be composite if its essence and existence differ, if its essence is not just to be or exist. Correspondingly, therefore, he holds that something might be simple if its very essence is to exist.

So in the SCG Aquinas argues that God is simple in that (1) God is not a body, (2) God and God's essence are not distinct, and (3) God is not something having existence conferred on it as the kind of thing it is. But Aquinas also draws out two other senses of "simple" and "composite" so as to deny that God is composite.

The first turns on a distinction between substance and accident. Largely under the influence of Aristotle, Aquinas holds that any particular naturally occurring thing in the world is an individual having a definite nature or essence. He thinks that such naturally occurring things are substances of various kinds. Now, in Aquinas's view, a substance retains its nature or essence for as long as it exists; for example, I am a human being throughout my entire life. As we know, though, things like me can acquire and lose various genuine features without actually ceasing to exist as what they are essentially or by nature. Hence, for example, I can become thin and then fat while still being me, while still being a human being. Or I can have a full head of hair and a smooth face at one time while proceeding to be bald and have wrinkles. So Aquinas generally takes substances to be things having what he calls "accidents." That is to say, he takes them to have features that they can acquire or lose while still being the substances that they are. So he claims that something might be composite just because it is a combination of substance and accidents. Correspondingly, Aquinas thinks that something lacking accidents can be thought of as, in a sense, simple.

The second distinction Aquinas draws out concerning composition and simplicity is grounded in the notions of genus and species.

Aquinas believes that it is possible to identify some things as members of a genus or species and as sharing a nature with other things. This leads him to suppose that members of a genus or species are composite in that the individuals that they are can be distinguished from the nature that they have. Correspondingly, Aquinas holds that something that just is its nature is simple in a way that members of a genus or species are not.

So, in terms of Aquinas's SCG thinking, X might be composite for any of the following reasons: (1) X is a body with parts; (2) X is an individual having a nature distinct from itself; (3) X is something having existence considered as derived from what is distinct from its nature; (4) X is something with accidents; (5) X is a member of a genus or species. Correspondingly, in terms of Aquinas's SCG thinking, X might be simple, even if not *entirely* simple, for any of the following reasons: (1) X is not a body with parts; (2) X is not an individual having a nature distinct from itself; (3) X is not something having existence considered as derived from what is distinct from its nature; (4) X is not something with accidents; (5) X is not a member of a genus or species.

All of the above theses concerning composition and simplicity run through what Aquinas writes in SCG 1,20–27, and they lead him to deny that God is composite. In reaching this conclusion, which, as I have said, is floated in SCG 1,18 and 19, Aquinas draws heavily on his distinction between act and potency. His presiding idea is that if God is the immutable first cause (see

SCG 1,13–17), then God is not changeable, not something to be strictly classified together with other things, and not something whose existence derives in
any way from something other than God. I shall leave it to you to pick through
SCG 1,20–27 so as to see how Aquinas defends this idea in detail and with an
eye to various objections to it with which he is familiar, but we can represent
the main stages of the argument of these chapters as follows.

1. Every body has parts, is moved, is potentially divisible, and is something
   than which we can think of something greater. But God does not have
   parts, is not moved, is not divisible, and is absolutely perfect. So God is not
   a body (SCG 1,20).
2. Something that can be distinguished from its essence is related to what is
   not identical with it, this being an essence that it can share with some other
   things. It is also something with accidents, since accidents cannot enter into
   a definition of what something is essentially. So such a thing has something
   that can be distinguished from it considered as the individual that it is, and
   it is, therefore, something with a potential for change. But God is not material, has no parts, is immutable, and does not depend for existence on anything else. So for God to exist is for him to exist as whatever his essence is,
   not as something having an essence shareable with other things (SCG 1,21).
3. God, whose essence or nature is not distinguishable from God or shareable by
   anything, has to be that whose essence or nature is to exist. What does not
   belong to something because of its essence has to be derived from what is
   other than it. Yet God does not depend for existence on anything other than
   God. So it is God's nature or essence to exist. For God to be what he is and for
   God to exist amount to the same thing, this meaning that God is pure being
   with no potentiality for nonexistence and no potentiality for change (SCG 1,22).
4. If nothing can be added to what God's essence amounts to, there are obviously no accidents in God. If God lacks the ability to undergo change, then
   accidental change cannot be ascribed to the divine nature since the existence of accidents in a substance depends on the subject being able to
   change by the agency of something else. But God is unchangeable and is
   not caused to change by anything (SCG 1,23).
5. If God is just pure being, then God cannot be a member of a genus or species. To classify in terms of genus or species is to circumscribe or identify
   a *way* of being, while God is pure being and is, therefore, not something
   classifiable along with things that can be categorized in terms of genus and
   species (SCG 1,24 and 25).
6. God is not what all things are insofar as they exist. God is not the "formal
   being" of all things and is, therefore, neither a substance nor an accident.

God is not mixed up in the being of things in the world and is not a part of what is other than God. Rather, God is the distinct and simple cause of all that is not divine and, as such, is above all of them (SCG 1,26).

7. God is not the form of any body but is Being Itself (*ipsum esse*), unlike the form of a body (SCG 1,27).

4.5 *Comments on Aquinas on Divine Simplicity*

It cannot be sufficiently stressed that what Aquinas says in SCG 1,18–27 represents a line of thinking that is fundamental to the SCG as a whole. Aquinas draws on it continually. Indeed, his SCG thinking on simplicity is central to almost all of his major writings. So perhaps I should make some comments on it so as to help you to reflect on it, especially since it currently seems to be out of favor in many philosophical and theological circles.[16]

To start with, then, let me note a number of criticisms that have been leveled against it.[17] We can summarize them as follows.

1. Aquinas's notion of divine simplicity conflicts with the picture of God conveyed by the Bible, which portrays God as an individual person undergoing change and interacting with things in the world. Talk about God as immutable, as not distinct from his nature, and as "pure being," is foreign to the Bible and incompatible with what we read about God in it.

2. Aquinas's account of divine simplicity seems to leave him saying that God is just a property, which is not what people who believe in God commonly take him to be. In the words of Alvin Plantinga: "If God is identical with each of his properties, then, since each of his properties is a property, he is a property.... Accordingly God has just one property: himself.... This view is subject to a difficulty both obvious and overwhelming. No property could have created the world; no property could be omniscient, or, indeed, know anything at all. If God is a property, then he isn't a person but a mere abstract object; he has no knowledge, awareness, power, love or life. So taken, the simplicity doctrine seems an utter mistake."[18]

3. God cannot be the same as his nature since that would mean that the different things said about God would, if true, be synonymous. Those who believe in God hold, for example, that God is both powerful and knowing. Yet "powerful" and "knowing" differ in meaning. It cannot be that God's power and knowledge are both what God is since God's power and knowledge would then just be God and would not be distinct, as power and knowledge actually are.

4. To say that it is God's essence to exist is erroneously to suppose that existing is a property that some individual can have. And to say that God's essence is to exist is erroneously to assume that God can be identified with this property.

5. Those who believe that God exists insist that God is free to act as he does. But God cannot be free to act as he does if Aquinas is right about divine simplicity. He holds that God is immutable and is what he eternally is, while something that is free to act as it does is capable of being different from what it is.

If these criticisms are good ones, then, as David Hume might have said, much of the SCG can be committed to the flames as containing nothing but sophistry and illusion.[19] Yet I think that they are not, in fact, very good criticisms.

1. It is true that the Bible does not provide an account of divine simplicity such as Aquinas offers in the SCG and elsewhere. Indeed, it often portrays God in very human terms. According to the book of Genesis, God once took a walk in the garden of Eden.[20] According to Exodus, "the Lord used to speak to Moses face to face, as one speaks to a friend."[21] In the Old Testament we find God described as having hands, eyes, ears, and a face.[22] He laughs, smells, and whistles.[23] He also undergoes emotions such as hatred, anger, joy, and regret.[24] Then again we have the New Testament referring to God as our father and as loving us as such.[25] It is obvious that the Bible frequently talks about God as if he were a kind of "top person" to be ranked higher than all the people we know.

Yet the Bible contains many texts that point in a different direction, one implying a profound difference between God, people, and anything else. While various biblical texts ascribe physical attributes to God, others insist that God is not physical. A notable text here is John 4:24, which says that God is spirit and thereby echoes a long-standing Old Testament line of thought according to which God is not a bodily thing but the maker and organizer of physical objects. Another text worth noting is Colossians 1:15 in which Christ is said to be "the image of the invisible God." Yet another text worth noting is 1 Timothy 1:17, according to which "the only God" is "invisible." And while the book of Exodus tells us that God spoke to Moses face-to-face, it quickly goes on to provide a serious qualification as it reports God as saying to Moses "You cannot see my face; for no one shall see me and live."[26] In Exodus 33:23 God tells Moses that the best that he can hope for is to see his backsides.

And there are biblical texts that seem to insist that God is radically different from all that he has made. A classic one is Isaiah 40:25: "To whom then will you compare me, or who is my equal? says the Holy One." The text continues: "Lift your eyes on high and see Who created these?...Have you not known? Have you not heard? The Lord is the everlasting God, the creator of the ends of the earth. He does not faint or grow weary; his understanding is unsearchable."[27] The book of Isaiah obviously does not take God to be a being among the beings in the world with which we are familiar. Nor does it think of God as something that we can imagine to be like us or like anything else in the world. So I take it that the Bible, while sometimes speaking of God as being like a human person, also says things that should lead us to deny that God is seriously such a thing.

Sometimes the Bible talks about God in anthropomorphic terms. Sometimes it does not.[28] How are we to deal with these apparent discrepancies? If our interest in biblical texts merely extends to noting what they appear literally to say verse by verse, then we can do just that and not worry about interpretation. But we might, as Aquinas did, think of the Bible as helping us to some understanding of God and ourselves, in which case we have to introduce what I can only call philosophical reasoning.

Does God have a body or not? There are biblical texts that can be cited on both sides here. So, what if we claim that God is a body? Then we presumably need nonbiblical arguments, philosophical arguments, for supposing that God is indeed corporeal, and that anything in the Bible that suggests otherwise should be regarded as figurative or not literally true. Again, what if we think that God does not have a body? Then we presumably need to appeal to nonbiblical arguments for supposing that God is indeed incorporeal and that anything in the Bible that suggests otherwise should be read as figurative.

This is how Aquinas proceeds. He was deeply immersed in biblical texts and recognized very well that if they are all taken literally, then some of them effectively, even if not formally, contradict each other. Yet he also thought that one can give nonbiblical reasons for reading some biblical texts literally and for reading some of them as being figurative, and this thought is at work in SCG 1,18–27. Here Aquinas is trying to elaborate on matters that, in his view, should help us better understand the Bible or, at least, better appreciate what biblical texts can be taken to imply if thought about.

One might still, of course, insist that "God is a person" is fundamental to the nature of belief in God and that Aquinas is casting this proposition aside because of an unbiblical taste for philosophical argument. Yet how fundamental to belief in God is the claim "God is a person"? It has been said that it is utterly fundamental.[29] In point of fact, though, "God is a person" is a relatively recent mantra. I gather that its first occurrence in English comes in the report of a trial of one John Biddle (b. 1615), who in 1644 was brought before magistrates in Gloucester, England, on a charge of heresy. His "heresy" was claiming that God is a person, which was taken at the time to be a Unitarian slogan favored by people wanting to deny the Christian doctrine of the Trinity, according to which God is three persons in one substance (and certainly not three persons in one person).[30] You might think that all who believe in God take God to be personal in some sense since knowledge and will can be ascribed to him. As I will show, however, Aquinas does not deny that there is knowledge and will in God. Indeed, he argues that there has to be.

2. Plantinga takes a property to be an "abstract object," a nonmaterial individual that cannot fail to exist and is not created by God. Plantinga also believes that there are many abstract objects. As well as properties, he takes propositions and "states of affairs" to be abstract objects, and he claims that all of them exist independently of God and independently of what we would normally think of as any individual thing. I take my cat to be an individual thing, an individual cat. Plantinga would agree that my cat is, indeed, something individual; but, he would add, to say that my cat is a cat, or that he is black and white, or that he is agile, is to say that he "exemplifies" or "instantiates" properties ("being a cat," "being black and white," "being agile"), which exist necessarily and independently of him. Plantinga seems to be asserting that Aquinas is wrong on divine simplicity since God is not an uncreated abstract object.

This line of thinking, however, does not engage with what Aquinas says as he develops his account of divine simplicity in the SCG. Unlike Plantinga, Aquinas does not believe in uncreated abstract objects, so he is manifestly not claiming that God is one of them. He would never say that there is an uncreated property called "being a cat" that preexists the coming-to-be of all cats. He would say that to call something a cat is to ascribe a nature to what actually exists without having to exist by nature. Therefore, when Plantinga suggests that Aquinas's teaching on God's simplicity is erroneous since it implies that God is what Plantinga thinks of as a property, he is talking past Aquinas rather than at him.

Friends of Plantinga when it comes to divine simplicity might argue that, when Aquinas says that there is no distinction in God of subject and nature (that God is his essence), he must mean that, for example, to say "God is good" and "God is living," though seeming to ascribe different attributes to God, is merely to ascribe one attribute to him, an attribute identical with God. Such friends of Plantinga might then go on to suggest that this account of God is wrong since different attributes are different and since God is not an attribute. But Aquinas does not hold that to say, for example, "God is good" and "God is wise" is to ascribe one and the same attribute to him. He denies that "God is good" and "God is wise" mean the same, are synonymous.[31] In *this* sense, he agrees that God has different attributes. For Aquinas, however, to make this point is only to say that we have different ways in which we speak of God, who is not to be distinguished from what we ascribe to him as we talk about him. It is not to say that God is an individual having different attributes in the sense that we can think of my cat having different attributes. And Aquinas certainly does not think of God as being what we mean when referring to a creaturely attribute.

3. The merit of criticism 3 lies in the evident truth that, when things in the universe exhibit different attributes, the attributes in question are really distinct from each other. My cat's agility is a reality in him that might well survive his being inquisitive. Or, as Aquinas would say, my cat's agility is an "individualized form" possessed by him, as is his inquisitiveness. Agility and inquisitiveness can be had by many different things and are, considered as such, universal rather than particular. But when agility and inquisitiveness come to be possessed by an individual, then individual instances of a universal arise: the agility of X, say, or the inquisitiveness of Y. These, for Aquinas, are unique realities, not one and the same reality.

Yet we can assume that Aquinas is not abandoning this line of thinking when ruminating on divine simplicity. So we can suppose that, when he defends the claim that God is simple, he is not telling us that there is something in which different attributes are actually one and the same attribute. Indeed, it is clear that he is not doing so.

As I have stressed, what he is doing, and what he says he is doing, is *denying* something of God. He is maintaining that God, unlike my cat, is not a being with distinct attributes or properties. Aquinas, of course, is aware that people who believe that God exists often speak as if God were a being with different attributes. He is aware that they utter subject/predicate sentences like "God is good" and "God is powerful": sentences that would be naturally taken to be ascribing different attributes to something if they did not have the word "God" in them. However, thinks Aquinas, what this should lead us to say is not that God has different attributes but that the simple reality of God is often spoken of in a way that fails to capture the reality in question. Aquinas thinks that there are reasons for employing different words, and meaning them literally, when talking about God. He thinks, for example, that there are reasons for speaking of God as literally both omnipotent and good.[32] However, he also thinks that there are reasons for not taking God to be an individual exhibiting a variety of attributes, and he wishes to give weight to all the reasons in question here. So he concludes that goodness and power in God do not amount to different realities. One might, of course, now complain that Aquinas is making God seem terribly mysterious or vastly different from the things with which we are acquainted in day-to-day life. But Aquinas would not regard this complaint as undermining his position, for his final verdict, of which his teaching on divine simplicity is a part, is that God *is* terribly mysterious and *is* vastly different from the things with which we are acquainted in day-to-day life.

4. Criticism 4 has been defended in one form or another by many philosophers, but I take the most rigorous statement of it to be found in the writings of C. J. F. Williams (1930–1997).[33] According to Williams, "___ exist(s)" cannot meaningfully be asserted of individuals. Rather, says Williams, here echoing things said by the famous logician Gottlob Frege (1848–1925), existence is a property of concepts.[34] On this account, to say, for example, that readers of Aquinas exist is not to tell us anything about any particular reader of Aquinas. It is to tell us that "___ is a reader of Aquinas" is truly affirmable of something or other. Or, in Williams's language, which also echoes what we find in the writings of Immanuel Kant (1724–1804), "existence" or "being" is not a property of individuals.[35]

To say of some individual that it exists is, thinks Williams, unintelligible, and with this thought in mind he turns to Aquinas on simplicity. He argues that what Aquinas says on this topic wrongly presupposes that existing is a property of individuals and then, ludicrously, identifies this property with God in an attempt to tell us what God is.[36] The idea here is that Aquinas has no business saying that God brings it about that various individuals simply exist, and that Aquinas has no business identifying God with a property of existence had by these individuals.

One of Williams's arguments for the view that it is nonsense to ascribe existence to an individual holds that if existence were attributable to individuals, then we could never, as we surely can, intelligibly say things like "Readers of Aquinas do not exist."[37] Why not? Because if existence *were* intelligibly attributable to individuals, to say, for example, that readers of Aquinas *do not exist* is to say that they *lack* a certain property, while to say this is implicitly to assert that they *exist*. In other words, according to Williams, if existence is a property of individuals, then statements like "Readers of Aquinas do not exist" is true only if it is false. This argument, however, wrongly assumes that negative existential assertions (assertions like "Readers of Aquinas do not exist") have to be taken as presupposing the existence of their subjects and to be denying something of them. To say that readers of Aquinas do not exist is not to suppose that nonexisting readers of Aquinas lack a property of some kind. It is to deny that anything can be truly said to be a reader of Aquinas.

Williams also argues for his position by claiming that sentences ascribing existence to individuals are ones for which we have no use "outside philosophy."[38] He means that we do not normally say things like "I exist" or "President X exists." But this also seems to be a poor line of argument. People would, doubtless, be puzzled were I to accost them and assert "I exist." They would probably be equally puzzled if, out of the blue, I announce "President X (you can supply a name here) exists." But would anybody seriously take me to be talking nonsense were I to say, for example, "The great pyramid at Giza exists, but the Colossus of Rhodes does not," or "You and I exist, but we will not exist if a giant meteorite hits the earth tomorrow"? Contrary to what Williams suggests, "exists," as affirmed of an individual, is hardly some esoteric piece of meaningless baggage. To be sure, and as Aquinas recognized, what it is for one thing to exist might be different from what it is for something else to exist. For my cat to exist is for him to be a cat. For me to exist is for me to be a human being. For a cabbage to exist is for it to be (what else?) a cabbage. And cats, humans, and cabbages are obviously things of different kinds. But individual examples of these kinds can surely, and as individuals, be sensibly thought of as existing.[39]

Williams, I presume, would have replied that in answer to the question "What is God?" it makes no sense to say that God is existence or Being Itself. Yet Aquinas's account of divine simplicity in the SCG is not an account of what God is. It is an account of what God *cannot* be. When saying that there is no distinction in God of essence and existence, Aquinas is not seeking to describe God. He is noting that, *whatever* God is, he *cannot* be something the existence of which is derived. And why does he do so? Because he thinks that there are things the existence of which does not derive from what they are (their essence), things that, therefore, have to be caused by what is distinct from them when it comes to essence and existence. Drawing on the Bible, and on what he finds in the writings of various theologians, and noting that nothing we take to be part of the universe exists by nature, Aquinas thinks that "God" is the obvious word to use so as to name what accounts for the existence of the universe. And why should he not? It would be fallacious to argue that since everyone has a mother the entire human race must have one. But Aquinas's case for God being simple is not like this argument. He is not saying that the existence of everything in the universe has a cause and that the universe as such therefore has a cause. And, as I have explained, he thinks that the causes of what confront us now might, as far as philosophers can prove, depend on a series of causes going infinitely backward in time. In his defense of divine simplicity, Aquinas is saying that the existence of anything that does not exist by nature has to be caused by what does exist by nature. He is saying that the existence of the entire universe has to be caused no matter when we take it to be existing.

5. Criticism 5 supposes that people have freedom of choice, and that, when they do such and such freely, they are also freely not doing something or other. The idea here is that freedom of choice is bound up with the notion of different courses of action, and also bound up with different ways in which a human agent can be described. With this idea in mind, 5 is suggesting that Aquinas's doctrine of divine simplicity should be rejected since God is free to create or not to create, and that he is free to create worlds of many different kinds.

The argument goes like this: (1) God has freedom to create or not to create; (2) God is free to create different kinds of worlds; (3) If (1) and (2) are true, then God could be different from what he is; (4) But if God could be different from what he is, then he cannot be simple, for to say that God is simple is to say that he and his nature are changelessly one and the same, which is to say that God cannot be different from what he is.

This argument is sometimes advanced using the notion of a "contingent property," a property that something that exists might have or lack. When my cat has eaten, he is not hungry. When I forget to feed him, he becomes hungry. We might put this by saying that being full or being hungry are contingent properties of my cat, and we might add that many of its properties are not contingent since they are properties that it has to have in order to exist at all. Since it is a cat, it is a mammal, so being mammalian is a necessary property of it. Now, so it has been suggested, according to Aquinas's claim that God is simple, God has no contingent properties. Yet God must have contingent properties if he is free to create or not to create, and if he is free to create worlds of different kinds. Why? Because, without ceasing to be God, he is different from how he could be. If he had not chosen to create, he would have been different from what he is given that he chooses to create. If he had chosen to create a world without cats, he would be different from what he is given that he has created cats.

The merit of this argument lies, I think, in the fact that freedom and difference, or freedom and contingent properties, do come together when we are thinking of people. I and my teeth would have come to be different from what I and they were last night had I chosen not to brush my teeth before going to bed. The problem with the argument, however, lies in the fact that if God is, in Aquinas's sense, the first cause, then he cannot be thought of as able to be different from what he is, and he cannot be thought of as having contingent properties.

When Aquinas speaks of the order of things produced by God, he is thinking about everything involved in the world of being and becoming. So he resists the suggestion that God is a being who comes, or could come, to be different as time goes by. For him, such a being would just be part of the spatiotemporal universe, not its cause. As I will show, Aquinas wants to assert (1) that God is free to create or not create, and (2) that God does not have to create a world just like ours.

By (1), however, he means that God's nature *does not* compel him to create, that he is *not* forced into creating given what he is essentially. He also means that there could be nothing distinct from God that, so to speak, pushes him into creating. Given what we are by nature, we cannot but urinate, or breathe, or vomit if digesting certain substances.[40] According to Aquinas, however, divinity has no need of creatures and does not come with an inbuilt compulsion to create. If it did, then it would, contrary to fact, make no sense to say of any creature that it might not exist.[41]

As for (1), Aquinas's meaning is that, logically speaking, lots of things that do not exist could exist, and that they would exist only if God made them to be. I live in the United States. Could I live in Russia? There seems to be no logical impossibility in the suggestion that I might live in Russia. So the world could be different in that I could live in Russia rather than in the United States. But Aquinas takes this point to mean no more than that there is no logical impossibility when it comes to my living in Russia.

Applying all of this to the objection to divine simplicity now in question, it seems fair to observe that, for Aquinas, to say that God is free to create or not create, or that he is free to create a world different from what we find ourselves in, is not to suggest that God might be different from what he essentially is, or that he might acquire "contingent properties." Aquinas's "God is free to create" is a comment on what God *is not*. God is *not* something whose nature forces him to create. It is also a comment on what exists in the world and on what can be thought to exist without logical contradiction.

An objector to Aquinas on simplicity might reply "But if God had not created Davies's cat, God would be different from what he is now." But why suppose that God creating or not creating my cat makes for any difference in God? To suppose that it might would be to think of God as a spatiotemporal individual who is modified as he lives his life and makes *these* choices rather than *those* choices. If Aquinas's approach to God is right, however, to think of God in that way is just not to think of God. For, so Aquinas would say (and here note the following negations), God *is not* part of space and time, *is not* (in a serious sense) an individual, and *does not* live a life consisting of many changes. If we had lived our lives differently, then we would be different from what we are now. But why suppose that God is something with a life history that could have taken a different course?

You may, of course, disagree with what I have been saying in response to the five criticisms of the SCG's account of divine simplicity noted above. Even if you do, however, it is incontestable that Aquinas sees what he says about divine simplicity in the SCG as primarily an account of what God is not. SCG 1,18–27 is a treatment of what has sometimes been referred to as God's "negative attributes."[42] In that case, however, it surely cannot be taken as a proper account of God since those who believe that God exists frequently speak of God by seeming to ascribe positive characteristics or attributes to him. Yet, as I will begin to show in the next chapter, Aquinas is aware of this fact and himself wishes to speak of God in positive or nonnegative terms.

5

Talking about God (SCG 1,28–36)

I HAVE STRESSED that in SCG 1,14–27 Aquinas lays emphasis on God being different from what is not God and that he makes much of what he calls "the way of remotion." For Aquinas, we should pay special attention to noting what God is *not* since we do not know *what* God is. Yet those who believe in God frequently seem to want to speak about God in ways that are positive and informative. They say, for example, that God is perfect and good. So what would Aquinas think of us positively ascribing certain attributes to God, of us asserting that, say, "___ is perfect" or "___ is good" can meaningfully be tacked on to the word "God" so as to result in true propositions?

From what we find in SCG 1,14–27, you might suppose that Aquinas would disapprove of us doing this. But he does not, as we can see from SCG 1,36, in which he asserts: "Although God is absolutely simple, it is not futile for our intellect to form enunciations concerning God in his simplicity by means of composition and division."[1] We "compose and divide," thinks Aquinas, when we pick out a subject and either affirm or deny something of it, as when we say "John is musical" or "John is not musical." So Aquinas believes that we can make true statements by using expressions of the form "God is X" or "God is not X." He thinks that, as well as being able truly to deny that God is such and such, we can make positive assertions concerning what God is. What, however, is his rationale for thinking this? In SCG 1,28–36 he explains what he takes it to be. In this chapter, therefore, I try to indicate what it amounts to in general terms. Then I turn to some details.

5.1 The General Picture

Aquinas's SCG approach to talking positively about God relies on some matters to which I drew attention in chapter 3. These are: (1) Aquinas's distinction between univocal and equivocal causes, (2) his view that an efficient or agent cause can contain its effects "virtually," and (3) his claim that the action of an agent is present in its effect. According to Aquinas, the effects of efficient causes derive from those causes, which act in their effects and also have the power to produce them, even if they do not look like them or resemble them strongly in some way. As Aquinas observes in SCG 1,29: "Effects that fall short of their causes do not agree with them in name and nature. Yet, some likeness must be found between them, since it belongs to the nature of action that an agent produce its like, since each thing acts according as it is in act."[2] My cat, as becoming fed by me, does not even belong to the same species as I do and might be said to "fall short" of me in terms of power and intelligence. But Aquinas holds that I am at work in my cat becoming fed by me and that what I am is being shown forth in my cat. By the same token, he argues, the existence of things depending on God can be thought of as somehow showing forth what God is, as being somehow like him.

Aquinas does not think that God is literally *like* anything that depends for its existence on him. That he does not think this should be clear from SCG 1,14–27, and especially from his claim that God is simple. But Aquinas does not, therefore, rule out the idea that we might be able to speak of God in positive terms, that we might be able truly and literally to say that "God is X," "God is Y," or "God is Z," where "X," "Y," and "Z" are words with which we are familiar from ways people speak about things that are not divine.[3] Aquinas does not think that any words have come into being so as to signify what only God is.[4] He takes language to have evolved as people encountered things in the world and tried to communicate with each other concerning them. For Aquinas, all the words and sentences we use when attempting to say what God is are borrowed, as it were, from their day-to-day use. Yet Aquinas also thinks that some words can be used in order to construct literally true propositions concerning God, not just figurative or metaphorical ones.

He thinks this because he holds that some words do not have a meaning built into them that would prohibit us from using them so as to say what God truly is. If I say that my cat is hungry, I am talking about it having a property that can only be had by an animal, as God is not. Again, if I say that Mary is tall, I am talking about her having a property that can only be had by something physical, as God is not. Yet what if I say that something is, for example, perfect or excellent? Do "perfect" and "excellent" have a meaning built into them that prohibits us from using them so as to say what God literally is? Aquinas does not think that they do. He also believes that there are other words that can be used to speak literally of God, words that do not, in his view, have what we might call a "creaturely limitation" as part of their meaning.

When concluding along these lines in the SCG, however, Aquinas always keeps in mind his teaching that God is simple. So, while saying that God can be positively and truly spoken of or described using certain words and sentences, he evidently has to make some distinction between the use of words and sentences to talk about God, considered as simple, and the use of words to talk of what is composite. Aquinas, though, is aware of this fact, and the distinction he employs is that between "what is signified" and "mode of signification."

This distinction is a technical one. It is not, however, all that complicated. Aquinas maintains that when talking of God we naturally do so as if he were composite. Since Aquinas denies that God is composite, however, he also holds that our way of talking about God is always going somehow to fall short of the reality of God. In other words, though Aquinas holds that we can sometimes speak truly and literally of God, he also holds that, when we do this, the way in which we speak signifies the divine reality imperfectly since it picks God out as if he were composite. For Aquinas, there are words that genuinely latch on to a reality in God. Yet Aquinas also thinks that we use them in sentences whose form was never designed to lay hold of divinity but to talk about composite things. "By means of a name," says Aquinas, "we express things in the way in which the intellect conceives them. For our intellect, taking the origin of its knowledge from the senses, does not transcend the mode which is found in sensible things, in which the form and the subject are not identical owing to the composition of form and matter."[5] By "name" (*nomen*) here Aquinas is referring to any word that picks something out or describes it.[6] So his point is that when we speak of God we express ourselves in a way fitted for the picking out and describing of what exists in the world and is composite, not simple. Aquinas therefore thinks that there is always going to be a kind of mismatch between the way we speak of God and the simple reality that God is. He does not, however, therefore conclude that we cannot speak about God so as, albeit imperfectly, to express what God positively is.

At this point, of course, you might want to say that Aquinas has to be wrong here since we can easily understand what, say, "God is good" means. We know what is being said when, for example, a human being is described as good. So why not just suppose that exactly the same thing is being affirmed when it is said that God is good? Aquinas would reply that the goodness of a human being cannot be just like God's goodness since God is entirely simple. If God is good, that cannot be because God possesses a property distinguishable from himself, a property that might be had by many different things. So (1) "Nothing can be predicated univocally of God and other things."[7] Yet Aquinas also asserts: (2) "Not everything predicated of God and other things is said in a purely equivocal way."[8]

By (1) here Aquinas means that "God is X," where "X" is a term or word that we also use when talking of what is not divine, should not be thought to signify or mean that God is *exactly like* what we take what is nondivine to be when saying that it is X. And by (2) Aquinas means that "God is X," where "X" is a term or word that we also use when talking of what is not divine, should not always be thought to signify or mean that God is in *no way* like what we take something nondivine to be when saying that it is X. According to Aquinas, when it comes to at least some sentences of the form "God is X," we can take "X" to have a meaning related to what it has when used to talk of what is not God. Or, as Aquinas puts it, the same words can sometimes be used to talk of God and of what is not divine because "they are said analogically."[9] He means that, for example, the word "good" can be used in "Fred is good" and "God is good" without it being the case that there is no related meaning at all in what "good" signifies in each case. Aquinas does not think that we can understand what it is for God to be good since he does not believe that we can understand what God is. But neither does he think that "God is good" cannot be thought of as literally true, even though the sentence must fail to express what God is since God is entirely simple and since God cannot exhibit goodness in a way that anything that is not divine might.

In short, the main points Aquinas makes in SCG 1,28–36 are:

1. Since God is entirely simple, our human way of talking always falls short when we speak about God. That is because our human way of talking engages with or reflects an understanding of what is composite.
2. Yet some words we use when talking of what is not divine can be used to speak truly and literally of God even though they signify what God is imperfectly because God is entirely simple.

But let us now see how Aquinas actually gets to these conclusions in his text.

5.2 *SCG 1,28–36: Details*

1. SCG 1,28–36 employs some distinctions concerning predication that run throughout his account of talking about God. For he speaks of words being used "univocally," "equivocally," and "analogically," and the differences he has in mind here need explaining.

Suppose that I say "John is a man" and "Henry is a man." Here, "man" seems to mean exactly the same thing in both sentences. Aquinas would make this point by saying that, in "John is a man" and "Henry is a man," the word "man" should be understood univocally.

However, suppose that I say "I keep my pen in my pocket" and "I keep my pigs in a pen." Here, "pen" seems to mean something completely different in both sentences. It is an accident of the development of the English language that we have one word that serves both to refer to a writing instrument and to a place in which pigs can be housed. Aquinas would make this point by saying that, in "I keep my pen in my pocket" and "I keep my pigs in a pen," the word "pen" should be understood equivocally and as having no meaning in common.

What though of "love" in "I love my wife," "I love my job," and "I love to visit Italy"? Love of a spouse is not exactly the same thing as love of a job or a place to travel. But I am surely not equivocating when using "love" in the three sentences just noted. There seem to be threads of connection between what we have in mind when thinking of love between spouses, love of a job, and love for a place to visit. Aquinas would make this point by saying that, in "I love my wife," "I love my job," and "I love to visit Italy," I am using the word "love" analogically.

In SCG 1,28–36, Aquinas is concerned to argue that, in sentences like "Fred is X" and "God is X," the word that we substitute for X in both sentences can be construed analogically, as not meaning exactly the same thing, while not meaning something completely different.

2. Aquinas begins his SCG discussion of our talking about God by discussing divine perfection (SCG 1,28). "The mode of a thing's excellence," he writes, "is according to the mode of its being. For a thing is said to be more or less excellent according as its being is limited to a certain greater or lesser mode of excellence."[10]

Here Aquinas is saying that "perfect" is, in a sense, a relative term. He does not think that "X is perfect" merely expresses a speaker's *feelings* toward X. He does not think that perfection is merely "in the eye of the beholder" and is, therefore, always totally subjective. He holds that, even if we do not always recognize this, some things can be truly said to be perfect or to have perfections or excellence in themselves. Yet Aquinas understands "perfect" to be an adjective of a certain kind. He thinks, for example, that "perfect" is not the same kind of adjective as is "wooden."

"X is a wooden horse" tells us two distinct things about X, each understandable on their own. It tells us that X is wooden and, in addition, that X is a horse. But "perfect" does not work like "wooden." I can know what something is if told only that it is wooden and not what kind of wooden thing it is. But I will not know what X is like if all I am told is that X is perfect. When saying that something is perfect or excellent we do so for reasons that can differ hugely depending on what we are talking about. What we count as perfection or excellence in a mathematician, say, will be different from what we count as perfection or excellence in a surgeon or an opera singer or a parent. In this sense, perfection and excellence are relative, though not subjective, since they differ in things of different kinds, things with different ways of being.

So in SCG 1,28 Aquinas does not argue for "God is perfect" as if perfection in everything amounted to exactly the same kind of descriptive property, as "being wooden" amounts to exactly the same kind of descriptive property in everything that is wooden. Rather, he settles for a general account of perfection and excellence according to which something is perfect insofar as it possesses being or existence to some degree. He also says that "if there is something to which the whole power of being belongs, it can lack no excellence that is proper to some thing."[11] On this basis, Aquinas holds that God, "who is his being…has being according to the whole power of being itself."[12] He also claims: (1) God is perfect since imperfection involves an absence of being of some kind, while God is Being Itself; (2) imperfect things proceed from what is perfect in some way, and God is perfect as that from which all that is not divine proceeds; (3) perfection follows from being in act, not being in potency, and God is perfect since God lacks potentiality and is fully in act; (4) something acts insofar as it is "in act," and God is perfect since he acts so as to bring about all actuality in what is not divine.

3. SCG 1,29 turns to how "a likeness to God is and is not possible in things."[13] Things can be said to be like God, says Aquinas, insofar as they proceed from God as their first efficient cause. But, he adds, this does not mean that they do not fall short of what God is as they reflect him as working actively in them. He observes: "God gave things all their perfections and thereby is both like and unlike them."[14] Here Aquinas is drawing on the notions of univocal causation and equivocal causation mentioned above, and he is claiming that, as efficiently caused by God, all that is not divine must be somehow like God even though God is not like something else as, say, a mother is like her daughter.

4. What terms or words used to talk about what is not divine can be properly used when talking about God? In SCG 1,30 Aquinas answers this question by saying that they are terms signifying perfections, though not perfections that can be had only by what is creaturely. He writes: "Since it is possible to find in God every perfection of creatures, but in another and more eminent way, whatever names unqualifiedly designate a perfection without defect are predicated of God and of other things: for example, goodness, wisdom, being, and the like. But when any name expresses such perfections along with a mode that is proper to a creature, it can be said of God only according to likeness and metaphor."[15] Aquinas has no problem with speaking

of God metaphorically. Indeed, he notes that metaphorical talk about God abounds in the Bible. But he does not take metaphorical talk of God to be literally true, while he does think that some talk of God is literally true, that it is, for example, literally true to say that God is "the highest good" or "the first being."[16]

5. However, Aquinas also maintains that our words or "names" always signify imperfectly when used to speak about God (SCG 1,30). Here we come to the distinction between "thing signified" and "mode of signification."

Some "names," says Aquinas, "signify a perfection without defect."[17] But they do so "with reference to that which the name was imposed to signify; for as to the mode of signification, every name is defective." Why so? Because we talk of and understand even perfect creatures as if they were composite, while God is not composite.

Take, for example, our talk about what is good and about goodness itself as present in different things. Aquinas holds that when we speak of goodness we are not referring to what subsists as a thing in its own right; we are not talking about a "subsistent form." Yet God is something that subsists in its own right; God is a subsistent form. Again, when we speak of things being good we are always talking about composite creatures, not something wholly simple. "As a result," says Aquinas, "with reference to the mode of signification there is in every name that we use an imperfection, which does not befit God,... And so with reference to the mode of signification no name is fittingly applied to God."[18]

Here Aquinas means that our understanding of what we say about something created cannot carry over into talk about God that resembles it at what we might call a "surface" level. He means that what we say can sometimes be misleading when it comes to what we are talking about, and not just because we might be lying. In paragraph 64 of his *Philosophical Investigations* Wittgenstein distinguishes between "surface grammar" and "depth grammar." He refers to "surface grammar" as "what immediately impresses itself upon us about the use of a word" given "the way it is used in the sentence structure, the part of its use—one might say—that can be taken in by the ear."[19] By "depth grammar" Wittgenstein means "what might be philosophically teased out from 'what can be taken in by the ear' so as to arrive at a better understanding of what is being said." Consider the sentences "I have a key in my pocket" and "I have a pain in my back." At the "surface" level, these sentences are alike since they are grammatically comparable. But we would surely be wrong to think of pains as being like physical objects such as keys. Thinking along somewhat similar lines, Aquinas suggests that when we speak truly of God we signify imperfectly and should be thought of as trying to speak of God as if God were a composite creature, which he is not.[20] Aquinas holds that when using such talk we are in a serious sense trying to say more than we can mean. As Herbert McCabe (1926–2001) once said: "St Thomas thought that things in some way pointed beyond themselves to something which is not a thing, which is altogether outside the universe of things and cannot be included in any classification with them. Given this idea it is not too difficult to understand his notion that words can point beyond their ordinary meanings, and this he thought is what happens when we talk about God. We can use words to mean more than we can understand."[21]

6. People use different words when "describing" God. They say, for example, that God is good and powerful. So, how can this fact be squared with the idea that God is simple? Aquinas deals with this question in SCG 1,31 while arguing that "the divine perfection and the plurality of names said of God are not opposed to his simplicity."[22] We can attempt to say what God is because God is active in different things and can be named from them. But it does not follow from this that God is anything composite. "Through his one simple being," says Aquinas, "God possesses every kind of perfection that all other things come to possess, but in a much more diminished way." He continues: "From this we see the necessity of giving to God many names. For since we cannot know him naturally except by arriving at him from his effects, the names by which we signify his perfection must be diverse, just as the perfections belonging to things are found to be diverse."[23] Here, of course, Aquinas is saying that we can talk about God, who is simple, by noting different things that he has produced. What something produces, thinks Aquinas, might be various, but this does not mean that the producing thing is composed of different parts.

7. The thesis of SCG 1,32 is that "nothing is predicated univocally of God and other things."[24] By now you may realize why Aquinas thinks this. For the record, however, his arguments are: (1) the effect of an agent cause that is not what the cause is specifically cannot be said to be univocally the same as its cause, even if comparisons between the cause and its effect can be made for some reason or other; (2) "There is nothing in God that is not the divine being itself, which is not the case with other things";[25] (3) when we predicate of different things univocally we do so by predicating a genus or a species or a difference or an accident or a property. But God is not a member of a genus to be distinguished from other members of that genus, and there are no accidents in God; (4) "Nothing is predicated of God and

creatures as though they were in the same order, but, rather, according to priority and posteriority. For all things are predicated of God essentially."[26] Basically, Aquinas is here saying that nothing can be predicated of God and creatures univocally since creatures are composite and God is not. My cat and your cat can both be univocally referred to as feline. You and I can both be univocally referred to as human. According to Aquinas, however, God is not one of a kind, and there is no distinction between the individual that God is and the nature that God has, which Aquinas takes to mean that God cannot share any feature that a creature might have so as to have this feature as the creature does.

8. If terms used when talking of God and creatures are not to be understood univocally, however, does it follow that they are all to be understood in a purely equivocal way? That it does so follow is something that Aquinas denies in SCG 1,33, in which we find several arguments. In SCG 1,33 Aquinas rejects the idea that F in "X is F" and "God is F" always has to be construed as so utterly different in meaning as, say, "pen" is in "I keep my pen in my pocket" and "I keep my pigs in a pen." And, in his defense of this position, the following arguments surface: (1) to say that X and Y are F purely equivocally is to note that they are totally unalike; yet God can be named from creatures as being a cause that accounts for creatures existing as somehow resembling what God genuinely is; (2) "There is a certain mode of likeness of things to God"; (3) we can actually express some knowledge that we have of God by using words that we employ when talking of other things; (4) "Equivocation in a name impedes the process of reasoning"[27]—but we can reason to true conclusions concerning God using language that we normally employ without reference to God; (5) "If names are said of God and creatures in a purely equivocal way, we understand nothing of God through those names; for the meanings of those names are known to us solely to the extent that they are said of creatures."[28] In arguments 1–5 here Aquinas is saying that it is possible to argue philosophically for some truths concerning God and that it would be impossible to do so if all that is said of God and of what is not God should be construed as being purely equivocal. In Aquinas's view, even our feeble attempts to show that God exists as a first cause would fail if "cause," used when talking of God, means something totally different from what it means in other contexts.

9. And now we come to Aquinas on analogy, the topic discussed in SCG 1,34. Here Aquinas concludes that "the names said of God and creatures are predicated neither univocally nor equivocally but analogically, that is, according to an order or reference to something one."[29] Aquinas is suggesting that we can sometimes literally apply to God a term normally

predicated of a creature, and that we can do so in the light of reasoning from what can be thought of as an effect of God. In being able to do this, says Aquinas, we do not start from a knowledge of God but from a knowledge of what is creaturely. Then, having known and "named" the creature, we can apply that name to God while thinking of God as the cause of all creaturely perfections. So: "Because we come to a knowledge of God from other things, the reality in the names said of God and other things belongs by priority in God according to his mode of being, but the meaning of the name belongs to God by posteriority. And so he is said to be named from his effects."[30]

10. What though of the fact that God is "named" by different names? Aquinas would say that, for example, God is good and that God is powerful while taking "good" and "powerful" to be different names. Yet if God is entirely simple, should we not conclude that different names used of God are in fact just equivalent or synonymous? In SCG 1,35 Aquinas argues that different names said of God are "not synonyms because they do not signify the same notion."[31] Yes, thinks Aquinas, God is simple. So God is not something with a range of different properties, and goodness and power, say, are not different attributes that God happens to have. But the words "good" and "powerful" are different words, and the fact that we might want to use them when talking about God does not take away from that fact and, therefore, does not make them synonymous. What happens, thinks Aquinas, is that we sometimes take words with different meanings and then apply them to God while realizing that what these words signify somehow exists in God even though God is simple. Or, as Aquinas says in SCG 1,36: "Although, as we have said, our intellect arrives at the knowledge of God through diverse conceptions, it yet understands that what corresponds to all of them is absolutely one."[32] To be sure, Aquinas agrees, God is simple, and our attempts to describe God from creatures in sentences like "God is good" or "God is powerful" fall well short of the reality that we are trying to talk about. They signify God imperfectly since they wear the appearance of talk about composite things, while God is simple. And yet, Aquinas thinks, it is not "futile for our intellect to form enunciations concerning God in his simplicity by means of composition and division."[33] Because of how we think and talk about creatures, we employ different notions when referring to God, and what we say about God is inevitably going somehow to misrepresent the reality of God, who is wholly simple. Yet it remains that there can be reason for saying certain even apparently different things of God because God is the cause of all that is not divine.

So Aquinas holds that God is simple and that we can have reason to make certain statements about God in which words used of God and creatures are to be understood analogically. That is the teaching of SCG 1,18–36 in one sentence. But you might find this teaching to be highly abstract since in SCG 1,18–36 Aquinas talks in general terms. He says enough for us to see why he thinks that certain words signifying perfections can be truly and not just metaphorically used when we speak about God. Yet, you might ask "When in the SCG is Aquinas going to tell us how he thinks we can be justified in making particular concrete statements about God, statements like 'God is good'?"

The question is a fair one, and the answer to it is: "As soon as he is done with SCG 1,36." I say that because in SCG 1,37–102, Aquinas embarks on a series of discussions concerning what are sometimes called "the attributes of God." In SCG 1,18–36 Aquinas is *scene setting*. From SCG 1,37 onward he gets down to specifics, starting with an account of what he thinks can be said about the goodness of God. In the next few chapters I shall try to follow him as he makes his way through discussions, not only of God's goodness, but also of God's knowledge, will, and life. However, before I conclude this chapter I should, perhaps, say something about problems that people have had concerning the teaching of SCG 1,28–36.

5.3 *How to Assess SCG 1,28–36?*

If you uncritically assume that Aquinas is always making philosophical sense, you might be happy to suppose that all that he says in SCG 1,28–36 is correct. Yet these chapters do raise serious questions, chiefly, I think, because of the way in which they rely on conclusions that Aquinas takes for granted given previous chapters of the SCG. As I have shown, SCG 1,28–36 draws heavily on the conclusion that God is simple. Yet if Aquinas is wrong when it comes to divine simplicity, then he is obviously wrong in much of what he says in SCG 1,28–36. Yet suppose, for the sake of argument, that Aquinas is right about divine simplicity. Does it follow that we can talk sense about God as Aquinas thinks that we can?

One reason for thinking that it does not would lie in the idea that if God is as different from creatures as Aquinas takes him to be, then we cannot say anything that is literally true about God since we cannot really know what we are saying. As Herbert McCabe notes, an obvious objection to Aquinas on literal talk about God "is that in e.g. *God is good*, 'good' must either mean the same as it means when applied to creatures or something different. If it means the same, then God is reduced to the level of creatures; if it does not mean the same, then we cannot know what it means by knowing about creatures, we should have to understand God himself; but we do not, hence we do not understand at all—we only have an illusion of understanding because the word happens to be graphically the same as the 'good' we do understand."[34]

This line of criticism is one with which many philosophers of religion seem to sympathize. So we often find it argued that terms used of God and creatures should, abstracting from figurative usage, always be thought of as univocal in meaning.[35] The idea here is that, when it comes to literally true discourse concerning God, words have to retain their ordinary or mundane meaning on pain of becoming incomprehensible or meaningless. Defenders of this approach happily concede that, say, goodness in God amounts to something different from goodness in me. At the same time, however, they typically hold that the difference here is only a matter of degree. Mary may be a better person than John because she generally behaves better than John usually does, but this does not mean that Mary and John are not both good in the same sense. What it means is that Mary has more of the same quality that John has in something like the way in which bag X might have more of the same stuff in it as does bag Y.

This line of thinking will evidently not appeal to someone who thinks that Aquinas is right about divine simplicity. Such a person will, with Aquinas, note that a word cannot be used of God and a creature univocally since, unlike creatures, there is no distinction in God between individual and nature. Even without recourse to the notion of divine simplicity, however, there is, perhaps, a case to be made for refusing to accept that when it comes to meaning we are faced with a stark alternative between "univocal" and "equivocal." For why suppose that a word must either mean exactly the same when used of different things or else mean something quite different? Why not instead say that a word can be used of two different things with related meanings? After all, we do seem able to use words in this way. What Aquinas means by "analogy" is very prevalent in our use of language. Someone might say that his wife and his dog are both faithful. Such a person does not mean that his wife and his dog belong to the same species and have faithfulness univocally. He means that there is some reason to say that "faithful" is what his dog and his wife can be said to be. He means that we can speak of wives and dogs being faithful without supposing that what they are as faithful amounts to exactly the same thing even when it comes to matters of degree. Should we suppose that a wife and a dog should be ranked on a scale so that we might award them marks when it comes to their faithfulness? Surely, we cannot do this, though it does not therefore follow that it is nonsense to say of a dog and a wife that both of them are faithful. We might say that there are limits when it comes to faithfulness and that not just anything can be thought of as faithful, and so on for adjectives other than "faithful." Yet what Aquinas says in SCG 1,28–36 does not argue otherwise. His main concern seems to be to suggest that if we are going to speak of God truly, and without resorting to metaphor, we can use words that we employ when talking about creatures without assuming that God is an individual with properties distinct from himself, as God would not be if thought of as entirely simple. Why does Aquinas think this? The answer is: "Because he holds that certain words used when talking of creatures can be used when talking of God for particular reasons."

To some extent I have already shown what Aquinas has in mind in taking this view. That is because I have already shown that he generally believes that terms signifying perfections that have no creaturely meaning built into them can be used when talking of God since God, though entirely simple, is that from which all creaturely perfections derive. In the SCG, however, Aquinas turns at length to the task of explaining why particular reasons can be given for saying why certain words that we already employ when talking about creatures can also be used when we try to talk about God. As I have noted, in SCG 1,37 he begins to do this by focusing on the assertion that God is good. So let me now try to follow him as he discusses this assertion.

Goodness, Oneness, and Infinity
(SCG 1,37–43)

PSALM 136 BEGINS: "Give thanks to the Lord, for he is good." The psalm does not construe God's goodness as a matter of universal beneficence. It takes God's goodness to amount to conformity to his covenant promises to Israel and is happy to note how much woe and destruction God has brought on Israel's enemies. Still, Psalm 136 speaks of God as good, and that God can be called good is bluntly asserted in other biblical texts. In the New Testament we are even told that *only* God is good.[1] What biblical authors mean by the goodness of God is debated by Old and New Testament scholars, but there is no denying the fact that God's goodness is proclaimed in the Bible. It has also been championed by postbiblical authors, even if not all of them have construed "God is good" in exactly the same way.

So you will not be surprised to find that in SCG 1,37–42 Aquinas speaks of God as good. You might, however, be puzzled to find that these chapters never refer to God as being good in a way that many people do. I say that since it is often assumed that "God is good" means that God is *morally* good or *perfectly morally* good and since Aquinas does not say that God is this in SCG 1,37–42 (or anywhere else in the SCG for that matter). Instead, he focuses on goodness as bound up with perfection and as being what all things desire.

6.1 Why Is It True That God Is Good? (SCG 1,37)

In SCG 1,37 Aquinas has four arguments for the truth of "God is good." They run as follows:

1. That by which something is called good is a virtue that belongs to it. But a virtue is a kind of perfection. So something is good from the fact that it is perfect. Yet God is perfect. So God is good.
2. God is the totally unmoved mover. Some movers can be thought of as self-moved because they act as attracted to certain ends and are not moved by things in the world around them. Such self-moved movers, however, are

still moved by objects of desire while a completely unmoved mover moves as being an object of desire. God is such an object and is therefore good.

3. "Good is that which all things desire," as Aristotle says in book 1 of his *Nicomachean Ethics*. Now all things, though in different ways, desire to exist and shun their destruction; so being actual is desirable and, therefore, good. Yet God is fully actual and has no potentiality.

4. When things act they bring about goodness in other things since they bring it about that there is some kind of actuality in them. In order to do this, they have to be good or actual in some way. God acts so as to bring about the being and goodness of all that is not divine. So God is good, as the Bible declares.

6.1.1 Comments on SCG 1,37

When reading the above arguments as they occur in the SCG, it will help if you bear the following points in mind.

1. Aquinas is clearly not thinking of "good" as an adjective used so as to indicate that something has a particular physical property or a particular characteristic that sets it off from other things. "John is fat" tells us that John has a particular physical property or attribute. "John is intelligent" tells us that John has a characteristic that some people lack. But Aquinas does not understand "God is good" as comparable to "John is fat" or "John is intelligent." In SCG 1,37 he is thinking in general terms and saying that God is good since God can be thought of as perfect or desirable. The word "perfect" is not a descriptive adjective like, say, "wooden" (see SCG 1,28). Nor is the word "desirable" a straightforwardly descriptive adjective since different things might be taken to be desirable for different reasons. Yet Aquinas thinks that anything good or perfect has to be actual in some way. He also thinks that anything good or perfect is somehow desirable. It is with these thoughts in mind that he argues that God is good.

2. The word "virtue" in the first argument of SCG 1,37 should not be construed in moral terms. We speak of moral virtues such as prudence, courage, and justice, and we commonly describe people, and not other things, as having virtues. But "virtue" (*virtus*) in SCG 1,37 means "power" or "ability." Aquinas is thinking that a good thing is something the powers of which are somehow in order and not inhibited. It is on this basis that he reasons to the conclusion that God, considered as purely actual and as totally simple, is good as lacking nothing needed for his perfection.

3. The second of the above arguments might make sense to you if you bear in mind what Aquinas says in SCG 1,13. As I have shown, he there accepts that some things move themselves in that, like dogs, say, they run around on their own. As I have also shown, however, Aquinas does not think that such self-movers are totally unmoved. He thinks that they are moved by what they desire, that they are drawn to what they find attractive in some way (as, say, a dog is drawn to a bone). So, thinks Aquinas, objects of desire can move movers that seem to be self-moving, and such an object accounts for movement in them. He goes on to say: "This object is higher, in the order or motion, than the mover desiring it; for the one desiring is in a manner a moved mover whereas an appetible object is an absolutely unmoved mover."[2] In SCG 1,37, therefore, Aquinas is proceeding from the idea of being desired to being an unmoved mover, as he takes God to be.

4. In SCG 1,37 Aquinas is not taking "desire" to be ascribable only to people with intelligence who can desire on the basis of what they know to be the case or on the basis of what they might hope to be the case. "Desire" (*appetitus* in Aquinas's Latin) might be thought of as inclination or tendency. A cat may pounce on a mouse because it has it in it to be drawn to mice considered as food. With this fact in mind, Aquinas would say that cats "desire" mice since they are inclined to grab them when they see them, or since they have a tendency to do so. Again, Aquinas would say that everything seeks or desires to be itself because, in the absence of interference, it "does its own thing" as the being that it is, whether conscious, like us, or nonconscious, like a plant. It is in this sense that Aquinas holds that the good is what all things desire. They desire it, are inclined to it, or tend to it, just because they are. In SCG 1,37 Aquinas says that "each thing according to its nature resists corruption." I take him to mean that everything tends to go on existing unless something else interferes with it. So I take him to think that all things "desire" goodness since they tend to continue to exist with the goodness that they have for as long as they exist.

6.2 Is God Goodness Itself? (SCG 1,38)

Some people speak of God's goodness as an attribute or property that God has, one that he possesses to a high or maximal degree. Aquinas, however, does not talk like this. As I have shown, he thinks that "God is good" is true. As I have also shown, however, Aquinas also holds that God is totally simple and that what God is and the individual that God is are not distinct. Not surprisingly, therefore, Aquinas follows SCG 1,37 with a defense of the claim that

God is not just a good thing but is goodness itself (*sua bonitas*). In SCG 1,38 he offers four main arguments for this conclusion.

First, God is his very act of being (see SCG 1,22). "God is, therefore, goodness itself, and not only good."[3]

Second, God's perfection is not something added to God. It is God's very substance. It is what God is.[4]

Third, God has to be goodness itself since goodness is not something in which God participates. It is what God's essence is. God is Being Itself and, as such, "can participate in nothing."[5]

Fourth, if God is entirely simple, then what God is has to be God, in which case God is goodness if God is good.[6]

As I say, what Aquinas argues in SCG 1,38 comes as no surprise since he draws heavily on what we find earlier in the SCG, especially SCG 1,18, 22, and 37. However, the third argument just noted calls for a bit of explanation because of its appeal to participation. The notion of participation features briefly prior to SCG 1,38. You can find it, for example, in SCG 1,22. I have not, however, offered any explanation of what Aquinas has in mind by the word "participation," and I should do so now.

For Aquinas, something can be said to participate in F if it is F or has F-ness and if it is something alongside others all of whom are F or who have F-ness.[7] I am human, and so are you. Aquinas would put this by saying that we both participate in humanity somehow. Here, of course, Aquinas is trying to do justice to the evident truth that many different things can be somehow the same while also being completely different things. His final position is that this can only be so because there is genuinely something distinguishable from them as individuals, something in which they can be said to share, or to "participate."

In what sense does Aquinas take the F-ness of X and Y to be different from X and Y? He certainly does not think of it as lying in the fact that the F-ness of X and Y is a substance eternally existing in addition to X and Y, as Plato has been credited to have held. Rather, he holds that we cannot straightforwardly identify individuals in the world with the natures or properties that they have in common or might be said to share. Though I am human, it would be odd for me to declare that I am human nature or that I am humanity. After all, human nature was, presumably, somehow around before I was born, and it will remain around when I am gone. So is there not, therefore, a sense in which human nature can be distinguished from me even though I cannot exist if I cease to be a human being?

Aquinas thinks that there has to be and that human nature, though not a substance, can be distinguished from me as being what I share in but am not to be identified with. He claims that human nature is *commonable* or *shareable* even if it is no distinct substance. You might ask how human nature can *be* anything if it is not a distinct substance or a particular accident had by a human being. Yet Aquinas does not think that "being a substance" or "being an accident" exhausts the possibilities for being. He does not think that God is a particular substance or accident, yet he thinks that God exists. Indeed, as I have shown, he thinks that God is subsisting being (*esse*). He also thinks that something like human nature can be said to exist since it is exemplified by many things not identical with each other or with the natures that can be ascribed to them.

Now back to the third argument I noted in SCG 1,38. We can represent it thus:

1. Something that is not goodness itself is called "good" with reference to what is distinct from the individual that it is, something "prior" to the good thing in question, something the goodness of which is *received* by the good thing in question. (Since Aquinas takes it that things can ultimately receive goodness only from what does not itself receive goodness from another, he consequently argues that God, as first cause, cannot be thought of as merely sharing in what good things have but is "good through its own essence.")[8]
2. God is pure being or Being Itself. But Being Itself is not potential or derived from another. So, if God is good, then God is goodness itself and not something that is good by sharing in what other things have as derived from God.

6.3 Is there Evil in God? (SCG 1,39)

If you think that God is "goodness itself," then you are hardly likely to suppose that there is evil or badness in God. You will think, as Aquinas does at the start of SCG 1,39, that "it is quite evident that there cannot be evil in God."[9] However, in the same chapter Aquinas spells out a number of arguments for this supposition. Here I shall summarize them very briefly since, as you will note, they just elaborate on what Aquinas takes to be implications of what he has been saying in the SCG up to this point.

1. If God is goodness itself, then there can be no nongoodness in him.
2. If God's essence is goodness, then there can be no evil in God unless God ceased to be God, which is impossible since God is eternal, as noted in SCG 1,15.

3. Since God does not have his being as existing alongside other things (as something that participates in being and is not Being Itself), then, if there is evil in God, it follows that God is essentially evil. But nothing can be essentially evil since evil arises in what exists, and is therefore good to some extent.

4. Evil is "the opposite of good."[10] But goodness involves perfection, and God is perfect without qualification (see SCG 1,28). So there is no evil in God.

5. An imperfect thing fails somehow when it comes to being actual. "Evil is a privation or includes privation." But "the subject of privation is potency, which cannot be in God. Neither, therefore, can evil."[11]

6. Things sometimes suffer from evil because something is thwarting them in some way. But nothing can mess around with God since God is wholly simple and is the reason why anything other than God exists and acts.

6.4 God as the Good of Every Good and as the Highest Good (SCG 1,40–41)

In chapter 2 of book 8 of his *De Trinitate* (*On the Trinity*), St. Augustine of Hippo refers to God as being "not good with some other good, but the good of every good." Augustine seems to be saying that God is not a good such and such but is goodness itself. He writes: "Take away this and that and see God, not good with some other good, but the good of every good."[12] In SCG 1,40 Aquinas picks up on the phrase "good of every good" (*omnis boni bonum*). Goodness, he says, is what God is, and good things in the world receive any goodness they have from the goodness that God essentially is. In SCG 1,41 Aquinas follows up this thought by insisting that God is the highest good (*summum bonum*) since (1) God is the good of every good, (2) God is good essentially, (3) all goodness in creatures derives from God, and (4) there is nothing evil in God.

6.5 Oneness and Infinity (SCG 1,42–43)

Given what Aquinas argues in SCG 1,37–39, the contents of SCG 1,40–41 are somewhat predictable. In SCG 1,42 and 43, however, Aquinas breaks new ground while arguing that God is one and that God is infinite.

Actually, to say that Aquinas breaks *new* ground in SCG 1,42–43 is a bit of an overstatement since, in his view, the contents of SCG 1,42 follow from what he has already written in the SCG. He writes: "From what has been shown it is evident that God is one."[13] But how so? Here is a summary of the arguments provided in SCG 1,42.[14]

1. There cannot be two highest goods since "that which is said by superabundance is found only in one being."[15] Yet God is the highest good.

2. There cannot be more than one absolutely perfect being since there is no way in which members of a class of absolutely perfect beings could be differentiated from each other.[16]

3. If something can be brought about by one thing, it is best to suppose that it is one thing that has brought it about. Yet "all things are sufficiently fulfilled by a reduction to one first principle" and "there is, therefore, no need to posit many principles."[17]

4. As first mover, God is a perfect, single, and continuous mover. God cannot be a collection of movers moving together. Nor can he be one of a group of movers not moving together. Neither can he be a mover who is not always moving in a regular way.[18]

5. There is no physical motion apart from the first mover, who is incorporeal. But by "God" we mean "first and incorporeal mover." So there is only one God.[19]

6. God is the first ordering cause active in all things considered as a whole and considered as a unit containing diverse things that interact in a nonaccidental way, thereby implying a single governing cause. So "there is only one governor for all things, whom we call God."[20]

7. If there are two absolutely necessary beings, they must be distinct in some way even if they are both absolutely necessary. But if X and Y are distinct from each other while each being absolutely necessary, then one or both of them must be composite. Yet God is totally simple.[21]

8. There cannot be many beings each of whom by itself is absolutely necessary in the sense of existing without the activity of anything external to it. If there are two necessary beings, it cannot be their being necessary that distinguishes them since they share this. So they will be different as having different accidents. In that case, however, neither of them is absolutely necessary since accidents require causes and causes imply something totally uncaused. Absolute necessity in something has to belong to it by nature, meaning that what is absolutely necessary is something whose very nature is to exist, not something with accidents that are somehow added to it considered as what it is by nature.[22]

9. If we speak of there being many gods, we are using the word "god" either univocally or equivocally when saying that one of them is god and that another is as well. If we use the word univocally, then our many gods will be

exactly the same insofar as they are gods, meaning that "there must be in both one nature."[23] But this nature is either derived from something else, or it is not. If it is not, then it is had by only one thing the very nature of which is to exist, as is the nature of God. "There cannot be one being for two things that are substantially distinguished."[24] So things that can be substantially distinguished are not things the essence of which is to exist, as is the essence of God.

10. What makes something *this* thing as opposed to *another* thing cannot be shared by many things. But being absolutely necessary is what God is, and, since he is entirely simple, his being necessary is not to be distinguished from the individual that he is. So the nature of God, which is God, is therefore not something that can be shared by other individuals any more than the individuality of a particular thing can be.[25]

11. If there were two gods, then the divine nature would not be identically the same in each and something else must be added to effect the distinction. But nothing can be added to the nature of God considered as wholly simple.[26]

12. The being that is proper to something is one. But God is his being since he is totally simple.[27]

13. A thing has being insofar as it has unity. But God is Being Itself and is therefore not subject to division.[28]

14. Things belonging to a genus have some one thing or principle running through them, something that is one and not a multitude. Now, all things that exist have being in common, and the principle of being in things must be one, not many.[29]

15. Rulers desire unity, and "one to whom rulership belongs should have unity." So "God, who is the cause of all things, is absolutely one."[30]

When it comes to God's infinity, Aquinas focuses on the notion of infinite perfection. He agrees that God cannot be infinite as comprising an infinite number of things or as being infinite in terms of bodily quantity. That God is not infinite in either of these senses follows from the fact that there is but one God and from the fact that God is incorporeal. Yet Aquinas sees no harm in asking whether God is infinite in power, goodness, or perfection, and he maintains that God is infinitely powerful, good, and perfect. There is "no terminus or limit to his perfection."[31]

What follows this remark is a restatement of what Aquinas has already said in the SCG concerning God's perfection. He notes, for example, that God somehow contains the perfections of everything other than God. Again, he reasons that God is supremely independent and unlimited since "He is his own being" and contains no potentiality since he is "infinite in his actuality."[32]

Yet again, he maintains (1) that God is not a being limited by what causes it, since God is the cause of the being of all that is not God, (2) that nothing better than God can be imagined since God is essentially perfect and is his own goodness, and (3) that God accounts for the existence of everything that can be thought of as finite.

6.6 A Note on Aquinas's "God Is Good" and "There Is No Evil in God"

Polytheism (belief in many gods) is not an option for Aquinas since he reads the Bible as teaching that God is one (meaning that there is only one God, not that God has a property of "oneness"). Polytheism is also not an option for Aquinas since he thinks of God as the source of the existence of whatever can be counted together with other things, as the reason why there is a world in which one can distinguish between individuals of the same kind. At the end of SCG 1,42 Aquinas notes that the Bible contains passages in which the word "god" is used in the plural and in reference to what is not divine.[33] But he claims, surely rightly, that such passages do not say that anything is God as is the one true God. Rather, they employ the word "god" to refer to what is not divine but which displays some perfection that one can associate with divinity (compare describing the object of one's love as an "angel").

Polytheism does indeed seem to be ruled out if we accept Aquinas's frame of reference and think of God as the simple, eternal, unchanging source of everything that has being and that is not Being Itself. The same can surely be said when it comes to belief in God as finite. If God is the simple, eternal, unchanging source of everything that has being, and if Aquinas is right about "God is perfect," then, in certain senses of "finite," being finite is not readily attributable to God. In the SCG, Aquinas does not consider "infinite" to be a positive descriptive adjective like, say, "square." He thinks of it in negative terms, as *denying* finitude to God. Indeed, in SCG 1,43 he explicitly says that "in God the infinite is understood only in a negative way, because there is no terminus or limit to his perfection."[34]

So, even if you disagree with some of the arguments in SCG 1,42 and 43, you might sympathize with what Aquinas seems basically to be saying in these chapters concerning God's oneness and infinity. You may not, however, sympathize with what he says about God's goodness and lack of evil in SCG 1,37–41, because you might think that Aquinas should be explaining in these chapters how God is morally good. As I have noted, Aquinas does not speak of God as being morally good in SCG 1,37–41. But should he not have done so? Should he not also have tried to defend the proposition "God is good" while citing ways in which God might be morally exonerated for permitting the evils that we encounter? In what follows, I want briefly to defend the way in which Aquinas does and does not proceed in SCG 1,37–41.

6.6.1 Why Aquinas Might Be Thought to Be Wrong in SCG 1,37–41

It is not hard to see why one might conclude that SCG 1,37–41 is off-beam and misguided because of its lack of attention to God's moral goodness. As I have noted, people often take it to be axiomatic that "God is good" means that God is morally good. Yet we find nothing about God's moral goodness in SCG 1,37–41. So, if "God is good" means that God is morally good, something must be wrong with SCG 1,37–41 since it says nothing about God's moral goodness. How, one might ask, can Aquinas hope to have offered a decent account of God's goodness without mentioning God's moral goodness? And how can Aquinas hope to have offered a defense of "God is good and not evil" without taking note of the evils in the world? If God accounts for the existence of the universe at any time, then he presumably accounts for the evils that exist. Yet how can God do this without being bad in some way? And is Aquinas not just being insensitive to the force of this question as he goes about his business in SCG 1,39, in which he claims that there is no evil in God? How can there be no evil in God if God allows people to suffer? How can there be no evil in God if he allows children to suffer? How can there be no evil in God if, for example, he allows for the occurrence of war, murder, genocide, and pain in general? After all, is not God a person? And are good persons not people who do their best to fight against moral evil and evils that inflict us because of how things work in nature? Yet in SCG 1,37–41 Aquinas says nothing about God being good as people are good.

6.6.2 Responses to the Above

One problem with the above line of argument is that it assumes that "good" always means "morally good," which it does not. "Good" is a general term of commendation, and we employ it when praising things of various kinds for different reasons.

We speak of good people, of course. We say that so-and-so is a good man or that so-and-so is a good woman, and when we do that we are typically referring to them as morally praiseworthy. It is in our general references to people as being good that the notion of moral goodness has its home. But we use the word "good" even when not commending people morally. We speak of good restaurants, good teachers, good books, good doctors, good music, good pia-nists, good refrigerators, good scientists, good radios, and good philosophers and theologians.

In short, we call all sorts of things good, and for much of the time when we do this we are not thinking of moral goodness at all. Good restaurants, good books, good music, good refrigerators, and good radios are not *morally* good. Again, even when we apply the word "good" to teachers, doctors, pianists, scientists, philosophers, and theologians, we need not be thinking in moral terms. To be sure, we might agree that, for example, good teachers are people who behave ethically toward their students and employers. However, when commending someone as a good teacher we would normally be thinking of teaching skills, not moral excellence. Again, we might readily concede that someone who is morally wicked can be a good, indeed brilliant, doctor or pi-anist or philosopher. Something can be good under one description and bad under another. Fred might be a great scientist but a bad husband. Mary might be a wonderful opera singer but a bad wife.

"Good" resembles "perfect." It is what Peter Geach (1916–2013) calls a log-ically attributive adjective. It gets its sense from the nouns to which it is at-tached. So goodness in teachers, say, amounts to something different from goodness in pianists or refrigerators. Good teachers are individuals who edu-cate well, engage with students in a lively way, care for their students, prepare their classes, and so on. By contrast, good refrigerators are things that keep food cool, do not make noise, conserve energy, have plenty of room in them, and so on. This is not to say that we have to be equivocating when calling dif-ferent things good. It is not to say that there is nothing at all common to eve-rything we call good. But it cannot be any particular property had by things of one kind, as, say, being mammalian is a property shared by dogs, cats, and whales. As Geach observes: "There is no such thing as being just good or bad, there is only being a good and bad so-and-so."[35]

Some philosophers have suggested that when we call things good we are not describing them but expressing a reaction to them. On this account, "X is good" should be understood to mean something like "I approve of X." This view has been criticized on the ground that "good" is an adjective. Yet we sometimes use adjectives when we are merely expressing a reaction of some kind. Americans often speak of things as being "awesome." When doing so, they are chiefly saying how wonderful or amazing they find something to be. They are not ascribing a distinct attribute to it, as they would if they said, for example, that X is a plastic bag rather than a paper one. Again, "astonishing" is an adjective, but one would only seriously call something astonishing be-cause one finds it to be unexpected or unusual, not because it contains in itself an attribute of astonishingness together with the other attributes that it possesses. In short, the fact that "good" is an adjective does not mean that it is always used to describe.

Yet "good" is grammatically an adjective, and there would seem to be a question of fact involved in its correct usage. If I return a radio to a store, I might say that the radio is bad or no good, and I might well be expressing my feelings or reactions to the radio. My retailer, however, will want me to prove that the radio I bought is defective in some way. Again, if my retailer insists that the radio I bought is good, I will expect him to demonstrate that he can, for instance, make it work properly. The words "good" and "bad" may be context- or noun-sensitive, but they are genuinely descriptive.

Can we, however, say what is common to everything that is genuinely good? Several times over in his writings, Aquinas responds to this question by quoting Aristotle, according to whom something is good insofar as it is desirable.[36] Aquinas thinks that we call something good because we take it to have features that we want it to have or that it needs to have considered as the thing that it is. And this conclusion makes sense. We will say that someone is a good teacher because he or she matches up to expectations that we have and find desirable in teachers. Or we will say that X is a good radio because it matches up to expectations that we have and find desirable in radios. Or we will say that something is in a good way insofar as it flourishes considered as what it is. Hence, for example, though my cat will not be in a bad way because it cannot function as a radio does, it will be in a bad way if its lungs are congested or if it has cancer. In general, we take things to be good insofar as they are working well considered as what they are.

What, though, if we say that God is good? If Aquinas is right in his teaching on divine simplicity, then we cannot mean that God is functioning well considered as something in the world. We cannot even mean that God is functioning well considered as the kind of thing that he is. We might say that God is beneficent in that he provides certain goods for creatures. Yet this will not commit us to the conclusion that God is morally good as people can be morally good. For we surely commend people as being morally good while thinking of them as spatiotemporal individuals who do what they ought to do in circumstances in which they find themselves or who, in the circumstances in which they find themselves, display virtues of the kind listed by Aristotle, virtues such as courage, temperance, justice, and prudence. Yet why should we suppose that God is morally good in these senses?

Aquinas does not do so because he takes God to be the source of all things that we can label as being "good" as members of a kind. He also does not do so since he thinks of God as goodness itself, not as someone trying to do the right thing in some particular context. As I will show when we come to SCG 1,93, Aquinas is prepared to say that God has "moral virtues." As I will also show, however, he thinks that there are moral virtues in God only insofar as God is what accounts for there being moral virtues in people, not because he thinks that God is morally virtuous as people are virtuous—as individuals who exist in time, who tend to do what makes for their fulfillment as human beings. You might say that if God is good then he is a good person. As I have already noted, however, Aquinas is not mesmerized by the nonbiblical formula "God is a person." He thinks that God accounts for the sheer existence of what we have in mind when we use the word "person" when talking of human beings. We can get our mind around persons of our acquaintance so as to understand what they are and whether they are well behaved or badly behaved. As I have noted, however, Aquinas does not think that we can do anything comparable when it comes to God. He does not even think that we understand what God is, and almost all of SCG 1 proceeds on the assumption that, if we are to know anything about God, we have to know it on the basis of what God has produced, not on the basis of some prior understanding of God. And if Aquinas is right in thinking along these lines, then he is right to focus on the goodness of God while not starting with the idea that God must be good as morally good human beings are good. If God, as Aquinas says in the SCG, is the first cause of all things and the simple and eternal and unchangeable source of there being something rather than nothing, then God's goodness can hardly be what we might affirm or deny while thinking about moral goodness in people. One might even suggest that to do this would be to engage in idolatry, to take God to be a creature of some kind.

It is with thoughts such as these in mind that Aquinas says what he does about God's goodness in SCG 1. Understandably, therefore, he does not defend the proposition "God is good" by trying to show that God is morally justifiable for allowing badness or evil to exist. Philosophers discussing the problem of evil frequently imply that we cannot say that God is good unless we have explained what God's good moral motives are for allowing evils. Aquinas, however, seems to think that such philosophers would be mistaken since (1) they assume that if God is good then God is morally good, and (2) they assume that, while abstracting from evils in the world, it is impossible to defend the claim that God is good. Aquinas does not think of God as a morally good person. But he does think that he can offer a defense of the proposition "God is good," and his defense of this proposition should be considered on its merits and not cast aside because it does not engage with reasons for supposing that God might be morally bad. As I will show, Aquinas goes on in the SCG to talk about what causes evil and what evil or badness are in general and in particular. In SCG 1,37–41, however, he is talking about God and goodness without claiming that God is a good thing of some kind. Insofar as he is doing this, there is something seriously wrong with criticisms of SCG 1,37–41 based on the idea that God, if he exists, is a morally good person who needs to be defended accordingly.[37]

6.7 *Moving On*

I have now shown how Aquinas argues that God exists as first mover and first cause. I have also shown him maintaining that God is perfect, though not a perfect such and such, and that God is good, though not a good member of a class of beings. As I have noted, Aquinas additionally claims that God is eternal, incorporeal, and simple, and that we do not understand what God is even though we can truly proclaim, without equivocation, that God is perfect and good.

Yet those who believe in God tell us that he has knowledge and acts with will or freedom, and, in spite of what he says about divine simplicity, Aquinas is of their mind. You will have surmised by now that he cannot take God to know by having investigated so as to arrive at a true conclusion on the basis of evidence or by being informed by someone. In SCG 1,44–96, however, he has much to say about God's knowledge and God's will. So let me now try to explain how he understands these.

God's Knowledge (SCG 1, 44–71)

I HAVE NOTED that Aquinas regards the words that we use when speaking about God as inevitably borrowed from their everyday nontheological employment (see chapter 5, section 1 here). And he does so when turning to the topic of God's knowledge. Though Aquinas ascribes knowledge to God, therefore, we should not assume in advance that we have grasped what he means by doing so. We need to read him on his own terms.

From what I have already shown of SCG 1, we might expect Aquinas to think that knowledge is different as it exists in God from what it amounts to in people or other things in the world. Yet, from what I have also shown of SCG 1, we might equally expect him not to think "knowledge" or "knows" as purely equivocal when ascribed to or said of God and of what is not divine. And we shall find both of these expectations to be fulfilled as we read SCG 1,44–71. Aquinas certainly does think that God's knowledge is not exactly like what knowledge is in anything other than God. He does, however, find connections between knowledge in God and in what is not divine. So, turning to what Aquinas says about God's knowledge, I am first going to note how, in general, Aquinas thinks of knowledge as had by things that he takes to be made by God. Then I shall try to explain why and how he takes knowledge to be ascribable to God. Finally, I shall offer some comments on what Aquinas says of knowledge in general (without reference to God) and on what he says as he speaks in the SCG about knowledge in God.

7.1 Aquinas on Knowledge

The verb "to know" occurs in sentences in which it surely does not mean exactly the same thing. Consider, for example, "I know that someone is ringing my doorbell," "I know that Paris is the capital of France," "I know that most people die before they reach the age of 100," "I know that it was once fashionable for Englishmen to wear spats," "I know that there are three letters in the word 'cat,'" "I know what a cat is," and "I know that 'God' translates the Latin 'Deus' into English." What is going on with me as I "know" all these things seems to be varied. To know that someone is ringing my doorbell is just to register the fact that my doorbell is ringing, and not of its own accord. Knowing that Paris is the capital of France is to grasp something precise concerning something particular. Again, knowing something about "most people" is to be aware of a generalization, not a fact about anyone in particular, as is knowing that spats were once fashionable in certain circles. And, while knowing that "cat" contains three letters is knowing something about a word, knowing what a cat is presumably involves knowing what it takes for a cat to exist at all, while knowing that the word "Deus" can be translated as "God" is to have some ability to read both Latin and English.

So "knowledge" does not always signify exactly the same thing, and Aquinas is aware of this fact. He does, however, think that knowledge always involves a cognition or awareness of some kind, an assimilation of what can be flagged by a possibly true proposition, even if the proposition is actually false.[1] When it comes to people, whom Aquinas takes to be the highest and best understood knowers of our acquaintance, knowledge is always the result of an *intellectual* contact with material things.

When I sit on a chair, the chair and my backside make contact, but not intellectually. What, though, if I observe a chair and am able to talk about it? Then I and the chair seem to come together as two contiguous physical things do not.

Again, what if my cat looks at a book the pages of which I present to it so that it can rub its nose into them? Again, there is contact. But is it intellectual?

Aquinas thinks that when it comes to people there is more than mere physical contact involved in the coming about of knowledge, however varied the objects of knowledge are, however different might be what we put after the word "that" in sentences like "I know/believe/recognize that ___."

According to Aquinas, knowledge is what things with intellect (*intellectus*) possess or can possess. Aquinas would agree that, for instance, my cat can be said to know that I am its source of food, though my cat lacks intellect. But he would have taken this "knowledge" on the part of my cat to be nothing but a reaction to me based on previous experience and its nature as a food-seeking feline: instinct married to habituation, not understanding or cognition in a more developed sense, not what Aquinas refers to as *intellectus* and ascribes to people when using the verbs *intelligere*, *scire*, and *cognoscere*, all of which can be translated as "to know."

Things with *intellectus*, says Aquinas, can have *scientia* or *cognitio*, both of which terms can be translated by "knowledge." Aquinas thinks of *scientia*, which he views as a kind of cognition, as knowledge in the fullest or highest sense, for he takes us to have *scientia* when we thoroughly understand what something is by nature, what its essence amounts to (see chapter 2, section 1 here). For Aquinas, to have *scientia* is to have followed a demonstration through to its necessary conclusion. It also involves grasping the truth of the premises that entail such a conclusion. But *cognitio* is also important for Aquinas since he thinks of it as at work when we take in the world around us by sensation and as we frame, or even entertain or accept, propositions that we understand, even if they do not amount to what we have demonstrated, or even if they do not amount to what Aquinas would have considered to be universal truths or real definitions of actually existing things.

Sometimes Aquinas speaks of knowledge occurring as we "receive" the forms of material things "immaterially." This may strike you as an odd or even unintelligible idea, but Aquinas takes it to be obviously right. Material things, he says, have forms in that they are things of a certain natural kind or in that they have accidents that really inhere in them. So, thinks Aquinas, my cat is a cat since being a cat is what it is by nature, and my cat is black and white since its coat is black and white. Aquinas takes this to mean that my cat has a certain *substantial form* (what it takes for it to exist as a cat) and various *accidental forms* (features that it happens to have but could lose without ceasing to be a cat). For Aquinas, my cat's substantial and accidental forms are real and ascribable to my cat, which *has* them just by being what it is substantially or accidentally. But what must be going on if I understand what a cat is? Then, says Aquinas, what exists in a cat substantially or accidentally must somehow exist in me even though I am not a cat.

The thought here is that in knowing what something is there has to be an intellectual taking in of what the thing actually is. There has, in the knower, to be something of what the thing known is. If there is not, thinks Aquinas, then the knower and thing known will not truly relate to each other or make contact with each other as knower and known. Aquinas is clear that things can be related to each other in different ways. He thinks that people can be related to each other by virtue of their respective physical positions or by virtue of the fact that one person is having some kind of effect on another one. Again, he would agree that X can be thought of as related to Y because X has some kind of sensory contact with Y, as, for example, my cat does with me as it lies on my lap. For Aquinas, however, knowing what something is cannot be equivalent to physical relation or sensory relation since it amounts to intellectually grasping what the thing truly is in itself, while there need be no such grasping when two things are physically related to each other or when one thing senses another. So, Aquinas concludes, I know what a cat is by having what it takes to be a particular cat formally without myself being an actual cat, and he takes this to mean that what exists in a cat materially comes to be in me without belonging to a material cat. Aquinas holds that one can only know what is intelligible and that physical things are potentially intelligible insofar as what they are can be understood. But the coming to be understood of potentially intelligible physical things, he says, can only occur as what exists in them formally comes to be in the intellect of a knower as form without matter.

We can distinguish between the questions "What does it mean to be a cat?" and "What does the word 'cat' mean?" What it means to be a cat is to exist as whatever a cat is. Yet understanding what "cat" means cannot be that. Understanding what a cat is has to be different from being a cat, even though it must involve the intelligible factor in cats coming to exist in one, and Aquinas would say the same when it comes to understanding what anything at all is. For him, anything potentially intelligible comes to be understood as it exists in knowers as understood, as what is potentially intelligible comes to be without being confined to matter. Hence his idea of knowledge occurring as we receive or are informed by the forms of material things immaterially. For Aquinas, knowledge or intellect is had by something only insofar as its way of being includes existence unrestricted by matter, insofar as it has received various forms without matter.[2]

7.2 *Aquinas on God's Knowledge (SCG 1, 44–71)*

When it comes to God's knowledge, Aquinas's main claims are:

1. God has intellect or understanding (SCG 1,44).
2. God's act of intellect is his essence (SCG 1,45).
3. God understands by nothing except his essence (SCG 1,46).
4. God understands himself perfectly (SCG 1,47).
5. Primarily and essentially, God knows only himself (SCG 1,48).
6. God knows things other than himself (SCG 1,49).
7. God has a proper knowledge of all things (SCG 1,50).
8. There is no habitual knowledge (*habitualis cognitio*) in God (SCG 1,56).
9. God's knowledge is not discursive (*discursiva*) (SCG 1,57).
10. God does not understand by composing and dividing (*componentis et dividentis*) (SCG 1,58).
11. God knows truths that we articulate by composing and dividing (SCG 1,59).
12. God is not only truth but the purest truth and the first and highest truth (SCG 1,60, 61, and 62).
13. God knows singulars, things that are not, future contingent singulars, the thoughts of the mind and the motions of the will, infinite things, lowly or trifling things (*vilia*), and evils (*mala*) (SCG 1,65–71).

7.2.1 God as Intelligent (SCG 1,44)

Aquinas's first set of arguments for God having intellect or being intelligent draws on his thinking about motion in SCG 1,13. Aquinas says that God must have intellect since God is the first self-moving being. He notes that self-moving things in the world are not completely self-moved since they are moved by appetite and knowledge. So, he reasons, the first unmoved mover must have in itself what corresponds to desire or knowledge in secondary movers. It cannot possess desire considered as an appetite for what is pleasing to the senses, but it can desire what is good without qualification. In that case, however, it must have knowledge of what is good without qualification. Indeed, Aquinas goes on to say, this conclusion follows even if we start by taking God to be not "a first self-moving being" but "an absolutely unmoved mover."[3] Why so? Because "the first mover is the universal source of motion" and because "since every mover moves through a form at which it aims in moving, the form through which the first mover moves must be a universal form and a universal good."[4] Aquinas holds that a form does not "have a universal mode except in the intellect," thereby drawing the conclusion that "the first mover, God, must be intelligent."[5] He goes on to observe that God must also be intelligent since there are many intelligent movers in the world all of which are instruments of God, and since it is never the case "that an intellectual mover is the instrument of a mover without an intellect."[6]

Following these motion-oriented arguments, Aquinas defends the claim that God is intelligent with four others not drawing on motion.

The first applies Aquinas's claim that intellect as active involves the existence of form without matter.[7] We read: "Forms that are understood in act become one with the intellect that understands them in act. Therefore, if forms are understood in act because they are without matter, a thing must be intelligent because it is without matter. But we have shown that God is absolutely immaterial. God is, therefore, intelligent."[8]

In the second argument Aquinas holds that, since God contains the perfections of creatures while being totally simple, God must contain the perfection of intellect, which, as Aristotle says, extends to all things and can contain them in understanding.[9]

In the third argument Aquinas maintains that God sets ends for things in nature, which implies intellect on his part. God "could not set an end for nature unless he had understanding. God is, therefore, intelligent."[10]

Finally, argues Aquinas: (1) the perfect is "prior" to the imperfect as act is prior to potency, (2) forms existing in particular things are imperfect since they are limited by that in which they exist, (3) such forms must derive from unlimited forms, which can only exist as objects of understanding "since no form is found in its universality except in the intellect,"[11] (4) if such forms were to exist as subsisting things, they would be intelligent, and (5) therefore, God, "Who is the first subsistent act, from whom all other things are derived, must be intelligent."[12] I should note that Aquinas is not here saying that there are many subsistent forms in which things in the world "participate" in some way. He does not believe that there are, and he rejects Plato's theory of forms as it is commonly construed, as holding that forms exist as objects in a non-material realm (see section 7.2.1 above). In SCG 1,44 he is arguing that forms limited by existing in particular material things must derive from a form not so limited, a form that, if it were to subsist, would have to do so as having intellect, as Aquinas takes God to have.

7.2.2   "God's Understanding Is the Divine Essence" (SCG 1,45)

You will, I hope, not be confounded to find Aquinas saying in SCG 1,45 that God's understanding is his essence. Given his SCG explication of divine simplicity, he could hardly say anything else. Aquinas holds that all that is in God is God, that there is no distinction between the individual God is and the nature that God has, and that there is no distinction between God's essence (*essentia*) and existence (*esse*). Such a position seems to entail that if God has knowledge, that knowledge is not an attribute that God has but is nothing other than the being or essence of God. As Aquinas writes in SCG 1,45: "Whatever is in God is the divine essence. God's act of understanding, therefore, is his essence, it is the divine being, God himself. For God is his essence and his being."[13] This line of thought runs through all of the arguments in SCG 1,45, so I shall not here try to represent each of them in detail.

7.2.3   God Understanding through the Divine Essence and as Understanding God (SCG 1,46–48)

As I have said, Aquinas thinks that we understand as forms come to be in us immaterially at least partly because of the sensory impact on us of things in the world.[14] He refers to these forms as intelligible *species* (ideas) by which we understand, so he regards them as causing us to know or understand.[15] With this notion in mind, in SCG 1,46 Aquinas denies that God understands by means of intelligible species as these come to be in people. Why? Because he takes God to be totally simple and lacking in parts that might help him to function in some way or other. We understand by means of intelligible species, he thinks, but he also argues that, given divine simplicity, God's understanding has to be what the divine essence is, not something deriving from what is in God while being distinguishable from the divine essence. Or, as Aquinas says in SCG 1,46, if "the divine intellect understood by an intelligible species other than the divine essence, something other would be added to the divine essence as principle and cause."[16] In SCG 1,46 Aquinas goes on to argue that God can only understand through his essence since there is no actualized potentiality in God and since there are no accidents in God. According to Aquinas, we *come to* know by means of intelligible species, which are *accidents* that arise in us, but there is no *coming about* in God, which means that God's understanding is, so to speak, a function of his essence, or that God's understanding is his essence. He writes: "God's understanding, as we have shown, is his essence. If, therefore, God understood through a species that was not his essence, it would be through something other than his essence. This is impossible. Therefore, God does not understand through a species that is not his essence."[17]

In short, the "big idea" in SCG 1,46 is that God cannot understand because something that comes to be in him causes him to do so. For Aquinas, there is understanding in God just because the divine essence exists. And because he thinks this, Aquinas proceeds in SCG 1,47 and 48 to argue that God must understand himself perfectly and that what God knows by essence or through himself (*per se*) is himself. If the divine essence is what stands to God as a source of knowledge comparable to intelligible species in people, says Aquinas, then this essence must be "perfectly conformed to the thing understood" and must be "perfectly joined to the intellect."[18] Yet Aquinas continues: "The divine essence, which is the intelligible species by which the divine intellect understands, is absolutely identical with God, and it is absolutely identical with his intellect. Therefore, God understands himself most perfectly."[19] Again, Aquinas argues, "that by which God understands is nothing other than his essence. Therefore, the primary and essential object of his intellect is nothing other than God himself."[20] Aquinas believes that God understands things other than himself, but he denies that it belongs to God to do so *primarily* or *essentially (per se)*.[21] In SCG 1,48 Aquinas offers seven arguments for this conclusion, but central to his thinking in this chapter is the idea that God does not have to know what is not divine in order to be God, who knows himself perfectly through his essence. In Aquinas's view, though God does in fact know or understand what is not divine, his doing so is not required for him to exist as knowing. Basically, the reasoning here is: (1) God could exist without knowing what is not divine, but (2) he could not exist without knowing himself perfectly, so (3) primarily and essentially God knows only himself.

7.2.4 God's Knowledge of What Is Not God (SCG 1,49–50)

How, though, does Aquinas think of God as knowing things other than God? One often finds it said, especially by those who favor the formula "God is a person," that God's knowledge of what is not divine arises by observation, by taking a look at things in some way. Such, however, is not Aquinas's view. When we know things by observing or looking at them we gain or acquire knowledge on the basis of sensory experience. So knowledge grounded in observation amounts to the actualizing of a potentiality and is caused in us by what is distinct from us. As I have shown, however, Aquinas denies both that there is potentiality in God and that anything in God is caused by what is not divine. When it comes to God's knowledge of other things, therefore, the line Aquinas takes in SCG 1,49 is that God knows other things by knowing himself as their cause.

In understanding himself, says Aquinas, God must understand himself as the cause of what he produces, the cause of all creatures, for that is what God is.[22] God "is through his essence the cause of being for other things."[23] He adds: "Since he has a most full knowledge of his essence, we must posit that God also knows other things."[24] Again, says Aquinas: "Since, then, God knows himself perfectly, he knows himself to be a cause. This cannot be unless he somehow knows what he causes. This is other than God, since nothing is the cause of itself. Therefore, God knows things other than himself."[25] Since God is intellectual, Aquinas also reasons, the likenesses of creatures must exist in God intelligibly as he knows and must therefore be known by him. Indeed, Aquinas adds in SCG 1,50: "God knows all other things as they are distinct from one another and from himself....God knows whatever is found in reality. But this is to have a proper and complete knowledge of a thing, namely to know all that there is in that thing, both what is common and what is proper."[26] One might naturally suppose that if all things other than God exist in God as known properly and completely, then God is made up of many things and is not entirely simple. However, having alluded to this supposition in SCG 1,51, Aquinas dismisses it while arguing that things other than God do not exist as individual things in God but do so in a single act of understanding by which God understands himself and what he produces (SCG 1,53 and 55).

7.2.5 What God's Knowledge Is Not (SCG 1,56–58)

I have now shown why Aquinas attributes knowledge to God in the SCG and why he thinks that in knowing himself perfectly God knows all that derives from him. Yet what Aquinas says about God knowing or understanding only through his essence clearly shows that he thinks that though we have reason to say that God knows, we also have reason to suppose that knowledge in God differs significantly from knowledge in us. And, as we proceed to SCG 1,56–58, we will find Aquinas noting other ways in which divine knowledge differs from human knowledge. For in these chapters we find him denying that God's knowledge is habitual, discursive, or arrived at by "composing and dividing."

By "habitual" knowledge Aquinas means "knowledge that we have without always drawing on it or bringing it explicitly to mind." We know a lot because we have learned and not forgotten what we learned. But we do not always have these truths in mind since sometimes we fall asleep and sometimes we think about all sorts of different things. We can recall what we have learned, but we do not always have in mind everything that we have learned. According to Aquinas, however, God lacks habitual knowledge. He says: "Where there is habitual knowledge not all things are known together; some are known actually, and some habitually. But, as we have proved, God has actual understanding of all things together. There is, therefore, no habitual knowledge in him."[27] In Aquinas's view, to possess a habit (*habitus*) is to have what we might call a disposition or ability on which we can draw as needed, which means that those with habits are things that are potentially thus and so in some way. Yet, says Aquinas, "the divine intellect is in no way in potency."[28]

When he refers to "discursive knowledge" in SCG 1,57, Aquinas is alluding to knowledge arrived at through a process of reasoning or ratiocination. Such a process, however, depends on there being potentiality in the reasoner while, according to Aquinas, there is no potentiality in God, and "his knowledge, therefore, is not ratiocinative or discursive, although he knows all discourse and ratiocination."[29] Again, says Aquinas, "God knows all things by one operation" and not by first considering this and then moving on to grasping that.[30] In God, Aquinas maintains, there is only "natural" knowledge—meaning "knowledge not arrived at by a process of reasoning." Ratiocination, says Aquinas, "is a certain motion of the intellect proceeding from one thing to another."[31] Yet God is the only truly unmoved mover, and so must be his intellect as it knows. Among other things, Aquinas goes on to argue that God's knowledge is not discursive since having to reason to conclusions indicates an imperfection of a kind while God is absolutely perfect. In short, Aquinas thinks that God does not have to strive to know by seeking to figure things out.

As for his denial that God understands by "composing and dividing" (*compositio et divisio*: literally "putting together and taking apart"), Aquinas's main point is that God having intellect does not mean that he is able to link or unlink a subject and predicate in a sentence expressing a truth. I might understand what a cat is. I might also understand what being black amounts to. Yet suppose I discover and declare that some cat is black. Or suppose that I recognize that some cat is not black. Then I bring together or separate concepts that I have formed independently of each other. According to Aquinas, however, God's intellect does not work by attaching discrete predicates to subjects whether in thought or in language. Neither does it work by detaching discrete predicates from subjects. According to Aquinas, God is not a language user and does not acquire concepts over time while bringing them together or separating them for purposes of expressing what he knows. God knows by knowing his essence and by knowing all things while being simple and, therefore, immutable.

In short, Aquinas maintains that God's knowledge is an "all at once" affair. In his view, as expressed in SCG 1,58, what chiefly has to be said when it comes to God not understanding by composing and dividing is: (1) God knows himself as noncomposite; (2) what God knows in knowing himself is not the result of knowing different things or grasping different concepts and bringing them together or separating them for purposes of assertion or denial; (3) there is no before and after in God. In SCG 1,59 Aquinas accepts that God is not ignorant of truths that we express by linking subjects and predicates together in propositions that we affirm or deny. But he denies that God's knowledge is arrived at by composing and dividing. He says that truth in an intellect is a matter of the intellect grasping how things are, and he goes on to say that God's intellect does this without arriving at true propositions as we do. God, thinks Aquinas, can grasp truth that we come to know over time and by reasoning or bringing concepts together. Yet his doing so does not depend on his thinking and arriving at truth as we do. Indeed, Aquinas holds in SCG 1,60 and 61, God himself *is* truth (*veritas*) and is the purest truth (*purissima veritas*), containing no falsity or deception. Aquinas maintains that "truth is a certain perfection of understanding or of intellectual operation"; so God is truth as being perfect understanding and intellect. He goes on to argue: "Truth is not compatible with falsity, as neither is whiteness with blackness. But God is not only true, he is truth itself. Therefore, there can be no falsity in him."[32] In SCG 1,62 Aquinas adds that God is the first and highest truth since he is the first and most perfect being who is truth by his essence and whose intellect and what it understands are totally united.

7.2.6 Some Specifics Concerning What God Knows Other Than God (SCG 1,63–71)

Although SCG 1,49–50 argues in general that God knows what is not divine, those chapters do not descend to details. As I have shown, Aquinas holds that

God knows what is not divine by being its maker. But Aquinas is aware of a series of objections to the view that God knows what is not divine, and he draws attention to them in SCG 1,63 while going on to rebut them in SCG 1,65–71. In his rebuttal he claims that God knows singulars (i.e., particular and existing created things), that God knows things that do not exist, that God knows future contingent singulars (i.e., things in the future that do not have to exist as they do), that God knows the thoughts and willings of intellectual creatures, that God knows infinite things, that God knows lowly things, and that God knows evils. Yet why does Aquinas think that God knows these things?

In SCG 1,65 Aquinas argues that God knows singulars, which are all God's effects, since "He makes them to be in act." Aquinas adds (1) that God, as the creator of everything, must, by his essence, know the individuality of things composed of matter and form since he makes all that has form and matter, (2) that God must know individual things in the world since, by being their creator, he knows how they break up into members of a genus or species, (3) that God would not be perfectly knowing if he were ignorant of singulars, (4) that God's knowing power (*vis cognoscitiva*) exceeds that of human beings, meaning that God, though simple, can know singulars that we come to know by our knowing powers, (5) that God knows particular things since his knowledge is perfect and since he makes things as the particulars that they are, rather as we sometimes bring particular things about by precisely knowing what we plan to bring about, (6) that God must know singulars by being their first mover acting through intellect, (7) that "the likeness of a form in the divine intellect, by reaching to the least of things to which its causality reaches, extends to the singularity of sensible and material form,"[33] and (8) that if God were ignorant of singulars, he would be more ignorant than we are since we can know particular things in their particularity.

SCG 1,66 maintains that God, like us, can know what does not exist insofar as God, like us, can understand what something that could exist would be if it did exist. In this connection Aquinas notes (1) that God, like a craftsman, can know what he plans to make even though it does not always exist, (2) that God knows himself perfectly and therefore knows exactly what he can bring about even if what he brings about does not always exist, (3) that, just as we can know what something is even if examples of it are destroyed, God, as maker of all things, can know what particular things that do not now exist were or will be since God has knowledge that we can express by means of propositions, (4) that God as the maker of all things must know what will come to be even if it does not currently exist, and (5) that God as creator must know all that comes to be in the course of time even though there is no change or successiveness in him and that "the divine intellect, therefore, sees in the whole of its eternity, as being present to it, whatever takes place through the whole course of time."[34]

In SCG 1,67 Aquinas says that God knows future contingent (i.e., nonnecessitated) singulars in that God knows all that takes place in time "from all eternity" insofar as "it is present" to him.[35] If I know that you will run tomorrow, that might be because your running tomorrow is already predetermined by causes operating now of which I am aware; but it does not follow that if you are running now, your running is necessitated in some way, and my knowing that you are running now is compatible with you freely running now. By the same token, Aquinas argues, God can know what is future but not necessitated since God knows the future as present to him. In SCG 1,67 Aquinas also argues as follows:

1. Things or events can be necessary or contingent. God knows whether or not they are necessary or contingent. That is because his knowledge must extend to "the being" that things have in themselves (i.e., it must extend to them being necessary, if they are necessary, and contingent, if they are contingent).

2. God's knowledge would be imperfect if it did not extend to matters of contingency and necessity. But God knows all things and their causes. So God knows what is both contingent and necessary.

3. Contingent and changing effects can proceed from what is first and necessary, and contingent effects can be known to God even though he is the first and immutable cause that cannot not be.

4. Nothing is future to God since, in his eternity, God unchangeably knows all that was, is, or will be. That is so even though we, who are not eternal, speak of God as knowing what is future to us in a way that might seem to imply that God's knowledge of events precedes them in time and therefore implies that they cannot not be.

5. It is true that "God knows that such and such is the case" entails that such and such is the case. But this proposition does not entail that the such and such in question is necessary in itself. So God's infallible knowledge of what was, is, and will be does not rule out the possibility that some things are but might not be, or might not be as they are.

In SCG 1,68 Aquinas ascribes to God knowledge of "motions of the will."[36] He does so because he thinks that such things exist and must be known to God as the creator of all that is not divine. "There is," he says, "a certain being in the soul and a certain being in things outside the soul," and "God, therefore, knows all these differences of being and what is contained under them."[37]

Furthermore, Aquinas argues, "God knows all things to which his causality extends," and "it extends to the operations of the intellect and the will."[38] Aquinas also reasons that "just as God, by knowing his being knows the being of each thing, so by knowing his understanding and willing he knows every thought and will."[39]

In SCG 1,69, and relying on a line of argument with which we are now very familiar, Aquinas argues that God knows infinite things, if there are such things, since he is their cause and knows the extent of his power, which is infinite and extends to what is potentially infinite (as, Aquinas thinks, the universe is potentially infinite, though containing a number of finite things, since it might, logically speaking, never have had a beginning). He goes on to argue: (1) There "always remains a new way in which some copy is able to imitate the divine essence" and "nothing prevents God from knowing infinite things through his essence";[40] (2) God knows what is infinite since his knowing, like his being, is infinite, and since God, who is infinite, must know himself perfectly; (3) No intellectual perfection can be lacking to God since God is perfect; so God must know what is infinite; (4) Even we can recognize that there may be a potential infinite (e.g., a potentially infinite number of objects); so God must also grasp this fact; (5) We are unable to count an infinite number of things since we cannot go through an infinite process of counting; but, since there is no successiveness in God, he can know the infinite as well as the finite; (6) God can know finite and infinite objects equally well since his knowledge, which is infinite and simple, extends over both of them.

When it comes to God's knowledge of lowly things, Aquinas again appeals to the idea that God's knowledge must extend to all that God brings about. Aquinas discusses the topic of God's knowledge of lowly things while bearing in mind the suggestion that it would somehow detract from God's excellence if he were to be familiar with what is of little account. His response to this suggestion is to argue that it is because of his greatness that God knows even the most trivial of things. So, we read:

> Since God is of an infinite power in understanding...his knowledge must extend even to the most remote things....If God knows something other than himself, however supreme in nobility it may be, by the same reason he knows anything whatever, however exceedingly lowly it may be called....He especially knows the order of the universe. But this order cannot be known without a knowledge both of the things that are more noble and of the things that are more lowly....The lowliness of the things known does not of itself redound to the knower....The knowledge of lowly things, therefore, does not detract from the divine

nobility, but rather belongs to the divine perfection according as it pre-contains all things in itself.[41]

God knows evil things, says Aquinas (SCG 1,71) since God knows what is good, implying that he knows its opposite, evil. Aquinas also argues that if God knows what is true, and if God's knowledge is perfect, then God must know evils since it is true that there are evil things or things that are bad. God, he says, must know how things differ from each other or are contrary to each other, which must involve him knowing that some things are bad or in a bad way. Again, he argues, God must know evil since God knows matter and since material things can suffer privations that amount to evil in them. In SCG 1,71, Aquinas ends up saying (1) that God must know dangers that threaten things because he knows what is best for things, and (2) that it does not count against God's perfection that he knows of what is evil since knowledge of evil is not blameworthy unless it leads one to give in to or to pursue evil, which is impossible when it comes to God since God is immutable. Aquinas concedes that since God, unlike us, knows by his essence, God's knowledge of evil does not exist in him as it comes to exist in us since we have potentiality as we come to know while God lacks potentiality. God, says Aquinas, knows of evils because he understands himself and in doing so understands other things, including what is potential or privative as well as what is actual. Yes, says Aquinas, God knows only himself as he knows the good that he is. Yet, Aquinas adds, "because in knowing Himself, He knows the beings that are by nature subject to privations, He must know the privations and the evils that are opposed to particular goods."[42]

7.3 *Thinking about SCG 1,44–71*

If you take Aquinas to be wrong in what he says about divine simplicity, you will think that there is little of value in SCG 1,44–71. That is because so many of its arguments presuppose that God is simple in the way that Aquinas takes him to be in SCG 1,16–25.

Again, you will find SCG 1,44–71 totally misguided if you are a thoroughgoing materialist and suppose that knowing or thinking or understanding is nothing but a material process undergone by particular physical things.

Yet again, you will reject SCG 1,44–71 if you are a philosophical idealist, if you think that there are no material things and that all we can know is our knowing, not things existing apart from us.[43] That is because Aquinas's account of knowledge in people arises because of an encounter with things in a material world, things that exist apart from us that can be known for what they are.[44]

I have already commented to some extent on Aquinas on God's simplicity, and this is not the place to try to adjudicate between philosophers of mind who disagree about whether knowledge is material or between philosophers who argue as to whether or not there is a material world. Yet, if nothing else, Aquinas's account of God's knowledge strongly coheres with much that he has previously said in the SCG. Indeed, it seems to follow from what precedes it with a kind of inevitability.

Aquinas clearly has no time for philosophical idealism since, as is evident from SCG 1,13, he takes it as obvious that there is a material world in which various changes occur. While idealists typically hold that all that we know are ideas in us, Aquinas maintains that we know by means of ideas, some of which put us in touch with what is material and distinct from us. So it is not surprising that what we find in SCG 1,44–71 bears no trace of idealism, and it is equally unsurprising that these chapters make the distinctions they do between human knowledge and divine knowledge.

On the commonsensical assumption that there really are material objects, it would seem that we come to know having not started life with any knowledge at all while acquiring it somehow on the basis of encountering things physically, listening to or reading those who have better acquaintance with things in the world than we have, just believing what informed people tell us, or reasoning things out for ourselves. So, given the reality of material objects, knowledge in us arises over time, and at least partly because of the effects in us of what is other than us. Knowledge in us frequently arises on the basis of observation, as when, for example, I see you doing something; so there is often a looking of some kind involved when it comes to us acquiring knowledge. Yet Aquinas cannot think that God has knowledge as we do since he has already denied that there is potentiality in God and since he has already (whether successfully or not) defended the claim that God is the first cause who is not causally acted on by anything.

You might suppose that it makes no sense to say that God's knowledge differs from human knowledge as Aquinas takes it to do since in "I know" and "God knows" the verb "to know" has to be understood univocally. As I have shown, though, Aquinas thinks that some words can be used analogically to speak of God and creatures. And in SCG 1,44–71 he is providing an account of how this is so when it comes to "knows." He certainly thinks that there is something in common between knowledge in us and knowledge in God because he takes knowledge to arise as form comes to exist immaterially. So Aquinas takes the move from "God is immaterial" to "God knows" to be a relatively unproblematic one. What he manifestly takes to be problematic is the move from "God knows" to "God has knowledge exactly as people do."

How unproblematic is the move from "God is immaterial" to "God knows"? A lot here depends on the worth of Aquinas's claim that knowledge as it actually occurs is nothing but form liberated from matter. Yet there presumably has to be some isomorphism when it comes to what is in me when I know what a dog is and what is there in the dog. And since all that is in a dog would seem to be what it takes for something to be a real dog and not the idea of a dog, and since I am not a dog when I know what a dog is, it makes sense to speak as Aquinas does when he says that to know what something material is amounts to sharing what it is without being the physical thing that it is.

We might, perhaps, try to make this point by focusing on the word "meaning." What it means to be a dog, say, is just to exist as a dog. So, it is confined exclusively to dogs. Yet I can meaningfully say that dogs are beings of a certain kind. So what it means to be a dog can enter into our world of thought and be expressed by language. We can have in mind what it means to be a dog. Yet our doing this can hardly amount to any of us being a dog, even though all of us can, in principle, understand what a dog is. So what can it amount to if not form or meaning not existing in a particular physical thing?

It would be odd to say that meaning exists in us individually or privately since meaning is expressed in language and since language is something shared. One cannot mean on one's own as one can brush one's teeth on one's own, and one cannot declare that a word has meaning just by personal fiat. Meaning is essentially commonable or shareable. But the things in the world that we understand and can speak about meaningfully are not commonable or shareable. They are what they are as material individuals, and what it means to be them is to be the material individuals that they are. So, insofar as we understand what things in the world are, insofar as these things become part of our knowledge as expressible linguistically, what is in them comes to exist in a way that is not confined to particular physical existence in some physical thing. And Aquinas seems to have recognized this point in what he says about knowledge, form, and liberation from material existence.[45]

Aquinas believes that some things are purely material, and it never occurs to him to suggest that they have knowledge or understanding. Why not? Because he thinks that their being what they are amounts to them just being physical things having nothing but the material forms that they have. Nevertheless, he believes that some things are not merely physical. People, he holds, can talk, reason, and understand. People, he says, can assimilate other things intellectually without becoming anything other than what they are physically, even if their doing so involves them in somehow physically changing.[46] Aquinas expresses this conclusion by claiming that we come to know as the thinkable or the knowable comes to exist in things that can contain in themselves a multitude of material things without being any of them.

You may, of course, think that Aquinas is wrong to make this claim. Yet it is, perhaps, not an idiotic or wholly indefensible one. At any rate, it has surfaced in various forms in the writings of many well-known philosophers. Aristotle defended it, and Aquinas is evidently indebted to what he says about it. But the claim can be seen to be there in what most philosophers have said insofar as they have subscribed to the view that thinking a thought is not a material process that can, therefore, be divided into material parts. Material things with parts go through physical processes that can be clocked. But can thinking a thought, or simply understanding what something is, be thought of as a material process divisible into parts spread out in time? Arguably not. Peter Geach once observed: "One may say that during half an hour by the clock, such-and-such thoughts occurred to a man; but I think it is impossible to find a stretch of physical events that would be just simultaneous, or even simultaneous to a good approximation, with one of the thoughts in the series. I think that Norman Malcolm was right when he said at a meeting in Oxford that a mental image could be before one's mind's eye for just as long as a beetle took to crawl across a table; but I think it would be nonsense to say that I 'was thinking' a given thought for the period of the beetle's crawl."[47] Geach goes on to argue that thinking cannot be the activity of the brain or any bodily organ since "the basic activities of any bodily part must be clockable in physical time in a way that thinking is not" and since "no physiological discoveries could establish that thoughts occurred precisely when certain brain-processes occurred."[48] What Geach says here is not offered by him in defense of Aquinas on the immateriality of knowing, but it seems to support it.

8

God's Will, Life, and Blessedness
(SCG 1,72–102)

AQUINAS ROUNDS OFF SCG 1 with discussions of God's will, life, and blessedness. You will not be surprised to find him arguing that there is will in God, that God is alive, and that God is blessed. Yet what does Aquinas mean by "will," "life," and "blessed"? In this chapter I shall first try to answer that question. Then I shall explain Aquinas's reasons for ascribing will, life, and blessedness to God. As you will see, Aquinas's procedure in SCG 1,72–102 is similar to what we found in his treatment of divine knowledge. He argues that will, life, and blessedness can be positively ascribed to God, but then he proceeds to explain how he thinks that they must exist in God in different ways from the ways in which they exist in what is not divine.

8.1 Aquinas on Will

Aquinas regularly connects knowledge with will. People, he says, can cognize, but they can also be moved by what they cognize in that they can be attracted or drawn to it. For Aquinas, therefore, will (*voluntas*) involves being drawn to what one somehow perceives or knows. He thinks that we will insofar as we find something we cognize to be desirable. He thinks of will as, so to speak, appetite in action. As I noted in chapter 6, Aquinas agrees with Aristotle's claim that the good is what everything desires, and his understanding of willing in people is connected with this claim.

Aquinas takes will to be a faculty or power in people, one that he strongly connects with their ability to know. It is commonly said that knowing and willing are to be sharply distinguished, but Aquinas does not rigidly distinguish between them. He thinks that distinctions can be drawn. He does not deny, for example, that one can know that such and such is the case yet be indifferent to the fact or not act on it in any way. And he thinks that will depends on knowledge in that we will to act on the basis of how we take things to be. In other words, he thinks that willing has a cognitive grounding. On the other hand, he also holds that judging something to be good amounts to being drawn to it somehow or in being attracted to it in some way. And he thinks that our knowledge can arise under the influence of desire.

As Herbert McCabe nicely puts it, Aquinas's position is that "there is no operation of the reason which is not also an operation of the will, and vice versa." According to Aquinas: "There is an interweaving of understanding and being attracted that cannot be unraveled in practice. We think of what we are *attracted* to thinking of, and we are attracted to what we *think* of."[1] Aquinas does not mean that we just believe what we want to. His point is that we pay attention to what we want to attend to.

You may think that there is a rigid distinction to be made between knowing or understanding on the one hand and willing on the other, and you may think so because of the effort that can sometimes be involved in doing what we know to be good. Doing what we know to be good can sometimes be difficult. Most people have to "force" themselves to pay regular visits to a dentist even though they know very well that it is good for them to do so. Yet, assuming that people go to a dentist voluntarily, they have to desire to visit a dentist, even though the thought of sitting in a dentist's chair comes with what we might call "mixed feelings." Thinking of some course of action as good, and therefore desiring it, does not necessarily mean liking it as one might, say, unequivocally and without reserve like to eat ice cream. Aquinas is conscious of this fact, and something that helps him to be so is his view of things not being good except under some description. As I have shown, Aquinas takes "good" to be a logically attributive adjective whose sense is noun-dependent. So he can perfectly well distinguish between dental visits being good *as a means to oral well-being* and bad *as a source of physical discomfort.* And if we drag ourselves to the dentist, thinks Aquinas, that will be because we value oral well-being more than we value never experiencing physical discomfort.

The role of desire in willing comes out strongly in some accounts that Aquinas frequently provides of voluntary or willed action. Aquinas never wrote a full-scale treatise on the topic of freedom and determinism, but he says plenty to indicate that his view is that a genuine human action, as opposed to a process through which our bodies might go that has nothing to do with our desires, is always something with respect to which one can raise the question "With a view to what?"

If I fall because someone pushes me, it would be idiotic for you to ask me "With a view to what are you doing that?" since I am not really *doing* anything. I am not willing anything. I am merely going through a process of change caused by something other than me.

Yet what if I decide to feed my cat? When doing that I walk into my kitchen, pick up a tin of cat food, transfer its contents to a bowl, and place the bowl in front of my hungry cat. At any stage in this process you can sensibly ask me "With a view to what are you doing that?" And I can give you an intelligible answer, which will refer to some good end that I am striving to bring about, something that I want or take to be desirable.

Now, according to Aquinas genuine human action, as opposed to a knee-jerk reaction or something like that, is always aimed at what the actor, rightly or wrongly, regards as good.[2] He therefore thinks that genuine human actions are always voluntary since they express or reflect the desires of the agents whose actions they are. That is why he takes will to be present when goodness is desired. He knows that we can desire things without trying to get them, but he thinks that there is will insofar as there is a being drawn to what is good, or to what is believed to be good, even if this does not always result in action.[3] I may be attracted to a particular human being while concealing my feelings. Yet Aquinas would say that I might still love or desire that person, or maybe just the good of that person; and loving or desiring, regardless of degree, is at the heart of Aquinas's notion of human willing.

8.2 Aquinas on Life

What is the difference between something that is alive and something that is not alive? Aquinas's answer to this question is that living things, unlike non-living things, are self-moving and have within themselves an active principle of movement, or an ability of their own to move themselves or others.

You might think that nonliving things can move since they can cause other things to undergo motion in any of the senses of *motus* that I noted Aquinas to subscribe to when I was explaining his understanding of *motus* in chapter 3. Yet Aquinas does not suppose otherwise, as we can see from the ways in which he speaks of agent causation in general. Of course, he thinks that a tennis ball can be moved by a nonliving tennis racket, and so on. But he does not think of a tennis racket as being self-moving.

Yet have we not now seen that Aquinas does not think of anything other than God as being a wholly unmoved mover? Indeed, we have. So what sense of "self-moving" does Aquinas have in mind when thinking of things in the world as living as opposed to nonliving? It is the sense in which something can be said to undergo change, or to initiate change in something else, without being pushed around by something else in the world. It is the sense in which, and forgetting about God, something might literally be said to be an automobile, even if it is not a car.

Aquinas accepts that things other than human beings are alive. He also thinks of nonhuman animals and plants as having life. In his view, all of these can operate or go through various changes by virtue of what they naturally are, as he thinks that nonliving things cannot. You might say that things that have died can go through changes because of what they are, that corpses, for instance, can decay. Yet, so Aquinas would reply, corpses are not what living things that become corpses are. On his account, when I die, then I cease to exist as a human being. My corpse, he thinks, is not the living thing that I am, and the corpse of a cat or what remains of a once living plant is neither a cat nor a plant. Corpses and the remains of plants obviously undergo change. But this, for Aquinas, is not a change in a human being or a cat or a cabbage, or whatever. It is change in what used to be a human being or a cat or a cabbage but is not now.

In saying this kind of thing Aquinas is drawing on his notion of substantial form. For him, "X is a cat" is true if X has what it takes to be a cat as opposed to something else. Or "X is a human being" is true if X has what it takes to be a human being. Since Aquinas does not regard a dead cat as a cat or a dead human being as a human being, he does not think of feline corpses as cats or of dead human beings as human beings. He thinks that something is a cat or a human being or a cabbage because it has a particular substantial form, and his distinction between living and nonliving things relies on this view. Living things, he says, are things with a certain kind of substantial form, things with a certain way of being or existing.

What kind of substantial form? As I presume you will appreciate, Aquinas thinks that an ideal observer's list of what exists with particular substantial forms is going to be incredibly long. That is because he thinks that many different things exist with different substantial forms. Yet he also thinks that the list can be divided into things that are alive and things that are not alive since some things move of themselves while others do not. He thinks, for example, that cats are alive because they can prowl around without being dragged or tinkered with by something else in the world. Correspondingly, he thinks that the corpse of a cat is not alive since any movements or changes it undergoes are not initiated by it in any sense but are explicable in terms of what is acting on it from outside. Aquinas certainly holds that a living cat is not a totally unmoved mover and that no living thing in the world is wholly unmoved. That is because he thinks that behind all movement or change is the mover he refers to as God, whom he takes to be the primary unmoved mover. Nevertheless, Aquinas holds that we can distinguish between cats, people, and cabbages on the one hand and desks, rugs, and stones on the other. The former, he holds, move of themselves in various ways, while the latter do not. He maintains that cats, people, and cabbages can undergo changes explicable in terms of what *they* are, not changes only explicable in terms of things *other* than them acting *on* them and thereby indicating what *they* are. So, for example, in *Summa Theologiae* 1a,18,1 he writes, echoing Aristotle:

> We first say that an animal is living when it begins to have movement of itself, and we judge it to be alive so long as this kind of movement appears in it. When it no longer has any movement of itself, but is moved only by another, we say that life has failed and that the animal is dead. So, it is clear that only things which move themselves with one or another kind of movement are, properly speaking, alive.... Thus, we call "living" those things which produce in themselves some kind of movement or operation. It is only metaphorically that we can say that things whose nature does not contain that power are living things.[4]

I should add that, corresponding to our distinction between "animate" and "inanimate," Aquinas, like Aristotle, holds that anything living has a soul (*anima*), meaning, and *only* meaning, that souls come to exist in the world as *any* living things come to exist in it.

8.3 Aquinas on Blessedness

Aquinas thinks that to be blessed (*beatus*) is to be happy, but in a unique way. Latin has two words that can be rendered into English as "happiness." These are *felicitas* and *beatitudo*, both of which are terms Aquinas frequently employs in his writings. Yet he takes them to flag significantly different concepts, though he sometimes writes as if he regards them as equivalent or synonymous. Primarily, Aquinas refers to *felicitas* when alluding to happiness that people can enjoy before they die—"earthly happiness," as we might call it. So, Aquinas thinks that, all things being equal, *felicitas* can be obtained by enjoying food and drink, by being with friends, by having wealth, by having sex, by having good health, or by having the admiration of other people. By *beatitudo*, however, Aquinas has in mind perfect and unending happiness, or perfect fulfillment to which nothing can be added or removed. *Beatitudo*, for Aquinas, is the ultimate good for people, which he takes to be union with God after death by those enjoying the beatific vision, a knowledge of and delight in God not normally obtainable in the present life (see chapter 2, section 3.2 here). Aquinas does not claim to be able to demonstrate that there is any such thing as the beatific vision. He is quite clear that, until one has it, one can only adhere to belief in it on the basis of faith in divine revelation. Still, Aquinas does believe in the beatific vision, and he thinks that it is enjoyed by the saints in heaven who grasp God's essence, albeit without completely comprehending it.[5]

8.4 Aquinas on Will in God (SCG 1,72–96)

SCG 1,72–96 defends these theses:

1. God has will.
2. God's will is God's essence.
3. God principally wills the divine essence.
4. In willing himself God also wills other things.
5. God wills himself and other things by one act of will.
6. God's willing different things is compatible with him being totally simple.
7. God's will extends to particular or singular goods.
8. God wills even things that do not yet exist.
9. God wills his own being and goodness of necessity.
10. God does not will other things of absolute necessity.
11. God cannot will what is in itself impossible.
12. God's will is no threat to there being contingency in things and does not impose necessity on them.
13. Reason can be assigned to God's will.
14. Nothing can cause God to will.
15. God has free choice.
16. God does not have passions arising from appetites.
17. There is delight and joy in God even though God is perfect.
18. There is love in God.
19. Virtue can be ascribed to God.
20. There are moral virtues in God having to do with action.
21. There are contemplative virtues in God.
22. God cannot will evil.
23. God hates nothing.

That is a long list of theses. If you compare them with those defended in SCG 1,44–72, you will notice a certain similarity in the progression of Aquinas's reasoning as he writes SCG 1,72–96 and SCG 1,44–72. In his discussion of God's knowledge, Aquinas asks whether God has knowledge, whether God's knowledge is his essence, whether God knows what is not divine, whether God's knowledge imposes necessity on things, whether God knows singulars, whether God knows what is contingent, and whether God knows evils. In

SCG 1,72–96 Aquinas raises comparable questions when it comes to God's will, and the way he answers them can be compared with the way he previously deals with God's knowledge. So I am now going to note how Aquinas defends the fifteen theses just noted while trying not to repeat myself too much when it comes to what I have said in chapter 7.

8.4.1 There Is Will in God (SCG 1,72)

Aquinas thinks that there being will in God follows from God having intellect. God, he says, understands what is good, and "the understood good is the proper object of the will."[6] Indeed, he adds, "all sensing and understanding beings have appetite and will."[7] Furthermore, says Aquinas, everything seeks its perfection, and intellectual beings do so through will; so in God there is will "by which his being and his goodness are pleasing to him."[8] Aquinas also argues: (1) with perfection of understanding comes delight, yet God understands perfectly; (2) God produces things by his intellect, so God must have will; (3) will is the first moving power in things with intellect, so God must have will; (4) freedom involves acting on one's own voluntarily, but God is the first agent acting through himself; (5) as knowing himself to be supremely good, God must desire the divine goodness as an end by means of will.

8.4.2 God's Will Is God's Essence (SCG 1,73)

Aquinas says that God's will is God's essence since God has will insofar as he has intellect and since God has intellect or understanding by his essence (see SCG 1,45 and 46). Furthermore, argues Aquinas: (1) God's understanding is his being (*esse*), as must be his willing; (2) God acts through his essence and must therefore will through his essence; (3) God cannot have will as an accident since God is simple; so the divine will is not something added to the divine essence.

8.4.3 God Principally Wills the Divine Essence (SCG 1,74)

Aquinas holds that what God principally understands is the divine essence (see SCG 1,48). So, he argues, this is what God principally wills. He also argues: (1) God cannot principally will something other than God since that would mean that there is something greater than God; (2) if God principally willed something other than himself, then something other than God would cause his willing, which is impossible; (3) things with will principally will their ultimate good while willing other things as a means of obtaining it; but the ultimate good is God (see SCG 1,41), so God is the principal object of the divine will; (4) powers in things are directly related to and measured by their principal objects, so the principal object of the divine will is the divine essence and all that it amounts to.[9]

8.4.4 In Willing Himself God Wills Other Things (SCG 1,75)

I have shown that Aquinas takes God to know what is not divine by knowing himself as their cause. In SCG 1,75 he argues that God wills what is not God by willing himself while making to exist things that are ordered to him as to an end. He also argues: (1) we will goodness or perfection for things that we love for their own sake; yet God wills what God is for its own sake, and in doing so wills things other than God insofar as they reflect what is in God; (2) to love (will) something in itself and for its own sake is to love everything in which it is found; but God loves his own being in itself and for its own sake; so God loves what shares in God's being by reflecting it and being made by him, and God loves what preexists in him as a model or pattern in the light of which he makes things to be; (3) in willing the divine essence, God can will things directed to it as drawn to it, even if they are not divine, and this means that God, being perfect in power, is something that wills whatever exists apart from God as being drawn to goodness; (4) God understands other things in himself, so "he principally wills himself, and wills all other things in willing himself."[10]

8.4.5 God Wills Himself and Other Things by One Act of Will (SCG 1,76)

Obviously Aquinas has to say that there is but one act of will in God because he takes God to be simple and immutable. His account of God earlier in the SCG says that God is eternal and does not have any before and after in him. So Aquinas is committed to there being nothing successive in God when it comes to willing. For him, all that is in God is the simple divine essence that is God. As you will see if you work through them, all of the arguments in SCG 1,76 seem to be grounded in this thought, so I shall not now try to summarize them in detail.

8.4.6 That God Wills Many Things Does Not Undermine God's Simplicity (SCG 1,77)

Many times over in SCG 1, and elsewhere in the SCG, Aquinas begins chapters by declaring that what he is about to say in them follows from what he has previously shown, and he does so at the start of SCG 1,77. Maybe I should have mentioned this before, but I do not take Aquinas, when writing the SCG, to suppose himself to have already established certain conclusions that he goes on to defend before he tries to defend them. If he thought that he had done that, then he could have spared himself the trouble of offering particular arguments for conclusions he proceeds to defend. What he seems to mean while beginning chapters with phrases like "from this it follows" or "from this it is apparent" is that what he has previously said can be drawn on while arguing for conclusions not specifically defended previously. That this is so seems clear from SCG 1,77.

Here Aquinas first says: "From this it follows that the multitude of the objects of the will is not opposed to the unity and simplicity of the divine substance."[11] But Aquinas then goes on to explain why this is so by giving arguments that he has not already presented in SCG 1. These arguments presume that God is simple and that God has knowledge and will, but they add to what Aquinas has previously said about God presuming that God wills many things. And the arguments are: (1) If God's will is but a single thing, the fact that God wills many things does not entail that there is complexity in him; (2) God wills other things by willing his own goodness, yet "all things in his goodness are one, since other things are in him according to his way,"[12] and since God's will and intellect exist in God, who is totally simple. In addition, says Aquinas, "that something be related to many is not opposed to its simplicity, since unity itself is the principle of numerical multitude."[13]

8.4.7 God's Will Extends to Singular Goods (SCG 1,78)

God's simplicity, Aquinas holds, does not prevent him willing many particular things since the complexity involved in many things being willed by God lies in them, not in God, who is the first and best thing. Again, says Aquinas, each particular good thing deriving from God derives its being and goodness from God, meaning that God's will extends to every particular good thing. Yet again, argues Aquinas: (1) God as the source of all that is divine must will their end and must will each of them as directed to it; (2) if God did not will singular goods, then the good of order in the universe would have arisen by chance whereas it actually arises by virtue of God's action; (3) since God understands particular goods, God must will particular goods.

8.4.8 God Wills Things That Do Not Yet Exist (SCG 1,79)

Having noted some reasons why it might be thought wrong to suppose that God can will what does not yet exist, Aquinas maintains that God can do this as eternally willing a world in which things arise in time. God can do this, he says, even if things come to exist over time.

8.4.9 God Wills His Being and Goodness of Necessity (SCG 1,80)

In SCG 1,80 Aquinas argues that since desire or will cannot but home in on what is absolutely perfect or good, God must will himself and his goodness of necessity since God is absolute perfection and goodness. Aquinas knows that we sometimes turn our backs on certain goods. His explanation of this is that we do so because we take some goods to be greater than others, as when I value dental hygiene more than a few moments of comfort away from a dentist's chair. On the other hand Aquinas thinks that if we knew what is absolutely good without any qualification, we would will it since it belongs to will to be drawn to goodness as such. So in SCG 1,80 he reasons that God wills or loves his own goodness with no possibility of failing to do so. That, Aquinas thinks, is because there can be no good perceived by God as a rival to the good that God is. This good, says Aquinas, is what God principally wills (see SCG 1,74), and he wills other things as ordered to it.

8.4.10 God Does Not Will Other Things Necessarily (SCG 1,81)

Does the line of thought in SCG 1,80 imply that God has to will things other than himself? Aquinas says that it does not. God wills other things as directed to his goodness, but God's perfect goodness does not depend on there being any creatures ordered to God. "Since the divine goodness can be without other things," Aquinas observes, "it is under no necessity to will other things from the fact of willing its own goodness."[14] Aquinas goes on to note that there could be many more good and different things than there are, which he takes to imply that God does not necessarily will what actually exists other than him. In this connection Aquinas argues that since God's goodness is infinite, as God is, it can be shared in an infinite number of ways and in ways other than the ways it is shared in by creatures that now exist. He continues:

If, then, as a result of willing his own goodness, God necessarily willed the things that participate in it, it would follow that he would will the existence of an infinity of creatures participating in his goodness in an infinity of ways. This is patently false, because, if he willed them, they would be, since his will is the principle of being for things.[15]

Given this conclusion, one might ask: "If, in understanding and willing himself, God understands and knows other things (see SCG 1,49 and 75), how can God necessarily know what is not divine without willing it of necessity?" Aquinas's answer is that God's goodness does not require that other things exist, so God can will his own goodness without being compelled to will other things, even though God knows what he could create as ordered to his goodness but does not create. In Aquinas's view, God does not will "all the things that can have an order to his goodness," but "God knows all things that have any order whatever to his essence, by which he understands."[16] In SCG 1,82 Aquinas notes arguments to the effect that there is some impossibility entailed by the thesis that God does not necessarily will what is other than himself (e.g., that if this is so, then God is indifferent when it comes to what he does and therefore contains potentiality or is moved to will by something other than himself). Yet Aquinas responds to these arguments by reiterating his reasons for concluding that God does not necessarily will what is other than himself. In SCG 1,83, however, he accepts that God wills something other than himself with what he calls "the necessity of supposition" (*ex conditione vel suppositione*). Since God is immutable and eternal, says Aquinas, then what he wills cannot not be. Yet, he adds, this does not mean that God from eternity has to will things other than himself. If he wills them, then they are inevitable, but only on condition of his willing them.

8.4.11 God Cannot Will What Is in Itself Impossible (SCG 1,84)

The main idea running through SCG 1,84 is that God cannot will what is impossible since what is impossible cannot exist and, therefore, cannot be willed into existence by God. "In so far as a thing is opposed to the nature of being as such," says Aquinas, "there cannot be preserved in it the likeness of the first being, namely the divine being, which is the source of being."[17] Aquinas accepts that God can will to exist what is able to exist. Yet he denies that God can make to exist what cannot possibly exist. He does not use this example in SCG 1,84, but he is clearly thinking that, for example, there cannot be a square triangle since "square" and "triangle" cancel each other out in "There is a square triangle," which, therefore, does not amount to a coherent thought about anything that might exist.

8.4.12 God's Will Does Not Abolish Contingency in Things and Does Not Impose Absolute Necessity on Them (SCG 1,85)

In SCG 1,85 Aquinas is arguing that God makes things to be what they are, whether contingent or necessary, whether able to be or not to be, or whether not able to be or not to be. Here we need to remember that Aquinas holds that some creatures are contingent and that some are necessary. He thinks that some creatures are contingent since they do not always exist. He also thinks that some creatures act without being necessitated or determined to act as they do by other things in the world. In addition, he thinks that there are things that always exist since they are not generated and cannot perish in the course of nature. Yet, he maintains, all of these things are what they are and only exist because of God, the first cause of everything, even of what is contingent in some way. God, says Aquinas, "wills whatever is required for a thing that he wills...but it befits certain things, according to the mode of their nature, that they be contingent and not necessary."[18] Aquinas agrees that if God wills something, it will be. But he does not therefore conclude that everything that God wills to be has to be something necessary.

8.4.13 A Reason Can Be Assigned to the Divine Will (SCG 1,86)

In defending what he does in SCG 1,86, Aquinas is ascribing *ratio* to divine willing. The Latin word *ratio* can be understood in various senses, but in SCG 1,86 it means something like "aim" or "end" or "goal" as intended by what has intellect. So, in SCG 1,86 Aquinas reiterates what he has said about God willing with a view to a good, this, as I have shown, chiefly being the goodness that is God and the goodness had by creatures reflecting God's goodness. Aquinas, therefore, thinks that God delights in, or wills, himself as perfect goodness, and that God wills to share this goodness with creatures that reflect it as things whose good exists in God before it exists in them. Aquinas holds that God is supremely good, that God makes creatures to share in goodness, and that God, so to speak, has in himself a blueprint of what creatures are and what is good for them. In this sense, Aquinas thinks of God as the beginning and end of creatures by being their cause and by being what they aim at as creatures of God. So he thinks that what is in God, who is entirely simple, is what God aims at both for himself and for what he has created, and he argues that this has to be the goodness that God is willing, that it has to be its *ratio*. So in SCG 1,86 we read: "The end is the reason for willing things that are for the sake of an end. But God wills his own goodness as the end, and other things he wills as things that are for the sake of the end. His goodness, therefore, is the reason why he wills the other things which are different from himself."[19] Aquinas makes it clear in SCG 1,86 that God sometimes wills what falls short in goodness in some ways (though, as I have shown, he takes everything to be good insofar as it merely exists). Yet, he thinks, in willing as he does when it comes to creatures, God's aim is to produce what shares somehow in his goodness, and he takes goodness as it exists in God and is shared by creatures in different ways to be God's *ratio* when it comes to willing.

8.4.14 Nothing Can Be the Cause of God's Willing (SCG 1,87)

One might expect to find Aquinas arguing in SCG 1,87 that nothing causes God's will because God's will is God and God is the first cause. Yet that is not quite what he explicitly argues in this chapter. He begins by saying that though a certain reason can be given for the divine will, this does not entail that anything is the cause of God's willing since the cause of the will willing is the end willed and because the end willed by God is God's own goodness and his act of will. Aquinas adds that no object willed by God causes God's willing, though one of them can be thought of as causing another to be ordered to God's goodness, in which case God wills one thing for the sake of another. In addition, Aquinas argues, there is in God's willing no discursiveness (*discursus*), no running through a process of reasoning (see SCG 1,57). "By means of one act," Aquinas says, "God wills his goodness and all other things, since his action is his essence."[20]

8.4.15 There Is Free Choice in God (SCG 1,88)

By "free choice" (*liberum arbitrium*) Aquinas means the power to choose not from necessity but of one's own accord, and he argues that this has to exist in God since God wills other things without being compelled to do so (see SCG 1,81). In SCG 1,88 Aquinas also argues: (1) that people exercising free choice will by reason, not by the impulse of nature, while "towards the things to which it is not determined by nature"[21] the divine will is inclined through intellect; (2) that we freely will ends by electing or choosing what is for the sake of an end, while God wills himself as an end and other things for the sake of this end; and (3) that people with free choice are masters of their acts, while God is supremely this since his action depends on nothing other than himself.

8.4.16 There Are No Passions of the Appetites in God (SCG 1,89)

By "passions of the appetites" (*passiones affectuum*) Aquinas means desires arising from things that can be sensed. So in SCG 1,89 he dismisses the suggestion that passions of the appetites exist in God since God is noncorporeal, immutable, and lacking potentiality. All of the arguments in SCG 1,89 are variations on this master argument.

8.4.17 There Is Delight and Joy in God (SCG 1,90)

Aquinas holds that delight (*delectatio*) and joy (*gaudium*) exist in God because God rests content with the goodness that God is.[22] There can, Aquinas concedes, be delight and joy that amounts to a passion had by physical beings such as us, and he is clear that there cannot be delight and joy of this kind in God. But, he observes, delight and joy can be intellectual and not grounded in "sensible appetite," and there is nothing to prevent God having delight and joy in the intellectual sense. Aquinas goes on to say that God, who principally wills himself as goodness without reservation, must be "supremely at rest in himself, as containing all abundance in himself."[23] He adds that God perfectly understands and must be full of delight because of this, and that God takes joy in every good as people take joy in good things unless they threaten them in some way. "Every good is a likeness of the divine good," he says. He adds, "Nor does God lose any good because of some good."[24]

8.4.18 There Is Love in God (SCG 1,91)

By now you will not be expecting Aquinas to say that love exists in God as an enduring passion sparked off by physical contact with something (emotional love, as we might call this). But he does hold that there can be love insofar as one thing wills the good of something else as its own good, and with this thought in mind Aquinas argues that there is love in God since God does will the good of other things as their own good, for the sake of these other things. "God," he says, "wills his own good and that of others" and "wills the good of each thing according as it is the good of each thing."[25] The remaining arguments of SCG 1,91 are variations on this argument coupled with appeal to the Bible as saying that there is joy and delight in God. It is, says Aquinas, "apparent from what has been said that, from among our affections, there is none that can properly exist in God save only joy and love; although even these are not in God as passions, as they are in us."[26]

8.4.19 Virtues Can Be Ascribed to God (SCG 1,92)

Aquinas thinks that people, considered as voluntary agents and as able to make discrete choices, can come to acquire certain virtues over time. And he thinks of these virtues as dispositions that we have toward acting well as human beings, dispositions, indeed, that we need in order to be good as things of the kind to which we belong.[27] Given what I have now shown him arguing in the SCG, Aquinas cannot think that God has virtues as we have them, for he takes God to be eternal, immutable, noncomposite, and lacking in potentiality, which we are not, and which nothing can be if it has acquirable dispositions or dispositions that can be lost. Yet in SCG 1,92 Aquinas argues that God can be thought to have virtues insofar as he is totally good and the source of goodness in creatures. "Virtue is a certain goodness in the virtuous," he observes. He adds: "Therefore the divine goodness must contain in its way all the virtues."[28] Note, however, that Aquinas takes the qualification "in its way" very seriously. God, he insists, cannot have virtues considered as dispositions or habits (*habitus*). In short, Aquinas is clear in SCG 1,92 that God is not morally virtuous as we can be and that there are human virtues that cannot possibly be ascribed to God precisely because they are dispositions that *people* need in order to display goodness as *people*. Again, therefore, the principal thesis of SCG 1,92 is, and only is, that God is perfectly good and contains in some sense the goodness enjoyed by anything that has goodness. As I shall now show, however, Aquinas still thinks that some specific virtues can be ascribed to God.

8.4.20 In God There Are Moral Virtues That Deal with Actions (SCG 1,93)

Aquinas begins SCG 1,93 with this sentence: "Now, there are some virtues directing the active life of people that do not deal with passions, but with actions: for example, truth (*veritas*), justice (*justitia*), liberality (*liberalitas*), magnificence (*magnificenia*), prudence (*prudentia*), and art (*ars*)."[29]

In SCG 1,93 Aquinas regards these virtues as embodying goodness related to action. And he thinks that they can be ascribed to God in "his way," not "our way," because of what God has brought about or made to exist. So, Aquinas argues: (1) art can be said to be in God since God makes things to be in accordance

with an understood plan; (2) God guides things by his knowledge, so prudence can be ascribed to him; (3) God variously wills that things should have
what they need, so justice, considered as giving something that it needs, can
be ascribed to God; (4) God distributes goodness to things without seeking
gain for himself, so there is liberality in him; (5) the virtue of truth is had by
someone who does and says what the person is, yet "all things that receive
being from God must bear his likeness in so far as they are, are good, and
have their proper models,"[30] so there is truth in God. As he concludes SCG
1,93, Aquinas touches on ways in which God cannot have some of the virtues
to which he has just referred. He notes, for example, that God cannot be prudent because he takes advice from people who might know more than he
does. Again, he says that God cannot possess commutative justice (i.e., the
justice involved in paying back what one owes) since God has not received anything from anyone.

8.4.21 There Are Contemplative Virtues in God (SCG 1,94)

In SCG 1,94, Aquinas is concentrating on wisdom and understanding, which
he takes to be virtues in people but which he also takes to exist in God, in "his
way" for reasons that I have now shown in some detail.

8.4.22 God Cannot Will Evil (SCG 1,95)

Aquinas begins SCG 1,95 by saying "From what has been said it can be shown
that God cannot will evil."[31] In fleshing out this comment Aquinas argues: (1)
God cannot will what is evil since God is entirely good; (2) will aims at evil
only because of error since the object of will is the good as understood, yet
there is no error in God; (3) God's will cannot be turned from willing the good
that God is. No surprises in this chapter, therefore, or in SCG 1,96 for
that matter.

8.4.23 God Hates Nothing (SCG 1,96)

Since Aquinas takes hating something to mean willing badness for it, he
thinks that God can hate nothing since his will is always turned to the goodness that he is and to the goodness of things existing as created by him. So,
he says, "If the will of God cannot be inclined to evil.... It is impossible that he
should hate anything."[32] If God truly hated something, adds Aquinas, then he
would will it not to exist. But God makes everything that exists to exist, so
"God wills good to each thing" and therefore "hates nothing."[33] You may think

that God hates some things because he permits various evils to exist, and, as I will show, Aquinas turns to a discussion of God and existing evils in SCG 3. In SCG 1,96, however, he is arguing that God cannot directly will evil as an end in itself and, therefore, cannot be said to hate anything, to target it specifically as something in which he wills evil to exist. He agrees that God sometimes wills there to be things that eat away at the good of other things. But he does not take this to mean that there are real or actual things that God hates. Again, Aquinas concedes that God wills certain goods that "cannot be without the loss of some lesser good."[34] Yet he does not take this to mean that God positively hates anything. He takes it to mean that God sometimes wills goods that are necessarily bound up with there being evils of certain kinds.

8.5 Aquinas on God's Life (SCG 1,97–99)

When it comes to God's life, Aquinas picks up on his general view of what is common to living things as I noted it above. "To live," he says in SCG 1,97, "is attributed to some beings because they are seen to move themselves, but not to be moved by another."[35] On this account, Aquinas goes on to say, God is supremely alive since "He does not act from another, but through himself, since he is the first agent."[36] Aquinas also argues that God is alive since God understands, wills, and "comprehends every perfection of being."[37] And God, Aquinas maintains, must be his life since God is entirely simple and since all that is in God is God (SCG 1,98). Since Aquinas takes God to be eternal, he goes on in SCG 1,99 to add that God's life is without end. He writes: "Nothing ceases to live except through separation from life. But nothing can be separated from God, since every separation takes place through the division of something from something. It is therefore impossible that God cease to live, since God is his life."[38] Again, says Aquinas, anything that exists at some time and that does not exist at another has a cause of its existence, while God has no cause and does not live at some time and not at other times. God, Aquinas finally argues, has to live eternally since God exists *tota simul*, without successiveness (see SCG 1,15) and since God is wholly immutable. God, Aquinas observes, "neither began to live, nor will cease to live, nor in living does he suffer any succession. Therefore his life is everlasting."[39]

8.6 God's Blessedness (SCG 1,100–102)

In the light of what I noted above concerning Aquinas on happiness as *beatitudo*, Aquinas obviously has to say that God enjoys beatitude, and this is what he does in SCG 1,100. God, maintains Aquinas, knows and wills the perfect goodness that God is. So God enjoys blessedness or perfect happiness. Given divine simplicity, Aquinas adds in SCG 1,101, God's blessedness has to be God himself. Then, in SCG 1,102, Aquinas concludes SCG 1 by claiming that God's blessedness or happiness is perfect and unique and, therefore, greater than that of any creature.

The nearest thing to blessedness is blessedness itself, says Aquinas. So, he reasons, since God is blessedness itself, "God is in a unique way perfectly blessed."[40] Human beings may look forward to *beatitudo* and may, indeed, achieve it. But they do not eternally possess blessedness as actual and as constituting what they are by nature. Again, says Aquinas: (1) God delights in himself immeasurably since he is perfectly at one with himself and wills himself as the highest good; (2) blessedness is a perfection enjoyed by what has intellect, "but no other intellectual operation can compare with God's operation . . . because by one operation God knows himself as perfectly as he is perfect"; (3) God's blessedness, unlike that of creatures, is eternal; (4) God's happiness lacks the weariness and various cares that accompany what happiness we might ever achieve in this life; it is also happiness deriving from what is much greater than what tends to make us happy (such as physical pleasure, riches, temporal power, honor, and fame); (5) God's happiness is that of one who perfectly enjoys what God is; so it is joy in what is divine and in all that is made to exist by what is divine.

At this point, Aquinas concludes SCG 1 with the words "To him, then, who is singularly blessed, be honor and glory unto the ages of ages. Amen."[41]

8.7 Some Comments on SCG 1,72–102

Like his account of God's knowledge in SCG 1,44–71, Aquinas's discussion of God's will, life, and blessedness in SCG 1,72–102 relies heavily on the notion of divine simplicity and would, therefore, seem to stand or fall depending on the cogency of that notion. But, and also like his SCG treatment of God's knowledge, Aquinas's SCG discussion of God's will, life, and blessedness strongly coheres with what precedes it and seems unproblematic given certain premises.

The coherence is most evident in the role that divine simplicity plays in the arguments of SCG 1,72–102. And if, for example, Aquinas is right to say that will follows on knowledge and is, indeed, bound up with it, then it is hard to see how one could rightly deny that God has will if one accepts that God has knowledge, for they seem to come as an inseparable pair.

Again, if one agrees that to be alive is to be self-moving, then it surely has to be true that God is alive if God is the first unmoved mover and the maker of the universe who has intellect and will. And it must also be true that if God is what is enjoyed by people in the beatific vision, then God must be blessed if God knows what God is and wills and willingly rests or delights in what God is.

You may want to dissent from some details in the arguments of SCG 1,72–102, but these chapters have a relentless and inevitable flow to them given their reliance on SCG 1,13–71 and given the truth of the premises to which I have just referred. It has, however, been argued that what Aquinas says about God's will in SCG 1,72–96 ought to lead him to deny that God has freedom to create. Aquinas asserts that God is free not to create both in his SCG discussion of God's will and at other points in the SCG, not to mention passages in works other than the SCG. Yet, as I say, it has been suggested that some reasoning in SCG 1,72–96 should have left Aquinas concluding that God lacks freedom when it comes to creating. So let me now say something about that line of argument.[42]

If God wills himself of necessity, as Aquinas claims in SCG 1,80, and if God wills himself and creatures in a single act of will, as Aquinas claims in SCG 1,76, then does not God necessarily will himself as the creator of what is not divine? And if God does that, then how can God fail to will that creatures should exist? In other words, if God, from eternity, wills what God is, and if God from eternity wills there to be creatures, then God must surely not be free not to create. So, one might think, Aquinas's account of God's will conflicts with what he says in SCG 1,81–83, where he denies that God has to create while noting that God is never constrained to choose some particular way to achieve what is good. In circumstances in which I might find myself, I may have no option but to take a plane in order to arrive somewhere by a certain time. Yet, thinks Aquinas, God cannot be thought ever to be constrained by options in this way. According to Aquinas, God unfailingly wills what is good without having to will a means to what is good. But if God unfailingly wills himself, and if God eternally wills to create what is not divine, how can God fail not to will what is not divine?

So, one might think, Aquinas really ought to be denying freedom to God when it comes to creating. Yet there are reasons to think otherwise, and these largely lie in what Aquinas says in the SCG concerning what cannot be true of God.

Aquinas does not think of God as needing creatures in any significant way. I need to eat so as to survive, but Aquinas's account of God in the SCG clearly rules out the idea of God depending on something in order to survive. It also rules out the idea of God being forced to do something by an agent acting on God. So, thinks Aquinas, we cannot suppose that God, by nature or causal influence, is compelled to create. Aquinas, as I have shown, develops his philosophy of God in the SCG by asking why there is motion and why there is something rather than nothing. In doing so he reasons that God has to act in or on things without being efficiently caused to do so. He, therefore, concludes that what God produces can only be thought of as what God has chosen to produce, which seems to entail that God does not have to create a world of creatures. To be sure, Aquinas accepts that God has eternally willed to create. But, as Aquinas points out in SCG 1,83, this only means that it is necessary that God has created on the supposition that God, from eternity, has decreed to create. It does not mean that God is compelled to create. As I have shown, in SCG 1,37 Aquinas supports the idea that "the good is diffusive of itself and of being."[43] But he does not take this thesis as entailing that God has to make good things other than himself to exist. He thinks of the thesis as stating that what is good always attracts those able to recognize it and share somehow in it. He does not take it to mean that a good thing is compelled to produce another good thing, and he does not think that God has to create what is good just because he is good. Aquinas maintains that God is good and that he wills creatures to exist so as to share in his goodness insofar as creatures can be thought to share in what God is by existing and being good. But he does not say anything to suggest that God has to create creatures or that God is compelled to do so by nature or anything outside him, and it is not at all obvious that what he does say in the SCG ought to force him to conclude that God has to create. Quite the opposite.

In this connection we should also remember that the natural theology of SCG 1 is something that Aquinas develops on the basis of premises that he thinks we can take to be true on the basis of observation coupled with other premises that are not based on observation. So, among other things, he notes that there are things that do not exist by nature, things that he thinks might never have existed, and he thinks that their being able not to exist has nothing to do with God but consists in what they are by nature. Hence the question "Why do they exist if what they are does not guarantee their existence at all times?" That things in the world do not have to exist is a critical premise in the natural theology of the SCG. So Aquinas can hardly be dismissing it when he writes as he does concerning God's will. As he does so, he is (1) assuming that there might have been nothing at all since the existence of things in the world is not explained by noting what they are, and (2) presuming that what exists but does not do so by nature has to have a cause that wills it into being. In the SCG Aquinas never says anything to suggest that the "able not to exist" aspect of creatures should be thought to lead us to conclude that God cannot but create. If Aquinas thought this, then his natural theology in the SCG would be totally undermined since it depends so heavily on the idea that creatures, who do not have to exist by nature, have to derive from what does exist by nature. In short, conclusions about what God has to produce should surely take account of whether or not what God has actually produced is, regardless of theological considerations, something that cannot but exist. Or so Aquinas thinks.

8.8 Moving on to SCG 2

I have shown that in SCG 1 Aquinas chiefly deals with the existence and nature of God. He has some things to say in SCG 1 about what is not divine since he speaks of God as the cause of the existence of creatures and since he draws on what he takes to be truths about certain creatures as he treats of God's activities of understanding and willing. Yet in SCG 1 Aquinas's focus is on God in himself, what God is and does simply by existing as God.

For Aquinas, however, God is the creator, and his action or "operation" (*operatio*) not only includes what is internal to himself, as Aquinas takes God's understanding and willing to be. In Aquinas's view God "operates" or acts as a maker, albeit not out of some necessity. So in SCG 2,1 he says that "for a complete study of divine truth, the second operation, whereby things are made and governed by God, remains to be dealt with."[44] This "second operation" of God is the subject matter of SCG 2, in which Aquinas turns to God as active in creatures as their maker and sustainer and in which he turns to human beings and angels considered as things of special interest in the order called into being by God. In the next chapter I will show how he gets started on this project.

God as Omnipotent Creator
(SCG 2,1–29)

WHY IS IT worth reflecting on God's works, on the things that God has made and governs? In SCG 2,2 Aquinas offers four reasons: (1) Doing so helps us to admire and reflect on God's wisdom, which is partially displayed by creatures; (2) doing so leads us to admire God's power and inspires reverence for God in us; (3) doing so incites us to love of God's goodness; (4) doing so endows us with "a certain likeness to God's perfection."[1] In SCG 2,3 Aquinas goes on to say that knowing about God's creatures can serve to lead us away from errors concerning truths of faith, errors that are "inconsistent with true knowledge of God."[2] What sort of errors does Aquinas have in mind here? He mentions four: (1) Wrongly taking creatures to be the first cause when, in fact, they derive their being from God; (2) wrongly attributing to creatures what belongs only to God; (3) wrongly conceiving of God's power through ignorance of the nature of creatures; (4) wrongly evaluating the dignity of people so as to suppose them to be subject to things to which they are not subject. In short, Aquinas declares, it is evident that "the opinion is false of those who asserted that it made no difference to the truth of the faith what anyone holds about creatures, so long as one thinks rightly about God."[3]

So, in SCG 2,5, Aquinas explains that he is going to embark on SCG 2 by considering "first, the bringing forth of things into being; second, their distinction; third, the nature of these same things, brought forth and distinct from one another, so far as it is relevant to the truth of faith."[4]

9.1 The Bringing Forth of Things into Being (SCG 2,6)

In SCG 2,6 Aquinas reiterates, and elaborates on, some key teachings of SCG 1 while drawing attention to the fact that he is doing just this. He begins by declaring that God is the first unmoved mover and that God is "the cause of being to many things." He says that it belongs to God as a being in act "to enact some being in act, to which he is the cause of being."[5] Again, he observes, since God is perfect (see SCG 1,28), we know that he is able to produce what is like him somehow (see SCG 1,75): that it belongs to God "to produce something actual, like himself, so as to be the cause of its existence."[6] Given that we know that God is perfect, Aquinas goes on to say, we know that God "does not lack the power of communicating his being to a thing by way of likeness" and that God will thereby be the cause of its being.[7] In this connection Aquinas notes that God, as pure act containing no potentiality, is able to produce effects and is able to be the cause of being.

9.2 Power in God (SCG 2,7–10)

Aquinas distinguishes between (1) passive power and (2) active power. On the one hand, he thinks, what exists might be able to (have the "power" to) be acted on by something other than itself. Thus, for example, I can be, or am able to be, carried around by people stronger than myself. On the other hand, though, Aquinas holds that what exists might have the ability or "active power" to act on or in something other than itself. Hence, for example, I might be able to carry my cat around.

From what he says in SCG 1, you will realize that Aquinas denies that there is passive power in God, and you will realize why he does so. In SCG 2,7, however, he emphasizes that God has active power considered as "the principle of acting upon another as such." He adds: "But it is proper to God to be the source of being to other things. Therefore, it pertains to him to be powerful."[8] In SCG 2,8 Aquinas argues that God's power is God's very substance since (1) there is no potentiality in God, (2) since God is his own being, (3) since perfection in God (including power) is contained in God's very being (see SCG 1,28), (4) since there are no accidents in God (see SCG 1,23), and (5) since "God is agent through his very self."[9] Working with these thoughts in mind, Aquinas argues in SCG 2,9–10 that God's power is his action. He means that God, who is simple, is not to be distinguished from his acts of willing, whether that involves willing his own goodness or willing, and thereby bringing about, the existence of creatures. Strictly speaking, says Aquinas, God's active power does not belong to him by essence since God does not have to act so as to bring about what is not divine. We can, thinks Aquinas, only attribute active power to God on the basis of him making things exist. Still, Aquinas is clear that God has active power, which is not an accident in him or something added to him. Active power belongs to God insofar as he is eternally able to go out of himself, as it were, and bring about the existence of effects that are not divine.

9.3 God and Relations (SCG 2,11–14)

Since Aquinas thinks that God has power with respect to his effects, he thinks that we can speak of God as related to them. And, since Aquinas holds that God's effects derive from God, he maintains that creatures can be said to be related to God. He also thinks that God produces what is somehow like God, that God knows his effects, that God moves things, and that God is first among beings. So in SCG 2,11 Aquinas is happy to say that "something is said of God in relation to creatures."[10]

In SCG 2,12, however, we find Aquinas (curiously, you might think) maintaining that "relations predicated of God in reference to creatures do not really exist in him."[11] Here I take him to mean that, whatever we might hold to be true of God as the creator of his creatures, his relation to them does not involve any modification or change in him. If I feed my cat, I act as an agent cause with respect to it, and my doing so involves certain changes in me. I move around, procure cat food, place it before the cat, and so on. These changes really exist in me. They are changes that I undergo. So my being the feeder of my cat includes my undergoing changes, meaning that I am related to my cat as its feeder as something undergoing change. As I have shown, however, Aquinas denies that God really changes since he takes God to be pure act and as lacking potentiality. So when it comes to relations predicated of God in reference to creatures, Aquinas's position is that these should not be thought of as relations involving changes in God.

Yet, thinks Aquinas, we can say that God is my creator and is the cause of any changes that I undergo. In this sense, he concedes, God is related to me. But not as modified by being so. For Aquinas, God is the eternal and unchangeable divine essence. So he thinks that language by which we truly express how creatures stand to God as their cause should not be taken to imply that the truth that it expresses implies that God is first like this and then like that, that God undergoes change. Aquinas presumes that we often have to talk about God as if he were an object in the world related to other things as things in the world are related to each other. He presumes that because he recognizes that we are stuck with talking of the totally simple as if it were somehow composite (unless we spend time noting the differences between God and creatures that Aquinas flags in SCG 1). Yet Aquinas also thinks that reflection should lead us to recognize that, say, affirming that God is my creator should not be taken to suggest that God somehow became different from what he eternally is when I came to exist. In other words, while Aquinas thinks that something true can be said of God in relation to creatures, he does not believe that what God brings about when it comes to creatures involves God becoming different from what he eternally is. I cannot be the feeder of my cat without going through certain processes. Yet, thinks Aquinas, God can be, or even be truly said to *become* to be, the creator of me without himself changing in any real way. Such is the basic argument of SCG 2,11–14, which views relations predicated of God in reference to creatures as being true because of what is going on with creatures as made to be by God, not because of a series of events in the life or being of God as he wills to create and as what he wills to create exists.

9.4 *God as Creator (SCG 2,15–21)*

Aquinas states the presiding thesis of SCG 2,15–17 right at the start of SCG 2,15: "Everything besides God derives its being from him."[12] According to Aquinas, everything nondivine is being made to exist for as long as it exists. Or, as he goes on to say: "Everything which is in any way at all must then derive its being from that whose being has no cause.... God is being in the highest mode. Therefore, he is the cause of all things of which being is predicated.... Above all causes, then, there must be a cause whose proper action is to give being.... Everything that is must, therefore, be from God."[13]

In SCG 2,15 he offers the following arguments for this thesis.

9.4.1 Argument One

1. What does not belong to something as such belongs to it through a cause.
2. Nothing can as such belong to two things since what belongs to something *as such* is limited to that thing, as, for example, having three angles equal to two right angles is proper only to triangles.
3. "So, if something belongs to two things, it will not belong to both as such."[14]
4. So nothing can be predicated of two things "so as to be said of neither of them by reason of a cause."[15]
5. Being is predicated of everything that exists.
6. So there cannot be two things neither of which has a cause of its being; either both must exist through a cause, or the one must be the cause of the other's being.
7. Yet God is the being whose existence has no cause (see SCG 1,13).

In this argument "belonging to something as such" means "belonging uniquely to something," as, say, being feline is unique to cats, or as, to take Aquinas's example, having three angles equal to two right angles is unique to triangles. So Aquinas is arguing that what does not belong uniquely to something has to derive from something outside it. He is then arguing that being is predicable of everything that exists, which he takes to mean that, unless it belongs to that the existence of which has no cause (that which exists "as such"), it does not belong to anything "as such."

9.4.2 Argument Two

1. Whatever something possesses essentially or by nature cannot be diminished or deficient in it; otherwise it would completely cease to exist.

2. If what it takes for something to exist remains in it intact, and if the thing is somehow diminished, the diminution must be caused by something other than the nature of the thing.

3. So what belongs to one thing less than to other things does not belong to it because of its nature; it belongs to it because of some other cause.

4. So "that thing of which a genus is chiefly predicated will be the cause of everything in that genus."[16]

5. But God is being in the highest degree (see SCG 1,13); so God is "the cause of all things of which being is predicated."[17]

9.4.3 Argument Three

1. Causes and effects are ordered to each other.

2. What is common among effects derives from a common cause.

3. Being is common to everything that exists, so there must be a cause able to give being.

4. God is the first cause (see SCG 1,13). So everything that exists must derive from God.

9.4.4 Argument Four

1. "The cause of everything said to be such and such by way of participation is that which is said to be so by virtue of its essence."[18]

2. God is being by his essence, so everything that exists participates in God's act of being, which belongs only to God (see SCG 1,42). So God causes being in all other things.

9.4.5 Argument Five

1. What is equally able to exist or not exist must be caused to exist by something else, for what is able to exist or not to exist is, by itself, "indifferent" when it comes to being or not being.

2. There must, therefore, be something that has to exist and that causes to exist all that can be or not be, and that even causes the existence of things not able to be or not to be while deriving their necessary existence from something else. This is what God is: a necessary being that causes to exist all things that can either exist or not exist, and a necessary being that is necessary of itself.[19]

9.4.6 Argument Six

1. God's actuality somehow includes the perfections of all things (see SCG 1,28).
2. So God is the maker of all things—bearing in mind that nothing other than God is able to exist without deriving from God.

9.4.7 Argument Seven

1. Imperfect things have their origin in what is perfect.
2. But God is the most perfect thing and the highest good (see SCG 1,28 and 41).

9.5 Creation "from Nothing" (SCG 2,16)

In SCG 2 Aquinas is thinking that for God to create is for him to account for things existing at any time. When we make things, we work on what preexists our actions of making. For us, making is a matter of transforming in some way. In SCG 2,16, however, Aquinas argues that God's act of making all things exist cannot be a modification of something that precedes this act. So he concludes that, as creator and absolute first cause, God makes, *but not out of anything*.

In defending this conclusion Aquinas offers a number of arguments, but they are all variations on the thinking I have just noted. They all indicate why, in Aquinas's view, God cannot make things exist by *first* getting to work on something and *then* bringing it into existence. In rounding off SCG 2,16 Aquinas notes that some "ancient philosophers" took matter to have no cause because things seem always to come about from other things and because "from nothing, nothing comes."[20] These philosophers, Aquinas accepts, were right insofar as they were thinking about how things in the world come to be because of the activity of other things in the world. Yet, he adds, they were wrong because they did not reflect on the coming about of everything that exists or has being while not being pure being, as God is. In short, Aquinas holds that, as well as asking what in the world accounts for this or that, we need to ask "Why is there something rather than nothing?" He also claims that God is the only possible answer to this question insofar as the question is construed as seeking an agent cause.

9.6 Creation Is Not a Motion or a Change (SCG 2,17–19)

If for God to create is for God to make things to be, period, and if God's act of creating is not an operation on what preexists it, then, Aquinas reasons, coming to be created is not to undergo a change of any kind.

Here, his argument is that all motion or change depends on things having potentiality of some kind while to be created is not to be changed from being in one state or from being a thing of some kind. It is to be caused to exist, but not out of anything. "In the action which is creation," Aquinas says, "nothing potential pre-exists to receive the action.... Therefore, creation is not a motion or a change."[21] Or, as he goes on to observe in SCG 2,18: "Creation is not a change, but the very dependency of the created act of being upon the principle from which it is produced. And thus, creation is a kind of relation."[22]

Aquinas admits that we inevitably tend to think of creation as a kind of change since we conceive of one and the same thing as first not existing and then as existing. But that, he adds, only reflects our way of understanding; it does not correspond to what actually goes on as God makes things exist. For a thing to be made to exist by God is not for it to undergo a change. And this, Aquinas adds in SCG 2,19, means that there is no successiveness when it comes to being created. Here he says that something undergoes successiveness by going through *motus*; but to be created is not to undergo *motus*, nor is God's act of creating to be construed as producing a change in anything.

9.7 *What Can Create? (SCG 2,20–21)*

From all that Aquinas says in SCG 1 and SCG 2,1–19, you will, presumably, be assuming that he holds that only God can create, and, in concluding his discussion in SCG 2,20-21, he makes it perfectly explicit that this is indeed what he thinks.

Could it be that something material is able to create? In SCG 2,20 Aquinas argues that no body is capable of creative activity in the sense that he has been discussing it. He says, for example, that bodies only act as moved, and they are only moved in time: that bodies only bring things about that come to be as a result of successiveness, while creation is successionless. Again, Aquinas argues that bodies act by changing other bodies, while creation is not the bringing about of a change in anything.

In SCG 2,21, Aquinas maintains that only God can create by making these points:

1. Creation is the first action that depends on no other action, while all other action depends on things being created. But God is the first agent.
2. There is nothing not caused to be by God, so only God can create.
3. The cause of existence in things has to be the first agent acting in all things, and this is what God alone is as making the difference between there being something rather than absolutely nothing.

4. The existence of everything other than God is caused, so nothing other than God could cause the existence of something other than itself except by acting as an instrumental cause. Yet instrumental causes always cause as things that are caused in some way by other things, and they cause by bringing about change. To be created, however, is not to have undergone a change. And instrumental causes act on things, while creation is "from nothing." Also, instrumental causes act so as to carry out what they are caused to do, while God is not caused to do anything by anything.

5. Nothing that is acted on causally as having a nature is the cause of the nature it has; otherwise it would be the cause of itself. But such a thing can account for something else having a nature, as, for example, parents bring it about that their children exist as human beings. Parents, though, do not bring it about that human nature exists. They communicate to others a nature that all of them share. But to create is to bring things to be from nothing. It is not to pass on something that already exists in some way. So nothing created can cause something else by creating it.

6. Finite causes produce effects that flow from them as the particular kind of things that they are, and their effects have a particular form.[23] But to create is to produce something common to everything, namely, existence. So only God, who belongs to no genus or species, can create because he is pure being by nature or essence.

7. Only the first being causes being *as being*, as opposed to being *in a certain way*. And God alone is the first being who makes things to be from nothing preexisting.

9.8 *God as Omnipotent (SCG 2,22–29)*

It is sometimes said that God is omnipotent because God can do anything. It is also said that there is no omnipotent God since one can easily think of things that God cannot do. If God is incorporeal, for instance, then God obviously cannot eat an ice cream; and it would therefore seem that there are things that God cannot do.[24]

As we can see from SCG 2,22, however, Aquinas does not construe "God is omnipotent" as "God can do everything." In other words, he does not think that God is omnipotent because we can tack onto "God can ___" any possible feat we care to mention. His view is that since God is the source of the being of things, since God is pure being and able to create, then God can make to exist anything the existence of which is possible. So, says Aquinas:

Every perfect power reaches out to all those things to which the effect possessed by it through itself and proper to it can extend; whatever can have the character of a dwelling falls within the range of the art of building, if it is perfect. Now, God's power is through itself the cause of being, and the act of being is his proper effect, as was made clear above [cf. SCG 2,21]. Hence, his power reaches out to all things with which the notion of being is not incompatible; for if God's power were limited to some particular effect, he would not be through himself the cause of a being as such, but of this particular being. Now, the opposite of being, namely non-being, is incompatible with the notion of being. Hence, God can do all things which do not essentially include the notion of non-being, and such are those which involve a contradiction. It follows, then, that God can do whatever does not imply a contradiction.[25]

In the last two sentences of this passage, "can do" (*potest*) clearly means "can bring about" or "can cause to exist" or "can create." Aquinas does not suppose that God can do anything that something other than God can do, such as eat an ice cream. But he does think that God can make to exist what can be thought to exist absolutely speaking. As he goes on to say, "God is perfect act, possessing in himself the perfections of all things.... His active power, therefore, is perfect, extending to everything not repugnant to the notion of that which is in act; namely to everything except that which implies a contradiction. God, then, is omnipotent as regards all but this."[26]

In SCG 2,25 Aquinas happily concedes that there are things that fall outside God's power but do not fall outside the power of some agents. He argues, for example, that God cannot be a body and cannot be changed. Again, he says, God cannot undergo privation, or forget, or have passions, or sin. In short, Aquinas maintains that it is *because* God is omnipotent that God cannot eat an ice cream. And, so he also thinks, by virtue of his omnipotence God always acts in conformity to the perfect goodness that God is. God's acting as a maker, he says, is always directed to the goodness of God. This is the thesis of SCG 2,24, in which Aquinas says: "It is by the wisdom of his intellect, therefore, that God brings things into being."[27]

Yet might it not be thought that God's intellect is limited in its effects as God acts? And might it not be thought that God's will is limited in the same way? Aquinas turns to these questions in SCG 2,26 and 27. In these chapters he argues:

1. Since God understands all that can proceed from him by understanding his essence (see SCG 1,49 and following), and since God's power is not

limited to producing certain particular effects (see SCG 2,22), God's intellect is not limited to certain particular effects.

2. God is infinite in essence, unlike anything else (see SCG 1,43). But God's intellect knows the divine essence perfectly and is therefore "not necessarily confined to these or those effects."[28]

3. Since God knows infinite things (see SCG 1,69), and since God brings things into being through his knowledge, "the causality of the divine intellect is not restricted to the production of finite effects."[29]

4. God knows "even those things which never are, nor will be, nor have been" (see SCG 1,66). So "it is not by any necessity on the part of his intellect or his knowledge that God works."[30]

5. God's knowledge stands to what he makes as the knowledge of a craftsman stands to what he makes. But God's craftsmanship extends to making things to exist; it extends to being (see SCG 2,15). So God's intellect "is not restricted to the production of certain determinate effects."[31]

6. Since God's intellect is not restricted to certain effects, God's will is not "necessitated to produce certain determinate effects."[32]

7. God wills nothing by absolute necessity (see SCG 1,26), so no effects proceed from God's will by necessity.

One might think that, in creating, God brings into being what, if he is just, he *ought* to bring into being. Yet, says Aquinas in SCG 2,28, God cannot be thought to create because he owes something to anyone or anything. If God had never created, he observes, nothing would be wronged by this fact since it would not exist in the first place. And nothing can lay claim to being owed anything by God since it has nothing of its own unless God provides it by creating. Again, says Aquinas, to owe something to another is to depend on that other in some way; yet God depends on nothing and can benefit from nothing. Aquinas notes the suggestion that God can only do what he does since "he can do only that which he ought to do." But, he observes, "God does not produce things from a debt of justice."[33] Yes, he agrees, God is obliged to make such and such if he is to make what depends on there being such and such. So God must make the sun and the moon if he is to make the world *in which we live*. Yet, Aquinas adds, it does not therefore follow that God, absolutely speaking, is obliged to make the sun and the moon, for God might never have created at all.

9.9 Some Comments on SCG 2,1–29

You will obviously want to dismiss much that Aquinas says in SCG 2,1–29 if you think that he has not previously shown that God exists as first mover and first cause, or if you reject his claim that God is entirely simple. Yet even if you agree with Aquinas on God's existence as first mover and first cause, and even if you agree with what Aquinas says about divine simplicity, you might have reservations with SCG 2,1–29. You might, for example, think that there has to be something wrong with its claim that, while creatures are really related to God, God is not really related to creatures. Or you might think that Aquinas is wrong to speak of God as omnipotent. In concluding this chapter, therefore, let me briefly say something about Aquinas on God and relations and God as omnipotent.

9.9.1 Relations

It would seem to be absurd to suggest that, among the relations that there *are*, some are real while some are not. But I do not think that this is what Aquinas suggests in the SCG. He does, however, say that, while creatures are really related to God, God is not really related to creatures. And this suggestion makes sense if we focus on how it can be said that something undergoes change without undergoing what we might call a "real" change.

Let us suppose that I come to hate you. My coming to hate you would, surely, amount to a real change in me. But would it amount to a real change in you? Surely not. You would certainly be affected by my trying to strangle you because I hate you. But my coming to hate you need have no impact on you at all. Indeed, I might come to hate you while doing nothing that might show by my behavior that I am anything other than well disposed to you. So we can distinguish between what Peter Geach calls "real change" and "merely Cambridge change."

By "merely Cambridge change," Geach means what is flagged by assertions like "John has come to be hated by Mary" or "Mary has come to be loved by John." Both of these could well be true assertions, and they seem to imply "Mary has come to hate John" and "John has come to love Mary." But "John has come to be hated by Mary" and "Mary has come to be loved by John" do not signify any real process of change in John or Mary. John may know nothing of Mary and may be entirely unaffected by the fact that she has started to hate him. Similarly, Mary may know nothing of John and might be changed in no way by the fact that John has begun to love her. On the other hand "Mary has cut her finger" and "John has broken his leg" do ascribe real changes to Mary and John.

So we can think of a merely Cambridge change as "a matter of contradictory attributes holding good of individuals at different times."[34] And we can distinguish merely Cambridge changes from real ones. Armed with these thoughts, we can now note that we might have perfectly true statements relating one thing to another without it being true that both things undergo real change, which is what Aquinas seems to be supposing when he says that, though creatures are really related to God, God is not really related to creatures. Aquinas certainly seems to think that, for example, *both* (1) "God has brought it about that Moses has a beard" and (2) "Moses has a beard brought about by God" can be true. Yet he does not think that the truth of (1) and (2) here entails that God undergoes any change, though Moses certainly does so as his beard grows. Aquinas thinks that "some relational propositions latch onto reality in a way that others do not."[35] And I think that he is right to do so. You may think that he is not since you may think that God has to undergo real change. On the supposition that God is changeless, however, what Aquinas says about how God is not related to creatures, while creatures are related to God, makes sense. For, as Geach observes:

> If we may after all regard a relational proposition as making predications about the related things A and B,[36] then it will make sense (whether it is true or not) to suppose that when we take the proposition as a predication about A, there is some actuality in A answering to the predication, but that when we take the same (or a logically equivalent) proposition as a predication about B, there is no actuality in B answering to the predication. And in concrete examples we can make it plausible that this is true. Take "Edith envies Herbert," for example: if Edith comes to envy Herbert, it is natural to regard this as a change in Edith rather than a change in Herbert (his "coming to be envied"); and it is very natural to regard a state of envy as an actual condition of Edith, but very unnatural to regard a "state of being envied" as an actual condition of Herbert. This gives a plausible content to the statement that, when Edith envies Herbert, this involves a "real" relation on Edith's side but not on Herbert's.[37]

Yet what if we focus not on causal propositions, like "God came to give Moses a beard" or "Moses came to have a beard by virtue of God," but on propositions like "God knows that Moses is asleep" or "God wills that Moses is sleeping"? Should we not suppose that propositions such as these, if they are true, are not always true, and that their truth implies that a real change can come about in God?

Here, I think, Aquinas would say that God eternally knows or wills what Moses is doing at any time, though he does not know or will it in some time frame to be related to that of Moses, that he does not *now* know or will that Moses is now asleep. For Aquinas, God's knowledge and will is unvarying and would exist even if there were nothing whose existence and changes could be clocked or written about in a historical book. Yet, he thinks, since God is the creator, then God can know what his creatures are in time and how what they are in time relates to what other things are in time. In Aquinas's view, God's knowledge and will do not stand to what God knows and wills as our knowledge and will stand to what we know and will. We know and will as creatures that interact at various times with other things in the world. According to Aquinas, however, God eternally knows and wills creatures in nonsuccessively knowing and willing himself as their creator. And, if Aquinas is right to think this, then he is right to suppose that the creaturely objects of God's knowledge and will do not bring about any change in God as they come to be what they are as creatures of God, even though God knows and wills them, and even though they stand in a real relation to God by actually having all that they are from God.

9.9.2 Omnipotence

Belief in divine omnipotence has been frequently criticized. As I have noted, some have said that if God is omnipotent, then God can do anything, while there are obviously lots of things that God, if nonmaterial, cannot do. Again, it has been suggested that there cannot be an omnipotent God because of a so-called paradox of omnipotence. Can God make something too heavy for him to lift? If he can, then it would seem that there is something that God cannot do, namely, lift the stone. If he cannot, then again it would seem that there is something that God cannot do, namely make something too heavy for him to lift.

By now, however, you will be aware of how Aquinas would reply to objections to divine omnipotence of these kinds. He would say that "God is omnipotent" should not be taken to mean that God can do anything you care to mention. He would say that God has power insofar as he can make anything to exist that could possibly exist. And, with regard to the paradox of omnipotence, he would say that God does not and cannot lift things (as we often try to do), while adding that God can bring about the levitation of anything that can rise.

You might suppose that God can hardly be omnipotent if he cannot make contradictories to be true. So you might think, for example, that God cannot be omnipotent if he cannot produce something that is both square and circular. Yet Aquinas does not think that divine omnipotence extends to making what is both square and circular. He would say, and surely rightly, that "X is both square and circular" is not a possibly true proposition, that there can be nothing producible that is both square and circular. As I have said, his view is that if "X exists" is possibly true, then God, as the source of the existence of all things, can make it to be that X exists. You might suppose that logical laws such as "Nothing can be both a square and a circle" are revisable. But can we say what a nonlogical world would be or be described to be?

Can we determine whether or not "X exists" is possibly true? This is a difficult question, and proofs of logical consistency are often hard to come by. Can there be something that has traveled through time? Can there be something that exists without a cause? Can human beings live after they have died? These are questions that philosophers have debated for centuries. Fortunately, though, when evaluating Aquinas's account of divine omnipotence, we do not have to worry about them. When holding that God is omnipotent, Aquinas is not offering an account of what is and is not possible when it comes to X, Y, or Z as existing. All he is saying is that *if* it is absolutely impossible for X, Y, or Z to exist, then God cannot make it to exist. If you think that it is impossible for X to exist, and if you can prove your case, then Aquinas would say that God cannot make X to exist. And so on for Y and Z. In other words, Aquinas's account of omnipotence in the SCG does not depend on analyses of what might or might not be. All it does is to assert that if something can be, then God can make it to be.

I find this assertion convincing if Aquinas is right in what he says in the SCG concerning God as the first cause who makes things to exist as one who does not *have* being but *is* being and is the cause of there being anything that does not have to exist because of what it is. One might think that God cannot bring about all that he brings about as existing together or at the same time, and that God is, therefore, not omnipotent. Yet there being everything that can be existing at the same time does not seem to be logically possible. For example, I cannot exist as my long dead ancestors existed since I am descended from them and since I came to be after they ceased to be. So, though "God might be able to create what he can create" is true in a trivial sense, it cannot be true as taken to imply that God can make creatures to exist without them and their actions being distinguishable from a temporal viewpoint.

You might, of course, now want to say that God can do what people can do since, according to Christian doctrine, God became incarnate and walked around and did various things that people can do, like eating. And if you want to say that, Aquinas would agree with you, as I will show when we come to SCG 4. In SCG 2, however, Aquinas is concerned with what is true of the divine essence, whether or not God became incarnate. In SCG 4 Aquinas will distinguish between what can be true of Christ *as* man and true of Christ *as* God. In his discussion of God's power in SCG 2, however, he is focusing on what God *as* God can do, on what the divine nature, which might never have created at all, might be thought of as able to produce.

Necessity in Creatures, the Eternity of the World, and Distinctions among Creatures (SCG 2,30–45)

IF CREATURES DEPEND on God's will, does it follow that there can be no necessary beings other than God? Might we not say that "there are some things in the universe whose being is simply and absolutely necessary"?[1] You might suppose that we cannot say this if only God is Being Itself who exists uncaused. Yet Aquinas actually does think that some creatures are "simply and absolutely necessary," as we see from SCG 2,30.

10.1 Can There Be Created Yet Necessary Things? (SCG 2,30)

According to Aquinas something is "simply and absolutely necessary" if it is not able *to be or not to be*. One might think he regards all creatures as able to be or not to be and that he should, therefore, assume that no creature exists of absolute necessity, and Aquinas is clear that no creature has to exist by nature (since its nature and existence can be distinguished from each other, and since its existence must be caused by God). However, Aquinas does think that some things created by God have a necessity that does not conflict with the fact that what they are by nature does not entail that they exist as God does: as eternal, simple, and underived.

Philosophers have often spoken about contingency and necessity by appealing to certain propositions and then applying what they have said when it comes to things that exist. Consider the proposition "No triangles are square." That seems to be logically necessary. But also consider the proposition "Australia exists." That you might think is not true of logical necessity. Indeed, if you thought that it was true of logical necessity, then you would suppose that Australia has always existed and could not possibly cease to exist. So let us say that "Australia exists" is not true of logical necessity as is "No triangles are square." In that case, Australia would seem to be something contingent, something that does not exist of logical necessity. So, it has consequently been said, there are things of two kinds: things that are logically necessary (the existence of which it would be contradictory to deny), and things that are contingent (the existence of which it would not be contradictory to deny). Yet, though Aquinas is perfectly aware of the distinction between propositions that are logically necessary and propositions that are not, he thinks that there are creatures of God that are necessary while other ones are contingent.

That is because Aquinas takes necessary creatures to be ones that (1) do not arise by a process of generation, and (2) cannot be annihilated by what exists in the material world. He says:

> Some things are so created by God that there is in their nature a potentiality to non-being; and this results from the fact that the matter present in them is in potentiality with respect to another form. On the other hand, neither immaterial things, nor things whose matter is not receptive of another form, have potentiality to non-being, so that their being is absolutely and simply necessary.[2]

Aquinas's distinction between creatures that are necessary and creatures that are contingent is not the distinction between what is logically necessary and logically contingent. It flags a difference between actually existing things created by God, and Aquinas, therefore, does not think that there being necessary created things conflicts with the view that all creatures depend for their existence on God's will.

You might think that if creatures come to be from nothing, then none of them can be necessary. However, though Aquinas accepts that all creatures derive from God, and though he is certain that God might never have created since (1) God does not need creatures and since (2) no agent can compel God to do anything, he does not think it therefore follows that there can be no created necessary things. Such things, Aquinas holds, are just beings of a certain kind, beings that could be and that, therefore, can be created by God. "To be simply necessary," says Aquinas, "is not incompatible with the notion of created being; for nothing prevents a thing being necessary whose necessity nevertheless has a cause, as in the case of the conclusions of demonstrations. Hence, nothing prevents certain things being produced by God in such fashion that they exist in a simply necessary way; indeed, this is a proof of God's perfection."[3]

10.2 Must Creatures Always Have Existed? (SCG 2,31–38)

If there are necessary creatures caused to be by God, however, should we not suppose that at least some creatures have always existed? Aristotle held that the world had no beginning, and other philosophers, especially ancient ones, have argued to the same effect.[4] So might we not indeed suppose that creatures have always existed, or that the physical universe, at any rate, never began to be?

Aquinas turns to these questions in SCG 2,31. To start with, he argues that it is not necessary for creatures always to have existed (SCG 2,31). In subsequent chapters he notes and comments on arguments for and against the conclusion that the universe has always existed (SCG 2,32–38). His overall view is: (1) it cannot be proved that the universe has always existed; (2) it cannot be proved that the universe began to exist; (3) God must account for the existence of the universe whether or not it had a beginning. As I noted in chapter 3, Aquinas did believe that the universe had a beginning since he took this to be taught by the Old Testament book of Genesis. However, in several of his writings, including the SCG, he views the teaching that the world began to be as a truth of faith, not something demonstrable as some of his contemporaries took it to be.[5]

When it comes to the thesis that it is necessary for creatures always to have existed, Aquinas's position is that creatures only exist because God wills them to exist, implying that there might not have been any creatures at all, let alone ones always existing. This is the argument of SCG 2,31. Here Aquinas says:

> Nothing proceeding from a will is absolutely necessary, except when it chances to be necessary for the will to will it. But, as we have shown [see SCG 2,23], God brings creatures into being not through a necessity of his nature, but voluntarily. Nor, as proved in Book 1, does he necessarily will the existence of creatures [see SCG 1,81]. Hence, it is not absolutely necessary for the creature to be, and therefore neither is it necessary for creatures to have existed always.[6]

Why might one think that the world has existed always and of necessity? Or why might one think that it cannot always have existed? With respect to the first question, Aquinas notes arguments of three kinds: (1) those taking their stand on what God is, (2) those taking their stand on what creatures are, and (3) those taking their stand on what is involved in making. Aquinas spells out these arguments in SCG 2,32–34, while replying to them in SCG 2,35–37. With respect to the question "Why suppose that the world cannot always have existed?" in SCG 2,38 Aquinas lists arguments in favor of the claim "The world is not eternal" while also maintaining that, though they are "not devoid of probability," they "lack absolute and necessary conclusiveness." In this chapter of the SCG, Aquinas insists on the fact that belief that the world began to be is to be held by faith alone.

So what are the arguments that Aquinas notes in favor of the claim that the world must always have existed? They run as follows. (And when reading my summaries of them, remember that they are arguments that Aquinas goes on to *reject*.)

10.2.1 Arguments Based on What God Is (SCG 2,32)

1. God is not moved at all. So he always acts in the same way. Since God and his will are eternal, God must therefore make creatures that always exist, since God is eternal, as is his will.
2. God's action is eternal, so things created by God must always have existed.
3. God is a cause that has it in him to produce creatures and cannot be thwarted from doing so should he do so willingly. So, given that God causes creatures, and given that God is eternal, creatures will always exist.
4. Voluntary agents do not delay in carrying out their purposes unless they are prevented from doing so. But God is eternal, and nothing within himself or outside himself can impede his action. So if the eternal God wills creatures to exist, they will always exist.
5. Agents with intellect do not choose one thing over another unless motivated by preferable differences of some kind in what they might choose. But there is no difference between two things neither of which exist. So God cannot be motivated to produce creatures that begin to exist as opposed to creatures that do not begin to exist. Indeed, if God eternally wills that creatures exist, creatures always exist.
6. Creatures willed by God are directed to God as an end. They are directed to goodness that exists in God before it exists in them. But God's goodness is unchangeable, so creatures are willed by God from eternity and must, therefore, always exist.
7. God's goodness is infinite, so God must will some creatures always to have existed in order to share always in God's goodness.

10.2.2 Arguments Based on What Creatures Are (SCG 2,33)

1. Some creatures are necessary beings (see SCG 2,30). So some creatures have always existed.
2. Some creatures have a power to exist forever, so they exist always, which means that they never began to exist.
3. When something begins to be changed there has to occur change of some kind either in what changes or in what is changed. So every change is

either eternal or is preceded by some change, which means that change and things changed have always existed given that God is immutable.

4. Things that generate other things aim to keep their species in being. "Now, it is impossible that natural desire should be futile. The species of generable things, therefore, must be perpetual."[7]

5. If time is everlasting, then so is change, and so are created substances. Yet time is everlasting since what is "now" is always preceded by a previous time, and since to deny that time always exists involves supposing a time before it existed and a time after it ceases to exist.

6. Some propositions are such that to deny them is to assert them. For example, to deny that truth exists is to assert that something is true. Yet such propositions and what follows from them are everlasting, which means that there is something other than God that is eternal.

10.2.3 Arguments Based on What Is Involved in Making (SCG 2,34)

1. If something is made, it has to be made from something. Now, God is not made. But everything that is made must be made from something, which means that something other than God is eternal.

2. "A movable subject must exist prior to anything made" and "since to proceed to infinity in this matter is impossible, we must come to a first subject not newly originated but always existent."[8]

3. If something begins to exist, then before it existed it was possible for it to exist. So, before anything begins to exist, there must be something that is "potentially a being," and since an infinite regress is impossible in this connection, there is some primary subject that did not begin to exist.

4. Nothing permanent exists while it is being made. Yet while something is being made, there must be something that is in process of being made. So "whatever is made has some pre-existing subject."[9] Since this cannot go on to infinity, there must be a first and everlasting unmade subject, and there must, in that case, be something other than God that is eternal, since God is not something being made and since God is not changed by anything.

10.2.4 Aquinas's Responses to the Arguments Based on What God Is (SCG 2,35)

As I have said, Aquinas rejects all the above arguments, and in response to those found in SCG 2,32, he replies as follows (the numeration below corresponds to that in section 10.2.1).

1. God need not be changed in any way as his effects begin to exist; and something coming to be does not entail that there is any coming to be in God.

2. The fact that God is eternal does not mean that his effects are eternal. That is because God makes creatures voluntarily and can decide when something begins to exist. "Nothing, therefore, prevents our saying that God's action existed from all eternity, whereas its effect was not present from eternity, but existed at that time when, from all eternity, he ordained it."[10]

3. God may suffice to bring things into being, but the fact that God is eternal does not imply that his effects are eternal. God's willing that something should exist does not mean that the thing has to exist eternally, as does God's will.

4. "Within the scope of God's will fall not only the existence of his effect but also the time of its existence."[11] The effects of God's will are not delayed even though they do not always exist, and that a creature should exist at a certain time is not delayed even though God wills it to be from eternity.

5. "Nothingness has neither measure nor duration."[12] And there are no parts in God, who is immutable. So we should not think of the beginning of creatures as something God produced because he acts with an eye on what it would be good for him to produce in some context in which he finds himself. Nor should we think that the coming to be of creatures has to be related to time or place, as a thing coming to be in the world has to be related to a particular time and place since there has to be a reason why it comes to be at some particular time and in some particular place. So we do not need to seek a reason explaining why and when a creature came to exist. "We have only to ask why it was not always produced, or why it was produced after not being or with some beginning."[13]

6. God eternally wills his own goodness, and he does not act so as to bring this about as we might act so as to bring about ends that we desire. God is eternal and immutable, so he gains nothing by his willing of creatures. Therefore, if God wills creatures to exist, he does so in order that they might somehow share in his goodness, and in doing this God does not have to create what has always existed.

7. In order to share his goodness with creatures, God does not have to create things that are eternal as he is. Indeed, God creating a world which has a beginning "makes it perfectly clear that all things other than God have God as the author of their being."[14]

10.2.5 Aquinas's Responses to the Arguments Based on What Creatures Are (SCG 2,36)

In response to the arguments summarized by Aquinas in SCG 2,33, Aquinas replies as follows (the numeration below corresponds to that in section 10.2.2).

1. Created necessary beings are created by God willingly, so they might never have existed.

2. Even if a creature has a power to exist always, it is still a creature that exists only by God's will. Even a creature with a power to exist always might not be eternal.

3. Creatures do not exist because of a change in God, who can will something to begin to exist and can will that the thing in question is not eternal. Creatures exist by God's simple will, which can extend to the bringing about of change having a beginning.

4. Natural agents may aim to perpetuate their species, but they have to exist in order to do that. So the argument from perpetuation of species does not settle whether or not there are creatures that have existed from eternity.

5. The fifth argument *presupposes* that change is eternal; it does not prove that change is eternal.

6. If time had a beginning, it would exist having previously not existed. Yet time might never have existed in the sense that there might never have been any change. So the fact that time might never have been does not entail that there have to be eternal creatures.

7. "The truth of propositions whose denial entails their affirmation…possesses the necessity of that order which obtains between predicate and subject. By such necessity, therefore, a thing is not compelled to exist everlastingly, except perhaps the divine intellect, in which all truth is rooted" (see SCG 1,62).

10.2.6 Aquinas's Responses to the Arguments Based on What Is Involved in Making (SCG 2,37)

In response to the arguments summarized by Aquinas in SCG 2,34, Aquinas replies as follows (the numeration below corresponds to that in section 10.2.3).

1. "Nothing comes from nothing" is true in the sense that things in the world that arise over time depend on there being something that precedes them. Yet the existence of any creature at all derives from God considered not as a being in the world acting so as to modify things somehow but as the source of there being any creatures at all rather than nothing. "Now, in this production of all being from God it is impossible for anything to be made from some other pre-existing thing; otherwise, this procession would not consist in the making of all created being."[15] In general, making involves change; but we can extend the meaning of the word "make" so as to recognize that "anything at all whose essence or nature originates from something else is made."[16]

2. "Since that which in no way exists is not in any particular state, the idea of motion used in the argument does not warrant the conclusion that, when a thing begins to be, it is *in another state now than it was before.*"[17]

3. There need be no passive potentiality preceding the existence of all created being. When things come about because of a process of change, there is something potentially able to be changed prior to the change in question. Yet creation is not a matter of a change occurring. Creatures, which might never have existed, were always able to be since God, from eternity, is able to make creatures. This, however, does not mean that creatures have always existed with a passive potentiality.

4. "In things made by way of motion, *to be made* and *to be* are not simultaneous, because the production of such things involves succession. But in things that are not made by way of motion, the making does not precede the being."[18]

10.3 Proving That the World Is Not Eternal (SCG 2,38)

Aquinas concludes SCG 2,37 by summarizing his findings concerning the thesis that the world has always existed. He writes: "In the light of all this, then, it is clear that nothing stands in the way of one's holding that the world has not always existed—a truth which the Catholic faith affirms."[19] Yet how should we respond to the claim that it can be proved that the world is not eternal? In SCG 2,38 Aquinas notes six arguments in defense of this claim, though he finds none of them persuasive.[20]

The arguments noted by Aquinas run thus.

1. If God causes all things, he must precede in duration the things that he produces.

2. If all being is created by God, it cannot be made from something and must be made from nothing. So it must have being after not being.

3. "An infinite number of things cannot be traversed."[21] But if the world has always existed, an infinite number of things would have been traversed by now.

4. One cannot add to the infinite. However, on the supposition that the world has always existed, infinity would seem to be added to daily as one event or process follows another.

5. If the world has always existed, there can be an infinite series of efficient causes. But there cannot be such a series.

shown [see SCG 2,15], all beings are from one first being. But we have just proved that the cause of a thing's being, and of its distinction from other things, is the same [see SCG 2,24]. Diversity of agents, therefore, cannot possibly be the first cause of the distinction among things.[30]

In SCG 2,41, however, Aquinas has some fairly precise targets at which he aims when denying that differences in the created order derive from different things. For he knows that some have claimed that there is a good cause for good things and a bad cause for bad things. He is aware that it has been said that "all good things proceed from a good principle and evils from an evil principle."[31] Aquinas takes this line of thinking to have been defended by certain ancient philosophers. He alludes, for example, to Empedocles (c. 495–430 B.C.), who taught that all things in nature are moved by two opposing causes: Love and Strife. Aquinas also thinks that, since the rise of Christianity, the notion of there being two opposing principles behind things in the world was especially championed by the Manicheans.[32] So in SCG 2,41 Aquinas comments critically on there being a good principle (first cause) of what is good and a bad principle of what is bad.

He argues that there cannot be one first principle of all evils since such a thing would be evil by essence and since nothing can be evil by essence because evil amounts to privation of some kind in what is good to start with (see SCG 1,39). He writes: "Everything that is must necessarily be good in so far as it is a being.... It is, therefore, impossible for the distinction among things to proceed from two contrary principles, the one good, the other evil."[33] Aquinas does not mean that everything that exists is *entirely* good. Indeed, he thinks that many things are bad or defective in various ways. Yet he also thinks that, in order to be a bad such and such or a defective such and such, something has to succeed in being what it takes to exist as the kind of thing that it is. It is in this sense that he holds that everything is good insofar as it has being. So he maintains that the very being of something (what it is essentially) cannot consist only of badness.

In SCG 2,41 Aquinas goes on to make these points:

1. If agents act insofar as they have goodness to some extent, something evil of itself could never be an agent. So, "every agent, as such, is good," and nothing can be the first principle of evils if it is evil of itself or by nature.[34]

2. Since evil amounts to nonbeing, and since efficient causes produce what reflects them, there cannot be an efficient cause of nonbeing. "No cause that is of itself active in character can be assigned to evil as such. Evils cannot, then, be referred to one first cause that is of itself the cause of all evils."[35]

3. Something that comes about without being aimed at by anyone or any-thing comes about accidentally. Since all agents aim at what is good, there-fore, evil can only arise in their effects without being aimed at. "Evil, therefore, has no essential cause, but occurs accidentally in the effects of causes. Hence, there is no question of maintaining the existence of one first principle of all evils."[36]

4. We have no reason to explain the difference between good and evil in things with reference to contrary agents (agents that, though different, might both exist) since contrary agents have contrary actions and since "contrary principles are not to be attributed to things produced by one action."[37] Yet good and evil are produced by the same action.[38]

5. Something lacking being entirely is neither good nor evil, while whatever has being is somehow good. So "a thing must be evil so far as it is a non-being."[39] Therefore, what is evil as such is deprived of being and cannot be an active agent cause in the coming about of what is evil or bad.

10.4.4 The First Cause of the Distinction in Things Is Not the World of Secondary Agents (SCG 2,42)

In SCG 2,42 Aquinas rejects a line of thinking that can be represented as follows.

1. Since God is one and simple, he produces just one effect.
2. This effect is not equal to God when it comes to simplicity, but it can pro-duce differences of some kind.
3. From this scenario a series of causes results that represents degrees of falling away from divine simplicity, and diversity in things derives from the activity of causes other than God.

Aquinas seems to think that something like this was the view of Avicenna.[40] Whether it was or was not, however, Aquinas rejects it for several reasons.

For example, he says, God's power is not limited to producing only one effect (see SCG 2,22), and this conclusion does not contradict the teaching that God is entirely simple. So "it is not necessary to say that because God is one and absolutely simple, no multiplicity can proceed from him unless it be through the mediation of certain things lacking in the simplicity proper to himself."[41] Again, says Aquinas: "It was shown above [see SCG 2,21] that God alone can create" and that all that is not God has to derive from God and not anything else.[42]

10.4.5 Distinction Does Not Result from a Secondary Cause Introducing Forms into Matter; Nor Does It Result from Differences in Merit or Demerit (SCG 2,43 and 44)

With SCG 2,43 and 44 we find Aquinas rejecting some rather arcane and implausible views over which I do not intend to linger. Just for the record, though, these views are (1) that God created matter, but an angel gave it different forms, and (2) that God made all spiritual and rational creatures equal; some of these fell away from God; this led God, out of justice, to establish divergent grades of spiritual substances and different grades among corporeal substances.[43] With respect to the first view, Aquinas, among other things, argues (1) that there are beings that cannot have been formed out of matter (here he is thinking of heavenly bodies), and (2) that to be is to have form, implying that, as cause of all that has being, God is the first cause of all forms. With respect to the second view, Aquinas maintains that diversity among creatures has to derive not from choices made by creatures but from the intention of the first cause willing the great good of a universe consisting of different things. Aquinas recognizes that Origen's theory, as reported in SCG 2,44, was offered by him since he thought that diversity in things must, if justice is to be preserved, be connected, somehow, to diversity of merit. But he goes on to say:

> Origen seems not to have taken into consideration the fact that when we give something, not in payment of a debt, but as a free gift, it is not contrary to justice if we give unequal things, without having weighed the difference of merits; although payment is due to those who merit. But, as we have shown above [see SCG 2,28], God brought things into being, not because He was in any way obliged to do so, but out of pure generosity. Therefore, the diversity of creatures does not presuppose diversity of merit.[44]

10.4.6 The True First Cause of the Distinction of Things (SCG 2,45)

So what is the true first cause of the distinction among things? Obviously, Aquinas thinks that this is God, and he argues to this effect in SCG 2,45, to which I referred above. He concludes the chapter by saying: "The diversity and inequality in created things are not the result of chance, nor of a diversity of matter, nor of the intervention of certain causes or merits, but of the intention of God himself, who wills to give the creature such perfection as it is possible to have."[45] Given his view of God as developed previously in SCG 1 and 2, Aquinas surely has to reach such a conclusion.

10.5 Some Comments on SCG 2,30–45

Ancient and medieval thinkers devoted a lot of time to discussing the question "Has the world existed for ever?"[46] Aquinas was among their number, and what he says in SCG 2,31–38 is one of his more detailed discussions of the question. But is Aquinas right in what he argues here?

Like all of his Christian contemporaries, Aquinas believed that the universe began to exist. He did so on the basis of Genesis 1 and because of what the Catholic Church officially taught from the time of the Fourth Lateran Council.[47] Yet Aquinas did not think it inconceivable that the universe might never have had a beginning, while some of his contemporaries thought it possible to prove that it had to have had a beginning. So do we have reason to think that the universe must have had a beginning? And does Aquinas say enough to show that the universe might not have had a beginning?

You may think that nothing Aquinas argues serves to show that the universe might never have had a beginning since it now seems to be scientifically established that it did. Here, of course, I am referring to the big bang theory, which is currently accepted by many scientific cosmologists.

Hence, for example, Richard Swinburne can say: "There is no doubt that the models best substantiated today are ones which show the Universe expanding from a 'big bang' some 14,000 million years ago. These models successfully predict not merely the density and rate of recession of the galaxies, but the ratio of the various chemical elements to each other and to radiation in the universe, and above all the background radiation."[48]

Of course, even if we accept the big bang theory in some form, there presumably remains the possibility that the big bang did not amount to an absolute beginning of things and might in some way have followed what preexisted it materially. Defenders of the big bang theory would typically say that they have given us reason to suppose that we can trace the history of the universe to a certain point. Yet is that enough to warrant us supposing that there was, in no sense, a material "before" prior to that point with respect to which the big bang might be an effect or result? As far as I can gather, it is not at all uncommon for contemporary cosmologists to admit that they are ignorant concerning whether the beginning of the universe as we know it, considered as expanding and filled with matter that has cooled, marks an absolute physical beginning.[49]

On the other hand, though, the universe, *as Aquinas conceived of it*, does seem to have had a dateable beginning. Aquinas's cosmology takes the earth always to have been at the center of a stable arrangement of things in which stars form a perimeter. So you may think that his claim that the universe cannot be shown to have had a beginning has been falsified by science since his day since it rests on a view of the universe that is now antiquated. Suppose, however, that we forget about scientific arguments concerning the start of the universe and focus on philosophical ones of the kind in which Aquinas engages in his discussion of the eternity of the world in SCG 2. Who wins when it comes to the question "Can it be proved that the universe had a beginning"?

As Aquinas notes, it has been argued that the universe must have had a beginning since if past time is infinite, an infinity of events would (impossibly) have to have elapsed or been traversed before today. Yet this argument, as J. L. Mackie observes, "just expresses a prejudice against an actual infinite."[50] As Mackie goes on to say: "It assumes that, even if past time were infinite, there would still have to have been a starting-point of time, but one infinitely remote, so that an actual infinity would have had to be traversed to reach the present from there. But to take the hypothesis of infinity seriously would be to suppose that there was no starting-point, not even an infinitely remote one, and that from any specific point in past time there is only a finite stretch that needs to be traversed to reach the present."[51]

As you will realize, this is what Aquinas argues in response to the third argument he discusses in SCG 2,38. You might reject it by saying that there is something problematic with the claim that the universe never had a beginning since, if that were correct, then it would, in principle, be possible for someone truly to say "I have just finished counting backward from infinity." Yet counting involves taking a starting number, while if the universe never began to exist there is no starting number from which to start counting backward.

You might say that an infinite number of past years cannot have occurred before the present since that would mean that infinity has an end. Yet an infinite number of past years might have elapsed if, in an infinite number of past years, there is no beginning or starting year. And if there is no beginning or starting year, then "we cannot imagine that the beginningless series of past years has been subjected to counting in any straightforward way, for it has no first member to match the first number used in counting."[52]

You might say that what is infinite cannot have an end and that the past ended just now. But there is no reason to suppose that an infinite series cannot have *one* end. After all, the series of positive whole numbers has an end at zero.

You might say that, while there might be an infinity of future events with no end to them, there cannot have been an infinity of past events since an infinite future is potential while an infinite past must be completed by now. Yet to suppose an infinite number of past years is not to suppose that they have two termini, one of which is the present moment and one of which is way back in time. Past years do not start from now, even if our thoughts about past years do so; and if the universe had no beginning, then past years did not have a starting point and do not have a finishing point, meaning that today could have arrived after infinite past time and that there can be days or moments after today. If past time had a starting point, then it would be impossible for an infinite number of days to have been fitted in between then and now. But if there is no starting point to the history of the universe, there is nothing to be fitted in between a first point and today.

This is not a book on cosmology and infinity, but I would like to conclude this chapter by suggesting that it is not obvious that to suppose that the world never had a beginning leads to manifest absurdities and that a case can be made in defense of Aquinas's SCG claim that it has not been proved that the world had a beginning.

As I have noted, however, Aquinas, unlike Aristotle and many ancient Greek philosophers, did think that the universe began to be.[53] Contrary to people who assume that "Does God exist?" means "Was there a God who got the universe going some time in the past?" Aquinas thinks that God exists as making things to exist at any time, and whether or not the world began to be. So Aquinas's natural theology in the SCG is not committed to theological claims to the effect that the universe had a beginning. In Aquinas we have a theologian who is taken by many Christians to be a highly orthodox thinker. It is not for nothing that he has been proclaimed by the Catholic Church to be a doctor of the faith. We might, therefore, wonder whether it is true, as some have said, that one cannot be a Christian if one thinks that the universe never had a beginning.

Once again, though, Aquinas *did* think that the universe began to exist. And he takes it to contain creatures of different kinds. Also, as I have shown, in SCG 2,5 Aquinas says that he intends in what follows to write (1) about the bringing forth of things into being, (2) about distinctions among things, and (3) about "the nature of these same things, brought forth and distinct from one another, so far as it is relevant to the truth of the faith."[54] In SCG 2 Aquinas deals with (1) and (2) in chapters 6–45. In SCG 2,46 Aquinas begins to follow up on his promise concerning (3). So let us now follow him as he does so.

Intellectual Creatures (SCG 2,46–101)

AS WE SAW in chapter 9, Aquinas says that in SCG 2 he is going to consider "first, the bringing forth of things into being; second, their distinction; third, the nature of these same things, brought forth and distinct from one another."[1] In SCG 2,6–29 Aquinas deals with the bringing forth of things into being, and in SCG 2,30–45 he deals with distinctions among them. So it remains for him to consider the nature of created things, which is what he starts to do in SCG 2,46–101.

You might think that this stated aim would lead Aquinas immediately to embark on an enormous treatise on the natures of all creatures. You might think, for example, that his readers can now expect extensive discussions from him on geology, chemistry, anatomy, physics, geography, botany, zoology, and so on. Yet in SCG 2,46–101 all that Aquinas talks about is intellective creatures (*creaturae intellectuales*).[2]

Why so? For one thing, Aquinas was not a natural scientist, so he was in no position to put on a scientific hat and lecture us in encyclopedic fashion on the business of natural scientists.

Then again, the subject matter of SCC 2 is theological. So in SCG 2,5 Aquinas speaks of himself as dealing with the nature of created things "so far as it is relevant to the truth of faith."[3] Nice though it might be to have an account of the workings of the kidneys of zebras or the structure of the spines and eyes of iguanas, such an account would not, in Aquinas's view, be relevant to the truth of Christian faith as proclaimed in texts like the Apostles' Creed. He thinks that the Christian faith proclaims truths to be believed. He also thinks that knowledge in its most advanced form can only be attributed to what has understanding or intelligence.

When turning to things that God has created, therefore, he finds it natural to focus on creatures that have understanding or intelligence. Indeed, he finds it natural to focus on what is involved in being a creature with understanding or intelligence *just insofar* as it has understanding or intelligence. On the assumption that we are physical human beings with intellectual abilities, an account of what we are could, of course, easily include an account of our various anatomical features and their ways of working. Yet in SCG 2, Aquinas, who certainly accepts that people are intellective beings, is not interested in things like the structure of the human heart or pancreas. He is interested in people as things with understanding or intelligence, things able to know God and to react to him, things produced by God for a special purpose, things that might be thought to reflect God and to be united with God in a particular way.

Yet, I should now note, Aquinas did not believe that people are the only creatures of God with intellect. He believed in the existence of angels, whom he took to be purely immaterial. Hence it is that Aquinas provides a long discussion of angels in *Summa Theologiae* 1a,50–64. In this he refers to biblical texts that refer to them. He also says that angels lack composition of form and matter; that they can act freely; that each angel amounts to a species in itself; that angels are immortal since, being incorporeal, they cannot die; and that angels can have effects in the physical world. In the *Summa Theologiae,* Aquinas presents an account of angels according to which they are more like God than any other creature. As you would expect, he affirms that no angel is such that there is no difference between its existence (*esse*) and its nature. But he does say that there is no distinction in an angel between individuality (*suppositum*) and nature. He also says that the knowledge of angels far exceeds that of human beings, that it exists in each angel "all at once" and does not arise from a process of reasoning, that it is not derived from sensory experience, and that it is not something on which angels draw from time to time having formerly come to learn.

So, to repeat, Aquinas thinks that not all intellectual creatures are human beings. In SCG 2,46–101, therefore, he has things to say about angels as well as about people. To start with, however, his discussion of intellectual creatures is highly general and proceeds independently of the belief that, as well as there being people with understanding, there are also angels with understanding. Having raised the question "Why should there be any creatures with intellect?" he goes on to ask "What is it to be something with intellect?" and the discussion draws on what Aquinas thinks we can say about people considered as having intellect.

11.1 Why Intellectual Creatures? (SCG 2,46)

From what I have shown him saying so far in the SCG, Aquinas cannot possibly think that God is compelled to create creatures with intellect. But he does think that there being such creatures would allow God to show forth his goodness more than he would have been able to do had he not created things with understanding. For one thing, he believes, if knowledge and will exist in God, then a created order containing things with knowledge and will is bound to reflect what God is more than a universe containing nothing with knowledge and will. Again, for Aquinas, God's act of creating, though uncompelled, is, so to speak, revelatory; it declares what God is (as Psalm 19:1 puts it). Yet for there to be anything you might call "revelation," there has to be something able to recognize it for what it is, which would seem to suggest that if God is to show himself forth or to declare himself to best effect, then there will have to be intellects able to recognize that he is doing this.

So Aquinas thinks that God's showing forth of his goodness to best effect requires that there should be creatures with intellect. He writes:

> The only thing that moves God to produce creatures is his own good-ness, which he wished to communicate to other things by likening them to himself, as was shown in Book 1 of this work. Now the likeness of one thing is found in another thing in two ways: first, as regards natural being—the likeness of heat produced by fire is in the thing heated by fire; second, cognitively, as the likeness of fire is in sight or touch. Hence, that the likeness of God might exist in things perfectly, in the ways possible, it was necessary that the divine goodness be communi-cated to things by likeness not only in existing, but also knowing. But only an intellect is capable of knowing the divine goodness. Accordingly, it was necessary that there should be intellectual creatures.[4]

Aquinas cannot here mean that intellectual creatures cannot but exist abso-lutely speaking, for he has already denied that God wills any creatures to exist by absolute necessity (see SCG 2,23). What he is saying is that if God's like-ness is to exist in created things as perfectly as is possible, then it will exist in what has intellect since likeness "only in existing" is less perfect than likeness in understanding. Or, as Aquinas also writes:

> It is according to the form of the effect pre-existing in the agent that the effect attains likeness to the agent, for an agent produces its like with respect to the form by which it acts. Now, in some cases the form of the agent is received in the effect according to the same mode of being that it has in the agent; for the form of fire has the same mode of being as the form of the generating fire. But in other cases the form of the agent is received in the effect according to another mode of being; the form of the house that exists in an intelligible manner in the builder's mind is received, in a material mode, in the house that exists outside the mind. And the former likeness clearly is more perfect than the latter. Now, the perfection of the universe of creatures consists in its likeness to God, just as the perfection of any effect whatever consists in its likeness to its efficient cause. Therefore, the highest perfection of the universe requires

not only the second mode in which the creature is likened to God, but also the first, as far as possible. But the form through which God produces the creature is an intelligible form in Him, since, as we have shown above [see SCG 2,23 and 24], God is an intellectual agent. Therefore, the highest perfection of the universe demands the existence of some creatures in which the form of the divine intellect is represented according to intelligible being; that is to say, it requires the existence of creatures of an intellectual nature.[5]

The two arguments I have just quoted from SCG 2,46 are distinct arguments. Yet they are bound together by the idea that God cannot show himself forth in the created order, or be reflected in it as well as is possible, unless he creates creatures with intellect. In this sense, Aquinas thinks of creation as an act of revelation requiring things able to receive it as such.[6]

11.2 What Can Be Said of Intellectual Substances in General? (SCG 2,47–55)

Given that there are created intellectual substances (whether angelic or human), what must they have in common?[7] This is the question to which SCG 2,47–55 is devoted, and Aquinas deals with it by pretty much saying what I reported him as holding in chapters 7 and 8 concerning human knowledge and will. So in SCG 2,47–55 we find Aquinas defending these theses:

1. SCG 2,47: Intellectual substances have will (they are *volentes*).
2. SCG 2,48: Intellectual substances have freedom of choice in acting (*liberi arbitrii in agendo*).
3. SCG 2,49: An intellectual substance is not something bodily (*non sit corpus*).
4. SCG 2,50: Intellectual substances are immaterial (*immateriales*).
5. SCG 2,51: An intellectual substance is not a material form (*forma materialis*).
6. SCG 2,52: Created intellectual things are not simple as God is since what they are does not guarantee that they exist (their *esse* and their *quod est* are distinct).
7. SCG 2,53: Created intellectual things contain a distinction of act and potency.
8. SCG 2,54: Our ability to distinguish between what something is and that it exists is not equivalent to our ability to distinguish between something's form and its matter, and the form/matter distinction is inapplicable to created immaterial things.
9. SCG 2,55: Intellectual substances are incorruptible (*incorruptibiles*).

11.2.1 Will (SCG 2,47)

Given what I said about Aquinas on will in chapter 8, you will not be surprised by thesis 1 in this list, and you will not be surprised to find him saying that things with intellect focus on goods to which they are attracted, which means that they have will, considered as desire in action. I cannot be drawn to anything unless I have some understanding of it, even a wrong understanding, and to understand, rightly or wrongly, always involves some kind of reaction for or against. So, it would seem, to know is to be related to things considered as desirable or undesirable, which seems to entail that knowledge involves will. To be sure, I can know that 2 + 2 = 4 without having any desires at all with respect to this fact. Yet it makes sense to say that beings with knowledge (which itself results from paying attention and which is also something one can choose to ignore) may react to what they know with delight or aversion. This is what Aquinas means when he says that if something has knowledge or understanding (*intellectus*), it must have will. For Aquinas, will is what exists in something only because the thing is intellectual and can act on its desires in ways that express what it is rather than what is forced on it. So we find Aquinas adding: "The form understood, through which the intellectual substance acts, proceeds from the intellect itself as a thing conceived.... Intellectual substances, then, move themselves to act, as having mastery of their own action. It therefore follows that they are endowed with will."[8]

11.2.2 Freedom of Choice (SCG 2,48)

Much the same point is what lies behind the position of SCG 2,48, though this time it is expressed with reference to freedom of choice (*liberum arbitrium*).

In many of his writings Aquinas distinguishes between will (*voluntas*) and freedom of choice (*liberum arbitrium*). Things with freedom of choice, he thinks, are voluntary agents and, therefore, have *voluntas*. Yet Aquinas also thinks that voluntary agents are not always making discrete decisions concerning some particular good to be obtained. When I run to catch a bus I am aiming or willing to get on the bus. But I am also performing a number of distinct actions as I leap forward placing one foot in front of the other many times over, and I might not be paying special attention to any of them considered as distinct actions. I am aiming to get on the bus, but I need not be discretely choosing each of the movements of my legs as I do so. If I were to do that, I would probably miss the bus. Yet, Aquinas thinks, we can make distinct choices based on what we take to be desirable and based on what we think will enable us to obtain what we desire. And, to have this ability is to have what

Aquinas calls *liberum arbitrium*, which we might think of as choosing on the basis of reason.

Aquinas holds that people with intellect can figure out how to get what they want and act on the way they have been thinking. So he takes *liberum arbitrium* to be part of what any voluntary agent must possess. Intellectual substances, he says, "are endowed with freedom of choice in acting." He continues: "That they act by judgment is evident from the fact that through their intellectual cognition they judge of things to be done. And they must have freedom if, as just shown, they have control over their own action. Therefore, these substances in acting have freedom of choice."[9] Aquinas goes on to say:

> So far as matters of action are concerned, whatever things possess judgment that is not determined to one thing by nature are of necessity endowed with freedom of choice. And such are all intellectual beings. For the intellect apprehends not only this or that good, but good itself, as common to all things. Now, the intellect, through the form apprehended, moves the will; and in all things mover and moved must be proportionate to one another. It follows that the will of an intellectual substance will not be determined by nature to anything except the good as common to all things. So it is possible for the will to be inclined toward anything whatever that is presented to it under the aspect of good, there being no natural determination to the contrary to prevent it. Therefore, all intellectual beings have a free will, resulting from the judgment of the intellect. And this means that they have freedom of choice, which is defined as *the free judgment of reason.*[10]

Here Aquinas is arguing that, while we cannot but desire goodness in general, we can distinguish between goods and opt for some of them as opposed to others. He thinks that desire or appetite is fixed in certain directions in what lacks intellect. He thinks, for example, that nonhuman animals act by instinct coupled with sense perception—that, for example, cats will, all things being equal, naturally run after mice that catch their attention.[11] But he also maintains that intellectual beings can recognize that there are different goods at which they might aim. Suppose that I like fried chicken, which I take to be something good and, therefore desirable. Do I have to gobble up fried chicken as automatically as a cat might pounce on a mouse? Well, Aquinas would reply, that will depend on other things I like and might also recognize as within my grasp. Suppose that I like to have low cholesterol. In that case, I might think twice about eating fried chicken. Or suppose that I want my beloved, who is a vegetarian, to approve of me. Then again, I might refrain from fried chicken. So, Aquinas holds, intellectual beings have freedom of choice because they can recognize that there are different goods that can compete for their attention as they act. This freedom of choice, in Aquinas's view, depends on the ability to understand how different things can be thought of as good.

11.2.3 Body (SCG 2,49)

In SCG 2,49 Aquinas notes that bodies contain what they are in quantitative fashion. He means, for example, that a plant or a cat is a material thing with physical dimensions. Yet he goes on to say: "An intellect does not, in terms of any quantitative commensuration, comprehend a thing understood, since by its whole self it understands and encompasses both whole and part, things great in quantity and things small. Therefore, no intelligent substance is a body."[12] Here we have Aquinas articulating a position of his that I noted in chapter 7: that knowledge comes about as forms are received immaterially. This position runs throughout SCG 2,49, so I shall not dwell on it now, though I shall return to it before the end of this chapter.

11.2.4 Immateriality (SCG 2,50)

Aquinas takes it to follow from the reasoning of SCG 2,49 that intellectual substances are immaterial. As I have noted, however, he thinks that people can be thought to have intellect, though he does not think that people are immaterial. So, what is Aquinas driving at in SCG 2,50?

He seems to be assuming that there is a distinction between *what has* intellect and what *intellect is as active,* and he is focusing on what intellect is as active whether or not intellect might be ascribed to what can be thought of as having a body as well as having intellect. So, given what he has argued in SCG 2,49, Aquinas says that, if no intelligent substance is a body, "such a substance is not composed of matter and form" and is, therefore, immaterial.[13] Aquinas agrees that something with intellect that also happens to be a composite of matter and form will understand things in the same way that something that is essentially corporeal does. But he does not think that the intellect in something that is composed of matter and form is, therefore, something material. Or, as he puts it: "Forms are not received in the intellect as in matter or a material thing. Clearly, then, intelligent substances are immaterial, even as they are incorporeal, too."[14]

Here, I should note, Aquinas is effectively rejecting some opposite positions that philosophers over many centuries have defended concerning the nature of human beings. Some of them (Plato and Descartes are outstanding and distinguished examples) have held that people are essentially thinking and incorporeal things.[15] Descartes, of course, lived long after Aquinas, and it is Plato whom Aquinas targets in the SCG as wrongly thinking that we are essentially immaterial beings. Yet Descartes is a classic source for the view that people are essentially intellectual and nonmaterial. As I have noted, though, many philosophers have argued that people are entirely physical and that knowledge or understanding is nothing but a physical process to be investigated and reported on as we might, say, investigate and report on what is going on with a piece of cheese as it becomes moldy.[16] In SCG 2,50 Aquinas is implying that something might be essentially corporeal while having an immaterial component. As I will soon show, Aquinas takes human beings to be both essentially corporeal and things with a subsisting part that is not material because it is intellective.

11.2.5 Intellectual Substance and Material Form (SCG 2,51)

By "material form" Aquinas means form as depending on matter because it is the form of something material. He would say that in the case of a dog, the substantial form of caninity exists in it as the material thing that it essentially is. For Aquinas, for a dog to cease to be canine would amount to it ceasing to exist. In this sense, he thinks, caninity in a dog depends on matter or material configuration. Yet, Aquinas reasons, if an intellectual substance acts through itself, it cannot be a form that depends for its existence on matter. It must be something subsisting (existing as a thing in itself) immaterially. This is the thesis of SCG 2,51, in which we find Aquinas saying:

> Forms dependent in being on matter do not themselves have being properly, but being properly belongs to the composites through their forms. Consequently, if intellectual substances were forms of this kind, it would follow that they have material being, just as they would if they were composed of matter and form.... Forms that do not subsist through themselves cannot act through themselves; rather the composites act through them. Hence, if intellectual natures were forms of this sort, it would follow that they do not themselves understand, but that it is the things composed of them and matter which understand. And thus, an intelligent being would be composed of matter and form; which is impossible, as we have just shown [see SCG 2,50].[17]

Notice that Aquinas is here considering what must be true of any created intellect. Having previously argued that a created intellect must have will and freedom of choice, and having suggested that a created intellect is not a body but something immaterial, he is now claiming that a created intellect must exist in its own right as something nonmaterial.

11.2.6 Created Forms as Not Divine (SCG 2,52)

Given his teaching on divine simplicity, Aquinas has to say that created intellects are not such that their essence is to exist. And this is what we find him saying in SCG 2,52. Aquinas has agreed that created intellects are not corporeal, not composites of form and matter, and not things that exist in matter as material forms do. In SCG 2,52 he is noting that, though created intellects share in God's simplicity to some extent, they are still creatures who derive their being from God and are not, therefore, pure Being Itself (*ipsum esse subsistens*), as Aquinas takes God to be. He writes: "Now, we have shown in Book 1 that God is his own subsisting being [see SCG 1,22]. Hence, nothing beside him can be its own being. Of necessity, therefore, in every substance beside him the substance itself is other than its being."[18]

11.2.7 Act and Potency (SCG 2,53)

The logic of SCG 2,53 is similar to that of SCG 2,52. In SCG 1 Aquinas argues that only God is pure being, so in SCG 2,52 he concludes that created substances are not pure being, not such that what they are entails that they exist. Since in SCG 1 Aquinas has argued that only God lacks potentiality, he argues in SCG 2,53 that created intellects have act and potency, that they exist but are potentially nonexistent.

11.2.8 Substance, Being, Form, and Matter (SCG 2,54)

As I have shown, Aquinas thinks that we can speak of there being composition of substance (*substantia*) and being (*esse*) in all creatures that have substantial forms. I have also shown that he thinks that some creatures have composition of form (*forma*) and matter (*materia*). In SCG 2,54 Aquinas is concerned to stress that the substance/being distinction is different from the form/matter distinction.

Why does he bother to emphasize that at this stage in the SCG? I presume that he does so because he was saying in SCG 2,53 that there is act and potency in created intellects and because he does not want his reader to assume that the fact that this is so means that intellectual creatures have composition of matter and form. He seems to want to stress that, though created intellects are potentially nonexistent, this does not entail that they have composition of matter and form. In his own words:

> Composition of act and potency has greater extension than that of form and matter. Thus matter and form divide [sc. render composite] natural substance, while potentiality and act divide common being [sc. all that has being but is not being itself]. Accordingly, whatever follows upon potentiality and act, as such, is common to both material and immaterial created substances.... Yet all that is proper to matter and form, as such, as to be generated and to be corrupted, and the like, are proper to material substances and in no way belong to immaterial created substances.[19]

The last sentence here is clearly intended by Aquinas as linking on to what he immediately goes on to say in SCG 2,55.

11.2.9 Created Intellects as Incorruptible (SCG 2,55)

If created intellects do not have matter and form, then they cannot perish in the course of nature as material things do, which is Aquinas's thesis in SCG 2,55. "From what has just been said," he observes, "it is clearly shown that every intellectual substance is incorruptible."[20] Aquinas takes perishing by corruption to be a material process. So, he claims again and again in SCG 2,55, created intellects cannot perish by corruption. All of his arguments in this chapter hammer home the point that if something is not material, it cannot perish as material things do and for the reasons that they do.

You might say that a thing might cease to exist in that God might withdraw his creative action from it, and Aquinas concedes that there is a possibility worth noting here. He says: "There is no potency with respect to their non-being [sc. the non-being of intellects] except in the first agent, inasmuch as it lies within God's power not to pour being into them (*non influere eis esse*)."[21] Strictly speaking, this remark of Aquinas only says that, for example, God might never have created me, considered as having intellect. But it might be taken as recognizing that God has power to make me cease to exist, and that this reading is correct seems clear from what Aquinas goes on to say. For, having asserted what I have just quoted him as saying, he claims that God would not take from things that which is "proper to their natures" (*quod est proprium naturis earum*), which seems to imply that God *could* do this. However, such "decreation" of something that exists would not amount to the thing *perishing* by being *corruptible*, and, as I have now explained, Aquinas denies that created intellectual things can perish by physical corruption. In short, Aquinas's view is that, while a car can squash a cat, nothing can demolish that which is not material.

11.3 Soul and Body in People (SCG 2,56–90)

I have noted that Aquinas does not take created intellect to be confined only to people. He thinks that angels are created intellects, and in SCG 2,91–101 he has several things to say about them. Before he discusses angels, however, in SCG 2,56–90 he has a lot to say about human beings and what intellect amounts to in them. These chapters consider a number of questions, yet by the time Aquinas has finished writing them he has presented an overall account of intellect in people that it would be good to grasp as a whole before working through some of its details. So, I shall now try to explain what that account basically has to say. Then I shall draw attention to some details to be found as Aquinas develops it.

11.3.1 Intellect and People: The Overall Account

As I have said, Aquinas does not think of human beings as totally immaterial things. He does not think that I am something that exists as a self-contained incorporeal substance, albeit one attached in some way to a body that I have. Descartes held that people, or the "selves" that people are, must be essentially immaterial, and he spoke of them as interacting with their bodies. On his account, what happens in my body can affect me in that, for example, my bodily sensations can lead me to know about things in the physical world. Again, on Descartes's account, I can affect my body by, say, deciding to get my legs moving. Yet Descartes's position is that I am not my body. For Descartes I am an essentially incorporeal and thinking thing.

Aquinas, by contrast, thinks it obvious that people are not incorporeal objects that are acted on by, and that can act on, bodies that they own or to which they are connected. Descartes ended up thinking of himself and others as he did because he thought it necessary to show that there are some things that we can certainly know to be the case, and he took the primary and incontrovertible truth to be "If I am thinking, then I exist, even if I do not have a body, as some skeptics have argued." Descartes gets to the certainty that he exists while temporarily entertaining skeptical thoughts about the existence of bodies. Aquinas, however, has no doubts about the existence of bodies. He thinks it obvious that we live among physical things that act on us as much as we act on them. He thinks as a typical scientist does. Scientists would be out of business

if they doubted the reality of a material universe. They take the reality of physical things for granted, and they see themselves as trying to understand such
things and their ways of working. So Aquinas (rightly or wrongly) starts with
what I suppose most of us would say: that there is a material world and that
some of the things in it are human beings.

As I have said, however, Aquinas thinks that human beings have understanding. He holds that intellect can be ascribed to people.[22] As I have also
shown, he holds that understanding cannot be a process in something material. I may perspire out of fear when I see a tiger in front of me. Yet, thinks
Aquinas, understanding what a tiger is cannot be a physical event, though it
may follow such an event. As we might put it, to understand what a tiger is
amounts to having formed a concept of something. Yet concepts in the mind
cannot be physical replicas of that of which they are concepts. To understand
what it is to be a tiger is to have the form (the whatness) of a tiger in one
without being a tiger. Or so Aquinas thinks.

In his view, therefore, people exist in the material world, but they are also
able to operate at a nonmaterial level because they have intellect. Indeed,
thinks Aquinas, the human intellect is a subsisting immaterial thing, like
any other intellect. On the other hand Aquinas does not want to say that
people are just their intellects. He thinks that people are intellect plus body,
the two making up a whole. Or, as Aquinas often says, people have both a body
and a soul.

At this point you might suppose that in taking this view Aquinas is holding
that a person is two distinct things yoked together somehow, as Descartes
takes people to be. But that is certainly not what Aquinas maintains. He says
that a living human being is a composite of soul and body. So he thinks of soul
and body as essential parts of one thing: the living human being. Some religious people have spoken of the human soul as if it were a human being, the
idea being that the person goes where the soul goes. For Aquinas, however, if
my soul and body are separated, then I cease to exist since what I am is a
human being, and a human being is a composite of soul and body. In that
case, however, how does Aquinas view the relationship between body and soul
in people? He argues that the human soul and body are related as form is
related to matter.

Throughout his writings, Aquinas takes form to correspond to an account
of what something is. And, as I have noted, Aquinas distinguishes between
substantial forms and accidental forms. In Aquinas's view substantial forms
are primary while accidental forms are secondary. To specify something's substantial form is to talk about what the thing is essentially; to specify something's accidental forms is to talk about what something happens to be but

can cease to be without ceasing to be what it is essentially. For Aquinas, there-fore, something with an essence or nature has a substantial form to which accidental forms may be added or subtracted. And when Aquinas says that the human soul stands to the human body as form stands to matter as actualizing it in some way, he means that the human soul informs the human body as a substantial form informs anything bodily or material. Or, rather, he means *something* like that.

Here we need to note that when he is not talking about people (or about angels or God), Aquinas takes himself, when he is referring to substances, to be speaking about what is purely material: distinct physical things having a nature distinguishable from the individuals that they are. So he takes the world to consist of many material things having substantial forms that make them to be what they are. These forms, he thinks, are displayed in matter (in what can undergo substantial or accidental change without itself having form) but are not themselves material. They *inform* matter, and they are, in princi-ple, shareable by different individuals. In holding to this position, Aquinas does not mean that, say, the substantial form of my cat is an independently existing nonmaterial thing. He means that my independently existing cat is made up of matter formed in a feline way, formed so as to constitute a cat, as opposed to a dog, or a crocodile, or whatever. Aquinas thinks that material things exist as displaying or having particular substantial forms that, so to speak, shape them. In this sense, says Aquinas, form gives being to what is material—not by creating it or by conferring some ethereal property called "being" to it but by constituting material things as different and existing things. So he thinks that for my cat to exist is just for it to be something feline, something with a feline nature, something having the substantial form of a cat.

Now, when it comes to material substances, Aquinas holds that substantial form informs matter just because the matter of material substances is formed in a certain way—meaning that form and matter in material substances are both material. Yet (1) he does not take this view when it comes to human beings. Nor (2) does he take it when it comes to living things in general. Since (2) here might seem to contradict what I have just been saying concerning Aquinas on form and matter, let me dwell on it a little before returning to (1).

As I noted in chapter 8, Aquinas takes all living things to have souls, to be animate as opposed to inanimate. Yet he also takes some living things (e.g., plants and cats) to be purely material, which leaves him with this question: Why are some material things animate while others are not? Aquinas thinks that, for example, cats are living things. But he does not think that stones are alive. So what makes cats different from stones when it comes to being alive? Aquinas's answer is that cats have a principle of movement in them, unlike stones. And, he reasons, this principle cannot be a material thing, otherwise anything material would be a living thing. So, he says, the principle of life in a living yet material thing cannot be a body or a bodily part of something wholly material. It has to be the form of that material thing, which cannot itself be a material thing.

Aquinas, therefore, believes that even in wholly material living things there is a component that cannot just be described as a material thing. For that reason, it is, strictly speaking, wrong of me to have said that, for Aquinas, form and matter in material things are both material. Aquinas's whole form/ matter distinction is denying that form and matter are both material. On the other hand we also need to bear in mind that Aquinas does not think of purely material living things as being anything but material, which is why it is not totally misleading for me to say that form and matter in material things are, for Aquinas, both material. When Aquinas says that the principle of life in a wholly material living thing is not something bodily, he is not arguing that, say, plants are at some level spiritual or incorporeal. He is claiming that one cannot fully explain why they are alive by noting some physical bits of them, since if something physical were a principle of life (a soul or vital principle) it seems hard to understand why all physical or material things are not alive.

When it comes to people, however, Aquinas does believe that we are dealing with what is not purely material since he takes people to have intellect, and he thinks that substantial form in people is not something physical. As I have shown, Aquinas thinks that an intellect (any intellect, whether human, angelic, or divine) is immaterial, is not a form that depends for its existence on matter and must therefore subsist (exist as a thing). So when he tries to compare soul and body in human beings to form and matter in general, he is not committing himself to the idea that the human soul is entirely like the substantial form of a wholly material thing. He is regarding the principle of life in human beings (their substantial form or soul) as a subsistent immaterial thing. More precisely, he is thinking of the human soul as informing the body by acting in and through it.

Aquinas does not think that the human intellect is united to the human body by being mixed up with it as, say, tea leaves and hot water get mixed up so as to become a cup of tea. That is because he does not think of an intellect as something material. Tea leaves and water are material things that we can mix together. Yet Aquinas does not think that what is not material can be mixed with something material. Nor does he think that the human intellect can be united to the human body by bodily contact, as I can be united to you by, say, holding your hand. For, once again, Aquinas does not think of intellect as something corporeal. Yet he does think that there is something to note about how physical things connect with each other that provides a model for trying to figure out how an intellectual substance (an individual intellect) can be united to a body. The something in question here is the fact that one physical thing can act on something else and be active in the operation of the something else in question.

As I noted in chapter 3, Aquinas thinks that agent causes are at work in what they bring about. He does not think of an agent cause as different from its effect as, say, two billiard balls that bounce off each other are different from each other. Of course, he thinks that there is a distinction to be made between agent causes and their effects. Yet he also thinks that an agent cause is active *in* its effect. He thinks, say, that, when I am grooming my cat, my cat's being groomed and my grooming my cat are not two actions but one action viewed from different points of view (that of the agent and the patient). I can cheerfully say "Well, it's me that is grooming my cat, not someone else." And my cat, if he could talk, might say, "Well, I am being groomed by Davies and not by anyone else." Yet my grooming my cat and my cat being groomed by me are one and the same thing.

Here we have cause and effect united as one thing is working in or on another. And, thinks Aquinas, this is what we have when it comes to the human soul and what human bodies do as things with intellect. For Aquinas, the human soul, which is a subsisting intellectual thing, is united to the human body as acting in it, as governing its motions and reactions from beginning to end.[23] Aquinas thinks that my body is moved by my soul (my intellect) without also thinking that I am my soul. In his view, my body, though often out of my control, is something that I need in order to exist as a human being. He also thinks that my voluntary bodily movements derive from my intellect and willing. Aquinas's view is that people act by virtue of intellect, which, he says, is immaterial but able to produce effects in that to which it is united as subsisting form to existing matter.

Does all of this mean that Aquinas was a mind/body dualist, as Descartes is commonly taken to have been? In a sense, yes. But in a sense, no. Like Descartes, Aquinas sharply distinguishes between understanding, thinking, and willing (on the one hand) and the occurrence of bodily processes (on the other). Unlike Descartes, however, Aquinas does not think that he is an incorporeal mind or a thinking thing. Aquinas takes himself to be a human being and, therefore, something essentially bodily. And he thinks of his mind or intellect as a part of himself that accounts for what he does physically as something with intellect, something with will, something that can understand and make choices.

At this point, however, I should note that Aquinas does not just say that people have intellect. He says that they have an agent intellect (*intellectus agens*) and a receptive or possible intellect (*intellectus possibilis*). What does he mean by speaking in this way? He does not mean that the human intellect is an object consisting of parts as, say, an apple pie is something that is made up of both apples and pastry. Aquinas's agent/receptive intellect distinction should be understood as comparable to the distinction we might make between a computer being able to deliver results that we are searching for and a computer being able to "remember" that for which we have been searching. But I offer this comparison only as an analogy since, as we know, Aquinas does not think of intellect as being something material, like a computer.

When saying that people have an agent intellect, Aquinas is not so much trying to explain what human understanding amounts to and how it arises as saying what has to be the case if human beings can understand what things are. I can understand that your cat and my cat are both cats. So it seems as though I can form a concept of "cat" without meaning, by my concept, what any individual cat is, considered as the individual material thing that it is. Or, so you might say, the meaning of a word cannot be an object that it names. Yet Aquinas thinks that knowledge in human beings arises on the basis of sensory experience. We are not, he believes, born with knowledge. We arrive, as it were, with a blank slate that needs to be written on as the world around us acts on us. This fact, however, leads Aquinas to ask how we can have knowledge expressible in sentences in which concepts and not individuals frequently feature.

If I know that cats have feline properties shared by all cats, then my knowledge seems to be knowledge of what things of a kind are, not just knowledge about some particular cat. The word "cat" is not the proper name of any cat, even if one might call one's cat "Cat." The word "cat" is used in sentences like "Sweetie is a cat" so as to assign Sweetie to a class of which there are many members. Yet a class of things is not a particular individual in the world with which we can interact, and if our knowledge arises on the basis of sensory experience of things, it seems natural to ask how we can move from contact with particulars to knowledge of what is not a particular individual. And, having raised this question, Aquinas replies that we do so not because of input from outside but because of the fact that we have an ability to abstract from particular things so as to form general concepts like "cat."

It is in this connection that Aquinas speaks of us as having an "agent intellect," an intellect that can process empirical data so as to be able to understand substantial and accidental forms in general. These, he thinks, exist, but only as possessed by particular material things. So, he argues, our intellect must have the ability to form concepts or ideas that are not particular material things. Hence the agent intellect. Or, as Anthony Kenny says, Aquinas's position on agent intellect is this:

> Substances in the physical world are in themselves only potentially thinkable, because they are individual and thought is universal. To make potentially thinkable objects into actually thinkable objects, we need an intellectual analogue of light in the visible world. And it is this intellectual analogue of light which is the agent intellect. One can think of the agent intellect as like the lantern a miner carries in his helmet, casting the light of intelligibility upon the objects a human being encounters in his progress through a mysterious world.[24]

Aquinas thinks of the agent intellect as an ability or capacity or power that belongs to individual thinkers. It is something that each of us has.[25] And it is something that allows us to think abstract thoughts, to talk about things in general, and, therefore, to acquire what we might take to be scientific knowledge (which is never about particular material individuals but which groups things together so as to say, for example, that if you have a cat on your lap, then you have on your lap something the nature of which can be documented and understood by many people).

When it comes to receptive or possible intellect (*intellectus possibilis*), Aquinas thinks of this as our ability to retain what we have learned. I have learned loads of things in my lifetime, but I do not always call them to mind. Yet I can call at least some of them to mind, and I am obviously doing this as I speak and employ concepts. I have an ability to retain and employ concepts and beliefs that I have acquired over time. And it is this ability that Aquinas has in mind when he speaks of people having a "receptive intellect," which he thinks of as a storehouse of ideas acquired over time. According to Aquinas, we do, in a sense, make the world that we live in because we have agent intellects. He does not mean that we create the world or that all that we know are ideas that we have formulated on the basis of sense experience. He thinks that we know a world that is there to be known because it acts on us physically so as to enable us to know about it. But he also thinks that things in the world leave traces in us, so to speak. So he thinks that, as the understanding things that we are, such traces exist in us to draw on as we continue to think. In short, he thinks that while our agent intellect allows us to form thoughts or concepts, our receptive intellect provides them with somewhere to live. Or, as Kenny says, reporting on Aquinas's thinking about agent and receptive intellect, "If the function of the receptive intellect is as it were to provide room for thoughts, the function of the agent intellect is to provide furniture for that room, that is to create objects of thought."[26]

11.3.2 Intellect and People: Some Details

All of the above ideas can be found in SCG 2,56–90, but they are sometimes presented by Aquinas while he is rejecting certain positions on the human intellect. For example, in SCG 2,57 and 58 he spends time trying to refute what he takes to be Plato's view of soul and body, and in SCG 2,59–61, as well as SCG 2,73 and 75, he examines and rejects a series of arguments that he attributes to Averroes (1126–1198). Again, in SCG 2,62 and 76 we find Aquinas contradicting Alexander of Aphrodisias (fl. 200) concerning the receptive or possible intellect.[27] Yet again, in SCG 2,63 Aquinas takes issue with Galen (130–200) while in SCG 2,74 and 76 criticizing Avicenna for saying that intelligible forms are not preserved in the possible intellect. At this point, however, I am not going to try to explain why Aquinas disagrees with the people I have just mentioned or what he takes them to have said.[28] Instead, I shall briefly note points in SCG 2,56–90 at which we see emerging the general view on human intellect that I have noted above.

A critical text is SCG 2,56. Here we find Aquinas arguing that an intellectual substance, though not a body, can be united to a body by acting on it. He says:

> Intellectual substances, being immaterial and enjoying a higher degree of actuality than bodies, act on the latter and move them. This, however, is not a contact of quantity, but of *power*....The intellectual substance, then, can be united to a body by contact of power.[29]

Does contact like this make intellect and body just one thing when an intellect is united to a body? Aquinas goes on to argue in SCG 2,57 that it can if we think of an intellectual substance being the substantial form of a body. We read:

> That by which something becomes a being in act from a being in potency is its form and act. But it is through the soul that the body becomes a being in act from being potentially existent, for living is the being of a living thing. Now the seed before animation is living only in potency, and, through the soul, becomes living in act. Therefore, the soul is the form of the animated body. In addition, since being as well as operating belong neither to the form alone, nor to the matter alone, but to the composite, to be and to act are attributed to two things, one of

which is to the other as form to matter. For we say that someone is healthy in body and in health, and that they are knowing in knowledge and in their soul, knowledge being the form of the knower's soul and health a form of the healthy body. Now, life and sensation are ascribed to both soul and body, for we are said to live and to sense both in soul and body. But we live and sense by the soul as the principle of life and sensation. The soul is, therefore, the form of the body.[30]

One might want to say that the soul has to be a body since there is nothing that is not a body, a position Aquinas turns to in SCG 2,65. Yet he distances himself from this conclusion. For example, he comments:

> Since living things are physical realities, they are composed of matter and form. Now, they are composed of a body and a soul, which makes them actually living. Therefore, one of these two must be the form and the other matter. But the body cannot be the form, because the body is not present in another thing as its matter and subject. The soul, then, is the form, and consequently is not a body, since no body is a form. It is, moreover, impossible for two bodies to coincide. But, so long as the body lives, the soul is not apart from it. Therefore, the soul is not a body.... Also, the soul is separate from the body, not as a thing touching from a thing touched, but as form from matter, although, as we have shown [see SCG 2,56], that which is incorporeal does have a certain context with the body.[31]

Aquinas recognizes that some have argued that intellect and sense are the same and that intellect is, therefore, somehow bodily. Yet Aquinas insists that intellect and sense are very different. Lots of animals have sensation, he says, but they lack intellect, and sensation takes in particular things while intellect takes in what is intelligible and universal. He observes:

> Sense is found in all animals, whereas animals other than man have no intellect. This is evident from the fact that the latter perform diverse and opposite actions, not as though they possessed intellect, but as moved by nature, carrying out certain determinate operations of uniform character within the same species.... Therefore, intellect is not the same as sense. Moreover, sense is cognizant only of singulars; for every sense power knows through individual species, since it receives the species of things in bodily organs. But the intellect is cognizant of universals.... Therefore, intellect differs from sense.[32]

When he speaks of nonhuman animals acting uniformly within a species (*in eadem specie*), Aquinas uses the word "species" as we would when saying, for example, that cats are a species of mammal, that they are mammals of a certain kind. But he is not using the word species (*species*) in this sense when he speaks of sense powers knowing through individual species (*per species individuales*). In the second use, Aquinas takes a *species* (which you should regard as a technical philosophical term in Aquinas's vocabulary) to be what, in the present context, can be taken in by sensation, like the feeling hot arising from contact with something hot.[33] And the point that he is making is that sensation is a physical effect of something particular acting on a body, while intellect grasps or takes in what is true of many things, even incorporeal ones. He means that, for example, I should not confuse my feeling of my cat on my lap with my understanding of what a cat is.

So, as I say, Aquinas's view is that an intellect can be the form of a body, and that it is so when it comes to people. And having disposed, to his satisfaction, of arguments to the contrary in SCG 2,57–67, he reiterates his position in SCG 2,68–90 and makes these points:[34]

1. In people, soul is the "principle of the substantial being of the thing whose form it is."[35]
2. In people, form and matter are joined in one act of being. A human being's intellect and body make up a composite that is one thing: a human being.
3. Soul and body in people are distinct, though together they form one composite substance, and when separated from each other neither of them amounts to a human being.
4. The human soul is "on the *horizon* and *confines* of things corporeal and incorporeal in that it is an incorporeal substance and yet the form of a body."[36]
5. In people, "body and soul are not two actually existing substances; rather the two of them together constitute one actually existing substance."[37]
6. We can distinguish between the essence of the human soul and its powers. By its essence the soul makes a body to be a living body of a certain kind. By its power it performs certain operations that are bodily ones—as when it enables people to see with their eyes. Yet the soul's power also extends to operations that do not depend on anything bodily—as when it understands. "The human soul is not a form wholly embedded in matter, but among all other forms occupies a most exalted place above matter. That is why it can produce an operation without the body."[38]
7. If the soul is united to the body as its form, it is not united by some kind of intermediary. As the form of the human body, the soul, strictly speaking, is just what makes a human being to be what he or she is as a human being.

8. The whole soul is in the whole body and in each of its parts since the human soul is not just the soul of one bit of a human being but of the whole human being and "is, therefore, in the whole body, and not merely in one part, according to its essence whereby it is the body's form."[39]

9. There is no reason why the possible and agent intellect cannot exist together in the human soul since "nothing prevents one thing from being in one respect potential in relation to some other thing, and actual in another respect."[40]

10. The human soul does not perish when the body perishes since it is not material and cannot, therefore, corrupt physically. "Every intellectual substance is incorruptible. But man's soul is an intellectual substance, as was shown [see SCG 2,56–68]. It therefore follows that the human soul is incorruptible."[41] Aquinas refers to the soul continuing to exist after the death of a person as a "separated soul."[42]

11. If a human being dies while his or her soul continues to exist, the soul in question, which is but a part of a human being, will not be able to function as it does when united to a human body. Human souls, as they inform living human bodies, gain knowledge by attending to things in the world around the bodies that they inform, which leaves them with impressions of material things.[43] So, a human soul is not able to gain what we might think of as empirical knowledge if it does not exist as informing a human body. "It must be borne in mind that the soul understands in a different manner when separated from the body and when united to it. . . . Indeed, although the soul, while united to the body, enjoys absolute being not depending on the body, nevertheless the body is the soul's housing (*stramen*), so to speak, and the subject that receives it."[44] Yet a human soul surviving the death of the body it once informed cannot lose its inherent ability to understand and to will.[45]

12. Nonhuman animals lack intellect, so their souls "are incapable of any operation that does not involve the body"; and "since every substance is possessed of some operation, the soul of a brute animal will be unable to exist apart from its body; so that it perishes along with the body."[46]

13. "The human soul begins to exist when the body does."[47]

14. The human soul is created by God and not made of God's substance as some seem to have thought.[48]

15. The human soul is directly created by God since it begins to be yet is not something material and emerging from something that is material; it is not made from anything, so it is created by God and is not brought about by anything else.[49]

11.4 Created Intellects That Are Not United to Bodies (SCG 2,91–101)

SCG 2,91–101 is clearly concerned with angels, though in these chapters Aquinas tends to use the expression "separate substances" (*substantiae separatae*) and expressions similar to that.[50] As I have shown, Aquinas takes human souls to be immaterial; but he also thinks that they exist as informing human bodies and as being deprived of certain ways of working if these bodies perish so that they no longer inform them. Might there, however, be created intellects that are not composites of form and matter, intellects that are purely immaterial while not informing bodies? Aquinas believed angels to be intellects of this kind, and in SCG 2,91 he argues philosophically that they exist and that there are a lot of them. He then proceeds to say what he thinks they have to be (or cannot be) and how they function (SCG 2,93–101).

You might find it surprising that Aquinas attempts to argue philosophically for the existence of angels since Christian belief in angels is commonly grounded in biblical texts that refer to them and since you might expect Aquinas only to view them as things the existence of which has been revealed by God.[51] As I have shown, though, Aquinas thinks that a number of biblical texts can be defended without invoking the notion of faith, without appealing only to what he calls "the articles of faith." And in SCG 2,91–92 he argues that this is so when it comes to belief in angels.

Here are just three of the arguments he presents in SCG 2,91:

1. Intellect is naturally something that exists apart from bodies. Intellect in people exists as conjoined to what is bodily not because it is essentially (*per se*) intellect but because it happens accidentally (*per accidens*) to be conjoined to what is bodily. This means that intellect as such is not inevitably united to a body so as to form a composite thing. So there are intellectual substances that are not united to a body.[52]
2. Intellect is something that is of itself subsistent; yet what subsists of itself is not essentially united to something else even if it is the case that the human intellect is united to the human body. So some intellectual substances are not united to a body.[53]
3. God creates so as to impart being to things. If created intellect only exists as soul informing matter in human beings, then there would be a huge gap in being between people and God since there could be intellect that resembles God by being wholly immaterial. So it is reasonable to think that God has filled that gap. "All possible natures are found in the order of things; otherwise, the universe would be imperfect.... Therefore, below the first substance,

God, who is not in a genus (as was shown in Book 1 of this work), and above the soul, which is united to a body, there are some substances subsisting without bodies."[54]

So in SCG 2,91–92 Aquinas takes himself to have given reasonable grounds for believing in the existence of angels. Yet what does he take angels to be? His views on this question, as provided in SCG 2,93–101, can, I think, be quickly summarized as follows (note that they mostly amount to conclusions as to what angels *cannot* be if they are totally immaterial and not the substantial forms of a body, as Aquinas takes the human soul to be).

1. Each angel constitutes a distinct species since angels, considered as subsisting things, cannot be individuated as instances of some material kind. "Subsisting quiddities are subsisting species. Therefore, several separate substances cannot exist unless they be several species. Moreover, things specifically the same but numerically different possess matter. For the difference that results from the form introduces specific diversity; from the matter, numerical diversity. But separate substances have no matter whatever, either as part of themselves or as that to which they are united as form. It is therefore impossible that there be several such substances of one species" (SCG 2,93).[55]
2. Angels do not belong to the same species as the human soul since, for example, each angel is a species on its own and since angels are not human souls united to bodies as form to matter (SCG 2,94).
3. Although each angel constitutes a species, angels can be grouped together as separate substances differing in rank from each other (SCG 2,95).
4. Angels, being wholly immaterial, do not gain knowledge based on sensory experience and do not have agent and possible intellects; nor do angels exist as knowing intellects existing in time (if time is what things are "in" insofar as they undergo material changes) (SCG 2,96).[56]
5. The intellect of an angel is always actually understanding; since the being of an angel is not measured by time, it is not sometimes potentially understanding and sometimes actually understanding. Understanding in angels "is not intermittent, but continuous" (SCG 2,97).
6. Angels understand what is actually intelligible and distinct from matter, not what is potentially intelligible. So angels, who are actually intelligible and wholly immaterial, understand each other and God (SCG 2,98).
7. Angels can understand what is intelligible in material things since they are things the nature of which leads them to understand what is intelligible (SCG 2,99).

8. Angels know material things in their individuality since their knowledge extends to what is real in what can be understood and since material things, as individual things, are real. We understand things in terms of genus and species but have to rely on bodily contact to individuate things. Angels differ from us in this respect and have understanding of material individuals without having bodily contact with them. "The likeness existing in the separate substance's intellect as a certain single and immaterial thing is of more universal power [sc. than it is in us as we receive the forms of things immaterially and thereby come to understand] and, consequently, is able to lead to the knowledge of both the specific and individuating principles, so that through this likeness, residing in its intellect, the separate substance can be cognizant, not only of the generic and specific natures, but of the individual nature as well" (SCG 2,100).[57]

9. Only God knows all things at once (*tota simul*) in knowing himself (see SCG 1,55). So angels do not know things as God does (SCG 2,101).

11.5 *Reflecting on SCG 2,46–101*

If you start with the assumption that only material things exist, you will obviously have to reject almost everything Aquinas says in SCG 2,46–101.[58] And if you think that you can prove that nothing nonmaterial exists, then you will take yourself to have good reason to suppose that SCG 2,46–101 is seriously wrongheaded since its arguments assume the possibility of there being immaterial intellects. So if a rigidly materialistic account of reality is all that we can safely rely on when thinking about what exists, Aquinas is just wasting his time in SCG 2 while trying to think about what intellect is in general and how it is that intellect can be ascribed to people and to angels. That is because lying behind everything he writes in SCG 2,46–101 is the supposition that not all that exists is material.

For Aquinas, that not all that exists is material is not a supposition or assumption. It is something that he takes himself to have established in his SCG arguments for the existence of God. And if you think that these arguments have merit, then you will come with an open mind to SCG 2,46–101 since you will not think that it is absurd to suppose that something can exist while not being physical or material. On the other hand, however, you might, while accepting that God exists as wholly immaterial, wonder whether Aquinas's SCG account of immateriality in human beings makes sense. And you might wonder whether Aquinas has given us grounds to believe in the existence of angels.

If we do not embrace a totally materialistic account of what people are, then we might be prepared to say that people are souls or selves attached to bodies (1) because they understand and think, (2) because thinking is not a bodily process, and (3) because we are our souls. Plato seems to have been of this view. And so have many philosophers since his time. I have already referred to Descartes as thinking that we are essentially incorporeal things, and defenders of Descartes on the distinction of mind and body remain to this day.[59] And, you might think, if Descartes's position on mind and body is defensible, then there is much to be said for what Aquinas argues concerning the human soul.

Yet I do not think that this conclusion would be true since Aquinas does not think that I am my soul. He thinks that my soul is but a part of me and that I am a composite of body and soul.[60] Aquinas's position on soul and body in people seems to be at odds with what Plato and Descartes defend—this being commonly referred to nowadays as "substance dualism." For Aquinas, I am not two distinct substances. He certainly speaks of my soul as subsisting. But he does not take it to be a substance. He takes it to be a part of me that is not something physical operating in a physical way. As for my body, Aquinas thinks that in the absence of my soul my body is not a human being, not a human substance.

You may, perhaps, think that arguments in favor of substance dualism are so many nails in the coffin of Aquinas's position on soul and body in people. Yet some of them seem to me to be good arguments.

Substance dualists typically maintain that it is ludicrous to suppose that mental events can be straightforwardly reduced to physical events since they are not empirically observable, since, for example, no empirical investigation can capture the occurrence of a thought. And this conclusion strikes me as correct. It certainly makes sense to say that one can see people thinking since their bodily behavior is often a good guide to what they are believing, surmising, expecting, doubting, and so on. Yet it also seems hard to disprove that people can know what they are thinking in having certain particular thoughts that they have. And it also seems hard to show that a person's privileged access to his or her thoughts is something empirically observable. I can take you to be morally disreputable without indicating so by what I say or do. And even if what I say or do indicates that I take you to be morally disreputable, my saying or doing here only indicates what I am actually thinking.

Understanding and thinking is often said to be what brains do. But statements like "My brain understands" or "My brain thinks" seem pretty weird. It is people, not brains, who think and understand, even if thinking and understanding depend on having a brain. Also, of course, it seems hard to believe that an examination of a living human brain is going to enable the examiner to conclude "This one is thinking that Paris is nicer than New York" or "That one is thinking that Wales is full of memories for me," and so on. In what sense can any brain state be thought to be numerically identical with any thought? The sentence "The present that I passed on to Paul is the same as the present that I received from Mary and wanted to get rid of" makes sense because we can say what it is that I wanted to get rid of. Yet can we make sense of "My recognizing that bats are mammals is the same as process X in my brain"? The question that cries out for answer here is "The same what?" and I do not see what answer can be given to this question.[61] You might say that the correct reply to the question is "Same thing." But "thing" does not specify what something is. We are not given any answer to the question "What is X?" if it is just said that X is a thing. Everything, you might say, is a thing.

Yet one can concede that there are mental events not reducible to physical ones without arguing that people are essentially immaterial. If you look around you, you will find people to be physical things because they have bodies. And if you find them to be that, then you will be agreeing with Aquinas. So you will not suppose that people are purely immaterial things. On the other hand you may think that there is more to people than can be described in an empirical account of them. And if you think that, then you might suppose that people are pretty unique in that they operate at both a material and an immaterial level, which Aquinas also takes to be the case. You might suppose that there can be no connection between what is material and what is not material. But why so? Aquinas would say that there can be a causal connection between what is immaterial and what is material. You will reject this thesis if you think that all causation *has* to amount to one material thing bringing about a change in another material thing. But why suppose that? Has this thesis been demonstrated to be true?

Aquinas obviously thinks that the thesis has not been demonstrated because of what he takes himself to have argued concerning the existence and nature of God. Yet he would also contest the thesis on the basis of his view of understanding as amounting to the reception of form immaterially—something that I explained and discussed a bit in chapter 7. Let me now, however, say a little more on that view.

Aquinas is quite clear that people are not immaterial substances. Yet he is also clear that understanding is a nonbodily operation. What he has in mind here can be illustrated by an example.

Someone wearing blue eyeglasses fails to see what someone wearing colorless ones sees since such a person cannot, for example, distinguish between white and pale blue. Someone who can distinguish all colors cannot be looking through glasses that are colored. Similarly, thinks Aquinas, a being that can, at least in principle, understand all bodily things cannot itself possess the nature of any bodily thing—meaning that understanding is not a bodily function of a bodily thing. Yes, thinks Aquinas, something bodily (a cow, say) can possess its nature bodily, and must, indeed, do so. But he also thinks that we could never understand (be informed by) every bodily nature if understanding amounted to having any bodily nature in the way that bodily things naturally possess it. Aquinas's position, as I said in chapter 7, is that we understand what something is by having its form in mind. He thinks, for example, that the nature signified by the word "cow" exists in a cow naturally because it is a cow; yet he also thinks that it exists in me as I understand what a cow is.

As Herbert McCabe says:

> This doctrine will be totally misunderstood if it is not recognized that it is intended to be *obvious*. It is not a description of a process by which we understand, if there is any such process. It is a platitude; it says "What I have in mind when I know the nature of a cow is the nature of a cow and nothing else." Now in case someone says "But if the nature you have in your mind is that of a cow, surely your mind must be a cow—for to have the nature of an X simply means to be an X," St Thomas merely replies that to understand the nature of a cow is to have this nature precisely *without* being a cow, and this is what is made clear by saying that one has the nature *in mind*.[62]

The platitude to which McCabe here refers does, indeed, seem to be a platitude. So understanding what something is would seem obviously to have that something in one in a nonmaterial way, which favors Aquinas's account of intellect in SCG 2,46–101. One might think of our minds as physical things in which concepts or understandings are lodged. Or, again, one might think of them as physical objects that perform certain physical functions. On this basis one might say that we understand what something is because we have a likeness or picture of it in mind in some physical sense. Yet as McCabe goes on to observe:

> One of the characteristic things about a picture is that it is first of all something in its own right—a piece of canvas or wood—and then it resembles something. Now it is just the things that the picture has in its own right that must be forbidden to the picture in the mind. If it were a picture on wood, it would not serve to distinguish a cow from a cow painted on wood; if it were made of cast iron, it would not help to tell a

cow from a cast iron lawn-cow. There is no *mental stuff* that the picture could be made of—it must have everything the cow has and nothing else. It cannot *resemble* a cow because anything except the sheer resemblance will be an alien element like wood or cast iron. It must be simply everything that a cow has and nothing else. And what is this except to be the nature of the cow?[63]

So, perhaps, what Aquinas says about immaterial human intellect is not entirely off-beam. And, taken as part of his account of what people are, it steers a delicate balance between concluding that we are wholly immaterial or wholly physical. Substance dualists will say that we are wholly immaterial, which seems patently false since we are human beings and since human beings exist as living objects in the spatiotemporal world. Hardheaded materialists will say that we are nothing but what is physical, which also seems false since it is hard to believe that thoughts are always physically detectable or identical with brain processes, and since understanding what something is cannot be a physical operation at all. Aquinas on the other hand positively affirms that people are essentially material things without thereby concluding that they are nothing but what is material, that there is nothing in them but that which can be thought of as entirely physical. So maybe his position on soul and body in people at least preserves something of the best in dualistic accounts of people and of material accounts of what people are.

Aquinas's SCG arguments on angels and angelic intellects, though, are perhaps somewhat implausible. Aquinas believed in angels independently of philosophical arguments because of his reading of the Bible. But you might well find his nonbiblically based arguments for the existence of angels in SCG 2,91–92 less than conclusive.

Consider the three arguments I highlighted earlier in this chapter.

The first one seems dubious since, even if intellect is not necessarily united to body, it does not follow that there are angelic intellects not united to bodies.

The second argument moves too quickly from the idea that intellects exist as subsisting to the conclusion that there are intellects that are created intellects not united to bodies.

The third argument rests on the idea that God could not create without making a world containing wholly immaterial things. Yet, while one might agree that if God wills to confer being on creatures as manifesting the being of God, who is able to create anything that can be thought to exist, it does not seem obvious that God must create angels so as to fill the gap between people, considered as partly immaterial, and God, considered as wholly immaterial while being that which exists of necessity because it is uncreated.

One might, of course, want to say that God, considered as Being Itself, might want to create as much as could possibly reflect him considered as such. And, unless you think that everything that could exist has to be something material, it seems true enough that wholly immaterial beings created by God could be part of a created world. But I do not see why God, as able to create all that can be, has to create all that can be. As I have shown, Aquinas does not think that God has to create at all. So the third argument for angels that I have noted can hardly suppose otherwise and must, I think, be understood as a probable argument based on some notion of what it would be fitting for God to produce if he wants to pour forth being into things of many possible kinds. But I do not find the argument definitively to establish that there have to be angelic intellects. You, of course, might think differently.

11.6 Moving On

Aquinas's intention in SCG 2 is to follow up SCG 1's discussion of the existence and nature of God with an account of what God has brought into being as the omnipotent source of all creaturely being. So, having first discussed what God's power amounts to, SCG 2 proceeds to consider what it means for there to be creatures of God and then goes on to talk about intellectual creatures, considered as the only created things capable of knowing something about God. Yet Aquinas thinks that God, as well as creating things, also governs them in various ways. So he is prepared to make a distinction between God's making of creatures and his directing of them. As I have shown, Aquinas thinks that God creatively acts as one in whom there is will. He also thinks that what agents produce by will are directed to ends that are intended by what produces them. But what might be the ends to which God directs creatures? And how might they succeed or fail to arrive at these ends? These are the primary questions raised by Aquinas in SCG 3.

Agents, Ends, Evil, and Good (SCG 3,1–15)

CHAPTER I OF SCG 3 amounts to a taking stock and a looking forward. First, Aquinas reminds us that he has previously dealt with God as "possessing the full perfection of the whole of being" and as being "the universal maker of the whole of being."[1] Then Aquinas repeats that God acts with will, and he goes on to note that things produced through the will of an agent are "directed to an end by the agent."[2] So, says Aquinas, God is the "Ruler of all beings" and "as he is perfect in being and causing, so also is he perfect in ruling."[3] Since there are creatures of different kinds, however, Aquinas recognizes that God's ruling or governance of creatures will be shown forth in different ways: that it will be one thing in creatures with understanding and something else in creatures that lack understanding. God's governing of creatures, God's providence, starts from God, however, and it is this governing that Aquinas wishes to focus on in SCG 3. Or, as he puts the point himself:

> Since we have treated of the perfection of the divine nature in Book One, and of the perfection of his power inasmuch as he is the Maker and Lord of all things in Book Two, there remains to be treated in this third Book his perfect authority or dignity, inasmuch as he is the End and Ruler of all things. So, this will be our order of procedure: first, we shall treat of God, according as he is the end of all things [see SCG 3,1–63]; second, of his universal rule, according as he governs every creature [see SCG 3,64–110]; third, of his particular rule, according as he governs creatures possessed of understanding [see SCG 3,111–163].[4]

12.1 Agents and Ends (SCG 3,2–3)

The notion of governance seems bound up with the notion of intention. Governors govern with ends in mind. Thus, for example, parliaments or monarchs go about governing their countries while seeking to bring about definite results. They act in order to achieve what they, rightly or wrongly, take to be good. Given that in SCG 3 Aquinas is concerned with God's governance of creatures, therefore, he has to bear in mind that creatures can be led to certain ends by God. Since he does not think that God can be fallible when it comes to what is good, he also has to think that God leads or governs things so as to result in what is truly good.

Yet how is God supposed to do this? One can readily understand how parliaments or monarchs might govern a country: by setting up laws and putting into place people and organizations able to enforce them, or by providing money for the welfare of various individuals. As I have shown, however, Aquinas does not think of God as a spatiotemporal being acting as something within the created order, which would seem to mean that he needs to think of God as governing things by creating them as the things that they are, which is what he does indeed think. According to Aquinas, God governs creatures by acting in them creatively, by making them to exist in various ways. So he holds that God brings about what is good partly by making creatures geared to what is good, though he recognizes that some creatures might reach what is good for them at the expense of others. As I have shown, Aquinas thinks that everything that exists is to some extent good. So he holds that even an ailing creature, whose ailing might contribute to the good of another creature, is still somehow good. Nevertheless, Aquinas views God's governing of creatures in terms of God's leading them to a range of goods by making them to be what they are and sometimes by helping them in special ways.

This point of view commits Aquinas to the view that all created things must have a divinely inbuilt tendency to what is good. Aquinas accepts that people often freely aim at what is morally wrong. Yet he also thinks that even a vicious person is acting so as to achieve what he or she takes to be good in some sense, and he takes nonthinking created agents always to act for a good end.

It is not, perhaps, hard to see why Aquinas might think that people always act for ends that they take to be good. If it makes sense to ask someone "Why are you doing that?" then it makes sense to suppose that the person is acting so as to achieve some desirable end or goal. Yet it might not seem so obvious that nonthinking creatures act for an end. We can, perhaps, happily concede that cats chase after mice while acting for an end. What, however, of other nonthinking things in the world? What about plants? What about stones?

Aquinas thinks that plants are living things and, therefore, have a principle of movement within them (see chapter 8, section 2 here). Yet he also thinks that plants, left to themselves and suitably provided for, consistently act in predictable ways, and he wonders why that should be so. He does not think that a physical analysis of plants will entirely explain why they act as they do since such an analysis will just describe what plants are materially. Nor does he think that the activities of plants can always be explained in terms of agent causes other than them. To be sure, plants grow from seeds, and Aquinas believes that agent causes are needed to account for the seeds being there; but he does not think that the agent cause or causes accounting for a particular plant can explain why the plant acts as it does. He holds that plants act as nonthinkingly aiming at what they strive for as existing plants. And he takes the same line when it comes to stones. We might, he supposes, be able to explain why a particular stone came into existence. And we might provide a scientific account when it comes to what a stone is. But then, thinks Aquinas, we might ask why stones in certain contexts bring about certain effects and were potentially able to do so beforehand. His answer to this question is twofold and is not confined to questions about plants or stones. It is an answer that he takes to apply to anything at all that can be thought of as acting, as moving from being potentially thus and so to becoming actually thus and so. And his answer is that (1) every agent acts for an end, and (2) every agent acts for a good (the theses defended in SCG 3,2 and 3).

Yet why should we believe that every agent acts for an end? Aquinas's answer is that every agent acts in ways that reflect its substantial form, and that things with substantial forms have tendencies to operate in particular ways, tendencies to move toward certain ends rather than others. Aquinas does not think that all substances tend to ends as things with intellect recognizing ends and gravitating toward them accordingly. He recognizes, for example, that while people can set about aiming for a good that they want and reason about how to obtain it, nonthinking things are incapable of acting in this way. However, he also thinks that it is not by accident that acting things actualize potentialities in themselves or others. He would say, for example, that it is not accidental that the motions of hearts produce circulation of blood, or that it is not accidental that sulphuric acid burns skin onto which it is poured. Aquinas's view is that acting things, given their natures, whether intellectual or not, have inclinations or tendencies to operate in various ways and to bring about certain effects that reflect their natures.[5] As he says in SCG 3,2: "Every inclination of an agent tends towards something definite. A given action does not stem from merely any power, but heating comes from heat, cooling from cold."[6] Aquinas goes on to observe that "in the action of all agents, one may find something beyond which the agent seeks nothing further. Otherwise, actions would tend to infinity, which is impossible.... Therefore, every agent acts for an end."[7] He means that acting agents act as directed not to an infinity of ends but to some end, one that they are actually capable of reaching. So, he reasons, "There must be something which satisfies an agent's desire when it is attained. Therefore, every agent acts for an end."[8]

Aquinas is not here saying that every agent that acts always achieves the end or ends with respect to which it acts. The operations of anything created, whether intellectual or not, can, he accepts, be thwarted. He does, however, think that agents, both with and without intellect, tend to ends and arrive at them unless prevented from doing so by something else, something acting for an end in its own way. So, he argues:

> Just as the entire likeness of the result achieved by the actions of an intelligent agent exists in the intellect that preconceives it, so, too, does the likeness of a natural resultant pre-exist in the natural agent; and as a consequence of this, the action is determined to a definite result. For fire gives rise to fire, and an olive to an olive. Therefore, the agent that acts with nature as its principle is just as much directed to a definite end, in its action, as is the agent that acts through intellect as its principle. Therefore, every agent acts for an end.[9]

If this were not the case, Aquinas suggests, we would never be complaining that something has gone wrong when it comes to the actions of created agents. If we think that something has gone wrong as an agent acts, that is because we have unfulfilled expectations when it comes to the agent and its action. If my cat tries to feed, but ends up vomiting and expiring, then something seems to have gone wrong. But wrong with respect to what? Presumably with respect to an end that we expect when it comes to functioning cats. Or, as Aquinas says: "There is no fault (*peccatum*) to be found, except in the case of things that are for the sake of an end. A fault is never attributed to an agent, if the failure is related to something that is not the agent's end."[10]

If you believe that the only kind of causation there is amounts to what Aquinas calls "agent" or "efficient" causation, you will reject what I have just reported as his thinking. For in SCG 3,2 he is saying that final causality is all-pervasive in the created order, that there are final causes as well as efficient ones (see chapter 2, section 1 here). In his view (see chapter 2, section 1 here), we might try to explain what something is by noting what it is made of, what its substantial form is (if it has one), what brought it into being, and what it aims at (where "aims" is obviously to be construed analogically). And in SCG 3,2 Aquinas is ramming home his conviction that final causality has to be acknowledged when it comes to all created substances.[11]

In SCG 3,3, however, he goes a stage further while developing this thesis. Here he argues that "every agent acts for a good."[12] In defense of this thesis he offers these arguments:

1. What agents tend to "in a definite way" must be something appropriate (*conveniens*) to them. Yet what is appropriate for something is good for it.[13]

2. When arriving at an end an agent is at rest. Now, "good" means a terminus for appetite since "the good is that which all desire." So "every action and motion are for the sake of a good."[14]

3. Action and movement are somehow directed to being either for the preservation of the agent or its species or for the acquisition of something. Being, however, is good in and of itself, which is why all things tend to or desire it.

4. Action is for some perfection, yet perfection is good.

5. "Every agent acts in so far as it is in act, and in acting it tends to produce something like itself. So, it tends toward some act. But every act has something of good in its essential character."[15]

6. Agents with intellect always act as pursuing ends thought of by them as good. Agents without intellect act on the basis of inclination drawing them to certain ends desirable in some way for them.

7. Everything shuns evil, which means that, when acting, things move to what is good in some way.

8. "What happens in the workings of nature is either always, or mostly, for the better." This does not come about by chance since chance events are not ones that occur always or for the most part. "Therefore, the natural agent tends toward what is better, and it is much more evident that the intelligent agent does so."[16]

9. Whatever is moved ends up as it is because of a mover or agent. So movers and things moved tend to the same thing. Yet movement involves a progression from potentiality to actuality, which is good.

In presenting these arguments, Aquinas is not denying that bad things can happen because of what agents or movers do. He is not, for example, denying that people suffer when wolves prey on them. Rather, he is commenting on action in general and suggesting that agents always act as drawn to some good, something they find desirable in some sense. They do this, he believes, as governed by God providentially.

12.2 Evil (SCG 3,4–15)

Aquinas's discussion of evil in SCG 3,4–15 leads him to present a number of conclusions and to consider and reply to a lot of objections. So it is possible to fail to grasp what Aquinas is fundamentally driving at in SCG 3,4–15 just by working through these chapters consecutively. When proceeding through

SCG 3,4–15 it is possible to miss the forest for the trees. For this reason, I shall now try to explain the essential reasoning and conclusions of this section of the SCG before turning to some of its details.

12.2.1 The Big Picture in SCG 3,4–15

In SCG 3,4–15 Aquinas is concerned with what he calls *malum*. This word can be translated into English as "evil," but it can also be translated as "badness." We tend to distinguish between evil and badness by saying that, for example, genocide or cancer is an evil, but a "white" lie or a mild headache is bad. Writing in Latin, however, Aquinas had only one word to cover badness in all its forms and degrees: *malum*. In SCG 3,4–15, therefore, he is concerned with badness of any kind, whether slight or humongous. His topic is badness in general.

Why so? Because he has previously claimed that God is good and creates only what is good. If that is so, then an obvious question arises when it comes to the view that God acts providentially in the order created by him. We can hardly deny that there is badness in the world since people act badly and since many things suffer or become diminished. There are and have been many moral monsters, and there is and has been a lot of pain and suffering arising from nonhuman agents. So if Aquinas is going to claim that everything that exists derives from God's will as providential, he is going to have to say something to explain why the fact that there is badness in the world does not count against this conclusion, which is what he tries to do in SCG 3,4–15.

In these chapters he is clearly working with the understanding of "good" that I noted in chapter 6. Aquinas thinks that goodness is what is desirable. Correspondingly, he thinks that badness is what is undesirable. As I have shown, though (see chapter 6, section 6.2 here), Aquinas regards "good" and "bad" as relative in the sense that something might be a good X but a bad Y (a good architect, say, but a bad plumber). Aquinas also holds that goodness exists insofar as something is actual; insofar as a form, whether substantial or accidental, is real; insofar as something is actually a substance of a certain kind; or insofar as it has some positive property or accident inhering in it. So Aquinas thinks that something is good just because it exists and succeeds in having a substantial form. As I have shown, he does not think that God is good in this way. He holds that God does not *have* his divine form but *is* it. When thinking of creatures, however, he takes goodness to consist in a form that is not impeded or defective.

How might form in creatures be impeded or defective? Well, I might lose my eyesight, which would obviously amount to a serious and impeding lack of accidental form in me.[17] But what if I act badly from a moral point of view? I might be perfectly happy in what I am doing, and I will certainly be aiming at what I take to be good. Yet Aquinas would say that I am failing since I am settling for a good for which I should not settle. For Aquinas, morally bad action is detrimental to a human being since it renders people less good than they could and should be. He thinks that there are ways of behaving that people need to pursue so as to be good or happy considered as human beings.

So Aquinas holds that evil or badness may be divided into two kinds: (1) the badness that is in people (or, indeed, in angels) who choose to act badly, and (2) the badness that arises as material things act on other material things so as to result in a diminishment of goodness in them. You might think that this is a distinction without a difference since you might think that a bad person is just someone who brings about bad effects of some kind. Yet Aquinas thinks that we should not confuse what is bad in itself with what is bad as suffering because of something acting on it.

With the best and most moral intentions, I might inadvertently bring about what is bad. For example, in war I might rush to help a comrade while unintentionally setting off a mine that wounds many of my comrades. Their suffering is a bad thing, but I am not bad for having been the cause, or one of the causes, of it. I was aiming at something good, which would seem to mean that we should not evaluate people morally simply with respect to what they happen to bring about. Yet, of course, I might maliciously will that someone should be in a bad way, and I might deliberately act so as to bring it about that this comes to pass. With an eye on such a scenario, Aquinas would say that I am certainly bringing it about that someone is in a bad way; but, he would add, there is a big difference between my willing evil to people and my inadvertently ending up killing people while trying to save others. In what does the difference consist? It cannot consist in a difference between what is brought about, since that might amount to something bad in both cases. Aquinas thinks that moral evil is only in the agent who is morally evil. It is not in the effects that the morally bad agent brings about. On the other hand, Aquinas also thinks, when things suffer or become bad because of the action of something in or on them, something becomes defective as that which is not defective, or not totally defective, is exerting itself at its expense.

Let us call the badness or evil present when we have moral evil "evil done." And let us call the badness or evil present as something fails due to the operation of something acting in or on it "evil suffered."[18] In that case, Aquinas's view is that evil done is only in the agent willingly intending some evil, whether one that merely affects the agent or one that affects something other than the agent.[19] And he thinks of evil suffered as badness coming about in something that is acted on by something else in a way that diminishes it. So Aquinas takes evil done to be present in an agent willing, aiming at, or tending to what is morally bad, or bad for some special theological reason. And he takes evil suffered to be in a patient; he takes it to be what is brought about as one thing adversely affects another thing. Sometimes, of course, and as Aquinas is aware, both kinds of evils can come about simultaneously. Thus, for example, there can be evil done and evil suffered as I choke someone to death so as to steal her money.

Yet what is evil or badness? As I have just been saying, Aquinas thinks that there is both evil done and evil suffered. But does he also think that they have something in common? At one level he does, though at another level he does not.

As I noted in chapter 6, Aquinas thinks of evil or badness as a matter of privation. His view is that, just as something is good insofar as it possesses form in some way, something is bad insofar as it somehow lacks form. So, for example, he thinks of living things as good, or as having goodness, just because they are alive, even if they are also ailing in some way. And he thinks of living things as bad or as displaying badness insofar as they lack form of some kind. I should stress that it is not Aquinas's view that evil amounts to a lack of any form you care to mention. He does not think that a spider is in a bad way because it cannot suckle its young like a mammal. Nor does he think that my cat is in a bad way because it cannot fly like a bird. His view is that there is badness in something insofar as it lacks what it needs considered as what it naturally is. So he thinks that blindness is an evil in people since by blindness they lack sight, which is desirable in people but not, say, in tulips. Again, he thinks that willing immorally is an evil in people since he thinks that it renders them less good than they ought to be. In other words, Aquinas takes all evil to amount to an absence of goodness (*privatio boni*), an absence that can be reasonably lamented, an absence that amounts to something achieving less than what is desirable for it considered as what it is.[20]

On the other hand, however, Aquinas also thinks that there is a critical difference between evil done and evil suffered. He is clear that both of these amount to privation of goodness or being in some way.[21] Yet, he maintains, while evil done has no concomitant good, evil suffered *always* has such a good. Aquinas's view is that if, say, I willingly murder you, then nothing benefits from this except accidentally. Of course, my murdering you might hypothetically lead someone to recognize the evil of murder and to devote themselves to preventing murders occurring. But that would be an accidental spin-off from my actually going about the business of murdering you. If I do this, thinks Aquinas, there is nothing but failure or privation. I display privation since I fail to act as I should; and you display privation by being acted on by me as I am killing you.[22] In the case of evil suffered, however, Aquinas thinks that there always has to be an explanation in terms of something that by being good in its way is bringing it about that something else is bad in its way. He thinks that all evil suffered involves badness + concomitant good.

It is not very difficult to offer a simple example illustrating what Aquinas has in mind here. If a cheetah jumps on a zebra so as to feed on it, the zebra is in a bad way immediately and is soon likely to become a corpse. Yet the cheetah is clearly flourishing and doing just what you would expect a healthy and thriving cheetah to do. Here we have badness or evil + concomitant good. One thing is flourishing at the expense of something else. One thing is suffering privation while another is being all that we expect it to be. A cheetah that succeeds in feeding on a zebra might be ailing in some way. But a cheetah that succeeds in feeding on a zebra is still doing well to some extent, an extent from which the zebra is doing badly.

Yet Aquinas does not try to make his case for evil suffered as involving concomitant good by providing examples of things doing well at the expense of other things doing badly. He does not offer an extensive inductive argument. His line is that there has to be a natural explanation for all cases of evil suffered, that instances of evil suffered should not be thought of as so many miracles, as events lacking causes in the world. And, with this thought in mind, he suggests that every case of evil suffered has to derive from something in the world that is at least good enough to inflict the evil in question, something that displays the goodness that it has as it brings about this evil.[23] My sick cat might yet be well enough to pounce on a mouse and to feed on it. If it manages to do so, then, Aquinas thinks, defect in the mouse comes about because of flourishing of a kind in my cat; and he thinks the same for comparable examples. If you believe in miracles, you might suggest that evil suffered could come about as God brings it into being without employing any creaturely and secondary cause. But Aquinas would not agree with you here, largely because he does not think that evil suffered has being that can be brought about by God. Indeed, he does not think that any evil or badness is something that God can create.

Why does Aquinas think along these lines? Because he does not think that evil is a substance with an essence, or a real accident in a substance having an essence. You might say that he therefore denies that evil exists. Yet that would be a misleading way of expounding his take on evil. If I were to assert that evil does not exist, you would likely take me to be mad. For how can one plausibly deny the reality of evil or badness, whether great or small? There have been philosophers who have denied all sorts of things that most of us take to be obviously true. Yet did any of them really believe that they never had a head-ache? And can anyone speaking in good faith seriously deny that people suffer from diseases? And is "Nobody ever acts badly" a credible belief? At any rate, Aquinas is confident that evil is real in that various things are now, and in the past have been, in very bad ways. He does not want to commit himself to the thesis "Evil does not exist."

Yet he does want to commit himself to the thesis that evil does not have an essence. He thinks that evil or badness can only be attributed to substances that fail in some way. He does not deny that bad things can successfully bring about badness in other things or in themselves, or that things that are good in various ways can bring about badness in other things. Yet he does not counte-nance the idea that there is such a thing as badness, considered as an inde-pendently acting substance with an essence. He thinks that there is subsisting goodness since he thinks that God exists and is goodness itself (see chapter 6 here). But he only holds that there is goodness itself because he thinks that there has to be a source of all that is good, a source that is not just a good thing of a kind but the source of all creaturely goodness. As I have shown, though, Aquinas thinks that what exists is good, and I have now shown that he main-tains that evil does not exist as a substance or accident having *esse*.

When he speaks of creaturely *esse* (being), Aquinas is talking about what actually exists as a substance or a positive accident had by a substance. So he finds it unproblemmatic to say that God, whom he takes to be subsisting *esse* and the cause of *esse* in creatures, is not a substance that has *esse*. Yet he finds it equally unproblematic to say that evil is not a substance that has *esse*. He thinks of evil or badness in substances as what can be attributed to substances insofar as they lack something that makes for well-being in them. In thinking in this way, Aquinas is not denying that evil or badness has one or more causes. He thinks, for example, that someone can be morally bad (evil done) by acting with some end or ends in mind (final cause). He also thinks that something can be a victim of evil suffered because one or more things are acting on it so as to bring about harm in it (efficient or agent causality).

But how is God causally related to evil done or suffered? Aquinas does not deal with this question in SCG 3,4–15, though he turns to it later in SCG 3. Given what I have now shown him arguing, however, he must surely think that God causes all the good in evil suffered and none of the bad in evil done, which is exactly what he does think. Since he holds that God accounts for the sheer existence of things and their various positive features, as opposed to their lack of certain positive features, he thinks that God causally accounts for all that is good in creatures. So he maintains: (1) God causally brings about all that is good in me insofar as I act well; (2) God is not causing the evil in me as

I act badly, even though he is causing me to exist as I choose to act badly; (3) God causes all the concomitant good in evil suffered, and causes none of the evil except indirectly, as one thing fails because of the well-being of another; (4) only good is the cause of evil, and that indirectly; (5) evil does not wholly destroy good.

12.2.2 SCG 3,4–15: Some Details

1. SCG 3,4–15 begins with a bold thesis: "Evil occurs in things apart from the intention of the agents."[24] What unintentionally comes about as the result of an agent acting, says Aquinas, "clearly happens apart from intention," while every agent intends what is good.[25] Aquinas obviously takes this conclusion to be bound up with his previous claim that every agent acts for a good (SCG 3,3). Defect in action, he says, arises from defect in the power of acting had by an agent. He continues:

> An agent acts in keeping with the active power that it has, not in accord with the defect of power to which it is subject. According as it acts, so does it intend the end. Therefore it intends an end corresponding to its power. So, that which results as an effect of the defect of the power will be apart from the intention of the agent. Now this is evil. Hence, evil occurs apart from intention.[26]

You may wonder whether people might not sometimes have evil as an intended end. But Aquinas is not at this point meaning to say that it is impossible for freely acting agents deliberately and successfully to will what is, in fact, evil. He is not denying that, for example, people can sometimes be hell-bent on revenge and doing wrong to people whom they hate. He is stressing that agents strive for what seems good to them and that if what they strive for fails to come about, or if something suffers because of their action, that is not because of what they intend or aim at in acting. "That which terminates in a privation," says Aquinas, "is apart from intention." He continues: "It terminates in a privation inasmuch as it attains the form which it intends, and the privation of another form is a necessary result of this attainment."[27] Here Aquinas seems primarily to have evil suffered in mind. But he quickly goes on to consider what might result from the action of things with understanding. We read:

> All intelligent agents tend towards something in so far as they consider the object under the rational character of a good.... So, if this object is not good but bad, this will be apart from their intention. Therefore, intelligent

agents do not produce an evil result, unless it be apart from their intention. Since to tend to the good is common to the intelligent agent and to the agent that acts by natural instinct, evil does not result from the intention of any agent, except apart from the intention.[28]

In other words, even if I aim at what is objectively bad, I am aiming at what I take to be good, not at what I take to be bad.

2. In SCG 3,5 Aquinas notes some arguments against what he has been claiming in SCG 3,4; and in SCG 3,6 he replies to these arguments. Here are the arguments noted in SCG 3,5:

a. What does not come about by virtue of intention must come about by chance, which is rare. Yet evil is not rare and is explicable in terms of what agents, whether intelligent or otherwise, aim at.
b. People sometimes willingly perform acts that are wicked.
c. Corruption, which involves privation, occurs in the natural world and is intended by nature. So nature intends privation.

And here is what Aquinas says in SCG 3,6:

a. Evil can exist in a substance or in its action. It exists in a substance if what it ought to have is lacking in it. So, for example, it is bad or evil for a human being to lack hands, while it is not bad or evil for a bird to lack hands.
b. If evil exists in a subject, then it is evil in an unqualified way. And evil in an action is also unqualifiedly evil.
c. "Not everything that is apart from intention is necessarily fortuitous or a matter of chance."[29] People who end up with hangovers due to alcohol consumption do not intend or aim at the pain of the hangover; they aim at enjoying drinking alcohol. Yet hangovers do not happen by chance.
d. So corruption in natural things, though not something aimed at by anything in nature, is "an invariable consequence [sc. of agents in nature acting in certain ways], for the acquisition of one form is always accompanied by the privation of another form."[30] It does not occur by chance.
e. There can be badness in the action of natural agents because of some defect in their power of acting. So, for example, I might limp while trying to walk because my power to walk is affected by a leg injury. But I am not intending my limping as I try to walk, and my limping will not come about by chance unless it happens to have come about because of chance events bringing it about that I am someone who ends up having to limp while trying to walk.[31]

f. Voluntary agents aim or intend with a view to a particular good. If they choose to act so as to deprive something or someone of well-being in some way, they do not do so by chance. Adulterers know what they are aiming at when having intercourse, and adultery is not something that happens by chance, though, of course, someone might, say, inadvertently kill someone while aiming to shoot a bird.

g. Moral evil is the result of voluntary action since it comes about as someone wills a good that results in privation in some way, either in the agent or in something else. "Though evil [sc. evil as wickedness] be apart from intention, it is nonetheless voluntary.... People will to do a disorderly action for the sake of some sensory good to be attained; they do not intend the disorder, nor do they will it simply for itself, but for the sake of this result."[32]

h. "Privations are not intended by nature in themselves, but only accidentally; forms, however, are intended in themselves."[33]

i. "What is evil in an unqualified sense is completely apart from intention in the workings of nature.... On the other hand, that which is not evil in the unqualified sense, but evil in relation to some definite thing, is not directly intended by nature but only accidentally."[34]

3. Is anything essentially evil? In SCG 3,7 Aquinas argues that nothing is essentially evil; and, having, in SCG 3,8, noted arguments against this position, he continues to defend it in SCG 3,9.[35] Evil, he maintains,

is simply a privation of something which a subject is entitled by its origin to possess and which it ought to have.... Now, privation is not an essence; it is, rather, a negation in a substance.... What is evil in itself cannot be natural to anything. For it is of the very definition of evil that it be a privation of that which is to be in a subject by virtue of its natural origin, and which should be in it. So, evil cannot be natural to any subject since it is a privation of what is natural. Consequently, whatever is present naturally in something is a good for it, and it is evil if the thing lacks it. Therefore, no essence is evil in itself.[36]

Aquinas goes on to note (1) that a substance has being by virtue of its essence, (2) that being is good, (3) that everything is good insofar as it possesses being, (4) and that good and evil are contraries. So, Aquinas concludes, "nothing is evil by virtue of the fact that it has an essence" and "no essence is evil."[37] Again, he reasons, "everything is either an agent or a thing that is made"; yet evil is not an agent or something made since a thing acts insofar as it is good in some way, and since what is made possesses form and, therefore, goodness.[38] Yet again, he argues, every being intends a good when acting (see SCG 3,3), so "no being, as being, is evil."[39] In addition, Aquinas notes: (1) what has an essence is or has form, and form is good since it is a principle of action; (2) being is actual or potential, and actuality is good since something is good to the extent that it is actual, while potentiality is good since it tends toward actuality; (3) every act of being comes from God (see SCG 2,15), and God is perfect goodness (see SCG 1,28 and 41); yet evil cannot be the product of what is good; so no being, as a being, is evil.

4. So what causes evil? In SCG 3,10 Aquinas insists that both evil in evil suffered and the evil in evil done are "caused only by the good," but caused only "accidentally."[40] He says that what comes about has to proceed from what is good since it comes from a real and acting agent, which evil is not. "What does not exist," he observes, "is not the cause of anything. So, every cause must be a definite thing. But evil is not a definite being, as has been proved [see SCG 3,7]. Therefore, evil cannot be the cause of anything. If, then, evil be caused by anything, this cause must be the good."[41]

When it comes to evil suffered, Aquinas argues, this can be either in an agent or in what an agent brings about. It is in an agent if the agent is somehow defective in power and, therefore, defective in action, this resulting in bad effects. Yet, says Aquinas, the bad effects here are spin-offs from an ability to act, which is, in and of itself, good. When it comes to evil suffered and what an agent brings about, Aquinas goes on to say, this may come about either because what is being acted on is "not well disposed to the reception of the agent's action on it" or because it is rendered defective by the goodness in what is acting on it.[42] When it comes to the second possibility, Aquinas claims that "from the point of view of the form of the effect, evil occurs accidentally because the privation of another form is the necessary concomitant of the presence of a given form."[43]

Yet, Aquinas goes on to say, this analysis of evil does not work when it comes to the evil in evil done. Those who do evil, he thinks, are not suffering from a defect of power, and "moral fault is noticed in action only, and not in any effect that is produced.... Moral evil is not considered in relation to the matter or form of the effect, but only as a resultant from the agent."[44] "The root and source of moral wrongdoing," Aquinas claims, "is to be sought in the act of will."[45] He takes this conclusion to mean that beings with intellect and will, while always aiming at what they take to be good, can choose to ignore other possible goods that they might and ought to pursue. He writes:

When the will inclines to act as moved by the apprehension of reason, presenting a proper good to it, the result is a fitting action. But when the will breaks forth into action, at the apprehension of sense cognition, or of reason presenting some other good at variance with its proper good, the result in the action of the will is a moral fault.[46]

So, says Aquinas, "a defect of ordering to reason and to a proper end precedes a fault of action in the will." This defect in ordering is, he claims, voluntary, "for to will and not to will lie within the power of the will itself."[47] He goes on to say that something with will is able to reason or not reason, or to pay attention or not pay attention to what might properly be considered when reasoning concerning an action. Aquinas therefore seems to think that people acting badly are voluntarily aiming at goods, implying, so he thinks, that their being morally bad springs from a good source in them that allows them to refuse to pay attention to what right moral reasoning requires. Their being morally evil results from them positively aiming at what they take to be good while not thinking rightly when it comes to their actions. In this sense, Aquinas thinks, the evil in evil done comes about accidentally since it results from an inappropriate good being sought.

5. The thesis of SCG 3,11 is that evil is always based on some good. Since it lacks an essence, says Aquinas, it cannot exist independently and must be in a subject. Yet, he reiterates, every substance is good just by existing, and "the privation which is evil is present in a good thing, as in a subject."[48] Again, he argues, evil causes injury, but only as injuring what is good and only because it is, therefore, in what is good. Also, he says, since evil is only caused accidentally by what is good, and, since what is accidental is reducible to what exists by itself, "with a caused evil which is the accidental effect of the good, there must always be some good which is the direct effect of the good itself, and thus this good effect is the foundation of the evil" since "what exists accidentally is based on that which exists by itself."[49] Aquinas acknowledges that someone might find it improper or unreasonable (*inconveniens*) to say that good is the subject of evil, that evil is grounded in goodness. Yet he thinks it proper to say that nonbeing can be present in a being as in a subject. He notes that any privation amounts to nonbeing grounded in what is to some extent good.

6. Can evil wholly destroy good? In SCG 3,12 Aquinas argues that it cannot since it always exists in what is to some extent good.

7. SCG 3,13 and 14 return to the notion of evil having a cause. Here Aquinas offers the following conclusions, which he takes to be inferable from what he

has previously been saying: (1) since what exists in something must have some cause, and since evil does exist in subjects, evil has some kind of cause; (2) since evil is always a privation of a certain kind, it must have a cause; (3) since evil is always a privation of a certain kind, it exists in things as foreign to their nature, as not due to what the things essentially are; so it must have a cause; (4) every evil is a consequence of a good; yet every good other than God has a cause; so "every evil has a cause";[50] (5) "Evil, though not a direct cause of anything by itself is, however, an accidental cause" since its presence in an active cause amounts to its being present accidentally in what that cause causes;[51] (6) defects in causes lead to defects in effects, yet a defect in a cause is an evil, even though it is not an independently existing (*per se*) cause as is an existing substance.

8. Aquinas thinks that God is the highest good and the source of all created goods. In SCG 3,15, however, he denies that there is any highest evil that is the first source or principle of all evils (a position he ascribes to Manicheans). A highest evil, he observes, would have to be entirely disconnected from goodness, as God is entirely separate from evil; yet evil depends on there being goodness of some kind. Again, he says that a highest evil would have to be evil by essence; yet evil has no essence (see SCG 3,7). Yet again, he argues: (1) first principles do not have causes, but every evil is caused by a good; (2) first principles act through their own power, but evil acts only through the power of what is somehow good; (3) first principles cannot be accidental; yet evil arises only accidentally; (4) all evils have accidental causes, while first principles have no cause; (5) first principles are genuine beings acting causally, yet evil is only an accidental cause.

12.3 Some Comments on SCG 3,1–15

One problem that some people will have with SCG 3,1–15 is its notion that nonthinking things can be thought of as acting for ends. Another problem some people will have with SCG 3,1–15 is the way it relies so heavily on the claim that evil is a privation or absence of being. So, at this point, let me say something about Aquinas on acting for ends and Aquinas on evil as privation.

12.3.1 Acting for Ends

According to Aquinas, all agents act with a view to an end, that is, all action is goal-directed. I have shown him maintaining this position in SCG 3,1–15, and it is one he continued to embrace in later writings. Hence, for example, in

Summa Theologiae 1a2ae,1,2 we read: "All efficient causes must needs act for an end. In an ordered system of causes, strike out the first, and the others have to go too. And the first of all causes is the final cause or end."[52] In short, as well as looking for efficient or agent causes when accounting for what happens, Aquinas continually looks for final causes. Indeed, as the above quotation makes clear, he takes final causation to be somehow more fundamental than efficient or agent causation since he takes the latter to presuppose or reflect the former. He thinks that efficient or agent causes achieve what they do as acting for ends, as being goal-oriented. In his view, efficient causes are oriented to particular effects or ends. He does not mean that efficient causes act so that certain ends will come about of necessity. As I have said, he allows for the operations of things to be thwarted by the actions of other things. Yet he does believe that all things are goal-oriented in their action, whether or not they are interfered with. In his view, all things tend to certain effects as they act.

As I said above, few of us will have problems with this thesis if we take it to be confined to a comment on human beings acting with reasons. But can the thesis be reasonably extended so as to cover the activity of nonthinking or nonchoosing things? It obviously cannot if all tending to an effect is confined to rational agents. The question, however, is "Should all tending to an effect be construed as the seeking of an effect by a rational agent?" Clearly, Aquinas thinks that it should not. Or, as he says in his *De Principiis Naturae*, "Natural agents can tend to goals without deliberating, where tending towards is simply having a natural bias towards something."[53] But this is a position that is often denied on the ground that efficient causation only occurs just as one thing makes contact with another and modifies it somehow. The idea here is that we do not have to invoke final causality or goal-directed activity when noting efficient causality. We just have to note what changes what in some way, and it is nothing but brute fact, or even accidental fact, that some things result in certain effects coming about.

Yet, while trying to formulate what we might call natural laws concerning the behavior of things, we specify what powers various things have so as to bring about various results. And to do this is surely to note what tendencies things have. It seems to amount to noting that what is subject to human understanding, while being thought to have definite ways of acting, is, in fact, aiming in some sense and is not just pushed around by something else.

If we want to cite a cause that would refute Aquinas's claim that nonthinking things act in a goal-directed way, we would need to note something whose effect would not come about barring intervention. Yet to note the causal powers that things have is just to note what they will bring about unless interfered with. It is to note how things in the world tend to act, activity that seems to suggest that, even in nonthinking things, there is what Aquinas calls "acting for an end." In the long run, Aquinas takes such acting to be governed or ordered by God. But when making the claim that all things act for an end in SCG 3, Aquinas is not relying on his belief in God. He is saying, as Aristotle did, that we cannot sensibly think of acting things except as tending to ends, that we cannot understand X efficiently causing Y if we do not view X as acting in a goal-directed way given its nature, as acting so that its effect, once we have figured things out, is not surprising given the nature of its cause and its way of acting. And, to say the least, this is not an unreasonable position.

One might claim that laws of nature can be expressed only by noting regularities in the world, by noting that such and such regularly follows the occurrence of such and such. Yet appeal to regularity explains nothing, for we surely want to know "Why do the regularities occur?" and simply noting that they do occur just fails to engage with this question. We cannot explain laws of nature just by referring to regularities. Instead, it seems, we have to refer to how things act given their natures, and to do this would seem to commit us to accepting that even nonthinking things operate in a goal-directed manner. As Edward Feser observes:

> If we say that a law of nature is simply a kind of regularity, then we are lead into either a vicious circle or a vicious regress, since the regularity of connection between A and B is what we're trying to explain in the first place. For to explain regularities in nature in terms of efficient causal necessitation, efficient causal necessitation in terms of laws of nature, and laws of nature in terms of regularities, would be to go around in a circle; while if, to avoid this circularity, we say that the regularity enshrined in a law of nature is of a *higher order* than the sort we started out trying to explain, then we will now need an account of this higher-order regularity, and will thereby have pushed the problem back a stage rather than having resolved it.[54]

12.3.2 Evil and Privation

We do not tend to think of evil or badness as something unreal. We think of it as very much there in the world. We might readily accept that what is bad is not good, which is true enough, even if subject to the qualification that what is bad might be good in some respect. Yet can "What is bad is not good" mean that evil is always an absence of being, an absence or lack in something actually existing, a privation in Aquinas's sense of "privation" as *privatio boni*? Arguably not.

For consider the occurrence of pain. This is, surely, perfectly real. People and other animals experience pain, and experiences are real since they exist in people that have them. So how can it be plausibly maintained that pain lacks real existence or is a privation of goodness? You might say that to be in pain is not to be in a good state, and it seems hard to dispute that suggestion. Yet is being in pain not being in a positively bad state? And, therefore, is Aquinas not entirely misguided in saying that badness or evil is always a privation of being? It is, perhaps, easy enough to see why he might think that, say, blindness is nothing but the absence of sight, or that lameness is nothing but the inability to walk well. But can a similar account plausibly be given when it comes to pain? And can a similar account be plausibly given when it comes to the badness of wicked people? Can someone boiling and seething with unjustified anger, someone hell-bent on unjustly inflicting retributive harm, be seriously thought of as lacking something while being angry and vengeful? Do not such persons have positively bad properties, ones that exist in them?

In response to these questions, I presume that Aquinas, who must have experienced pain, and who certainly recognized that there are people who can truly be said to be bad, would ask us to consider why we take certain things to be bad. And he would, I think, say that we would have no notion of badness if we did not start off with some notion of goodness.[55]

To call something bad is to deny that it is good, but we do not need some notion of badness in mind when saying that something is good. When a mother nurses her healthy newborn child, she rejoices; but not because she is looking at it as something that lacks all the various ailments that children can be born with or acquire. She might know little of these and would probably not be able to list them. She just notes how well her child is. Worries about her child come later, and are grounded in what she knows of her child as a healthy one. Without knowledge of her child as healthy, she has no basis for considering it to be ailing or in a bad way. And so, it would seem, is the case with any evaluation of something as bad. To call something bad is to say that it does not match up to certain expectations that we have, and these expectations have to be grounded in our understanding of things being good. "It's bad" makes no sense unless some criteria for being good is provided for the "it" in question.

So if "X is bad or in a bad way" is true, that presumably has to be because X lacks what makes for goodness in it, because it lacks what we want it to have, or what we think it ought to have in order to flourish. Badness, therefore, is obviously an absence of goodness. But is it nothing but this? Again, what about pain, which seems real enough, and which makes for badness in those who endure it? You might say that pain is just an absence of pleasure, but that seems a somewhat implausible thesis if only because people and other animals really do feel pain and are, surely, not suffering from an illusion or delusion when they do so. Someone in pain is, surely, not just not enjoying pleasure but actually undergoing pain.

We must surely concede that pain is real and that it would be wrong just to describe it as an absence of pleasure. For people and other things do experience pain, and, if you wish to deny that this is so, I would not know what to say to you. That there are and have long been things suffering pain is, I would suggest, as certain a conclusion as any premises in a deductive argument that might be devised in order to disprove it. And pain cannot just be an absence of pleasure since there are things that are not even capable of pleasure that do not undergo pain. If I furiously beat my car with a stick because it is not working properly, it undergoes no pain, but it is also not being deprived of pleasure. If I beat you with a stick, however, you will feel pain, and you will feel pain if your teeth decay to a certain point without treatment, or if you break your leg.

At the same time, though, it seems odd to speak of pains as if they were substances of some kind. I can count the number of clocks in my apartment, but can I, in any comparable sense, count the number of pains there might be in that particular space? Perhaps I might be able to do so if you and I are the only sentient beings in my apartment and if both of us are suffering from a headache. There is my headache, and there is your headache. So maybe we should conclude that there are two pains. Yet pains are not substances or objects as people are. If we are going to make any sense of "There are two pains in my apartment because two people in my apartment have a headache," that will be because we recognize that there are two people in my apartment who are in pain, each of them suffering at the same time. Pains do not exist so as to be individuated and counted. Rather, it is people in pain who can be individuated and counted.

So what is going on when people are in pain? Clearly, they are ailing in some way. Some state of well-being that we and they look for in them is somehow being knocked out. Though pains are real and are felt, it is people who feel pain, and we deem them to be in a bad way while doing so because we are lamenting the lack of a certain state of well-being in them. Yet this thought would seem to be in line with Aquinas's claim that evil is always a privation of a certain good.

As I have noted, Aquinas does not think that his privation thesis is equivalent to "There is no evil or badness" or "Evil or badness does not exist." He holds that "John is in a bad way" would be true if John is in pain, regardless of how he comes to be in pain. But he also thinks that there is no badness that is a substance that is present in John if he is in pain. He thinks that John is undergoing various sensations because something that is a substance or thing, in the way that a pain is not, is acting in or on him so as to bring about these sensations in him, sensations that we call bad because we have some understanding of what well-being amounts to in people considered as what they essentially are.

So, I suggest, the reality of pain does not disprove what Aquinas says when claiming that badness or evil consists only in a privation of goodness. We are not talking nonsense when we speak of the reality of pain, but "reality" is a peculiar word in that almost anything you care to mention can be thought of as "real." The reality of God, so Aquinas would have said, is significantly different from, say, the reality of a stone. He would also have said that the reality of pain is significantly different from the reality of any spatiotemporal object or substance. Its reality, he thinks, lies in something, for whatever reason, ailing at a sensory level. And, as I have noted, he looks for some physical explanation of such a thing doing so.

Yet should Aquinas not have taken pain to be unqualifiedly bad? I do not think that he did so since in some of his writings he says that pain that we suffer might lead us to improve ourselves in some way.[56] Be that as it may, though, in the SCG he denies that evil suffered is unqualifiedly bad since he takes it to be an absence of good. Yet would he have been wrong if he thought that pain is unqualifiedly bad?

Those who suggest that pain refutes the claim that badness or evil is a privation of goodness typically assume that any right-minded person would accept that pain is unqualifiedly bad, and in the last paragraph I said that someone in pain is ailing in some way. But we might also note why pain might not be thought to be bad.

We might reasonably say that pain is bad because it grieves us, because being in pain amounts to being uncomfortable to a lesser or greater degree. Physical sensations of pain amount to discomfort in those who experience them. On the other hand there would be something wrong with us if we did not experience pain given the presence in or on us of what causes us to feel pain. You might not take yourself to be thriving if you burn your hand and thereby experience pain. Yet I would not be thriving if I did not feel pain when something very hot touches me.

There is a rare medical condition called congenital analgesia, and it is a bad thing. People who suffer from it do not experience physical pain. So they daily risk the danger of doing themselves damage. Why so? Because while the rest of us immediately seek to distance ourselves from what inflicts physical pain on us, victims of congenital analgesia do not, or do not always, do so. They can fail, for example, to notice that they have boiling water pouring over their hand, or that their teeth have decayed beyond repair, or that they are on the verge of a heart attack. So while pain amounts to unpleasant sensations, it might also be thought of as natural and beneficial and not unqualifiedly bad. Pain is a reaction to what is threatening in some way, so it is good even if the experience of pain is not attractive or desirable—good because the lack of it would amount to a sentient being just not functioning well. Congenital analgesia is a defect in a human being.

You might say that, though pain often instrumentally helps us to avoid certain evils, it is still bad and is of no use at all to someone suffering pain from a terminal disease. Yet this does not mean that pain should be thought of as refuting the idea that badness amounts to privation of goodness. The badness of pain arises as something working well falls victim to something else; it does not exist as a substance or thing in its own right. People and other sentient beings suffer pain as a natural consequence of what is acting in or on them to diminish them, which is what Aquinas thinks.

One objection to this suggestion would be the claim that pain is intrinsically evil, something evil or bad by nature. It would be a substance the essence of which is to be evil. As I have shown, though, Aquinas does not think that there is anything the essence of which is to be evil. Is he right to think this? I suggest that he is, since if evil is a falling away from what is good, and if to be actual is to be good in some way, we cannot make sense of the idea that there is something the essence of which is to be nonactual. This is not to say that pain does not exist. It is just to say that if someone is in pain, which can sometimes help us to thrive, the pain that the person has can be rightly described as a privation of goodness in them.

Pain, of course, is not always a matter of sensation. We speak of ourselves as being in pain because we have lost a loved one or have failed to achieve some goal at which we were aiming. Here "pain" means an intellectual awareness accompanied by an emotion. Why do we speak of pain arising from the loss of a loved one, or pain felt when we have not succeeded in what we were trying to do? I assume that our primary sense of "pain" is physiological. When we think of pain we think first of all of someone undergoing various unpleasant physical sensations. So, in the language of Aquinas, we apply the word "pain" to talk about grief and disappointment while doing so analogically (see chapter 5, section 1 here).

For Aquinas, though, analogical predication, if it makes sense, has to rely on there being some likeness between two things described as being analogically X or Y. And there is a likeness between pain as a matter of pure sensation and pain consisting in grief or disappointment. For one thing, the pain of grief or disappointment is not totally devoid of physicality. We feel grief in our bodies, and we also feel disappointment in our bodies. Grieving people, who are not to be thought of as angels, do not just react to the death of a loved one as if it were something to be considered purely intellectually. They cry, or try to stop themselves crying. They feel tense. Their blood pressure or heartbeat is different from what it would be were they ecstatically happy. Sometimes they display symptoms of depression, and they often undergo other physical changes. Grief cannot be properly understood without reference to physiology, even though some grieving people might seem to be totally unmoved physically.

In his long discussion of emotion in *Summa Theologiae* 1a2ae,22–48, Aquinas argues that emotions (*passiones animae*) always involve some physical factor, so he thinks that, if they are painful, that is because the person undergoing the emotion is suffering in some way. Yet what would it be for someone to be suffering emotionally? Surely, it would be for them to be woundingly agitated or unhappy. To be in that state, however, would be for them to lack well-being of some kind considered as human beings. Of course, certain emotions might lead us to help ourselves. My feeling fear when I confront a bear might lead me to run and get out of danger. So emotions can enable us to thrive. Insofar as they can be thought of as being painful, however, they are what amounts to us lacking goodness of some kind, which seems to square with Aquinas's account of evil as privation.

What I have just said, though, needs to be considered together with what Aquinas thinks about goodness in general. Abstracting from what he says about God as goodness itself, he does not think that there is any such thing (substance) as goodness any more than he thinks that there is any such thing (substance) as badness. He does not think of created goodness as being a distinct substance. He thinks that there are created substances that are good in various ways.

We know what is being said when it is said that X, Y, and Z are all yellow. But we do not, in the same sense, know what is being said when told that X, Y, and Z are *either* good or bad (see chapter 6, section 6.2 here). X might be a good desk, while Y might be a good pumpkin, and Z might be a good human being. X might be a bad parent, while Y might be a bad (i.e., defective or sick) dog or cabbage, and Z might be a bad human being. As I have shown, Aquinas thinks that the adjective "good" is noun-dependent in that we will only understand what "X is good" means when we know what "X" stands for. To be sure, Aquinas thinks that there is a general account of "good" to be given in terms of which "good" means "desirable" or "attractive." But "desirable" and "attractive" are as noun-dependent as "good" when it comes to us knowing what precisely they amount to given that they can be applied to very many things and to things coming under different descriptions.

In general, Aquinas thinks that something is desirable in that it is succeeding or flourishing in some way, in that it actually displays particular properties or attributes that it needs in order to be in good shape considered as what it is essentially. Correspondingly, he takes "badness" to signify some lack of such actual properties. He is not, of course, thinking of badness as a vacuum filled with nothing. That is because he generally takes badness to be ascribable to actual spatiotemporal things, not things with holes of nonmatter in them. In speaking of evil as privation, he is referring to what is not there in something in which it should be there, the absence of being here being something for which he thinks there might be any number of reasons, though all of them based on goodness of some kind. When it comes to pain, he thinks that this is always a diminishment in something brought about by something acting in or on it.

So perhaps Aquinas's notion of badness as privation has something to commend it. It accords with our natural inclination to say that being bad or in a bad way is to be lacking or defective. It also accords with our natural inclination to suppose that if something is in a bad way, there has to be something accounting for this. And it accords with Aquinas's view that goodness is a matter of actuality, not a lack of form. It might be criticized for supposing that what is real is not real at all but somehow nonexistent. Yet Aquinas does not think that all that is real has to be an existing substance; nor does he think that what is real but not an existing substance cannot amount to a lack of being in something. He thinks that something can be in a bad way because of the presence in it of something that causes it to be deficient in various ways. This is obviously so since viruses can badly affect people and since glue poured into a computer will truly screw it up. In Gilbert and Sullivan's *Iolanthe*, the Fairy Queen chides her subjects for falling in love with mortals. This, she says, is weakness. The fairies reply: "We know it's weakness, but the weakness is so strong." Aquinas knows well enough that there are weaknesses that can be thought of as strong and, therefore, positive—pain being an obvious example. But this does not lead him to conclude that such weaknesses are existing substances. Accepting that they amount to weaknesses, he seeks a causal explanation for them in something that does not display weakness as it goes about its work. And why should he not do so?[57]

You might think that he should not, and you might completely disagree with what I have said in defense of the drift of SCG 3,2–15. Now, though, I need to try to help you to understand, and perhaps think about, SCG 3,16–25.

13

The End of All Things and of People in Particular (SCG 3,16–63)

AS I HAVE shown, Aquinas spends time early in SCG 3 arguing that all agents act for good ends. Following the discussion of evil in SCG 3,4–15, he returns to the notions of goodness and ends in SCG 3,16–25 and then proceeds to say what he takes to be the ultimate end of human beings. You may wonder why Aquinas introduces his treatment of evil where he does. Indeed, you may take it to amount to a rather long digression pointlessly stuck into a discussion of goodness and ends. Yet there is a definite flow of thought at work here. If everything acts for a good end (SCG 3,2–3), then how can evil be aimed at as an end? In SCG 3,4–15 Aquinas is evidently trying to answer this question by saying that evil is not, in fact, aimed at as an end and that it is not something positive or actual that aims at some end. With those points made, he feels that he can return to actually existing things aiming at good ends, as he does from SCG 3,16 onward.

SCG 3,16–25 is arguing that all creatures tend to, or aim at, the goodness that is God. This thesis, though, might strike you as puzzling or downright unintelligible. Does a cabbage aim at God's goodness? Does my cat? Do atheists? How could they? What would it mean to say that they could? In SCG 3,16–25, however, Aquinas is obviously aware that people might raise questions like these since he engages with them, at least implicitly. So at this point I shall try to explain what Aquinas is driving at when maintaining that all creatures aim at God, whom he believes to be goodness itself.

13.1 Creatures Aiming at God (SCG 3,16–25)

When Aquinas says that creatures aim at, tend to, or intend an end, he means that they ultimately operate as seeking what is good.[1] In thinking this, however, he is reasoning analogically.

We would have no problem with statements like "John was aiming to please Mary by buying her flowers," or "When buying her flowers, John was intending to please Mary," or "John was seeking to please Mary by buying her flowers." The verbs "to aim," "to intend," and "to seek" are quite at home when it comes to referring to what people do. Indeed, when we speak of something aiming or intending or seeking, we first of all think of the something in question being human.

As I have shown, however (see chapter 5, section 2 here), Aquinas holds that one and the same word can be used in different but related senses given certain connections between what it signifies when used to talk about different things. We might spontaneously think that only people aim or intend or seek. Yet cats can surely be thought of as aiming at mice when trying to pounce on them, and arrows can surely be said to be aiming at a target when directed to one by an archer. And, though intention might be taken to be only ascribable to thinking things, tending to an end can be ascribed to nonthinking things, as when we say that cats tend to chase mice, or that daffodil bulbs tend to produce yellow flowers, or that acid tends to burn. Again, while it might be thought that people are the highest class of seekers in the world, it makes sense to say that, as tending to certain ends, other things in the world can be spoken of as seeking. Cats seek food. Plants seek moisture as they extend their roots.

In other words, as substances of different kinds can be thought of as having certain ways of working, so can they be thought of as tending in various ways: tending, Aquinas thinks, in ways that benefit them. Of course, not all *tending to* benefits things that tend since disaster can strike something tending to an end, and Aquinas is obviously aware of this. On the other hand, though, he thinks that, unless interfered with, substances tend to what is objectively good for them. You might say that people often tend to what is objectively bad for them. Again, though, Aquinas is aware of this and would say that people tend to what they intellectually take to be good.

So Aquinas thinks that many different things aim, tend to, and seek. His view is that, by virtue of having characteristic ways of behaving, all naturally occurring things that operate or act also aim, tend to, or seek. But why should they be thought of as aiming at God or as tending to God or seeking God? For Aquinas, they do so because God is their maker.

At this point, consider human beings who make things. What are they doing? They are bringing about something that they intend to bring about, something that they think of as good. If I want to make a clock, then I will normally want to make a good clock.[2] Human makers intend to bring about what is good in some way, and their succeeding in doing so both fulfils their intention as makers and results in something that amounts to goodness or perfection in what they produce. The goodness of what I might make is in what I make as reflecting what is in me as aiming at it.

Yet now consider naturally occurring things. For example, consider my cat Sweetie. Can he be said to be good as reflecting an aim intended by the maker of cats? Aquinas thinks that he can. He thinks that Sweetie is a good cat insofar as he reflects what God aims at in making good cats. Sweetie, of course, can be thought as being made by its parent cats. Yet these obviously cannot be thought of as makers that determine what cats are, for they are themselves cats. I can determine what some artifact I produce is; but no cat can determine what a cat is. All it can do is reproduce itself. If anything can be thought of a maker of cats, it cannot be a cat; it must be something that makes it be that there are cats that can make other cats.

Now, Aquinas holds that God is the ultimate maker since God is the maker of all things, the creator of everything that is not divine. So, he thinks, the actions of all things reflect God's intention for them as their maker, rather as a clock can reflect the intentions of a clockmaker. Their aiming at what is good amounts to an embodiment of a blueprint in God's mind, so to speak. What they aim at is in God before it is in them: in God before being in them because they are reflecting what God intends them to be. For Aquinas, the goodness at which creatures aim, and their aiming at this goodness, is in God as their maker. In seeking their goodness, they are seeking what God intends.

In this sense, thinks Aquinas, even Sweetie is seeking God. For, thinks Aquinas, when aiming for ends, he is seeking what is in the intention of God as his maker. In Aquinas's view, what creatures tend to derives from and is in God. He therefore thinks that, since God is the primary maker, creatures acting for ends are always seeking what is in God as making them. As Herbert McCabe succinctly observes, according to Aquinas:

> God is the ultimate maker, and, as such, the ultimately desirable, the ultimate good. Every creature, just in naturally tending to its own goodness, is seeking God as what ultimately intends it, as its maker. And this is what, for Aquinas, the goodness of God is first of all about: it is the goodness, the attractiveness or desirability inseparable from being Creator. God is the *omega* because he is the *alpha*, the end because he is the beginning. God is good because he is the Creator; not, first, in the moral sense that it was very good of him to create us and we should be grateful, but in the metaphysical sense that, being Creator he must be the ultimate object of our desire, without which we would have no desires. Aquinas puts this point by saying that each creature tends to its own natural perfection, but God "contains the perfections of all things," meaning not that he *is* all things, but that, as maker, he intends their perfections. God has these perfections, says Aquinas, "in a higher way," in the way that they are in the intention of the *maker* before they are in the *thing made*—not before in time but in the sense that the presence of

these perfections in the made things *depends on* them being the intention of the maker.[3]

McCabe did not intend to do so, but I take him in this passage to provide an admirable paraphrase of the reasoning in SCG 3,16–24. In these chapters Aquinas is not asking us to believe that all creatures consciously act with God as their end, as I might act so as to be united with someone I love. In SCG 3,19 he says that all things "tend to become like God" (*quod omnia intendunt assimilari Deo*); but he does not mean that Sweetie has pretensions to divinity. Aquinas is clear that no creature can be what God is. Or, as he says in SCG 3,20, "Creatures do not attain goodness in the same measure as it is in God, though each thing imitates divine goodness according to its measure."[4] He means that creatures can be thought of as like God, but only for particular reasons. Hence, for example, in SCG 3,21 he notes that acting creatures have causal power and exhibit goodness to different degrees. In the same chapter he says that "the effect tends to the likeness of the agent," and "the agent makes the effect like to itself, for the effect tends toward the end to which it is directed by the agent."[5]

The "big idea" in SCG 3,16–24 is indeed what McCabe presents as Aquinas's thinking in the quotation above. When reading through these chapters you might be perplexed by some things that Aquinas says that clearly depend on cosmological views that are now outdated. In SCG 3,22, for example, he talks about "celestial bodies" and their movements in ways that no physicist would today. Again, in SCG 3,23 he refers to the motion of the heavens (*motus caeli*) deriving from an intellectual principle (*a principio intellectivo*). At the same time, however, he is maintaining that any creature that acts for an end is aiming to act in conformity with what God intends. In doing so, of course, he is not claiming that all creatures always act in conformity with God's will. He is not, for example, denying that people can act sinfully. His point is that created agents always act for ends, and that their doing so amounts to them aiming at certain goods.

However, Aquinas evidently thinks that there is a serious difference when it comes to the actions of nonthinking things and the actions of thinking things. He holds that the actions of nonthinking things are directed to God insofar as they cannot but aim at what God, as their maker, intends them to be. But he also maintains that agents with intellect can choose to diverge from goodness that God intends for them, goodness that they aim at while operating at a purely physical and nonthinking level. Such agents, he thinks, are not merely things without intellect aiming at God as being made by God so as to conform to what God intends them to be, as is my cat. Such agents, he suggests, have an ability to turn away from what God intends even though they nonintellectually act for ends and, in doing so, tend to the goodness that is God.

In other words, Aquinas subscribes to the following theses in SCG 3,16–24: (1) nonthinking things tend to what God is as they exist and act as created by God; (2) thinking things do the same, but they do not always do so as they reflect on their actions or operations and make choices; (3) thinking things can aim or fail to aim at God because they are able to make choices. According to Aquinas, everything physical tends to God as seeking its good. But he also thinks that there are physical things (i.e., human beings) that do not always operate or act at a purely physical level. These things, he holds, can deviate from what is truly good for them.

What, however, does Aquinas take to be truly good for us? In SCG 3,25 he says that the end of everything with intellect is to understand God. My cat, Aquinas thinks, has arrived at its end, and has somehow become God-like, just by existing and acting as God intends it to act. In addition, however, Aquinas thinks that beings with intellect would be frustrated if there were something to know that they do not know. I do not mean that Aquinas supposes that I would necessarily be in a bad way if, for example, I do not know what is going on in my local supermarket as I am cooking my dinner, or if I do not always know what my friends are doing. His position is that knowers are made by God to understand, to lay hold of what is intelligible. And, since he takes God, as pure form, to be supremely intelligible, he thinks that not to have some understanding of God would be an impediment or privation in something with intellect. So he concludes that such a thing must aim at understanding God—somehow. As he says in SCG 3,25:

> Each thing intends, as its ultimate end, to be united with God as closely as is possible for it. Now, a thing is more closely united with God by the fact that it attains his very substance in some manner, and this is accomplished when one knows something of the divine substance, rather than when one acquires some likeness of him. Therefore, an intellectual substance tends to divine knowledge as an ultimate end....The more a person knows, the more is he moved by the desire to know. Hence, human natural desire tends, in the process of knowing, to some definite end. Now this can be nothing other than the most noble object of knowledge, which is God. Therefore, divine knowledge is the ultimate end of human beings.[6]

This ultimate end Aquinas refers to as felicity (*felicitas*) or happiness (*beatitudo*). He says: "The ultimate end of people, and of every intellectual substance, is called felicity or happiness, because this is what every intellectual substance desires as an ultimate end, and *for its own sake alone.* Therefore, the ultimate happiness and felicity of every intellectual substance is to know God."[7] But in what does felicity or happiness consist? This question is Aquinas's concern in SCG 3,26–63.

13.2 Ultimate Felicity for Humans (SCG 3,26–63)

In SCG 3,37 Aquinas bluntly says: "Our ultimate felicity consists only in the contemplation of God."[8] He means that perfect human happiness amounts to a "vision of the divine substance," as he puts it in SCG 3,57.[9] Before he discusses this vision of God, however, Aquinas spends time ruling out possible candidates for the title "That in which human felicity ultimately consists."

13.2.1 What Ultimate Human Felicity Is Not: 1 (SCG 3,26–36)

According to Aquinas, ultimate human felicity does not consist in an act of will (*in actu voluntatis*) (SCG 3,26). Nor does it consist in bodily pleasures (*in delectationibus carnalibus*) (SCG 3,27), in honors (*in honoribus*) (SCG 3,28), in glory (*in gloria*) (SCG 3,29), in riches (*in divitiis*) (SCG 3,30), in worldly power (*in potentia mundana*) (SCG 3,31), in goods of the body (*in bonis corporis*) (SCG 3,32), in sensory experience (*in sensu*) (SCG 3,33), in acts of the moral virtues (*in actibus virtutum moralium*) (SCG 3,34), in being prudential (*in actu prudentiae*) (SCG 3,35), or in acting creatively as an artist (*in operatione artis*) (SCG 3,36).

In denying that ultimate human felicity consists in an act of will, Aquinas is concerned to stress that it lies in knowing, not in being attracted or desiring. He is convinced that we become united to God by willing in certain ways. Yet, he argues, as beings capable of knowing, it is in knowing God that our ultimate happiness must lie.[10] So, he says:

> Since happiness is the proper good of an intellectual nature, happiness must pertain to an intellectual nature by reason of what is proper to that nature. Now appetite is not peculiar to intellectual nature; instead it is present in all things, though it is in different things in different ways. And this diversity arises from the fact that things are differently related to knowledge. For things lacking knowledge entirely have natural appetite only. And things endowed with sensory knowledge have, in addition, sense appetite.... But things possessed of intellectual knowledge

also have an appetite proportionate to this knowledge, that is will. So, the will is not peculiar to intellectual nature by virtue of being an appetite, but only in so far as it depends on intellect. However, the intellect, in itself, is peculiar to an intellectual nature. Therefore, happiness, or felicity, consists substantially and principally in an act of the intellect rather than in an act of the will.[11]

And to this argument Aquinas adds some others, the main ones being these:

1. What we will is prior to our willing it; we move to what we perceive as desirable. So the object of our willing is something known, something that leads us to want it. Therefore, "no act of will can be the first thing that is willed."[12] Yet happiness, as the ultimate end, is the first thing that is willed; so an act of will cannot be happiness or felicity. In other words: by will or appetite we are drawn to something; yet it is not an act of will that we are drawn to; it is something we desire.
2. Willing can be misconceived insofar as we can will what is not truly good. So ultimate human happiness has to amount to understanding rather than willing.
3. By willing we tend to what we desire but might lack. So our ultimate happiness cannot just lie in willing or desiring or loving. It must consist in obtaining what we will or desire or love, on condition that this is something supremely good, something than which nothing greater can be willed, desired, or loved.

When it comes to what else Aquinas thinks ultimate human happiness cannot be, a major notion governing his discussion is that if X is to be ultimate human happiness, then it has to be an end beyond which no other can be thought desirable. It cannot be a good that is a means to an end. It must be ultimately desirable, first among what is desirable for people, something desirable for its own sake. With this idea in mind, therefore, Aquinas argues as follows.

1. Human felicity cannot consist in bodily pleasures, such as food and sex, since these are ordered to ends not identical with them—such as bodily preservation or the generation of offspring. In SCG 3,27 Aquinas also argues: (1) since ultimate happiness is not an act of will, it cannot lie in bodily pleasures which belong to sensory desire; (2) bodily pleasures are enjoyed by nonhuman animals, so distinctively human happiness cannot lie in them; (3) the final end for people must involve what is ultimately best

for them, which cannot be enjoying certain physical sensations but rather lies in understanding of some kind; (4) ultimate human happiness cannot lie in union with something inferior to what is human; yet sensory plea-sures derive from union with what is inferior to human beings; (5) some-thing that is not good unless it is moderated is not good of itself; yet the enjoyment by human beings of bodily pleasure has to be in moderation so that people are not damaged; so bodily pleasure is not the ultimate good for people; (6) if bodily pleasures were goods in and of themselves, then enjoy-ing them as much as possible would be good for people; yet excessive en-joyment can be positively and physically harmful; (7) if ultimate human happiness consisted in bodily pleasures, it would be wrong ever to display temperance concerning them; but it is sometimes virtuous to do so, and temperance is a virtue; (8) if the ultimate end of everything is God (see SCG 3,17), the ultimate end for people must be that by which they are brought closest to God; yet sensory pleasures can impede union with God since they can drag people down to wallowing among bodily things.[13]

2. "That which is good and desirable on account of something else is not the ultimate end. But honor is of this sort. A person is not rightly honored unless it be because of some other good that is present in that person. And this is why people seek to be honored, desiring, as it were, to have a witness to some good feature present in them."[14] In SCG 3,28 Aquinas also argues: (1) honors are conferred on one by others; they do not amount to a perfect way of functioning, the possession of perfect happiness; (2) people attain perfect happiness as a result of being virtuous; but having an honor conferred on one is not something one can bring about by choosing to act well; (3) even evil people have honors conferred on them; so ultimate human happiness, in which there can be no evil, cannot lie in honors.

3. By "glory," Aquinas means "a widely recognized reputation" accompa-nied by praise.[15] With this understanding in mind, he denies that ultimate human happiness lies in glory since people seek glory so as to be honored. He adds: "If honor is not the highest good, much less is glory."[16] In SCG 3,29 he also argues: (1) we praise those who are on the way to arriving at a good end, not those who have achieved ultimate human happiness; so ultimate human happiness cannot chiefly consist in praise; (2) it is better to know than to be known; so ultimate human happiness cannot amount to being well known; (3) it is good to be known for good things one has done; yet these good things are better than being well known, from which it follows that it is not the case that the highest good is being widely known; (4) our highest good should be perfect, but the knowledge that comes about as one is well known comes with

uncertainty and error; (5) our ultimate good should be something abiding; yet glory comes and passes away, and "nothing is more variable than opinion and human praise."[17]

4. Our highest good or happiness cannot lie in riches or wealth since these "are only desired for the sake of something else; they provide no good of themselves but only when we use them."[18] In SCG 3,30 Aquinas also argues: (1) one can hardly take our highest good to lie in having things from which we chiefly benefit only when we get rid of them; (2) that which gives human beings ultimate happiness must be better than them; but people are better than riches or wealth since these "are but things subordinated to our use";[19] (3) whether or not we obtain wealth or fortune does not always depend on what we choose to do; there is an element of chance involved in the acquisition or losing of wealth or fortune; yet our highest good cannot consist in what can be acquired or lost by chance.

5. Nor can it lie in worldly power since chance frequently plays a big role in our acquiring or losing this. Also, great worldly power can be had by people who are bad. Yet "people are deemed good chiefly in terms of the highest good" and "are not called good, or bad, simply because they have power."[20] In any case, power is relative, while perfect human happiness must be intrinsic to those who enjoy it; and power can be used for good or ill, while this cannot be true of ultimate human happiness. In addition, of course, human power is fragile; it comes and goes and depends on various things; yet nothing like this can be that in which ultimate human happiness consists.

6. Our highest good cannot consist in goods of the body since such goods can be had by both bad and good people. They are also unstable and largely beyond our control. By "goods of the body," Aquinas is not thinking of the sensory delights to which he refers in SCG 3,27. As he says himself, he is thinking of goods such as health, beauty, and strength, and he denies that ultimate human happiness can lie in these, not only because they can be had by both good and bad people but also because they can be had by nonhuman animals, some of which possess them to a greater degree than we do.

7. Ultimate human happiness cannot lie in goods to be attributed to people because their senses are working well. The sense powers of nonhuman animals often work well, yet nonhuman animals cannot attain the ultimate happiness that is proper to human beings. In any case, "Intellect is better than sense. So, the good of the intellect is better than the good of the senses. Therefore, our highest good does not lie in sense."[21]

8. Ultimate human happiness cannot lie in actions performed by people with moral virtues since these are just means to acquiring happiness.

Aquinas writes: "Human felicity is incapable of being ordered to a further end, if it is ultimate. But all moral operations can be ordered to something else....Therefore, our ultimate felicity does not lie in moral operations."[22] Aquinas means that, for example, we act with bravery so as to obtain victory, and we act with justice so as to preserve peace. Yet, he suggests, our ultimate happiness or end cannot consist in a virtuous striving for something other than it. In general, Aquinas argues in SCG 3,34, ultimate human happiness does not consist in striving to be virtuous. Rather, it amounts to having arrived at some final perfect state. Since he thinks this, in SCG 3,35 he takes it to be obvious that ultimate human happiness cannot consist in the acting on the basis of the virtue of prudence. "The act of prudence," he says, "is only concerned with things that pertain to the moral virtues." He continues: "Now our ultimate felicity does not lie in the acts of the moral virtues [see SCG 3,34], nor, then, in the act of prudence."[23]

9. Ultimate human happiness does not lie in acting creatively as an artist since "the knowledge that pertains to art" is "practical knowledge."[24] Aquinas means that the knowledge that pertains to art is knowledge that helps one to bring about a result, like a wonderful building or a beautiful painting. So, he thinks, it is knowledge ordered to an end and cannot be the ultimate end for people. In any case, he adds, art only results in artifacts, "which cannot be the ultimate end of human life."[25]

So, in SCG 3,37 Aquinas concludes:

> If the ultimate felicity of people does not consist in external things which are called the goods of fortune, nor in the goods of the body, nor in the goods of the soul according to its sensitive part, nor as regards the intellective part according to the activity of the moral virtues, nor according to the intellectual virtues that are concerned with action, that is, art and prudence—we are left with the conclusion that the ultimate felicity of people lies in the contemplation of truth.[26]

The contemplation of truth, says Aquinas, is an operation unique to human beings; other animals do not engage in it. Furthermore, he adds, the contemplation of truth "is ordered to nothing else as an end, for the contemplation of truth is sought for its own sake."[27] And what truth does Aquinas have in mind as that the contemplation of which provides human beings with ultimate happiness? He thinks that it is God. "Our ultimate felicity," he says, "consists in the contemplation of wisdom, based on the considering of divine matters...[and]...our ultimate felicity consists only in the contemplation of God."[28]

13.2.2 What Ultimate Human Felicity Is Not: 2 (SCG 3,38–48)

Having arrived at this verdict, Aquinas embarks on another set of arguments designed to show what ultimate human happiness cannot be. More precisely, he moves on to argue that ultimate human happiness cannot be something achieved by people prior to their death.

As I have shown, Aquinas thinks that people do enjoy some knowledge of God in the present life (1) since there is some vague awareness of God present in people by nature (see SCG 1,11), (2) since "God exists" is demonstrable (see SCG 1,13), and (3) since we can demonstrate that certain perfections should be attributed to God and that certain ways of being should not (see SCG 1,14–102). Aquinas also holds that Christians are able to assent to truths about God by faith even if they are not able to demonstrate them (see SCG 1,5–8). In SCG 3,38–40, however, Aquinas denies that ultimate human happiness amounts to knowledge of God in any of these senses.

To start with, he takes what he calls the "common and confused knowledge of God which is found in practically all people" to be imperfect and to admit of error.[29] Yet, says Aquinas, human happiness cannot be defective.

Again, he argues, while certain propositions concerning God are demonstrable, not everyone is able to arrive at demonstrative knowledge of God (see SCG 1,4), and even those who can still lack a knowledge of what God is (see SCG 1,14). Such "proper knowledge as we have of God through demonstration," says Aquinas, "is not sufficient for our ultimate felicity."[30] Why not? Because it "still remains in potency to something further to be learned about God, or to the same knowledge possessed in a higher way."[31] Even when we have managed to achieve some knowledge of God by demonstration, Aquinas laments, "we still remain ignorant of many things" and lack ultimate happiness.[32]

As for what he calls "the knowledge of God which is through faith" (*cognitio Dei quae est per fidem*), Aquinas takes this to be imperfect since it does not amount to knowledge even if what the believer holds to by faith is true. Yes, Aquinas agrees, by faith we lay hold of what is true. But, he adds, we remain with a lack of understanding. He writes:

> In the knowledge of faith, there is found a most imperfect operation of the intellect, having regard to what is on the side of the intellect, though the greatest perfection is discovered on the side of the object. For the intellect does not grasp the object to which it gives assent in the act of believing. Therefore, neither does our ultimate felicity lie in this kind of knowledge of God.[33]

We often say that seeing is believing. Yet Aquinas takes mere believing to be needed precisely when there is a lack of sight or understanding. So he regards faith as intrinsically inferior to knowledge and thinks that our ultimate happiness cannot lie only in having faith. Ultimate happiness, he says, puts an end to natural desire. Yet, he goes on to observe, "The knowledge of faith does not bring rest to desire but rather sets it aflame, since all people desire to see what they believe."[34]

13.2.3 Ultimate Human Happiness and Separate Substances (SCG 3,41–46)

Aquinas therefore thinks that ultimate human happiness consists in a knowledge of God that goes beyond any knowledge of God that we can have in this life. He is, however, aware of lines of argument that might be thought to suggest otherwise—lines of argument that claim that, in this life, we can know or understand separate substances (i.e., purely intellectual beings as considered in SCG 2,96–101) and thereby enjoy a fulfilling knowledge of God.

Why would someone say that a knowledge or understanding in this life of separate substances would provide us with some fulfilling knowledge of God? Because such a person might think that understanding separate substances would involve an understanding of God that is superior to the ways of knowing God that Aquinas refers to in SCG 3,38–40. And it is thinking along these lines that Aquinas is concerned with in SCG 3,41.

In SCG 3,41 Aquinas refers back to the SCG's previous discussion of separate substances. Then he says this:

> A separate substance, in knowing its own essence, knows both what is above and what is below itself, in a manner proper to its substance. This is especially necessary if what is above it is its cause, since the likeness of the cause must be found in the effects. And so, since God is the cause of all created intellectual substances...then separate intellectual substances, in knowing their essence, must know God himself by way of a vision of some kind. For a thing whose likeness exists in the intellect is known through the intellect by way of vision, just as the likeness of a thing which is seen corporeally is present in the sense of the viewer.[35]

If this line of thinking is correct, then understanding a separate substance would seem to involve a grasp of what that substance knows. And if separate substances know God as Aquinas takes them to do (if they enjoy some kind of vision of God), then it would seem that if we can understand separate substances, we thereby gain some vision of God ourselves. But can we understand separate substances in this life?

Aquinas raises this question in SCG 3,41, and he then goes on to note and discuss arguments coming from three thinkers, two of them Arabic:[36] Avempace (1095–1138), Alexander of Aphrodisias, and Averroes. Aquinas presumes that each of these authors asserts that we can in this life understand separate substances. Since his discussion of them running through SCG 3,41 to SCG 3,44 is detailed and, I suspect, only of interest to specialists in the history of philosophy, I am not going to try to talk you through it. Instead, I shall note where it leads Aquinas.

His conclusion is that the arguments he has been discussing are flawed, that we cannot understand separate substances, and, therefore, that we do not in this life have a knowledge of separate substances that gives us a knowledge of God that is superior to the general knowledge of God had by most people, to the knowledge of God derived from demonstration, and to the knowledge of faith. "A thing is futile," says Aquinas, "which exists for an end which it cannot attain."[37] Then he argues:

> Since the end of people is felicity, to which their natural desire tends, it is not possible for our felicity to be placed in something that we cannot achieve. Otherwise it would follow that we are futile beings, and our natural desire would be incapable of fulfilment, which is impossible. Now, it is clear from what has been said that we cannot understand separate substances on the basis of the foregoing opinions. So, our felicity is not located in such knowledge of separate substances.[38]

In SCG 3,45–46 Aquinas asks whether there is any way in which people can understand separate substances in this life. In SCG 3,46, for example, while citing texts from St. Augustine, and while assuming that the human soul is not material, he wonders whether human beings, just by being what they are, might directly or immediately understand what is incorporeal. Yet, he argues, though we can know *that* we exist just because we are thinking things, we do not know *what* we are, and what a human soul is, just by existing as things going through various intellectual operations. Knowing what we are, he says, depends on thinking hard concerning how we function and what we aim at. It is not to be gained simply by being human, and "the soul does not understand itself through itself in this life."[39] Here Aquinas means that we do not understand nonmaterial things just by having a human soul.

So, in SCG 3,47, Aquinas ends up saying that, in this life, we cannot "see God through his essence" (*quod non possumus in hac vita videre Deum per essen-*

tiam).⁴⁰ We do not know God's essence and, therefore, do not know what God is (see SCG 1,14–27). According to Aquinas, the essence of God is not something we can know or understand in this life as we might be able to understand what the essence of something in the spatiotemporal world might be. So, he argues, ultimate human happiness is not to be found in any knowledge of God that we have in this life, given the fact that, in this life, our knowledge of what things are is crucially dependent on sensory experience. In SCG 3,47 Aquinas notes passages in the writings of St. Augustine that might be thought to present a different view; but, rightly or wrongly, and while citing some other texts of Augustine, he argues that they should not be thought to do so. When it comes to our understanding of God in this life, Aquinas takes Augustine to be on his side. He reads Augustine as saying that our present understanding of God latches onto what God is rather as our reflection in a mirror matches what we are. A mirror image does not capture the full reality of the one looking into it; it is only a reflection. By the same token, says Aquinas, the knowledge of God that we have in this life fails to capture what God is. Continuing to pursue the mirror analogy, and with Augustine still in mind, he claims that God cannot be seen by us in his essence but can only be seen "through a glass in a dark manner," as St. Paul says in 1 Corinthians 13:12. Consistently with what he has been arguing earlier in the SCG, Aquinas goes on to say:

> Although this mirror, which is the human mind, reflects the likeness of God in a closer way than lower creatures do, the knowledge of God which can be taken in by the human mind does not go beyond the type of knowledge that is derived from sensible things, since even the soul itself knows what it is as a result of understanding the natures of sensible things.... Hence, throughout this life God can be known in no higher way than that whereby a cause is known through its effect.⁴¹

So, says Aquinas in SCG 3,48, "Our ultimate felicity does not come in this life." Given what he has just been arguing, you might think that Aquinas has already given reason enough for making this assertion. Be that as it may, however, SCG 3,48 spells out a number of other reasons as to why we cannot be ultimately happy in this life. I summarize them as follows.

1. Our ultimate human end satisfies us so that we seek nothing more. In this life, however, there is always something more to seek; in this life we do not understand everything.
2. Perfect happiness is stable and enduring. When people attain felicity they "attain stability and rest, and that is why this is the notion of all people

concerning felicity, that it requires stability as part of its essential character."[42] In this life, though, there is no certain stability, however happy we are. We are continually dogged by illness and misfortune.

3. Death overcomes us before we have reached ultimate happiness.

4. True and ultimate happiness cannot be mixed up with evil. In the present life, however, we can never be entirely free from evil, both physical and psychological.

5. We naturally shrink from death and have sorrow because of it. But we cannot achieve freedom from it in this life, so we cannot be ultimately happy in this life.

6. Ultimate happiness is a doing, not a tendency to act in certain ways. "But it is impossible to perform any action continuously in this life."[43]

7. All human happiness in this life comes with sorrow attached. We cannot have perfect happiness in this life since we can always lose what happiness we have because of death or sickness. The best we can have is an imperfect happiness of some kind.

8. If we are to arrive at ultimate or perfect human happiness, and if we cannot arrive at it in this life, we must arrive at it after death.

9. Everyone coming to grasp truth is tending to perfection, but nobody ever arrives at full knowledge. In this life, we are always in the process of learning and are never in the state of having reached an ultimate end. "Thus, since our ultimate felicity in this life seems mainly to consist in speculation, whereby the knowledge of the truth is sought...it is impossible to say that people achieve their ultimate end in this life."[44]

10. We do not in this life actually understand all things. So in this life we are not ultimately happy as we would be if enjoying a knowledge of God that is clearer and more perfect than we have in this life.

13.2.4 Beatitude (SCG 3,49–63)

Aquinas, therefore, thinks that people can only be ultimately happy, can only reach their highest end, by knowing God after death more clearly than they are able to in this life. To be happy in this way, he says, is to enjoy beatitude or ultimate happiness. But what is involved in beatitude? Can something more precise be said about human beatitude than anything that Aquinas has already maintained in the SCG? Aquinas clearly thinks that there is more to be said about ultimate human happiness. Hence, SCG 3,49–63.[45]

In SCG 3,49–63 Aquinas is concerned to maintain that the souls of human beings are, after death, able to achieve what we might call a direct or noninferential knowledge of what God is (i.e., God's essence, which, as I have shown, Aquinas says we cannot at all know in this life).[46] He does not claim that souls enjoying beatitude are able fully to comprehend what God is; he holds that only God can do this. Yet he does claim that God's essence is known by what enjoys beatitude, even though he thinks that some of the blessed might understand what God is better than others. He speaks of this beatific knowledge as a *seeing* (*visio*) of some kind, though not one that people can achieve by reflecting on themselves in this life, and not one that they can arrive at without God's help. He thinks of beatitude for human souls as a miracle, as brought about only by God.

Is it certain that any human soul will enjoy beatitude? You may think that it is not, since even if we concede that God exists, we are not thereby committed to the view that God will leave anything that is part of a human person in existence after the person has died. In the SCG, however, Aquinas is evidently supposing that no natural desire can exist in something unless the thing were able, in principle, to have it satisfied.[47] So he finds it evident that if God has made us such that it is a knowledge of God that makes for our happiness, then God will certainly give our souls a beatific knowledge of God, unless we do something to leave ourselves unworthy of it. And he thinks that God can do this by enlightening our intellects and bringing it about that God's form is received in them directly and without intermediaries. According to Aquinas, the very form of God can be received by the soul of a human being in a way that allows it to know the essence of God.

In working toward this conclusion, Aquinas makes these points:

1. The souls of the dead cannot understand what God is just by understanding what they are. One might understand what the cause of an effect is by understanding the effect. But in understanding what they are as effects of God, human souls cannot understand what God's essence is, if only because, as effects of God, creatures of God do not fully show forth what God is as their creator. It is "not possible for the divine substance to be understood through a created likeness."[48] The ultimate happiness of human souls "does not lie in the knowledge of God in which they know him through their substances, for their desire still leads them on toward God's substance."[49]

2. God knows himself by being himself, and God's knowledge is God. Human souls can come to see God by sharing in God's knowledge. God's essence is both the object and that by which one who sees God actually does see God. Human souls see God as the pure form that God is brings about knowledge of it in them. They see God as the very form of God, which brings about

understanding in them. "Thus, then, shall we see God face to face, in the sense that we shall see him without a medium, as is true when we see a person's face."[50]

3. "No created substance can, by its own natural power, attain to the vision of God in his essence."[51] "No intellectual substance can see God through his divine essence unless God is the agent of this operation."[52]

4. The beatified human soul benefits from "an influx of divine goodness," which may be compared to a light that illumines something in darkness. "This disposition whereby the created intellect is raised to the intellectual vision of divine substance is fittingly called the light of glory, not because it makes some object actually intelligible, as does the light of the agent intellect, but because it makes the intellect actually powerful enough to understand."[53]

5. The light of glory "falls far short of the clarity of the divine intellect. So, it is impossible for the divine substance to be seen as perfectly by means of this kind of light, as it is seen by the divine intellect itself....It is impossible for any created intellect's vision to be equal to the seeing of the divine substance."[54]

6. "There is no created intellect so low in its nature that it cannot be elevated to this vision [sc. the vision of God]."[55] That is because the light of glory is not something that any creature naturally possesses; it comes about only by God's action, and "what is done by supernatural power is not hindered by diversity of nature, since divine power is infinite."[56]

7. "It is possible that one of those who see God may see him more perfectly than another, even though both see his substance."[57]

8. The vision of God is the final end of intellectual beings. Yet such beings naturally desire to understand what things are in the world and how they relate to each other. So human souls who see the divine substance will have such desire satisfied. This, however, does not mean that any created intellect can see all that God knows in knowing the divine essence.[58]

9. To see God by the light of glory is not to see in successive stages. That is because God is one single and simple thing rather than a book whose pages can be turned over as we seek to learn more. Therefore, the soul as seeing God shares to some extent in God's eternal life, in which there is no successiveness (see SCG 1,15). "So, this vision is perfected in a sort of participation in eternity. Moreover, this vision is a kind of life, for the action of the intellect is a kind of life. Therefore, the created intellect becomes a partaker in eternal life through this vision."[59] "This vision consists in a participation in eternity, as completely transcending time."[60] It follows from this that those who see God will never cease to see God. The vision of God,

since it lacks successiveness, is not in time. "So, it is impossible for people to lose it, once they have become partakers of it."[61]

10. When the soul of a human being arrives at the vision of God, all the desires of that person are fulfilled. Since God is Truth, our desire for truth is satisfied in the vision of God. Our desire to live in accord with reason will also be satisfied by this vision since reason, "having been enlightened by the divine light," will have arrived at what it ought "so that it cannot swerve away from what is right."[62] We crave honor and renown, yet souls enjoying the vision of God "are raised through this vision to the highest peak of honor, because they are in a sense united with God"; and such souls enjoy renown insofar as they are recognized for what they are by God and all who are united with God by seeing him.[63] People also desire wealth, pleasure, and continued existence. However, souls seeing God enjoy "a plenitude of all goods" by enjoying God, "who contains the perfection of all good things."[64] And the vision of God gives great pleasure and is more pleasurable than "the delight of the sense" and comes with no fear of loss.[65] As for being preserved in existence, that is built into the soul's vision of God since this exists as lacking successiveness.

13.3 The Value of SCG 3,16–63

How shall we evaluate the positions adopted by Aquinas in SCG 3,16–63? We shall obviously take them to be worthless if we cannot follow Aquinas in holding that God exists and if we cannot follow him so as to think that people are more than what is purely material. We might, perhaps, readily concede that, as Aquinas holds, ultimate human happiness cannot consist just in the enjoyment of bodily pleasures and the like. After all, Aristotle, who did not share Aquinas's notion of God, and who had no belief in life after death, was at one with Aquinas when it comes to the idea that human beings are most happy when engaging in contemplation or understanding.[66] Yet why should we assume that anyone will be ultimately happy in the sense of "ultimately happy" that Aquinas has in mind in SCG 3,25–48?

You might say that, as a Christian theologian, Aquinas is entitled to suppose that we shall live having died and that God will ensure that we do so. In SCG 3, however, Aquinas seems not to be presuming Christian doctrine. He appears to reason philosophically, albeit that he frequently peppers his discussions with quotations from the Bible. SCG 3 seems to be following up on Aquinas's promise in SCG 1,9 to consider, while following "the way of reason" (*per viam rationis*), what can be known of God, the coming forth of creatures from God, and the ordering of creatures to God as their end. But does it do so successfully?

It does not if we take it to rest on demonstrations to the effect that our souls will survive the death of our bodies. Nor does it do so if we take it to rest on demonstrative arguments concluding that any human soul enjoys the beatific vision. But Aquinas does not attempt to demonstrate either that our souls will survive our bodily death or that anyone is guaranteed to enjoy the beatific vision. As I have shown (see SCG 2,55), he argues that our souls are not perishable as are physical objects. He does not, however, take this conclusion to be equivalent to "Our souls have to survive the death of our bodies." Whether they do or not is, for Aquinas, a matter of faith, as is the belief that some souls enjoy the beatific vision. When it comes to SCG 3,16–63, therefore, the question "Has Aquinas proved that our souls survive our death or that any human soul enjoys the beatific vision?" is irrelevant. More to the point would be the questions "Has Aquinas shown that we have a natural desire for the vision of God?" and "Has he shown that nothing short of the beatific vision can give us ultimate happiness?"

That people have a natural desire for what Aquinas calls "ultimate happiness" has been denied since to say that they do seems to imply that, by nature, people can arrive at a knowledge of what God is. The idea here is that we can provide no account of human nature that would make it seem capable of what Aquinas means by "ultimate happiness." Why not? Because, so it has been argued, human beings cannot lift themselves up to the vision of God by themselves, because only God can tell us what our destiny is, and because this destiny cannot be deduced from what we know of ourselves by human reasoning. Yet Aquinas does not seem to be denying any of these points in SCG 3,16–63. In these chapters he never claims that people have an ability to secure the beatific vision by means of their natural capacities. Nor does he deny that our future is in the inscrutable hands of God, or that our going forward to enjoy the beatific vision is something we can deduce to take place from what we might know of ourselves as reflecting on human nature without benefit of divine revelation. In SCG 3,16–63 what Aquinas claims is that we have an unlimited desire to know, and that this desire would be frustrated if we could never know what God is.[67] He does not assert that we are as guaranteed to enjoy the beatific vision just by desiring it as, all things being equal, we might take ourselves to be guaranteed to nourish ourselves should we choose to drink milk. He thinks that if we come to enjoy the beatific vision, that has to be because of God raising us to it by what he calls "the light of glory" (see SCG 3,53). In SCG 3,16–63 Aquinas is not offering an account of human beings that depicts them as inevitably gaining beatitude. He is noting that people, given what we know of them, can only be ultimately happy *if* beatified. He is also noting how goods less than the beatific vision cannot ultimately satisfy them. In doing so, he proceeds philosophically and in a way that he thinks ought to be appreciated even by non-Christians.

Along with some famous theologians such as Karl Barth, you might say that philosophical reflection can do us no good before the Christian God since that God is beyond reason and can only be approached as one addressing us in revelation (see chapter 2, section 3.1 here). Yet, like Barth, Aquinas believes in divine revelation. For him, that truly declares what is and what is not the case when it comes to our future. On the other hand, however, he does not think that divine revelation can conflict with what we know to be true independently of it. For Aquinas, truth cannot contradict truth. And, he thinks, it is not hard to see, apart from divine revelation, that we are naturally inclined to knowledge of the kind that he has in mind when he speaks about the beatific vision. And, when defending this conclusion, he surely makes some good points. For it makes sense to say that *if* we are to be ultimately happy, that has to be because certain natural desires that we have will be satisfied. More precisely, it makes sense to say that if we are to be ultimately happy, that cannot be because of our possession of what we can obtain by our efforts in this life, that it cannot be because of what Aquinas discounts as amounting to ultimate human happiness in SCG 3,26–44. Even an atheist can agree that physical pleasures and so on can leave one unsatisfied. Aquinas, of course, is no atheist. But he does think that what atheists can truly perceive deserves to be granted a hearing when it comes to understanding what we might be before God in the long run. And perhaps he is not wrong to do so if truth cannot contradict truth.

Is he, however, right to home in on knowledge as our final end, as that which will make us truly happy? Aquinas's account of ultimate human happiness seems to be austerely intellectual. Yet might one not argue that ultimate human happiness cannot come about without there being other kinds of satisfaction? For why should intellectual joy (the vision of God as Aquinas thinks of it) be the only thing that might make us happy in the long run? Why not intellectual joy accompanied by physical joy? After all, we are not just things able to know. We are things able to be happy at a sensory level. So how can it be said that sensory enjoyment cannot be part of our ultimate happiness? Why focus only on understanding? Why not say that we cannot be ultimately happy unless we are also satisfied at the sensory level?

As I will show, in SCG 4 Aquinas holds that the dead shall be raised in bodily form. In SCG 3,16–63, however, he focuses only on happiness considered as a matter of knowledge, which he takes to be wholly incorporeal. But should he have done this? Should he not, instead, have argued that our ultimate happiness must consist both in our knowing God and in us enjoying bodily satisfactions?

You will see why he does not do this while noting his arguments to the effect that ultimate human happiness cannot consist in X, Y, or Z (see in particular SCG 3,27–32). According to Aquinas, bodily pleasure cannot be our final end, cannot amount to perfect happiness, since it is something we share with other animals and since intellectual joy is superior to physical joy. But in SCG 3,16–63 Aquinas does not seem to note how much a desire for physical pleasure makes us be what we are. If we were to become creatures without interest in physical pleasure, then we would, presumably, have turned into things that we are not. So how can our ultimate happiness consist *only* in something intellectual—the vision of God?

Aquinas seems to think that there has to be but *one* final end for people when it comes to their happiness. Yet, without denying that the vision of God will satisfy us to a high degree, might one not suggest that if we enjoy the beatific vision without physical satisfaction, then it is not really we who enjoy that vision? Aquinas, of course, thinks that it is only the souls of the blessed who enjoy the beatific vision. So one can see why he concentrates on the idea of the vision of God being that which gives ultimate happiness to what is left of us when we have died. Be that as it may, his confidence in SCG, 3,16–63 in it being only a matter of knowledge in which ultimate human happiness consists might be regarded as suspect since it seems to disregard much that we physically enjoy and hope to enjoy in the future.

I remember offering some presents to a child and saying "You can have only one of them." The child replied "I want all of them." In SCG, 3,16–63 Aquinas seems to think that, when it comes to ultimate happiness, there is only one present on offer. Yet perhaps he might have thought better when it comes to this conclusion while reasoning philosophically, as he clearly is in SCG 3,16–63. Later in the SCG, and relying on what he takes to be divine revelation, Aquinas declares that our bodies shall be raised from the dead as incorruptible and immortal. While making this point, Aquinas says that "only the occupation of the contemplative life will persist in the resurrection" (SCG 4,83).[68] Yet he also argues that, come our resurrection, we shall "have bodies one can handle, composed of flesh and bones."[69] And, he adds, our bodies will be "immune from every evil."[70] In other words, in SCG 4 Aquinas takes our final end to include physical happiness or well-being. This, I think, ought to make us wonder why in SCG 3 he so resolutely homes in on intellectual happiness as constituting our ultimate well-being.

You might suggest that he does so because in SCG 3 he is not relying on divine revelation so as to establish the theses that he defends. Yet if it is philosophically plausible to say that physical well-being cannot be lacking if people are to be ultimately happy, to claim that people will have to enjoy physical well-being in order to be ultimately happy is not to rely on revelation. It is to rely on what might be thought to be necessary for ultimate human happiness *should* people be granted it.

In response to this point Aquinas might observe that, in SCG 3,25–48, he is merely concerned with what can make us ultimately happy with respect to our status as having intellect. Yet in these chapters he frequently refers to ultimate happiness as what can be achieved by human beings, not just pure intellects. He speaks of *felicitas humana* (human happiness). If, however, it is this that he is concerned with in SCG 3,25–48, then he surely ought not only to conceive of it as something intellectual since human beings are not just intellectual substances. In short, though one might well see the force of SCG 3's denial that ultimate human happiness can lie in honors, glory, riches, and so on, one might reasonably feel that an account of ultimate human happiness that presents it as only a matter of seeing God intellectually, only a matter of understanding, cannot really be taking full account of the word "human" in the phrase "ultimate human happiness."

In SCG 3,63 Aquinas declares that "our every desire is fulfilled" in the beatific vision. As I have shown, he defends this conclusion while noting that sensory delight, which even nonhuman animals enjoy, is inferior to intellectual enjoyment. What he does not seem to consider, though, is that human beings are not just intellects and that, if sensory pleasure is lacking to them, one might wonder whether they remain as human beings. As I noted in chapter 11, Aquinas does not think that a human soul is a human being. So why, in SCG 3, does he resolutely proceed to report on what he takes ultimate human happiness to be only by confining it to understanding? Might one not suppose that something important has dropped out of the picture in his claim that ultimate human happiness is only to be found in knowing? Might one not think that, even if Aquinas is right to say that, among creatures in the spatiotemporal world, only human beings stand out as able to know, it does not follow that human beings will be ultimately happy only by knowing?

Be that as it may, though, by the end of SCG 3,63 Aquinas takes himself to have shown that God is the end of all things, including people. But he still takes himself to need to explain how God governs creatures, what divine providence amounts to both in general and with respect to people. Aquinas starts on this task in SCG 3,64. So let us now follow him as develops his arguments.

Providence at Work (SCG 3,64–110)

"FROM THE POINTS that have been set forth," says Aquinas at the start of SCG 3,64, "we have adequately established that God is the end of all things."[1] If God is that, however, then God must govern or rule all things. God must provide for them or exercise providence over them. So, starting at SCG 3,64, Aquinas turns directly to the topic of God's providence, a subject that will occupy him until the end of SCG 3. In discussing it, he breaks his treatment into two parts while following up on what he promises in SCG 3,1 concerning his order of procedure for SCG 3,64–163. First, he talks about providence in general, insofar as it amounts to God's governing of all creatures (SCG 3,64–110). Then, in SCG 3,111–163, he turns to providence with an eye on "creatures possessed of understanding."[2] What he says in SCG 3,64–110 is the topic of this chapter. I shall turn to the arguments of SCG 3,111–163 in the following one.

That God governs all things seems obvious to Aquinas given his previous claims that everything created derives from God in its entirety and that all creatures are ordered to the goodness that is God. If these conclusions are true, he says, then God clearly governs all creatures. Soldiers in an army, he observes, have the good of their commander as an end and are governed by their commander. By the same token, Aquinas presumes, "Since all things are ordered to divine goodness as an end...it follows that God, to whom this goodness primarily belongs...must be the governor of all things."[3] Again, he says that if God is the first unmoved mover, then God must operate in all that moves, and must do so by understanding. Yet, Aquinas notes, "to rule or govern by providence is simply *to move things toward an end through understanding*"—meaning that "God by his providence governs and rules all things that are moved toward their end."[4] As I have shown, Aquinas thinks that even nonthinking things move toward ends. And this, too, is something that leads him to say that God governs creatures. For, he reasons (reintroducing a line of thinking to be found in SCG 1,13):

> It is impossible for things that do not know their end to work for that end, and to reach that end in an orderly way, unless they are moved by someone possessing knowledge of the end (*nisi sint mota ab aliquo*

habente cognitionem finis).... So, the whole working of nature must be ordered by some sort of knowledge. And this, in fact, must lead back to God....Therefore, God governs the world by his providence.[5]

Aquinas notes that some ancient philosophers held that "all things come about as a result of material necessity, the consequence of which would be that all things happen by chance and not from the order of providence."[6] Yet, he insists, if the universe is of God's making, it is governed by understanding and is not just composed of what acts blindly or randomly with no goal or purpose behind it.

14.1 *God as Acting in All Things (SCG 3,65–70)*

To start with, Aquinas goes on to say that God governs things just by making them to exist as tending to goodness (SCG 3,65). Creatures cannot tend to goodness unless they exist, Aquinas argues, since "to the extent that they exist, they bear the likeness of divine goodness which is the end for things."[7] God, says Aquinas, not only makes things to be by making them to begin to exist; God also makes them to be for as long as they exist. So God's creative causality is at work in the sheer existence of creatures at any time, and God "preserves all things in being through his intellect and will."[8] Unlike something in the world producing its like, Aquinas argues, God makes creatures to be while not being one of them. God does not generate creatures. As the first cause of all things, God creates, which means that he "preserves things in being through his operation."[9] Echoing much that I have already shown him to be saying in SCG 3,65 Aquinas, is clear that "it is impossible for the being of a thing to continue except through divine operation" and that "all natural things are preserved in being by nothing other than the power of God."[10] This conclusion, in turn, leads Aquinas to maintain (SCG 3,66) that, insofar as a creature can be thought to produce what exists, it does so only as acting by God's power. "It is," says Aquinas, "as a result of divine power that a thing gives being."[11] He adds: "The first agent is God. So, since being is the common product of all agents, because every agent produces actual being, they must produce this effect because they are subordinated to the first agent and act through its power."[12] Aquinas, of course, does not mean that created agents produce being from nothing as does God. Yet he does think that they bring it about that real things or situations come about; and his point is that they do so by virtue of God's creative power.

From all of this Aquinas thinks it safe to conclude (SCG 3,67) that God causes the operations of all things that operate. He means that all acting creatures act as made to exist by God when acting as they do and that God, therefore, operates in every creaturely operation. "Every operating agent," he says, "is a cause of being in some way, either of substantial or accidental being. Now, nothing is a cause of being unless by virtue of its acting through the power of God.... Therefore, every operating agent acts through God's power."[13] He continues: "Every power in any agent is from God, as from a first principle of all perfection. Therefore, since every operation results from a power, the cause of every operation must be God."[14] It is sometimes said that, once God has established something in existence, the thing can continue to function on its own. But this is certainly not what Aquinas thinks. For him, no creature can do anything unless God brings it about that it does so. He writes:

> Just as God has not only given being to things when they first began to exist, and also causes being in them as long as they exist, conserving things in being.... So also has he not merely granted operative powers to them when they were originally created, but always causes these powers in things. Hence, if this divine influence were to cease, every operation would cease. Therefore, every operation of a thing is traced back to God as to its cause.[15]

And if that is true, Aquinas immediately concludes, God must be everywhere (SCG 3,68). Given that he takes God to be immaterial, Aquinas is not suggesting that God is in all places as occupying them dimensively. He means that God is present everywhere as causing the operations of the things the existence of which constitute places. "The mover and the thing moved," he notes, "must be simultaneous.... But God moves all things to their operations.... Therefore, God is in all things."[16] Here Aquinas is invoking the principle that the action of an agent is in the patient (see chapter 3, section 4.3 here) so as to claim that if God acts in the operations of creatures, then God is in them as an agent cause is present in its effect.

In that case, however, does it not follow that creatures do not actually produce anything? If God brings about the existence and operations of creatures, how can it be that there is any causal agent other than God? Given the arguments of SCG 3,65–68, should Aquinas not conclude that created things are never really causes at all? These questions do seem to arise given what Aquinas claims in SCG 3,65–68, and he is aware of arguments, mostly coming from Muslim philosophers, holding that created things do not genuinely act if God is actively at work in them. He alludes to these arguments in SCG 3,69. Yet he is unconvinced by them. Why? Because, for a number of reasons spelled out in SCG 3,69, he thinks it would be foolish to deny that created causes do have causal efficacy, that, for example, it would be wrong to say that chefs do not produce meals or that bullets have never killed people. God, he asserts, is the maker of all things; but this does not entail that there are no secondary causes (created causes acting by God's power while also being true causes). If I push the trigger of a gun that emits a bullet that wounds someone, the fact that I do so does not mean that the bullet is not, in fact, wounding the person. By the same token, Aquinas reasons, God's action as primary cause in the operations of creatures does not mean that the creatures are not acting. "We do not," he says, "take away their proper actions from created things, though we attribute all the effects of created things to God, as an agent working in all things."[17]

Aquinas acknowledges how it might seem difficult "to understand how natural effects are attributed to God and to a natural agent."[18] He notes, for example, that it might seem odd to say that one action can proceed from two agents. He also says that if something can be brought about by one thing, there would appear to be no need for other agents to be invoked for the coming about of the thing in question. Again, he observes that one might suppose that "if God produces the entire natural effect, then nothing is left of the effect for the natural agent to produce."[19] Nevertheless, Aquinas sticks to his claim that God moves and empowers created agents to act and that they do genuinely act even though this is so. He says:

> The same effect is not attributed to a natural cause and to divine power in such a way that it is partly done by God, and partly by the natural agent; rather, it is wholly done by both, according to a different way, just as the same effect is wholly attributed to the instrument and also wholly to the principal agent.[20]

What Aquinas means here is that created agents act and get things done even though their power to act derives from God working in them. For Aquinas, creatures are always secondary causes as they bring about effects. They are secondary, not primary, because all created activity derives from God. Yet Aquinas believes that secondary causes are genuine causes. They have power; so they act. Their power derives from God acting in them; so what they bring about by their power is also what God is bringing about while acting in them. Or, as Aquinas argues prior to what I just quoted from him:

> In every agent, in fact, there are two things to consider: namely, the thing itself that acts, and the power by which it acts. Fire, for instance, heats by means of heat. But the power of a lower agent depends on the power of the superior agent, according as the superior agent gives this power to the lower agent whereby it may act; or preserves it; or even applies it

to the action, as the artisan applies an instrument to its proper effect, though he neither gives the form by which the instrument works, nor preserves it, but simply gives it motion. So, it is necessary for the action of a lower agent to result not only from the agent by its own power, but also from the power of all higher agents.... And just as the lower agent is found immediately active, so also is the power of the primary agent found immediately in the production of the effect. For the power of the lower agent is not adequate to produce this effect of itself, but from the power of the next higher agent; and the power of the next one gets this ability from the power of the next higher one; and thus the power of the highest agent is discovered to be of itself productive of the effect, as an immediate cause.[21]

Here Aquinas is thinking of a primary agent as something the action of which runs through what the agent brings about by means of secondary causes. He is thinking of causal series comparable to the example I gave in chaper 3, section 1.2 in which a book moves as resting on a moving book that is, in turn, moved by my hand acting as I will it to move. So, he reasons, if the actions of creatures amount to actions that are empowered by God as they occur, creatures that bring about effects are instruments of God yet, for all that, causes in their own right.

14.2 What Divine Providence Does Not Exclude (SCG 3,71–74)

Given what Aquinas has so far been saying about God's providence, should we, perhaps, suppose that certain real things cannot exist? More precisely, should we not conclude that if Aquinas is right about God's providence there could not be, as there appear to be, (1) instances of evil, (2) contingency in things, (3) freedom of choice, and (4) fortune and chance? Aquinas thinks not. In SCG 3,71–74 he maintains that (1)–(4) here are not excluded by divine providence.

14.2.1 Evil (SCG 3,71)

As I noted in chapter 12, Aquinas agrees that some things are bad or evil, but in SCG 3,71, he maintains that this fact does not conflict with belief in God's providence. God's governing of things, he holds, is quite compatible with some things failing in certain respects. Such governing, he says, does not rule out secondary causes that are defective in their action, or secondary causes that bring about defects in other things. Nor is it contrary to there being evil in one thing resulting from the flourishing of another, or there being degrees of goodness in things (implying the existence of what is less than perfect). Again, Aquinas reasons, "Many goods are present in things which would not occur unless there were evils." He continues:

> For instance, there would not be the patience of the just if there were not the malice of their persecutors; there would not be a place for the justice of vindication if there were no offenses; and in the order of nature, there would not be the generation of one thing unless there were the corruption of another. So, if evil were totally excluded from the whole of things by divine providence, a multitude of good things would have to be sacrificed.[22]

Indeed, Aquinas goes on to say, certain human goods would be lacking if there were no evils. He writes:

> If no evils were present in things, much of the good of people would be diminished, both in regard to knowledge and in regard to desire and love of the good. In fact, the good is better known for its comparison with evil, and while we continue to suffer certain evils our desire for good grows more ardent. For instance, how great a good health is, is best known by the sick; and they also crave it more than do the healthy.[23]

In this connection Aquinas goes so far as to say that if someone says "God does not exist since there is evil," one might reasonably reply "If evil exists, God exists" since "there would be no evil if the order of good were taken away, since its privation is evil."[24]

14.2.2 Contingency (SCG 3,72)

By "contingency" Aquinas means "what is able to be or not to be, what is not there by absolute necessity, what is not guaranteed always to exist." As I have shown, he accepts that some things come about that are not intrinsically necessary or causally necessitated by other things in the universe. So he finds no difficulty in saying in SCG 3,72 that a world governed by God can contain what is not causally necessitated. His view is that God makes things to be what they actually are.[25] He therefore reasons that if some things or processes are contingent, they have been established as such by God. He agrees that if God has willed to create something, the something in question cannot but exist. Yet, he

suggests, the something in question need not be necessary given the operation of various created causes. Why not? Because some creatures can be impeded in their activity by others and because some things can come about that
are not determined by the activity of any secondary cause (secondary to God,
that is). "Since there are many things among proximate causes that may be
defective," says Aquinas, "not all effects subject to providence will be necessary, but a good many are contingent."[26]

One might, of course, think that a truly provident God would create a
world lacking contingency. Yet, observes Aquinas, such a world would lack
diversity when it comes to ways of being and would not be a world in which
things of different kinds interact while reflecting the power of the creator to
make things of different kinds with different abilities. "Every necessary
thing," he says, "as such, always exists in the same way. It would be incompatible, then, with divine providence, to which the establishment and preservation of order in things belongs, if all things came about as a result of
necessity."[27] Here Aquinas seems to be saying that a world containing
nothing but what is necessary would hardly be a world that could be thought
to be governed at all. It would be something that always has to be just
what it is.

14.2.3 Freedom of Choice (SCG 3,73)

In SCG 3,73 Aquinas is considering the view that, given God's providence, no
creature can be said to act freely. He rejects this view in the light of his idea
that secondary causes can be genuine causes and that not all secondary
causes are necessitated by things in the world to bring about certain effects.
Nonintelligent agent causes, he notes, operate in a regular way and invariably
bring about certain effects unless something interferes with them. But, he
adds, reasoning creatures (i.e., human beings) can deliberate and decide between alternatives, even though they act as governed by God and even though
their very being is God's doing. And, says Aquinas, freedom to choose is a
good that is utterly compatible with God's governing of creatures to good
ends. "Whatever pertains to perfection," he argues, "is to be preserved by
providence rather than what pertains to imperfection and deficiency."[28] He
goes on to say: "The fact that the will is a contingent cause arises from its perfection, for it does not have power limited to one outcome but rather has
the ability to produce this effect or that; for which reason it is contingent in
regard to either one or the other."[29] In general, Aquinas reasons in SCG 3,73,
freedom of choice is a reality, and it is good that it should exist in a world governed by God.

14.2.4 Fortune and Chance (SCG 3,74)

There is fortune or fortuitousness (*fortuna*) and chance (*casus*), thinks Aquinas, when something comes about that is not directly the result of a single cause or a set of causes working together for one end. It is not, he would have said, fortuitous or a matter of chance that arsenic administered in large doses kills people, or that carts move when people push them; but it would be fortuitous or a matter of chance if two people who had not seen or thought about each other for years suddenly bumped into each other in a place that neither of them had visited before, or if I missed an appointment because I inadvertently took a wrong turn on the way to it. Aquinas does not deny that fortuitous or chance events lack causes, but he thinks of such events as not necessitated by a single cause or a group of causes exercising their power in a typical way. And in SCG 3,74 he claims that fortuitous or chance events can occur in a world governed by God. Indeed, he argues, "it would be contrary to the essential character of divine providence if all things occurred by necessity."[30] Things that happen rarely, he says, can be just as much present in a world made by God as can things that happen with regularity (see SCG 3,72); and things can come about apart from what agents aim at. In short, Aquinas reasons that there being what is, to us, unexpected, and there being what is unintended, is what we might actually expect in a world made by a God who is not bringing about a scenario in which every event is rigidly determined by prior ones.

14.3 Providence and Singulars (SCG 3,75–76)

Continuing with somewhat the same theme, in SCG 3,75–76 Aquinas maintains that God's providence extends to individual things that are able to be or not to be (*quod providentia dei sit singularium contingentium*) and that it extends to them immediately (*quod providentia dei sit omnium singularium immediate*). His point is that God does not just govern things that are not generated or corruptible, and that God governs what is generated and corruptible without having to rely on intermediaries. As I have noted, Aquinas distinguishes between created things that are contingent and created things that are necessary; and, as we saw in chapter 8, he holds that things of these two kinds can exist in a world willed by God. In SCG 3,75 he is basically just repeating himself when it comes to there being created contingent things, while adding in SCG 3,76 that God governs contingent created things directly by making them to exist with the powers that they have. It cannot, Aquinas reasons, be that God lacks direct and perfect knowledge of contingent things. Nor can it be that God does not will them to be as the individuals they are with the powers that they have. So, he says, just as God knows contingent created individuals by virtue of his omniscience, he "must also establish order for them immediately."[31] Aquinas agrees that God can use secondary causes to bring about what he wills. He remains clear, however, that secondary causes operate as willed to exist and act by God. He notes that human governors employ people to carry out their plans and that this might lead one to think that God governs created contingent causes by, so to speak, handing on the work to assistants. Yet, so he argues, human governors "pass the buck" because they lack knowledge and power, as God does not. In Aquinas's view, God's creating and governing of creatures is not the activity of one who needs any help from another. As we read in a particularly clear section of SCG 3,76:

> In the case of things regulated by human providence we find that a certain higher overseer thinks out the way in which some of the big and universal matters are to be ordered, but this overseer does not personally think out the ordering of the smallest details; rather, that business is left to be planned by agents at a lower level. But, as a matter of fact, this is so because of the overseer's deficiency; either because he or she does not know the circumstances for the individual details, or because he or she is not able to think out the order for all, by virtue of the effort and length of time that might be needed. Now, deficiencies of this kind are far removed from God, because he knows all singular things, and he does not make an effort to understand, or require any time for it; since, by understanding himself he knows all other things [see SCG 1,46]. Therefore, God plans even the order for all singular things.[32]

14.4 Providence and Secondary Causes (SCG 3,77–83)

I have already shown that Aquinas thinks that God governs creatures by operating through secondary causes. But he returns to this conclusion in SCG 3,77–83 so as to spell out some additional details concerning it. In doing so, he adopts a rather hierarchical notion of causality, one that I have already shown surfacing in SCG 3. He argues that God rules some creatures by means of other ones that are superior to them. The idea that God should do this seems to be one that Aquinas derives from the thought that God would bring it about that a world that best reflects God as the source of all being would be one in which all possible ways of being are to be found. This thought, in turn, leads

Aquinas to say that, should God choose to create, God can be expected to make a world containing various things that depend for their activity on things greater than them in certain ways.

Aquinas's development of this idea might seem to you unobjectionable to some degree since part of it amounts to him only saying that beings with intelligence frequently direct things that lack it. As we read in SCG 3,78: "Of all creatures the highest are the intellectual ones.... Therefore, the rational plan of divine providence demands that the other creatures be ruled by rational creatures."[33] Things become murkier, however, as Aquinas develops this thought.

In SCG 3,79, for instance, he claims that "the lower ones of an intellectual nature must be governed by the higher ones."[34] This conclusion leads him to hold that there are intellectual things that govern intellectual beings such as us, if only by helping them in some way. In SCG 3,80 he refers to angels as "spiritual things" that know God better than we do and share in God's governing of creatures. In SCG 3,82, Aquinas, using arguments that will seem archaic to many people now, says that the planets (the celestial bodies, as he calls them) can have an enormous influence on earthly events.[35]

Whether or not we swallow what Aquinas says about angels and heavenly bodies as causal agents, however, it is clear what he is chiefly driving at in SCG 3,77–83. This is the thesis that "as far as the planning of the order to be imposed on things is concerned, God disposes everything by himself."[36]

With a view to angels and heavenly bodies, we also need to notice that, while Aquinas attributes serious causal efficacy to them in SCG 3,80 and 82, and again in SCG 3,91, he resolutely *denies* (1) that celestial bodies can coerce our intellects (SCG 3,84), (2) that they are the causes of our willing and choosing (SCG 3,85 and 87), (3) that corporeal effects on earth come about from celestial bodies of necessity (SCG 3,86), and (4) that angels or any other intellectual substance can directly cause our choosing and willing (SCG 3,88). In defending these denials, Aquinas draws on arguments he has previously offered to the effect that our intellects are immaterial so as to develop criticisms of thinkers whom he takes to dispute them. God, Aquinas insists, "is the first principle of our acts of counsel and of will."[37] He agrees that we might be aided by what secondary causes bring about in us while operating under God's governance (this point is underscored in SCG 3,92); but he denies that all events come about as necessitated by them as they so operate (this point is emphasized in SCG 3,92, in which Aquinas eschews talk about fate, considered as the subjection of all things "to the necessitation of the stars").[38] For Aquinas, it is God's providence that rules the created order, not the causality of secondary agents empowered by God.

14.4.1 Some More Objections to Belief in Divine Providence (SCG 3,94–96)

In SCG 3,94, however, Aquinas raises five objections to this conclusion.

The first runs: "If all things that are done here below, even contingent events, are subject to divine providence, then, seemingly, either providence cannot be certain or else all things happen by necessity."[39] The idea here seems to be (1) that if there are contingent events, then God cannot guarantee what will happen, which would undermine belief in divine providence, and (2) that if all that happens falls under God's providence, then everything that happens is determined or necessitated to happen.

The second and third objections appeal to God's knowledge. According to the second, if God foresees what will happen, then it has to happen. More precisely:

> If divine providence is certain, then this conditional proposition must be true: *If God foresees this, then this will happen.* Now, the antecedent of this conditional proposition [i.e., "God foresees this"] is necessary, for God is eternal. Therefore, the consequent [i.e., "this will happen"] is necessary, for every consequent in a conditional proposition must be necessary when the antecedent is necessary. So, the consequent is like the conclusion of the antecedent, and whatever follows from a necessary proposition must be necessary. Therefore, it follows that, if divine providence is certain, all things must occur by necessity.[40]

According to the third objection, "it is either necessary, if all things are foreseen by God, that divine providence be not certain or else that all things happen by necessity."[41]

> Suppose that something is foreseen by God; for example, that a certain man will become a ruler. Now, it is either possible that he will not rule, or it is not. But, if it is not possible that he will not rule, then it is impossible for him not to rule; therefore, it is necessary for him to rule. However, if it is possible that he will not rule, and if, given the possible something impossible does not follow, then it does follow that divine providence will fail; hence, it is not impossible for divine providence to fail. Therefore, it is either necessary, if all things are foreseen by God, that divine providence be not certain or else that all things happen by necessity.[42]

As for the fourth objection, the argument is: if God foresees all things, then fate, not God, accounts for what happens, there is no choosing done by anything, and "free choice is taken away if divine providence be certain," as are all contingent causes.[43] And, according to the fifth objection: "Divine providence does not exclude intermediate causes, as we showed above [see SCG 3,77]. But, among causes, some are contingent and capable of failing. So it is possible for an effect of providence to fail. Therefore, God's providence is not certain."[44]

The objections to the certainty of divine providence that Aquinas notes in SCG 3,94 are not stupid ones, and some of them are still pressed by contemporary philosophers. We should, therefore, not be surprised to find Aquinas considering them as he proceeds with SCG 3,94. We might suppose that he will reject them largely because he thinks that he has already established the reality of divine providence and has also shown that what is not necessary can fall under it. And in this supposition we would be correct. Indeed, having presented the objections now in question, Aquinas first says that "for the purpose of answering these arguments, we must repeat some of the observations put down before."[45] And at the end of SCG 3,94 he remarks: "Those arguments in favor of the necessity of effects foreseen by God, which might be drawn from the certainty of knowledge, are solved above, where we treated of God's knowledge [see SCG 1,63 and following]. Yet in SCG 3,94 Aquinas does have some precise responses directly aimed at the arguments against the certainty of divine providence noted in that chapter.

For one thing, he maintains that nothing can prevent God's foresight, which extends to both necessary and contingent things and events. He continues:

> So, it is obvious that, though divine providence is the direct cause of an individual future effect, and though it is so in the present, or in the past, indeed from eternity, it does not follow... that this individual effect will come about of necessity. For divine providence is the direct cause why this effect occurs contingently. And this cannot be prevented.[46]

Again, Aquinas argues: "It is also evident that this conditional proposition is true: *If God foresees that this event will be, it will happen.*... But it will occur in the way that God foresaw that it would be. Now he foresaw that it would occur contingently. So, it follows that, without fail, it will occur contingently and not necessarily."[47] Yet again, says Aquinas, something in the future that is foreseen by God may be something able not to be; yet "it is not possible for the order of providence to fail in regard to its coming into being contingently...[and]...it can be maintained that this man may not become a ruler if he is considered in himself, but not if he be considered as an object of divine foresight."[48] With the fourth and fifth objections above in mind, Aquinas argues (1) that causes and ways of being are as subject to providence as effects, so "it does not follow that, if everything be done by divine providence, nothing is within our power" because "the effects are foreseen by God, as they are freely produced by us," and (2) that it is appropriate to God's providence "sometimes to permit defectible causes to fail, and at other times to preserve them from failure."[49]

14.5 *Providence and Prayer (SCG 3,95–96)*

If God's providence is unchangeable, however, what room is left for the practice of asking God for things? How can belief in the appropriateness of petitionary prayer be reconciled with the claim that divine providence is what it is and cannot be thwarted? Should asking God for things not be dismissed as pointless? Or should we, perhaps, say that, because prayer is not pointless, divine providence can be changed by what we do?

These are Aquinas's questions in SCG 3,95–96, and his answers to them maintain both that prayer (*oratio*) is appropriate and that divine providence can be changed by nothing created since God is immutable. I should, however, stress that, when Aquinas uses the word "prayer" in SCG 3,95–96, he is only referring to asking God for things. He is not concerned with prayer as worship or adoration or as anything other than presenting our needs to God as able to satisfy them. Writers on prayer have often construed it in very broad terms. In the SCG, though, Aquinas does not. Nor does he maintain, as some people do, that prayers are always answered. Indeed, the purpose of SCG 3,96 is to note that they are not always answered and why that might be so.

By now you will realize that Aquinas is definitely going to rule out any notion of prayer that takes it to be something by which we coerce God. He thinks of prayer as causal insofar as he thinks that God grants us some things *because* we have prayed for them. He does not think of prayer as changing God in any way. For one thing, he does not think of it as informing God of our needs, for he takes God to be omniscient. For another, Aquinas does not regard God as moved or changed by our prayers as effects of agent causes can be moved or changed by them. In Aquinas's view, both answers to prayer and our prayers themselves are part of what comes about by God's providence.

Given this idea, however, what sense can Aquinas make of prayer? His position is that prayer is appropriate since, when praying, we are asking for what we know that God can bring about.[50] He thinks that it is good for us to ask for things from God since that amounts to recognizing what God is and acting accordingly. At the same time, however, he holds that prayer has to be an activity brought about by God. So, he argues: (1) God from eternity wills that the

created order should be as it was, is, and shall be; (2) the created order includes free and rational creatures who can and do ask for things that they need
from God; (3) it also contains what free and rational creatures have asked for
from God; (4) so it contains both people who pray and positive responses to
things that people seek in prayer. For Aquinas, God does not answer prayer as
a temporal and mutable human being might be swayed to grant a request, but
he does providentially work so as to produce people who turn to him for help
and so as to bring about what they ask him to provide.

Aquinas therefore says that "prayer is not established for the purpose of
changing the eternal disposition of providence, since this is impossible, but so
that people may obtain from God the object they desire."[51] Just as God's providence does not impose necessity on things, it does not prevent us freely asking
God for what we want. And, says Aquinas, it is as possible for God to bring
about what we ask for as it is for God to bring about what we intend for ourselves as we act so as to help ourselves. You might say that, given divine providence, there is no point in asking for things from God. Yet, reasons Aquinas,
that would be like saying that there is no point in walking so as to get to some
place at which we want to be. He writes:

> Divine providence does not exclude other causes; rather it orders them
> so that the order which providence has determined within itself may be
> imposed on things. And thus, secondary causes are not incompatible
> with providence; instead, they carry out the effect of providence. In this
> way, then, prayers are efficacious before God, yet they do not destroy the
> immutable order of divine providence. So, it is the same thing to say
> that we should not pray so as to obtain something from God, because
> the order of his providence is immutable, as to say that we should not
> walk in order to get to a place, or eat so as to be nourished; all of which
> are clearly absurd.[52]

In short, thinks Aquinas, God, in accordance with his goodness, "fulfills the
holy desires which are brought to completion by means of prayer."[53] Aquinas
holds that good desires come from God and that there is nothing to prevent
God fulfilling them as expressed in prayer. Indeed, he says, the fulfilling of
our desires by God is a case of friendship and love since friends want what
people they love want and since God's answering prayer amounts to him
willing what people desire.

What, though, of requests in prayer that are not granted by God? As I have
said, Aquinas is not of the view that God always answers prayers by giving
people what they ask for. You might say that God always answers prayers in

that God always provides what is good for those who pray. Yet Aquinas proceeds in SCG 3,96 on the assumption that there is something wrong with this view. He certainly thinks that God can give us what is good for us without us asking for it specifically. But he does not take this as amounting to God giving us what we have asked for. He takes it to amount to God not doing so. He seems to be supposing that if I ask you for X, and if you do not give me X while giving me something else, or something better than X, then you have not given me what I asked for. So he readily concedes that some prayers are not granted by God, while adding that it is appropriate or fitting (*conveniens*) that this should be so.

Why might God not give us what we ask for? Here are Aquinas's answers to this question in SCG 3,96 (all of them presented together with biblical quotations, which I shall not reference):

1. Sometimes people do not ask God for what is truly good.
2. Sometimes people do not persevere in praying for what they want, this indicating a lack of desire on their part or a lack of confidence in God.
3. Sometimes people ask for things from God while lacking humility toward him or affection for him.
4. Sometimes people who pray are not holy, not in tune with what God is all about, not desiring of God's good will as acting with them to obtain good results.
5. Sometimes people pray for the welfare of those who do not deserve it.
6. Sometimes people pray for what God knows to be harmful to them. And they sometimes pray for what is not as good for them as something else would be.

So, in SCG 3,96, Aquinas goes on to say that divine providence accords with reason in that it works for good in various ways even as it extends to creatures who differ in goodness. As I have shown, diversity among things that exist is, for Aquinas, a sign of God's goodness because it shows that God wants things of various kinds to be, things with different strengths and weaknesses. While we might instinctively suppose that God would produce something lacking no perfection (a best possible world, as it were), Aquinas invites us to consider the many ways of being, and of being good, that can be brought about by God, considered as the source of all possible things. In a passage presenting a thought that runs through SCG 3, he writes:

> Since every created substance must fall short of the perfection of divine
> goodness, in order that the likeness of divine goodness might be more

perfectly communicated to things, it was necessary for there to be diversity of things, so that what could not be perfectly represented by one thing might be, in a more perfect fashion, represented by a variety of things in different ways.... Perfect goodness which is present in God in a unified and simple manner cannot be in creatures except in a diversified manner and through a plurality of things.[54]

And, thinks Aquinas, diversity is going to give rise to there being some things that are better in various ways than others. Diversity, for him, guarantees inequality brought about by God's providence. Yet might God not somehow act apart from the order established by his providence in general? This is the question with which Aquinas is concerned in SCG 3,98–102.

14.6 Miracles (SCG 3,98–102)

14.6.1 Preliminaries (SCG 3,98–100)

So far in SCG 3, Aquinas has presented a view according to which God acts so as to establish a world that, though deriving from God, has its own way of working. He has been arguing that created things in it operate in different ways, sometimes by necessity and sometimes not. He has also been arguing that created things regularly operate in certain ways so as to achieve certain ends. Yet Aquinas knows very well that some of his Christian colleagues, not to mention some of his Jewish and Islamic ones, believe that God can somehow override the order of nature (in which X regularly follows from Y, and in which some events that have occurred cannot be produced by the God-given natural powers of creatures). In short, he is aware of belief in miracles, to which he turns in SCG 3,98–102. The word "miracle" does not actually occur in SCG 3,98–100. It comes to the forefront only in SCG 3,101. Yet SCG 3,98–100 is clearly working up to a defense of the claim that miracles can occur or might have occurred—this being a claim that one would expect Aquinas to accept if only given what we read in the New Testament, which seems to report events that we might take not to be explicable scientifically.

The "working up" stage of Aquinas's discussion of miracles argues as follows:

1. God creates by will, not necessity. Therefore, God can make things that are other than what he makes while governing things as a whole by his providence.
2. "God can do nothing that does not fall under the order of his providence, just as he can do nothing that is not subject to his operation. Nevertheless, *if his power is considered without qualification*, he can do other things than those

which are subject to his providence or operation, but, *because of the fact that he cannot be mutable,* God cannot do things that have not been eternally under the order of his providence."[55]

3. There is a general order in created things such that some of them causally depend on other ones. But God, who acts from will, not necessity, can act apart from this order by, for example, bringing something about that causally derives only from him, not from something created. "The very perfect artisan can produce any kind of work that the less perfect artisan could make. Now, God operates through will, and not through natural necessity.... Therefore, he can produce immediately, without special causes, the smaller effects that are produced by lower causes."[56] God, by his essence, "is able to produce immediately every effect that any particular agent can bring about."[57] God "is able immediately to move anything to any effect without intermediate causes."[58]

4. Although the order established by providence represents God's goodness, it does not do so perfectly since no creature is equal to God. "But that which is not perfectly represented by a given copy may again be represented in another way besides this one.... Therefore, the divine will is not limited to this particular order of causes and effects in such a manner that it is unable to will to produce immediately an effect in things here below without using any other causes."[59]

5. We can sometimes make ourselves to be well or ill, to be in a good way or a bad way, by imagination and emotion that override bodily principles working in us. So it is possible for God to produce effects in creatures "without using the causes that are naturally brought into being for the purpose of producing such an effect."[60]

6. The order imposed on things by providence results in various events occurring—for the most part, but not always, for sometimes things fail in their actions for naturalistically explicable reasons. But if the natural order can produce what occurs rarely, then "it is more certain that divine power can sometimes produce an effect, without prejudice to its providence, apart from the order implanted in natural things by God."[61] God's doing this, indeed, "makes it evident that the order of things has proceeded from him, not by natural necessity, but by free will."[62]

7. For God to bring about what a created secondary cause cannot produce is not for him to act against nature (*contra naturam*) even though it is for him to act apart from the order found in nature. That is because God brings it about that something comes to be as subject to the divine will, which is appropriate for something in nature to be. By bringing about an effect lacking a natural cause, God is not doing violence to anything or offending against the status of something that is there in the natural world.

14.6.2 Miracles Directly (SCG 3,101–102)

With these observations made, Aquinas proceeds to a head-on discussion of miracles while noting: "Things that are at times divinely accomplished, apart from the generally established order in things, are customarily called *miracles*."[63] So you can now, I hope, see why I take SCG 3,98–100 to be concerned with miracles, even though Aquinas does not use the word "miracle" in these chapters. Indeed, SCG 3,98–100 effectively presents and completes his SCG defense of the claim that miracles are possible.[64] All that SCG 3,101 seeks to show is how miracles might be differently categorized even though "those things must properly be called miraculous which are done by divine power apart from the order generally followed in things."[65] And all that SCG 3,102 maintains is that only God can work miracles.

In SCG 3,101 Aquinas notes that there are three kinds of miracle.

First, he says, there are ones "in which something is done by God which nature never could do."[66] In this connection, he instances the sun reversing its course, or standing still, and a sea opening up to allow people to pass through it.[67]

Second, says Aquinas, there are "those events in which God does something which nature can do, but not in this order."[68] In this connection, Aquinas instances animals living after being dead, seeing having been blind, and walking having been paralyzed. Nature, Aquinas notes, can bring about living, seeing, and walking people. But it cannot bring them to be living having been dead, seeing having been blind, or walking having been paralyzed.

Finally, says Aquinas, there are miracles in which "God does what is usually done by the working of nature, but without the operation of the principles of nature."[69] Here he means that God might bring about what can be brought about by created things, though without them being involved in the occurrence of what comes about.

In SCG 3,102 Aquinas argues that only God can work miracles since, by definition, a miracle is something that a creature cannot bring about. As I have shown, Aquinas takes all creatures, no matter how exalted, to be secondary causes existing and acting by the power of God. Creatures, for Aquinas, make up the world of things with different natures acting under God's providence so as to produce effects commensurate with those natures. So he finds it obvious that creatures cannot function so as to bring about what can only result from God. Or, as he says: "Whatever is completely confined under a certain order cannot work above that order. But every creature is established under the order which God has put in things. So, no creature can operate above this order; but that is what it means to work miracles."[70] We may, Aquinas goes on to say, be frequently astonished by things that occur by the powers of created things. But these are not miracles. They are what ought to lead us to improve our scientific knowledge. It is, Aquinas notes, "the prerogative of God alone to work miracles. Indeed, he is superior to the order in which the whole of things is contained, just as from his providence this entire order flows. Moreover, his power, being utterly infinite, is not limited to any special effect or to the production of a particular effect in any limited way, or order."[71]

14.7 Magic and Demons (SCG 3,104–110)

In SCG 104–110 we find chapters that, I suspect, would be of no interest to contemporary philosophers and theologians. For in them Aquinas solemnly discusses how magicians might be empowered by bad immaterial substances to bring about what they do. In this context, Aquinas is obviously not thinking of magicians as the conjurers we applaud as their quickness of hand or their use of physical objects deceives our eyes. He is thinking of them as able to bring about effects in the world by incantations or rituals, and as helped in their "art" of magic by demonic forces. Since I take SCG 104–110 to be mostly of historical interest, I am not going to try to follow through its somewhat convoluted reasoning. Instead, having noted that Aquinas feels moved to write about magic and demons while talking about God's providence, I shall proceed to what he says about rational creatures as subject to providence in a special way—his concern in SCG 3,111–163. This is the topic of the following chapter. Before concluding this one, however, I would like to make some comments on the reasoning of SCG 3,64–110.

14.8 Is Aquinas Right about Divine Providence?

If we are not just concerned to arrive at an accurate understanding of what Aquinas says about providence in SCG 3,64–110 (a commendable aim in itself), we shall want to consider whether it has anything useful or believable to offer. Does it?

As I have noted at the end of several previous chapters, our evaluation of various sections of the SCG will depend on what we make of what Aquinas says prior to them. And so it is when it comes to SCG 3,64–110. We shall reject almost all that he says here if we reject his reasons for belief in God given in SCG 1,13, or if we think that God does not or cannot exist. We shall do the same if we adopt a notion of God at odds with Aquinas's defense of divine simplicity as presented in SCG 1,14–27 or if we think of God's creative activity in a way that is different from what Aquinas presents in SCG 2,1–29.

Even so, however, there are questions that can be raised concerning SCG 3,64–110 without reference to truths that Aquinas might be thought to have established previously in the SCG. I shall say something about three of them.

14.8.1 Creaturely Causality and Human Choosing

If I seem to close a door, but if God actually causes me to close it, how can I have really closed the door? Should it not, instead, be said that God has closed the door? As I have shown, Aquinas is conscious that questions like this might be raised against his account of divine providence. Yet does he deal with them successfully? Does he show that created causes can be real causes? And does he show that God's providence does not rule out creaturely free choice?

You may say that he does not since it is obvious that if something brings something about while acting under the influence of a cause that is making it do what it does, then the thing in question is being pushed around and is not doing anything of itself. Yet it would surely be wrong to say that what is being pushed around so as to effect some change or whatever is not acting causally even if it does not initiate its movements. Even if I am being pushed into water by someone, it still remains that I cause effects in the water. It is, of course, with thoughts like this in mind that Aquinas holds that secondary causes are still real causes. So I think we have good reason to think, as does Aquinas, that secondary causes are real causes. In thinking this, Aquinas seems to be saying that secondary causes that are secondary to one or more agent cause can be genuinely causal, which seems obviously true since if X, an agent cause, causes Y, an agent cause, to cause Z, it has to remain that Y causes Z.

Yet what about people choosing to do things? If I am coerced to close a door, I still act causally so as to get the door closed. But do I get it closed willingly? Well, I surely do not if I am forced to close the door by someone manipulating my body or by someone holding a gun to my head. So how can it be that if, as Aquinas says, all creatures do what they do by virtue of God's causality, there is any such thing as human freedom? Many philosophers have denied that people have freedom since they have thought that all that we do is the result of physical events of some kind, whether external to us or internal to us. In doing so, they seem to be assuming that causation always amounts to necessitation, which is not obviously true, as Aquinas says and as some recent philosophers have argued.[72] Yet let us, for the sake of argument, allow that people have freedom of choice, as Aquinas argues they do in SCG 2,48. In that case, how can their freedom not be abolished by God acting in them by virtue of providence?

This question seems to be an odd one since if people actually do have freedom of choice, then God's providence cannot abolish it. If it is the case that such and such is so, then it is so regardless of what else we might want to enter into the equation for purposes of discussion. Now, Aquinas has argued that people have freedom of choice, so he can hardly allow that considerations concerning God's providence should lead us to conclude that they do not. Yet we might think that, given that people have freedom to choose, God is not operative in all things, as Aquinas says that he is. Why might we think this? Some would say that we should do so because if an action is performed freely, it cannot be caused by anything, not even God.

One can see the force of this suggestion on the supposition that God exists alongside creatures while acting on them so as to move them in this or that direction. For if God is like that, then he would seem to be always coercing creatures. If I move a jug, the jug has no say in its move. If I slip on the ice, I have no say in my slipping. So one might think that if God always causes me to act as I do, then I have no say in my action and that all of my actions are determined by God. Yet, of course, Aquinas does not conceive of God as something alongside creatures acting on them so as to move them in this or that direction. He thinks of God as creating creatures to be whatever we truly take them to be without reference to God. In a serious sense, Aquinas thinks that God makes no difference to things.

Of course, he thinks that God makes all the difference since God accounts for there being something rather than nothing. But he does not regard God's doing that as involving a modification of anything. As I have shown, in SCG 2,17–19 he argues that for God to create is not for him to change something preexisting his creative action. The whole drift of Aquinas's philosophy of God in the SCG pulls away from the view that God exists alongside things as something able to interfere with them in some way. For Aquinas, God makes things to be what they truly are.

In his discussion of God's providence, therefore, Aquinas claims that if some things do not come about as causally necessitated by other things, they are not causally necessitated even though they come about by God's power at work in them. You may say that if God accounts for something coming about, then God is rendering it to be necessitated. Yet that view surely has to mean that God is compelling or forcing it in some way, and Aquinas would reply that God cannot force or compel anything by creating it to be what it is. He would claim that things are what they are, whether necessitated or not necessitated, not in spite of God but because of God. And one can, I think, readily see why he arrives at this view given the account of God, God's nature, and the notion of creation that Aquinas takes himself to have defended prior to his discussion of providence.

If you start with the idea that providence is a matter of God messing around with all things, then you will naturally conclude that providence is a threat to freedom or contingency in any form. But Aquinas does not start with that idea of providence because he takes it to be incompatible with a true understanding of God. His point is that God from eternity has willed to make a world in which some things come about of necessity (e.g., as when death inevitably occurs following a massive trauma) while others do not (e.g., as when I freely decide to go on holiday). You may say that when we act freely, we act independently of God. Consistently with his understanding of God in the SCG, however, and consistently with his understanding of providence, Aquinas would reply that we can never act independently of God even though we can act independently of certain creatures. Would he be right to reply in this way? I suggest that he would since if all creatures owe their existence to God, then God must be the source of free human actions and other contingencies since these exist as opposed to there being nothing at all. Whatever freedom or contingency means, it cannot mean not depending on God considered as the maker of things in the way that Aquinas argues that he is.[73]

If we want to reject what Aquinas says about God working in all creatures by providence, we are going to have to abandon the considerations that lead him to speak of God as the creator of the universe. We shall have to settle for the view that God is just one more thing among the things that exist. Aquinas, of course, does not deny that God exists. Nor does he deny that God is distinct from creatures. But he does deny that God is an individual thing having a nature deriving from anything (this is the drift of his teaching on divine simplicity). He also denies that God is spatiotemporal. So he does not think of God as something alongside creatures. In other words, we might say that he denies that God and the universe can be added up so as to make for a number of beings plus God as an additional one. For he clearly does not think of "being" as a word specifying a kind of thing, and he would deny that God can be included in a list of things belonging to different kinds members of which can be thought of as able to coerce things like or unlike them.

14.8.2 God's Knowledge and What It Might Be Thought to Necessitate

In SCG 3,94 Aquinas, as I have shown, denies that God's knowledge poses a threat to his view of providence. Is he right to do so, however? For is it not clear that if God knows what is the case, then it has to be the case?

Actually, it is not clear that this is true. In fact, it is evidently false since "X knows that-p" does not entail that p is something that could not fail to be. It is true that if I know that you are painting a wall, then you are painting a wall. But it does not follow that you cannot but be painting a wall. "X knows that-p" guarantees that-p, not because of something determining the truth of p, but because of the meaning of "know." We cannot know that-p if it is not the case that-p (though we might believe that-p without it being the case that-p). But, though "Fred knows that I am painting a wall" cannot be true if I am not painting a wall, nothing follows as to whether or not I am constrained to paint the wall.

Yet what if we change "Fred knows that I am painting a wall" to "Fred knows on Monday that I will paint a wall on Tuesday"? Then it might seem far from obvious that my painting on Tuesday is something over which I have any control. And, applying this thought when reflecting on God's knowledge, we might be tempted to conclude that if God foreknows all that will come to pass, then all that comes to pass, including what people do, comes about inevitably. As Richard Sorabji succinctly says, echoing what many others have argued since Aquinas's time:

> If God were not *infallible* in his judgement of what we would do, then we might be able so to act that his prediction turned out *wrong*. But this is not even a possibility, for to call him infallible is to say not merely that he *is* not, but that he *cannot* be wrong, and correspondingly we *cannot* make him wrong.... The restriction on freedom arises not from God's infallibility alone, but from that coupled with the *irrevocability* of the past. If God's infallible knowledge of our doing exists *in advance*, then we are *too late* so as to act that God will have had a different judgement about what we are going to do. His judgement exists *already*, and the past *cannot* be affected.[74]

This is an interesting line of thinking, yet it is not very effective considered as a refutation of Aquinas's conclusion that God's knowledge does not render what comes to pass as doing so inevitably. For one thing, and as Aquinas says in SCG, if God knows that something comes about without doing so inevitably, then the thing comes about without doing so inevitably. This fact is not abolished even if we think of God knowing that something or other will come to be the case before it comes to be the case. If God knows on Monday that I will freely paint a wall on Tuesday, then what God knows is that I will *freely* paint a wall on Tuesday, and God *cannot* be knowing that my wall painting on Tuesday is somehow necessitated. As William Lane Craig observes:

> The reason that God foreknows that Jones will mow his lawn is the simple fact that Jones will mow his lawn. Jones is free to refrain, and

were he to do so, God would have foreknown that he would refrain. Jones is free to do whatever he wants, and God's foreknowledge logically follows Jones's action like a shadow, even if chronologically the shadow precedes the coming of the event itself.[75]

Even without relying on this argument, however, a defender of Aquinas can resist the conclusion that God's knowledge necessitates what he knows by noting that, for Aquinas, God does not literally foreknow anything. As I have shown, Aquinas takes God to be outside time. His view is that God knows all that occurs in time by knowing himself as the eternal and nontemporal creator of all things. So his view is that if we want to cast around for an inadequate image of what God's knowledge of creatures amounts to, we should think in terms of someone just knowing what is there before them. If I see you painting a wall, it does not follow that you could not but be painting the wall. For Aquinas, God knows the course of created history in one eternal glance that is not prior to the coming about of creatures in the sense that my knowing that Jones will mow his lawn is prior to Jones mowing his lawn. And this view of his rightly, I think, leads him to suppose that God's knowledge cannot, by itself, impose necessity on creatures. You may think of God as being in time. You may think that we can write a biography of God given tips from God's literary agents. In that case, you will think that the best that can be said in favor of the view that God's knowledge does not entail that everything that happens is necessitated amounts to the obvious point that, if what God foreknows is something that does not have to be, then what God foreknows is something that does not have to be. Yet if, with Aquinas, you also think that God's knowledge of creatures can never be constituted by what God derives from looking ahead to time future to God, if you think that what occurs in time is known to God from eternity, then you will naturally think that it imposes no necessity on creatures, just as our knowing what is before us does not impose necessity on what is before us.

14.8.3 Miracles

The discussion of miracles in SCG 3,98–102 is a bit of a puzzle in that Aquinas does not make it clear what he is doing in it. Is he holding that miracles have occurred? You might think that he is because of the biblical allusions in SCG 3,101. But Aquinas does not specifically argue in that chapter that certain miracles have taken place. What the chapter seems to offer is a fairly thorough account of kinds of miracles that are possible, and the discussions in SCG 3,98–100 and SCG 3,101 do not seem to presume that there have been any miracles. What they argue is that miracles would not be impossible given divine providence and that, if anything is a miracle, it could only be brought about by God. This hesitancy of Aquinas bluntly to declare that certain miracles have occurred might be due to his purpose in SCG 1–3 not to go beyond what he takes rational reflection, as distinct from divine revelation, to deliver. Yet it is not obvious that the occurrence of miracles cannot be argued for independently of divine revelation, and in SCG 1–3 Aquinas is happy to cite biblical texts as backing up what he has been saying. So perhaps one might feel that SCG 3,98–101 is somewhat blurry when it comes to its aim. That said, however, it is obvious that in these chapters Aquinas is defending the possibility of miracles, and one might ask whether he has done this successfully.

Some will think that he cannot have done so since miracles are manifestly impossible. You can find this claim presented in what is probably the most famous philosophical discussion of miracles—chapter X of David Hume's *An Enquiry Concerning Human Understanding* (originally published in 1758 but revised by Hume until his death in 1776). Hume defines "miracle" as "a violation of the laws of nature," and at one point he says that miracles cannot occur. He does this when noting certain miracles supposed to have taken place at the tomb of Francis of Paris (1690–1727). Having noted testimony to their occurrence, Hume says: "And what we have to oppose to such a cloud of witnesses, but the absolute impossibility or miraculous nature of the events which they relate. And this surely, in the eyes of all reasonable people, will alone be regarded as a sufficient refutation."[76] In chapter X of the *Enquiry Concerning Human Understanding* Hume mostly expresses skepticism concerning miracles based on a sophisticated argument concerning testimony and probability.[77] He argues that we always have good reason to disbelieve accounts to the effect that a miracle has occurred. Yet, in the passage I have just quoted, he asserts that miracles cannot happen; and others have agreed with him on this score.

If miracles are simply impossible, then Aquinas is wrong in his discussion of them. Yet it is hard to see why we should think that miracles are impossible. We might not believe that any miracles have occurred. And, like Hume, we may think that the evidence against them having occurred must always be deemed to outweigh the conclusion that they have occurred. But we surely should not therefore conclude that miracles are to be ruled out *a priori*. After all, miracles, as Aquinas understands them, are occurrences in the universe, albeit ones directly brought about by God. They are not events describable in terms that involve some logical contradiction. It cannot be that numbers have sprouted leaves since numbers are not things in the biological realm and since "being a number" is logically incompatible with sprouting leaves. Yet the miracles that Aquinas seems to have in mind in SCG 3,101 are not occurrences that seem to be reportable only on the condition that one is contradicting oneself while attempting to report them. One might say that miracles are not possible given the powers that creatures have. But Aquinas does not deny that. He presumes it. And even Hume says things that cohere with Aquinas's position here. In the *Enquiry Concerning Human Understanding* he observes: "Whatever is intelligible and can be distinctly perceived, implies no contradiction, and can never be proved false by any demonstrative argument or abstract reasoning *a priori.*" So, Hume continues:

> It implies no contradiction that the course of nature may change, and that an object, seemingly like those which we have experienced, may be attended with different and contrary effects. May I not clearly and distinctly conceive that a body, falling from the clouds, and which, in all other respects, resembles snow, yet has the taste of salt or feeling of fire? Is there any more intelligible proposition than to affirm that all the trees will flourish in December and January, and decay in May and June?[78]

What Hume thinks he can clearly and distinctly perceive in this passage seems to be akin to what Aquinas has in mind when he talks about miracles. Admittedly, Hume is only saying that we cannot guarantee that nature will always operate in the same way. Yet that concession seems to leave the door open to the possibility of things occurring in the universe that cannot be ruled out given how things in nature regularly behave so far as we can determine. And Aquinas defends this possibility in his SCG discussion of miracles. Given that this discussion is to be read as, to a great extent, only arguing that miracles are possible, that is a point worth noting.

Also worth noting is that Aquinas does not claim that miracles are violations of natural laws. Those who refer to natural laws usually take themselves to be noting ways in which things have to behave given our knowledge of their natures. Thus, one might say that potatoes have to soften when placed in boiling water for half an hour. To speak in this way, however is to suppose that the natural world is a closed system on or in which nothing can act so as to bring about what does not normally happen given the natures of things in the world. Yet, as we see throughout the SCG, Aquinas does not think of the natural world in this way, and his account of miracles reflects this fact. So, one might hold, he has done something outside SCG 3,64–110 to defend what he argues there, and one need not evaluate these chapters entirely on their own.

15

Providence in Relation to Rational Creatures (SCG 3,111–163)

AT THE OUTSET of SCG 3,111 Aquinas takes himself to have shown "that divine providence extends to all things."[1] But he still wants to explain "that there is a special meaning for providence in reference to intellectual and rational creatures."[2] This is the task he devotes himself to in SCG 3,111–163.

He begins by arguing that rational creatures, by which he now chiefly means human beings, differ from other creatures. Then he claims that people are governed by God providing laws directing them in their actions. Divine law, he holds, "looks to the ordering of people toward God."[3]

So Aquinas next considers how people are ordered to God in different ways and by various courses of action. He maintains that God orders us to act in accordance with reason concerning physical matters. He then spends several chapters talking about fornication, marriage, and the use of food. He also offers discussion of those in his day who attacked voluntary poverty and perpetual abstinence from sexual activity.[4]

Having noted that what we do is punished or rewarded by God, Aquinas then spends time discussing punishment in general and punishment by God in particular. Yet, returning to his claim that God can help people to attain ultimate happiness (see SCG 3,53), he goes on to reflect on how God might aid some people by grace (*gratia*) while withholding it from others. Aquinas clearly thinks that God might not give grace to some people. But he also believes that God does not have to give grace to anyone. He therefore views grace as given to rational creatures by God's will and mercy, not because of desert.

15.1 Rational Creatures and Providence (SCG 3,111–113)

According to Aquinas, two things make people unique in terms of God's providence in the spatiotemporal world. First, they have the ability to act freely. Second, their end is the "knowing and loving of God."[5] Given these facts, Aquinas thinks that "there is one orderly plan in accord with which rational creatures are subjected to divine providence, and another by means of which the rest of creatures are ordered."[6]

Aquinas argues that freely acting people are "principal agents," not mere instruments. This means that they need to be guided by God as agents that provide for themselves. They have value in their own right and not just as a tool does only insofar as it gets a job done for one who uses it. "Intellectual creatures," says Aquinas, are "controlled by God, as objects of care for their own sakes; while other creatures are subordinated, as it were, to the rational creatures."[7] According to Aquinas, special government is needed for people just because they have freedom when acting. So "through divine providence provision is made for intellectual creatures on their own account."[8] Things with freedom, says Aquinas, need to be governed differently from things that lack it. Therefore, things without freedom are governed by God for the sake of those with it. All nonfree things "are divinely ruled by providence for the sake of intellectual substances."[9] Why so? Not only for their individual good but also for the good of the whole universe, since that requires the perfection of intellectual creatures.

On this picture, people are directed to God as choosing individuals, not just things sharing a nature with other things. Aquinas therefore goes on to argue that people are governed by God as able to provide for themselves.[10] They "receive direction from God in their acts, not only for the species, but for the individual."[11] Members of a species may be helped by what other members of it do, and divine providence may see to it that they are so helped. Yet people must be governed by God, not only as contributing to the good of their species, but as acting as able to make choices.

God takes care of each nature according to its capacity: indeed, he created singular creatures of such kinds that he knew were suited to achieving the end under his governance. Now, only rational creatures are capable of this direction, whereby their actions are guided, not only specifically, but also individually. For they have understanding and reason, and consequently they can grasp in what different ways a thing may be good or bad, depending on its suitability for various individuals, times, and places. Therefore, only rational creatures are directed in their acts by God, individually as well as specifically.[12]

15.2 People and Laws: The General Picture (SCG 3,114–116)

How can we be governed by God as free individuals? Aquinas's answer to this question is "by law." He writes:

Just as the acts of irrational creatures are directed by God through a rational plan which pertains to their species, so are the acts of people directed by God inasmuch as they pertain to the individual....But the acts of irrational creatures, as pertaining to the species, are directed to God through natural inclination, which goes along with the nature of the species. Therefore, over and above this, something must be given to people whereby they may be directed in their own personal acts. And this we call law.[13]

In Aquinas's view, law is "nothing other but reason and rule" (*lex nihil aliud sit quam quaedam ratio et regula operandi*). He regards such a plan as goal-directed, as aiming at what is good. Since he takes the end and good for people to lie in God, therefore, he concludes that "it is appropriate for law to be given to people by God."[14]

Not surprisingly, Aquinas next claims that God's law for people chiefly orders them to God. "The end for human creatures," he says, "is to cling to God, for their felicity consists in this, as we have shown above [see SCG 3,37]. So, the divine law primarily directs people to this end: that they may cling to God."[15] Aquinas takes this conclusion to mean that the end of divine law is the love of God. He thinks that people can cling to God only by intellect and will, and he holds that it is through will that we rest in what our intellect grasps. He notes, however, that we can willingly adhere to something because of love or fear. We will do so because of fear if we take our doing so to be a means of avoiding what we do not like. But we will adhere to something by love "for the sake of that thing." Furthermore:

> What is valued for its own sake is of greater importance than what is for the sake of something else. Therefore, the adherence to God in love is the best possible way of clinging to God. So, this is what is chiefly intended in the divine law.[16]

But where are we to look so as to discover God's law for us? Aquinas ends SCG 3,114–116 with biblical quotations, which seems to suggest that, at this point in the SCG, he is going beyond what he takes reason to be able to discover apart from revelation. Indeed, right at the end of SCG 3,116 he says: "The New Law, as the more perfect, is called the *law of love*, while the Old Law, as less perfect, is the *law of fear*."[17]

In SCG 3,116 Aquinas does not explain his sudden introduction of a distinction between the Old Law and the New Law except to say that the latter is superior to the former. We can, though, understand his thinking at this point by noting some of the things he says in his *Summa Theologiae*. In this, he makes it clear that he believes the Old Law to consist in commands, precepts, and prohibitions given by God to people in Old Testament times.[18] He also makes it clear that he takes the Old Law to be superseded by the New Law, considered as God working in us so as to unite us to God by means of grace and by means of the life, death, and resurrection of Jesus of Nazareth.[19] So, by SCG 3,116, Aquinas is explicitly arguing as a Christian theologian talking to Christians. He cannot primarily be addressing Jews or Muslims. They would not for a moment have bought into talk about there being a New Law, as Aquinas understands it, that is superior to an Old Law.

That said, however, having finished with SCG 3,116, and continuing frequently to cite Scripture, Aquinas appears to proceed to talk about what divine law requires of people as if this could be determined without the benefit of Christian revelation. So let us now follow him as he does so. As I will show, he often appeals to that which is "according to reason" (*secundum rationem*) as settling what God's providence intends for us.

15.3 Love of Neighbor, Right Faith, Worship of God, Marriage, Sex, Food, and Nature (SCG 3,117–129)

In SCG 3,117–128 Aquinas argues for these conclusions:

1. God's law requires us to love our neighbor, considered as someone with whom we share a common end (SCG 3,117).
2. God's law requires us to believe truly concerning God, this being something that depends on "right faith" (SCG 3,118).
3. Since we rely so heavily on our senses, providence arranges that we should employ physical objects and physical rituals when approaching God or trying to think about him (SCG 3,119).
4. God's law requires that only God be worshiped (SCG 3,120).
5. God's law is given so that we may make proper use of bodily and sensible things (SCG 3,121).
6. Male human beings should not commit fornication, and they should not engage in sex except with a view to possible procreation (SCG 3,122).
7. Sex belongs within marriage, which (1) should last as long as both partners are alive, (2) should be monogamous, and (3) should not take place between close relations (SCG 3,123–125).
8. Not all sexual intercourse is sinful. Sexual intercourse is proper, and in accordance with reason, as long as it is open to conception (SCG 3,126).
9. The use of food is not sinful if guided by reason and aimed at bodily preservation. People may also rightly make use of money so as to take care of themselves and others (SCG 3,127).

10. We are social animals who depend on each other in various ways. So we need to be governed by divine law in order to live with each other on the basis of reason (SCG 3,128).

11. Some human acts are right according to nature (*secundum naturam*), not just as ordered by law (SCG 3,129).

It seems clear that Aquinas regards these conclusions as rationally defensible. As I have said, in SCG 3,117–129 he frequently cites the Bible. Indeed, in SCG 3,120 he bluntly asserts that "the divine law is promulgated" in Exodus 20, where we find the Ten Commandments listed.[20] However, SCG 3,117–129 should, I think, be read as an exercise in moral philosophy to which scriptural quotations serve as a kind of divinely authenticated backup. Aquinas holds that God governs us by means of our reason. In SCG 3,117 he also says that "divine law is offered to people as an aid to natural law" (*lex divina profertur homini in auxilium legis naturalis*).[21] By "natural law" he seems to mean directions for action based on what is natural or instinctive to all people as made to exist by God, this to be taken as giving us reason for embracing or avoiding certain ways of behaving.

What reasons does Aquinas give in defense of conclusions 1–11?

15.3.1 Loving Our Neighbor (SCG 3,117)

The arguments here are:

1. We share a common end, so we "should be united with each other by a mutual love."[22]

2. God loves human beings in that he directs them to the beatific vision. If someone loves God, therefore, that person should love all people as directed to God by God.

3. We are social animals, so we should get on together and will the good of others.

4. We need some peace and quiet if we are to attend to God. Love between people makes for this.

5. "It is natural for all people to love each other."[23] This is obvious from the way we spontaneously come to the help even of people we do not know.

15.3.2 Right Faith (SCG 3,118)

The arguments here are:

1. We can only enjoy the vision of God if we are guided by faith. "Therefore, we must be led to the right faith by the divine law."[24]

2. In order to be totally and perfectly subject to God, people must not believe something false about God. "Therefore, people are ordered to the right faith by divine law."[25]

3. Someone in error concerning God cannot love God or desire God as an end. Therefore, people "must be bound by divine law to hold a right faith concerning God."[26]

4. False opinion is a kind of vice since it deflects us from truth, which we need to lay hold of as good for us given that we are intellectual beings. So divine law prohibits "false opinions about God and matters concerned with God."[27]

15.3.3 Our Dependence on Our Senses and the Worship of God (SCG 3,119–120)

In writing SCG 3,119–120 Aquinas is concerned with what we might call "religious observances." He is thinking of ritual, liturgical events, cultic practices, veneration, and devotional behavior; and he argues that these are means by which divine providence draws us close to God given our bodily nature. He writes:

> Since it is connatural for us to receive knowledge through our senses, and since it is very difficult to transcend sensible objects, divine provision has been made for us so that a reminder of divine things might be made for us, even in the order of sensible things. The purpose of this is that the intention of people might be better recalled to divine matters, even in the case of someone whose mind is not strong enough to contemplate divine things in themselves.[28]

Aquinas is clear that our use in worship of physical things and bodily practices does not derive from any need in God. For example, with respect to "sensible sacrifices," he says that their purpose is to remind us that we owe what we are and what we have to God as "Creator, Governor, and Lord of all."[29] He continues:

> Certain blessings using sensible things are provided for us, whereby we are washed, or anointed, or fed, or given drink, along with the expression of sensible words, so that we may be reminded through sensible

things that intelligible gifts come to us from without, and from God, whose name is expressed in sensible words. So, certain sensible works are performed by people, not to stimulate God by such things, but to awaken us to divine matters by these actions, such as prostrations, genuflections, vocal ejaculations, and hymns.... We do these things for our sakes, so that our attention may be directed to God by these sensible deeds and our love may be aroused. At the same time, then, we confess by these actions that God is the author of soul and body, whom we offer both spiritual and bodily acts of homage.[30]

In short, Aquinas thinks that people owe God homage, worship, and adoration by bodily behavior.

15.3.4 *Latria* (SCG 3,120)

Aquinas uses the word *latria* to signify the adoration or worship of God, and in SCG 3,120 he stresses that *latria* is due only to God. He does so since he is aware that some have said that certain things that are not divine should be worshiped. Indeed, in SCG 3,120 he gives examples of claims to this effect, though he rejects all of them while concluding:

It is unreasonable for people who maintain only one, separate, first principle to offer divine cult to another being. For we render cult to God, as we have said [see cf. SCG 3,119], not because God needs it, but so that a true opinion concerning God may be strengthened in us, even by means of sensible things. But an opinion on the point that God is one, exalted above all things, cannot be established in us through sensible things unless we honor God with something unique, which we call *divine cult*. So, it is evident that a true opinion concerning the one principle is weakened if divine cult is offered to several beings.[31]

15.3.5 Bodily and Sensible Things (SCG 3,121)

The thesis of SCG 3,121 is that God requires us to govern our love and use of bodily things by reason. In defense of this thesis Aquinas offers four arguments.

First, he notes that, just as our minds can be raised to God by physical things if we use them in a proper way, the improper use of physical things can lead us to focus, to a greater or lesser degree, on what is less than God.

Second, he maintains that our bodies are subject to God and should, therefore, be directed by our reason. He observes: "It pertains to divine providence, of which divine law is but a rational plan proposed by God to us, to see that individual things keep their proper order. Therefore, we must be so ordered by divine law that our lower powers may be subject to reason, and our bodies to our souls."[32]

Third, he says, good law promotes virtue, and "virtue consists in this: that both the inner feelings and the use of corporeal things be regulated by reason."[33]

Finally, Aquinas argues that good lawmakers legislate in accordance with reason and that divine law must, therefore, command us to submit to what is reasonable.

15.3.6 Fornication and Marriage (SCG 3,122–125)

At the end of SCG 3,121 Aquinas claims that this chapter has "refuted the error of some who say that those acts only are sinful whereby one's neighbor is offended or scandalized."[34] He means that one can act against reason without doing harm to anyone since one's actions can be unreasonable in themselves even if they involve people happy to go along with them. In SCG 3,122–125 Aquinas develops this thought with an eye on sexual activity, the purpose of which he takes to be procreation.[35]

Here are some of the arguments presented in these chapters.

1. Fornication is essentially sinful since it involves a man ejaculating without intending to produce offspring and to provide for them. "The emission of semen ought to be so ordered that it will result in both the production of the proper offspring and in the upbringing of this offspring."[36]
2. Every emission of semen is contrary to human goodness except in cases when a man has sex with a woman while being open to the conception of a child. So it is sinful and "contrary to nature" (*contra naturam*) for a man to ejaculate deliberately without intending to conceive and to provide for a child, unless, for example, he does so while knowing that the woman with whom he is having sex is sterile.[37]
3. A man prone to fornication might have sex having abandoned his wife and having conceived a child with her. Yet "it is appropriate to human nature that a man remain together with a woman after the generative act" and not engage in fornication. This is the case whether or not a woman abandoned by a man is able to fare well for herself and her child.[38]
4. It takes a lot of time and effort to rear children, to provide for them physically, and to educate them. So "it is natural to the human being for the man to establish a lasting association with a designated woman, over no short

period of time.... Therefore, marriage is natural for people, and promiscuous performance of the sexual act outside marriage is contrary to human good."[39]

5. It is a grave sin, second only to homicide, "for a man to arrange for the emission of semen apart from the proper purpose of generating and bringing up children" since "the inordinate emission is incompatible with the natural good; namely the preservation of the species." "After the sin of homicide, this type of sin appears to take next place, for by it the generation of human nature is precluded."[40]

6. People should remain married for life since "it is natural that the father's solicitude for his son should endure until the end of the father's life" while "the natural order demands that father and mother in the human species remain together until the end of life."[41]

7. Divorce would be against justice when it comes to women since "the female needs the male, not merely for the sake of generation... but also for the sake of government, since the male is both more perfect in reasoning and stronger in his powers."[42] Women are there for men for purposes of generation, and it would be wrong for a man to disown a once beautiful woman he married were she to have aged, lost her looks, and be no longer able to conceive.

8. Wives are subject to their husbands. "So, it would be against the natural order if a wife were able to abandon her husband. Therefore, if a husband were permitted to abandon his wife, the society of husband and wife would not be an association of equals, but, instead, a sort of slavery on the part of the wife."[43]

9. Fornication can result in a man fathering a child without knowing who his child is. But fathers of children have "a certain natural solicitude to know their offspring."[44] Moreover, "if a husband could put away his wife, or a wife her husband, and have sexual relations with another person, certitude as to offspring would be precluded.... So, it is contrary to the natural instinct of the human species for a wife to be separated from her husband."[45]

10. Polygamy is contrary to reason.[46] That is because all animals able to reproduce sexually have an inbuilt instinct to resist promiscuity and because "all animals desire to enjoy freely the pleasure of the sexual act, as they also do the pleasure of food; but this liberty is restricted by the fact that several males may have access to one female, or the converse."[47] Also, "Men naturally desire to know their offspring, and this knowledge would be completely destroyed if there were several males for one female. Therefore, that one female is for one male is a consequence of natural instinct."[48] To be sure, "certainty as to offspring is not precluded if one male has relations

with several women."[49] But the freedom to have sex with one spouse at will is taken away from both men and women by the practice of polygamy.[50]

11. Friendship (*amicitia*) consists in equality of some kind (*in quadam ae-qualitate consistit*), which would be lacking between spouses if they had more than one spouse at the same time. "So, if it is not lawful for a wife to have several husbands, since this is contrary to certainty as to offspring, it would not be lawful, on the other hand, for a man to have several wives, for the friendship of wife and husband would not be free, but somewhat servile.... For among husbands having several wives the wives have a status like that of servants."[51]

12. Reason suggests that close relatives should not marry since "there is in matrimony a union of diverse persons," not people united by physical origin.[52] "Those persons who should already regard themselves as one because of having the same origin are properly excluded from marriage, so that in recognizing themselves as one in this way they may love each other with greater fervor."[53] Also, "because the acts performed by husband and wife are associated with a certain natural shame (*quandam naturalem verecundiam habeant*), it is necessary that those persons to whom respect is due because of the bond of blood should be prohibited from performing such actions with each other."[54]

15.3.7 Is Sexual Intercourse Intrinsically Sinful? (SCG 3,126)

The word "sin" (*peccatum* for Aquinas) is usually taken to mean an offense against God, and one's view of what constitutes sin will obviously depend on what one takes God to will. In SCG 3,126, however, Aquinas still appears to be arguing in defense of various positions on the basis of reason, not revelation or any particular view when it comes to what God is. He is obviously doing so as one who thinks that what reason indicates is backed up by what we find taught in the Bible; so the reference to sin in SCG 3,126 alludes to what Aquinas takes the Bible to teach when it comes to offense against God. That said, however, SCG 3,126 seems to be arguing that reason tells us that not all sexual intercourse (understood as between a man and a woman) is wrong.[55]

Why, though, does Aquinas take sexual intercourse to be something that people can sometimes engage in while respecting what reason requires? He does so because he thinks that people can have sexual intercourse with a view to possible conception, that they can do so "in a manner which is suited to the generation and upbringing of children."[56] "Carnal union," he says, "is the end of certain bodily organs," and "that which is the end of certain natural things cannot be evil in itself."[57] Aquinas views sexual intercourse to be directed to the perpetuation of the human race. So he denies that sexual intercourse is always sinful, though he is clear that it is sometimes sinful depending on who is doing what with whom, for what reason, and in what context.

15.3.8 Food (SCG 3,127)

The line of thought in SCG 3,126 carries over into SCG 3,127 so as to argue that there is nothing intrinsically wrong or sinful in the consumption of food, as long as we eat in accordance with reason. "The proper end of taking food," says Aquinas, "is the preservation of the body by nutrition."[58] It is right to eat to keep ourselves alive. Aquinas accepts that we might fail to eat in a healthy way, and he thinks that we might be culpable on this score. He also thinks that we might be blamed for other reasons when it comes to our eating habits. But he is clear that "to use either plants or the flesh of animals for eating or whatever other utility they may have for us is not a sin in itself."[59] This conclusion, in turn, leads Aquinas to argue that the use of possessions other than food is licit insofar as we use them according to reason. If we are going to procreate, then we need to support ourselves financially. With that thought in mind, Aquinas concludes that "the possession of wealth is not in itself illicit, provided that the order of reason be respected."[60] He goes on to say that what he has noted in SCG 3,127 refutes the errors of people (unspecified) who entirely reject the institution of marriage and who reject those who have acquired wealth on which they draw.

15.3.9 Human Relations (SCG 3,128)

As I have shown, SCG 3,117 maintains that divine law requires us to love our neighbor. SCG 3,128 develops this point so as to conclude that living in harmony with others is necessary for our fulfilment. For one thing, says Aquinas, we are better off working together than on our own, and people can be of assistance to each other by instructing each other well and by aiding each other in other ways. He also argues that we need to be at peace with each other and to give each other what justice requires. In this connection he appeals to Exodus 20:12–17, according to which we should honor our parents and refrain from murder, adultery, theft, false witness, and covetousness.

15.3.10 "According to Nature" (SCG 3,129)

In SCG 3,129 the thesis is: "Things prescribed by divine law are right, not only because they are put forth by law, but also because they accord with nature."[61]

It is obviously Aquinas's view that God's law has been declared by God in the Bible. Yet it is equally obvious that Aquinas also believes that divine law accords with reason, and SCG 3,129 shows him trying to justify this belief by specifically appealing to human nature. So we find him saying that "the things prescribed by divine law are naturally right in themselves."[62] Again, he observes: "There are certain operations that are naturally suitable to people, and they are right in themselves."[63]

According to Aquinas, if something has a nature, "there must be definite kinds of operations which are appropriate" to it and are consequent to it.[64] Aquinas also thinks that "it is obvious that there is a determinate kind of nature for people."[65] Consequently, he reasons that "there must be some operations that are in themselves appropriate to human beings."[66] What kind of operations? Aquinas is evidently thinking of those approved in SCG 3,117–128: loving our neighbor, acting in accord with right faith, engaging in religious observances, worshiping God, governing bodily and sensible things by reason, and living in harmony with each other.

15.4 Divine Counsels (SCG 3,130–138)

When reading SCG 3,130–138 we need to bear in mind that Aquinas distinguishes between precepts and counsels. He takes a precept to be an order to do or not do something, and he takes a counsel to be a directive that is not binding, one we are free to act on only if we choose to do so. There is a difference between saying to someone (1) "You must pay what you owe," and (2) "It is good to give money to charities." Again, there is a difference between (1) "You must not commit murder," and (1) "It is good to spend one's life working to save people's lives." Now Aquinas takes divine law to contain a number of precepts, such as those found in the Ten Commandments. Yet he also thinks that there are counsels as well as precepts on which people might act. He takes precepts to be things that people have to act on so as to conform to divine law. But he also believes that there are counsels that might be embraced by some people seeking a union with God that goes beyond what can be achieved just by doing what God positively commands all to do, or by refraining from doing what God absolutely forbids.

Theologians in Aquinas's day commonly acknowledged that this precept/ counsel distinction can be found in texts such as Matthew 19:16–22. Here we read of a rich man who came to Jesus and said, "Teacher, what good deed must I do to have eternal life?" Jesus replies, "You shall not murder; You shall not commit adultery; You shall not steal; You shall not bear false witness; Honor your father and mother; also, You shall love your neighbor as yourself."

The man then says to Jesus, "I have kept all these; what do I still lack?" To this question Jesus responds, "If you wish to be perfect, go, sell your possessions, and give the money to the poor."[67] By Aquinas's time, biblical texts like this in sense were understood to mean that there are certain lifestyles that, without needing to be embraced by all people, are good ways of living. More precisely, some were saying that perfection consists in embracing voluntary poverty, chastity, and obedience as a member of a Christian religious order.

Aquinas accepts this notion of perfection, which is why he distinguishes between precepts and counsels. So, at the start of SCG 3,130, we find him saying:

> Since the best thing for us is to become attached in our minds to God and divine things, and since it is impossible for us intensively to busy ourselves with a variety of things in order that our minds may be applied to God with greater liberty, counsels are given in the divine law whereby we are withdrawn from the busy concerns of the present life as far as is possible for one who is living an earthly life. Now, this detachment is not so necessary to us for justice that its absence makes justice impossible; indeed, virtue and justice are not removed if we use bodily and earthly things in accord with the order of reason. And so, divine law admonitions of this kind are called *counsels*, not *precepts*, inasmuch as we are urged to renounce lesser goods for the sake of better ones.[68]

What counsels does Aquinas have in mind? He is thinking of the counsels to be poor, chaste, and obedient. He makes this clear in SCG 3,130, while working up to the conclusion that, since poverty, chastity, and obedience are "dispositions to perfection and are the effects and signs of perfection, it is fitting that those who pledge themselves to them by a vow to God should be said to be *in the state of perfection*."[69] At this point in the SCG, the discussion, once again, can hardly be addressing Jews or Muslims. It is an "in house" one directed at Christians familiar with the precept/counsel distinction while also aware of religious orders whose members vow themselves to poverty, chastity, and obedience. But it is certainly not a discussion that amounts to "preaching to the choir," so to speak. That is because Aquinas was aware of Christians in his day who opposed voluntary poverty, chastity, and obedience embraced in the institutional context of religious orders.

Why did they do so? You will get a sense of what Aquinas took them to be saying as you read through SCG 3,131–138. I am, however, not going to go through these chapters in detail because they are a contribution to a debate that is now of interest only to historians. Suffice it to say that in SCG 3,131–138, and in response to various arguments, for which he does not cite references, Aquinas insists on the value of voluntary poverty and chastity and on the value of taking vows as a member of a religious order.

15.5 Rewards and Punishments (SCG 3,142–146)

The notion of law seems to be bound up with that of reward and punishment. A legally appointed judge might declare that we should be compensated or punished in some way. Laws are typically enforced in human societies with a view to reparation and retribution. It is, therefore, not surprising that in SCG 3,142–146 Aquinas turns to reward and punishment. If there is such a thing as divine law, are there rewards for acting in accordance with it? And does not acting in accordance with divine law come with retribution? These questions are what Aquinas has in mind in SCG 3,142–145, while in SCG 3,146 he discusses punishment inflicted by human beings on other human beings.

He begins by claiming that "not all rewards and punishments are equal" (*quod non omnia praemia et poenae sunt aequales*).[70] By this he means that rewards and punishments should match that to which they stand as rewards or punishments. If you care for my cat for a week, I might reasonably reward you by, say, taking you out to dinner. But I can hardly be expected to reward you by giving you all the money that I possess. Again, you may think that I should be punished for stealing your cat. Yet would you think that I should be hanged for doing so? Presumably not. So you might think, as does Aquinas, that rewards and punishments should be varied and admit of degrees, which is the thesis of SCG 3,142.

In SCG 3,143, however, and with the notion of punishment in mind, Aquinas turns to a distinction between what he calls "mortal" and "venial" sin. Its biblical basis lies in 1 John 5:16–17, where we read: "If you see your brother or sister committing what is not a mortal sin, you will ask, and God will give life to such a one—to those whose sin is not mortal. There is sin that is mortal; I do not say that you should pray about that. All wrongdoing is sin, but there is sin that is not mortal." The author of these verses is evidently thinking that some sins are very grave, while some are less grave, and this is what Aquinas has in mind when distinguishing between mortal and venial sin.

It is possible, he says, to sin in two ways.

One way is such that the mental intention is entirely broken away from the order to God, who is called the ultimate end of all good people; and this is mortal sin. The second way is such that, while the ordering of the human mind to the ultimate end remains, some impediment is brought in whereby one is held back from freely tending toward the end; and this is called venial sin.[71]

In short, Aquinas takes mortal sin decisively to separate those who commit it from God, while he takes venial sin to be less disastrous in its consequences.[72] In his view, mortal sin warrants those who commit it to be "cut off from the end of human beings," while venial sin does not.

Aquinas recognizes that someone who sins mortally might repent and get back on course when it comes to conforming to the law of God.[73] He is clear, though, that there is no room for repentance after death. Why so? Because he thinks that death deprives people of their human capacity to aim for their ultimate end. He says: "The soul needs a body for the obtaining of its end, in so far as it acquires perfection through the body, both in knowledge and in virtue. But the soul, after it has been separated from its body, will not again return to this state in which it receives perfection through the body."[74] In SCG 3,144, therefore, Aquinas maintains that to die in mortal sin is to be eternally deprived of the beatific vision. He agrees that punishment inflicted on human beings by other human beings can be intended as corrective and, therefore, should come to an end. Yet, he insists, those who die in mortal sin are deprived of the context in which they can correct themselves. He also notes that some people are legally executed, though not with a view to their improvement. One is not, thinks Aquinas, forced to admit "that all punishments are purgatorial and terminable."[75] In fact, he says, those who die in mortal sin "are not only to be punished by their exclusion from perpetual happiness, but also by the experience of something painful."[76] He continues:

> Punishments are inflicted for faults so that people may be restrained by the fear of these punishments.... But we do not fear to lose what we do not desire to obtain. So, those who have their will turned away from the ultimate end do not fear to be cut off from it. Thus they cannot be restrained from sinning simply by exclusion from the ultimate end. Therefore, another punishment must also be used for sinners, which they may fear while they are sinners.... This punishment is due to sinners, that from those things in which they set their end they receive affliction and injury.[77]

What though of punishment inflicted on people by people? Is this justifiable? Aquinas argues that it can be since we might be deterred from acting unjustly given laws that allow judges to punish us for so acting. He also maintains that "divine providence requires the good to be rewarded and the evil to be punished" and that "people who are in authority over others do no wrong when they reward the good and punish the evil."[78]

Yet what about capital punishment? Is that permissible? We might agree that society needs laws that come with penalties for those breaking them. It is not hard to appreciate why Aquinas is not against punishment as such, especially given his view that there is such a thing as divine law that aims to draw people to what is humanly good. But should anyone condemn someone else to death? And should anyone execute someone else? Aquinas's answer is that capital punishment is defensible.

He bases his argument on the notion of there being a common good that can override that of an individual. This common good, he thinks, justifies the existence of laws that come with penalties attached. He also thinks that not executing certain people might endanger the good of others. So his approach to capital punishment is preventative. He holds that capital punishment is justified insofar as it protects people. Many have said that capital punishment is required by justice since people can commit crimes that obviously require that they die for committing them.[79] But that is not Aquinas's line. He thinks that capital punishment is justified with an eye on avoiding harm that might be done by the one scheduled for execution. We therefore find him arguing:

> The common good is better than the particular good of one person. So, the particular good should be preserved in order to preserve the common good. But the life of certain pestiferous people is an impediment to the common good which is the concord of human society. Therefore, certain individuals must be removed by death from human society.... The ruler of a state executes pestiferous people justly and sinlessly in order that the peace of the state may not be disrupted.[80]

In SCG 3,146, Aquinas's approach to capital punishment is not retributive. It is defensive. He thinks that some people should be put to death so that others may be protected from them. He does not, as we might, consider the possibility of guaranteeing, with some reason, that certain people who have done certain things can be ensured never again to be able to harm others. However, Aquinas did not live in a world that contained the high-security jails with which we are now familiar. He lived in a world in which "pestiferous" people might easily be expected to escape confinement so as to return to being "pestiferous."[81] At the end of SCG 3,146 he notes that those about to be executed might express contrition for what they have done. Yet, he drily observes: "The danger that threatens from their way of life is greater and more certain than the good which may be expected from their improvement."[82]

15.6 Grace (SCG 3,147–163)

So Aquinas thinks that final human happiness results from conforming to God's law. But how does this conformity come about? Evidently, by people acting in certain good ways aiming at the goodness that is God. Yet where does this acting come from? Can it be attributed only to people acting by their natural powers? In SCG 3,147 and following, Aquinas maintains that in order to arrive at beatitude, people need divine help, which he refers to as grace.[83]

Why so? Because "our ultimate end is fixed in a certain knowledge of truth which surpasses our natural capacity" and because "if we are ordered to an end which exceeds our natural capacity, some help must be divinely provided for us, in a supernatural way, by which we may tend toward our end."[84] This point is repeated over and again in SCG 3,147.[85]

However, Aquinas does not think that God's help in leading people to beatitude coerces them. That is because he takes people to have freedom of choice, even though he believes that all that people are and have is from God (see SCG 2,47 and following). For Aquinas, God's creative activity in people is not a threat to their ability to choose; it makes them able to choose; it is a condition of them choosing. "God by his help," says Aquinas in SCG 3,148, "does not force us to right action....God also causes our works in us in accord with our measure, which means that we act voluntarily and not as forced....Forced acts are not acts of the virtues, since the main thing in virtue is choice, which cannot be present without voluntariness to which violence is opposed. Therefore, people are not divinely compelled to act rightly."[86]

From what he says in SCG 3,147 and 148, Aquinas takes it to be obvious that people cannot merit God's help in advance—the thesis of SCG 3,149. We cannot move ourselves to obtain God's help; rather, "we are moved by God to obtain it."[87]

> The movement of the mover precedes the movement of the movable thing in reason and causally. Therefore, divine help is not given to us by virtue of the fact that we initially move ourselves toward it by good works; instead, we make such progress by good works because we are preceded by divine help.... The soul cannot prepare itself to receive the influence of divine help except in so far as it acts from divine power. Therefore, it is preceded by divine help toward good action, rather than preceding the divine help and meriting it, as it were, or preparing itself for it.[88]

In SCG 3,150, Aquinas calls God's help in leading us to beatitude "sanctifying grace," and he takes it to be present in those who have it even when they are not consciously acting. It must be something that endures even when people who have it are, for example, asleep. It must be a "special goodness and perfection" in people.[89] "The help of grace which we obtain from God in order to reach the ultimate end," Aquinas adds, "designates a form and perfection present in us."[90] And in SCG 3,151, he goes on to maintain that sanctifying grace causes us to love God. He writes:

> Sanctifying grace is an effect in people of divine love. But the proper effect in us of divine love seems to be the fact that we love God. Indeed, this is the principal thing in the lover's intention: to be loved in turn by the object of love. To this, then, the lover's main effort inclines, to attract the beloved to love of the lover; unless this occurs, the love of the lover must come to nothing. So, this fact that we love God is the result in us of sanctifying grace.[91]

Again, we read:

> The ultimate end, to which people are brought with the help of divine grace, is the vision of God's essence, which is proper to God alone. Thus, this final good is shared with people by God. So, we cannot be brought to this end unless we are united with God by the conformation of God's will. And this is the proper effect of love, for "it is proper to friends to approve and disapprove of the same things, and to be delighted in and to be pained by the same things."[92] Hence, by sanctifying grace people are established as lovers of God, since they are directed to it by the end that has been shared with them by God.[93]

In SCG 3,152 and 153, Aquinas maintains that grace also brings about faith and hope in people. In his *Summa Theologiae* he lays emphasis on faith as belief in the key Christian doctrines, and he takes hope to be for what Christian doctrine promises.[94] In SCG 3,152 and 153, however, he is not concerned to discuss faith and hope in detail and in specifically Christian terms. His biblical quotations in these chapters make evident where he finds his authority to lie when it comes to faith and hope; and one can recognize from SCG 1,1–6 what he means by "truths of faith." But in SCG 3,152 and 153 he refers to faith only as faith in God as able to raise us to the vision of God. And he takes hope only to be hope that God will do this.

So, he says, those who look forward to beatitude do so by God-given faith, since we do not know what God is and since the beatific vision is not within our natural power to grasp. "It is," Aquinas argues, "necessary that, above our natural knowledge, there also be added to us a knowledge which surpasses natural reason. And this is the knowledge of faith, which is of the things that are not seen by natural reason."[95] He continues:

> We are directed by the help of divine grace to our ultimate end [see SCG 3,147]. But the ultimate end is an open vision of the First Truth in Itself [see SCG 3,50 and following]....Therefore, before it comes to this end, our intellect must be subject to God by way of belief, under the influence of divine grace which accomplishes this.[96]

When it comes to hope, Aquinas's line in SCG 3,153 is that the faith he has just been speaking about leads those who have it to hope, by virtue of grace, for the vision of God. So, he argues:

> If by grace someone is made a lover of God, there must be produced in that person a desire for union with God, according as that is possible. But faith, which is caused by grace, makes it clear that the union of people with God in the perfect enjoyment in which happiness consists is possible. Therefore, the desire for this fruition results in us from the love of God. But the desire for anything bothers the soul of the desirer, unless there be present some hope of attainment. So, it was appropriate (conveniens) that in people, in whom God's love and faith are caused by grace, there should also be caused a hope of acquiring future happiness.[97]

In SCG 3,154 Aquinas goes on to speak of gratuitous grace (gratia gratis data). He takes this to be grace provided so as to convey to others truths about God that cannot be demonstrated. He describes such grace as including an ability to teach divine truth, an ability to preach truly to the accompaniment of genuine miracles (not just events that seem amazing), and an ability inspired by God infallibly to predict (prophesy) future events. In short, Aquinas takes gratuitous grace to be given by God when revealed divine truth is truly preached, sometimes accompanied by events that can only be brought about by God. He also argues that the preaching of divine revelation needs people graced so as to interpret it and discern what is and what is not true when it comes to what is presented by others as being divine revelation. He finds this approach to gratuitous grace to be found in 1 Corinthians 12:8–10.[98]

Given what he has been saying in SCG 3,147–153, we will not be surprised to find Aquinas maintaining in SCG 3,155 that people need grace to persevere in what is good or with a view to their ultimate good. "In order that we may immovably continue in the good, which is to persevere," says Aquinas, "we need divine help."[99]

For that which surpasses the power of free choice, we need the help of divine grace. But the power of free choice does not extend to the effect of final perseverance in the good.... The power of free choice applies to those things which fall within the scope of election. Now, what is chosen is some particular operation that can be performed. But such a particular operation is what is here and now present. Hence, that which falls under the power of free choice is something that is to be done now. But to persevere does not mean something as now operable, but the continuation of an operation throughout time. Now, this effect, of persevering in the good, is beyond the power of choice. Therefore, we need the help of divine grace to persevere in the good.[100]

Can someone who falls away from the pursuit of God and goodness come back to it? In SCG 3,156 Aquinas responds to this question in the affirmative, while noting that such a return to God will be the work of grace. He says:

It pertains to the same power to maintain the continued salvation of a person and to restore it when it has been interrupted, just as health is continually maintained by the natural power in the body, and an interruption of that health is repaired by that same natural power. Now, people persevere in the good by means of divine grace, as we showed [see SCG 3,155]. Therefore, if one has fallen as a result of sin, that person may be restored by means of the same grace.[101]

This line of thinking leads Aquinas to go on immediately, though briefly, to argue that we cannot be freed from sin without divine grace (SCG 3,157). He clearly takes this conclusion to be implied by what he has just said, as it indeed seems to be.

Yet how are people freed from sin? Aquinas's answer, given in SCG 3,158, is that we are freed from sin as we move away from it, as we refrain from it. He means that our turning to God, and away from what conflicts with union with God, is *itself* God's grace at work in us. He also means that we are freed from sin by acknowledging and accepting punishment due to sin, or by making up for our sin in some way.[102] This punitive or retributive tone features a lot in SCG 3,158, and it does so because Aquinas thinks that wrongdoing needs to be compensated for if justice is to prevail. Indeed, in SCG 3,158 Aquinas explicitly says that "the order of justice demands that a punishment be assigned for a sin."[103] We should, however, notice that the punishment emphasis in SCG 3,158, considered as something imposed on repentant sinners from without, becomes somewhat muted as the chapter proceeds. I say this for two reasons.

First, in SCG 3,158 Aquinas does not seem to be thinking along the lines "If God makes me suffer, then that frees me from sin." Rather, his idea seems to be "If I repent of what I have wrongly done, then I shall myself want to make up for my wrongdoing somehow."

Second, he goes on to say that repentance might not require any punishment at all, whether willed by sinners on themselves or not. Thus, we find him arguing:

> When the mind is turned away from sin the displeasure with sin can be so forceful, and the attachment of the mind to God so strong, that no obligation to punishment will remain.... The punishment that a person suffers after remission of sin is necessary so that the mind may adhere more firmly to the good; since people are chastised by punishments, these punishments are, then, like remedies. It is also necessary so that the order of justice may be observed, in the sense that one who has sinned must stand the penalty. But love for God is enough to set the mind of someone firmly in the direction of the good, especially if this love is strong; and displeasure for a past fault, when intense, brings great sorrow. Consequently, through the strength of one's love for God, and one's hatred of past sin, there is removed the need for punishments of satisfaction or purification. Moreover, if this strength is not great enough to set aside punishments entirely, nevertheless, the stronger it is, the smaller will be the punishment that suffices.[104]

So, in SCG 3,158, Aquinas's position seems to be that our embracing penalties for doing what we have done can be a sufficient but not a necessary condition of us being freed from sin.

Suppose, however, that someone does not turn toward God. Can that person be held responsible even though grace is required for turning toward God? This question is the topic of SCG 3,159, and Aquinas's answer is yes.

He begins by noting that it might seem as though one should not be held responsible for lacking grace since "someone cannot merit the help of divine grace, nor turn toward God unless God converts that person, for no one is held responsible for what depends on another."[105] But he goes on to say:

> We ought to consider that, although one may neither merit in advance nor call forth divine grace by a movement of free choice, people are able to prevent themselves from receiving grace.... And since this ability to impede or not impede the reception of divine grace is within the scope of free choice, not undeservedly is responsibility for the fault imputed to those who offer an impediment to the reception of grace.[106]

Here I take it that Aquinas regards the choice to sin as impeding grace. He does not mean that anyone can block grace as, say, a boulder can block one's attempt to enter a cave. Given his notion of divine omnipotence, and given his claim that grace is God at work in us, he cannot think of an impediment to grace as physically resisting God's activity. As I have shown, though, he does think that people are able freely to sin and that divine causality does not negate human freedom. So he thinks of choosing to sin as culpable and as stepping out of the way of grace since sin is no work of grace and is nothing caused directly by God. Sin, he holds is an "obstacle" (*impedimentum*) to grace because it amounts to a turning away from God and is incompatible with grace. One cannot be both wet all over and dry all over. One's being wet obstructs one's being dry. By the same token, Aquinas maintains that sinning obstructs one's being in grace. And sin, he thinks, is chosen by us in the face of God, so to speak. He writes:

> Those alone are deprived of grace who offer an obstacle within themselves to grace; just as, while the sun is shining on the world, people who keep their eyes closed are held responsible for their fault, if as a result some evil follows, even though they could not see unless they were provided in advance with light from the sun.[107]

In Aquinas's view, a will turned to sin is turned away from God, even though all that is good comes from God. Or, as he says in SCG 3,160:

> Whenever someone's mind swerves away from the state of rectitude, it is evident that the person has departed from the order of their proper end. So, what should be the most important thing in their affection, the ultimate end, becomes a less important object of love than that object to which their mind is inordinately turned, as if to an ultimate end. So, whenever anything comes up that is in agreement with the inordinate end but incompatible with their proper end, it will be chosen, unless they are brought back to their proper end, so that they favor this end above all things, and this is the effect of grace. However, in so far as they choose something that is incompatible with their ultimate end, they offer an impediment to grace, for grace gives direction to the end.[108]

As I explained in chapter 12, Aquinas believes that to sin is freely to turn away from a good that one ought to pursue, that it is grounded in love of what is not really good for the sinner. In line with this belief, he argues in SCG 3,160 and 161 that sinners culpably turn away from God and culpably remain in sin unless turned from it by God.

Can they be turned from sin to God? Aquinas thinks that they can. In SCG 3,161, he suggests that, just as God can work miracles, God can bring sinners back to seeking their ultimate end. But he adds that God does not always do so, just as he does not always bring it about that the blind miraculously receive their sight. This, Aquinas thinks, is obvious, for there are people who persevere in sin to the end. You might, of course, immediately ask "Why is this so?" Yet, while Aquinas partly replies to this question by saying "So that we might appreciate how God can be merciful," his final answer is that we do not know, any more than we know why God has made the world to be as it is in all its diversity. Conversion of sinners, he says, depends on God's will alone, "just as it resulted from his simple will that, while all things were made from nothing, some were made of higher degree than others."[109] Clearly, Aquinas does not think that God is obliged to make all people to be saints any more than he is obliged to make all living things to be creatures with understanding and the power to choose.

Inveterate sinners might reply that God is culpable for not making them to be saints. In SCG 3,162, however, Aquinas notes that sinners choose to sin and that God does not cause sin in anybody. Continuing to maintain his privation account of evil as I explained it in chapter 12, and continuing to maintain that human beings have freedom to act as they do, in SCG 3,162 Aquinas holds that sin is not directly caused by God. It is a defect that results from the moving power of the sinner. He says:

> Every sin stems from a defect in the proximate agent, and not from the influence of the primary agent: as the defect of limping results from the condition of the leg bone and not from the motor power, for, in fact, whatever perfection of motion is apparent in the act of limping, it is due to this power. But the proximate agent of human sin is the will. Therefore, the defect of sin comes from the will of human beings and not from God, who is the primary agent; from God, however, comes whatever pertains to perfection of action in the sinful act.[110]

Having noted some biblical texts that seem to agree with this line of thinking, Aquinas also notes others that might be thought to point in the opposite direction.[111] He argues, however, that the second group of texts should be understood only as teaching that "God does not grant to some people help in avoiding sin, while to others God does grant it."[112] He adds (1) that there are various ways in which divine providence keeps us away from circumstances that might tempt us to sin, and (2) that God has given us reason and other abilities that allow us to turn away from sin.

Winding up his SCG 3 discussion of grace, and drawing on other things he has said about providence, Aquinas concludes SCG 3 by alluding to predestination (*praedestinatio*), reprobation (*reprobatio*), and election (*electio*). These are biblical notions, and in SCG 3,163 Aquinas cites Scripture so as to register this fact. In this final chapter of SCG 3, however, he does not engage in detailed biblical commentary. Nor does he embark on a full-blown discussion of predestination, reprobation, and election. Instead, he contents himself with briefly observing that what leads up to SCG 3,163 has shown that "some of us are directed by divine working to our ultimate end as aided by grace, while others who are deprived of the same help of grace fall short of their ultimate end, and since all things that are done by God are foreseen and ordered from eternity by divine wisdom…the aforementioned differentiation of people must be ordered by God from eternity."[113] So, says Aquinas, "it appears that predestination, election, and reprobation constitute a certain section of divine providence, according as people are ordered to their ultimate end by divine providence."[114] Echoing what I have shown him saying about divine causality and contingency in what God has created (see chapter 8, section 4.12 and chapter 14, section 2.2 here), he notes that predestination, election, and reprobation do "not take away contingency in things."[115] If we are brought to the beatific vision, that is not because of some merit that we have prior to God giving us grace. Our coming to be beatified derives from grace, while "there can be no cause of the divine will and providence, although, among the effects of providence, and likewise of predestination, one may be the cause of another."[116]

15.7 Some Reflections on SCG 3,111–163

If you believe that God exists, and that God's nature is as Aquinas takes it to be in SCG 1, you will not think it odd that in SCG 3,111–163 Aquinas pursues the topic of providence while taking people to be governed by it. And you might applaud him for doing so on the ground that people are different from other things in the spatiotemporal world. Aquinas singles us out as able to make choices and as able to know and love God. If he is right to do so, then he would seem right to claim that, if God exists, he must govern us in a special way.

You might also think that God's governing of people has to involve promulgating divine law to us, that God has to instruct us how to behave and how not to behave. For if good law aims at human well-being, then must we not be taught what divine law is so as to aim at the beatific vision? And how can we be taught how to achieve beatitude unless informed of this by God? If we want to arrive at a certain destination, then we need to be told how to get there; and if God is our final end, then we would seem to be lost if we have not been instructed how to get to God. Instruction, of course, can take different forms. Hence, for example, I might give you precise instructions when it comes to getting from London to Munich, or I might educate you so that you can work out on your own how to make the trip. Either way, though, you are being guided by me so as to arrive at what you seek. If we seek beatitude, therefore, and if this is obtainable, it seems plausible to suppose that God will guide us to it either by explicitly telling us what we need to do so as to arrive at it or by making this clear by some other means.

Yet in SCG 3,111–163 this is exactly what Aquinas claims that God has done. In these chapters he speaks of guidance to beatitude given to us by divine revelation (as in the Ten Commandments and the teaching of Jesus). But he also speaks of guidance given to us by reason. As well as saying that God has revealed what is needed for beatitude, he says that God has conveyed divine law to us by giving us reason, which he takes to show us what we should and should not do if we are to be united with God.

Is Aquinas convincing when he speaks in SCG 3,111–163 of what God has taught us under the guidance of reason? Some people will respond to this question by wondering whether there is any such thing as reason, considered as an entity to be understood. Indeed, from the time of Plato to the present, philosophers have asked whether we can know what reason might be and what it might lead us to know. Aquinas, though, has no doubt that reason is real enough in the sense that we can think well so as to be intellectually justified in reaching conclusions on the basis of true premises that entail them. As I have also shown, he thinks that reason can lead us at least to know what is in accord with divine law and what conflicts with it when it comes to our behavior. Hence SCG 3,117–129.

Much of what Aquinas says in these chapters would today, I assume, be thought of as largely uncontroversial. We should justifiably feel uneasy with his sweeping claim that men are more perfect than women when it comes to reasoning (see SCG 3,123). Yet it seems hard to deny that people need to get on together so as to flourish as individuals (see SCG 3,117). And Aquinas is surely talking practical sense while reflecting on how engaging in polygamy could lead people to be unhappy in certain ways. We might doubt his claim that all men naturally desire to know their offspring, but we can surely appreciate his point that polygamy might lead to pain for both women and men who practice it. We might especially agree that women married to one man might end up being treated as servants of the man rather than his equals. Circumstances may differ, of course, so it is not inconceivable that the many wives of one man might all end up being equally valued by their husband. But they might not.

Aquinas's insistence that *latria* should be given only to God is something else that makes sense. Even an atheist can acknowledge that nobody should worship anything less than what Aquinas takes God to be. When speaking of *latria*, Aquinas is talking about reverence due to God as creating us and as giving us all that we have. If God is the creator of all things, then it would surely be stupid to bow down in worship to one of God's creatures. It also makes sense to say (see SCG 3,118) that union with God depends on right belief concerning God. If we take union with God to involve loving and worshiping God, then seriously wrong belief about God would seem to impede such love and worship. That is because to love X and to worship X, while being seriously mistaken about what X is, can mean not loving or worshiping X. Love and worship resemble support. I may claim to support someone: a political figure, say. But if my beliefs about that person are sufficiently off the mark, it is not that person whom I am supporting, no matter how much I might protest to the contrary. Similarly, if my beliefs about an object of my love or worship are sufficiently off the mark, the object of my love or worship is not what I take it to be.[117]

Remembering, however, that in SCG 3,117–129 Aquinas is concerned to explain how we should act or not act by virtue of reason, we might wonder whether he has successfully made a good case for all that he says in these chapters. In particular, one might wonder whether he has proved his case in what he says about sexual activity in SCG 3,122–126.

Much of this turns on the claim that sexual relations, or sexual activity in general, needs to consist in behavior open to procreation. It is not Aquinas's view that someone sterile should not have sex with another person. He rejects this position.[118] He does, however, claim that sex is intended by God for the production of children. If sexual activity is not engaged in as open to procreation, he says, it is "against nature" because the end of sexual activity is the preservation of the species (see SGC 3,122). Yet why should we suppose that this is the only right end for sexual activity? Obviously, human beings would disappear if everyone permanently refrained from sexual activity. So sexual activity is a necessary condition for the survival of the human species. But does it therefore follow that sexual activity not open to procreation is unnatural and, therefore, wrong?

If we take what is natural to be whatever occurs in the realm of nature, then sexual activity not open to procreation is evidently natural since it occurs. If we want to know what is natural, then all we have to do is note how things in the world behave, and some of them have sex, or use their sexual organs, with no possibility of procreation resulting.

Evidently, though, Aquinas is thinking of "natural" as an evaluative term, not a purely descriptive one. He claims that there is something wrong, and therefore against nature, in sexual activity not geared to procreation. And he does so because he thinks that sexual activity is necessary for the survival of our species. Even if it is, however, why should we conclude that sex not open to procreation is always wrong? If I need to do X in order to obtain Y, why should my doing X without wanting to obtain Y be thought of as a mistake of some kind? I need to eat in order to live. But might I not sometimes reasonably eat without a view to survival? Might I not, for instance, consume a piece of chocolate just for the pleasure of it? And when it comes to our survival as a species, good though this might be, why suppose that sexual activity not geared to procreation is a threat to it? Human beings will continue to exist whether or not some of them engage in sexual activity not open to procreation. In Aquinas's day, infant mortality rates were high, so one might understand why he thought that people should behave sexually so as always to aim at procreation. Even in the time of Aquinas, however, there was no chance of the human race dying out because people sometimes engaged in sexual activity with no possibility of conception occurring.

Could it be that nonreproductive sexual activity is against nature since all people are drawn to have sexual intercourse that might result in conception? Could it be that it is against nature since all animals are sexually drawn in this way? Aquinas does not raise these questions in SCG 3,122–126. Yet in *Summa Theologiae* 1a2ae,94,2 he says:

> There is in human beings a bent towards things which accord with their nature...that is in terms of what they have in common with other animals; correspondingly those matters are said to be of natural law which nature teaches all animals, for instance the coupling of male and female, the bringing up of young, and so forth.[119]

One can, I think, safely assume that this line of thinking lies behind what we find in SCG 3,122–126. And in SCG 3,122 Aquinas specifically claims that the purpose of the sexual act is directed to generation, which indicates that there is just one sexual act under discussion in this chapter, one that all people and other animals want to engage in: heterosexual intercourse.

However, not all nonhuman animals want always to engage in this.[120] Neither do many people. That many people do not seems obvious and is witnessed to by the governments in the world that have now found it right to acknowledge same-sex marriage. So why conclude that if even a majority of people are spontaneously drawn to have heterosexual sex, it follows that there is one sexual act to which all people are drawn, this being a reason to argue that sex not open to procreation is against nature?

It might be suggested that people who have nonreproductive sex are really attracted to reproductive sex and perversely engaging in nonreproductive sex just for the sake of pleasure. Yet the evidence these days seems to be against that suggestion. Given recent research on homosexuality, and given the testimony of people declaring that they have never been attracted to sexual activity leading to procreation, the suggestion seems questionable. It might be said that people not attracted to heterosexual intercourse are ill or ailing in some way, and I suspect that this is what Aquinas thought while arguing that sexual activity can have only one proper or legitimate end. But he does nothing in the SCG to show that people not attracted to heterosexual intercourse are sick or ill. He seems to proceed on the assumption that all human beings naturally desire heterosexual sex.[121] Given that assumption, one might understand why he thinks that God has given us sexual organs only for the purpose of procreation, or that all human beings are naturally directed only to reproductive sexual activity. Has he, however, successfully shown by *reason* that the use of our sexual organs must always to be accompanied by an intention to allow for conception?

There is a long Christian tradition that holds that our sexual appetites can only be properly satisfied by heterosexual intercourse open to procreation. And Aquinas is a major contributor to this tradition, not only because of what he says about sex in the SCG but also because of what he says about it in his *Summa Theologiae*. Yet does he, in SCG 3,122–126 (and more specifically in SCG 3,122) prove by reason that this tradition is solidly grounded? You may think that he does. Yet there is surely a topic for debate here.[122]

At this point I leave you to think on this matter and on other arguments offered by Aquinas in SCG 3,122–126. For I now need to proceed to SCG 4, in which Aquinas writes about the doctrine of the Trinity, the doctrine of the Incarnation, Christian sacraments, and the resurrection of our bodies.

Father, Son, and Holy Spirit
(SCG 4,2–26)

IN SCG 1–3, Aquinas argues for certain conclusions concerning God while noting what errors are set aside by them and while showing "how the truth that we come to know by demonstration is in accord with the Christian religion."[1] However, with SCG 4 it is what Aquinas takes to be divine revelation that comes to the forefront. In this book, he introduces arguments based on reason only so as to try to make some sense of what he believes on faith, never to refute arguments complaining that this has not been philosophically proved to be true. Since Aquinas holds that divine revelation is primarily given in the Bible, therefore, SCG 4 provides biblical quotations in abundance while presenting them as proof texts. It continually appeals to Scripture as settling what is to be believed on certain topics. More specifically, it does so with respect to the Christian doctrines of the Trinity, the Incarnation, and the resurrection of people from the dead. It also does so while turning to the sacraments of the Catholic Church.

To repeat what I have already stressed (see chapter 1, section 4 here), Aquinas makes a sharp distinction between faith and reason. He thinks that there are some things that people may know to be true since their truth can be demonstrated. Yet he also thinks that there are truths that cannot be demonstrated. Among this second set of truths Aquinas includes the articles of faith, which he takes to be grounded in Scripture and to be formally presented in texts like the Apostles' Creed, the Nicene Creed, the Nicene-Constantinopolitan Creed, and the definition of faith coming from the Council of Chalcedon.[2] Running these creeds together, we find what Aquinas took to be the doctrine of the Trinity, the doctrine of the Incarnation, and the doctrine that the dead shall be raised. It is these doctrines that Aquinas is concerned with in SCG 4, and, since he does not take them to be demonstrable, his initial procedure is to defend them with reference to the Old and New Testaments. So a lot of SCG 4 is devoted to citing scriptural passages that Aquinas regards as teaching what he takes these doctrines to maintain. SCG 4 is, therefore, very much an exercise in biblical interpretation proceeding on the assumption that the Bible should be thought of as inspired by God. It also proceeds on the assumption that biblical texts should be read in a literal sense unless there is some reason for taking them to be only figuratively true.[3]

Aquinas's way of reading the Bible is not that of contemporary biblical scholars, so you should not expect SCG 4 to read like modern, academic biblical commentaries.[4] You can, however, take it for granted that, rightly or wrongly, Aquinas believes that the doctrines of the Trinity and the Incarnation are grounded in biblical texts. You can also take it for granted that he thinks the same when it comes to belief in the resurrection of the dead and to what he means by the word "sacrament."

All of this becomes obvious in the foreword that Aquinas provides for SCG 4, in which there are echoes of what we find in SCG 1,1–9 (see chapter 1, section 4 here). This foreword is partly a reflection on Job 26:14 and partly a reiteration of what Aquinas has previously said or implied in the SCG concerning faith and reason. "There is in people," says Aquinas, "a threefold knowledge of things divine." He continues:

> Of these, the first is that in which people, by the natural light of reason, ascend to a knowledge of God through creatures. The second is that by which the divine truth—exceeding the human intellect—descends on us in the manner of revelation, not, however, as something made clear to be seen, but as spoken in words to be believed. The third is that by which the human mind will be elevated to gaze perfectly upon the things revealed.[5]

Aquinas goes on to concede that by reason we attain only an imperfect knowledge of God, albeit one "in keeping with reason's native capacity."[6] We should not, he says, suppose that divine revelation gives us perfect knowledge of God. We read:

> What has been passed on to us in the words of sacred Scripture may be taken as principles, so to say: thus, the things in those writings passed on to us in a hidden fashion we may endeavor to grasp mentally in some way or other, defending them from the attacks of the infidels. Nonetheless, that no presumption of knowing perfectly may be present, points of this kind must be proved from sacred Scripture, but not from natural reason. For all that, one must show that such things are not opposed to natural reason, in order to defend them from infidel attack.[7]

So Aquinas declares that the purpose of SCG 4 is to treat of matters concerning God that are taught by revelation.

We must treat of the things about God which surpass reason and are proposed for belief: such is the confession of the Trinity; second, of course, the things which surpass reason that have been done by God, such as the work of the Incarnation and what follows thereon; third, however, the things surpassing reason which are looked for in the ultimate end of people, such as the resurrection and glorification of bodies, the everlasting beatitude of souls, and matters related to these.[8]

The "confession of the Trinity" (*confessio trinitatis*) is the topic of SCG 4,2–26.

16.1 Aquinas's General Approach to the Trinity in SCG 4,2–26

Since Aquinas denies that the doctrine of the Trinity can be proved by philosophical reasoning, his discussion of it in SCG 4,2–26 amounts only to a defense of it based on biblical texts together with arguments intended to suggest that the doctrine is not intrinsically absurd. In grounding his account of the Trinity on Scripture, Aquinas is aiming to refute those who reject what he takes to be orthodox Trinitarian doctrine while taking their stand on the Bible. In arguing that the doctrine of the Trinity is thinkable or not incoherent, however, he seems to have a more philosophical readership in mind.

In accordance with what he takes to be Christian orthodoxy, Aquinas holds that God is Father, Son, and Holy Spirit.[9] He believes that, though there is but one God, there is also distinction within God. He takes the Bible to teach that Jesus is divine and is the Word that is God from eternity (see John 1:1–14). He also takes the Bible to teach that Jesus spoke of God as his father so as to teach that Jesus and his father are distinct, while also being one in some sense (see John 10:30). In addition, Aquinas thinks of the Bible as telling us that there is that which is divine though distinct from God the Father and God the Son—this being the Holy Spirit (see John 15:26 and John 16:1).

Aquinas does not mean that there are three Gods. He believes that the divine nature is shared by three who can be distinguished from each other without implying the truth of polytheism and without implying that the three that constitute God are three parts of God or three distinct features possessed by God. Yet what three does Aquinas take there to be in the one God? His answer, derived from the theological tradition he inherited, is "Three persons." God, for him, is a trinity of persons: Father, Son, and Holy Spirit.

Aquinas does not think that the persons of the Trinity are three human beings, or even three distinct centers of consciousness, as three people might be thought to be. His approach to divine simplicity clearly prevents him from doing that (see chapter 4 here). So he argues that "person," when it comes to the Trinity, signifies a relation. He says that the divine persons are subsistent relations that exist in God. In doing so, he thinks of God the Son as what God the Father has eternally conceived as knowing the divine nature. And he thinks of God the Holy Spirit as the love that is eternally there in God as God knows and wills the divine nature.

If I form a concept of myself, that concept is in me, as would be my willing or loving of myself based on that concept.[10] Aquinas does not think that God forms concepts as we do or that God wills as we do. He does not, for example, think of God forming concepts or willing over time while being able to lose concepts or to lose the ability to will or love. He does, however, think that God understands the divine nature and is drawn to it. So, with the doctrine of the Trinity in mind, he speaks of the eternal life of God with respect to understanding and willing. He says that God from eternity knows and wills the divine nature (see SCG 1,45–48 and 1,74). He also suggests that, though God is entirely simple, God's knowledge and will exist in God and are not just constructions of our minds when thinking about God. So, he argues, God's knowledge of God and God's willing of God can, in the light of divine revelation, be thought of as relationally distinct.[11] Yet given his thinking on divine simplicity, which entails that all that is in God *is* God, he also argues that what is relationally distinct in God *is* God. On this basis, he maintains that distinction can be intelligibly thought to be in God (albeit eternally) as God knows and loves what is divine. And he takes the doctrine of the Trinity as teaching that this is so. His view is that God is Father, Son, and Holy Spirit insofar as there are *real* relations *in* God. As I noted in chapter 9, section 3 here, Aquinas holds that "relations predicated of God in reference to creatures do not really exist in him" (SCG 2,12). So he is obviously prepared to distinguish between real and nonreal relations. Yet he takes the persons of the Trinity to be real relations, ones that exist *in* God.

When it comes to relations predicated of God with respect to creatures, Aquinas seems to be saying that, though God makes creatures to exist, God is not modified because changeable creatures exist over time as created by God. Aristotle's *Categories* provides a famous and influential discussion of relations, but it does not consider them with an eye on what Aquinas takes God to be considered as the first cause of things in all their ways of being.[12] Aquinas thinks that creatures undergo real changes and can be thought of as related to God on that basis since we can talk of them in sentences that use tenses. So Moses might have said "God is creating me," and I might say "God was creating Moses." But do these statements imply that God has undergone a change between being the creator of Moses and being the creator of me? Aquinas thinks not. He holds that God, though unchangeable, can be talked of by us as if undergoing change, as if coming in and out of various relationships between things. So, he thinks, we can truly say that God came to be my creator when I came to exist, or that God became incarnate at some time while not having been incarnate beforehand. But he does not think that God undergoes any real change as history proceeds. Even when it comes to the Incarnation of God in Christ, he insists that the change here is on the side of what is created. For him, "The Word became flesh" (John 1:14) does not mean that the Word went through a process. It means that something unprecedented occurred in the world: the birth of a child united to God in a special way, as the Son of God incarnate.

Yet Aquinas does think that there can be real relations in God, and he begins to defend himself by noting how it is that will and knowledge can exist in us while being distinct. My knowledge of you can be distinguished from my delight in you, my loving of you. So Aquinas thinks that there can be knowledge and will in God even if God has no creaturely objects to know and to deal with providentially. And he thinks that there being knowledge and will in God, without reference to creatures, is reason to think that the doctrine of the Trinity is not nonsensical. He argues that God can know and love God. He thinks that knowledge and will in God can be directed only to what God is. But, since he thinks that God's knowing and willing are not distinct from what God eternally is, he argues that God's knowledge and love of God cannot be anything other than God. He holds that all that is in God *is* God and that real relations in God *are* God.

We commonly take there to be relations insofar as certain physical things in the world are connected to each other in various ways. Hence, for example, we can readily speak of my heart as related to my hands since it pumps blood through my body. Again, I might be thought of as related to my cat as being its owner, or I might be thought of as related to you with respect to spatial position: me standing on your right, say, while you are to my left. Yet again, I might be related to someone by being that person's child, or I might be related to you as being the person to whom I owe money. However, there are other ways in which things can be thought of as related to each other. For example, the number 4 is related to the numbers 3 and 5 by being the successor of the former and the predecessor of the latter. Not all relations are between physical objects, and Aquinas holds that the persons of the Trinity can be thought of as distinct insofar as the relations between them are real, insofar as each person of the Trinity exists as related in some way to the others. This distinction between the divine persons is not, he says, such as to make them three Gods or three aspects of God. The divine persons are distinct as real and subsistent relations.

How are they distinct? Aquinas's answer is: (1) the Father is distinct from the Son because the Father brings forth (or, as Aquinas says, "generates") the Son; (2) the Son is distinct from the Father because the Son is generated by the Father; and (3) the Holy Spirit is distinct from the Father and the Son because the Holy Spirit is the love between the Father and the Son. Aquinas makes these points while appealing to the notion of procession. If X proceeds from Y, then X comes from Y in some sense. But Aquinas cannot possibly think of there being a coming forth of one thing in God from another as, say, there is a coming forth of a human child from its parents. So he takes procession in God to be eternal and not a matter of one thing bringing about another new individual thing distinct from itself, as is the case with human generation. For Aquinas, procession is internal to God and is nontemporal. The Son, he says, eternally proceeds from the Father as the Father eternally forms something like a concept or idea of the divine nature. And, he adds, the Holy Spirit eternally proceeds from the Father and the Son as being the love between them produced by them.[13]

In saying all this, Aquinas is drawing on what he takes to be inadequate analogies: knowledge and love in people. We can come to know by understanding what something is. So, says Aquinas, we can think of God as knowing what God is. We can also come to love what we know. So, says Aquinas, we can think of God as loving what God is. Yet he is very much aware that these comparisons between people and God are seriously flawed when used to articulate the doctrine of the Trinity. I can come to know or form concepts; but only as a creature, which God is not. Again, I can come to love; yet Aquinas does not think that my knowledge and my love are me. He thinks that they are aspects or properties of me (in his terminology, they are accidents in me), and he thinks that they are temporal, transient, and finite, as God is not. Nonetheless, despite the inadequacy of the comparisons he draws on when talking about the Trinity in SCG 4,2–26, Aquinas regards them as adequate enough to sustain the conclusion that people are not talking nonsense when professing the doctrine of the Trinity.

His reasoning is: (1) knowledge and will (love) exist in people; (2) there is, from eternity, knowledge and will in God to be distinguished from God's knowing and willing of creatures; (3) this knowledge and will is the divine nature, not attributes of it to be distinguished from the individual that God is; (4) nothing *in* God is distinct from the divine nature that God *is*; (5) so knowledge and will in God can be "internal" to God, and both are what God essentially is; (6) in knowing the divine nature, God must love it since the divine nature is pure goodness that has to be loved by one who is perfectly good and who truly knows all that can be known; (7) it is not contrary to reason to suppose that, in knowing the divine nature, God knows it and loves it; (8) since all that is in God is God, it is also not contrary to reason to suppose that there could be relations in God between God as knowing and loving God and between what God knows when knowing God and what God loves when loving God; (9) these have to be real relations in God if what God knows of God comes from God's knowledge and if God's love of God comes from God's knowledge; (10) a real relation, however, is a relation to something else; (11) so it is not against reason to suppose that in God there are real and distinct relations that are divine, though there is nothing in God that is not God.

Once again, I should stress that when arguing in this way, Aquinas is not trying to prove that the doctrine of the Trinity is true. He does not think that it is entailed by anything he has said in SCG 1–3. He is only saying that it is not refutable by reason. He believes the doctrine of the Trinity to hold that the Second Person of the Trinity proceeds from God the Father and that the Holy Spirit proceeds from God the Father and God the Son. That there should be such proceeding, amounting to three eternal divine persons, is not a conclusion that he holds to be rationally demonstrable. In SCG 1–3 we see what he views as knowable about God by reason, and the doctrine of the Trinity does not feature in these books.[14] It emerges for discussion only in SCG 4,2–26, in which Aquinas defends it by means of quotations from the Bible and by arguing that it is not contrary to reason. His SCG discussion of the Trinity does not spring from his natural theology. It is prompted by his Christian belief, based on his reading of the Bible, that God is somehow both one and three. It is also, of course, prompted by his belief that the doctrine of the Trinity comes with impeccable ecclesiastical credentials as enshrined in texts such as the Nicene-Constantinopolitan Creed.

Can we summarize Aquinas's SCG teaching on the Trinity in terms that he would have ratified? We can, since he provides such a summary himself in SCG 4,26. Here we read:

> One must hold that in the divine nature three persons subsist: the Father, the Son, and the Holy Spirit; and that these three are one God, distinguished from one another by relations only. For the Father is distinguished from the Son by the relation of paternity and innascibility (being unbegotten); the Son from the Father by a relation of sonship; the Father and the Son from the Holy Spirit by spiration, so to say; and the Holy Spirit from the Father and the Son by the procession of love; by this the Spirit proceeds from each of them.[15]

16.2 SCG 4,2–26: Some Details

16.2.1 Scripture and the Second Person of the Trinity (SCG 4,2–9)

Is the doctrine of the Trinity as Aquinas defends it biblical? Aquinas maintains that it is, and in SCG 4,2–9 he argues for this conclusion with respect to God the Son and with specific reference to passages in both the Old and New Testament. "Sacred Scripture," he says, "hands on to us the names of 'paternity' and 'sonship' in the divinity, insisting that Jesus Christ is the Son of God."[16] In defense of this judgment, Aquinas cites texts such as Psalm 2:7, Proverbs 30:4, Matthew 11:27, John 3:35, Romans 1:1–3, and Hebrews 1:6. He concludes, "we are taught from sacred Scripture that the Son of God, begotten of God, is God."[17]

Yet, notes Aquinas, certain people "perversely presumed to measure the truth of this doctrine by their own comprehension of it," thus embracing "opinions both vain and various."[18] In this connection, Aquinas singles out Cerinthus (fl. c. 160), Ebionites (early second century), Paul of Samosata (third century), Photinus (fourth century), Sabellius (possibly third century), and Arius (d. 336). In SCG 4,4–9, Aquinas maintains that all of these stand condemned on biblical grounds.

He lumps together Cerinthus, the Ebionites, Paul of Samosata, and Photinus as teaching that Jesus was only a human being and was God's son only by adoption, not by nature. When attacking this position, Aquinas appeals to biblical texts such as Proverbs 8:24–30, John 1:3, John 3:13, and Philippians 2:6.

Aquinas takes Sabellius to hold that the phrase "God the Son" designates "not a subsisting person but a kind of additional property of a pre-existing person, for the Father himself, in that he assumed flesh from the virgin Mary, received the name of Son."[19] According to Aquinas, however, "Scripture makes the falsity of this position quite manifest" since it "does not call Christ merely the virgin's son, but also the Son of God."[20]

Teachings ascribed to Arius provoked a major controversy among Christians from around 325 to 381. Arius was resolute in defending the uniqueness of God as the indivisible and changeless source of creatures. Accordingly, he taught that the Son of God (Jesus), though much to be venerated, is a creature who, in some sense, had a beginning and is not eternal. Thinking of Arius as holding to this conclusion, however, in SCG 4,7 Aquinas bluntly observes: "That this opinion is manifestly repugnant to divine Scripture anyone can see who considers diligently what sacred Scripture says."[21] In SCG 4,6, Aquinas notes biblical verses that he thinks to have been cited in defense of the claim that the Son of God is a creature. In SCG 4,7 he presents a scriptural counter blast to this claim.[22] Verses Aquinas cites at this point include Romans 9:5, Colossians 2:9, Hebrews 1:5, and 1 John 5:20. In SCG 4,8, therefore, we find Aquinas saying:

> Since truth cannot be truth's contrary, it is obvious that the points of scriptural truth introduced by the Arians to confirm their error cannot be helpful to their teaching. For divine scripture shows that the essence and divine nature of the Father and the Son are numerically identical, and according to this each is called true God, it must be that the Father and Son cannot be two gods but one God. For, if there were many gods, a necessary consequence would be the partition in each of the essence of divinity, just as in two people the humanity differs in number from one to the other; and the more so because the divine nature is not one thing and God another thing [see SCG 1,21]. From this it follows necessarily that, since there exists one divine nature in the Father and the Son, the Father and the Son are one God.[23]

You will see from this quotation, and from other parts of SCG 4, that Aquinas brings to his reading of Scripture much for which he argues philosophically in SCG 1–3.

16.2.2 Could There Be Generation in God?
(SCG 4,10–14)

In SCG 4,2–9 Aquinas is arguing as a biblical commentator, albeit one approaching the Bible with certain philosophical views. In SCG 4,10–14, however, he is clearly anxious to explain how what he takes the Bible to say about God the Son is not unreasonable. So he begins SCG 4,10 by saying:

> When all things are carefully considered, it is clear and manifest that sacred Scripture proposes this for belief about the divine generation: that the Father and Son, although distinct as persons, are nevertheless one God and have one essence or nature. But one finds this far removed from the nature of creatures: that any two be distinguished as individuals while being one in essence; so, human reason, proceeding from the properties of things, experiences difficulties in a great variety of ways in this secret (*secretum*) of divine generation.[24]

What sort of ways? Continuing with SCG 4,10, Aquinas explains by summarizing these ten arguments:[25]

1. Generation in the world comes about as a result of change, and things that are generated perish. Therefore, there cannot be generation in God, "who is immutable, incorruptible, and eternal."[26]

2. If generation involves a change, then what is generated is first potentially thus and so and then actually thus and so. But there cannot be any move from potentiality to actuality in the immutable divine nature.[27]

3. If God the Son is begotten by God the Father, the nature that he receives cannot be that of the Father as is the nature had by the child of a human father since this would entail polytheism. Nor can God the Son receive numerically the same nature as the Father has since this would entail that the divine nature is divisible, which it is not. We might suppose that the whole of the divine nature is passed into God the Son. Were that so, however, "it ceases to be in the Father; and so, in generation, the Father is corrupted."[28] We might think that the divine nature flows from the Father as water flows from a spring into a stream. But this would imply division in God. So, "the Son of God is neither a true son, since the Father's species is not his; nor true God, since he does not receive the divine nature."[29]

4. If God the Son is the divine essence, and if the divine essence has real or subsistent being, then the Father and Son are one subsistent thing, as Sabellius said. But if the Son is not the divine essence, then, as Arius thought, the Son is not God.[30]

5. What individuates a thing, what makes it to be itself and not something else, cannot be in some existing thing other than it. What different things share cannot make them to be what they are individually. Yet God's essence individuates God, and this essence cannot be in the Son. So as Arius held, the Son is not God. Either that, or there is, as Sabellianism teaches, no real distinction between God the Father and God the Son.

6. If God the Father is distinct from God the Son, while being one when it comes to essence, "there must be in them something other than the essence by which they are distinguished, for a common essence is ascribed to each and what is common cannot be a distinguishing principle. Therefore, that which distinguishes the Father from the Son must be other than the divine essence."[31] However, this conclusion entails that neither the Father nor the Son is God, in whom there is no composition of individuality and nature.[32] One might say that Father and Son "are distinguished by a relationship only, inasmuch as one is Father, and the other is the Son."[33] But "what is predicated relatively...seems not to predicate *a something* in that of which it is said, but rather a *to something*."[34] Therefore, an eternal and real distinction between Father and Son cannot be defended by saying that Father and Son, as truly God, are distinct by relationship alone. When we

speak of X as being related to Y in some sense, we must suppose there to be both something of which we can say what it is in itself and something to which this thing can be related as other than it. Thus, for example, servants are individual people who have masters who govern them. In that case, however, the relationship between God the Father and God the Son has to amount to one thing being what it is in itself and another thing being related to it. So if God the Father and God the Son are related, either one or both of them have their being independently of each other, like a servant as related to a master, or they are identical in the sense in which something is identical with itself. In that case, however, "it does not seem possible that the persons of the Father and the Son are distinguished by relations only."[35]

7. The relation distinguishing the Son from the Father is either real or only in thought.[36] If it is the former, (1) it cannot be the divine essence since this is shared by both the Father and the Son, and (2) there will be something in the Son that is not his essence—meaning that the Son is not divine since God is God's essence. If, however, the relation distinguishing the Son from the Father is something only in thought, it cannot "distinguish the Son from the Father personally, for things which are personally distinguished must be really distinguished."[37]

8. "Every relative depends on its correlative. But what depends on another is not true God. If, then, the persons of the Father and the Son are distinguished by relations, neither of them is true God."[38]

9. If the Father is God and if the Son is God, the word "God" must signify their nature, not any accident they possess, for there are no accidents in God (see SCG 1,23). Now, there can be no plurality of subjects in one nature, even though different things might have a nature in common, as two people can be human. So, "if the Father and the Son are two persons, it seems impossible that they are one God."[39]

10. Plurality is presupposed when we ascribe to things predicates that are opposed to each other. Yet we do this when we say that the Father is unbegotten and generating while the Son is begotten. So the Father and the Son cannot be one God.[40]

It is in response to these arguments that Aquinas develops his account of God the Father and God the Son in terms of what reflects on itself and understands: the account I summarized in chapter 16, section 1. Having noted ways in which some living things are superior to others, he says: "The ultimate perfection of life belongs to God, in whom understanding is not other than being.... Accordingly, the intention understood in God must be the divine essence itself."[41] Aquinas means that what exists in God as God eternally knows the divine essence cannot but be God. He concedes that when we come to know or understand something we inevitably acquire something accidental to us, something that arises in us but not because of what we are essentially. But he denies that this is the case when it comes to what is in God as God knows the divine nature. So, he argues, if we think of God as able to have an understanding of divinity, that understanding will not be different from the divine nature, since all that is in God is God. He adds: "From these considerations we can somehow conceive how divine generation is to be taken."[42]

We cannot, says Aquinas, take it to be a matter of one thing springing from another as, say, a plant or an animal springs from another plant or animal. We can, however, intelligibly think of it as an eternal coming forth in God of what is God. He writes:

> It is manifest that God understands what God is [see SCG 1,47]. Now, whatever is understood should, as understood, be in the one who understands, for the significance of the very act of understanding is this: the grasping of that which is understood by an intellect; hence, even our intellect understanding itself is within itself, not only as belonging to one thing with a particular essence, but also as grasped by itself in the act of understanding. God, therefore, must be in God as what is understood by God.[43]

Aquinas believes that when we arrive at an understanding of something, there comes to be in us a "word" (*verbum*) in our minds. He holds that our speaking in words that can be written down or heard reflects what is conceptually in us even before we speak.[44] He also thinks that if I tell you what something is, I am passing on to you what is in my mind as a matter of understanding in me. So, drawing on the thought of there being a word in the mind of one who understands, he goes on to say that, reflecting on divine revelation, we might say that in God there is a word who is God.

Here Aquinas refers to the first chapter of the Gospel of John. He says that we can think of the word of God (i.e., God's understanding of God) as being the Word of which John 1 speaks when referring to that which was always with God and which was God while becoming incarnate in time. The being (*esse*) of this word, Aquinas goes to say, "is identical with that of the divine intellect and, consequently, with that of God, who is God's own intellect."[45] Aquinas accepts that when we understand ourselves, the understanding in us arises in time and is not a human being. It is a grasping by intellect of what a human being is. When it comes to God understanding God, however, matters are different.

The Word of God, precisely because he is God understood, is true God, having the divine being naturally, because the natural being of God is not one being and that of God's understanding another....The divine Word is not merely an intention understood, as our word is, but it is also a thing existing and subsisting in nature. For God is a true subsistent thing, since God is substantial being in the highest degree.[46]

Since God is entirely immaterial, Aquinas adds, it is "impossible that the divine nature be specifically one and numerically different. The Word of God, therefore, has a nature in common with God and has it with numerical identity. For this reason the Word of God and the God whose Word he is are not two gods but one God.... God is both the divine essence and the divine act of being."[47] So, Aquinas maintains, the Word of God eternally arising in God proceeds from God or is generated or conceived by God. In this sense it is God's offspring. In this sense it is God the Son. Obviously, in human generation there are temporal stages, and what is generated is spatially and physically distinct from its generator. However, Aquinas thinks that, if there is generation in God, conception, birth, and being present to a generator are simultaneous. He says: "The Word of God is at once conceived, brought forth, and present."[48]

Given what he has been saying about the coming forth in God of God the Son, should Aquinas not conclude that God the Son can form a concept of himself, thereby generating another son? Indeed, should he not conclude that generation in God goes on without end? In keeping with what he takes to be orthodox teaching on the Trinity, Aquinas holds that in God there is but one divine Son. In SCG 4,13, though, he does allude to the questions I have just raised. He writes:

It seems to follow from the foregoing both that the divine Word has another word and the divine Son another son. For it was shown that the Word of God is true God. Whatever, therefore, belongs to God must belong also to the Word of God. But God necessarily understands God. Therefore, the Word of God also understands the Word of God. If, then, one says that because God understands God there is in God a Word begotten by God, it seems to follow that in the Word so far as he understands himself one must allow another word. And thus there will be a word of the Word and a son of the Son. And that word, if divine, will again understand himself and will have another word. In this way, the divine generation will proceed to infinity.[49]

How does Aquinas deal with this difficulty to there being only one Word or Son in God? He does so by reminding his reader that God the Son is not another God distinct from God whose Word he is. God the Son, says Aquinas, is not an intellect distinct from the intellect of God the Father. God the Son is nothing but God's understanding of God, not something forming a concept of itself and, therefore, not something generating one or more divine sons. So, Aquinas argues: "Just as the Word is not another god, so neither is he another intellect; consequently, not another act of understanding; hence, not another word."[50]

What, though, of the ten arguments in SCG 4,10? In SCG 4,14 Aquinas says that they have been refuted by what he argues in SCG 4,11–13. Generation in God, he notes, does not involve material change or a move from potentiality to actuality. It is not the same as human generation of children, so it does not raise questions as to whether God the Father gives the divine nature to God the Son wholly or partially. Again, says Aquinas, distinction in God does not imply multiplication of deities. The Word of God is God and is the divine essence. There is distinction in God only because relations exist in God that subsist in the divine nature and are not accidents ascribable to God. These relations, Aquinas insists, are real (*secundum rem*) and "not in understanding alone" (*non solo intellectu*). God the Son is what God the Father generates, and God the Father is what generates God the Son. Here, uniquely, we have relation in what is but one essence. Or, as Aquinas puts this thought:

> From the fact that in God there is unity of essence and distinction of relations it becomes manifest that nothing stops one's finding opposites in the one God, at least those opposites which follow the distinction of relation: *begetting* and *begotten*, for instance, which are opposed relatively, and *begotten* and *unbegotten* which are opposed as affirmation and negation. For wherever there is distinction one must find the opposition of negation and affirmation. Things which differ in no affirmation or negation are entirely undifferentiated, for the first would have to be in every respect one with the second, and thus they would be thoroughly identified, and in no way distinct.[51]

Here Aquinas is saying that if everything said of one thing can be said of another, we lack reason for distinguishing between them just on the basis of what is said of them. But if we can say of X that it is distinguishable from Y, there is a real distinction between X and Y. And, thinks Aquinas, there is a real distinction between God the Father and God the Son since the Father and the

Son are distinguishable even though they are one in essence. Distinguishable how? With respect to their relation to each other.

16.2.3 The Holy Spirit as Divine (SCG 4,15–26)

In SCG 4,15 Aquinas observes that "the authority of the divine Scriptures not only tells us about the Father and the Son in divinity, but together with these also numbers the Holy Spirit."[52] Yet should Christians think of the Holy Spirit as being divine as are the Father and God the Son? In SCG 4,15–26, Aquinas argues that they should.

As with his discussion of God the Son, Aquinas begins his discussion of God the Holy Spirit by appealing to biblical texts (SCG 4,15–18). But, and again reflecting the progression of thought in SCG 4,2–14, he continues in SCG 4,19–26 to consider how we might take the claim that the Holy Spirit is God to be thinkable without just quoting from the Bible. He writes:

> Taught by holy Scripture, we maintain this firmly about the Holy Spirit: that he is true God, subsistent, personally distinct from the Father and the Son. But one ought to consider how a truth of this kind must be grasped somehow, in order to defend it from the attacks of unbelievers.[53]

When it comes to the Holy Spirit being God, in SCG 4,15 Aquinas cites Matthew 28:19, John 15:26, and 1 John 5:7. In SCG 4,16 he notes biblical texts that might be thought to suggest that the Holy Spirit is a creature; but in SCG 4,17 he denies that they do this while quoting yet more biblical texts that he thinks of as teaching that the Holy Spirit is truly divine. He takes it to be clear that Scripture tells us that the Holy Spirit is God and is something in God distinct from the Father and the Son: a point he reiterates in SCG 4,18.

Yet how can we understand the Holy Spirit if this teaching is true? In one sense, of course, Aquinas does not think that we can understand the Holy Spirit since he takes the Holy Spirit to be God and since he denies that we can understand what God is (see chapter 5 here). It is often said that the doctrine of the Trinity presents us with something more mysterious than the claim that God exists, but such is not Aquinas's view. He thinks that our powers of understanding have seriously broken down as soon as we entertain the assertion "God exists." Yet, just as he tries to beat against the barriers to our understanding when it comes to "God exists," he aims to indicate that people are not talking nonsense when they affirm the doctrine of the Trinity. Hence what we find in SCG 4,11–14, and hence what we find in SCG 4,19 and 23.

Here Aquinas begins by noting that something with understanding must also will or desire. He argues:

In every intellectual nature a will must be discovered. For an intellect is made to be in act by an intelligible form so far as it is understanding, as a natural thing is made to be in act in its natural being by its proper form. But a natural thing, through the form by which it is perfected in its species, has an inclination to its proper operations and to its proper end, which it achieves by operations...and it tends to what is fitting for itself. Hence, also, from an intelligible form there must follow in people who understand an inclination to their proper operations and their proper end. Of course, this inclination in an intellectual nature is the will, which is the principle of operations in us, those by which we who understand operate for an end. For end and the good are the will's object. One must, therefore, discover a will in everyone who understands.[54]

Here Aquinas is saying that, as understanding, we are drawn to what we think of as good for us. And he thinks that this being drawn is love in us. He holds that we love what we desire or are attracted to.[55] We are drawn to what we delight in. "To be affected toward something," he says, "is to love that thing."[56] He adds:

From the fact that we love something we desire that thing if it is absent; we rejoice, of course, if it is present; and we are sad when we are kept from it; and we hate those things which keep us from what we love, and grow angry against them.[57]

Aquinas then goes on to say that what is loved is in the intellect of the lover as well as in the lover's will. He takes it to be in the lover's will as an end to which the lover is drawn, and he thinks that if the lover attains such an end, then the will of the lover comes to be at rest as delighting in what it has gained.

Now, Aquinas is clear that there is intellect in God (see chapter 7 here). So, he has no problem in thinking of there being will in God (see chapter 8 here). Given his thoughts on divine simplicity, however, he cannot suppose that knowledge or will in God amount to accidents that come to exist in God as God moves from one way of being to another. Consequently, he argues that both knowledge and will in God are God and that love in God is God.

What, though, can God will just by being God and not by creating creatures to love? Obviously, thinks Aquinas, the answer to this question has to be that God as loving by essence has to love God. So, he argues, we can think of the Holy Spirit as the love that eternally comes forth as God the Father and God the Son know and love each other. Aquinas has already maintained that God the Son proceeds from God the Father by generation. He has said that God the Son is nothing but God as generated by God the Father and that God the Father is nothing but

God as generating God the Son. In SCG 4,19 Aquinas suggests that we can think of God the Holy Spirit as eternally coming forth as God the Father and God the Son love each other. We can think of there being in God not just generating and being generated. We can think of there being love as the Father loves the Son and as the Son loves the Father. This love, says Aquinas, is the Holy Spirit, which is not an accident in God but is what God eternally and unchangeably is. He writes:

> A thing's proceeding in order to be in the will as the beloved is in the lover is not a proceeding by way of generation, just as a thing's proceeding in order to be in the intellect does have the essentials of generation.... Therefore, God proceeding by way of love does not proceed as begotten.... But, because the beloved in the will exists as inclining, and somehow inwardly impelling the lover toward the very thing beloved, and an impulse of a living thing from within belongs to a spirit, this is suitable: that God proceeding by way of love should be called God's "spirit," as it were a kind of existing spiration.[58]

The idea here is that the Holy Spirit can be thought of as distinct in relation to its origin, as God the Son is distinct from God the Father when it comes to the relationship between generator and generated. Distinct how? Not as what is known can be thought of as distinct from a knower, but distinct as proceeding as love between things. Aquinas thinks that God the Father finds in God the Son a likeness of what God the Father is. He also thinks that it is not stupid to say that God the Father and God the Son can love what they see in each other, this love being the Holy Spirit. Aquinas takes this thought to commit him to saying that the Holy Spirit "proceeds" from the Father and the Son and not from the Father alone. As Herbert McCabe notes:

> It is essential to Aquinas's doctrine that the Holy Spirit proceeds from *both* the Father and the Son, and not merely from the Father. The reason for this is that the only distinction admissible in the Trinity is that of being at opposite ends of a relation based on a procession of origination. If the Holy Spirit does not proceed from the Son, there is no such relation between them and therefore no distinction between the Son and the Holy Spirit. Thus in Aquinas's account there are two processions in God, one of the intellect, God's knowing himself, which is generation, and one of the will, God's enjoying himself.... Each of these gives rise to a relationship with two (opposite) ends, the origin and the originated. There are thus four of these relations. This does not, however, result in four distinct persons, for in order to be distinct, a person must be at the

opposite end from both other persons. The Father is opposed to the Son by generating and to the Spirit by spiration. The Son is opposed to the Father by being generated and to the Spirit by spiration. The Spirit is opposed to both the Father and the Son by being spirated.[59]

In adopting this position Aquinas, of course, is taking sides on a matter that has divided Eastern Christian churches and the Western (Latin) church for centuries.[60] The belief that the Spirit proceeds from both the Father and the Son was defended by the Council of Lyons (1274) and the Council of Florence (1439) and was widely held in the West long before those councils. It features, for example, in the so-called Athanasian Creed (c. 381–428). However, this belief is not explicitly asserted in the Nicene Creed or in the original text of the Nicene-Constantinopolitan Creed. Nevertheless, Aquinas upholds it and turns to its defense in SCG 4,24–25.

He begins by arguing that it coheres with the New Testament and the teaching of eminent Christian theologians since New Testament times, such as St. Augustine. Then he says that the truth that the Spirit proceeds from the Son as well as the Father is "also clarified by straight reasoning" (*etiam evidentibus rationibus apparet*). He writes:

> Among things, with the material distinction gone (and in the divine persons such can have no place), one discovers no differentiation except by some opposition. For things which have no opposition to one another can be simultaneously in something identical; thus, no distinction can be caused by them. Take white and triangular. Although they are diverse, they can, because they are not opposed, be in an identical thing. But one must set down, according to the documents of the Catholic faith, that the Holy Spirit is distinct from the Son; otherwise there would not be a Trinity, but a duality of persons. Therefore, a distinction of this kind must take place through some opposition.[61]

Aquinas goes on to say that when it comes to the persons of the Trinity, opposition cannot be, for example, that of affirmation and negation, which distinguishes what is from what is not. Nor can it be opposition of contrariety (i.e., difference springing from what Aquinas refers to as "form" or "nature") since each divine person is divine and is but one form, that of God, whose nature is *ipsum esse subsistens* ("subsistent Being Itself"; see chapter 4 here). So, Aquinas concludes:

> One divine person is not distinguished from another except by the opposition of relation: thus, the Son is distinguished from the Father

consequently to the relative opposition of father and son. For in the divine persons there can be no relative opposition except according to origin.... Therefore, if the Holy Spirit is distinguished from the Son, he is necessarily from the Son.... The Son is from the Father and so is the Holy Spirit. Therefore, the Father must be related both to the Son and the Holy Spirit as a principle or origin to that which is from the principle or origin. He is related to the Son by reason of paternity, but not to the Holy Spirit; for then the Holy Spirit would be the Son, because paternity is a relation to nothing but a son. There must, then, be another relation to the Father by which he is related to the Holy Spirit; and we call this "spiration." In the same way, since there is in the Son a relation by which he is related to the Father, the name of which is sonship, there must also be in the Holy Spirit another relation by which he is related to the Father, and this is called *procession*. And thus, in accord with the origin of the Son from the Father, there are two relations, one in the originator, the other in the originated: that is, spiration and procession. Therefore, paternity and spiration do not constitute two persons, but pertain to the one person of the Father, for they have no opposition to one another. Therefore, neither would sonship and procession constitute two persons, but would pertain to one, unless they had an opposition to one another. But there is no opposition to assign save that by way of origin. Hence, there must be an opposition of origin between the Son and the Holy Spirit so that the one is from the other.[62]

Aquinas is not here denying primacy in the Trinity to God the Father. Nor is he suggesting that the Holy Spirit is inferior to the Father and the Son. He is arguing that if there is distinction in God as taught by the doctrine of the Trinity, the distinction has to arise (albeit eternally) from there being what is at opposite ends of a relation based on a coming forth. When it comes to the Holy Spirit, he thinks, this is a coming forth based on the generation of the Son by the Father, something that amounts to the love between them. For Aquinas, the Holy Spirit is not a likeness of God, as he takes God the Son to be as conceived by God the Father as knowing himself. Rather, the Holy Spirit is an enjoyment or delight that eternally exists as the Father and the Son love each other, and it is in this sense that Aquinas thinks of God the Holy Spirit as a person.

What, though, can it mean to say that there are divine persons? Aquinas knows that what he took to be orthodox theology speaks of there being three persons in God. When it comes to the Trinity, however, he is not remotely inclined to think that "person" has to mean "human being" or "center of consciousness" or something along those lines. Three thinking individuals (whether bodily or not) cannot be one thinking individual. Yet, says Aquinas, we can use the word "person" to note what Father, Son, and Spirit each are. He thinks that the Father is a person and that the Son and Holy Spirit are persons. Why so? Because he thinks that "person" can be used to mean "individual" *in some sense.*

There is a famous definition of "person" deriving from Boethius (c. 480–524), and Aquinas often quotes it with approval. According to this definition, a person is "an individual substance of rational nature" (*Persona est rationalis naturae individua substantia*).[63] It is, however, clear that, for Aquinas, the persons of the Trinity are (1) not individuals (considered as members of a kind), (2) not substances (considered as individually existing things that exist independently of other things), (3) not rational (as going through processes of reasoning), and (4) not things having a nature to be distinguished from what they essentially are.

When it comes to his discussion of the Trinity in SCG 4, it is not the Boethian understanding of "person" that is at the forefront of Aquinas's thinking. What is at the forefront is the notion of relation. In his discussion of the Trinity in the SCG, as well as in his discussion of it in the *Summa Theologiae*, Aquinas seems intent to show that there is a unique sense in which Father, Son, and Holy Spirit can be thought of as distinct even though they are not members of a kind, not individually existing things that exist independently of other things, not things going through processes of reasoning, and not things having a nature to be distinguished from what they are. As McCabe observes, "For Aquinas the key to the Trinity is not the notion of person but of relation."[64] As McCabe also notes, we should not read Aquinas as being sexually biased as he cheerfully talks about God the Father and God the Son. Aquinas inherits such gender language from the Bible; but when he talks about the Trinity, gender is not an issue. As I have shown, in SCG 4,24 he writes as though conception always results in a son. He says: "Paternity is a relation to nothing but a son," which is manifestly false. Yet one can hardly suppose that Aquinas seriously thought otherwise. He knew that there can be fathers of daughters. As he writes about Father and Son when it comes to the Trinity, he appears to be somewhat mesmerized by biblical texts in which God is said to have a son. He is also, I presume, influenced by the thought, common in his day, that women did not contribute physically to the human generative process. But his discussion of the Trinity in SCG 4 could, without losing anything of importance in its reasoning, be rephrased so as to leave Aquinas saying, for example, that God the Son is generated from God the parents. As McCabe notes when commenting on Aquinas's Trinitarian thinking, "the plural 'parents' would be no more misleading than is the sexual connotation of 'Father.'"[65]

16.3 Is Aquinas Right on the Trinity?

SCG 4,2–26 raise many questions. To start with, we might wonder whether Aquinas's citations of Scripture suffice to show that the doctrine of the Trinity is true in the sense that he understood it to be from his reading of the Nicene Creed, the Nicene-Constantinopolitan Creed, and the teaching of the Council of Chalcedon. Is what Aquinas believes to be the orthodox doctrine of the Trinity confirmed by the Bible? People who do not regard the Bible or church councils as having any authority will be unconcerned with this question. More likely, they will ask whether the doctrine of the Trinity can be proved philosophically or whether it is coherent. But Aquinas does take seriously the authority of the Bible and church councils. So one can reasonably ask whether he is right to hold that what church councils have said concerning the Trinity is a correct representation of what we find in the Bible.

We might think that it is not, since the doctrine of the Trinity as it emerges in the Nicene Creed, the Nicene-Constantinopolitan Creed, and what comes from the Council of Chalcedon is just not there in the Bible. These councils purported to be correctly clarifying the teaching of Scripture in opposition to readings of the Bible at odds with their understanding of it, and they would not have been doing that if the Bible unambiguously taught what the councils did concerning the Trinity. Yet Aquinas thinks that their reading of the Bible was correct insofar as it resulted in a formally stated doctrine of the Trinity. So was he right to think this?

I raise this as a serious question. Yet I am not able to offer an answer to it in this book. To do so would require me to present detailed analyses of the biblical texts Aquinas appeals to in SCG 4,2–26. Here, I think, we need to look to contemporary biblical scholars who have worked on the texts he cites and who have, drawing on the best historical and textual research now available, tried to understand what their authors might have meant when writing them. You might think, as I suspect Aquinas did, that we can lift verses from the Bible and correctly understand them as saying just what they seem to read to us as saying when taken in isolation and as so many words on paper.[66] And if you think that, then you might well find Aquinas to be victorious every time he cites Scripture in defense of the doctrine of the Trinity as found in the conciliar texts governing his discussion of it. If you do not think that, however, you will suppose that a lot of work needs to be done so as to show that Aquinas's many biblical references in defense of what he takes to be the doctrine of the Trinity show what he takes them to show. You might say that they do exactly this since Aquinas is reading the Bible in the light of orthodox church teaching and since that teaching should govern our understanding of what biblical texts mean. If you take that view, however, you will have little or no interest in how various biblical texts came to be written or in what their authors, in their various historical contexts, might have meant when composing them: a lack of interest that has been defended by some and castigated by others.

Abstracting from matters of biblical interpretation, however, there is another question that might be raised concerning what we find in SCG 4,2–26. This is a question that has been pressed by theologians who think that philosophy should not be governing theology as they take it to do for Aquinas.

As obvious as it is that SCG 4,2–26 is written by a Christian, and as obvious as it is that Aquinas never claims to demonstrate the truth of the doctrine of the Trinity, it is equally obvious that what this Christian says about the Trinity relies on a number of conclusions he holds to be philosophically demonstrable. The SCG is shot through with the conviction that, without benefit of revelation, we can reasonably conclude that God is entirely simple (see chapter 4 here) and that our best "name" for God is "He Who Is" (see chapter 5 here). Yet, one might ask, why should Aquinas turn to the doctrine of the Trinity in the light of conclusions that he has arrived at philosophically? Should he not have started with divine revelation and discarded his philosophy of God as presented in SCG 1?

This question has often been pressed, with respect not only to what Aquinas says about the Trinity in SCG 4,2–26 but also to what he writes about the Trinity in works other than the SCG—the *Summa Theologiae*, for instance.[67] But, I think, it is obvious how Aquinas would reply to it. First, he would say that truth cannot contradict truth. Then he would say that there are truths that we can know about God apart from divine revelation, truths that have to be borne in mind when reflecting on revelation. Perhaps he would add that we should not abandon what we know to be true about God when reflecting on what we believe to be true of God.

It is easy to sympathize with Aquinas as he thinks along these lines. If the natural theology presented by him in the SCG and elsewhere is sound, how else could he think? You might argue that Aquinas's natural theology is not sound, and if that conclusion is correct, then, perhaps, he should indeed rest what he says about the Trinity only on divine revelation as identified in some way and as contrasted with what can be known by reason or philosophical argument of the kind that he respected, this being deductive argument leading from evidently true premises to true conclusions entailed by them. Yet Aquinas thought that his natural theology was sound. So why should he not take it for granted when turning to the doctrine of the Trinity? Why should any people who think that they have established truths about God by reason not take these truths for granted when reflecting on the Trinity? Some would reply that we need to acknowledge that human beings are fallen and that their reason is always clouded and unreliable. If one really believes that, however, then one ought always to doubt what reason seems to declare, whether about God or anything else. If our reason is always clouded, then we have achieved no advances in knowledge since we first appeared on earth. But why believe that? And, if we do believe it, should we not refrain from trying to argue a case for it?

That said, however, is Aquinas right to speak about God while abstracting from the doctrine of the Trinity? He obviously does this. Hence, for example, the conclusions defended in SCG 1 are not ones that he takes to establish the existence of the Trinity. It is only in SCG 4 that he turns to the Trinity directly. But if God is Father, Son, and Spirit, does not talk of God that is not grounded in this doctrine effectively fail to be talk about God? And if that is so, should we not conclude that what Aquinas says about the Trinity in the SCG is theologically dubious since it appears to treat the doctrine of the Trinity as a kind of appendage to an otherwise self-contained account of what God is?

In response to this question, I would deny the premises on which it seems to rely. I take these to be (1) "We cannot truly talk about something without taking it to be all that it actually is," and (2) "Aquinas regards the doctrine of the Trinity as a kind of appendage to an otherwise self-contained account of what God is."

The first premise here is evidently false. We can speak truly of many things without explicitly alluding to all that they are. We can, for example, truly conclude that John is a thief without paying any attention to the fact that he is six feet two inches tall, or even being aware of this fact. Again, one can deduce that all cats are mammals without knowing, or alluding to, where they were born, what their coloring is, or even the breed of cat to which they belong.

The second premise is false since Aquinas obviously thinks that God is *essentially*, and not accidentally, Father, Son, and Holy Spirit. If he thinks that, he cannot possibly regard the doctrine of the Trinity as an appendage to a true account of what God is.

The fact that Aquinas is happy to speak about God in the SCG without bringing in the doctrine of the Trinity derives from his distinction between truths of reason and truths of faith. Much of the SCG is concerned with what we can know of God by reason, and as I have shown, Aquinas does not take that to amount to a knowledge or understanding of God's essence (see chapters 4 and 5 here). Nor does he take it to amount to knowledge concerning a distinction of persons in God. He does not claim that the doctrine of the Trinity is philosophically demonstrable. One should not conclude from this fact, however, that he does not positively believe that God is essentially Father, Son, and Spirit.

Indeed, it is clear from SCG 4 2–26 that Aquinas takes God to be just this while starting from what he believes to be divine revelation. Christian theologians with no interest in what might be established about God without benefit of revelation may, understandably, want to write nothing about God other than a series of books or articles on the Trinity based on the Bible. Aquinas, however, though revering what he took to be the doctrine of the Trinity as revealed in the Bible, also maintains that this doctrine can be discussed separately from the claim that there are creatures who depend from moment to moment on what is not a being among beings.

Why does he think this? Obviously, because he holds that reason tells us something about God without penetrating to the truth of the doctrine of the Trinity. Is he right to think so? He is if he is right to think that we can speak truly of God without having to conclude that God is Father, Son, and Spirit. And, given his claim that reason can only arrive at truths about God based on causal arguments (see chapter 2 here), he is right in thinking that we cannot by reason show that God is three persons. As Peter Geach says:

> Since all the propositions of natural theology tell us only what is true of a being by virtue of his being God, they cannot serve to establish any distinction there might be between two Persons both of whom were God and the same God. Thus, so far as natural theology goes, the question whether many distinct Persons can be one and the same God is *demonstrably undecidable*, on Aquinas's view.[68]

Or as Aquinas himself says in *Summa Theologiae* 1a,32,1:

> It is impossible to come to the knowledge of the Trinity of divine persons through natural reason. For...through natural reason we can know God only from creatures; and they lead to the knowledge of God as effects do to their cause. Therefore, by natural reason we can know of God only what characterizes God necessarily as the source of all beings.... Now the creative power of God is shared by the whole Trinity; hence it goes with the unity of nature, not the distinctions of persons. Therefore, through natural reason we can know what has to do with the unity of nature, but not with the distinction of persons.[69]

However, if God is simple, as Aquinas maintains, how can there be three who are God? As I have said, Aquinas's answer is that God is three subsistent relations within the divine nature. This nature, he thinks, is not multipliable; so there cannot be three gods as there can be three people or three cats. For Aquinas, the divine essence is God and is not multipliable. Yet, Aquinas argues, this does not mean that there could not be real distinction within God since such distinction could be within the divine essence and based on subsistent relations. But can we make sense of the notion of subsistent relations?

It is, I think, significant that Aquinas does not allude to subsistent relations except in his various discussions of the Trinity, and he does not cite non-Trinitarian examples of subsistent relations. Generally, he takes a real relation, as opposed to a notional one, to be an accident in a creature.[70] So, for example, he assumes that it is obvious that if John comes to think about Fred, John comes to be what he was previously not, that is, related to Fred as thinking about him. Yet Aquinas does not take subsistent relations in God to be accidents. So why does he introduce the idea of subsistent relations when talking about the Trinity?

He does so (1) because he thinks that revelation teaches that there is distinction in God, (2) because he does not want to say that there are three Gods, and (3) because he thinks that he has reason to deny that there are accidents in God. If there is distinction in God, Aquinas reasons, this cannot be because of distinguishable accidents that God has, for all that is in God is God, who is *ipsum esse* (see chapter 4, section 4 here). So Aquinas concludes that distinction in God has to be a matter of there being subsistent relations in God, and in doing so he introduces a notion of real relation that goes beyond the way that he understands this when talking philosophically about created things.

You might say that he should not do so. As you will by now have realized, though, Aquinas frequently employs what he takes to be familiar philosophical terms or words so as to use them in ways that go beyond their usual sense. Take, for example, his use of "agent cause" when talking about God as creator of all things from nothing (see chapter 9, section 5 here). Aquinas knows that the notion of agent cause arose because of reflection on things in the world that modify other things. However, with the notion of God as creator in mind, he speaks of God as an agent cause that makes things exist without thereby changing them. And when it comes to the Trinity, Aquinas uses the term "relation" so as to say that in God there can be relations that are subsistent and not merely accidents. In this context, Aquinas views the word "relation" as justified because of the teaching that God is Father, Son, and Spirit. He takes this teaching to imply that the Father is really distinct from the Son and the Holy Spirit, that the Son is really distinct from the Father and the Holy Spirit, and that the Holy Spirit is really distinct from the Father and the Son. Given his thinking on divine simplicity, he therefore concludes that relations in God cannot be accidents but must subsist in God and be all that God is. This might well be thought of as a natural conclusion for him to arrive at given his view of divine simplicity and given his conviction that orthodox Christian teaching holds to there being three persons in God. If God is entirely simple, as Aquinas holds, then there can be no question of there being three Gods or of there being accidents in God. Yet if there are distinct persons in God, these "persons" cannot be accidents in God. The divine persons have to be thought of only as subsistent relations existing in God. So there is a plausible logical progression that leads Aquinas from belief in God as *ipsum esse*, and from subscription to what he takes to be orthodox Trinitarian doctrine, to the conclusion that Father, Son, and Spirit can be thought of as real but subsisting relations in God based on relative opposition grounded in proceeding (the Son from the Father, and the Holy Spirit from the Father and the Son).

Some theologians and philosophers have rejected this conclusion while favoring what is commonly referred to as "Social Trinitarianism." This comes in different forms from different authors, but it basically seems to amount to the view that the Trinity is a group or society of three interacting beings working together as distinct centers of consciousness while relating to each other in something like the way people occasionally do. And some Social Trinitarians have partly defended their position by criticizing Aquinas on the Trinity. Hence, for example, William Lane Craig writes:

> It can be safely said that on no reasonable understanding of "person" can a person be equated with a relation. Relations do not cause things, know truths, or love people in the way the Bible says God does. Moreover, to think that the intentional objects of God's knowing Himself and loving Himself constitute in any sense really distinct persons is wholly implausible. Even if God the Father were a person, and not a mere relation, there is no reason, even in Aquinas's own metaphysical system, why the Father as understood and loved by Himself would be different persons. The distinction involved here is merely that between oneself as subject ("I") and as object ("me"). There is no more reason to think that the individual designated by "I," "me" and "myself" constitute a plurality of persons in God's case than in a human being's case.[71]

Craig here seems to be presupposing some univocal sense of "person" as an individual thinking thing that Aquinas is not employing in SCG 4,2–26. He also seems not to understand how Aquinas's talk of three persons in the Trinity is presented so as to cohere with his "metaphysical system," which positively commits him (see SCG 1) to insisting that the existence of God is not different from God's essence. Be that as it may, though, Craig ends up talking about the persons of the Trinity as if they were parts of some whole, which is why he declares himself to be a Social Trinitarian. God the Father, he says, "is not the whole Godhead," and "it seems undeniable that there is some sort of part/whole relation obtaining between the persons of the Trinity and the entire Godhead."[72] And, as I have said, other contemporary thinkers share this idea of the Trinity being a collection of things having a common nature that they share, as three human beings share the property of being human.[73] By now, though, you will realize why Aquinas would be suspicious of that suggestion. He would take it to be contrary to what God is as simple and lacking composition. He would think that it must somehow erroneously involve a commitment to tritheism, to there being three Gods.

In defense of what Aquinas says about the Trinity, some philosophers have claimed that identity should be understood in relative terms. The doctrine of the Trinity, as Aquinas understands it, says that Father, Son, and Spirit are different persons, each of whom is the one, true God. On the supposition that if X is identical with Y, then all that is true of X is true of Y, one might suppose that the doctrine of the Trinity has to be false since if Father, Son, and Spirit are distinct, they cannot all be the one, true God. Yet might not X and Y be the same even though different things are true of X and Y? It has been argued that they can.

The notion of identity seems to be the same as the notion of sameness. If X is identical with Y, then X is somehow the same as Y. Can we, however, sensibly think of sameness in the abstract? If we say that X is the same as Y, do we not have to provide an answer to the question "Same what as what, and in what respect?" Do we not at least need recourse to a noun when claiming that X and Y are the same? Arguably we do. "They are the same" means nothing unless we know what we are talking about. We can, though, make sense of statements like "The cat that jumped on my lap today is the same cat that jumped on my lap yesterday." We cannot understand what "X is good" means unless we know what it is we are talking about (see chapter 6, section 6.2 here). Similarly, we cannot understand what "X is Y" or "X is the same as Y" could mean unless we know what X and Y are supposed to be. In other words, we might think that identity is not something absolute but is relative somehow.

That we would be right to think this has been argued with much logical sophistication by Peter Geach. As an analysis of "There is but one God," he suggests "For some y, y is God, and, for any z, if z is God, z is the same God as y." Then he adds:

> It is important to notice that this would leave open the possibility of there being several Divine Persons; there would still be but one God if

we could truly say that any Divine Person was the same God as any other Divine Person. Now different Persons' being the same God is not manifestly impossible: for, in general, x and y may be the same F although different things are true of x and y.[74]

I should note, however, that the notion of relative identity has been criticized by a number of philosophers both considered in itself and as employed in order to talk about the Trinity.[75] I should also note that Aquinas does not develop a formal defense of relative identity when he talks about the Trinity in SCG 4,2–26. In these chapters he presumes, on the basis of revelation, that there is distinction in God. He does not speak of Father, Son, and Spirit being *the same God* in a way that might suggest that Father, Son, and Spirit are the same as I might be thought to be the same human being who wrote the sentence you read before the sentence you are now reading. What he says is that in the divine nature, which is "one" only because it is not multipliable, not something shared as, say, humanity is what is shared by different human beings, there can be distinction based on relative opposition.

At the end of the day, Aquinas thinks of the doctrine of the Trinity as a mystery, as revealed by God, as something that we can try to reflect on only so as to make some kind of feeble sense of it. In SCG 4,2–26 he argues that we can make sense enough of the orthodox doctrine of the Trinity so as to declare that it is taught in the Bible and so as to refute the idea that the doctrine is incoherent or nonsensical or unthinkable. But this is pretty much all that he does in the SCG. Some have suggested that the Trinity is something that falls within human experience, or the experience of some people, at least.[76] But Aquinas does not argue along these lines. Might he have done well to have considered the Trinity as an object of human experience, one to be understood on that basis? Given his understanding of our sources for truths about God as spelled out in SCG 1, Aquinas's reply to this question would, of course, be "Certainly not." There is just no room in the thinking of Aquinas for the idea that people can directly experience God and truly describe God on the basis of "seeing" or "perceiving" God somehow (see chapter 2, section 3.2 here). It is therefore to be expected that his SCG discussion of the Trinity never draws on it. You may think that it should have done so. But its failure to do so leaves Aquinas presenting an account of the Trinity that is at least consistent with what he has previously been saying concerning human knowledge of God. And consistency, after all, is a virtue, even if consistency displayed when lying is, arguably, not.

God Incarnate (SCG 4,27–49)

SCG 4,2–26 FREQUENTLY alludes to the Son of God, the Second Person of the Trinity, by referring to Jesus Christ. It does so because Aquinas takes Christ to be the Second Person of the Trinity. He does not think that, from eternity, the Second Person of the Trinity is a nameable human individual with physical properties. He does, however, hold that Jesus of Nazareth, whom many call "Christ," was a human being born in time who was and remains the Second Person of the Trinity incarnate.[1]

Here, as with his account of the Trinity, Aquinas is drawing on what he takes to be orthodox Christian teaching. More specifically, he believes what he presumed the Council of Chalcedon to have taught in its Definition of Faith. In this text we find the following:

> Following the saintly fathers, we all with one voice teach the confession of one and the same Son, our Lord Jesus Christ: the same perfect in divinity and perfect in humanity, the same truly God and truly man, of a rational soul and a body; consubstantial with the Father as regards his divinity, and the same consubstantial with us as regards his humanity; like us in all respects except for sin; begotten before the ages from the Father as regards his divinity, and in the last days the same for us and for our salvation from Mary, the virgin God-bearer, as regards his humanity; one and the same Christ, Son, Lord, only-begotten, acknowledged in two natures which undergo no confusion, no change, no division, no separation; at no point was the difference between the natures taken away through the union, but rather the property of both natures is preserved and comes together into a single person and a single subsistent being; he is not parted or divided into two persons, but is one and the same only-begotten Son, God, Word, Lord Jesus Christ, just as the prophets taught from the beginning.[2]

According to Chalcedon, Christ is one subject, individual, or person with two distinct natures: divine and human. Christ is truly God and truly human: God as being the Second Person of the Trinity; human as God the Son incarnate. For Aquinas, Chalcedon states the orthodox doctrine of the Trinity, though he does not think that the truth of this doctrine can be philosophically demonstrated any more than he thinks that the truth of the doctrine of the Trinity can be.

Aquinas turns to the doctrine of the Incarnation in SCG 4,27–49, which he thinks of as following on naturally from SCG 4,2–26. He writes:

> Since, of course, when divine generation was dealt with above, it was said of God the Son, our Lord Jesus Christ, that some things belong to him in his divine nature, and some in that human nature by the assumption of which in time the eternal Son chose to be incarnate, it now remains to speak of the mystery of the Incarnation itself.[3]

As I will show in the next chapter, SCG 4,53–55 turns to the question "Was it suitable (*conveniens*) for the Incarnation to have taken place?" So SCG 4,27–49 is not Aquinas's last word in the SCG concerning the Incarnation. But it amounts to a unity since its concern is with whether we can believe in the Incarnation and what we might take it to involve.

Right at the outset, Aquinas accepts that the Incarnation is a great mystery. "Among divine works," he says, "this most especially exceeds the reason."[4] But he is convinced that the doctrine of the Incarnation as expounded by Chalcedon is faithful to Scripture both with respect to what it says of Christ as God and with respect to what it says of Christ as human. So in SCG 4,27 we find the following, which will give you a sense of how biblically Aquinas takes himself to be thinking as he embarks on his discussion of the Incarnation in SCG 4.

> This marvelous incarnation of God, of course, which divine authority hands down, we confess. For it says in John 1:14: "The Word was made flesh, and dwelt among us." And the Apostle Paul says: "Who being in the form of God, thought it not robbery to be equal to God, but emptied himself, taking the form of a servant being made in the likeness of men, and in habit found as a man" (Philippians 2:6–7). This is also shown clearly by the words of our Lord Jesus Christ himself, since at times he says lowly and human things of himself, such as "The Father is greater than I" (John 14:28) and "My soul is sorrowful even unto death" (Matthew 26:38), which became him in his assumed humanity; but at times he says sublime and divine things, such as "I and the Father are one" (John 10:30) and "All things whatsoever the Father has are mine" (John 16:15), which certainly belong to him in his divine nature. Even the things which we read about what our Lord did show this. That he feared, that he was grieved, that he thirsted, that he died: these belong to the human

nature. That by his own power he healed the sick, that he raised the dead. That he effectively commanded the elements of the world, that he drove out devils, that he forgave sins, that when he chose he rose from the dead: these reveal the divine power in him.[5]

The structure of Aquinas's discussion of the Incarnation in SCG 4,27–49 strongly resembles the structure of his discussion of the Trinity in SCG 4,2–26. First (SCG 4,28–38), he singles out a number of authors whom he takes to be heretical and refutable with reference to Scripture (see SCG 4,4–9). Then (see SCG 4,40–49), he reflects on the Incarnation so as to say how we might think about it without talking nonsense (see SCG 4,10–25). In SCG 4,40 Aquinas notes a number of objections to belief in the Incarnation, and he replies to them in SCG 4,49. In between SCG 4,40 and SCG 4,49, he deals with questions related to what he ends up concluding in SCG 4,49. In doing all of this, he brings together arguments based both on reason and revelation, which you may now not find surprising given the way Aquinas proceeds from SCG 4,1 onward and given what he says in SCG 1,1–2 (see chapter 1, section 4 here).

17.1 The Incarnation and Heresy (SCG 4,28–39)

The people Aquinas singles out as heretical in SCG 4,28–38 include Photinus, Manicheans, Valentinus (second century), Apollinarius (c. 310–c. 390), Arius, Theodore of Mopsuestia (c. 350–428), Origen (c. 185–c. 254), Nestorius (after 351–c. 452), Eutyches, and Macarius of Antioch (seventh century).[6] According to Aquinas, all of these figures in one way or other deny that Christ is a divine person with two distinct natures, and all of them stand condemned by a variety of biblical texts.

Thus, for example, Photinus, whom Aquinas takes to have taught that Christ had only a human nature, is refuted by, for example, John 1:14, Philippians 2:6–9, and Ephesians 4:10 (see SCG 4,28).

Again, thinks Aquinas, Manicheans (whom he believes to have said that the body of Christ was an unreal "phantasy body") are refuted by New Testament texts, such as Luke 24:37–39 (see SCG 4,29).

In SCG 4,30 Aquinas turns to Valentinus, whom he presumes to have held that Christ's body was a heavenly one (*corpus caeleste*), not an earthly one. Yet that position is false, he argues, given texts such as Romans 1:3 and Galatians 4:4. Equally false, he adds, is the claim (which he ascribes to Arius) that Christ had no human soul and was united to the Word as a human body is informed by a human soul (see SCG 4,32). That claim, he says, is refuted by Matthew 26:38 ("My soul is sorrowful even unto death") and John 12:27 ("Now is my soul troubled"). The claim now in question is also, says Aquinas, refuted by the fact that God cannot be the form of a body (see SCG 1,23). So he suggests that one should recognize that "in Christ the soul was one thing and the divinity of the Son of God another."[7]

Might it be said that Christ had a sensitive soul (i.e., that Christ was able to desire and experience at a physical level) while lacking mind and intellect? That this should be said is a view that Aquinas attributes to Apollinarius in SCG 4,33; but he rejects it in the light of biblical teaching to the effect that Christ was a human being. If Christ was human, he declares, then he must have had a soul in the way in which we do; he must have been able to operate at both a sensory and intellectual level. "If in Christ there was a sensitive soul without reason, it was not of the same species with our soul, which does have reason. Neither, then, was Christ himself of the same species with us."[8]

Having in SCG 4,34–38 considered and rejected some other views about Christ that he takes to be heretical and not in accordance with Scripture, Aquinas, in SCG 4,39, offers a summary of what he takes to be orthodox teaching concerning Christ. He writes:

> It is clear that according to the tradition of the Catholic faith we must say that in Christ there is a perfect divine nature and a perfect human nature, constituted by a rational soul and human flesh; and that these two natures are united in Christ…in one hypostasis and one supposit (*secundum unam hypostasim et suppositum unum*)….One must say that there are in Christ two natures neither confused nor mixed….As in the Trinity there is a plurality of persons subsisting in one nature, so in the mystery of the Incarnation there is one person subsisting in a plurality of natures.[9]

Key terms in this passage are "hypostasis," "nature," and "person." These are words that we find in discussions of the Incarnation prior to Aquinas. But how does Aquinas understand them?

By "hypostasis" he means "individual," as in "I am one individual and you are another." Aquinas's "hypostasis" is equivalent to his term *suppositum* (see chapter 11 here). Naturally occurring things, as opposed to artifacts (such as computers) or as opposed to what we might call "beings of reason" (such as prime ministers) come in different kinds. Computers are made by people for purposes, but they are not naturally occurring substances even if they are built up from what occurs in nature. And prime ministers are not a naturally occurring kind of thing. They are, so to speak, social constructs.[10] Yet there are, for example, tons of things that belong to natural kinds, and my cat is one of them. But we can hardly identify my cat with the nature it has insofar as it is feline. My cat is not "sheer felinity." It is one cat among many. It is Sweetie and not Smokey or Felix. So my cat has individuality as well as nature or essence. And it is individuality in this sense that Aquinas has in mind when he talks about something being a "hypostasis" or *suppositum,* words that are broadly interchangeable with terms such as "subject" or "individual." According to him, you and I, for example, are not human nature. We are individual human beings. We are individuals or subjects in our own right, however much we might resemble each other. You are one thing, and I am another.

In fact, so Aquinas would say, you and I are individual persons. On Aquinas's account, the word "person" can be introduced at this point since an individual can be thought of as not just one thing as opposed to something else. For him, individuals, though unique, can be grouped in certain ways prior to being picked out as the individuals that they are; and some individuals are persons insofar as intellect and will can be ascribed to them. Hence, as I have shown (chapter 16), Aquinas is happy to say that God is a Trinity of persons since there is distinction in God without this resulting in God the Father, God the Son, and God the Holy Spirit failing to be what God eternally is, and Aquinas therefore holds that there are three who are God, and to each of these three he ascribes knowledge and will.

17.2 Reasoning Concerning the Incarnation (SCG 4,40–49)

With all of these thoughts in mind, Aquinas acknowledges that if Christ is both human and divine, it will be necessary to say things of him that are in opposition to each other. He also concedes that "opposites cannot be said truly of the same thing in the same way."[11] It would be absurd to claim that, for example, I am, without qualification, both suffering and incapable of suffering, or that I am unqualifiedly, both dead and immortal. So, Aquinas notes, "it is necessarily in different ways that the divine and human are predicated of Christ."[12]

In that last quotation, from SCG 4,39, Aquinas is working up to the view that we should distinguish between what can be truly said of Christ while paying attention to the distinction of natures in him. On the one hand, he thinks, we can say what is true of Christ insofar as he is divine. On the other, we can say what is true of Christ insofar as he is human. According to Aquinas, what we say of Christ insofar as he is divine is going to conflict with what it makes sense to say of a human being. If, for example, Christ is God, then Christ is omnipotent. But human beings are not by nature omnipotent. Again, if Christ is human, then Christ walked around and was capable of suffering. But the divine nature, which, for Aquinas, is God, is not able to walk around or suffer. What, though, if Christ is one subject with two distinct natures? Then, thinks Aquinas, it can make sense to say both that Christ walked around and was capable of suffering with respect to his human nature and that Christ was omnipotent or anything else that God is by nature.

Suppose that I am a US citizen and a car mechanic. My being a US citizen entitles me to vote in the United States while my being a car mechanic does not come with this right. Again, suppose that I am a professor of philosophy and a qualified dentist. *As a professor of philosophy* I am not entitled to extract people's teeth. Yet I am so entitled considered *as a qualified dentist*. Given certain qualifications, therefore, we can make sense of the idea that contraries might be consistently ascribed to one and the same thing, which is the thought that Aquinas has in mind when thinking about the Incarnation. He holds that we can consistently ascribe contraries to Christ while bearing in mind the distinction of natures in him, while noting what is true of Christ *as God* and what is true of him *as a human being*.

Obviously, the examples I have just given are going to be of only limited value when thinking about the Incarnation as Aquinas understands it. My being a US citizen and my being a car mechanic do not amount to me having two natures as Aquinas understands the word "nature." Generally speaking, he thinks that "nature" is equivalent to "essence." So he would say, for example, that something having a human nature is essentially human (has a human essence), though he would not say that anybody is essentially a US citizen or a car mechanic or a philosophy professor or a qualified dentist. Be that as it may, however, he does claim that, when it comes to the Incarnation, we can distinguish between what Christ is *as God* and what Christ is *as human*, or between what the Word is *as God* and what the Word is *as human*.

As I have noted, Aquinas accepts that the Incarnation, as a work of God, "most especially exceeds the reason."[13] But he is aware of certain arguments to the effect that the doctrine of the Incarnation, as he understands it, is positively unreasonable. In SCG 4,40, therefore, he lists them. Then he presents what he takes to be a true account of what should be said about the Incarnation (SCG 4,41) while going on to elaborate on certain aspects of the Incarnation (SCG 4,42–48). Finally, he explains why he takes the arguments noted in SCG 4,40 to be misguided.

17.2.1 Arguments against Belief in the Doctrine of the Incarnation (SCG 4,40)

Here are the arguments to which Aquinas refers in SCG 4,40:

1. If God is not corporeal, then God cannot become corporeal.
2. Something that acquires a new nature undergoes substantial change. So if God the Son acquired a new nature with the Incarnation, God the Son is, impossibly, substantially changed.
3. "If the hypostasis of the Son of God becomes by the Incarnation the hypostasis of human nature, the Son of God is not everywhere after the Incarnation since the human nature is not everywhere."[14]
4. To have a nature is to be something of a certain kind and not another. So one individual cannot subsist in two natures.
5. In God, nature and individuality are the same. God is the divine nature and the divine existence. "But human nature cannot be identified with a divine hypostasis. Therefore, it seems impossible that a divine hypostasis subsist[s] in human nature."[15]
6. A nature is more simple and formal than the thing that exists with a nature since something existing with a nature is material and, therefore, complex: it is composed of form and matter. If what is divine exists in human nature, therefore, that human nature is more simple and formal than a divine hypostasis, which is impossible on the assumption that God is entirely simple.
7. Every human individual is material; yet a divine being cannot be this.
8. Christ's soul and body were the equal of those of other human beings. But in other human beings soul and body make up one thing. So, given the orthodox doctrine of the Incarnation, the soul and body of Christ make up one thing: the person of the eternal Word. Yet this seems to mean that there are two persons in Christ if God is incarnate in him.
9. The soul and body of a human being make someone to be a particular human being. We should, therefore, conclude that, if Christ is God incarnate, God is two individual subsisting things.
10. Considered as having a soul and a body, Christ is a particular substance. So, just by being that, Christ is a hypostasis, and we do not need to talk about the Word as the only hypostasis present in the Incarnation.
11. If in Christ, considered as both human and divine, there is only one individual, "then in one's understanding of the man who is Christ there ought to be a divine hypostasis."[16] Yet particular human beings are not divine individuals. Therefore, and given the doctrine of the Incarnation, "___ is human" can be affirmed of Christ and other people only equivocally.

12. According to the doctrine of the Incarnation, in Christ there are body, soul, and divinity. But the soul informs the body or is the form of the body. So the soul is not the individual human being. In that case, however, neither is something divine an individual of human nature; "it is, rather, formally related to that nature."[17]

13. What comes to be in something after the thing has come into being is an accident of that thing. So if the Word comes to be flesh, this must amount to the Word acquiring an accident. Yet there are no accidents in God.

17.2.2 How to Understand the Incarnation (SCG 4,41)

The key thought in SCG 4,41 is that Christ is one individual with two natures. Aquinas holds that, in Christ, there is one subject with two natures. The subject is the Word: the Second Person of the Trinity. The natures are divine nature and human nature.

Aquinas begins to develop this understanding of the Incarnation by noting that the word "nature" is used in different ways. However, he settles on an understanding of "nature" that takes something with a nature to have an essence. He then argues that "nothing prevents some things not united in nature from being united in hypostasis or person."[18] He suggests that members of a species cannot conceptually or in reality have anything added to them that leaves them to be members of that species if what is added results in them becoming members of another species. So, for example, "if to animate substance one adds only *sensible*, one will have another species."[19] Aquinas nonetheless goes on to say that it is possible for something belonging to a species to have what other members of it do not. One human being, for example, might have musical talents while another might not. So, says Aquinas, "nothing prevents some things being made one in the individual which are not united in one integrity of species."[20]

I take it that Aquinas is at this point thinking with an eye on the fact that if Christ is one subject with two natures, then we will ascribe to him properties or attributes that do not all belong to something with one nature, properties or attributes that might even be thought to conflict with each other. Hence, if Christ is divine, then Christ is eternal and omnipotent. But if Christ is human, Christ is physical, changeable, mortal, and subject to things acting on him. Yet how can all of this be true? Aquinas replies that it can be true since it is possible for a subject to be more than what its nature implies and that Christ, who is human, can be more than what a human being essentially is. Christ could not be more than what a human being essentially is if Christ were merely human. Yet, thinks Aquinas, if Christ has two natures belonging to one subject (the Word), there is nothing to prevent him having properties or attributes that belong essentially to things of different natures (i.e., the divine nature and human nature). He recognizes that if, say, a particular dog has something that is not included in an understanding of what it takes to be canine (if, say, it has black hair), that something will be an accident. He does not, though, want to suggest that being human is an accident in God since he denies that God has accidents. He does, however, think that there can be a subject of which we can predicate what does not belong to a particular nature, which would seem to leave open the possibility of there being a subject that is both human and divine and of which different things can be said with an eye to different natures had by it.

When it comes to the Incarnation, therefore:

> The union of the Word and the man was such that one nature was not breathed together out of the two; and the union of the Word to the human nature was not like that of a substance—a man, say—to those externals that are accidentally related to him.... But let the Word be set down as subsisting in a human nature as in one made his very own by the Incarnation; and in consequence that body is truly the body of the Word of God, and the soul in like manner, and the Word of God is truly man.[21]

According to Aquinas, the Incarnation involves a union of two natures in one subject or person: the Word. The Word is divine, and Christ is both human and divine since Christ is the Word incarnate. Aquinas, of course, acknowledges that statements like "My cat is feline and canine" are self-contradictory. He agrees that things having only one nature cannot be what things having another nature are unless they can be subsumed under one genus. Obviously, if X is a mammal and if Y is a mammal, X and Y might be thought to be the same in some respect even though they differ when it comes to nature (differ when it comes to what Aquinas would call substantial form). Hence a cat and a whale, though both mammals, are different things with different natures. Nevertheless, Aquinas thinks that something with distinct natures can consistently be spoken of in seriously different ways because it is one subject of which we can assert all that might be properly asserted of things with different natures. So, he says, if Christ is divine, then all that is true of the divine essence can be affirmed of him. And if Christ is human, all that is true when it comes to what is human can also be affirmed of him. In Aquinas's view, the apparent conflict in what we might say of Christ with a view to his human and divine natures does not amount to self-contradiction since these natures are had by one subject. In his view, "Christ is God" and "Christ is human" affirm that one subject has two natures, not that one nature can be what another one is.

As he continues with SCG 4,41, Aquinas admits that the Incarnation presents us with something both unique and hard to fathom. He holds that the Incarnation is unique since, apart from Christ, there is nothing we can refer to that is one subject with two distinct natures. We can, he thinks, refer to things that are similar in nature. But things like these are not single subjects having two distinct natures. As for it being hard to fathom what is involved in the Incarnation, Aquinas holds that this is inevitable given our ignorance when it comes to what God is. As I have shown, he agrees that we can make various true statements concerning God (see chapters 5–9 here). As I have also shown, however, he denies that we have a grasp of what God is as we might have a grasp of what, for example, a cat is (see chapter 4 here). Given what we find in his SCG discussion of the Trinity (see chapter 16 here), Aquinas does not even think that we have some full-blown understanding of the persons of the Trinity comparable to our knowledge of three things in the world. Toward the end of SCG 4,41, however, he offers an analogy when it comes to the Incarnation. It is one that he derives from the Athanasian Creed, which he takes to teach that "as the rational soul and flesh are one man, so God and man are one in Christ."[22]

Aquinas obviously has to deny that the Second Person of the Trinity is just the soul of Jesus of Nazareth, a living human being. He thinks that our bodies are united to our souls as matter is united to form; but he does not want to say that Christ is just matter informed by God the Son. He believes that this suggestion would mean that there is but one nature made of God and what is human. Yet, he says, when thinking about human beings with souls, we might usefully note how the bodies of people can be united to their souls as instruments of them.

Suppose that I am driving a car. In that case, who is driving the car? It would obviously seem to be me. Yet how does the car stand to me as I drive it? It would seem to be something that I use as a means for traveling around. So let us say that my car is an instrument that I use so as to achieve an end that I have in mind.

But now let us suppose that I scratch my neck so as to get rid of an itch. If I scratch my neck to relieve an itch, I will use my hand, and my will is working through my hand. The movements of my hand seem directly under my control in a way that a car is not as I fiddle around with it. So might we plausibly think that Christ was God incarnate as united to God as I am united to my body as I will to act and to choose? Aquinas clearly thinks that there is something in this suggestion.[23] He writes:

> A pick-axe is not the soul's very own instrument, as one's hand is, for many people can wield one and the same pick-axe, but one's hand belongs to

one's soul in its very operation. For this reason the hand is an instrument of the soul united to it and its very own, but a pick-axe is an instrument both external and common. This is the way, then, in which even the union of God and human nature can be considered. For all people are related to God as instruments of a sort, and by these God works....But people in general are related to God as extrinsic and separated instruments, so to say; for God does not move them only to operations which are his very own, but to the operations common to every rational nature....But the human nature of Christ is assumed with the result that instrumentally he performs the things which are the proper operation of God alone....The human nature of Christ, then, is compared to God as a proper and conjoined instrument is compared (*sicut instrumentum proprium et coniunctum*), as the hand is compared to the soul....Therefore, nothing prevents our putting the union of the human nature to the Word in this way: that the human nature is, so to speak, an instrument of the Word—not a separated, but a conjoined, instrument: and the human nature, nonetheless, does not belong to the nature of the Word, and the Word is not its form; nevertheless, the human nature belongs to the person of the Word.[24]

One should notice, however, that having said all that, Aquinas observes that the comparison he has in mind at this point is not and cannot be exact. "One should understand," he says, "that the Word of God was able to be much more sublimely and more intimately united to the entire human nature [sc. of Christ] than the soul to its very own instrument of whatever sort."[25]

17.2.3 Some Elaboration on SCG 4,41 (SCG 4,42–48)

In drawing to the end of his account of the Incarnation, Aquinas makes six points.

1. It was fitting for the human nature of Christ to be united to the Second Person of the Trinity (SCG 4,42).
2. Christ's human nature did not preexist Christ's coming-to-be in time (SCG 4,43).
3. Christ's human nature was perfect in soul and body (SCG 4,44).
4. Christ had no human father (SCG 4,45).
5. The coming-to-be of Christ can fittingly be ascribed to the Holy Spirit, though not as a matter of physical generation (SCG 4,46 and 47).
6. Christ must not be called a creature (SCG 4,48).

As he presents these conclusions, Aquinas, more than anything else, seems to be intent on bringing into his discussion what he takes to be stated or implied by Scripture, while reasoning concerning what he takes Scripture to teach.

Scripture tells us that the Word became flesh. Since Aquinas takes the Word to be the Second Person of the Trinity, he argues that it is the Second Person of the Trinity who assumed the human nature of Christ. Or, rather, he argues that, for several reasons, it was *fitting* or *suitable* that it should have been the Second Person of the Trinity who assumed this nature. Aquinas does not claim to be able to demonstrate that it was the Second Person of the Trinity and not the First or the Third who became incarnate.

He does, however, claim to demonstrate that Christ's human nature could not have preexisted the Incarnation in time. Basically, he argues that Jesus of Nazareth could not possibly have preexisted himself. "Since the Word assumed the human nature," he says, "necessarily the human nature did not pre-exist before its union with the Word."[26] It had to be the case that the Incarnation did not involve a union between God and a human being who preexisted the Incarnation.

When it comes to Christ's perfect human nature in soul and body, Aquinas seems to be reasoning with an eye on his view of when it is that a fully formed human being comes into being. He did not believe that people begin to exist with a rational soul and a body straight upon conception. He thought that quite a bit of time elapsed between conception and the conceived having both a rational soul and a body.[27] Yet, he reasons, it must have been a fully formed human being with whom the Word became incarnate. In the very beginning of the conception of Christ, therefore, "the rational soul was united to the body."[28] Aquinas finds it unbelievable that anything less than a fully formed human being with a rational soul could be united to the Word so as to make for one subject with two natures: divine and human. He says: "Anything corporeal that comes into being is, *before its animation*, formless and still lacking the perfection of nature. It was therefore not fitting for the Word of God to be united to a body not yet animated. Thus, from the moment of conception, the soul of Christ had to animate Christ's body."[29]

Yet how could this have been if, as Aquinas thought, human conception does not immediately result in a fully formed human being? In SCG 4,45 Aquinas suggests that the conception of Christ must not have been an ordinary conception but one lacking a human father. Ordinary human conception, he says, depends on sexual intercourse, and it does not immediately result in there being a fully formed human being with a rational soul.[30] So, he reasons, if Christ was fully formed as a human being when conceived, there is a miracle to be acknowledged. The human mother of Christ cannot have conceived him as human mothers conceive their (not fully formed) offspring following sexual intercourse. Aquinas makes this point by saying that Christ was born of a virgin. That Mary, the mother of Jesus, was literally a virgin when she conceived him is not something that he attempts to demonstrate in SCG 4,45. He does, however, suggest that it was fitting that she should have been. Or as he puts it himself: "It became the Word of God, by whom all things are established and by whom all things are preserved in his wholeness, to be born so as to preserve his mother's wholeness in every way. Therefore, suitably this generation was from a virgin."[31]

In SCG 4,46, Aquinas proceeds to say that Christ was born of the Holy Spirit. I have shown how he maintains that everything that comes to pass in the created order is the work of the whole Trinity. Hence his objection to the claim that one can prove the doctrine of the Trinity with reference to what has been created by God (see chapter 16, section 3 here). All the same, Aquinas thinks that the Incarnation can be fittingly thought of as arising from what love is in God: this being the Holy Spirit. Here I assume that, though he does not quote it, Aquinas has in mind Luke 1:35, in which Mary, the mother of Jesus, is told: "The Holy Spirit will come upon you, and the power of the Most High will overshadow you; therefore the child to be born will be holy; he will be called the Son of God." Aquinas does conceive of the Trinity as a society or group of individuals acting so as to produce different things given the abilities or status of its members. So he does not believe that God the Father has a job in which God the Son is not involved. Nor does he think that God the Holy Spirit is somehow "doing his own thing" apart from what God the Father and God the Son are up to. But he does think that the Incarnation is a matter of love: love of God for people. Since he takes the Holy Spirit to be love as it exists in God, therefore, he finds it natural to say that Christ was born of the Holy Spirit, though not, for obvious reasons, with the Holy Spirit being a physical parent of Christ as Mary was.

Aquinas takes Mary, the mother of Jesus, to be a creature. He also supposes that Christ's human nature was a creature: something in time and space created by God. In that case, however, should Christ not simply be referred to as a creature? With this question in mind, Aquinas again appeals to the idea that Christ is one person with two natures. When we speak of Christ, we are not referring to what is merely human. We are talking about the Word, and the Word is not a creature even though what the Word assumed in the Incarnation was creaturely. "In Christ," Aquinas observes, "there is no other hypostasis or person save that of God's Word, and this person is uncreated.... Therefore, one cannot say without qualification: 'Christ is a creature,' although one may say it with an addition, so as to say 'so far as human' or 'in his human nature.'"[32]

17.2.4 Replies to the Arguments in SCG 4,40 (SCG 4,49)

With this general account of the Incarnation in place, in SCG 4,49 Aquinas finally returns to the arguments he noted in SCG 4,40. He maintains that these arguments are refuted by the discussion of the Incarnation in SCG 41–48. More precisely, he argues as follows.

1. The doctrine of the Incarnation does not assert that God was changed into something corporeal or that God is the form of what is bodily.

2. The doctrine of the Incarnation does not ascribe substantial change to the Word. It teaches that the Word came to be united to what is changeable (the human nature of Christ), not that the Word itself was in any way modified by the Incarnation.

3. "Nothing prevents the Word of God from being everywhere, although the human nature assumed by the Word is not everywhere."[33]

4. The Second Person of the Trinity exists just by being divine, not by being human as God incarnate.

5. The Word and the divine nature of the Word are the same, and the Word exists by virtue of the divine nature, not the human nature assumed in the Incarnation. So we do not have to think of the human nature of Christ as identical with the person of the Word.

6. "It is not necessary that the human nature [sc. of the Word] be more simple than the Word so far as the Word is the Word, but only in so far as the Word is this man."[34]

7. Considered simply as the Second Person of the Trinity, the Word does not have physical dimensions. Such dimensions can only be ascribed to the Word in the light of the Incarnation.

8. The doctrine of the Incarnation does not entail that the soul and body of Christ are anything other than what is united to or assumed by the one person of the Word. As assumed by the Word, the soul and body of Christ are united to what is better than a merely human person.

9. Christ, indeed, had a soul and a body. In the Incarnation, however, there was only one person, hypostasis, or *suppositum*: that of the Word.

10. Christ was a particular thing. But if we ask who Christ was, the answer is "the person of the Word." The hypostasis of Christ is just the Second Person of the Trinity, who in the Incarnation took on a human nature in the particular man Jesus.

11. We do not use "man" equivocally when saying that Christ is a man and Socrates is a man. But we do hold that Christ is a man the person or hypostasis of which is the uncreated Word.

12. The Second Person of the Trinity does not exist as being what makes a particular human being to be a particular human being. The Second Person of the Trinity is the eternal God who does not need to create anything. In the Incarnation, however, the Word takes on a human nature and is united to this as being one subject in two natures. "The hypostasis of the Word is the subject of the human nature so far as he draws this latter into his own subsistence."[35]

13. There can be no question of the human nature of the Second Person of the Trinity being an accident that God comes to possess. For God is eternal and, therefore, unchangeable. In the Incarnation, the Word is unchangeably united to what is human by becoming what is human without being essentially human.

17.3 Some Comments on SCG 4,27–49

It is important to keep in mind that SCG 4,27–49 is *Aquinas's* account of the Incarnation. In one sense, of course, it is obviously this since, undeniably, "Aquinas's account of the Incarnation is Aquinas's account of the Incarnation." Nevertheless, we should not assume that in SCG 4,27–49 Aquinas exactly affirms what others have held about the Incarnation, even though he might appear to do so. SCG 4,27–49 incorporates ideas that are characteristic of him. The fact that these chapters state that Christ is truly God and truly human should not automatically lead us to suppose that they are affirming what others are thinking when speaking in that way. Unlike many who believe that Christ is truly God and truly human, Aquinas takes God the Word to be a distinct person in a Trinity constituting one simple divine nature. He also thinks that we should focus on a distinction between subject and nature so as to allow for the Word being one hypostasis with two natures. In addition, of course, he has an understanding of human nature that not everyone shares. He is clear, for example, that to be human is to be a composite of body and soul, not an essentially incorporeal substance. SCG 4,27–49 should therefore be read in the light of thoughts that Aquinas articulates independently of what he says in these chapters. That Christ is truly God and truly human has been affirmed by many people, but not all of them are saying quite what Aquinas does in SCG 4,27–49.

It might even be suggested that what Aquinas maintains in SCG 4,27–49 is not what those who drafted the Chalcedonian position on the Incarnation were thinking. It is clear that he takes his stand on Chalcedon and that he refers to Christ as one person with two natures. But SCG 4,27–49 goes beyond the text of Chalcedon's definition of faith. Chalcedon does not elaborate on the meaning of "person" and "nature." Nor does it try to give an account of how we might think in detail when it comes to the union of divinity and humanity in Christ. It asserts that Christ is one person in two natures, fully God and fully human, and then it falls silent. It presents no detailed analysis of the terms that it employs. It does not offer an account of the divine nature such as we find in SCG 1. It makes no attempt to harmonize the statements "Christ is human" and "Christ is divine." Nor does it present a theological or philosophical discussion of the Incarnation. To be sure, Chalcedon claims to teach truly about the Incarnation. Yet it does not elaborate on what the Incarnation involves in the way that Aquinas does while trying to defend the language that Chalcedon employs. In this sense, SCG 4,27–49 is not just a bald reassertion of Chalcedon when it comes to the Incarnation.[36]

In order to evaluate these chapters, therefore, we should be treating them in their own right and not as contributions to a single discussion in which everyone is agreed when it comes to what has to be defended concerning the Incarnation. This, in turn, means that when evaluating SCG 4,27–49 we should ask questions like "Is Aquinas right to approach the Incarnation in the conviction that God is simple and unchangeable?" and "Is Aquinas right to think that what he calls a hypostasis or person can be both divine and human?"[37] In addition, perhaps, we need to ask whether Aquinas is right in his reading of the biblical texts that he cites when defending his account of the Incarnation. Again and again in SCG 4 Aquinas thinks of the Bible, and especially the New Testament, as teaching something like the doctrine of the Incarnation as defined by the Council of Chalcedon. But do we really find a Chalcedonian view of Christ in the Bible?

In one sense, we obviously do not since the Bible does not explicitly declare that Christ is one person with two natures. Yet Aquinas is perfectly aware of this fact. On the other hand he does believe that the New Testament presents Christ as being divine and that the Chalcedonian definition effectively summarizes what the New Testament says about Christ. Is he, however, right to believe this? For that matter, is he right to think, as he clearly does, that Christ claimed to be divine or thought of himself as such?

With respect to these questions, I suggest that you take a look at how biblical scholars these days write about the New Testament and the assertion that Christ is God. Some of them suggest that the New Testament does not provide backing for the blunt statement "Jesus of Nazareth is divine." Some of them also suggest that the notion of Jesus being divine does not reflect what he could himself have entertained. On the other hand, however, there are biblical scholars who find many New Testament verses that say or imply that Jesus is what Old Testament authors refer to as God.

N. T. Wright is a good example. He is aware of objections to the view that the New Testament teaches that Christ is truly divine, not just metaphorically or in a manner of speaking. On the other hand he provides reasons for saying that the New Testament contains much that claims divinity for Christ. Wright even gives reasons for supposing that, in doing so, the New Testament is reflecting what Christ himself taught and supposed.[38] Wright, of course, might be wrong in his reading of the New Testament and on what he infers on its basis. The fact, however, is that here we have a well-known and highly acclaimed biblical scholar talking about the Incarnation and the New Testament in ways that would have been congenial to Aquinas. So it is not *obvious* that the ways in which Aquinas appeals to the New Testament as he defends what he takes to be the Chalcedonian definition are clearly untenable.

Yet, one might say, SCG 4,27–49 as a whole is untenable since no sense can be made of its presiding thesis that Christ is truly divine and truly human. For is it not obvious that nothing can be truly both divine and human? Does not anything coming close to the Chalcedonian definition reek of self-contradiction? Is it not clear that Christ cannot be divine if Christ was human since God is not a spatiotemporal thing? Is it not equally clear that God cannot be identified with anything human since being human cannot involve what being divine involves?

Questions along these lines have been raised for centuries. And, although people raising them have not always attacked accounts of Christ such as we find in the SCG as being self-contradictory or logically impossible, some have. A quite famous example is John Hick (1922–2012). In the much-discussed book *The Myth of God Incarnate*, he says:

> Orthodoxy insisted upon the two natures human and divine. But orthodoxy has never been able to give this idea any content. It remains a form of words without assignable meaning. For to say, without explanation, that the historical Jesus of Nazareth was also God is as devoid of meaning as to say that this circle drawn with a pencil on paper is also a square."[39]

Even people sympathetic to what Aquinas says about the Incarnation have drawn attention to questions of coherence concerning it. Hence, for example, Eleonore Stump writes:

> There is certainly a *prima facie* case to be made for the objection that the doctrine of the Incarnation attributes contradictory properties to one and the same thing. On the doctrine of the Incarnation, one and the same thing is said to be limited in power and not limited in power, for

example. Being limited in power and not being limited in power are contradictory properties, and both properties are attributed to Christ. So, on the face of it, it seems as if the objection is right."[40]

Should we not therefore conclude that SCG 4,27–49 is effectively asking us to believe the impossible?

You might think that we should since in these chapters Aquinas does not present a full-blown proof of the consistency of the doctrine of the Incarnation as he understands it. He obviously thinks that the doctrine is consistent, but he does not formally try to prove that it is. This fact, however, might be taken as favoring his approach to the Incarnation since proofs of consistency are notoriously hard to come by. Given the work of Kurt Gödel (1906–1978), this seems to be evident in mathematics. Gödel is generally recognized by philosophers as having shown that one cannot prove a mathematical theory to be free of internal contradiction without having recourse to another theory resting on assumptions that are stronger and less reliable than the theory the consistency of which is being proved.

That said, however, we might still wonder whether it could possibly be true that one thing is both divine and human. "My cat is unqualifiedly a dog" cannot be true.[41] Yet Aquinas does not claim, *without qualification*, that Christ is human and divine. His claim is that, when it comes to the Incarnation, there is one subject with two distinct natures. He regards "___ is divine" and "___ is human" as predicating something of an individual. He does not think that these expressions stand for or refer to or name something or other. He thinks of them as telling us what is to be said about something.

Logicians sometimes refer to what is called the "two-name" theory of predication. According to this, sentences like "A is B" should be viewed as telling us that one class of things is included in another.[42] And if Aquinas subscribed to this theory, he would have to be thought to mean that "Christ is divine" and "Christ is human" tell us that Christ is included in the class of both divine things and human ones. But Aquinas did not subscribe to the two-name theory of predication. Instead, he recognized the serious logical difference between naming and predicating.

So he thinks that to say "Christ is divine" and "Christ is human" is to assert different things of one subject. He thinks the same when it comes to "the Word is divine" and "the Word is human." Hence his insistence on the Incarnation amounting to there being one hypostasis, person, or subject having two natures, not to there being two things of different kinds that are one thing as, say, two dogs are one thing because they share a nature. Two dogs can, indeed, share a nature. Two dogs, indeed, do share a nature since they are both canine. But Aquinas does not regard the Word as sharing a nature with what is human. He thinks of God as having two distinct natures: human and divine. He also thinks that, with the Incarnation, the divine nature of the Word and the human nature of the Word are had by one thing: the Second Person of the Trinity.

Yet is it not the case that "X is human and divine" cannot be true since "___ is human" takes away what is given by "___ is divine"? Is not "X is human and divine" like "X is square and circular"? Evidently, Aquinas thinks not, and that is because he takes seriously the distinction of natures in God incarnate. Hence, for example, when denying that Christ is a creature, he notes qualifications to be made when it comes to the natures of Christ. Yes, he says, "Christ is a creature" is true. But only if qualified by "so far as he is human" (*secundum quod homo*) or "in his human nature" (*secundum humanam naturam*).

In other words, Aquinas holds that different and indeed contrary things can be said of God incarnate as long as one bears in mind whether it is the divine or human nature of the Word that is under discussion. In his view, to single out a subject of predication is not to say anything about it. There is a "saying about" John only if some predicate is asserted of John. He also thinks that, when we speak of the Word, we need to be clear whether we are speaking with a view to its divine nature or its human one. If we speak about the Word only with reference to its divine nature, then we will say things that we would never say concerning something merely human. Again, if we speak of Christ (considered as God the Word incarnate) with reference to his human nature, we will say things that we would never say of the divine nature. Yet, Aquinas maintains, these different ways of talking are in order on the supposition that the Word has two distinct natures.

As becomes much clearer from *Summa Theologiae* 3a,16 than from SCG 4,27–49, Aquinas's approach to the Incarnation relies heavily on the idea that something can be said to be such and such considered under one description and something else considered under another. Without contradiction, one might, for example, say that, in virtue of being president of the United States, someone has control over the U.S. military even though that person does not have control of the U.S. military just in virtue of being a U.S. citizen. So one might consistently say (1) "X, as U.S. president, has control of the U.S. military," and (2) "X, as a U.S. citizen, has no such control." Similarly, thinks Aquinas, one can consistently say (1) "Christ, as human, is spatiotemporal," and (2) "Christ, as divine, is eternal and immaterial."

For Aquinas, it is the distinction of natures in God incarnate that allows both of the last two propositions to be possibly true. You might say that if Christ exists in space and time, and if Christ is eternal and immaterial, then

Christ is spatiotemporal, eternal, and immaterial, which cannot be so. However, Aquinas is not declaring that Christ is unqualifiedly spatiotemporal *and* eternal *and* immaterial. He is saying that in the Incarnation something with one nature took on another nature and that our talk about this thing (the Word) has to respect the difference of natures taught by the claim that in the Incarnation we have one subject with distinct natures.

One can understand why Aquinas takes this line. For, as Peter Geach observes:

> Instead of saying "Christ's human nature was passible, his divine nature impassible," we may say "Christ as man was passible, Christ as God is impassible": and so in other cases. But the feasibility of this depends, as Aquinas pointed out, on taking seriously the distinction of subject and predicate. The term "as" occurs predicatively—"Christ as man" means "Christ in so far as he is a man"; if we take the subject-predicate distinction seriously, we may therefore distinguish between what is predicable with truth of the subject "the man Christ" and what is predicable of "Christ as man." Such distinctions are indispensable in the theology of the Incarnation.[43]

Aquinas does not think of the human and divine natures of the Word as parts of God. Given his account of divine simplicity, how could he? He is not saying that, considering one part of God, we can assert "It is human" while saying of another part "It is divine." Once again, he is emphasizing that in Christ there is one subject with two distinct natures. He does not claim that we have exact parallels to the Incarnation to appeal to so as simply to say, "Well, the Incarnation is just another example of something with which we are familiar." What he claims is that it is not contradictory to say that Christ or the Word is such and such with respect to his human nature and that Christ or the Word is such and such with respect to his divine nature.

My example concerning the U.S. president might be thought to imply that Aquinas held that there being one subject with two natures is a commonplace. But he clearly does not think this. He does not believe that there is any straightforward parallel to the Incarnation. As I have noted, he does not even think that the analogy of a conjoined instrument gets us to the reality of the Incarnation without falling short. I intended the U.S. president example only to indicate how we might, without contradicting ourselves, speak of one thing in apparently contradictory ways without actually contradicting ourselves. President X can certainly be such and such as president and not such and such as a U.S. citizen. Of course, Aquinas does not think that predications like "___ is president" or "___ is a U.S. citizen" tell us what anything is by nature. Nor does he think of humanity and divinity as conventional. He maintains that to be human is to have a distinct essence. And, though he denies that God has an essence as human beings do (though he claims that God and God's essence are not distinct), he takes the divine essence to be a reality distinct from other essences. He does, however, think that if we focus on a distinction of natures, there is nothing to stop us saying that the Word is human and that Christ is divine.

One might object to this idea by saying that what we mean by "human" is "something created" and that something human cannot, therefore, be both human and divine. Thus, for example, Maurice Wiles (1923–2005) writes: "It seems to me not unreasonable to regard 'being created' as part of the *meaning* of man...and 'not being created' as part of the meaning of God."[44] And, if you agree with Wiles, you will think that anything human has to be created and that the doctrine of the Incarnation as Aquinas presents it is dubious. For if it is part of the meaning of "human" that anything human is created, then how can Christ be both human and uncreated? But there are problems with this line of thinking.

One is that it conjures up the specter of a novel and implausible proof of God's existence. This would run: (1) all human beings are created things; (2) if there are created things, then they have to be created by God; (3) so God evidently exists. Why, however, should any atheist think that all human beings are created? Why should an atheist think that anything is created? It would seem to be absurd to say that we can cogently prove the existence of God by insisting that "created" is part of the meaning of "human" and that anything created must be created by God. Doubtless, though, Wiles would not have wanted to commit himself to the argument I just derived from what he writes. His real point seems to be that to be human is to be something the essence of which involves being created, something that has an essential property of being created. Yet we can intelligibly deny that point since, even if God does exist, there is no essential property of being created. If things have essential properties, they exist with properties, attributes, or powers that belong to them and that mark them out as things of different kinds. Hence, for example, whales are essentially mammalian, and snakes are essentially reptilian. Essential properties distinguish things of one natural kind from another. But if God makes all creatures to exist, "being created" cannot be a distinguishing feature of any creature. "All creatures are created" is, of course, trivially true. But it is not true that being created serves to mark out one creature from another. As Herbert McCabe notes:

> Being created could not possibly be part of the meaning of man or of anything else (except, of course, "a creature"); being created could not

possibly make any *difference* to anything. If it did, creation would be impossible. God might set out cheerfully to create, let us say, a Nicaraguan Okapi, but he would never be able to do so; all he would be able to create would be a *created* Nicaraguan Okapi, which would on this hypothesis be different. But maybe all he ever proposes to create is a created Nicaraguan Okapi? Alas for the vanity of divine wishes; he would have to end up with a *created* created Nicaraguan Okapi, and that would be different again.[45]

What McCabe says here is in line with Aquinas's teaching that God's act of creating does not involve him bringing about a change in anything (see chapter 9, section 6 here). And, as McCabe goes on to say, if we can accept the point that Aquinas is making about creation not being a change, we should also be able to see that the point has a bearing when it comes to Aquinas's view of the Incarnation.

It is easy to see why Aquinas, for example, insisted that creation is not a change; being created cannot make any difference at all to what anything is any more than existence can; it could not enter into the description of anything. We could not ever say "If this is created, then it must be like this and not like that." This truth is not only of interest to logicians and metaphysicians; it also matters to theologians, because part of the doctrine of the Incarnation [sc. as Aquinas takes it to be] is that the person of Jesus is *uncreated*. Being uncreated doesn't make any difference either. Just as we cannot infer from the fact that Fred is created that he must be this kind of being rather than that, so we cannot infer from the fact that Jesus is uncreated that he is this kind of being rather than that. To be divine is not to be a kind of being, just as to be a creature is not to be a kind of being (the word "nature" is used only analogically in the phrase "divine nature"). To be a man, on the other hand, *is* to be a kind of being, and this is the kind of being that Jesus was and is.[46]

It has sometimes been suggested that Aquinas's overall position on the Incarnation does not seem to leave much room for the Son of God being a man. Indeed, Aquinas has sometimes been accused of Monophysitism, according to which the Son of God has only one divine nature, not two, as proclaimed by Chalcedon.[47] Yet that Aquinas denies that the Son of God is a man or that he, even inadvertently, has Monophysite tendencies, seems to be an odd suggestion. Aquinas viewed Monophysitism as attacking the doctrine of the Incarnation taught by Chalcedon. So it is highly unlikely that he ever thought of the Incarnation in Monophysite terms. His approach to the Incarnation takes Chalcedon to be the touchstone of faith concerning the

Incarnation. Admittedly, in the *Summa Theologiae*, much more than in the SCG, Aquinas elaborates on the Incarnation in ways that suggest that Christ was not like your average human being. In *Summa Theologiae* 3a,7, for instance, he says that Christ was always graced by God and had all the moral virtues that most of us merely strive to acquire. Again, in *Summa Theologiae* 3a,9 we find him ascribing the beatific vision to Christ.[48] However, even the *Summa Theologiae* account of Christ never affirms of Christ what cannot, in Aquinas's view, be affirmed of a human being, albeit one graced by God. And the account of the Incarnation in SCG 4,27–49 is at one with that in the *Summa Theologiae* when it comes to this matter. That, yet again, is because it insists on there being a real distinction of natures in God incarnate.

So what Aquinas is saying in SCG 4,27–49 is this:

1. God the Word exists from eternity sharing and being what all the Persons of the Trinity are by nature. The Word is not an instance of a natural kind but is the divine nature: something that is entirely simple or noncomposite.
2. At the conception of Jesus, God the Word took on a human nature with no change to his divine nature.
3. At the conception of Jesus, a human being was born who was the same person (hypostasis) as the Word.
4. The Incarnation was not a mixing together of things of different kinds or natures; it was not like a single item on a menu that a chef might bring to a table having followed various cooking recipes and having brought their ingredients together; it resulted in there being one individual with both the nature of God and the nature of a human being.
5. So when we say that Jesus is God, we mean that there is one subject with two distinct natures. There is one subject to refer to while predicating different things of it: things that we cannot consistently predicate of something having only one nature, but things that can consistently be predicated of Christ given the distinction of natures in God the Word and Christ.

You might suppose that if Aquinas takes the Word incarnate to be divine, then he cannot take it to be truly a man. But he does take the Word incarnate to be just this because of the predicate "___ is human" and because of what he thinks about distinction of person or hypostasis and nature. He does not take "person" or "hypostasis" to mean "a human individual with a center of consciousness," or something like that. He takes these words to signify "a subject of which things can be affirmed or predicated" with respect to its nature, and he does not believe that, apart from the Incarnation, there is one thing with two distinct natures. Nonetheless, he does think that the doctrine of the

Incarnation tells us that God has become a man and that a man is God. When he writes about the Incarnation and says things like "The Word is divine" and "Christ is divine," he always has in mind the question "Who is the Word?" and "Who is Christ?," not "What is the Word?" and "What is Christ?" And his answer to "Who is the Word?" and "Who is Christ?" is always "The Second Person of the Trinity." But, he thinks, "the Second Person of the Trinity" is a phrase that refers to a subject or individual (as "my best friend" might refer to Joe Smith, or as "my cat" refers to the animal I live with and have named "Sweetie"). "Joe Smith" and "Sweetie" are not words that state what anything is. They are names or subject terms to which we need to add descriptions or predications so as to end up making true assertions. Having singled out Joe as a subject for discussion, we might say that he is, for example, human, has Irish ancestors, and teaches theology. Similarly, we can make little of the name "Sweetie" unless we are told, for example, that Sweetie is feline and inclined to sleep for most of the day. Once again, we need to distinguish between what is referred to and what is said of it. We need to distinguish between subjects and predicates. And, thinks Aquinas, if we do this when it comes to Christ, we can truly and without inconsistency say things like "God (i.e. God the Son) was born and died" or "Christ (i.e. God the Son) is eternal and immutable." As McCabe puts it, Aquinas maintains that "to say 'Jesus is son of God' is to say something quite different from saying 'Jesus is son of Mary' because here 'son of God' and 'son of Mary' are in the predicate place. But to say 'The son of God died on the cross' is to make the same assertion as is expressed by 'The son of Mary died on the cross.'"[49] On this account, "The son of God died on the cross" and "The son of Mary died on the cross" are, as logicians would say, extensionally equivalent but not intensionally equivalent.

It has been suggested that, in order to claim "The Son of God died on the cross," we need unqualifiedly to ascribe change, pain, and development to God and should, therefore, reject Aquinas's claim that the divine nature is eternal and immutable. If God does not really suffer in Christ, it has been argued, then God is remote from us and our suffering.[50] On this account, the suffering of God who became flesh is real suffering and involves real change in God. The argument then is that Aquinas's approach to the Incarnation is wrong since it is presented by him together with the insistence that God is eternal and immutable. Yet Aquinas's approach to the Incarnation positively embraces the conclusion that God, the Word, can be truly and not metaphorically spoken of as undergoing suffering. Aquinas thinks that it is as true to say "God suffers" as it is true to say "God is immutable." Why? Because of the distinctions between subject and predicate and hypostasis and nature. If "God" in "God suffered" means that Christ (where "Christ" refers to the

Second Person of the Trinity) suffered, then Aquinas will agree that "God suffered" is literally and not metaphorically true just because Christ clearly underwent a great deal of suffering. But Aquinas does not think that this conclusion obliges us to give up on divine immutability. He thinks that God suffers since one person in two natures suffered, but he does not take this belief to mean that the divine nature undergoes suffering.

In other words, Aquinas can say that his account of the Incarnation does not deny that God really suffers. Of course, it denies that the divine nature is capable of suffering. Yet, following Chalcedon, Aquinas does not think that God incarnate has only one nature. So he maintains that God the Word incarnate really did have hard and painful experiences. Indeed, he effectively says that if one denies the Chalcedonian account of the Incarnation, then one has no legitimate way of inferring from the statement "Jesus suffered and died" that "God suffered and died" without recourse to a notion of God observing the sufferings of Jesus while undergoing some kind of mental discomfort concerning how people could treat someone like him. And, as I have shown (see chapters 4 and 5 here), Aquinas would regard the idea of God as observing, while reacting accordingly, to spring from an idolatrous view of the divine nature as one thing alongside other things, some additional item to register when compiling a list of things that exist that are not *ipsum esse subsistens*.

One might, however, think that Aquinas's way of presenting the doctrine of Chalcedon in SCG 4,27–49 could be improved on. I doubt, though, that Aquinas would have rejected that idea. Just as he read with interest accounts of the Incarnation expressed before his time, he would, I assume, have read with interest attempts to say what the Incarnation involves written since then. In recent years, many such accounts have been offered by both theologians and philosophers.[51] Some of them come very close to or are equivalent to what Aquinas has to say about the Incarnation. Some of them arguably discard what Chalcedon taught while purporting to take that council as laying down what is doctrinally binding. Others, again, proceed while assuming that "the Word became flesh" cannot be understood along Chalcedonian lines but has to be understood as metaphor or myth or a matter of God somehow giving up divine attributes. It is obviously impossible to be sure how, in detail, Aquinas would have reacted to such modern accounts of God incarnate. Yet we can, I think, be certain that he would have approached them while asking whether they positively deny what he takes Chalcedon to teach. That Jesus is one person with two natures is a theological interpretation of Jesus grounded in the teaching of Chalcedon; and one might reasonably surmise that theological interpretations of Jesus other than that of Chalcedon are possible. After all, Christians managed to profess belief in Christ as divine long before the

Council of Chalcedon; and there is no reason to suppose that they cannot do so these days without expressing how the Incarnation should be thought about in terms presented by Chalcedon. But it is one thing to use the same terms as Chalcedon, and it is another to deny the doctrine that it teaches. Were he alive now, therefore, I suspect that Aquinas would be open to new ways of talking about the Incarnation while resisting any of them that seem to imply, contrary to the language of Chalcedon, that Christ is not truly God and that God the Word is not truly a human being.

Yet, as I have shown, Aquinas takes the Incarnation to be beyond what human reasoning can fathom. He thinks that we can speak truly about God and can know ourselves to be doing so. In keeping with his claim that we do not know what God is, however, he denies that we can understand what the Incarnation amounts to. You might think that SCG 4,27–49 tries to describe God in clear ways; but you would be wrong to do so. In these chapters, Aquinas defends certain traditional formulae as cohering with Scripture and as not being inconsistent. The extent to which he succeeds in doing so is what we need to consider when reading SCG 4,27–49.

The Fittingness of the Incarnation, the Sacraments, the Resurrection, and the Final State of People and of the World *(SCG 4,50–97)*

AQUINAS BEGINS SCG 4,50 by saying that he has now shown "that what the Catholic faith preaches about the Incarnation of the Son of God is not impossible."[1] But was it suitable or fitting (*conveniens*) for God to become incarnate? That, Aquinas says, is the next thing to consider, and he goes on to consider it in SCG 4,50–55. Then, in SCG 4,56–78, he turns to a discussion of the sacraments of the Christian church while moving on to bring the SCG to a close by dealing with human resurrection, the last judgment, and the state of the world after the last judgment (SCG 4,90–97).

18.1 The Suitability of the Incarnation (SCG 4,50–55)

You may find it surprising that Aquinas begins his discussion of the suitableness of the Incarnation by launching into a defense of belief in Original Sin as he understands it. Yet he makes clear why he does so. He notes that St. Paul says that, while many became sinners because of the disobedience of one man, many are made right with God by the obedience of another (Romans 5:19). The disobedient man here is Adam as depicted in the book of Genesis. The obedient man is Christ. Paul thinks that Christ somehow reconciled sinners to God. Aquinas interprets this conclusion as teaching that the Incarnation was suitable because of Original Sin. He is aware that belief in Original Sin has been contested and that some have argued that the Incarnation was not suitable as a remedy for it. In SCG 4,50–55, therefore, he addresses the question "Was the Incarnation suitable?" by defending belief in Original Sin. With that defense concluded, he goes on to consider and rebut other reasons for denying the suitability of the Incarnation (SCG 4,53–55).

18.1.1 Original Sin (SCG 4,50–52)

By the time of Aquinas the notion of Original Sin was well established among Christian theologians, though it was sometimes presented in different ways. The biblical warrant for Original Sin was taken to be Romans 5:12–21 and 1 Corinthians 15:22. According to these texts, (1) the sin of Adam (see Genesis 3) brought condemnation and death into the world, yet (2) escape from sin and death has been made available through the activity of Christ. In time, and under the influence of figures such as St. Athanasius (c. 296–373), Tertullian (c. 160–c. 225), St. Ambrose (c. 339–397), and St. Augustine, these teachings came to be understood as holding that human beings inherit sin from Adam and are rescued, if at all, only by Christ. This understanding was confirmed by the Second Council of Orange (529).[2]

It is against this background that Aquinas drafts SCG 4,50–52. To begin with, he rehearses the narrative of Genesis 3, which he interprets as telling us that Adam, though not subject to death in Paradise, became so subject because of his sin.[3] He says that we should hold that death was a penalty inflicted on Adam for sinning, and he adds that, since we are all subject to death, we must all share in the fault of Adam and its consequences. Aquinas is clear that not every human being has consciously chosen to commit a sinful act. Young children, he thinks, do not choose to sin. Yet, he insists, sin is in all human beings and is "passed on to them in their origin."[4] It is passed on in this way, he thinks, since sometimes even babies die and since death is a penalty for sin. He also argues that there would be no point in baptizing babies if there were no sin in them for which baptism could be thought of as a kind of antidote. "If children not yet baptized cannot reach the kingdom of God, one must say that there is some sin in them."[5] "According to the tradition of the Catholic faith," Aquinas declares, "one must hold that people are born with Original Sin."[6]

With that point made, however, Aquinas notes a number of arguments that "adversaries of this truth" might be likely to raise. He does not agree with these arguments but presents them as reasoning as follows.

1. One cannot ascribe fault to someone because of what someone else has done. So "the sin of the first man is not imputed to the entire human race."[7]
2. The descendants of Adam were not actually in him. They stand to him only as originated by him. But sin is something that only an existing individual commits.
3. Sin is committed by individual people with human souls. Yet the human soul is not passed down from Adam. It is directly created by God (see SCG 2,86–89).

4. If Adam's sin is passed down to his descendants, then it is passed down to Christ. However, Christ was without sin.

5. "What follows on a thing from its natural origin is natural to that thing. But what is natural to a thing is not a sin in it."[8]

6. Let us suppose that sin flows from Adam to his descendants insofar as Adam is spoiled or failing in some way. In that case, sin would result from something in nature being defective. But "a sin does not flow from the first parent into his descendants by a spoiled origin."[9] In any case, "if by a spoiled origin sin flows from the first parent into his descendants, it will not flow into all, but into a few."[10] Also, something defective coming about because of something else failing in some way is not responsible for the defect it inherits. "Therefore, there is no way for a blameworthy failure to come down from the first parent to his descendants by origin."[11]

7. What has goodness by nature does not have it taken away by sin. There is natural good even in devils. But generation is an act of nature, so Adam's sin cannot spoil things so as to result in sin being passed on to his descendants.

8. People generate people, not what can be attributed to their offspring apart from their human nature. Yet sin is a defect in human beings, and it does not follow that, since people derive from Adam, they derive sin from him.

9. The parents of a particular human being might commit no sin in procreating that person. Therefore, we need not suppose that all people descended from Adam are born as sinners just because Adam sinned.

10. Adam sinned, but then he repented of his sin. We can, therefore, just as well ascribe his state of repentance to his posterity as we can his sin.

11. If Adam's sin was passed on to his descendants, then so were the sins of progenitors following Adam in time. This would seem to mean that the most recently born are burdened with more sin than their predecessors, which is false.

Aquinas begins his response to these objections by noting that we evidently suffer from woes of various kinds. We are beset by obstacles. We are frequently frustrated. We end up dead. Aquinas notes that we might put all of this down to naturalistic factors: to what we can expect given what we are by nature and given what the world in which we live is like. He goes on to say, however, that God could have arranged for us not to undergo the evils that beset us, and he suggests that this fact gives us reason to think they are penalties of some kind: penalties for sin. He writes:

> Although defects of these kinds may seem natural to human beings in an absolute consideration of human nature on its inferior side, nonetheless,

taking into consideration divine providence and the dignity of human nature on its superior side, it can be proved with enough probability that defects of this kind are penalties. And one can gather thus that the human race was originally infected with sin.[12]

With that thought in place, Aquinas responds to the objections he noted in SCG 4,51. In doing so, he makes the following points, which I list without intending them to correspond one-to-one with the arguments alluded to in SCG 4,51 as I summarized them above.

1. Individual human beings can be praised or blamed for the actions they perform. A species, though, can be affected by its origin, and the human species can be thought of as infected by the sin of Adam. "A sin, then, which is committed by an individual human being or person is not imputed as fault to anyone other than the sinner.... But, if there is sin which pertains to the nature of the species itself (*quod ipsam naturam speciei respiciat*), there is nothing inappropriate (*inconveniens*) in it being passed from one to another, just as the nature of the species is communicated through one to others."[13] Now, the sin of Adam deprived him of personal goodness. Yet it also deprived the human species derived from him of a certain goodness, that is, that which Adam had before he sinned. The fault imputed to Adam has been transmitted to all of his descendants, not as personal fault or culpability but as inherent in human beings fathered by Adam. Before he sinned, Adam was highly graced by God. Having sinned, he lost this grace, as did all of his descendants considered as being in Adam as a species. What Adam had to pass on to his heirs was a fallen state resulting from his personal sin. The descendants of Adam are born in a sinful state "so far as they belong to Adam's nature which was corrupted by sin."[14]

2. We do not have to suppose that descendants of Adam derive their rational souls from the semen of Adam. Original Sin is a flaw in the human species, but individual rational souls come into being following the copulation of individual members of the human species.

3. Christ was a descendant of Adam, but he received from Adam only what makes a human body to be a human body. He did not inherit the fault or sin of Adam. "The power to form Christ's body was not derived from Adam but from the power of the Holy Spirit" (see SCG 4,46).

4. Human nature has a defect passed on to it arising from Adam's sin. Yet this defect is natural to human beings considered as Adam's flawed descendants. Adam naturally passed on a state of being defectively human.

5. By sinning, Adam gave up what God conferred on him as a gift: unflawed human nature. This unflawed nature was, in a sense, natural since it was intended by God to be transmitted to Adam's heirs in a natural way. It was not, however, natural in the sense of being something that anything created could bring about by its power. Yet the claim that what follows on a thing from its natural origin is natural to that thing, while what is natural to a thing is not a sin in it, is no good objection to belief in Original Sin. This claim takes "natural" to mean what results from things in the world acting in accordance with what they are and the powers that they have as created things.

6. Defective things in the world arising from a defect in what gives rise to them occur rarely. However, the defect of Original Sin comes from something that results in a defect in all of Adam's heirs.

7. "Sin does not take away that good of nature that belongs to the nature's species. But that good of nature which grace added over and above nature could be removed by the sin of our first parent."[15]

8. If Adam had not sinned, he would have passed on to his heirs all that he had before he sinned: a graced life free from defect and death. As human, Adam was not naturally immune to defect and death. As graced, though, he was. Adam passed on to his descendants what he was as a sinner.

9. Christian baptism frees us from Original Sin. But this does not mean that we do not, as Adam's natural successors, start with the stain of Original Sin as conceived by people subject to it.

18.1.2 The Suitability of the Incarnation (SCG 4,53–55)

I have noted several times that Aquinas is fond of the word *conveniens*, which we can translate into English as "suitable," "fitting," or "appropriate." I have also noted that *conveniens* and its English equivalents are rather vague terms. Context can make them more precise. Hence, for example, we know exactly how it is suitable, fitting, or appropriate to behave when presented to the British monarch. We know this in the light of British royal protocol. In the absence of such a context, however, "suitable," "fitting," and "appropriate" are not words that are easily definable except with reference to each other, or with reference to terms that are equally hard to define.

On the other hand one might grasp what someone takes to be suitable, fitting, or appropriate given arguments that they provide for something *not* being such.[16] And in SCG 4,53 Aquinas summarizes a series of arguments to the effect that the Incarnation was not *conveniens*. In fact, he summarizes twenty-six arguments for this conclusion. Then in SCG 4,54 he explains why he takes the Incarnation to be suitable, while going on in SCG 4,55 to reply to the arguments listed in SCG 4,53. These, he says, are "disposed of easily" (*non difficile est solvere*).

18.1.2.1 Arguments against the Suitability of the Incarnation (SCG 4,53)

The drift of the arguments to which Aquinas thinks it easy to reply is as follows.

1. It hardly befits God to be united to a human nature, this being so much lower than God is.
2. If God were to become incarnate, something of use (*utilitas*) would have to come from it. Yet God can produce what is useful merely by willing it to be and without becoming incarnate.
3. If God cares for all things, then God should not have taken on only a human nature.
4. It would have been more appropriate for God to have taken on an angelic nature than a human one since angels are more like God than are human beings.
5. If God were to assume a human nature, people would be led erroneously to think that God is not "exalted above all bodies."[17]
6. Many errors have arisen concerning the Incarnation. So "it was not becoming human salvation that God should be incarnate."[18]
7. If the Incarnation occurred so as to save people, then it should have saved all people, while it appears to have saved only some people.[19]
8. If God became incarnate, his incarnation should have come with evidence of this fact going beyond the miracles of Christ, which it did not.
9. If the Incarnation was needed so as to free people from sin, then it should have occurred earlier than Christians claim that it did.
10. If the Incarnation was needed so as to free people from sin, then God incarnate should be in the world until the end of the world.
11. It would be good if people had an assurance of beatitude. But this assurance would have been better given to us if God had assumed "an immortal, impassible, and glorious flesh and had displayed this to everyone."[20]
12. God incarnate would have made use of wealth and honor, which, according to Christian teaching, he did not.
13. Christians say that Christ, though divine, suffered, and that all of us should recognize this fact. But the Incarnation of God in the suffering Christ positively obscures Christ's divinity.
14. It cannot be thought that Christ, as God incarnate, went to his death in obedience to God as his father, as Christians believe. That is because we

cannot think of God, considered as the father of Christ, wanting his son to undergo something contrary to what the divine nature is: something not able to die.

15. God does not will the death of human beings. He desires sinners to repent and live. So he could have hardly wanted Jesus, the most perfect person, to die.

16. It seems cruel to demand that an innocent human being should die on behalf of sinners, as God incarnate is said to have done.

17. It might be said that Christ's death was a wonderful demonstration of humility. However, one who is humble is so before one who is superior, and God has no superior.

18. Again, people can be verbally instructed when it comes to what humility is. They can also be instructed by human example. Therefore, it was not necessary for the Word to become flesh or to die.

19. It might be said that Christ died to cleanse us from sin. Yet it is only by God's grace that people are freed from sin.

20. It might be said that the death of the sinless Christ amounted to satisfaction for sin (i.e., to restitution for sin). To this claim, however, it can be replied that sinners should themselves satisfy for sins that they have committed.[21]

21. If something greater than human beings was needed to satisfy for human sin, an incarnate angel would have done as well as God.

22. Sin is not removed by sin. It is increased. So if Christ had to satisfy for sin by his death, this death should not have involved anyone sinning. It could have been a natural death.[22]

23. Since people frequently sin, Christ should have died many times over if his death is needed for the sins of human beings.

24. Bearing in mind the distinction of natures in the Word incarnate, the death of Christ no more satisfies for Original Sin than would the death of any other human being, for Christ died in his human nature, not his divine one.

25. If Christ satisfied for the sin of the human race, it seems unjust that people continue to suffer from the results of Original Sin: these being a tendency to sin, suffering, and death.

26. If Christ satisfied for the sin of the human race, there is no need to seek further remedies for the forgiveness of sin. Yet people keep on seeking such remedies.

Having listed these arguments, Aquinas concludes SCG 4.53 by observing: "These and similar points, then, can make it appear to someone that what the

Catholic faith preaches about the Incarnation has not been harmonious with the divine majesty and wisdom."[23]

18.1.2.2 *Why the Incarnation Was Suitable (SCG 4,54)*

As I have said, Aquinas replies to the above arguments in SCG 4,55. As I have also said, though, in SCG 4,54 he presents an independent case for the conclusion that the Incarnation was *conveniens*. Here are his arguments for this conclusion.

1. Perfect human happiness lies in beatitude (see SCG 3,48–63). Struck by the gulf between God and human beings, between the divine nature and human nature, people might naturally feel disheartened about their ability to achieve such a glorious status. But the Incarnation assures us that what is human can be united to what is divine by intellect and can grasp God immediately. The Incarnation shows that what is human can enjoy the immediate vision of God. Therefore, it provides us with grounds for hoping in our own beatitude.[24]

2. "This dignity of human beings—namely, that in the immediate vision of God their beatitude is to be found—was most suitably manifested by God by his own immediate assumption of human nature."[25]

3. The truths of the Christian faith (the "articles of faith") are not things that we can know to be true. We cannot demonstrate them to be true. We must settle for believing them in faith, which falls short of knowledge. But faith in what is true about God and beyond human reasoning has to be taught by one who knows without reasoning what God is and what he is doing. The truths of faith have to be delivered to us by nothing less than God, and they are so delivered by virtue of the Incarnation. For it is nothing less than the Word incarnate that passes them on to us. Only by becoming incarnate can God instruct us concerning what we need to believe but cannot prove by reason.[26]

4. Our perfect happiness consists in enjoying God, in coming to be like God by means of the beatific vision (again see SCG 3,48–63). Yet one can only enjoy something if one has developed a taste for it, if one loves it somehow. And the Incarnation can be seen as something that might stir up love for God in us. For in the Incarnation we find God loving us to a high degree. "God's love for people could be demonstrated to them in no way more effective than this: God willed to be united to human nature in person, for it is proper to love to unite the lover with the beloved as far as possible."[27]

5. We value and strive for friendship. However, friendship can only exist between things that are equal in some way.[28] Thus, we may think of the

Incarnation as giving us friendship with God because God became incarnate and, by doing so, came in human nature to treat us as an equal.

6. "It was necessary for people to be solidly grounded in virtue to receive from God made human both the teachings and the examples of virtue" so as to lead us to beatitude.[29] Over time, various people have given us examples of virtuous behavior. But all of them have somehow failed when it comes to achieving goodness, while God incarnate gives us the unqualifiedly best example of what it is to be perfectly good as a human being.

7. Sin is an obstacle to beatitude. So the human race needs a remedy for sin, and this remedy can only come from God as moving us to good and as remitting the offense against him in which sin consists. But if we are to be confident of God's forgiveness of our sins, then God must assure us regarding our forgiveness. It was, therefore, fitting for him to become incarnate so that people might be forgiven and be assured of forgiveness.

8. As the church has traditionally taught, justice "requires that God should not remit sin without satisfaction."[30] But it is beyond the power of any ordinary human being to satisfy for the sin of the whole human race. "Therefore, in order to free the human race from its common sin, someone had to satisfy who was both human and so proportioned to the satisfaction, and something above what is human that the merit might be enough to satisfy for the sin of the whole human race."[31] Yet only God is above human beings as able to bestow beatitude. "Therefore, it was necessary for our achievement of beatitude that God should become incarnate to take away the sin of the human race."[32]

18.1.2.3 *Replies to the Arguments in SCG 4,53 (SCG 4,55)*

With these points made in defense of the Incarnation's suitability, Aquinas replies to the arguments in SCG 4,53. I paraphrase his arguments as follows:

1. Human beings have God as their end and are born to be united to him by their intellect. The Incarnation provides us with a unique example of a subject that is exactly so united.[33]

2. The divine nature is not dragged down in any way because of the Incarnation. The Incarnation results in something creaturely being elevated to the status of being divine.[34]

3. God could have willed to bring about the good that comes from the Incarnation without having become incarnate. But doing so by becoming incarnate "was in harmony with human nature" (*congruebat humanae naturae*).[35]

4. Human beings are both immaterial and bodily. They are neither purely material nor purely immaterial. "Thus, it seems suitable that the universal

cause of all things assume that creature in which the cause shares more with other creatures."[36] From this it seems to follow that it was suitable for God to assume the nature of a rational creature rather than a nonrational one.[37]

5. Angels are unchangeable when it comes to their will. They have an "unchangeable choice" and cannot be converted from what they will.[38] People, however, can be so converted. Now, Scripture says that the chief aim of the Incarnation is the salvation of sinners. So it makes sense that God should assume a human nature rather than an angelic one.[39]

6. In the Incarnation it is a person (the Second Person of the Trinity) that assumes human nature. So it was more suitable for God to assume human nature than angelic nature since in people the nature is other than the person, which is not the case with angels.[40]

7. Angels know God better than human beings do. Unlike people, therefore, they can be "intelligibly instructed by God regarding divine truth."[41] For instruction concerning divine truth, however, people, whose knowledge derives from their senses, need someone in the world to hand this on to them. Such instruction was provided by God incarnate, who, as God incarnate, also provided human beings with grounds for hoping for union with God in spite of the immense difference between people and God. We might add that human beings are superior to everything in the spatiotemporal world, which makes it appropriate for God to assume a human nature so as "to finish a kind of circle in the perfection of things."[42]

8. The Incarnation does not lead people into wrongly thinking of God as not being greater than anything bodily. That is because it did not amount to God being just something bodily or something other than what is divine. In the Incarnation, there is one person with two distinct natures: divine and human.[43]

9. Since the Incarnation, lots of errors have arisen concerning it. But these errors have, over time, been corrected by sound Christian teaching.[44]

10. Human salvation is, indeed, a great good. And it derives from the Incarnation. But God's act of saving people needs to be accepted by them. So the Incarnation does not bring about salvation automatically. It only brings about salvation in those who willingly "cleave to the incarnate God by faith and love."[45]

11. The Incarnation did come with manifestations of Christ's divinity. For Christ performed many miracles. Furthermore, he did so in his own right and not as someone calling on God to bring about a miracle. And he gave others the power to bring about miracles *in his name*. Also, and through Christ, miracles of a nonphysical kind occurred, such as the

reception of the Holy Spirit and the coming about of charity in people (see Hebrews 2:3–4).[46]

12. There are reasons why the Incarnation should not have occurred earlier than it did. For one thing, it provided a remedy for sin, which means that it had to occur after people had sinned, acknowledged their failure, and looked to God for help. Again, by virtue of the Incarnation, God provided precepts that lead to perfection (see 15.2 here); but people have to be led gradually to such precepts, as children have to be instructed over time. So it was fitting for Christ to have taught us in the wake of what people were taught by the Old Testament. It was also fitting that, just as people of great dignity should be preceded by envoys preparing the way for them, Christ should have been preceded by the authors of Old Testament texts, which point to Christ as one to come.[47]

13. Had Christ lived among us until now, our reverence for him would have decreased because of his familiarity as one among many. Instead, he left us so that we might respect or revere him for what he is.[48]

14. The fact that God became incarnate as something with flesh and blood, something able to suffer and die, tells us that God wants to be united to people in a most intimate and, therefore, most loving way. Again, if God had not become incarnate, he could not, by virtue of the death of Christ (the death of God), have rescued us by satisfying for sin. Again, by becoming human, God was able to give us an example of virtuous behavior. Also, by uniting himself to what is human, Christ, by his resurrection, gave us an assurance of our own resurrection after death.[49]

15. It was appropriate for Christ not to have been someone with a lot of money or someone enjoying great worldly honors. That is because God became incarnate so as to teach us that our final end does not consist in earthly riches. Also, had Christ been someone with great financial backup, people might have supposed that we are saved by money and not by God.

16. Given what Scripture teaches, we can assume that Christ died while being obedient to God the Father. But Christ died for love of us. He embraced his death as an act of charity to us. So Christ was obedient to his father as he died. In being so, he did not compromise his divinity since he suffered and died in his human nature, not his divine nature.

17. God does not will death to people, but he does will the virtue of embracing death bravely and in charity. It is in this sense that God willed Christ's death.

18. God did not will Christ's death out of cruelty. He willed it insofar as it was an act of charity.

19. It is true that God lacks humility. That is because nothing is greater than God, while humility involves subjecting oneself to a superior. But it was

fitting for Christ to display humility in his human nature, and the humility of Christ gained value from the fact that Christ was also divine.

20. People can certainly be taught about humility. Yet deeds influence action more than words, and people are especially influenced by the deeds of people they recognize to be good. So it was fitting for God incarnate to set an example of humility for us to follow.

21. Christ's death provides an example of holding death in contempt while sticking to truth. But Christ also died to suffer the penalty due to the sin of human beings, to make satisfaction for sin. And, although God's grace suffices for the forgiveness of sin, satisfaction is also required. By dying out of charity, however, Christ satisfied for sin as neither people nor angels were able to do.

22. Sin is not removed by sin. But the efficacy of Christ's death derived from the charity of Christ embracing it on behalf of people. It did not derive from the sin committed by those who killed Christ.

23. Christ did not have to die just as many times as people sinned. His death dealt with all sin because of his charity and because of his dignity as both divine and human.

24. It is not evidently unfitting for the penalties due to Original Sin to remain even in those saved by Christ. The suffering of those saved by Christ allows them to be like Christ, who suffered and died on their behalf. Again, if the followers of Christ became immortal and incapable of suffering, others would come to follow Christ more for bodily benefits than spiritual good, which would run counter to Christ's desire to draw people from love of bodily things to love of what is spiritual. Also, if adhering to Christ automatically rendered one free from suffering and death, people would be pretty much coerced into adhering to Christ, which would not be desirable since faith in Christ is only meritorious if it is embraced freely.

25. Christ certainly satisfied for human sin. Yet people saved from sin by Christ still need to work at the business of staying conformed to Christ and his work of salvation. Therefore, each Christian should "seek to be regenerated through Christ" and should "undertake to do those things in which the power of Christ's death operates."[50]

By means of these arguments, Aquinas takes himself to have defended the conclusion that the Incarnation is *conveniens*, just as he takes SCG 4,40–49 to have defended the conclusion that the Incarnation is not impossible. Notice, however, that he does so somewhat modestly. He does not declare that he has intellectually fathomed what the Incarnation is and what its effects are. In concluding SCG 4,55, he says that "from what has been set down [sc. in SCG

4,40–55] it is to some extent (*aliquatenus*) clear that what the Catholic faith preaches about the Incarnation contains nothing impossible and nothing inharmonious."[51] The words "to some extent" here surely need to be taken seriously. Aquinas does not claim to have demonstrated that God became incarnate or that the logical coherence of the doctrine of the Incarnation can be formally proved. Nor does he claim to have fathomed the suitability of the Incarnation. All he claims to have done is to have shown that certain arguments against the possibility of God becoming incarnate are answerable, and that certain arguments holding that the Incarnation, as understood by orthodox Christians, was not suitable are also answerable. The remorseless and detailed way in which Aquinas argues concerning the Incarnation in SCG 4,40–55 should not blind us to the fact that he takes his achievement in these chapters to be a limited one coming from someone who does not yet enjoy the beatific vision.

18.2 Sacraments (SCG 4,56–78)

As he moves from his discussion of the Incarnation to a discussion of sacraments, Aquinas refers back to what he says toward the end of SCG 4,55. As I have shown, he thinks that people saved by Christ need to keep striving to conform themselves to Christ. Or, as he puts it, "it was necessary to show people some remedies through which the benefit of Christ's death could somehow be conjoined to them."[52] He goes on to say that the remedies required have to be "handed on with some visible signs."[53] And he takes these visible signs to be the sacraments of the Christian church as he understood them.

Aquinas thinks of sacraments as celebrated by ritual and as amounting to seven in number: baptism, confirmation, Eucharist, penance, extreme unction, holy orders, and matrimony. That there are just seven sacraments was not defined by the church in Aquinas's day. It was the Council of Basel (1431–1435) and the Council of Trent (1545–1563) that formally declared the number of sacraments to be seven. Yet belief in there being only seven sacraments was widespread in Aquinas's day, and he takes it for granted, though in SCG 4,58 he provides a brief defense of there being seven sacraments by comparing them with certain needs that people have just by being human.

In, *Summa Theologiae* 3a 60–90 we find a lengthy discussion of sacraments, one that was unfinished since Aquinas died having only just started to write on the sacrament of penance. By contrast with the treatment of the sacraments in the *Summa Theologiae*, the one to be found in the SCG is very short. Its main conclusions, however, are in line with what we find in the later *Summa*. Both works insist on the need for sacraments. Both think of sacraments as conferring grace and as bringing about certain effects as instruments of God. In addition, both of them contrast the sacraments of the Christian church with "sacraments of the Old Law," both of them maintain that sacraments do not depend for their validity and effects on the worthiness of the people who preside over their celebration, and both of them approach the sacrament of the Eucharist by suggesting that it involves a change of substance. Finally, the discussion of sacraments in the SCG and the *Summa Theologiae* both speak of sacraments as empirically observable processes that do not bring something about just by symbolizing nonempirically observable realities. For Aquinas, a sacrament actually effects what the celebration of it symbolizes: grace flowing from the life and death of Christ.

18.2.1 The Need for Sacraments (SCG 4,56)

In SCG 4,56 Aquinas argues that we need the Christian sacraments since they apply to individuals what Christ achieved for all people by his death: salvation from sin and union with God. According to Aquinas, Christ died to reconcile people to God. But he does not think of Christ's death as bringing about human salvation independently of how people react to it or act after Christ's death. A tidal wave will wash people away regardless of anything they do in the face of it. In Aquinas's view, however, the work of Christ has to be appropriated by individual people on a day-to-day basis, which is where the sacraments come in. These, he says, allow us to live our lives while doing specific things that free us from sin, keep us free from sin, or unite us to God in some way. In making this point, he does not offer an analogy to help us grasp what he is driving at. Yet it is not, perhaps, hard to provide one.

Consider a couple who marry. When they marry, they are, of course, married. But people have to work at marriages. And they have to do so as physical beings. So they will need to express affection in physical ways and continue to do so for as long as is possible. They will, for example, need to make love. And they will need to do something to get over disagreements. They will need, for example, to apologize to each other, and so on. The point I am making is that marriages succeed because of behavior. And, so it seems to me, Aquinas takes the "marriage" between God and people effected by the death of Christ to succeed on the same basis. He thinks that we have to work physically at being married to God. Or, in his words:

> Instruments must be proportioned to their first cause. But the first and universal cause of human salvation is the incarnate Word....Therefore, harmoniously the cure by which the power of the universal cause

reaches people had a likeness to that cause; that is, the divine power operates in them under visible signs.[54]

In short, Aquinas holds that people living their lives in conformity to Christ need to express this conformity in physical ways. And he thinks that the sacraments of the church provide them with such ways and are necessary for just this reason. He does not say that all Christians need the grace conferred by the celebration of all of the sacraments. So he does not say that all Christians need to be married or to be ordained as priests. But he does say that all Christians need to be baptized, and he clearly implies that if those who are baptized live long enough, then they will benefit from the sacraments of penance, the Eucharist, and extreme unction if they embrace them voluntarily and in good faith.

18.2.2 Sacraments of the Old Law and Sacraments of the New Law (SCG 4,57)

As I noted in chapter 15, section 2, Aquinas distinguishes between what he calls "the Old Law" and "the New Law." For him, the Old Law amounts to commands, precepts, and prohibitions to be found in the Old Testament, while the New Law is what is declared by God in the teaching of Christ and in his death and resurrection. According to Aquinas, the New Law is what is in force given the life and death of Christ. And, he argues, this New Law leads us to see that there are sacraments we would not have believed in while reading the Old Testament. He acknowledges that people in Old Testament times, Jewish people living before the birth of Jesus, celebrated rituals that helped them to conform to God's will for them. But, he says, these rituals only pointed toward the coming of Christ and do not draw on what Christ achieved by his life and death. So the rituals (sacraments) that we find noted in Old Testament texts should be thought of as things that people went in for while hoping for something better: human salvation through Christ. "The sacraments that preceded Christ's Incarnation," says Aquinas, "had to be such as signified and somehow promised salvation. But the sacraments which follow the suffering of Christ ought to be such as to deliver this salvation to people, not merely such as to point to it by signs."[55]

18.2.3 Baptism and Confirmation (SCG 4,59–60)

Aquinas thinks that baptism takes away Original Sin and all of the sin and guilt of someone prior to baptism. So he maintains that baptism leaves the baptized without the need to satisfy for sins that they committed before baptism. He adds that baptism is fittingly celebrated using water since water is good for getting rid of "filth in bodily things."[56] He also argues that, considered as "a spiritual generation," people should only be baptized once: a conclusion he takes to rule out the teaching of "Donatists or Rebaptizers."[57]

Aquinas's discussion of confirmation deals with that sacrament as celebrated in the West during his time. He thinks that it marks the mature and public embracing of grace while providing grace to continue to embrace it. Confirmation, he says, is "the sacrament by which spiritual strength is conferred on the one born again" and makes that person "a front-line fighter for the faith of Christ."[58] The celebration of confirmation, Aquinas adds, employs material and gestures that match the grace conferred by that sacrament.

18.2.4 The Eucharist (SCG 4,61–69)

In SCG 4,56–78, it is the sacrament of the Eucharist to which Aquinas devotes the most space, though the SCG discussion of the Eucharist is noticeably shorter than what we find in *Summa Theologiae* 3a,73–78. It begins by providing a brief account of what the Eucharist involves (SCG 4,61). Then, however, matters become more complicated and polemical as Aquinas proceeds to note "the errors of the infidels about the sacrament of the Eucharist" while offering a series of "solutions" to them (SCG 4,62–68).

The general account of the Eucharist in SCG 4,61 is fairly straightforward and amounts only to these points:

1. We need physical nourishment to help our bodies to grow and function well. Correspondingly, we need "spiritual nourishment" for "the spiritual life" so that "the reborn may both be conserved in virtues and grow in them."[59]
2. Spiritual nourishment should be provided sacramentally by what looks like human food and drink. So the celebration of the Eucharist makes use of bread and wine.
3. In the Eucharist, the Word incarnate is "contained in his substance."[60] It is the flesh and blood of Christ that nourish us in the Eucharist.

In saying all this, of course, Aquinas is presupposing what he takes to be New Testament teaching. In SCG 4,61 he only cites John 6:56 ("My flesh is true food and my blood is true drink"). But, as later chapters make clear, Aquinas approaches the Eucharist in accordance with a literal reading of Matthew 26:26, Mark 14:22, and Luke 22:19, in which Christ is said to have handed bread and wine to his apostles while referring to it as being his body and blood.[61] Aquinas takes these texts to mean that, before he died, Christ instituted the sacrament of the Eucharist in which people truly, not just figuratively or symbolically, take into themselves the body and blood of Christ. To the question "What is received by Christians who partake of the Eucharist?" Aquinas's answer is "The body and blood of Christ" or just "Christ." But he does not think that this is an easy idea to take on board or understand. Indeed, right at the start of SCG 4,63 he says that "the divine power operates with a greater sublimity and secrecy in this sacrament than a human being can search out."[62] Yet he resolutely sticks to the claim that Christ's body and blood are truly received in the celebration of the Eucharist.

Why should he not? Critics of Aquinas's approach to the Eucharist in the SCG have given many answers to this question, some of them based on their reading of the New Testament, some of them based on what they think it makes philosophical sense to say.[63] Working, however, from the literal way in which he reads New Testament texts that he takes to record Christ's institution of the sacrament of the Eucharist, Aquinas devotes SCG 4,62–68 to a discussion of it focusing on the philosophical possibility, or intellectual coherence, of what he takes it to be: the literal reception of the body and blood of Christ. As he says in SCG 4,68, he is out to explain that "what ecclesial tradition holds about the sacrament of the altar contains nothing impossible for God, who can do all things."[64]

I am not going to provide a summary of the arguments in SCG 4,62 that Aquinas cites as intended to cast doubt on the truth about the Eucharist as he understands it (there are five of them, though he presents these as suggesting several related subarguments). Instead, I shall try to give you a sense of what he does and does not take the Eucharist to be.

18.2.4.1 *What the Eucharist Is According to SCG 4,63–68*

Given his beliefs concerning Christian teaching on the Eucharist, and given that he thinks that people celebrating this sacrament can be nourished by what is truly the body and blood of Christ, Aquinas could, of course, just settle for repeating the formula "The body and blood of Christ is truly received in the celebration of the Eucharist." As I have shown, however, the SCG is shot through with what Aquinas takes to be illuminating thoughts coming from Aristotle, to whom he is indebted when trying to philosophize about the truth of the Catholic faith and how it might be expressed by "the wise person" mentioned in SCG 1,1–2 (see chapter 1, section 4 here). Unsurprisingly, therefore, he talks about the Eucharist while using Aristotelian terminology.

He says that if the bread and wine used in the celebration of the Eucharist become the body and blood of Christ, we can think of this as amounting to the coming-to-be of a substance without the accidents we usually associate with it. Christ comes to be in the Eucharist since "the substance of the bread is converted into the substance of the body of Christ, and the substance of the wine into the substance of his blood."[65]

On this account, there is no bread in the Eucharist following the words of consecration used in the sacrament.[66] The only substance present is Christ. Yes, says Aquinas, there are the appearances of what Aristotle would have called the "accidents" of bread and wine.[67] But these are but accidents (involving quantity, qualities, relations). They are not the accidents of any substance. They are not accidents inhering in bread and wine since, following the words of consecration, there is no bread and wine. And they are not accidents inhering in Christ since Christ does not have the accidents of bread and wine. In the conversion of bread and wine into the body and blood of Christ, Aquinas holds, "what takes place is the contrary of what takes place in natural mutations, for in these the substance persists as the subject of the mutation, whereas the accidents are varied; but here, conversely, the accidents persist, the substance passes."[68] In Aquinas's view, when it comes to the Eucharistic change God "conserves an accident in being, even after the removal of the substance which was conserving it."[69]

One might wonder how it can be that, as seems to be the case, and as Aquinas takes St. Paul to say in 1 Corinthians 11:21, people can be physically sustained over time just by eating lots of consecrated bread and wine. And in dealing with this puzzle one might suggest that there is a point at which the body and blood of Christ in the Eucharist turn back into bread and wine. Aquinas, however, prefers to think that the accidents of bread and wine remaining after the Eucharistic consecration are miraculously empowered to nourish us physically without being miraculously made to be the accidents of bread and wine. He writes:

> It seems better to say that in the consecration itself, just as the substance of the bread is miraculously converted into the body of Christ, so this is miraculously conferred on the accidents: that they subsist which is proper to substance, and, as a consequence, are able to do and to suffer the things which the substance could do and suffer if the substance were present. And so, without a new miracle, they are able to inebriate and to nourish, to be burned and to rot, in the same way and order they would if the substance of the bread and wine were present.[70]

Does this mean that the body of Christ is broken up as the bread used in celebrating the Eucharist is broken up or as the wine used is poured into different cups or chalices? To this question Aquinas replies in the negative since he takes Christ to be present in the Eucharist, not as divisible into bits but as wholly present in all that is dimensively perceptible on the altar used for the celebration of the Eucharist. For him, the body of Christ, in its glory following Christ's resurrection, cannot be divisible. It cannot be broken into parts. It cannot even be moved around. In his view, the body of Christ is present in the Eucharist sacramentally, not as a body with dimensions existing only in some particular place or in many particular places. We can, he holds, break up consecrated bread and wine, but we do not, thereby, break up the body and blood of Christ by anything that we do when celebrating the Eucharist. So, he says:

> Since the body of Christ is in the sacrament by reason of his substance into which the substance of the bread—the dimensions thereof remaining—has been converted, as the whole species of bread was in every part of its dimensions, so the entire body of Christ is in every part of the same dimensions. Therefore, that breaking or division does not touch on the body of Christ so as to be in it as in a subject, but the subject thereof is the persisting dimensions of the bread or wine.[71]

As I said above, Aquinas might have summarized his SCG theology of the Eucharist by simply saying "The body and blood of Christ is truly received in the celebration of the Eucharist." Instead, though, he uses Aristotelian language so as to suggest how we might think of the Eucharist as making sense of some kind. We should, however, notice that the "Aristotelian" notion of the Eucharist employed by Aquinas is not very Aristotelian. Aristotle, of course, had no notion of what Aquinas had in mind when writing about the Eucharist and did not try to defend this in terms of his own philosophy. More significantly, however, in his SCG discussion of the Eucharist Aquinas draws on Aristotle while saying things that Aristotle never asserted. For example, Aristotle never suggested that there could be accidents that are not those of an existing substance. Aristotle's account of substance and accidents rules out the idea of there being accidents that are not the accidents of a substance. So it is not surprising that many people have noted this fact and contested what Aquinas says about the Eucharist as being incompatible with the philosophy of Aristotle.[72]

A good example of a famous theologian resisting what Aquinas says about the Eucharist as non-Aristotelian is Martin Luther (1483–1546). He declared that Aquinas seems to know "neither his philosophy or his logic" since "Aristotle speaks of substance and accidents so very differently from St Thomas."[73] Yet

Aquinas is not concerned to be an "orthodox Aristotelian" in his discussion of the Eucharist in the SCG. He knows very well that Aristotle never thought of there being accidents that are not accidents of a substance. But he does think that we can take it to be possible for accidents to exist and to be observed as we celebrate the Eucharist, accidents not inhering in any substance. Just as he thinks that the Aristotelian notion of agent causation can be stretched so as to allow for an agent cause bringing about something from nothing as when God makes creatures to exist (to have *esse*), he thinks that God can bring it about that there is something (Christ) present in the Eucharist regardless of accidents that we might observe. Although Aquinas does not use the word "transubstantiation" when discussing the Eucharist in SCG 4, he is thinking of the Eucharist as involving a unique change of one substance into another one.[74] As Herbert McCabe notes, however, "Aristotle could have made no sense of the notion of transubstantiation. It is not a term that can be accommodated within the concepts of Aristotelian philosophy; it represents the breakdown of these concepts in face of a mystery."[75]

18.2.5 Penance (SCG 4,70–72)

When he writes about the sacrament of penance in SCG 4,70–72, Aquinas is thinking of what contemporary Roman Catholics are more likely to refer to as confession: the admission of sin to a priest followed by absolution and the carrying out of some penitential act in recompense for the sin or sins acknowledged. This practice takes its biblical mandate from texts such as Matthew 16:19 and 18:18, John 20:21–23, and James 5:16. The practice was endorsed in 1215 by the Fourth Lateran Council, which ordered that "all the faithful of either sex, after they have reached the age of discernment, should individually confess their sins in a faithful manner to their own priest at least once a year."[76]

On penance, Aquinas makes these points:

1. Although baptism, confirmation, and the Eucharist confer grace, people are always able to fall into sin this side of the beatific vision. We can act in ways that are out of step with a life lived according to virtue. Our desire can come to fail to be fixed on God. Ignorance and passion can always lead us into sin.[77]

2. However, we can always be reunited to God by God's grace. If we are always able to sin, we are always able to repent and return to being virtuous. If "sin takes place after grace is received, people can still be led back to the state of justice."[78] So much is taught by scriptural texts such as 1 John 2:1–2 and 2 Corinthians 2:6–7.[79]

3. The sacrament of penance is a remedy for sin committed after baptism. "If people sin after baptism, they evidently cannot have the remedy against their sin in baptism. And since the abundance of the divine mercy and the effectiveness of Christ's grace do not suffer them to be dismissed without a remedy, there was established another sacramental remedy by which sins are washed away. And this is the sacrament of penance, which is spiritual healing of a sort."[80] For the sacrament of penance to heal us, however, we need to be sorry for our sins as graced by God to be so. We also need to seek God's help concerning them while looking to Christ as redeeming us from sin if we value him and what he stands for. And we must make up for our sins in some way. So the sacrament of penance calls for us to be contrite, to cleave to God in Christ, to receive absolution of our sins from a minister of the church, and to make some amends for sins that we have committed—amends to be decided on by the minister to whom we confess, who represents the church.[81]

18.2.6 Extreme Unction (SCG 4,73)

The title of SCG 4,73 is "De Sacramento Extremae Unctionis." We can translate this as "On the Sacrament of Extreme Unction." But that translation needs some explanation. And here we need to note certain biblical texts. In James 5:14 we read: "Are any among you sick? They should call for the elders of the church and have them pray over them, anointing them in the name of the Lord." This text led Christians to anoint the sick with oil as a symbol of healing and of consecration to God, following Old Testament texts that speak of oil as healing or soothing and as consecrating.[82] And the church came to speak of this anointing as a distinct sacrament conferring grace and the forgiveness of sins, which is how Aquinas thinks of it.

But how sick do you need to be so as to receive the sacrament of the sick? Aquinas clearly thought that you need to be in danger of death so as to receive it and benefit from it. So we find him saying that "this sacrament is not to be given to anyone at all who is sick, but only to those who seem in their weakness to be approaching the end."[83] Here Aquinas is disagreeing with current Roman Catholic practice, which allows a priest to administer the "sacrament of the sick" to people who do not seem about to expire.

18.2.7 Orders (SCG 4,74–77)

When he refers to orders, Aquinas is thinking of ordination to ministry in the church, especially ordination to the priesthood and consecration to the office of bishop. In accordance with church tradition, he also recognizes as orders what are commonly referred to as minor orders. Contemporary Roman Catholic teaching diverges from Aquinas when it comes to the conferring of minor orders, which are not now taken by Roman Catholics to be sacramental.[84] Hence, we find the Second Vatican Council (1962–1965) referring only to bishops, priests, and deacons as being in holy orders. Yet Aquinas, unoriginally and given his context, thinks of the conferring of all ecclesiastical orders, including various "minor" ones, as amounting to the celebration of a sacrament. He says, "The bestowal of all these orders accompanies some sacrament."[85]

As he takes all sacraments to do, Aquinas takes the sacrament of Orders to confer grace on those who receive it properly.[86] He also argues that it is needed if the church is to exist as a visible institution passing on to people the teaching of Christ while, as the sum of its members, receiving the benefit of Christ's saving work. The sacraments, he says, "must be dispensed by visible people who have spiritual power," as, for example, angels are not.[87] It was, he suggests, "necessary that Christ should establish other ministers in his place who would dispense the sacraments to the faithful."[88] As we would expect, in making this point Aquinas cites a number of biblical texts, while going on to speak of those in orders as instruments of Christ working only through Christ's authority and power. In SCG 4,74 he also argues that there is need for people able to preside over the sacrament of penance and that of the Eucharist, which leads him to think of the priesthood as a "principal" order in the church.[89] Bishops, he thinks, come in as those with a "higher ministry which dispenses the sacrament of orders."[90] First among these is the bishop of Rome. Aquinas, whose approach to government is strongly monarchical, thinks of the pope as one person needed to govern the one true church. So, he writes:

> The best government of a multitude is rule by one, and this is clear from the purpose of government, which is peace; for peace and the unity of his subjects are the purpose of the one who rules, and one is a better constituted cause of unity than many. Clearly, then, the government of the Church has been so disposed that one is at the head of the entire Church.[91]

With that said, Aquinas references biblical texts that he takes to endorse the view that the pope is the one head of the church to whom obedience is due. But, I might note, at this point he just quotes chapter and verse without trying to argue that the texts he cites are best interpreted as saying that the papacy, in any recognizable form, was instituted by Christ. Nor does he offer a historical analysis of the origin of the papacy. He simply assumes that it is a good thing that the Catholic Church has its pope as the leader of all Christians, while taking this to accord with the biblical texts that he cites. And he concludes his discussion of orders while reiterating his anti-Donatist sentiments as presented in SCG 4,59. Ordained ministers of the church, he says, validly celebrate sacraments even if they are sinners. "The power of their orders persist in the ministers of the Church perpetually. Therefore, it is not taken away by sin. Therefore, even sinners and evil men, provided they have orders, are able to confer the sacraments of the Church."[92]

18.2.8 Matrimony (SCG 4,78)

Married people today will, perhaps, be astonished by SCG 4,78. For it is extremely brief and would not, by today's standards, pass muster as an essay on the theology of marriage. However, it is not presented as being such an essay. Its purpose is only to make some comments on marriage on the assumption that marriage is a sacrament that confers grace, as Aquinas takes all sacraments to do. So, in SCG 4,78, Aquinas settles for making some points that he takes to cohere with things that he has previously said in the SCG concerning our sexual organs and the use to which we might put them. He says that sexual intercourse is necessary if people are to survive as a species, from which it follows that "Matrimony, in that it consists in the union of a husband and wife purporting to generate and educate offspring for the worship of God, is a sacrament of the Church; hence, also, a certain blessing on those marrying is given by the ministers of the Church."[93] So, Aquinas concludes:

> There are three goods of matrimony as a sacrament of the Church: namely, offspring to be accepted and educated for the worship of God; fidelity by which one man is bound to one wife; and the sacrament, and in accord with this there is indivisibility in the marriage union, in so far as it is a sacrament of the union of Christ and of the Church.[94]

18.3 Resurrection, the Life to Come, and the End of the World (SCG 4,79–97)

With his treatment of the sacraments concluded, Aquinas is almost done with what he has to say in the SCG. For, he thinks, if we recognize what the sacraments are about, we have arrived at some grasp of what the Incarnation achieved: human freedom from sin and union with God. Since Aquinas regularly takes the created order to be geared to human salvation (looking forward in the SCG; see SCG 4,97), his discussion of sacraments, intimately tied as it is to his discussion of the Incarnation, amounts to a rounding off of his account of the end of the created order.

Yet Aquinas clearly thinks that there is still more of substance to discuss before bringing the SCG to a close, and he makes the necessary transition early in SCG 4,79. He writes:

> We have shown above that we have been freed by Christ from what we incurred by the sin of the first man; and, when the first man sinned, not only was the sin itself passed on to us, but also death.... It is, then, the effect of the death of Christ in regard to the remission of sin which we achieve in the sacraments.... But the effect of the resurrection of Christ in regard to our liberation from death we shall achieve at the end of the world, when we shall rise by the power of Christ.... It is, then, a necessary tenet of faith to believe that there will be a resurrection from the dead.[95]

Aquinas is in no doubt that the resurrection from the dead is clearly taught by Scripture. He refers, in particular, to Job 19:25–27, John 5:25–28, and 1 Corinthians 15:12–18. So he thinks that the realization of the end of the created order will involve the resurrection from the dead of all human beings, which he takes to be an event future to his writing the SCG and future to anyone reading it.[96] Hence SCG 4,79–90 is exclusively devoted to human resurrection. In SCG 4,90–95, Aquinas turns to a consideration of human souls immediately following death. Then he concludes the SCG by talking about how we, and the world as a whole, shall be after what he refers to as the Last Judgment, by which he means how all people stand in relation to God come their resurrection.

18.3.1 The Main Line of Thought in SCG 4,79–97

SCG 4,79–97 includes things that you may find very puzzling. You might, for example, find it hard to fathom what Aquinas is saying in SCG 4,81 when he discusses cannibalism. You might also feel perplexed by the degree to which Aquinas draws on the idea that planets are moved by souls of some kind.[97] But the basic drift of SCG 4,79–97, in which Aquinas draws heavily on scriptural texts when it comes to his speculations, seems clear enough, and the major points in these chapters, whether cogent or not, can be briefly summarized as follows.[98]

1. The bodies of human beings will rise from the dead and will be immortal. This is evident from Scripture.[99]

2. Apart from the testimony of Scripture, a reason for believing in human resurrection lies in the fact that, after death, a person's soul survives without animating a human body (see SCG 2,79). But the soul of someone who has died needs to be rejoined to the person's body. That is because the soul of a human being is incomplete if it is not animating a human body— meaning that it is "contrary to the nature of the soul to be without the body." But what is contrary to nature "cannot be perpetual."[100]

3. People tend naturally to happiness. Yet they cannot be fully happy without being bodily, for "the soul is naturally a part of human nature," and perfect human happiness cannot be achieved if the souls of people who have died are not reunited to their bodies.[101]

4. People deserve either reward or punishment for how they have chosen to act. But acting people are composed of soul and body. After death, therefore, people need to be rewarded or punished as things having both soul and body, which calls for the resurrection of the body.[102]

5. A number of arguments might be cited to the effect that there is an absurdity in belief in the resurrection of the body. According to these arguments:

   a. What is destroyed or corrupted in nature does not come back into existence numerically the same as before. But death brings about corruption in one who has died. So it seems impossible for a person who has died to return to life numerically the same.[103]

   b. Since having an essence involves having essential properties or principles, something losing an essential property or principle ceases to exist. Now when something is annihilated it cannot become numerically the same thing as it was before. Yet death seems to annihilate many of a person's essential properties or principles.[104]

   c. Continuity is required for identity over time. But death deprives us of existence, which suggests that we cannot live after death as the things that we are before death.[105]

   d. If our bodies return to life, then they should be restored with everything that belonged to them, which seems unseemly since it entails the resurrection of a huge and unseemly amount of waste matter.[106]

   e. Some people eat nothing but human flesh, and these people, nourished by human flesh, themselves have children. So the same flesh can be in different people. But it cannot rise again in several human beings, which it would have to if the resurrection gave us back what we had before death.[107]

   f. What is common to individuals in a species is natural to that species. But resurrection is not natural to human beings since no natural agent can raise all people from the dead.[108]

g. If we are delivered from sin and death by Christ, then, surely, only those redeemed by Christ should be raised from the dead. So not all human beings will be raised from the dead.[109]

6. In reply to these arguments, it should be said that when God created human beings he made them able to control and direct their bodies so as to avoid bodily corruption; he made them to be able to share in the perpetual life of the human soul. Human bodies were not created so as to corrupt, though human bodies are naturally corruptible unless grace renders them incorruptible. Human bodies fell victim to physical corruption as a result of sin. Considered from this point of view, however, death is accidental to human beings, not something they have to endure of absolute necessity just by being human. This accident, however, was taken away by Christ so that "by the divine power which gave the body incorruption the body may once again be restored from death to life."[110] Again, although nature cannot restore a corrupt body to life, God's power can do this. "Since the divine power remains the same even when things are corrupted, it can restore the corrupted to integrity."[111]

Also, no essential properties or principles of human beings become absolutely nothing after we have died. The form of our bodies (our souls) survives physical death, as does the matter of our bodies considered as having dimensions. "Therefore, by conjunction to a soul numerically the same, the human being will be restored to matter numerically the same."[112]

Furthermore, one can think of what is bodily as having the substantial form of a body. But the substantial form of a human being is the human soul as informing a body with dimensions. Also, the rational soul is above matter and there is continuity of soul that can be reunited to matter.

In addition, we should note that there is bodily continuity through life in spite of material difference. "People are not numerically different at different ages, although not everything which is in them materially in one state is also there in another. In this way, then, this is not a requirement of people's arising with numerical identity: that they should assume again whatever has been in them during the whole time of their lives; but they need to assume from that matter only what suffices to complete the quantity due, and that especially must be resumed which was more perfectly consistent with the form and species of humanity."[113]

As for the argument against resurrection alluding to cannibalism, we need to remember that for someone to be raised from the dead, there is no need for everything that was ever materially in that person to be raised when that person is raised. So human flesh consumed by Fred, say, can rise without being part of Fred, and Fred can rise with whatever he physically acquired from eating what was not human. And if Fred eats nothing but human flesh, he can rise again with what he received at birth. When it comes to human resurrection, we should think that "if something was materially present in many people, it will rise in someone to whose perfection it belonged most intimately."[114]

7. People raised from the dead will never die again.[115] This is taught by Scripture and the Christian tradition. It is also to be inferred from the fact that without resurrection to immortality there would, for example, given points 2 and 3 above, need to be an endless cycle of human deaths and human resurrections, which does not seem to fit with the idea that God creates things for an end rather than an ever recurring series of ends.[116]

8. People raised from the dead will have no use for food and sex. They will not need food since eating food is necessary for human survival, while resurrected people are immortal and have no need to digest what we have to do in order to survive. And they will not need to engage in sexual activity since that is intended by God so that children should be born in order to continue the human species, while no children shall be born come the resurrection of all human beings, at which human history comes to an end.[117] Sexual intercourse is geared to human life prior to the resurrection of all human beings. It is not needed and will not take place following the resurrection of all human beings (see Matthew 22:30).

9. Our resurrected bodies will be real human bodies of flesh and blood. They will be numerically identical with our present bodies, and they will also be like the resurrected body of Christ as described in the New Testament.[118]

10. Although our resurrected bodies will be human, they will, by God's power, have a different disposition (*dispositio*) from the bodies we have now. For they will be incorruptible, as is the human soul. Our resurrected bodies will also be perfectly subject to our souls.[119]

11. Both good and bad people will be raised from the dead, and their bodies will be equally incorruptible, though not everyone will enjoy the beatific vision. However, the resurrected bodies of those enjoying the vision of God will share in the glory of the souls which enjoy it. The resurrected bodies of the blessed will be effortlessly directed to what the souls of the blessed will for them. So they will have agility and power. They will also be free from any suffering.[120]

12. "Since the bodies of the risen will achieve the characteristics of heavenly bodies, they, too, will have a place in the heavens, or, rather, 'above all the heavens,' so as to be at once with Christ, whose power will lead them to this glory."[121]

13. The resurrected bodies of people will display sexual difference and will be male or female, even though the risen will have no use for sexual organs. The resurrection of people restores deficiencies of nature, so it reestablishes people in what they are physically; it restores "the integrity of the body." And "all must rise in the age of Christ, which is that of youth, by reason of the perfection of nature which is found in that age alone. For the age of boyhood has not yet achieved the perfection of nature through increase; and by decrease old age has already withdrawn from that perfection."[122]

14. The resurrected bodies of those who die as unrepentant sinners will be largely like those of the blessed. But the damned will be encumbered by carnal desire, and their bodies will not be subject to their will as shall the bodies of the blessed. Also, the bodies of the damned will undergo endless suffering and will be separated from the bodies of the blessed.[123]

15. Before their resurrection, the souls of the damned suffer, but not physically. Christ tells us that they suffer from fire (Matthew 25:41), but this teaching should be interpreted as meaning that the souls of the damned know that they are subject to something lower than them. Also, of course, the damned can suffer from general remorse and frustration.[124]

16. Our souls are rewarded or punished by God as soon as we die. Then, they either enjoy the vision of God forever, or they eternally lack it. The fate of our resurrected bodies depends on the state of our will at death. However, there can be people destined for heaven who die without being perfectly conformed to God. The souls of such people endure a period of purification (purgatory) prior to the beatific vision, as Scripture teaches.[125]

17. After death, our souls are fixed when it comes to willing. The souls destined to enjoy the beatific vision are fixed on God. The souls of the damned are not. "Souls immediately after their separation from the body become unchangeable in will, with the result that the will of people cannot further be changed, neither from good to evil, nor from evil to good."[126]

18. The resurrection from the dead will come at one time. Some will be raised to glory, others to punishment. This is what the Last Judgment amounts to, and it is Christ who will be the judge since his life and death lead people to eternal life, as John 5:27 says. Nonetheless, Christ will be assisted in his act of judgment by his apostles, as we gather from Matthew 19:28.

19. Following the Last Judgement, all generation and corruption in the universe will cease. For generation and corruption on earth exist with a view to the final end of all people, as St. Paul says.[127] Generation and corruption on earth is caused by the movements of heavenly bodies. So after the Last Judgment, the heavenly bodies will cease to move, though they will continue to exist. However, naturally perishable things, such as plants and

animals, will pass away, as 1 Corinthians 7:31 teaches. Such perishable things will be consumed by fire, as 2 Peter 3:7 says. However, the material world will inherit a kind of glory because of the glory of that for which it exists: the human being.

So, says Aquinas, at the end of time, there will be a great transformation in created things. And it is on this note that the SCG ends.

18.4 Some Comments on SCG 4,79–97

As he says at the outset of the SCG, Aquinas's concern in this work is to consider how reason, aided by revelation, can reflect on what Christians believe to be true. Aquinas is also intent on taking account of reasons presented to the effect that the Christian religion asks us to believe in a series of falsehoods or impossibilities. In doing so, he covers a great deal of ground and engages with key Christian doctrines and a large range of philosophical questions and topics. In SCG 4,79–97 the doctrines Aquinas touches on include the doctrine of original sin and the doctrine of the resurrection of the body. In concluding this chapter, therefore, I would like briefly to say something about Aquinas's treatment of these topics.[128]

18.4.1 Original Sin

As I have noted, Aquinas views Original Sin as providing a context for the Incarnation.[129] He thinks of the Incarnation as dealing with Original Sin. He also thinks of Original Sin as infecting the human race and as leaving people with a problem resolved only by Christ and Christian baptism. And the treatment of Original Sin in the SCG is highly traditional. It reflects what people such as St. Anselm and St. Augustine say on the topic. It also anticipates what the Council of Trent and the 1994 *Catechism of the Catholic Church* declare when it comes to Original Sin.

On the other hand, however, the SCG discussion of Original Sin is open to question. I say this because of the way in which it so firmly connects Original Sin with the fall from grace of Adam, considered as a historical individual from whom we have inherited sin and death. This historical emphasis in the SCG's discussion of Original Sin will pose no problem for Christians who believe in monogenesis and who read the biblical story of Adam and Eve literally. But it will pose a problem for the large number of contemporary scientists who favor an evolutionary over a monogenetic account of human beings. For modern evolutionary thinking about human origins ("paleoanthropology") denies that there could have been a unique founding pair of humans, "Adam and Eve." The argument is that the line leading to modern humans (*Homo sapiens*) broke off from other primates about six million years ago and that our species appeared in Africa about half a million years ago. On this account, humans today reflect the fact that separate groups at different times left Africa and moved to different parts of the world, where, under the influence of natural selection, the different characteristics we see in the human species evolved.[130]

Someone committed to the position I have just summarized might, of course, well believe that people are sinful creatures. G. K. Chesterton (1874–1936) once referred to the doctrine of Original Sin as "the only part of Christian theology which can really be proved."[131] He meant that it would be mad to deny that we have difficulty distinguishing between right and wrong, and that we seem, as a species, to veer, with remarkable regularity, to bad behavior and to the construction and maintenance of societies full of wrongdoing. However, that people often behave badly only coheres with what Aquinas says about Original Sin. It does not confirm his account of the origin of sin and the connection he makes between sin and death. So when reading the SCG discussion of Original Sin we need to bear in mind the following questions at least: (1) Can we reasonably believe in a historical Adam and Eve? (2) If we cannot, might we still be able to find something believable in what the SCG says about Original Sin?

(1) is actually more difficult to answer than, I presume, most of us take it to be. We live in a culture in which evolutionary accounts of the origin of human beings are generally taken to be broadly correct. Yet, of course, few of us are scientists, and few of us would know where to start when trying to demonstrate that belief in monogenesis has been definitively refuted scientifically. The point I am making here is that if you want rationally to reject the monogenetic picture of human beings that runs through the SCG account of Original Sin, the onus would seem to be on you to be scientifically up to speed on the scientific case against monogenesis. And even if you do the necessary scientific work, you might still find yourself wondering whether science has thoroughly disproved monogenesis since it has been argued that monogenesis is compatible with what contemporary scientists say about our origins. You might find yourself wondering this if, for example, you read something along the lines of Kenneth W. Kemp's article "Science, Theology, and Monogenesis."[132] Having sympathetically, and in detail, presented accounts of a number of evolutionary theories, Kemp suggests that a respectable scientist need not give up on some version of monogenesis. I, of course, am no respectable scientist, and I am unable to adjudicate when it comes to Adam and Eve and the scientists. But it does seem to me that if you want to pronounce on

this matter, you will need to do a fair bit of scientific research, as Kemp has clearly done.

In response to this point, some Christians defending belief in monogenesis will say that their faith requires them to do so. Christians committed to the view that the biblical account of Adam and Eve should be read literally will take this line. Again, some Roman Catholics will hold that they are committed to monogenesis given what the Council of Trent declared concerning Original Sin. For that Council rejected any approach to the topic of Original Sin that denies the historicity of Adam and Eve and the claim that the human race has inherited sin and death from Adam.[133]

Yet contemporary Old Testament scholars seem fairly agreed that it would be an exegetical error to suppose that the biblical account of Adam and Eve was intended to be read as historical in the sense that we expect biographies to be. And the Roman Catholic Church has, in fact, never officially asserted monogenesis in opposition to evolutionary accounts of the human race.[134] Like Aquinas, the Council of Trent speaks of Adam and Eve as if they were historical individuals. But Trent was not attacking any evolutionary theory since theories of evolution did not exist in the sixteenth century. I might add that, in recent years, the teaching office of the Catholic Church seems to have become increasingly open to the idea that people are the result of an evolutionary process. In his encyclical *Humani Generis* (1950), Pope Pius XII insisted on the truth of the doctrine of Original Sin but also left room for those engaging in research concerning human evolution. Again, in an address on evolution to the Pontifical Academy of Sciences delivered in 1996, Pope John Paul II said (1) that, in *Humani Generis*, Pius XII affirmed "that there is no conflict between evolution and the doctrine of the faith regarding man and his vocation, provided that we do not lose sight of certain fixed points," and (2) that "Today, more than a half-century after the appearance of that encyclical, some new findings lead us toward the recognition of evolution as more than an hypothesis."[135]

So perhaps we might consider reviewing what the SCG says about Original Sin on the supposition that Adam and Eve never existed as historical parents of the human race. I am not claiming that we have to do this since I lack the knowledge that might lead me to support such a claim in a scientifically informed way. And you might think that the Bible always trumps modern science and that it tells us that Adam and Eve were historical individuals. If you say that, however, you are contrasting modern science and the Bible in a way that Aquinas may not have wanted to do were he alive today. There is no knowing what he would have made of what biblical scholars argue now concerning the nature of the Genesis story of Adam and Eve. And he might well have concluded that evolutionary theories concerning the human race have to be taken seriously. He wrote theology while often relying on a number of what are now, I assume, refutable scientific assumptions. He thought, for example, that the sun moves around the earth. He also thought that what he called the "heavenly bodies" are incapable of perishing. And he knew nothing about what we now refer to as the Milky Way. In short, Aquinas, unsurprisingly, was unaware of what we now seem to know about the vastness of the universe, the galaxies in it, and what might have occurred in the universe light-years away. So what would he make of modern science, especially with respect to the notion of Original Sin? I find it hard to believe that he would have dismissed evolutionary theories out of hand since he believes that truth cannot contradict truth and that what we genuinely learn from scientific research should be taken very seriously. Nevertheless, it is impossible to be sure how his theology of Original Sin would read were he alive to develop it now.

However, suppose that we think it reasonable to speculate that he would not be pursuing it with the historical approach to Adam and Eve that he presents in the SCG. In that case, how might he present it? Perhaps along the lines that some theologians have done while knowing the writings of Aquinas very well and while greatly respecting them. Here I think in particular of Timothy McDermott and Herbert McCabe.[136] Both of these authors agree that there is no getting away from the idea of human evolution, and both of them agree that we cannot read the account of Adam and Eve in Genesis as historical. On the other hand both of them note that Aquinas thinks of Original Sin as something that infects us just by being born as human beings coming to exist in a world in which there prevails an opposition to what God is all about. And both of them think that we should understand Original Sin in the light of the Incarnation.

The line of thought here is: (1) though people often deny this, it seems evident that we are all drawn into a state of sin just by being born and brought up among creatures who are collectively disposed to sin; (2) it is Christ who presents us with an alternative to this state of alienation from God; (3) Christ did this by showing us that God actually wants us to share in the life of love that constitutes the Trinity, and he did so by willingly accepting and then forgiving what people did to him; (4) the death of Christ shows us what people are capable of as sinners while also declaring God's love for people.

On this account, we are all infected by sin since all of us come to birth in a world stained by it. Yet, on this account also, we are challenged to accept that God can redeem us by becoming one of us and can, thereby, show us that we can be what Adam, in the Bible, was supposed to be before he sinned. The presiding idea here is that human salvation should not be construed as the wiping out of some particular sin committed in the distant past. It should be thought of as God becoming human and accepting and rescuing people from what they are as prone to sin.

McDermott and McCabe are saying that we are, collectively, in a bad way and that God has offered us the chance of being united with Christ and what he did and said while, in his resurrection, having his life and death endorsed by God the Father. And that is certainly what Aquinas thinks in the SCG as he moves from his treatment of Original Sin to his account of the death of Christ. So perhaps his theology of Original Sin can be separated from his historical assumptions concerning Adam and Eve while leaving his notion of human salvation intact.

18.4.2 The Resurrection of the Body

Aquinas never claims to be able to demonstrate philosophically that we shall be raised from the dead corporeally. He does say that the souls of the dead will be permanently frustrated without being reunited to what is bodily and that this fact coheres with belief in bodily resurrection and gives us some reason to believe in it. But he does not claim that human resurrection in the future can be proved to occur.

Such philosophical modesty is, perhaps, appropriate since it is hard to see what argument can philosophically demonstrate that the dead shall be raised. It has often been said that the resurrection of Jesus is a well-established fact. But even if we agree with this conclusion, as many do not, nothing follows about the resurrection of all human beings—not without a number of theological premises, anyway. Unsurprisingly, therefore, Aquinas derives his confidence that the dead shall be raised from what he takes to be divine revelation. Yet why should he focus so emphatically on bodily resurrection? Why not, instead, think of life after death as nothing more than a matter of ongoing nonmaterial consciousness, the survival of a disembodied mind or soul?

Many people, some of whom self-identify as Christians, seem to think of life after death in nonmaterial terms. This position, however, conflicts with standard Christian teaching, which tells us that, like Christ, we shall be physically raised from the dead (see 1 Corinthians 15: 12–18). It is, of course, not Christian teaching that bodily resurrection amounts to the mere resuscitation of a corpse. The New Testament depicts the resurrected Christ as having abilities that no ordinary human body has. He appears and then vanishes (see Luke 24:36–50 and 1 Corinthians 15:4–9). He can miraculously enter a locked room (see John 20:19). Again, when St. Paul talks about the resurrection of all people he appeals to the notion of transformation. Although clearly not much interested in speculation concerning resurrected bodies (see 1 Corinthians 15:35–36), Paul compares our resurrected bodies with what springs from a seed that is planted in earth (see 1 Corinthians 15:37–38). He goes on to say that, when it comes to the resurrection of the dead, "What is sown is perishable, what is raised is imperishable. It is sown in dishonor, it is raised in glory. It is sown in weakness, it is raised in power."[137] With all of that said, however, the New Testament approach to life after death focuses on it being bodily, not the ongoing existence of a nonmaterial mind. It is not therefore surprising that Christians have never been asked to believe in the "immortality of the soul" in the sense in which philosophers like Plato seem to have done: as the ongoing nonmaterial existence of what constitutes a human person. In any case, the notion that we live after death only immaterially is questionable unless we assume that a human being actually is something nonmaterial.

Here, once again, we return to the notion of substance dualism to which I referred in chapter 11. According to this, we are essentially nonmaterial things, which implies bodily death presents no obstacle to belief in life after death. For if I am something the essence of which is incorporeal, then the corruption of my body does not entail that my life is thereby ended. Yet is it reasonable to suppose that we are essentially noncorporeal? Arguably not. For, as Aquinas notes, we so manifestly seem to be bodily even if we are not *merely* material (see chapter 11 here). Whatever else we might be, we are surely objects on which biologists can get their hands. That, presumably, is why we can refer to ourselves as, for example, seeing, hearing, and feeling: notions bound up with bodily existence. As Peter Geach observes:

> How do we eventually use such words as "see," "hear," "feel," when we have gotten into the way of using them? We do not exercise these concepts only so as to pick out cases of seeing and the rest in our separate world of sense experience; on the contrary, these concepts are used in association with a host of other concepts relating, e.g., to the physical characteristics of what is seen and the behaviour of those who do see. In saying this I am not putting forward a theory, but just reminding you of very familiar features in the everyday use of the verb "to see" and related expressions; our ordinary talk about seeing would cease to be intelligible if there were cut out of it such expressions as "I can't see, it's too far off," "I caught his eye," "Don't look round," etc....I am not asking you to believe that "to see" is itself a word for a kind of behaviour. But the concept of seeing can be maintained only because it has threads of connection with these other non-psychological concepts; break enough threads and the concept of seeing collapses.[138]

Being alive as a human being is not to be equated with being essentially immaterial, notwithstanding the arguments of philosophers who have said that all of us are essentially immaterial things. So it is perhaps to Aquinas's credit that he recognizes this in what he writes about resurrection in SCG 4.

Some people, of course, will argue that the notion of all human beings being raised from the dead is absurd. As I have shown, in SCG 4,80 Aquinas notes seven arguments to this effect. And the arguments have force. But Aquinas has replies to them that are also forceful.

For example, it seems reasonable to suggest that if God is omnipotent, then human resurrection is possible if the notion of human resurrection does not involve any logical impossibility. That we might not be able to understand how God can raise the dead surely does not prove that to raise the dead lies outside God's power.

Again, we might sympathize with Aquinas's claim that human resurrection must involve material continuity between people before death and people as raised from the dead if the dead as raised are personally identical with people who have died. The obvious objection to this claim is that resurrected human bodies cannot be materially identical with the bodies of those who have died since the bodies of those who have died corrupt and turn into other things. As Aquinas notes, however, material identity is not required for personal identity even if personal identity over time requires material continuity. Hence his observation: "People are not numerically different at different ages, although not everything which is in them materially in one state is also there in another. In this way, then, this is not a requirement of people's arising with numerical identity: that they should assume again whatever has been in them during the whole time of their lives."[139] This point is reiterated to some effect by Geach. He writes:

> If it is difference of matter that makes two bodies different, it may seem to follow that a body can maintain its identity only if at least some identifiable matter remains in it all the time; otherwise it is no more the same body than the wine in a cask that is continuously emptied and refilled is the same wine. But just this is the fallacy: it does not follow, if difference in a certain respect at a certain time suffices to show nonidentity, that sameness in the respect over a period of time is necessary to identity. Thus, Sir John Cutler's famous pair of stockings were the same pair all the time, although they started as silk and by much mending ended as worsted; people have found it hard to see this, because if at a given time there is a silk pair and also a worsted pair then there are two pairs. Again, it is clear that the same man may be in Birmingham at noon and in Oxford at 7 p.m. even though a man in Birmingham

and a man in Oxford at a given time must be two different men. Once formulated, the fallacy is obvious, but it might be deceptive if not formulated.[140]

You might think that the objection to belief in human resurrection based on cannibalism is pretty decisive. But it really is not. For, as Aquinas says, we do not have to assume that our resurrected bodies will be materially identical with everything that has been part of them prior to our death. What seems to be more important is material continuity. It has been suggested that continuity of memory suffices for personal identity and that if, after my death, someone is around who has my memories, then I live again.[141] But that suggestion is not cogent. As Joseph Butler (1692–1752) famously said, memory *presupposes* personal identity and cannot constitute it. Also, the attempt to secure personal identity only with reference to memory falls foul of an argument presented by the Scottish philosopher Thomas Reid (1710–1796). If I am who I am because of my memory, says Reid, then we might end up ludicrously affirming that someone may be, and at the same time not be, the person who did a particular action. He continues:

> Suppose a brave officer to have been flogged when a boy at school for robbing an orchard, to have taken a standard from the enemy in his first campaign, and to have been made a general in advanced life; suppose, also, which must be admitted to be possible, that, when he took the standard, he was conscious of his having been flogged at school, and that, when made a general, he was conscious of his having taken the standard, but had absolutely lost the consciousness of his flogging. These things being supposed, it follows…that he who was flogged at school is the same person who took the standard, and that he who took the standard is the same person who was made a general. Whence it follows, if there be any truth in logic, that the general is the same person with him who was flogged at school. But the general's consciousness does not reach so far back as his flogging; therefore…he is not the person who was flogged. Therefore the general is, and at the same time is not, the same person with him who was flogged at school.[142]

So one can see why it might be thought that if we are to live after death, then some bodily continuity is required, meaning that if we look forward to life after death, we should be thinking in terms of resurrection, as Aquinas does.

As I have shown, he believes that the resurrection of people will occur at the end of the world and with the Last Judgment. Some philosophers have argued that we should think of our resurrection as immediately following our death since this would get rid of certain worries concerning personal identity. If we are raised just when we die, then why should we doubt that it is we who are raised? Yet the idea that we are raised exactly when we die seems to smack more of the idea that resurrection is the resuscitation of a corpse rather than the transformation to glory of which St. Paul speaks in 1 Corinthians. It also seems to conflict with the fact that we have a lot of dead and buried people around us. If we can exhume a human body, then what sense can it make to say that the remains of the person we are exhuming has already been resurrected? It has been suggested that, when we die, God might resurrect us somewhere while leaving behind a body that looks as we did when we died.[143] This view, though, seems questionably to suppose that God can deceive us on a grand scale. Anyway, Aquinas does not concern himself with the notion of immediate resurrection after death. Why not? Because, I presume, and if he ever thought of it, he takes it to be out of accord with what the New Testament has to say about the resurrection of Jesus and the resurrection of all people.[144]

Yet might it not be reasonably claimed that what Aquinas says about human resurrection rests on antiquated views about the universe? It seems to do so given the way it is connected with his views about the heavenly bodies and what he takes to be physically "above" them. You might also think that what Aquinas says about resurrection in SCG 4 should be rejected because of what scientists now tend, though with conflicting voices, to predict about the end of the universe. For their expectations seem to be very different from those of SCG 4,97. Aquinas looks forward to an end of the world marked by a cessation of movement in certain heavenly bodies. Today, scientists talk about entropy, expansion, and cooling down. Or they talk about a "big crunch" and gravity leading to high density and high temperature.

However, we surely do not need to suppose that Aquinas's antiquated cosmology renders untenable what he is fundamentally striving to say at the end of the SCG. With the best cosmology available to him, he offers a picture of what even he must have thought to be unpicturable and unpredictable on empirical grounds. His eschatology, his account of the end of the world, is not futurology designed to provide us with a travel guide to the hereafter.[145] What motivates him when turning to eschatology is biblical talk about human resurrection and God bringing about a new world with graced and incorruptible human beings united to God. And, as Stephen T. Davis observes, such talk is not to be ruled out on scientific speculations concerning what is likely to happen in the universe over time. In Davis's words:

> The concern would be entirely appropriate if atheism or deism were correct, but resurrection points the way for us here. Christians do not

hold that the Resurrection of Jesus occurred, or that the general resurrection will occur, as natural consequences of the laws of physics. Rather, the idea is that, at a certain point, God will miraculously intervene and bring about an event that, absent divine intervention, would not have occurred. The universe is not a closed system. So Christians should not envision the end of all things as the nature and predictable result of the operations of the laws of nature. They should see the eschaton as the result of a mighty act of God.[146]

This is pretty much what Aquinas seems to think.[147] But, we might wonder, why he should be as concerned with resurrection as he clearly is in SCG 4. For is resurrection not redundant given what he says about ultimate human happiness in SCG 3? As I have shown, he there maintains that the vision of God is what alone truly fulfills us (see SCG 3,25–37 and chapter 3, sections 2 and following here). According to Aquinas, we are made perfectly happy only by contemplating God. In that case, though, what can be added to our happiness by bodily resurrection? In connection with this question it is important to remember that Aquinas believes that the souls of the dead can enjoy the vision of God and that many of them do. So what of significance can be added to them by the resurrection of their bodies?

That nothing can thereby be added has been argued by John Morreall.[148] According to him, if we can be beatified on death, we can be perfectly happy without our bodies being resurrected, which means that the notion of resurrection positively conflicts with that of the beatific vision. "If the blessed in heaven are perfectly happy right now in their condition as souls," he says, "it is hard to see what purpose the resurrection would serve.... If heaven does consist in our enjoyment of the beatific vision, the resurrection of the body would simply be otiose."[149] If Morreall is right here, there would seem to be something wrong with Aquinas's emphasis on the importance of resurrection. Indeed, Aquinas himself appears to be aware of an objection to belief in human resurrection resembling that of Morreall. In *Summa Theologiae* 1a2ae,4,6 he references an argument according to which our final happiness consists in seeing the divine essence (*in visione divinae essentiae*), an activity to which the body contributes nothing (*nihil exhibet corpus*).

Considered as an objection to Aquinas on resurrection, however, Morreall's conclusion is misguided since it rests on the view that people should be identified with their souls, which Aquinas does not accept.[150] Morreall asserts that Christian belief in the human soul is dualistic and Platonic.[151] Yet Aquinas is not Platonic or dualistic when it comes to what it is to be a human individual. As I have explained, he considers the human soul to be part of a body/soul composite, not a particular human being (see chapter 11 here). Unsurprisingly, therefore, he believes that the souls of the dead are not human beings and are seriously lacking prior to resurrection. Even if they see and delight in God, they exist in a state that is unnatural for them. That is why Aquinas thinks of resurrection as important. He holds that if we are soul/body composites, then we are not there in the fullness of our being without resurrection. What is there is what is but a part of us lacking that which it was created to inform. If I am my soul, then I might have all that I need to be happy come the beatific vision. But Aquinas does not think that I am my soul. And even if he did, he could argue that bodily resurrection might add something to my eternal happiness. For, as Richard Creel suggests, even a soul/body dualist ought to concede that the happiness of our souls can be increased by becoming connected again to our bodies.[152] We do not have to think of perfect happiness as equivalent to unsurpassable happiness since one can be perfectly happy without enjoying happiness that could not be possibly be augmented; so God could make something perfectly happy without making it unsurpassably happy.[153] Again, just as spices can enrich or enhance good and wholesome food, bodily pleasure might enhance the lives of people considered as essentially incorporeal.[154] Even on an austerely dualistic account of people as nonbodily things connected to bodies they have and as surviving the death of these bodies, there would seem to be room for additional happiness should they again become able to enjoy on a bodily basis.

Having presented his account of the final state of the world (SCG 4,97), Aquinas ends the *Summa Contra Gentiles* on a biblical note. He cites two scriptural texts and piously endorses them. We read:

> And hence, the saying of the Apocalypse (21:1): "I saw a new heaven and a new earth." And Isaiah (65:17–18): "Behold I create new heavens, and a new earth: and the former things shall not be in remembrance and they shall not come upon the heart, but you shall be glad and rejoice forever." Amen.[155]

This signing off may seem abrupt. One might look for a lengthier conclusion, one in which Aquinas sums up the *Summa Contra Gentiles* while brooding on its virtues and those of its author. Yet Aquinas's writings are conspicuously lacking in self-promotion and a display of his character. They typically present a series of arguments and then fall silent. In this respect, the final brief paragraph of the *Summa Contra Gentiles* is only what readers familiar with Aquinas would expect from him. As Anthony Kenny has said, the writings of Aquinas are the product of "a teacher invisible, standing out of the light so that others may see."[156]

Appendix

SCG AT A GLANCE

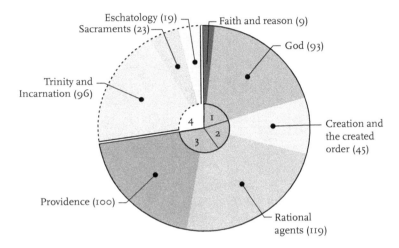

The numerals in parentheses indicate the number of chapters that treat the given topic; the numerals in the center indicate the book where the treatment occurs.

Book 4 is set apart to show that in contrast with the previous parts, Aquinas's treatment here relies mostly on biblical authority.

Notes

1. For a famous work displaying the structure of the *Summa Theologiae,* see the analysis to be found in the *Cursus Theologiae* of John of St. Thomas (1589–1644). This is available in English in John of St. Thomas, *Introduction to the "Summa Theologiae,"* translated and edited by Ralph McInerny (South Bend, IN: St. Augustine's Press, 2004).

2. *Saint Thomas Aquinas: "Summa Contra Gentiles"* (Notre Dame: University of Notre Dame Press, 1975). Volume 1 is translated by Anton C. Pegis. Volume 2 is translated by James F. Anderson. Volumes 3 and 4 are translated by Vernon J. Bourke. Volume 5 is translated by Charles J. O'Neil. The Notre Dame volumes are reprints of a text originally published by Hanover House (Garden City, NY) in 1955 under the title *On the Truth of the Catholic Faith.* The whole of this translation, with Latin-English facing text, is available for free online at http://dhspriory .org/thomas/ContraGentiles.htm. Note, however, that this online version lacks page numbers and contains many typographical errors absent in the text published by Notre Dame.

3. In 1924 an English edition of the *Summa Contra Gentiles* was published by the fathers of the English Dominican Province (London: Burnes Oates and Washbourne, 1924). This translation is now out of print, but it can be found online at http://www.saintwiki.com/index.php?title=Summa_Contra_Gentiles.

4. The Notre Dame edition of the SCG splits book 3 into two volumes, which I abbreviate as ND, 3/1 and ND, 3/2.

5. If you are able to read Latin, you should consult the Leonine Commission's version of the *Summa Contra Gentiles* (Rome, 1918–1930). This is a critical edition of the text, though some learned corrections to it have been provided by René-Antoine Gauthier in his *Somme Contre Les Gentils* (Paris: Editions Universitaires, 1993). For a Latin edition of the SCG online, see http://www.corpusthomisticum.org/.

CHAPTER I. THE *SUMMA CONTRA GENTILES* AND ITS CONTEXT

1. "Aquinas" in "Thomas Aquinas" seems to denote the name of his family (*de Aquino*), not the place of his birth. Aquinas was related to counts of that place. But these were flourishing long before Aquinas was born. In documents written during his lifetime and after his death he is often referred to as "Brother Thomas."

2. For scholarly biographies of Aquinas, see (in order of publication): (1) James A. Weisheipl, *Friar Thomas D'Aquino* (Oxford: Blackwell, 1974); *Albert and Thomas: Selected Writings*, edited by Simon Tugwell (New York: Paulist Press, 1988); (3) Jean-Pierre Torrell, *Saint Thomas Aquinas:* Volume 1, *The Person and His Work* (Washington, DC: Catholic University of America Press, 1996). For medieval accounts of Aquinas's life, see *Thomae Aquinatis vitae fontes praecipuae*, edited by Angelico Ferrua (Alba: Edizione Domenicane, 1968). Also see *The Life of Saint Thomas Aquinas: Biographical Documents*, edited by Kenelm Foster (London: Longmans, Green, 1959).

3. For discussions of the date of Aquinas's birth, see the works cited in the previous note. Historians differ when it comes to providing a chronology for Aquinas's life. You should bear this in mind when reading this chapter. If you look at the three works cited above, you will come to see where there is room for disagreement. For more on Aquinas's early life see Adriano Oliva, *Les Débuts de l'enseignement de Thomas d'Aquin et sa Conception de la "Sacra Doctrina"* (Paris: Vrin, 2006). Also see Adriano Oliva, "Philosophy in the Teaching of Theology by Thomas Aquinas," *Thomist* 76 (2012).

4. Books and articles on Aquinas these days sometimes refer to him as "Thomas," or "St. Thomas." In older publications one finds him frequently referred to as "the Angelic Doctor." In this book I follow a currently standard convention by referring to him as "Aquinas."

5. The current University of Naples bears an image of Frederick II on its crest.

6. Albert (c. 1193–1280) taught theology at the University of Paris and in Germany. He commented on almost all of Aristotle's works as well as on some highly influential theological ones. He was canonized in 1931.

7. Some scholars date the *De Principiis Naturae* to a period of Aquinas's life slightly later than the time of his stay in Cologne. Aristotle's dates are 385–322 B.C.

8. For an introduction to Peter Lombard, see Philip W. Rosemann, *Peter Lombard* (Oxford: Oxford University Press, 2004). Lombard's *Sentences*, written in the twelfth century, was the standard textbook for students and teachers of theology in Aquinas's day.

9. Aquinas's disputed question *De Veritate* (*On Truth*) dates from his time as Master of Theology starting in 1256.

10. For a fine historical account of the teaching context in which Aquinas worked, see Michele M. Mulcahey, *"First the Bow Is Bent in Study...": Dominican Education before 1350* (Toronto: Pontifical Institute of Medieval Studies, 1998).

11. For an analysis of the *Summa Theologiae*, see Brian Davies, *Thomas Aquinas's "Summa Theologiae": A Guide and Commentary* (Oxford: Oxford University Press, 2014). Also see Bernard McGinn, *Thomas Aquinas's "Summa Theologiae"* (Princeton, NJ: Princeton University Press, 2014).

12. I commend the following books to you as presenting an overview of Aquinas's writings: M.-D. Chenu, *Toward Understanding Saint Thomas* (Chicago: Regnery, 1964); Brian Davies, *The Thought of Thomas Aquinas* (Oxford: Clarendon Press, 1992); Brian Davies, *Aquinas* (London: Continuum, 2002); Edward Feser, *Aquinas: A Beginner's Guide* (London: Oneworld, 2009); Herbert McCabe, *On Aquinas* (London: Continuum, 2008); Ralph McInerny, *Aquinas* (Cambridge: Polity, 2004); Eleonore Stump, *Aquinas* (London: Routledge, 2003); Denys Turner, *Thomas Aquinas: A Portrait* (New Haven, CT: Yale University Press, 2013). Also see *The Cambridge Companion to Aquinas*, edited by Norman Kretzmann and Eleonore Stump (Cambridge: Cambridge University Press, 1993), and *The Oxford Handbook of Aquinas*, edited by Brian Davies and Eleonore Stump (Oxford: Oxford University Press, 2012).

13. Interest in Aquinas as a commentator on the Bible is steadily growing as I write this book, and with good reason, since Aquinas's biblical commentaries tell us much about both his theological and philosophical views. See *Aquinas on Scripture*, edited by Thomas G. Weinandy, Daniel A. Keating, and John P. Yocum (London: T&T Clark International, 2005).

14. Pseudo-Dionysius is the name usually used to refer to the author of a number of influential works thought in Aquinas's day to have been written by the disciple of St. Paul mentioned in Acts 17:34. Scholars today believe that they were written by an unknown author several centuries after New Testament times. For an English edition of the writings of Pseudo-Dionysius, see *Pseudo-Dionysius: The Complete Works*, translated by Colm Luibheid (New York: Paulist Press, 1987).

15. The *Liber De Causis*, once attributed to Aristotle, was, as Aquinas realized, a text derived from *The Elements of Theology* by Proclus (412–485), a Neoplatonic philosopher. For an English edition of Aquinas's commentary on the *Liber De Causis*, see *St. Thomas Aquinas: Commentary on the Book of Causes*, translated by Vincent A. Guagliardo, Charles R. Hess, and Richard C. Taylor (Washington, DC: Catholic University of America Press, 1996).

16. See Torrell, *Saint Thomas Aquinas*, 330 and following.

17. Torrell lists this as a "treatise," along with texts like *De Principiis Naturae*. I do not really understand why he does so since the *Compendium* amounts to a survey of theology comparable to the *Summa Theologiae*, albeit that it is much shorter.

18. For a catalogue of Aquinas's works, see Torrell, *Saint Thomas Aquinas*, 330–361.

19. See *Summa Theologiae* 2a2ae,1,8, in which Aquinas explicitly says that the articles of faith are proclaimed in the Nicene Creed.

20. *De Trinitate* 2,1.

21. SCG 1,3.

22. For discussions of Aquinas on faith and reason, philosophy and theology, see Frederick Christian Bauerschmidt, *Thomas Aquinas: Faith, Reason, and Following Christ* (Oxford: Oxford University Press, 2013), and Per Erik Persson, *"Sacra Doctrina": Reason and Revelation in Aquinas* (Philadelphia: Fortress Press, 1970).

23. Having argued philosophically for various conclusions, Aquinas, in the SCG, frequently cites biblical authority for what he has just been saying. Yet again and again in the SCG he spends a great deal of time arguing without appeal to revelation.

24. Norman Kretzmann, *The Metaphysics of Theism: Aquinas's Natural Theology in "Summa Contra Gentiles" 1* (Oxford: Clarendon Press, 1997), chapter 1.

25. Barth was *very* opposed to natural theology. I note texts of his that clearly indicate so, and I offer a discussion of his position in "Is God beyond Reason?" *Philosophical Investigations* 32, no. 4 (October 2009).

26. See Weisheipl, *Friar Thomas D'Aquino*, Tugwell, *Albert and Thomas*, and Torrell, *Saint Thomas Aquinas*. You should realize that we have a substantial part of the SCG written in Aquinas's own hand (from 1,22 up to 3,20, though with various gaps).

27. The Leonine Commission's critical edition of the SCG appeared between 1918 and 1930. Questions can be raised about its accuracy, though I have no intention of trying to pursue them in this book. For a technical discussion of textual problems concerning the SCG, and for some proposed corrections to the Leonine edition, see René-Antoine Gauthier, *Somme Contre Les Gentils* (Paris: Editions Universitaires, 1993). I am working on the assumption that the Notre Dame translation of the SCG, based on the Leonine edition of that text, takes us pretty close (Gauthier notwithstanding) to what Aquinas would have wanted English readers to be working from today when it comes to the SCG.

28. For an excellent introduction to problems concerning the ways in which writings by medieval authors such as Aquinas have come down to us, see Thomas Williams, "Transmission and Translation," which is chapter 14 of *The Cambridge Companion to Medieval Philosophy*, edited by A. S. McGrade (Cambridge: Cambridge University Press, 2003).

29. See Gauthier, *Somme*.

30. Aquinas did not read Greek. He relied on Latin translations when making use of Aristotle.

31. A *summa* ("summary") was an established literary genre by the time of Aquinas. A *summa* was a systematic, almost encyclopedic, discussion of a large range of theological questions with attention paid to arguments for and against various positions. Peter Lombard's *Sentences* would have been recognized as a *summa* by Aquinas, though it does not bear that title.

32. Reference to *Gentiles* appears in SCG manuscripts from around 1272. Note, however, that we cannot be sure that Aquinas himself named the SCG either

Summa Contra Gentiles or *Liber de Veritate Catholicae Fidei contra Errores Infidelium.* For an author highlighting apologetic elements in the SCG, see A. Patfoort, *Saint Thomas d'Aquin: Les Clefs d'une Théologie* (Paris: FAC éditions, 1983), chapter 5.

33. For Aquinas's familiarity with Islam, see Gauthier, *Somme*, 122.

34. See Gauthier, *Somme*, 172–173.

35. See Gauthier, *Somme*, 173.

36. ND, 1, 59 [1].

37. ND, 1, 60 [1].

38. ND, 1, 62 [2].

39. ND, 1, 62 [3].

40. ND, 1, 62–63 [4].

41. For a study of the SCG that emphasizes Aquinas's theological commitments when writing it, see Thomas S. Hibbs, *Dialectic and Narrative in Aquinas: An Interpretation of the "Summa Contra Gentiles"* (Notre Dame: University of Notre Dame Press, 1995).

42. Kretzmann, *The Metaphysics of Theism*, 24.

43. I discuss certain theological objections to natural theology in "Is God beyond Reason?" For a brilliant critique of the claim that natural theology conflicts with biblical teaching, see James Barr, *Biblical Faith and Natural Theology* (Oxford: Clarendon Press, 1993). I refer to Barr again in chapter 2.

44. ND, 1, 71 [1]. By "fitting argument" Aquinas means an argument that is plausible even though not demonstrative.

45. At this point in the SCG, Aquinas does refer to Islam. He offers a brief tirade against Mohammed in which he claims that Mohammed's teachings are grounded in the promise of carnal pleasure and that they are not supported by miracles. Aquinas also says that Mohammed gained support by force of arms and that his teachings conflict with the Old and New Testaments. This little anti-Islamic outburst of Aquinas, however, is hardly evidence that the SCG is focused on Islam or that its arguments are uniquely intended for Christian preachers in Islamic territory.

46. ND, 1, 74 [1].

47. ND, 1, 75 [7].

48. ND, 1, 77 [2].

49. ND, 1, 78 [3].

CHAPTER 2. APPROACHING THE QUESTION OF GOD'S EXISTENCE (SCG I,10–12)

1. Aquinas also discusses these questions in *Summa Theologiae* 1a,2. But the treatment of them in the SCG is considerably longer than the treatment in the *Summa Theologiae.*

2. I shall return to Aquinas's notion of substantial form. For now, I am trying to get some major points across as quickly as I can.

3. Ludwig Wittgenstein, *Philosophical Occasions 1912–1951*, edited by James Klagge and Alfred Norman (Indianapolis: Hackett, 1993), 373.

4. I quote from *Thomas Aquinas: Selected Philosophical Writings*, translated by Timothy McDermott (Oxford: Oxford University Press, 1993), 71–72.

5. ND, 1, 79. Like the translator of ND 1, I am taking "self-evident" to be an accurate rendering of Aquinas's phrase *per se notum* (literally, "known through itself," understood to contrast with "known by means of something else").

6. ND, 1, 79 [1].

7. Aquinas must have been thinking of particular writers when noting, in the SCG, arguments for the claim that "God exists" is self-evident. But he does not refer to any authors by name. However, the first and second arguments look very like what St. Anselm of Canterbury (1033–1109) offers in chapters 2 and 3 of his *Proslogion*, a text with which Aquinas was familiar. For Anselm's arguments see *Anselm of Canterbury: The Major Works*, edited by Brian Davies and G. R. Evans (Oxford: Oxford University Press, 1998), 87–88. In the *Summa Theologiae*, Aquinas cites St. John Damascene (c. 675–749) as someone who, rightly or wrongly, might be quoted in defense of what looks like the fourth argument for "God exists" being "self-evident." The *Summa Theologiae* reference to Damascene in this connection appears to be to his *On the Orthodox Faith*, 1,1.

8. ND, 1, 81 [1].

9. ND, 1, 82 [5].

10. From this text alone, though also from others in the SCG, I infer that Aquinas is presupposing that readers of the SCG would be, to say the least, students with a fair grounding in theology and philosophy as he understood it. This inference squares with what Patfoort argues in *Saint Thomas d'Aquin: Les Clefs d'une Théologie* (Paris: FAC éditions, 1983).

11. Aquinas himself accepts that God's essence is to be and that, in God, essence and existence are identical, and he goes on to argue for this conclusion later in the SCG. In SCG 1,12, however, he presumes that his readers are familiar with the conclusion and that the people he is talking about accept it. So, I shall refrain from an attempt to explicate it in detail until later in this book.

12. See Aristotle, *Posterior Analytics* II,9 (93b–28).

13. See Aristotle, *Metaphysics* IV,7 (1012a 23–25).

14. See Aristotle, *Posterior Analytics* I,18 (81a 38–39).

15. ND, 1, 85 [8]. By "middle term" Aquinas has in mind a term that allows us to proceed to a conclusion from at least two premises. He would, for example, have thought of "carnivore" as the middle term in the argument "All cats are carnivores; all carnivores eat meat; therefore all cats eat meat."

16. We might translate *demonstratio propter quid* by "demonstration why" and *demonstratio quia* as "demonstration that."

17. Aquinas does not think that we can never offer a demonstration *quia* that relies on some knowledge of what a certain cause is. His point is that a distinction can

be made between demonstration *propter quid* and demonstration *quia* so as to register the fact that we can reason causally while not understanding what a certain cause really is. For another example of *quia* reasoning as Aquinas understands it, consider the case of a door that normally opens as we push on it but gets stuck on some occasion since it is obviously meeting resistance of some kind from the other side. One would try to account for the door failing to open, but one might have little idea as to what exactly is resisting one's pushing against it. I mention this example since it fits in with the fact that Aquinas thinks that demonstration *quia* when it comes to God actually leaves us in a serious state of ignorance concerning God even though it can successfully be employed when arguing for the truth of "God exists."

18. Aquinas is contrasting knowledge and belief here since he thinks that knowledge involves understanding in a way that belief, or mere belief, does not. A scientist might know what gravity is while a nonscientist might just believe, on the say-so of the scientist, that gravity is real. By the same token, Aquinas thinks that someone might know that God exists while others might believe that this is so because they have been told that it is so.

19. The reference here is to *De Fide Orthodoxa* (*On the Orthodox Faith*), bk. 1, chapter 4. In this chapter John emphasizes the incomprehensibility of God. He writes: "It is clear that God exists, but what He is in essence and nature is beyond all understanding....As regards what God is, it is impossible to say what He is in His essence, so it is better to discuss Him by abstraction from all things whatsoever. For He does not belong to the number of beings, not because He does not exist, but because He transcends all beings and being itself." My quotations from Damascene come from the translation of *De Fide Orthodoxa* provided in *Saint John of Damascus, Writings*, translated by Frederic H. Chase, Jr., The Fathers of the Church (Washington, DC: Catholic University of America Press, 1958), 37:170–172.

20. I quote from *Aquinas: "Summa Theologiae," Questions on God*, edited by Brian Davies and Brian Leftow (Cambridge: Cambridge University Press, 2006), 23.

21. ND, 1, 85 [9].

22. In the Latin translation of Romans 1:20 that Aquinas used, the word rendered as "understood" by the New Revised Standard Version of the Bible is not one that would, for Aquinas, have meant "fully understood." Aquinas takes Romans 1:20 to be speaking of *some* knowledge of God derived from what God has made, not of a knowledge that he would regard as a matter of *scientia* concerning the divine nature. For Aquinas on different senses of "know," see Scott MacDonald, "Theory of Knowledge," which is chapter 6 of *The Cambridge Companion to Aquinas*, edited by Norman Kretzmann and Eleonore Stump (Cambridge: Cambridge University Press, 1993). Aquinas thinks that we can know something about God without grasping what God is essentially.

23. ND, 1, 84 [6].

24. The classic text here is A. J. Ayer, *Language, Truth and Logic*, 2nd ed. (London: Victor Gollancz, 1946), specifically 114–120.

25. David Hume, *An Enquiry concerning Human Understanding*, edited by Tom L. Beauchamp (Oxford: Clarendon Press, 2000), 123.

26. I take it that the death knell for logical positivism was sounded by Alonzo Church in his review of the second edition of *Language, Truth and Logic, Journal of Symbolic Logic* 14 (1949).

27. Davies and Leftow, *Aquinas: "Summa Theologiae,"* 24.

28. Davies and Leftow, *Aquinas: "Summa Theologiae,"* 26.

29. D. Z. Phillips, *The Concept of Prayer* (London: Routledge and Kegan Paul, 1965), 10.

30. *The Concept of Prayer*, 81.

31. D. Z. Phillips, *Religion without Explanation* (Oxford: Blackwell, 1976), 174 and 181.

32. In his highly influential *Meditations on First Philosophy*, René Descartes (1596–1650) argues that he is essentially a nonmaterial thinking thing. Many natural theologians have worked on the assumption that God is what Descartes takes himself to be, albeit more knowing, more powerful, and much better behaved. Hence, for example, Richard Swinburne begins *The Coherence of Theism*, rev. ed. (Oxford: Clarendon Press, 1993), by saying that God is "a person without a body" (1).

33. I defend this conclusion in some detail in my "D. Z. Phillips on Belief in God," *Philosophical Investigations* 30, no. 3 (2007).

34. Oxford: Clarendon Press, 1993.

35. Barr's point is endorsed and in some ways developed in Christopher Rowland, "Natural Theology and the Christian Bible," which is chapter 2 of *The Oxford Handbook of Natural Theology*, edited by Russell Re Manning (Oxford: Oxford University Press, 2013).

36. Acts 17:24.

37. Acts 17:28.

38. James Barr, *Biblical Faith and Natural Theology* (Oxford: Clarendon Press, 1993), 26.

39. Vatican I, *Dogmatic Constitution on the Catholic Faith (Dei Filius)*, chapter 2. The text I cite reads: "Eadem sancta mater Ecclesia tenet et docet, Deum, rerum omnium principium et finem, naturali humanae rationis lumine e rebus creatis certo cognosci posse: 'invisibilia enim ipsius a creatura mundi, per ea quae facta sunt, intellecta, conspiciuntur' (Rom 1,20)."

40. Barr, *Biblical Faith and Natural Theology*, 43 and following.

41. Psalm 19:1.

42. For the notion of a universal knowledge of God derived from the world, see especially Wisdom 13:5. Also see Barr, *Biblical Faith and Natural Theology*, 67: "Both Paul and Wisdom begin from creation and provide an account of the way

in which people, failing to recognize the reality of the creator God, entered into idolatry and then into the vilest immorality. Both say that God, the true God, was known to people, which is why their idolatry was disgraceful and inexcusable. Both hold it clear that God is knowable through the things that he has made (Wisd. 13:5; Rom. 1:20). The similarities are very great."

43. Barr, *Biblical Faith and Natural Theology*, 104.

44. For a review and criticism of a lot of them, see Graham Oppy, *Ontological Arguments and Belief in God* (Cambridge: Cambridge University Press, 1995).

45. The exception here is Alvin Plantinga, who offers a defense of an ontological argument, though not one that Aquinas considers, in *The Nature of Necessity* (Oxford: Clarendon Press, 1974), and *God, Freedom and Evil* (London: Allen and Unwin, 1974).

46. I try to explain them in chapter 7 of *The Cambridge Companion to Anselm*, edited by Brian Davies and Brian Leftow (Cambridge: Cambridge University Press, 2004).

47. For a more technical statement of this point, see Oppy, *Ontological Arguments*, 114–116.

48. William P. Alston, "Why Should There Not Be Experience of God?," in *Philosophy of Religion: A Guide and Anthology*, edited by Brian Davies (Oxford: Oxford University Press, 2000), 384. Alston extensively develops what I have quoted him as saying in William P. Alston, *Perceiving God: The Epistemology of Religious Belief* (Ithaca, NY: Cornell University Press, 1991).

49. Alston does not target Aquinas for criticism in what he says about perceiving God. However, his comments on the notion of perceiving God are obviously relevant to what Aquinas says about "God exists" not being "self-evident." For another contemporary philosopher arguing along lines similar to those of Alston, see Richard Swinburne, *The Existence of God*, 2nd ed. (Oxford: Clarendon Press, 2004), chapter 13.

50. See *Summa Theologiae* 1a,12,1. As I will show, Aquinas has things to say relevant to the beatific vision in SCG 2.

51. "Why Should There Not Be Experience of God?," 385.

CHAPTER 3. ARGUING FOR GOD'S EXISTENCE (SCG 1,13)

1. ND, 1, 85 [1].

2. So Aquinas actually ends up delivering less in SCG 1,13 than he might seem to be promising. The opening words of SCG 1,13 might be taken as suggesting that Aquinas is about to engage in an extensive history and defense of proofs of God's existence. But he does not do that. Why not? I suspect it is because he thinks that in SCG 1,13 he has said enough to demonstrate that God exists for his purposes at this stage of the SCG. In later chapters he has more to say when it comes to causal reasoning to the conclusion that God exists.

3. I am not concerned to enter into a discussion of whether or not Aquinas accurately represents Aristotle while drawing on him in SCG 1,13. I am not concerned to

discuss the accuracy of Aquinas on Aristotle at any point in this book. My aim
is to focus on what Aquinas thought Aristotle said and to follow him accordingly for purposes of expounding him. For an account of SCG 1,13 and Aristotle,
see J. Owens, "Aquinas and the Proof from the *Physics*," *Medieval Studies*
(1966). The passage in *Physics* VII that Aquinas seems to have especially in
mind in SCG 1,13 reads: "Everything that is in motion must be moved by something. For if it has not the source of its motion in itself it is evident that it is
moved by something other than itself, for there must be something else that
moves it. If on the other hand it has the source of motion in itself, let AB be
taken to represent that which is in motion of itself and not in virtue of the fact
that something belonging to it is in motion. Now in the first place to assume
that AB, because it is in motion as a whole and is not moved by anything external to itself, is therefore moved by itself—this is just as if, supposing that KL
is moving LM and is also itself in motion, we were to deny that KM is moved by
anything on the ground that it is not evident which is the part that is moving it
and which the part that is moved. In the second place that which is in motion
without being moved by anything does not necessarily cease from its motion
because something else is at rest; but a thing must be moved by something if
the fact of something else having ceased from its motion caused it to be at rest.
If this is accepted, everything that is in motion must be moved by something.
For if AB is assumed to be in motion, it must be divisible, since everything that
is in motion is divisible. Let it be divided, then, at C. Now if CB is not in motion,
then AB will not be in motion; for if it is, it is clear that AC would be in motion
while BC is at rest, and thus AB cannot be in motion in its own right and primarily. But *ex hypothesi* AB is in motion in its own right and primarily. Therefore
if CB is not in motion AB will be at rest. But we have agreed that that which is
at rest if something is not in motion must be moved by something.
Consequently, everything that is in motion must be moved by something; for
that which is in motion will always be divisible, and if a part of it is not in
motion the whole must be at rest." I quote from *The Complete Works of Aristotle*,
edited by Jonathan Barnes (Princeton, NJ: Princeton University Press,
1984), 407–408.

4. It has been suggested that in SCG 1,13 Aquinas only argues that something
moving is moved by another. Yet the best sense of what he says has him thinking
that what is moved (passive) is moved by another, not that anything in process of
movement is being moved by something else. See James E. Weisheipl, *Nature
and Motion in the Middle Ages* (Washington, DC: Catholic University of America
Press, 1985), 76–77. Aquinas takes "to be moved" as what Weisheipl calls "a passive capacity for someone else's action." He reasons that "someone else must do
the acting." As Weisheipl also says, "St. Thomas never said, *Omne movens ab alio
movetur* [Everything moving/in process of motion is moved by another]" or that
"everything that is in motion must be here and now moved by something" (78).

5. As should be clear, I am taking Aquinas's word *motus* to be translatable into English as either "movement" or "change." In what I go on to say about SCG 1,13, however, I shall largely stick with ND, 1's use of "move," "moved," "motion," and so on.

6. Some philosophers have argued that there is no world external to us considered as thinkers. If they are right, then we can regard most or all of the SCG to rest on a huge mistake. Since nobody acts on the assumption that the view I have just referred to is correct, I shall say nothing more about it in this book. Aquinas never discusses it in any of his writings. Perhaps the reason why is obvious. If you do not find it obvious, consider what you would be presupposing when trying to argue that there is no external world of which any of us have knowledge. For example, with what or whom would you take yourself to be arguing?

7. "Move" in English can be transitive or intransitive. I can move my cat or move out of my cat's way. In Latin, the passive form of the transitive verb *movere* is used to express the intransitive sense of "move." So "movetur" could equally mean "is moving/is in motion" or "is moved."

8. ND, 1, 86 [5].

9. ND, 1, 86 [5].

10. ND, 1, 86 [5]. Aquinas goes on to note that Plato thought that something might move itself without being a bodily thing. How so? By understanding or judging itself. However, Aquinas is here thinking of what moves itself as being what he is arguing for in SCG 1,13, something "absolutely unmoved" in the sense of these words that Aquinas takes Aristotle to be working with. As I will show, Aquinas thinks that there can be movement of a sort even in what is wholly unmoved since he draws a distinction between acts (movements) that remain in one and others that go "out of one" so to speak. I can reflect on myself, this, for Aquinas, not being an action that goes outside me. Or I can kick my cat, this being an action that, for Aquinas, definitely goes outside me (because there is something other than me involved in it).

11. ND, 1, 87 [6]. I am assuming that Aquinas is here saying that, for example, if I can be said to be at rest because a part of myself is at rest (since my foot, say, is not moving), then I am at rest only because a part of me is and I am, therefore, not at rest "primarily" and of my own accord but only because a part of me is at rest. And I am assuming that Aquinas is taking this point to imply that nothing primarily moves itself if it is moved by a part of itself.

12. ND, 1, 87 [7].

13. See Aristotle, *Physics* 8(254b–257b). By "inductive" Aquinas means "based on empirical investigation."

14. By "causes removing impediments" Aquinas is thinking, for example, of me permitting (and thereby causally accounting for) the water in my bath to flow away because I remove the bath plug.

15. ND, 1, 88 [9]. See *Physics* 8,5.

16. Anthony Kenny, *The Five Ways* (London: Routledge and Kegan Paul, 1969), 21.

17. See *Summa Theologiae* 1a,4,2. Here we read: "Any perfection found in an effect must also be found in the effective cause of that effect—either as it exists in the cause, when cause and effect are of the same sort (as when people beget people), or in a more perfect manner, when cause and effect are not of the same sort (as when the sun's power produces things having a certain likeness to the sun)." I quote from *Aquinas: "Summa Theologiae," Questions on God*, edited by Brian Davies and Brian Leftow (Cambridge: Cambridge University Press, 2006), 46.

18. John F. Wippel, *The Metaphysical Thought of Thomas Aquinas* (Washington, DC: Catholic University of America Press, 2000), 447. Wippel offers an analysis of texts of Aquinas on agent causation in "Thomas Aquinas on Our Knowledge of God and the Axiom that Every Agent Produces Something Like Itself," which is chapter 6 of John Wippel, *Metaphysical Themes in Thomas Aquinas II* (Washington, DC: Catholic University of America Press, 2007).

19. ND, 1, 89 [12].

20. Aquinas did believe that the world had a beginning, but, he says, this is a conclusion that has to be arrived at by people on the basis of faith in what the Bible says. It is not demonstrable. See *Summa Theologiae* 1a,46 and SCG 2,38.

21. ND, 1, 90 [14].

22. ND, 1, 90 [15].

23. Aquinas's "true by itself"/"true by accident" distinction amounts to the distinction between what is true of absolute necessity and what just *happens* to be true. If I am a human being, I am *necessarily* something with a body (the idea of having a body is built into our idea of being a human being). But if I am a human being, it is not necessary that I should have visited Hong Kong or have a tattoo of a penguin on my chest. If I have visited Hong Kong or have a tattoo of a penguin on my chest, that is just something that *happens* to be true of me though it might never have been true of me.

24. I take it that Aquinas would regard as "false and impossible" a proposition like "Some triangles have four sides." And I take it that he would regard a proposition that is "possibly true but actually false" to be one such as "Brian Davies, the author of this book, has a tattoo of a penguin on his chest." Some philosophers have claimed that what seems to be impossible cannot be captured in a genuine proposition. Others have said things to cast doubt on there being any genuine proposition captured by sentences with words like "this" in them (since "this," to put it mildly, is a very vague word). Even if you accept these theses, however, you will surely see what Aquinas is saying at this point in the SCG.

25. By "accidental feature" Aquinas means one that something might have but does not have to have given what it is by nature. So, I might be musical, but the fact that I am a human being does not guarantee that I am musical. As well as being musical, I might also be bald, which I do not have to be just because I am human (there are plenty of nonbald people). Now suppose that I happen to be

both bald and musical. Does it follow that I have to be both of these things? Apparently not. This is what Aquinas is saying at this point in the SCG.

26. The suggestion seems to be that, for example, though Fred, as it happens, is both musical and bald, it is probable that there is someone who is musical and not bald or that there is someone who is bald but not musical.

27. ND, I, 91 [19]. Here Aquinas is alluding to the fact that things can undergo different kinds of changes in the ways I mentioned above: change of place, change of quality, and change of quantity. So, he is saying, for example, that something moving locally (change of place) is either moved by what itself moves locally or by something undergoing change of quality or quantity.

28. ND, I, 91 [19].

29. ND, I, 95 [32]. In the present paragraph my summary of what Aquinas is saying at this stage in SCG 1,13 omits some twists and turns that Aquinas presents in his text. But I think that it conveys the sense of what he is driving at. For a more complicated analysis, see Norman Kretzmann, *The Metaphysics of Theism: Aquinas's Natural Theology in "Summa Contra Gentiles" 1* (Oxford: Clarendon Press, 1997), 72–83. Also note Wippel, *The Metaphysical Thought of Thomas Aquinas*, 427–431.

30. This argument is often referred to as the Kalām Cosmological Argument. For a defense of it, see William Lane Craig, *The Kalām Cosmological Argument* (London: Macmillan, 1979). For criticisms of the argument, see J. L. Mackie, *The Miracle of Theism* (Oxford: Clarendon Press, 1982), 92–95. For discussion of the argument by me, see my *An Introduction to the Philosophy of Religion*, 3rd ed. (Oxford: Oxford University Press, 2004), 48–54.

31. ND, I, 96 [35].

32. ND, I, 96 [35].

33. Referring to a passage in the *Summa Theologiae* in which Aquinas speaks about degrees of truth, P. T. Geach interprets Aquinas to be holding, somewhat absurdly, that, for example, "if one lie is a bigger lie than another, the truth opposed to one is a bigger truth than the truth opposed to the other." See G. E. M. Anscombe and P. T. Geach, *Three Philosophers* (Oxford: Blackwell, 1961), 116. I doubt that Geach is right here, but Aquinas's talk about degrees of truth is somewhat obscure.

34. What might Aristotle have made of SCG 1,13 (read in the context of the SCG as a whole) had he been able to read it? I do not know since I am not an expert on Aristotle, though there are doubtless experts on Aristotle today who might venture some guesses.

35. Aquinas thinks that there are beings that are both necessary and created. I elaborate on this notion in chapter 10.

36. My quotations from the *Summa Theologiae* here come from Davies and Leftow, *Aquinas: "Summa Theologiae,"* 25–26.

37. Dictionaries are full of what Aquinas would have thought of as nominal definitions of nonexisting things. Think about dictionary definitions of words like "chimera," "unicorn," "fairy," "elf," and so on.

38. See Kenny, *The Five Ways*, 18–19: "If a thing cannot be moved by itself, it does not follow that it must be moved by something else. Why cannot it just be in motion, without *being moved* by anything, whether by itself or anything else?"

39. See Kenny, *The Five Ways*, 28: "At any given time, the rectilinear uniform motion of a body can be explained by the principle of inertia in terms of the body's own previous motion without appeal to any other agent." Newton himself actually said: "Every body perseveres in its state of rest or of uniform motion in a straight line, unless it is compelled to change that state by forces impressed on it" (*Philosophiae Naturalis Principia Mathematica*, bk. 1 [1687]).

40. See Kenny, *The Five Ways*, 26–27. Also see C. J. F. Williams, "Hic autem non est procedere in infinitum," *Mind* 69 (1960). Williams suggests that Aquinas falls victim to fallaciously assuming that if something is a "secondary cause," there has to be a first cause—the conclusion here assuming what has to be proved given its introduction of the phrase "secondary cause." According to Williams, we are not entitled to claim to know that an infinite series of causes is impossible unless we first know that all movers are properly described either as first or second movers. Williams's argument is directed against what Aquinas writes in *Summa Theologiae* 1a,2,3, but I suspect that he would have taken it to apply to what we find in SCG 1,13. Kenny, at any rate, seems to take it to do so.

41. See Kenny, *The Five Ways*, 23.

42. Among others, Scott MacDonald does this in "Aquinas's Parasitic Cosmological Argument," *Medieval Philosophy and Theology* 1 (1991).

43. *The Metaphysical Thought of Thomas Aquinas*, 454. For a more detailed defense of this point, see "The Specter of *Motor Coniunctus*," which is chapter 5 of Weisheipl's *Nature and Motion in the Middle Ages*.

44. Edward Feser, *Aquinas: A Beginner's Guide* (London: Oneworld, 2009), 79.

45. Hume, *A Treatise of Human Nature*, bk. 1, sec. 3. For other relevant texts by Hume, see *An Enquiry Concerning Human Understanding*, secs. 4 and 5.

46. This is what Aquinas says in his commentary on Aristotle's *Physics*. I quote from *Thomas Aquinas: Selected Philosophical Writings*, translated by Timothy McDermott (Oxford: Oxford University Press, 1993), 83 and 84.

47. See *Summa Theologiae* 1a,22,2, ad.1.

48. *Aquinas*, 76.

CHAPTER 4. GOD AS ETERNAL AND SIMPLE (SCG 1,14–27)

1. ND, 1, 96 [1] (though I translate Aquinas's word *conditio* as "nature" rather than "properties").

2. ND, 1, 96 [2].

3. ND, 1, 98 [3].

4. ND, 1, 98 [4]. By "being everlastingly" Aquinas does not mean "existing in time without beginning to exist or ceasing to exist." He means existing eternally, without beginning or end.

5. This argument bears a resemblance to the third way of arguing for God's existence provided by Aquinas in *Summa Theologiae* 1a,2,3.

6. Once again, Aquinas is not offering a causal argument reaching into the past for a chronologically first cause. Toward the end of SCG 1,15 he clearly accepts the possibility of time and motion lacking a beginning. But he does add that if motion had a beginning, then there will have been a moving cause having no beginning.

7. ND, 1, 99 [5].

8. ND, 1, 99 [5].

9. ND, 1, 100 [3].

10. Aquinas acknowledges the existence of material things that do not pass away. He takes the heavenly bodies to be such things. But for present purposes I do not need to elaborate on that fact. For a detailed analysis of Aquinas on the material world, see Jeffrey E. Brower, *Aquinas's Ontology of the Material World: Change, Hylomorphism, and Material Objects* (Oxford: Oxford University Press, 2014).

11. For some discussion of matter by Aquinas, see the early sections of his *De Principiis Naturae*. Indeed, this text as a whole throws light on a number of terms that Aquinas employs in the SCG. For an English translation of the whole of *De Principiis Naturae*, see *Thomas Aquinas: Selected Philosophical Writings*, translated by Timothy McDermott (Oxford: Oxford University Press, 1993), 67–80. Notice also that in the SCG Aquinas distinguishes between the question "Is there matter in God?" and "Is God a body?" He does not try to deal with the second question here until SCG 1,20. Also note that Aquinas has a sense of "matter" in terms of which it makes sense to say that matter is measurable in terms of dimensions, as when a tailor measures people's waists so as to make up pants that will fit them. But this sense of "matter" is not, I think, at work in SCG 1,17. In that chapter, the key idea is "Whatever matter is, it is in potency" (ND, 1, 101 [2]).

12. ND, 1, 103 [2].

13. ND, 1, 105.

14. "Quod igitur est in fine nobilitatis omnium entium, oportet esse in fine simplicitatis." See ND, 1, 104 [6].

15. Indeed, the *Summa Theologiae* discussion of God's simplicity is generally more clearly organized and more streamlined than is the discussion of God's simplicity in the SCG, though the key moves in each of them are the same.

16. Note, however, that it has been very much in favor with various influential Christian authors. It can, for example, be found in the writings of St. Augustine of Hippo and St. Anselm of Canterbury. That God is simple was formally ratified by the Fourth Lateran Council and the First Vatican Council. For the conciliar texts, see *Decrees of the Ecumenical Councils*, edited by Norman P. Tanner (Washington, DC: Georgetown University Press, 1990), I:230 and II:805.

17. I am now focusing on five lines of criticism. Others have been offered that I have to pass over in silence for reasons of space. Still, the criticisms I focus on

are fairly standard ones. For detailed discussion of objections to Aquinas on simplicity, see Peter Weigel, *Aquinas on Simplicity* (Peter Lang: Bern, 2008) and James E. Dolezal, *God without Parts: Divine Simplicity and the Metaphysics of God's Absoluteness* (Eugene, OR: Pickwick, 2011).

18. Alvin Plantinga, *Does God Have a Nature?* (Milwaukee: Marquette University Press, 1980), 47.

19. See Hume, *An Enquiry Concerning Human Understanding*, edited by Tom L. Beauchamp (Oxford: Clarendon Press, 2000), 123.

20. Genesis 3:8.

21. Exodus 33:11.

22. See Genesis 3:8; Numbers 11:1; 1 Samuel 5:11; 2 Kings 19:16; Isaiah 52:10.

23. See Genesis 8:21; Psalm 2:4; Psalm 37:13; Isaiah 7:18.

24. See Genesis 6:6; Deuteronomy 16:22; Isaiah 61:8; Isaiah 62:5.

25. See Matthew 6:26, Matthew 18:12–14, Luke 6:35–36, Luke 12:32, John 16:27, Romans 8:15–16, and 1 John 3:1.

26. Exodus 33:20.

27. Isaiah 40:25–28.

28. For a discussion of anthropomorphic imagery in the Bible, see chapter 10 of G. B. Caird, *The Language and Imagery of the Bible* (Philadelphia: Westminster Press, 1980).

29. See Richard Swinburne, *The Coherence of Theism*, rev. ed. (Oxford: Clarendon Press, 1993), 1: "By a theist, I understand a man who believes that there is a God. By a 'God' he understands something like a 'person without a body (i.e. a spirit) who is eternal, free, able to do anything, knows everything, is perfectly good, is the proper object of human worship and obedience, the creator and sustainer of the universe.' Christians, Jews, and Muslims are all in the above sense theists." Again, see the quotation from Alvin Plantinga that I provide above.

30. See Philip Dixon, *Nice and Hot Disputes: The Doctrine of the Trinity in the Seventeenth Century* (Edinburgh: T&T Clark, 2003).

31. See SCG 1,35. Also see *Summa Theologiae* 1a,13,4.

32. See *Summa Theologiae* 1a,6 and 25.

33. See C. J. F. Williams, *What Is Existence?* (Oxford: Clarendon Press, 1981). Also see C. J. F. Williams, "Being," in *A Companion to the Philosophy of Religion*, edited by Philip L. Quinn and Charles Talliaferro (Oxford: Blackwell, 1997). Again, see C. J. F. Williams, *Being, Identity, and Truth* (Oxford: Clarendon Press, 1992).

34. For Frege on existence, see *The Foundations of Arithmetic*, translated by J. L. Austin (Oxford: Blackwell, 1980), 58 and following.

35. See Immanuel Kant, *Critique of Pure Reason*, translated by Paul Guyer and Allen W. Wood (Cambridge: Cambridge University Press, 1997), A592–602.

36. C. J. F. Williams, "Being."

37. Williams develops this argument in *What Is Existence?* and *Being, Identity, and Truth*.

38. *What Is Existence?*, 79 and following.

39. For a defense of this conclusion, see, for example, Colin McGinn, *Logical Properties* (Oxford: Clarendon Press, 2000), chapter 2.

40. Obviously, some people have problems urinating and breathing. But not by nature. Problems with urination and breathing arise as what humans are by nature is messed around with in some way. That is why the word "problem" is appropriate in this context.

41. Some would say that everything that Aquinas calls a creature actually has to exist. See Bede Rundle, *Why There Is Something Rather Than Nothing* (Oxford: Clarendon Press, 2004). In reply, Aquinas would appeal to his claim that we can distinguish between an individual's essence and its existence so as to conclude that what something is does not guarantee that it is.

42. See *Somme Contre les Gentils*, bk. 1, edited by Cyrille Michon (Paris: Flammarion, 2000), 104. I find the expression "negative attributes" to be somewhat mystifying since I take an attribute to be something that an individual positively has and not something that it lacks or is somehow negative while also being an attribute. And I suspect that Aquinas would agree with me here given what he says in general about substances and accidents. The point to stress, however, is that in SCG 1,18–27 Aquinas is repeatedly saying that God is not this and not that.

CHAPTER 5. TALKING ABOUT GOD (SCG 1,28–36)

1. ND, 1, 150 [1].

2. ND, 1, 138 [2].

3. Note that one can say that something is literally F without being committed to the view that it is, therefore, literally *like* some other thing that can be said to be literally F. That X and Y are both F does not entail the conclusion that they are literally *like* each other. A large flea and a large elephant are both literally large, but very unlike each other. I refer to this example below when following out what Aquinas has to say on "God is good."

4. In SCG 1,22 and in *Summa Theologiae* 1a,13,11 Aquinas says that "Qui est" ("He Who Is") is the appropriate name for God. He does so while appealing to Exodus 3:13, in which God, in the Latin version of the Bible that Aquinas was using (the Vulgate), tells Moses to say that his true name is *Qui est*. And, *Qui est* in Latin, like "He Who Is" in English, is an unusual phrase. Still, both of these phrases employ words that exist in Latin and English independently of talk about God.

5. ND, 1, 140 [3].

6. One could properly render Aquinas's word "nomen" as "term" instead of "name." We think of a name as chiefly being a proper name, like "Fred," but Aquinas does not.

7. ND, 1, 143 [1].

8. ND, 1, 145 [1].

9. ND, 1, 147.

10. ND, 1, 135 [2].

11. ND, 1, 135 [2].

12. ND, 1, 135 [2].

13. ND, 1, 138 [1].

14. ND, 1, 138 [2].

15. ND, 1, 140 [2].

16. ND, 1, 140 [2].

17. ND, 1, 140 [3].

18. ND, 1, 141 [3].

19. See Ludwig Wittgenstein, *Philosophical Investigations*, translated by G. E. M. Anscombe, P. M. S. Hacker, and Joachim Schulte, rev. 4th ed. (Oxford: Wiley-Blackwell, 2009), 167ᵉ and 177ᵉ.

20. I do not want to press the comparison between Wittgenstein on surface and depth grammar and Aquinas on signifying imperfectly. But there is a helpful comparison to be made here, one that contemporary students of philosophy might find useful.

21. Volume 3 of the Blackfriars edition of the *Summa Theologiae* (London: Eyre and Spottiswoode; New York: McGraw-Hill, 1964), 104.

22. ND, 1, 141 [1].

23. ND, 1, 143 [4].

24. ND, 1, 143.

25. ND, 1, 144 [3].

26. ND, 1, 145 [7].

27. ND, 1, 146 [5].

28. ND, 1, 146–147 [6].

29. ND, 1, 147 [1].

30. ND, 1, 148 [6].

31. ND, 1, 149 [1].

32. ND, 1, 150 [2].

33. ND, 1, 150 [1].

34. Volume 3 of the Blackfriars edition of the *Summa Theologiae*, 106.

35. For a defense of this conclusion, see Richard Swinburne, *The Coherence of Theism*, rev. ed. (Oxford: Clarendon Press, 1993), chapter 5. In this chapter Swinburne suggests that Aquinas really thinks that terms used of God and creatures can be understood univocally.

CHAPTER 6. GOODNESS, ONENESS, AND INFINITY (SCG 1,37–43)

1. See Mark 10:18, Matthew 19:17, and Luke 18:19.

2. ND, 1, 94 [28].

3. ND, 1, 152 [2].

4. ND, 1, 153 [3].
5. ND, 1, 153 [5].
6. ND, 1, 153 [6].
7. I am simplifying a bit here since Aquinas discusses participation in some detail in his writings and makes distinctions between what can be said to participate in what. For the details, see chapter 4 of John F. Wippel, *The Metaphysical Thought of Thomas Aquinas* (Washington, DC: Catholic University of America Press, 2000).
8. ND, 1, 153 [4].
9. ND, 1, 154 [1].
10. ND, 1, 155 [5].
11. ND, 1, 155 [6].
12. I quote from Saint Augustine, *The Trinity*, translated by Edmund Hill (New York: New York City Press, 1991).
13. ND, 1, 158 [1].
14. Some of the arguments are complicated and therefore hard to summarize. You should, therefore, check my summaries against the text of Aquinas so as to see whether or not I have caught the essentials of his arguments in SCG 1,42. I hope that I have.
15. ND, 1, 158 [2].
16. ND, 1, 158 [3].
17. ND, 1, 158 [4].
18. ND, 1, 159 [5].
19. ND, 1, 159 [6].
20. ND, 1, 159–160 [7].
21. ND, 1, 160 [8].
22. ND, 1, 160–161 [9].
23. ND, 1, 162 [12].
24. ND, 1, 162 [12].
25. ND, 1, 162 [13].
26. ND, 1, 163 [16].
27. ND, 1, 163 [17].
28. ND, 1, 163 [18].
29. ND, 1, 163 [19].
30. ND, 1, 164 [20].
31. ND, 1, 166 [3].
32. ND, 1, 166 [5 and 6].
33. See ND, 1, 164 [22].
34. ND, 1, 166 [3].
35. P. T. Geach, "Good and Evil," *Analysis* 17 (December 1956): 33.
36. *Nicomachean Ethics* 1,1,1094a3.
37. For a book-length discussion of Aquinas on God being good and evil being real, see my *Thomas Aquinas on God and Evil* (Oxford: Oxford University Press, 2011).

CHAPTER 7. GOD'S KNOWLEDGE (SCG 1,44–71)

1. See *Summa Theologiae* 1a,17,3.

2. For this line of thinking Aquinas clearly owes a debt to Aristotle. See *De Anima* 2,5,418a3–6; 2,12,424a17–21.

3. ND, 1, 171 [3].

4. ND, 1, 171 [3].

5. ND, 1, 171 [3].

6. ND, 1, 171 [4].

7. In *Summa Theologiae* 1a,14 the only reason given for there being knowledge in God hinges on God being nonmaterial. So Aquinas's discussion of why there is knowledge in God is more complex in the SCG than it is in the *Summa Theologiae*.

8. ND, 1, 171 [5].

9. For Aristotle here, see *De Anima* 3,8,431b21. Aristotle speaks of the intellect being in a sense all things since it can contain all things intellectually.

10. ND, 1, 172 [7].

11. ND, 1, 172 [8].

12. ND, 1, 172 [8].

13. ND, 1, 173 [2].

14. I say "at least partly" because Aquinas thinks that more enters into us coming to understand or know than mere physical contact with physical things. He maintains that we have an intellectual power to organize incoming sense data as we come to know.

15. Aquinas uses the word *species* in different senses, but I agree with Anthony Kenny that, when Aquinas speaks of intelligible *species*, the word is best rendered as "idea." See Anthony Kenny, *Aquinas* (Oxford: Oxford University Press, 1980), 69. For a sketch of the idea of intelligible species, see SCG 1,53.

16. ND, 1, 175 [2].

17. ND, 1, 176 [6].

18. ND, 1, 176 [2].

19. ND, 1, 176 [2].

20. ND, 1, 178 [2].

21. The phrase *per se*, which recurs in SCG 1,48, literally means "through itself." So, when he says that God only knows himself *per se*, Aquinas means that what God knows through his essence has first and foremost to be the divine essence (i.e., God), even if God's knowledge in fact extends to what is not divine. Note that Aquinas holds that God does not have to create anything for him to know. Given that he thinks that this is so, Aquinas naturally supposes that God can exist without knowing or understanding anything other than God.

22. Note that Aquinas does not think that God is essentially the cause of all creatures since he thinks that God might never have created anything. But Aquinas

does think that God is the cause of all creatures and must, therefore, understand himself as being so.

23. ND, 1, 180 [2].

24. ND, 1, 180 [2].

25. ND, 1, 181 [4].

26. ND, 1, 181–182 [1 and 2]. By "what is common" Aquinas means "what it shares with other things." By "what is proper" he means "what belongs to it alone."

27. ND, 1, 194–195 [2].

28. ND, 1, 195 [3]. What Aquinas says here, of course, implies that God cannot be said to have knowledge since he remembers what he once learned. It also implies that there can be no forgetting on God's part.

29. ND, 1, 196 [2].

30. ND, 1, 197 [3].

31. ND, 1, 197 [7].

32. ND, 1, 204 [2] and 205 [2].

33. ND, 1, 216 [9]. Here Aquinas is saying that God knows things by being their maker and that he must therefore have in him what is reflected by what he creates, this including what is singular even though it also includes what is shared by things that are singular.

34. ND, 1, 219 [7].

35. ND, 1, 221 [2]. You should note that in SCG 1,67 "contingent" and "necessary" do not mean "logically contingent" and "logically necessary." A proposition is logically contingent if it is true but could be false, and a proposition is logically necessary if it could not possibly be false. In SCG 1,67, however, Aquinas is thinking of what is contingent as being not in itself necessitated by causes and of what is necessary as being necessitated by causes.

36. ND, 1, 225.

37. ND, 1, 225 [2].

38. ND, 1, 225 [3].

39. ND, 1, 225 [4].

40. ND, 1, 228 [5].

41. ND, 1, 232–233 [3, 4, and 5].

42. ND, 1, 239 [14].

43. Perhaps the most famous philosophical idealist was George Berkeley (1685–1753). In this context, of course, "idealist" does not mean "someone who pursues noble principles."

44. Aquinas's approach to knowledge would be described by philosophers as a "realist" one since it holds that we can know what exists other than our thoughts or ideas. Since I take it that most people think that we can know what is other than us and our ideas, I presume that Aquinas's "realism" is not unusual or manifestly absurd. Indeed, one needs to be a certain kind of philosopher if one's position is that all that we know are our ideas. In fact, one would need to be a

philosopher who thinks that it makes sense to say "I know my ideas but I have no knowledge of dogs or cats existing independently of me, and of what they are considered as such." But can we make sense of this conclusion?

45. For more on this, see chapter 11.

46. Aquinas thinks that people are essentially physical since he thinks that people are human beings and that being human is to be physical. Yet Aquinas does not think that people are nothing but physical objects since, as I have shown, he takes them to be able to receive forms immaterially.

47. P. T. Geach, *God and the Soul* (London: Routledge and Kegan Paul, 1969), 36. Norman Malcolm (1911–1990) was a distinguished philosopher who taught at Cornell University and was a close friend and interpreter of Ludwig Wittgenstein.

48. *God and the Soul*, 37.

CHAPTER 8. GOD'S WILL, LIFE, AND BLESSEDNESS (SCG I,72–102)

1. Herbert McCabe, *On Aquinas* (London: Continuum, 2008), 79.

2. Aquinas distinguishes between what he refers to as *actus hominis* (an act of a human being) and *actus humanus* (a human action). By the latter he means an action deliberately intended and based on reflection of some kind, such as feeding one's cat because one knows that it is hungry. By the former he means a bit of bodily behavior that we go through without thinking it out, such as stroking one's chin when engrossed in conversation. If I engage in *actus humanus*, thinks Aquinas, then I can explain why I did what I did. But, Aquinas holds, I might not even have noticed that I have engaged in *actus hominis*. The distinction seems to be a reasonable one. See *Summa Theologiae* 1a2ae,1,1.

3. As I have noted, Aquinas thinks that nonthinking things can be said to desire or tend to certain goods, but he does not think of them as desiring or tending on the basis of knowledge or reflection on knowledge.

4. I quote from *Aquinas: "Summa Theologiae," Questions on God*, edited by Brian Davies and Brian Leftow (Cambridge: Cambridge University Press, 2006), 208. For Aristotle on life, see *De Anima* 3,7,431a6 and 1,4,408b6.

5. A classic text of Aquinas discussing the beatific vision is *Summa Theologiae* 1a,12, which consists of thirteen articles.

6. ND, 1, 239 [2].

7. ND, 1, 240 [3].

8. ND, 1, 241 [4].

9. I take it that, when Aquinas speaks of powers as related to and measured by their principal objects, he is thinking that, for example, the power of sight is related to visible objects and is judged to be weak or strong in relation to them. What he goes on to say indicates that he thinks that will in God, which he takes to be a power in God, has to be principally directed to the being and goodness of God.

10. ND, 1, 247 [7].
11. ND, 1, 250 [1].
12. ND, 1, 250 [3].
13. ND, 1, 251 [5]. Here Aquinas seems to mean that the many numbers that there are stand in relation to being one or indivisible.
14. ND, 1, 257 [2].
15. ND, 1, 258 [4].
16. ND, 1, 259 [7].
17. ND, 1, 265 [3].
18. ND, 1, 266 [2].
19. ND, 1, 268 [2].
20. ND, 1, 269 [4].
21. ND, 1, 270 [3].
22. Aquinas distinguishes between delight, as possession of a present good, and joy as a resting of the will when it comes to good that is not presently possessed. He draws attention to this distinction toward the end of SCG 1,90 while saying that God delights in the goodness that he is, but takes joy "both in himself and in other things" (ND, 1, 277 [7]). In SCG 1,90, as well as in SCG 1,91, Aquinas sometimes seems to treat "joy" and "delight" as virtually synonymous.
23. ND, 1, 276 [4].
24. ND, 1, 276 [6].
25. ND, 1, 277 [2 and 3].
26. ND, 1, 280 [12]. Aquinas thinks that when we experience passion we are literally moved by what is different from us, and, as I have shown, he does not think that God is literally moved by anything different from himself.
27. See *Summa Theologiae* 1a2ae,49–67.
28. ND, 1, 282 [1].
29. See ND, 1, 285 [1].
30. ND, 1, 287 [8]. Curiously, in SCG 1,93 Aquinas does not spell out why God can be said to have the virtue of magnificence. I presume that this is because he takes magnificence to be a kind of liberality, for which he does give reason for attributing to God in SCG 1,93. For Aquinas on magnificence, see *Summa Theologiae* 2a2ae,134,1–3.
31. ND, 1, 290 [1].
32. ND, 1, 292 [2].
33. ND, 1, 292 [3].
34. ND, 1, 293 [8].
35. ND, 1, 294 [3].
36. ND, 1, 294 [3].
37. ND, 1, 295 [4].
38. ND, 1, 296 [2].
39. ND, 1, 297 [5].

40. ND, 1, 301 [2].
41. ND, 1, 304 [9].
42. For a defense of this line of argument, see chapter 7 of Norman Kretzmann, *The Metaphysics of Theism: Aquinas's Natural Theology in "Summa Contra Gentiles" 1* (Oxford: Clarendon Press, 1997). For a polite and cogent criticism of Kretzmann, see John F. Wippel, "Norman Kretzmann on Aquinas's Attribution of Will and of Freedom to Create to God," *Religious Studies* 39 (2003).
43. ND, 1, 152 [5].
44. ND, 2, 30 [5].

CHAPTER 9. GOD AS OMNIPOTENT CREATOR (SCG 2,1–29)

1. ND, 2, 32 [5].
2. ND, 2, 32 [1].
3. ND, 2, 34 [6].
4. ND, 2, 36, chapter 5 [1].
5. ND, 2, 37 [4].
6. ND, 2, 37 [5].
7. ND, 2, 37 [6].
8. ND, 2, 38 [2].
9. ND, 2, 40 [6].
10. ND, 2, 42.
11. ND, 2, 43 [in the title of the chapter].
12. ND, 2, 46 [1].
13. ND, 2, 47 and 48 [2, 3, and 4].
14. ND, 2, 46 [2].
15. ND, 2, 46 [2].
16. ND, 2, 47 [3].
17. ND, 2, 47 [3].
18. ND, 2, 48 [5].
19. This argument strongly resembles that of the Third Way in *Summa Theologiae* 1a,2,3.
20. ND, 2, 53 [14].
21. ND, 2, 54 [2]. In SCG 2,17 Aquinas speaks of both "motion" (*motus*) and "change" (*mutatio*). He thinks of these as different from each other since he takes *motus* to be a change in something that goes through various changes while continuing to exist as the thing that it is, while he thinks of *mutatio* as a more radical kind of change, as when something is generated or as when something perishes, as when something acquires or loses a substantial form. Yet, for Aquinas, both *motus* and *mutatio* involve some move from potentiality to actuality; and he thinks that being created cannot involve that. To be sure, Aquinas holds that something created by God is *potentially nonexistent*. But he does not think that *being created* involves any progression from potentiality to actuality.
22. ND, 2, 55 [2].

23. Here I take Aquinas to be thinking along these lines: Human beings only generate human beings, or milk, when drunk, produces effects that reflect what milk is. This is the force of his assertion "Anything whose actuality is subject to generic, specific, and accidental determinations must have a power that is limited to effects similar to the agent as such; for every agent produces its like" (ND, 2, 63 [9]). As I have already explained, "Every agent produces its like" does not, for Aquinas, mean that the effect of every agent cause literally looks like its agent cause. It means that the effects of agent causes reflect the nature of their causes.

24. See D. Z. Phillips, *The Problem of Evil and the Problem of God* (London: SCM Press, 2004), 11–12.

25. ND, 2, 65–66 [3].

26. ND, 2, 66 [4].

27. ND, 2, 72 [3].

28. ND, 2, 77 [3].

29. ND, 2, 78 [4].

30. ND, 2, 78 [5].

31. ND, 2, 78 [6].

32. ND, 2, 79 [2].

33. ND, 2, 81 [7].

34. See P. T. Geach, "God's Relation to the World," *Sophia* 8 (October 1969): 4. Geach speaks of *Cambridge* change since some famous Cambridge philosophers, such as John McTaggart (1866–1925) said that change is what we have when, say, "Fred is happy" is true at time 1 while it is true at time 2 that "Fred is miserable."

35. Geach, "God's Relation to the World," 1.

36. Geach has previously argued that we can, indeed, do this, though some have denied that we can. See Geach, "God's Relation to the World," 2–3.

37. Geach, "God's Relation to the World," 4.

CHAPTER 10. NECESSITY IN CREATURES, THE ETERNITY
OF THE WORLD, AND DISTINCTIONS AMONG
CREATURES (SCG 2,30–45)

1. ND, 2, 85 [1].

2. ND, 2, 85 [2]. For Aquinas, examples of necessary created beings are angels and human souls. For reasons I cannot go into here, Aquinas also takes heavenly bodies to be necessary created beings. For a detailed account of Aquinas on heavenly bodies, see Thomas Litt, *Les Corps Célestes Dans L'Univers de Saint Thomas D'Aquin* (Louvain: Publications Universitaires, 1963).

3. ND, 2, 86 [5].

4. For Aristotle, see *Physics* 1,9 and 8,1, *De Caelo* 1,3, and *Metaphysics* 12,6. In his commentary on Lombard's *Sentences*, Aquinas argues that Aristotle did not really hold that the universe had no beginning. But he came to repudiate this reading of Aristotle, as seems clear from his commentary on Aristotle's *Physics*.

5. See *Summa Theologiae* 1a,46 and *De Potentia* 3,17. Also note Aquinas's *De Aeternitate Mundi*. Many of Aquinas's contemporaries held that it can be proved that the world began to exist. Such, for example, was the position of St. Bonaventure (c. 1217–1274), who, like Aquinas, taught at the University of Paris. Another notable contemporary of Aquinas who thought that the world cannot be eternal was John Pecham (c. 1230–1292), a student of Bonaventure and archbishop of Canterbury from 1279 to 1292. Norman Kretzmann, whose knowledge of medieval authors was considerable, says that Aquinas seems to have been the only person during Aquinas's lifetime to have contested the claim that it can be proved that the world began to be while also insisting, on the basis of faith, that it did begin to be. See note 14 on 148 of Kretzmann, *The Metaphysics of Creation: Aquinas's Natural Theology in "Summa Contra Gentiles" II* (Oxford: Clarendon Press, 1999). A notable premedieval Christian arguing against Aristotle's conclusion that the world has always existed was John Philoponus (c. 490–570). The work of his to note in this connection is *De Aeternitate Mundi Contra Aristotelem*. This comes down to us only in fragments, but for an English edition of it as a whole, see Philoponus, *Against Aristotle on the Eternity of the World*, translated by Christian Wilde (London: Duckworth, 1987).

6. ND, 2, 92 [4].

7. ND, 2, 98 [5].

8. ND, 2, 101 [3].

9. ND, 2, 101 [5].

10. ND, 2, 103 [3].

11. ND, 2, 103 [5].

12. ND, 2, 104 [6].

13. ND, 2, 105 [6].

14. ND, 2, 106 [8].

15. ND, 2, 110 [2].

16. ND, 2, 110 [3].

17. ND, 2, 110–111 [4].

18. ND, 2, 111 [6].

19. ND, 2, 111 [7].

20. As I noted above, Aquinas seems to have been unusual in his day in taking the position that he does on our ability to prove that the world cannot have always existed.

21. ND, 2, 112 [4].

22. ND, 2, 113 [10].

23. Aquinas thought that the sun revolves around the earth. So I have modified his example so that it might make sense to contemporary readers, all of whom I expect to think that the earth revolves around the sun.

24. ND, 2, 113 [12].

25. ND, 2, 113 [12].

26. ND, 2, 114 [13].
27. Something like this argument appears in paragraph 3 of ND, 2's rendition of SCG 2,39.
28. ND, 2, 116–117 [6].
29. ND, 2, 119 [3].
30. ND, 2, 121 [4].
31. ND, 2, 121 [5].
32. Manicheism was founded by a Persian teacher called Mani (216–c. 275). It thrived between the third and seventh centuries. At one time, St. Augustine of Hippo was an adherent of Manicheism, and he wrote about it in his *Confessions*. Central to Manicheism was belief in an ongoing struggle between a power for good and a power for evil, each of them responsible for some things in the world. For more on Manicheism, see Andrew Welburn, *Mani, the Angel and the Column of Glory: An Anthology of Manichean Texts* (Edinburgh: Floris Books, 1998).
33. ND, 2, 121 [5].
34. ND, 2, 122 [6].
35. ND, 2, 122 [7].
36. ND, 2, 122 [8].
37. ND, 2, 122 [9].
38. Here Aquinas seems to be thinking that evil always results accidentally from what something or someone aims at when seeking goodness of some kind. I might aim to save your life by pushing you out of the way of an oncoming car, only to find that I have inadvertently pushed you into the way of yet another oncoming car. Or I might aim to get rich by robbing a bank, only to find that I have inadvertently deprived my aged parents of the money they have invested in it. So Aquinas takes badness to be accidentally caused as good is aimed at by one or more agents and, therefore, sees no need to postulate several different agents when trying to account for the occurrence of goodness and badness in general. You might think that someone might aim at something bad directly and that badness is not, therefore, accidentally caused. Yet Aquinas thinks that aiming (whether on the part of people or other things) is always aiming at what seems (intellectually or by instinct or nature) good to what is aiming. Serial killers might revel in killing since it gives them a release or satisfaction of some sort. Yet serial killers are aiming at what seems to be good to them, something that, indeed, can be thought of as good (i.e., there is nothing intrinsically wrong with release or satisfaction). So even in this case Aquinas would say that evil results accidentally from a seeking of goodness of some kind.
39. ND, 2, 122 [10].
40. Aquinas seems to be thinking of Avicenna's *Metaphysics* 9,4. He says that Avicenna says "that God, by knowing Himself, produces one first intelligence, wherein there already exists potentiality and act; that this intelligence, by knowing

God, produces the second intelligence; by knowing itself as it is in act, produces the soul of the sphere; and by knowing itself as being in potentiality, produces the substance of the first sphere." Aquinas goes on to say: "And thus, proceeding from this point, [Avicenna] teaches that the diversity of things is the effect of secondary causes" (ND, 2, 128 [11]). I am not here concerned with the accuracy of Aquinas's reading of Avicenna. That is something on which scholars who know more than I do about Avicenna can advise us. For a solid and scholarly introduction to the thinking of Avicenna, see Jon McGinnis, *Avicenna* (Oxford: Oxford University Press, 2010).

41. ND, 2, 127 [8].

42. ND, 2, 127 [9].

43. Here Aquinas seems to be alluding to Origen's *Peri Archon* (*On First Principles*) 2. Origen (182–254) was a Christian Neoplatonist and, arguably, the first Christian author to engage in theology and philosophy in a systematic way. He taught in Alexandria and Caesarea. Ideas associated with Origen came in for much criticism among later theologians.

44. ND, 2, 135–136 [15].

45. ND, 2, 138–139 [9].

46. For ancient authors, see Richard Sorabji, *Time, Creation and the Continuum* (Chicago: University of Chicago Press, 1983). For medieval authors, especially Aquinas, see Richard C. Dales, *Medieval Discussions of the Eternity of the World* (Leiden: Brill, 1991). Aquinas's earliest discussion of the eternity of the world comes in his commentary on Peter Lombard's *Sentences*, bk. 2, distinction 1, question 1. For a translation of this text, see *Aquinas on Creation*, edited by Steven E. Baldner and William E. Carroll (Toronto: Pontifical Institute of Medieval Studies, 1997). The volume edited by Baldner and Carroll also contains a translation of Aquinas's *De Aeternitate Mundi* based on the 1976 Leonine edition of that text.

47. In 1215 the Fourth Lateran Council decreed that God created from "the beginning of time" (*ab initio temporis*) and thereby provided the first, formal, conciliar text asserting that the world had a beginning.

48. Richard Swinburne, *Space and Time,* 2nd ed. (London: Palgrave Macmillan, 1981), 258.

49. See Max Tegmark, *Our Mathematical Universe* (New York: Knopf, 2014).

50. J. L. Mackie, *The Miracle of Theism* (Oxford: Clarendon Press, 1982), 93.

51. *The Miracle of Theism*, 93.

52. Sorabji, *Time, Creation and the Continuum*, 219.

53. It has been suggested that the start of the book of Genesis does not say that God created the material universe from nothing or that the universe had a beginning brought about by God. But it does seem to do just this. Genesis 1:1 says: "In the beginning when God created the heavens and the earth, the earth was a formless void and darkness covered the face of the deep." So, you might think that

Genesis 1.1 is saying that, in creating, God acted on something. Yet, taken as a whole, Genesis does seem to teach that nothing other than God ever existed without God making it to be. Here I agree with Richard Sorabji when he says: "It makes no difference that it [Genesis, 1.1] (naturally) does not specify whether it is formless matter or the ordered universe, including its matter, that begins: in either case we should in effect have an absolute beginning to the material universe" (*Time, Creation and the Continuum*, 194).

54. ND, 2, 36, chapter 5 [1].

CHAPTER II. INTELLECTUAL CREATURES (SCG 2,46–101)

1. SCG 2,5. ND, 2, 36, chapter 5 [1].

2. In SCG 2,46–101 Aquinas also refers to "intellectively active creatures" (*creaturae intelligentis*), "intellective substances" (*substantiae intellectuales*), "intellectively active substances" (*substantiae intelligentis*), "intellective natures" (*naturae intellectuales*), "intellective beings" (*intellectualia*), "intellectively active beings" (*intelligentes*), and "intellects" (*intellectus*). I think that Norman Kretzmann is right to say that these different terms are more or less interchangeable for Aquinas. See *The Metaphysics of Creation: Aquinas's Natural Theology in "Summa Contra Gentiles" II* (Oxford: Clarendon Press, 1999), 233.

3. ND, 2, 36, chapter 5 [1].

4. ND, 2, 141 [6].

5. ND, 2, 140–141 [5].

6. Aquinas does not speak of revelation in SCG 2,46, and my use of "revelation" at this point does not correspond to the way in which Aquinas typically uses it. Aquinas thinks of revelation as amounting to a series of propositions that people cannot demonstrate to be true but must accept on the basis of faith. Still, he does think that, in the sense that I might reveal something of myself by leaving traces behind, God reveals something of himself by creating (on the principle that the effects of agent causes resemble them in some way). And SCG 2,46 seems to be working with this thought so as to suggest that the reason why there are beings with intellect lies in the fact that God's showing himself forth in the created order would stop seriously short if there were not creatures with intellect.

7. I use the phrase "or whatever" here since you might think that there are or might be creatures with understanding who are neither angelic nor human, since you might think that there are or could be intelligent extraterrestrials. Aquinas never discusses extraterrestrials and does not do so, I assume, because his medieval cosmology seems to rule them out. But I doubt that he would dismiss the possibility of such things were he working with the kind of cosmology that scientists favor today. On the other hand, I am sure that he would be offering

the same account of the intellect of extraterrestrials as he does of what he considers intellect in people to be in SCG 2, 56–90.

8. ND, 2, 143–144 [4].

9. ND, 2, 144 [2].

10. ND, 2, 146 [6].

11. Cats may not run after mice if they are blind, or have smelling or hearing disabilities. Nor will they run after mice if something or someone has introduced into them some aversion to mice. They will also not run after mice if they are tied up. And so on. Hence my use of the phrase "all things being equal."

12. ND, 2, 147 [2].

13. ND, 2, 149 [2].

14. ND, 2, 151 [8].

15. See *Meditations on First Philosophy* 2. Having argued that he certainly exists since he cannot consistently maintain that he does not exist as long as he is thinking, even while entertaining the thought that he might not exist, Descartes asks what it is that he is. Later in his *Meditations*, he goes on to argue that he is essentially, or by nature, an immaterial thinking thing since, while he can doubt that bodies exist, he cannot consistently doubt that he exists. My view is that Descartes is wrong here since, for example, the fact that I can doubt that there is something whose essential nature is not to think, while I cannot doubt that I exist, does not entail that I am a being whose essential nature is to think. Be that as it may, however, many philosophers from ancient times to the present have argued that people are essentially thinking and incorporeal things, albeit things with bodies to interact with. In several of his writings, including the SCG, Aquinas frequently ascribes this view to Plato, whom he takes to regard people as controlling their bodies as the captain of a ship controls his ship: the assumption being that the captain and his ship are distinct things.

16. For a recent example of this line of argument, see Alex Rosenberg, *The Atheist's Guide to Reality: Enjoying Life without Illusions* (New York: Norton, 2011). The assumption that all that exists is material is commonplace among many contemporary philosophers. If you start with this assumption then you will end up saying the kind of thing that Rosenberg does in the book I have just cited. Aquinas, of course, would ask why we should assume that all that exists is material. Can we demonstrate that all that exists is material? I doubt that we can do that while wondering what such a demonstration would look like (where "demonstration" means what Aquinas takes it to mean). We can presume or believe that everything that exists is nothing but material. But can we demonstrate that this is so? I may be wrong here, but the impression I get when reading people like Rosenberg is that they are assuming more than they can prove. If you start by supposing that everything that exists is bodily and made up of physical elements, then your view of things that exist will commit you to the conclusion that all that exists are physical things bouncing off each other insofar as they

connect causally and materially. But is it possible to demonstrate that this supposition is warranted? If it is possible to do this, what would the demonstration be? It might start with the premise "All that exists is material or bodily or physical." But why suppose that this premise is self-evidently true? As I have shown, Aquinas offers reasons in SCG 1 for supposing that it is not true.

17. ND, 2, 151 and 152 [2 and 3].

18. ND, 2, 153 [2].

19. ND, 2, 158 [10].

20. ND, 2, 158 [1].

21. ND, 2, 163 [14].

22. Aquinas does not deny that people can be born suffering from brain damage that results in them being unable to think or reason or understand. But he would not have denied that such people are living human beings. He would have said that they are living human beings who suffer from defects that render them unable to engage in activities that are characteristic of healthy human beings, as are people who have been knocked unconscious or exist while being in a coma.

23. Aquinas thinks that all human beings have souls. But, you might say, a newborn baby does not have intellect and will, from which it follows that not all human beings have a soul. Aquinas's response to this thought would be "Even babies have intellect and will since they are things with the power to understand and will even though they are not able to exercise these powers." In Aquinas's view, human understanding and willing, considered as actually occurring, follows from a process of interaction between people and what exists around them in the material world. Yet, he thinks, there could be no "following from" here without a power or ability to proceed to the acquisition of knowledge. So he thinks that babies born without defects already have it in them to understand and will.

24. Anthony Kenny, *Aquinas on Mind* (London: Routledge, 1993), 46–47.

25. Some medieval readers of Aristotle took the agent intellect to be something outside all people allowing them to understand, this implying that there is but one agent intellect by which people manage to understand. Aquinas has no time for this idea since he thinks that we understand as individuals and must be able to understand because of what we have in us individually.

26. Kenny, *Aquinas on Mind*, 43.

27. Hardly anything is known about Alexander's life, so only a rough dating for him is possible. In SCG 2,62 Aquinas takes Alexander to have taught that the receptive or possible intellect results from a blending together of physical things.

28. In SCG 2,56–90 Aquinas also contests what he takes to be various misreadings of Aristotle on soul. I am going to pass over these discussions in silence since they are technical and take us into problems of interpretation that I cannot engage with in this book.

29. ND, 2, 166 [8, 9, and 10].

30. ND, 2, 172 [14–15].
31. ND, 2, 199–201 [2–3 and 8].
32. ND, 2, 201–202 [2–3].
33. Aquinas also uses the word *species* to mean "idea," as in "I have the idea of a cat in mind." But in SCG 2,66 *species* refers to the having of a sensation produced by something acting on one's body.
34. In what follows I am briefly summarizing and not trying to follow the various twists and turns of Aquinas's detailed argumentation in SCG 2,68–90, in which he discusses and rejects all sorts of strange views. My aim is to help you to get a bird's-eye view of the thrust of SCG 2,68–90, not to talk you through it point by point.
35. ND, 2, 204 [3]. Aquinas means that human beings are rational animals and that it is their intellect that makes them to be that.
36. ND, 2, 205 [6]. Aquinas means that human bodies rank high among bodily things because they are capable of motion and have several ways of sensing. On the other hand, he thinks that people rank low among intellectual creatures since, depending on their bodies for knowledge, they are inferior to creatures that are pure intellects who do not need to acquire knowledge as people do.
37. ND, 2, 207 [2].
38. ND, 2, 208 [6]. In SCG 2,70 Aquinas refers to the view, which he ascribes to Aristotle (see *De Anima* 2,3), that heavenly bodies have intellect. Yet Aquinas does not commit himself to this view. He says: "As for the heaven being animate (*de animatione caeli*), we have spoken of this matter not as asserting its accordance with the teaching of the faith, to which the whole question is entirely irrelevant" (ND, 2, 211–212 [7]).
39. ND, 2, 213 [2].
40. ND, 2, 246 [2].
41. ND, 2, 254 [2]. In SCG 2,79 Aquinas presents several arguments for the incorruptibility of the human soul. Here I am noting what I take to be the line of thinking that seems to be operative in almost all of the arguments in SCG 2,79. One of the arguments in SCG 2,79 that does not appeal to the nonmateriality of the human substantial form maintains that people have to exist forever since "it is impossible that natural appetite should be in vain" and since "man naturally desires to live forever" and since "man attains perpetual existence as regards his soul, whereby he apprehends being unqualifiedly and in respect of every time."
42. See ND, 2, 265 [12].
43. Aquinas refers to these impressions as "phantasms," which he thinks of as what people, as composites of form and matter, acquire as they take in what they encounter by means of their senses and by virtue of their agent intellect resulting in what they end up with in their receptive or possible intellect.
44. ND, 2, 264 [12].
45. In the *Summa Theologiae* Aquinas appears to embrace a different position on the human soul after death from what we find in SCG 2,81. In SCG 2,81 he notes

that understanding in a separate soul cannot arise on the basis of bodily experience while it can come about as comparable to understanding had by essentially incorporeal creatures such as angels, to whom he refers in SCG 2,96–101. "When the soul shall be completely separated from the body," he says, "it will be perfectly likened to separate substances in its mode of understanding, and will receive their influx abundantly" (ND, 2, 265–266 [12]). In *Summa Theologiae* 1a,89,1, however, Aquinas plays down the comparison between knowledge arising in departed (separate) human souls and knowledge in totally incorporeal things (angels). As SCG 2,81 does not, *Summa Theologiae* 1a,89,1 highlights the idea that the nature of the human soul requires that it be united to a human body in order to be perfect and nondeficient considered as what it is. According to *Summa Theologiae* 1a,89,1, it is against nature (*praeter naturam*) for the soul to acquire understanding when not joined to a human body, implying that knowledge in separate substances such as angels is not a good analogy for knowledge arising in people. For more on this difference between SCG 2,81 and *Summa Theologiae* 1a,89,1, see Anton Pegis, "The Separated Soul and Its Nature in St. Thomas," in *St Thomas Aquinas, 1274–1974, Commemorative Studies*, edited by A. Maurer et al. (Toronto: Pontifical Institute of Medieval Studies, 1974), vol. 1.

46. ND, 2, 267 [2].

47. ND, 2, 272. In SCG 2,83 Aquinas cites a number of arguments contesting this conclusion, but he finds the arguments flawed and rejects them in SCG 2,83 and 84. For a comprehensive account of Aquinas on the origins of human life, see Fabrizio Amerini, *Aquinas on the Beginning and End of Human Life* (Cambridge, MA: Harvard University Press, 2013).

48. This is the thesis of SCG 2,85, in which Aquinas seems to be attacking what he takes to be Manichaean views concerning God being a body of some kind. In SCG 2,85 Aquinas also argues that human souls are not eternal, while God is, that God is not the form of anything, while the soul is the form of the body, and that God lacks potentiality, while something from which something is made has potentiality.

49. This is the thesis of SCG 2,87–89.

50. You can see that in SCG 2,91 and following Aquinas has angels in mind because of his reference to Pseudo-Dionysius toward the end of SCG 2,91. Aquinas says, "We conclude to the existence of a plurality of intellectual substances that are not united to bodies," and he then goes on to say: "With this conclusion Dionysius is in agreement when, speaking of angels, he says that 'they are understood to be immaterial and incorporeal'" (ND, 2, 315 [10]). The reference here is to *De Divinis Nominibus* 4. For a detailed study by Aquinas of separate substances, see his treatise *De Substantiis Separatis* (*On Separate Substances*), written some time after 1271. For an English edition of this text, see *Saint Thomas Aquinas: Treatise on Separate Substances*, translated by Francis J. Lescoe (West Hartford, CT: Saint Joseph College, 1959).

51. The word "angel" occurs close to three hundred times in the Bible. Belief in angels was declared to be a matter of faith by the Fourth Lateran Council, which speaks of God making "the angelic and the terrestrial" (*angelicum videlicet mundatum*).

52. See ND, 2, 312–313 [2]: "That which is through itself must be prior to that which is by accident. Therefore, there are some intellectual substances, prior in nature to souls, which, through themselves, enjoy subsistence without bodies." I assume that Aquinas is here saying that there have to be things with essences before there can be things that are accidentally thus and so.

53. See ND, 2, 313 [3]: "It is not of the generic essence of an intellectual substance to be united to a body, although this is of the essence of that intellectual substance which is the [human] soul. There are, then, some intellectual substances which are not united to bodies."

54. ND, 2, 314 [6]. In SCG 2,92 Aquinas argues that there are many "separate substances" (i.e., angels). Since SCG 2,92 relies heavily on what I take to be outdated cosmological or scientific views concerning heavenly bodies, which Aquinas derives from Aristotle (who never referred to angels), I am going to pass over this chapter in silence while assuming that you are not especially interested in antique cosmology. Yet it is interesting to find Aquinas disagreeing with Aristotle in SCG 2,92 concerning *how many* separate substances there are if one tries to count them with reference to heavenly bodies. Aquinas takes Aristotle to teach that there are as many separate substances "as the movements observed in the heaven" (ND, 2, 316 [1]). But, he argues: "The intellectual substances existing apart from bodies are much more numerous than the heavenly movements" (ND, 2, 317 [4]). So, Aquinas's discussion of angels is indebted to Aristotle at some remove from what Aristotle seems to have thought.

55. ND, 2, 321 [2–3]. By "quiddity" (*quidditas*) Aquinas means "what a thing is as signified by a definition." According to Aquinas the quiddity of a substance is its essence.

56. Aquinas writes: "Following upon local movement, time measures only such things as exist somehow in place" (ND, 2, 328 [10]).

57. ND, 2, 339 [2].

58. The belief that nothing exists except material things is sometimes referred to as naturalism. For an introduction and discussion of this, see Stewart Goetz and Charles Taliaferro, *Naturalism* (Grand Rapids, MI: Eerdmans, 2008).

59. See Richard Swinburne, *The Evolution of the Soul* (Oxford: Clarendon Press, 1986). For a good account of contemporary and previous views on mind and body, see William Jaworski, *Philosophy of Mind: A Comprehensive Introduction* (Oxford: Wiley-Blackwell, 2011). For defenses of a variety of positions on mind, body, soul, and self, see *The Mind-Body Problem: A Guide to the Current Debate*, edited by Richard Warner and Tadeusz Szubka (Oxford: Blackwell, 1994).

60. For good accounts and discussions of Aquinas on the human soul, see Gyula Klima, "Man = Body + Soul: Aquinas's Arithmetic of Human Nature," in *Thomas Aquinas: Contemporary Philosophical Perspectives*, edited by Brian Davies (Oxford: Oxford University Press, 2002). Also see Gyula Klima, "Aquinas on the Materiality of the Human Soul and the Immateriality of the Human Intellect," *Philosophical Investigations* 32 (April 2009).

61. See C. J. F. Williams, *Being, Identity, and Truth*, chapter 7.

62. Herbert McCabe, "The Immortality of the Soul," in *Aquinas: A Collection of Critical Essays*, edited by Anthony Kenny (Notre Dame, IN: University of Notre Dame Press, 1976), 304.

63. "The Immortality of the Soul," 304–305.

CHAPTER 12. AGENTS, ENDS, EVIL, AND GOOD (SCG 3,1–15)

1. ND, 3/1, 31 [1].
2. ND, 3/1, 31 [2].
3. ND, 3/1, 32 [3].
4. ND, 3/1, 33–34 [10].
5. Aquinas does not deny that an active agent can be thwarted in bringing something about. Nor does he think that an active agent always acts on other things so as to produce the same effect in all of them. So, he does not, for example, think that cocaine has the same effect when injected into a dead cat as it does when sniffed by a human being. Nevertheless, Aquinas does think that agent causes typically have predictable effects as they act.
6. ND, 3/1, 34 [2].
7. ND, 3/1, 35 [3].
8. ND, 3/1, 36 [4].
9. ND, 3/1, 36–37 [6].
10. ND, 3/1, 37 [7]. The Latin word *peccatum* can be translated into English as "fault," "error," or "mistake." It can also be translated as "moral failure" or "sin." In SCG 3,2 Aquinas is using *peccatum* as meaning failure in a general sense. I can hardly convict my cat for being sinful if it vomits after eating some food that I have given it. But there is a fault or an error or a mistake or a failure occurring in my cat if it ends up vomiting after having eaten. Something is going wrong with my cat if it vomits having been given good food to eat.
11. Aquinas takes it as obvious that explanation in terms of an end or goal has to be invoked in the case of artifacts since these are constructed by people with a definite aim in mind. But he also thinks that nonthinking things act with (analogically construed) aims since they have natures that reflect what they are insofar as they act.
12. ND, 3/1, 38 [1].

13. The Latin word *conveniens* means "appropriate," "fitting," "suitable," "seemly," or "becoming," and its meaning is as vague as are these English words (more on this in chapter 18). In SCG 3,3 Aquinas seems to be saying that if agents incline to a particular end, that end is one that matches their needs or tendencies so that there is a fit between end and agent.

14. ND, 3/1, 38 [3].

15. ND, 3/1, 39 [6].

16. ND, 3/1, 40 [9]. This argument strongly resembles part of the so-called Fifth Way of demonstrating God's existence that Aquinas presents in *Summa Theologiae* 1a,2,3. Notice that in neither the Fifth Way nor SCG 3,3 is Aquinas claiming that things in the world exhibit design as, say, artifacts might be thought to do. He is saying that things lacking intellect regularly strive for, and regularly, if not always, end up arriving at what is good for them in some way.

17. Accidental since, though it is normal for people to be able to see, I survive as a human being even if I become blind.

18. I derive the "evil suffered" and "evil done" terminology from Herbert McCabe, who seems to have invented it. See Herbert McCabe, *God Matters* (London: Geoffrey Chapman, 1987), chapter 3. By "evil suffered" and "evil done" McCabe was trying to flag a distinction that Aquinas draws between *malum poenae* (evil of punishment) and *malum culpae* (evil of fault), and there is something of a mismatch between what McCabe calls "evil suffered" and what Aquinas calls *malum poenae*. That is because behind Aquinas's use of *malum poenae* lies the view that pain and suffering are to be viewed as a punishment on the heirs of Adam for his primordial sin (see Genesis 3). On the other hand Aquinas certainly does take *malum poenae* to be evil as suffered by creatures by virtue of the actions on them of other creatures. And, though in SCG 3,4–15 he does not refer to *malum poenae*, he does make it clear that he has in mind what McCabe, and I now, refer to as "evil suffered."

19. By "evil that merely affects the agent" I mean badness or evil that arises only in the agent willing it. Aquinas would certainly have said that my freely committing suicide, while of sound mind and not overwhelmed by emotions beyond my control, amounts to me harming only myself. Of course, a person who commits suicide might cause psychological pain to his or her friends or family, should he or she happen to have any friends or family. Yet, in an obvious sense, to commit suicide is to perform an action that terminates only in harm to oneself. Again, Aquinas would say that willingly harboring hateful thoughts against someone is an evil in an agent, even if the agent does not act on the hateful thoughts so as to harm anyone else.

20. In the SCG and elsewhere, Aquinas regularly employs this understanding of badness or evil while focusing on naturally occurring substances (*entia per se*) rather than artifacts or what he refers to as *entia per accidens*. Yet he would certainly invoke the same understanding when it comes, say, to products of human

engineering. He would say, for example, that a computer is bad because it fails to function in the way that we expect it to, whether or not this is due to its lacking a part or to its being interfered with by something spilled into it.

21. Here remember Aquinas's connection between being and goodness that I noted in chapter 6.

22. I should note that, in the case of X murdering Y, Aquinas allows for there being success in X to some extent. Obviously, successful murderers have to have sufficient power so as to bring about the death of people they kill. So they succeed as physical agents able to bring about certain effects. Yet, thinks Aquinas, their physical success is displayed at the expense of a deep malfunction in them considered as moral agents.

23. Let us suppose that a mother accidentally stumbles on a balcony and that her baby ends up tumbling from it so as to die when landing on concrete below. It might seem absurd to say that the demise of the baby arises because the concrete is doing well at the expense of the baby and to think of this scenario along the lines of the cheetah and zebra example that I have noted. Yet I do not think that Aquinas would deny this. I think he would be saying: (1) the death of the baby is to be accounted for in terms of gravity and what concrete is; (2) it is the concrete that accounts for the death of the baby when falling on it; (3) so there is a scientific explanation for the baby's death to be given in terms of what it has landed on and what, by virtue of what it is as having the reality that it does, resulted in the death of the child. We might be uneasy with talk about concrete doing well. But should we be uneasy to think that concrete, given what it is when not interfered with, might be expected to have certain effects on things dropped on it? If it did not, would we not wonder whether it is really concrete but, say, a bed of feathers disguised as concrete?

24. ND, 3/1, 41 [1].

25. ND, 3/1, 41 [2].

26. ND, 3/1, 41 [3].

27. ND, 3/1, 42 [4].

28. ND, 3/1, 42–43 [5].

29. ND, 3/1, 45 [4].

30. ND, 3/1, 45 [5].

31. An actor might limp while trying to portray a limping person on stage. But such an actor will only be pretending to limp and will not be limping because of a genuine problem or deformity inhibiting power to walk, a problem or deformity that someone who has it would prefer to be without as he or she tries to walk. Or so Aquinas thinks.

32. ND, 3/1, 47 [9].

33. ND, 3/1, 47 [10].

34. ND, 3/1, 48 [11].

35. I am now going to pass over in silence the objections to SCG 3,7 that Aquinas lists in SCG 3,8. I am also going to say nothing about his replies to these objections

to be found in SCG 3,9. My intention is to try to make clear why Aquinas wants to defend the thesis of SCG 3,7.

36. ND, 3/1, 48 and 49 [2 and 6].
37. ND, 3/1, 48 [3].
38. ND, 3/1, 48 [4].
39. ND, 3/1, 49 [5].
40. ND, 3/1, 55 [1] and 61 [18].
41. ND, 3/1, 55–56 [3].
42. ND, 3/1, 57 [8]. Here Aquinas seems to be thinking of bad effects brought about by something good acting on what is not itself in a good way. He provides an example that appears to depend on antiquated biology, but his point, I think, would be illustrated by the example of someone reacting badly to medication because of weakness or injury of some kind.
43. ND, 3/1, 57 [9].
44. ND, 3/1, 58 [11]. Here Aquinas is emphatically denying that I am a bad person just because of what I bring about. I might be thought to be a bad author because I write bad books, or a bad painter because I produce aesthetically worthless pictures. But my badness as a person is, thinks Aquinas, something in me, not in my effects. So Aquinas's moral evaluation of people is not a consequentialist one. It does not depend on noting what they have managed to *bring about*. It rests on a recognition of what they *are* as willing agents, regardless of whether or not what they aim to bring about comes about.
45. ND, 3/1, 59 [13].
46. ND, 3/1, 60–61 [16].
47. ND, 3/1, 61 [17].
48. ND, 3/1, 62 [3].
49. ND, 3/1, 62 [5].
50. ND, 3/1, 67 [5].
51. ND, 3/1, 67 [1].
52. I quote from volume 16 of the Blackfriars edition of the *Summa Theologiae* (London: Eyre and Spottiswoode; New York: McGraw-Hill, 1968), 7.
53. I quote from *Thomas Aquinas: Selected Philosophical Writings*, translated by Timothy McDermott (Oxford: Oxford University Press, 1993), 72.
54. Edward Feser, *Scholastic Metaphysics: A Contemporary Introduction* (Heusenstamm: Editiones Scholasticae, 2014), 96. For another good defense of Aquinas on final causation, see Paul Hoffmann, "Does Efficient Causation Presuppose Final Causation?: Aquinas vs. Early Modern Mechanism," in *Metaphysics and the Good: Themes From the Philosophy of Robert Merrihew Adams*, edited by Larry Jorgensen and Samuel Newlands (Oxford: Oxford University Press, 2008).
55. Some philosophers have suggested that we have no more reason to say that badness is an absence of goodness as we have to say that goodness is an absence of badness. Yet Aquinas, rightly, I think, would say that this suggestion seems to

leave unexplained why we lament what is bad. We do so, he thinks, because we have some standard or desire or expectation in the light of which we complain that something is bad or in a bad way; and he thinks that this has to lie in our awareness of what something we call bad would be if it were good.

56. See Eleonore Stump, "Biblical Commentary and Philosophy," which is chapter 10 of *The Cambridge Companion to Aquinas*, edited by Norman Kretzmann and Eleonore Stump (Cambridge: Cambridge University Press, 1993).

57. For criticisms of the view that evil amounts to privation, see Todd C. Calder, "Is the Privation Theory of Evil Dead?," *American Philosophical Quarterly* 44 (October 2007); John F. Crosby, "Doubts about the Privation Theory That Will Not Go Away: Response to Patrick Lee," *American Catholic Philosophical Quarterly* 81 (2007); H. J. McCloskey, "God and Evil," in *God and Evil*, edited by Nelson Pike (Englewood Cliffs, NJ: Prentice Hall, 1964). For defenses of the view that evil amounts to privation, see M. B. Ahern, "The Nature of Evil," *Sophia* 5 (1966); Bill Anglin and Stewart Goetz, "Evil Is Privation," *International Journal of Philosophy of Religion* 13 (1982); Brian Davies, *The Reality of God and the Problem of Evil* (Continuum: London: 2006), and *Thomas Aquinas on God and Evil*, chapter 4; Patrick Lee, "Evil as Such Is Privation: A Reply to John Crosby," *American Catholic Philosophical Quarterly* 81 (2007); Herbert McCabe, "Evil," which is chapter 3 of McCabe, *God Matters*; Herbert McCabe, *God and Evil in the Theology of St Thomas Aquinas* (London: Continuum, 2010).

CHAPTER 13. THE END OF ALL THINGS AND OF PEOPLE IN PARTICULAR (SCG 3,16–63)

1. In SCG 3,2 Aquinas argues that every agent acts for an end. In SCG 3,3 he argues that every agent acts for a good. So, one might think that Aquinas takes acting for an end to be distinguishable from acting for a good. Yet he certainly does think that to aim for an end is always to aim at a good.

2. I might want to make a clock that is constructed so as to kill someone. Ordinarily, though, if people want to make a clock, they want to make a good clock, something that tells us the time and is not a weapon of destruction.

3. Herbert McCabe, *Faith within Reason* (London: Continuum, 2007), 118.

4. ND, 3/1, 77 [2].

5. ND, 3/1, 82 [5].

6. ND, 3/1, 97 [2] and 102 [13].

7. ND, 3/1, 102 [14] (emphasis added).

8. ND, 3/1, 125 [9].

9. ND, 3/1, 191 [1].

10. In SCG 3,26 Aquinas sets things up so as first to note arguments for supposing that ultimate human happiness consists in willing or desiring or loving and then to say why these arguments do not work. In my account of SCG 3,26

I focus on the main reasons that Aquinas gives for supposing that willing or desiring or loving cannot be the ultimate end for human beings.

11. ND, 3/1, 104–105 [8].
12. ND, 3/1, 105 [9].
13. At the end of SCG 3,27 Aquinas notes that the arguments of this chapter refute Epicurean philosophers, the teaching of the Cerinthians, and the teaching of those who insist that right human action is rewarded by physical pleasures. Epicurean philosophy derives from Epicurus (341–270 B.C.). The Cerinthians were a first-century sect who looked forward to a thousand years of physical pleasure following their resurrection from the dead.
14. ND, 3/1, 114 [3].
15. ND, 3/1, 115 [1]. Aquinas derives this definition of "glory" from Cicero (106–43 B.C.) and St. Ambrose of Milan (339–397).
16. ND, 3/1, 115 [2].
17. ND, 3/1, 116 [7].
18. ND, 3/1, 116 [2].
19. ND, 3/1, 117 [5].
20. ND, 3/1, 118 [2].
21. ND, 3/1, 120, chapter 33 [2].
22. ND, 3/1, 120–121, chapter 34 [2].
23. ND, 3/1, 122 [2].
24. ND, 3/1, 123, chapter 36 [2].
25. ND, 3/1, 123 [3].
26. ND, 3/1, 123, chapter 37 [1].
27. ND, 3/1, 124 [3].
28. ND, 3/1, 125 [8 and 9].
29. ND, 3/1, 125 [1].
30. ND, 3/1, 128 [1].
31. ND, 3/1, 128 [3].
32. ND, 3/1, 130 [7].
33. ND, 3/1, 131 [2].
34. ND, 3/1, 132 [5].
35. ND, 3/1, 133 [1].
36. So, at this stage in the SCG we do find Aquinas directly combating Islamic thinking, albeit highly technical Islamic thinking. See what I say in chapter 1 concerning the purpose of the SCG.
37. ND, 3/1, 148 [2].
38. ND, 3/1, 148–149 [2].
39. ND, 3/1, 154.
40. ND, 3/1, 158.
41. ND, 3/1, 161 [9].
42. ND, 3/1, 163 [3].
43. ND, 3/1, 164 [7].

44. ND, 3/1, 166 [12].
45. In SCG 3,49–63 Aquinas makes it clear that he believes that creatures other than human beings are able to know God as, or maybe even better than, people can be thought to do while enjoying their ultimate end. That is because he thinks that people finally enjoy God as intellectual beings and because, as I have shown (see chapter 11, section 4 here), he holds that there are intellectual beings other than human ones. That said, however, it is final human happiness or beatitude with which Aquinas is chiefly concerned in SCG 3,49–63.
46. Note that in SCG 3,49–63 it is the happiness of human *souls* after death with which Aquinas is concerned. As I have shown (see chapter 11), he thinks (1) that the souls of human beings can survive the deaths of the human bodies they inform, and (2) that a human soul is not a human being. Since Aquinas is not concerned in SCG 3,49–63 with what is to be said of human happiness following the resurrection of people's bodies, the focus in these chapters is happiness of the human soul considered as following straight after death. I should add that in these chapters Aquinas is not concerned with people who die whose souls have no hope of enjoying beatitude.
47. In SCG 3,51 Aquinas observes: "It is impossible for a natural desire to be incapable of fulfilment, and since it would be so, if it were not possible to reach an understanding of divine substance such as all minds naturally desire, we must say that it is possible for the substance of God to be seen intellectually, both by separate substances and by our souls" (ND, 3/1, 175 [1]).
48. ND, 3/1, 169 [7].
49. ND, 3/1, 174 [8].
50. ND, 3/1, 177 [5]. With his talk about seeing God face-to-face, Aquinas is picking up on 1 Corinthians 13:12, in which St. Paul says, "For now we see in a mirror dimly, but then we will see face to face." Aquinas interprets St. Paul metaphorically. He writes: "It is wrong to understand this in a corporeal way, picturing in our imagination a bodily face of the Divinity.... Nor is it even possible for us to see God with our bodily face" (ND, 3/1, 177 [5]).
51. ND, 3/1, 177.
52. ND, 3/1, 178 [2].
53. ND, 3/1, 182 [6]. For Aquinas on agent intellect, see chapter 11, section 3.1 here.
54. ND, 3/1, 186–187 [2 and 3].
55. ND, 3/1, 191 [1].
56. ND, 3/1, 191 [2].
57. ND, 3/1, 193 [1].
58. See ND, 3/1, 195–197.
59. ND, 3/1, 200 [2].
60. ND, 3/1, 201 [4].
61. ND, 3/1, 202 [2].
62. ND, 3/1, 207 [3].
63. See ND, 3/1, 207 [4].

64. ND, 3/1, 208 [6].
65. ND, 3/1, 208 [7].
66. So much is clear from books 1, 6, and 10 of the *Nicomachean Ethics*.
67. For a detailed account of Aquinas on the human desire for seeing God, one that documents the teachings on this topic coming from authors later than Aquinas, see Lawrence Feingold, *The Natural Desire to See God According to St. Thomas Aquinas and His Interpreters*, 2nd ed. (Naples, FL: Sapientia Press, 2010). Also see Thomas Joseph White, "Imperfect Happiness and the Final End of Man: Thomas Aquinas and the Paradigm of Nature-Grace Orthodoxy," *Thomist* 78 (2014). I think that White's article skillfully captures the sense of Aquinas's account of beatitude in the SCG while noting how it might be taken to be defensible against certain criticisms of it. Both Feingold and White provide copious reference to secondary sources on Aquinas on ultimate human happiness.
68. ND, 4, 319 [7].
69. ND, 4, 321 [3].
70. ND, 4, 326 [4].

CHAPTER 14. PROVIDENCE AT WORK (SCG 3,64–110)

1. ND, 3/1, 209 [1].
2. See ND, 3/1, 34 [10].
3. ND, 3/1, 210 [2].
4. ND, 3/1, 210–211 [4].
5. ND, 3/1, 211 [5].
6. ND, 3/1, 214 [13].
7. ND, 3/1, 214 [2].
8. ND, 3/1, 214 [3].
9. ND, 3/1, 215 [4].
10. ND, 3/1, 216 [5 and 6]. As the conclusion of SCG 3,65 indicates, Aquinas takes these conclusions to correct "the position of the exponents of the Law of the Moors"—these being Islamic thinkers whom Aquinas does not name but whom he takes to have held that things in the universe do not always and totally depend on God for their existence. So, here again (see note 37 to chapter 13), we have an allusion to ideas coming from Muslims, albeit one that is not developed by Aquinas or backed up by specific citations.
11. ND, 3/1, 218 [2].
12. ND, 3/1, 219 [3].
13. ND, 3/1, 220 [1].
14. ND, 3/1, 221 [2].
15. ND, 3/1, 221 [3]. Aquinas thinks that what he says here squares with biblical teaching. Among other texts, he cites Isaiah 26:12, John 15:5, and Philippians 2:13, all of which emphasize the causal role of God in the actions of people.

16. ND, 3/1, 223 [2].
17. ND, 3/1, 235 [29].
18. ND, 3/1, 235 [1].
19. ND, 3/1, 235 [4].
20. ND, 3/1, 237 [8].
21. ND, 3/1, 236 [5].
22. ND, 3/1, 239 [6].
23. ND, 3/1, 240 [8].
24. ND, 3/1, 241 [10].
25. It sounds platitudinous to say that God makes things to be what they are since a thing has to be whatever it is. What else could it be but what it actually is? But it is not platitudinous to say that God makes things what they are if one is talking to someone who says that everything that exists is what it is of necessity and that it always has to exist. To such a person one might reply "Well, some things that exist are things that do not have to exist, or are things that do not have to be what they happen to be"—which is Aquinas's main point in SCG 3,72.
26. ND, 3/1, 242 [2].
27. ND, 3/1, 243 [4].
28. ND, 3/1, 244 [2].
29. ND, 3/1, 244–245 [2].
30. ND, 3/1, 246 [2].
31. ND, 3/1, 254 [3].
32. ND, 3/1, 255–256 [5].
33. ND, 3/1, 261 [1].
34. ND, 3/1, 263 [1].
35. Aquinas, indebted to Aristotle, though also influenced by authors later than him, took the earth (considered as spherical and immobile) to be at the center of the universe. He also thought that the sun and the moon and a small number of planets (considered as noncorruptible and unchangeable) rotated around the earth, the whole, in turn, being moved by an orbiting outermost sphere consisting of fixed stars. This cosmology is incompatible with cosmology as we know it today and as emerging by the beginning of the eighteenth century. For more on it, see Edward Grant, *Planets, Stars, and Orbs: The Medieval Cosmos, 1200–1687* (Cambridge: Cambridge University Press, 1994). Also see appendix 3 of volume 10 of the Blackfriars edition of the *Summa Theologiae* (London: Eyre and Spottiswoode; New York: McGraw-Hill, 1967).
36. ND, 3/1, 277 [1].
37. ND, 3/2, 37 [7].
38. ND, 3/2, 50 [6].
39. ND, 3/2, 50–51 [1].
40. ND, 3/2, 52 [4].

41. ND, 3/2, 52 [5].
42. ND, 3/2, 52 [5].
43. ND, 3/2, 52–53 [6].
44. ND, 3/2, 53 [7]. As I have noted, Aquinas thinks that the word "cause" is not the name of a substance and that causes can only be thought to be acting insofar as they bring about effects. So, Aquinas is here evidently thinking of "causes capable of failing" as meaning "things able to cause that are somehow thwarted in doing so for some reason."
45. ND, 3/2, 53 [8].
46. ND, 3/2, 56 [12].
47. ND, 3/2, 56–57 [13].
48. ND, 3/2, 57 [14].
49. ND, 3/2, 57 [15 and 16].
50. In SCG 3,95–96 Aquinas does not consider prayer for what is logically impossible. He assumes that prayers are offered by people who have needs that they recognize could be met by God as able to bring about what could come about.
51. ND, 3/2, 58 [1].
52. ND, 3/2, 62 [8].
53. ND, 3/2, 58 [2].
54. ND, 3/2, 66–67 [2].
55. ND, 3/2, 74 [3].
56. ND, 3/2, 76 [2].
57. ND, 3/2, 76 [3].
58. ND, 3/2, 77 [4].
59. ND, 3/2, 77–78 [6].
60. ND, 3/2, 78 [7].
61. ND, 3/2, 79 [9].
62. ND, 3/2, 79 [9].
63. ND, 3/2, 81 [1].
64. Notice that in SCG 3,98–100 Aquinas does not argue that any miracles have occurred. All he argues is that miracles could occur. Even in SCG 3,101–102 he does not argue for the occurrence of any specific miracles, though he obviously has biblical texts in mind at certain points. SCG 3's discussion of miracles is largely hypothetical in the sense that it maintains (1) that miracles could occur (SCG 3,98–100), and (2) that if they occurred they could be classified in different ways and could only be brought about by God (SCG 3,101–102).
65. ND, 3/2, 82 [1].
66. ND, 3/2, 82 [2].
67. Here Aquinas clearly has in mind Isaiah 38:8, Joshua 10:13, and Exodus 14:21.
68. ND, 3/2, 82 [3].
69. ND, 3/2, 82–83 [4].
70. ND, 3/2, 83 [2].

71. ND, 3/2, 85–86 [8]. In SCG 3,103 Aquinas, with particular reference to Avicenna, accepts that there might be nonmaterial substances that can bring about effects in the world that make us marvel. But he denies that they should be taken to be miracles. He also denies that angels or saints can work miracles by their own power.

72. See Elizabeth Anscombe, "Causality and Determination," which is chapter 13 of volume 2 of Anscombe's *Collected Philosophical Papers* (Oxford: Blackwell, 1981). The title of the volume is *Metaphysics and the Philosophy of Mind*. Speaking in a way of which, I suspect, Aquinas would have approved, Anscombe notes: "If A comes from B, this does not imply that every A-like thing comes from some B-like thing or set-up or that every B-like thing or set-up has an A-like thing coming from it; or that given B, A had to come from it, or that given A, there had to be a B for it to come from. Any of these may be true, but if any is, that will be an additional fact, not comprised in A's coming from B." (Anscombe, "Causality and Determination," 136.)

73. This point is effectively made by James Ross. He writes: "The whole physical universe, all of it, is actively caused to be. Still, to say that freedom or human agency is thereby impeded is absurd. Nothing can be or come about unless caused to be by the creator. So the fact that God's causing is necessary for whatever happens cannot impede liberty; it is a condition for it. Similarly, in no way is our liberty impeded by the fact that God's causing is sufficient for the being of the very things that do the very things that we do. Nothing possible can be impeded by its necessary conditions." For this, see James F. Ross, "Creation II," which is chapter 5 of *The Existence and Nature of God*, edited by Alfred J. Freddoso (Notre Dame, IN: University of Notre Dame Press, 1983), 131. Also see Herbert McCabe, *God Matters* (London: Geoffrey Chapman, 1987), 14–15: "We are free not because God is absent or leaves us alone, we are free because God is more present—not of course in the sense that there is *more of God* there in the free being, but in the sense that there is nothing, so to say, to distract us. God is not acting here by causing other things to cause this act, he is directly and simply himself causing it. So God is not an alternative to freedom, he is the direct cause of freedom. We are not free in spite of God, but because of God."

74. Richard Sorabji, *Time, Creation and the Continuum* (Chicago: University of Chicago Press, 1983), 255.

75. William Lane Craig, *The Only Wise God* (Grand Rapids, MI: Baker Book House, 1987), 74.

76. Hume, *An Enquiry Concerning Human Understanding*, edited by Tom L. Beauchamp (Oxford: Clarendon Press, 2000), 94.

77. For a fine development of this point, see R. M. Burns, *The Great Debate on Miracles: From Joseph Glanville to David Hume* (Lewisburg, PA: Bucknell University Press, 1981).

78. Hume, *An Enquiry Concerning Human Understanding*, 31.

CHAPTER 15. PROVIDENCE IN RELATION TO RATIONAL
CREATURES (SCG 3,111–163)

1. ND, 3/2, 114 [1].
2. ND, 3/2, 114 [1].
3. ND, 3/2, 124 [2].
4. Obviously, there is a story here that I need to explain. I shall do so soon.
5. ND, 3/2, 114 [1].
6. ND, 3/2, 115 [1].
7. ND, 3/2, 115 [1].
8. ND, 3/2, 116 [2].
9. ND, 3/2, 117 [6].
10. Clearly, Aquinas is not here thinking of people born with disabilities that render them unable to think or act on the basis of reason.
11. ND, 3/2, 120 [1].
12. ND, 3/2, 121 [4].
13. ND, 3/2, 122–123 [1].
14. ND, 3/2, 124 [5].
15. ND, 3/2, 124 [3].
16. ND, 3/2, 126 [2].
17. ND, 3/2, 127 [7].
18. See *Summa Theologiae* 1a2ae,98–105.
19. See *Summa Theologiae* 1a2ae,106–108.
20. ND, 3/2, 140 [25].
21. ND, 3/2, 128 [6].
22. ND, 3/2, 127 [2].
23. ND, 3/2, 128 [6].
24. ND, 3/2, 129 [2]. Here Aquinas seems to be assuming that God, in his goodness, can provide us with right faith, which amounts to believing what we cannot know to be true on the basis of reason.
25. ND, 3/2, 129 [3].
26. ND, 3/2, 130 [4].
27. ND, 3/2, 130 [5].
28. ND, 3/2, 131 [1].
29. ND, 3/2, 131 [2].
30. ND, 3/2, 131–132 [3–4].
31. ND, 3/2, 134–135 [5].
32. ND, 3/2, 141 [2].
33. ND, 3/2, 142 [3].
34. ND, 3/2, 142 [6].
35. When reading SCG 3,121–126, it may help you to bear in mind that Aquinas, like most people in his day familiar with the writings of Aristotle on generation,

had a different understanding of the mechanics of human conception than we do now. He knew nothing about the female ovum and thought that conception occurs as semen goes to work on blood in the female so as to form a likeness of the male whose semen it is. Here I quote from Fabrizio Amerini: "The formation of the embryo or fetus—Thomas uses the two terms interchangeably—is the result of the action of the male (the father) on the female (the mother) by means of his semen. In terms of the four Aristotelian causes, the male is the efficient cause of the process, while the mother, through the menstrual blood, is the material cause. Except in cases where Thomas is not concerned to express himself precisely, he never considers the male semen as a material cause of the generative process.... The semen, on the other hand, is the formal cause, and it is in the semen that there exists a vital 'spirit' (*spiritus*), in which is found what the tradition calls a 'formative power' (*virtus formativa*)." See Amerini, *Aquinas on the Beginning and End of Human Life* (Cambridge, MA: Harvard University Press, 2013), 13–14. This account of conception explains the emphasis on semen in what Aquinas says about sex in SCG 3. It also goes some way to explaining what he says about "the inordinate emission of semen" and homicide in SCG 3,122.

36. ND, 3/2, 143–144 [4]. Why the focus on semen in SCG 3,122? I suspect it emerges since the now outdated biological position that Aquinas accepted took semen to be the dominating and formative factor in conception. Aquinas's view of the role of semen reflects that of Aristotle as found in his *The Generation of Animals*.

37. ND, 3/2, 144 [5].

38. ND, 3/2, 145 [6].

39. ND, 3/2, 145–146 [8].

40. ND, 3/2, 146 [9].

41. ND, 3/2, 147 [2].

42. ND, 3/2, 147 [3].

43. ND, 3/2, 148 [4]. This seems to be an odd argument. If a wife is subject to her husband as governing her, where is the equality between them to which Aquinas here refers? Possibly Aquinas is at this point presupposing the authority of 1 Corinthians 7, in which St. Paul, while saying that husbands have authority over the bodies of their wives, also goes on to say that wives have authority over the bodies of their husbands. In Colossians 3:18–19 we read: "Wives be subject to your husbands, as is fitting in the Lord. Husbands, love your wives and never treat them harshly." Maybe this text is also something that Aquinas has in mind when speaking of equality between husband and wife.

44. ND, 3/2, 148 [5].

45. ND, 3/2, 148 [5].

46. I speak here of polygamy as meaning a man having more than one wife or a woman having more than one husband. Yet under the heading "polygamy" we

can distinguish between polygyny (a man having more than one wife) and polyandry (a woman having more than one husband). In SCG 3,124 Aquinas is against both polygyny and polyandry.

47. ND, 3/2, 150 [1]. Note the phrase "or the converse" here. Also note that Aquinas does not deny that certain male animals have promiscuous relations with several females. He lists male dogs and chickens "and the like" (*et huiusmodi*) at ND, 3/2, 151–152 [3].

48. ND, 3/2, 151 [1].

49. ND, 3/2, 151 [2].

50. Aquinas concludes SCG 3,124 by saying that what he asserts in this chapter rebuts "the custom of those having several wives" (ND, 3/2, 152 [8]). Though he does not say so explicitly, I assume that he is here thinking of Islamic practice as he understood it, which allows for a man having more than one wife, as did Mohammed. Note, however, that Aquinas explicitly takes SCG 3,125 to refute what he takes Plato to say, presumably from a version of *Republic* 5 that came down to him in some form.

51. ND, 3/2, 152 [4].

52. ND, 3/2, 153 [2].

53. ND, 3/2, 153 [2].

54. ND, 3/2, 153 [3]. How close is *too close* for Aquinas when it comes to close relatives not being married to each other? He does not really specify. Indeed, he does not define "relative" (*propinquus*) at all. The Latin *propinquus* is as vague as the English "relative." But in SCG 3,125 Aquinas cites the examples of brothers marrying sisters and children marrying their parents. Perhaps he also has in mind canon law of his day defining affinity that prohibits marriage between certain people related in certain particular ways. He presumably does so since, as he must have realized, we can trace relations over time between loads of people who have ended up being married to each other without being related as sister or brother or parent or offspring.

55. When reading the SCG, we need to remember that Aquinas always maintains that truth cannot contradict truth. So he is always assuming that the ability to reason, when well exercised, has to conform with what divine revelation teaches.

56. ND, 3/2, 155 [1].

57. ND, 3/2, 155 [2].

58. ND, 3/2, 156 [1].

59. ND, 3/2, 157 [3]. It should be clear from this quotation that Aquinas has no problems with eating meat. He is not a philosophical vegetarian. These days, of course, many people argue that there is a moral case to be made against the consumption of animals slaughtered for the purpose of human consumption. See, for example, Peter Singer, *Animal Liberation* (New York: Random House, 1975).

60. ND, 3/2, 158 [7].

61. ND, 3/2, 162 [1].
62. ND, 3/2, 162 [2].
63. ND, 3/2, 163 [3].
64. ND, 3/2, 163 [4].
65. ND, 3/2, 163 [4].
66. ND, 3/2, 163 [4].
67. Aquinas cites this text in SCG 3,130.
68. ND, 3/2, 165 [1].
69. ND, 3/2, 167 [5].
70. ND, 3/2, 210.
71. ND, 3/2, 212 [1].
72. The same distinction between sins is taught in the 1994 *Catechism of the Catholic Church*, secs. 1854–1864.
73. See SCG 4,71, where Aquinas says, "As one can sin after grace is received, so also from sin, it seems, one can return to virtue" (ND, 4, 275 [2]). Note also that in SCG 3,146 Aquinas says that "the evil, as long as they live, can be corrected from their errors" and that even "at the critical point of death" they "have the opportunity to be converted to God by repentance" (ND, 3/2, 222 [10]).
74. ND, 3/2, 214 [2]. See SCG 2,44.
75. ND, 3/2, 217 [11]. In *Summa Theologiae* 2a2ae,64, Aquinas holds that capital punishment can be morally permissible in certain circumstances for the protection of other people. We find the same argument in SCG 3,146.
76. ND, 3/2, 218 [1].
77. ND, 3/2, 218–219 [2 and 4]. In this connection Aquinas appeals to Matthew 25:41.
78. ND, 3/2, 220 [2].
79. Here I am thinking of arguments like "If X murdered Y, then X deserves to die just for doing so," or "If I knock your eye out, you are entitled to demand that you should knock out one of my eyes." Such arguments are offered by defenders of what is usually called the *lex talionis*, or law of retribution, according to which a punishment should fit a crime and be equal to it. It can be found in texts as early as Babylonian times and seems to be subscribed to by many people today.
80. ND, 3/2, 220–221 [4 and 5].
81. Of course, even in high-security prisons there have been convicted murderers who have killed people in prison with them.
82. ND, 3/2, 222 [10].
83. The word "grace" (*gratia*) occurs in SCG 3,148 but is not really explained until SCG 3,150, in which Aquinas notes that "what is given people, without any preceding merit on their part, is said to be given *gratis*, and because the divine help that is offered to people precedes all human merit [see SCG 3,147], it follows that this help is accorded *gratis* to us, and as a result it quite fittingly took the name grace" (SCG 3/2, 230). Aquinas adds that we can also refer to God's help as grace since it brings us into God's good graces as being favored by God.

84. ND, 3/2, 224 [3].

85. Aquinas takes the point to rebut the teaching of Pelagius (c. 354–418), whom he regards as having held that people can merit union with God merely by their use of the power to choose.

86. ND, 3/2, 226–227 [2, 3, and 5].

87. ND, 3/2, 228 [1].

88. ND, 3/2, 228 [1 and 2]. In arguing like this, Aquinas once again takes himself to be rebutting Pelagius.

89. ND, 3/2, 232 [4].

90. ND, 3/2, 232–233 [7].

91. ND, 3/2, 233 [2].

92. Here Aquinas seems to be alluding to something that Aristotle says in *Nichomachean Ethics* 9,3. The allusion strikes me as unfortunate since friends can often disagree when it comes to what is good or bad, or whether something is delightful or not. Friends can differ in their political views (preferring one politician to another, say) and in their aesthetic preferences (preferring Puccini to Wagner, say, or rock music to classical music).

93. ND, 3/2, 234 [3].

94. See *Summa Theologiae* 2a2ae,1–22.

95. ND, 3/2, 236 [3]. One again, in SCG 3,152 Aquinas castigates Pelagius. This time, his objection is that Pelagius (or his followers) says that "the beginning of faith in us was not from God but from ourselves" (ND, 3/2, 237 [7]).

96. ND, 3/2, 236–237 [4].

97. ND, 3/2, 238 [3]. The use of the word *conveniens* in this passage indicates that Aquinas is not taking himself to demonstrate that God has given the grace of hope to all who desire what God is all about. Rather, he seems to be saying that it is appropriate for God to give hope to those in whom he has given the grace of faith, considered as belief in God as the ultimate end for people—a conclusion that, at the end of SCG 3,153, he supports by scriptural references that he takes to confirm what he has been saying in this chapter.

98. The 1 Corinthians text reads: "To one is given through the Spirit the utterance of wisdom, and to another the utterance of knowledge, according to the same Spirit, to another faith by the same Spirit, to another gifts of healing by the one Spirit, to another the working of miracles, to another prophecy, to another the discernment of spirits, to another various kinds of tongues, to another the interpretation of tongues."

99. ND, 3/2, 250 [2] (with slight modification).

100. ND, 3/2, 250–251 [3].

101. ND, 3/2, 253 [2].

102. Aquinas thinks that justice can require that a wrongdoer should be punished. But he also allows for what he calls "satisfaction," by which (broadly speaking) he means doing something that balances the wrongness that one has done. In

SCG 3,158 he also thinks that punishment might actually strengthen us in our desire to amend our ways. He says, "Just as the will is drawn toward consent to the sin by means of pleasure, so it is strengthened in the detestation of sin by means of penances" (ND, 3/2, 257 [1]).

103. ND, 3/2, 257 [4].

104. ND, 3/2, 258–259 [6].

105. ND, 3/2, 260 [1].

106. ND, 3/2, 260–261 [2].

107. ND, 3/2, 261 [2].

108. ND, 3/2, 261–262 [1].

109. ND, 3/2, 264 [2].

110. ND, 3/2, 265–266 [5].

111. He cites Exodus 10:1, Isaiah 6:10 and 63:17, and Romans 1:28.

112. ND, 3/2, 266 [7].

113. ND, 3/2, 267 [1].

114. ND, 3/2, 267 [2].

115. ND, 3/2, 267 [2].

116. ND, 3/2, 268 [3].

117. For an elaboration of this point, see P. T. Geach, *God and the Soul* (London: Routledge and Kegan Paul, 1969), chapter 8.

118. See ND, 3/2, 144 [5]: "If by accident generation cannot result from the emission of semen, then this is not a reason for it being against nature, or a sin; as, for instance, if the woman happens to be sterile."

119. I quote, with slight emendation, from volume 28 of the Blackfriars edition of the *Summa Theologiae* (London: Eyre and Spottiswoode; New York: McGraw-Hill, 1966), 81–82.

120. That not all nonhuman animals always desire or engage in sexual coupling with members of the opposite sex is nowadays well documented. See Joan Roughgarden, *Evolution's Rainbow: Diversity, Gender and Sexuality in Nature and People* (Berkeley: University of California Press, 2004), chapter 8.

121. The heterosexual/homosexual distinction with which we are now familiar was developed relatively recently: around 1892, if we believe the *Oxford English Dictionary*. But Aquinas did not have it to hand. He seems to have thought that all human beings are born seeking, as they develop, sex with partners of the opposite sex. So he takes "the sexual act" to be open to procreation unless interfered with or unable to result in procreation for some other reason.

122. For a critique of Aquinas's general approach to sex and sexual ethics, see Gareth Moore, *A Question of Truth* (London: Continuum, 2003). For a defense of it, see *The Catechism of the Catholic Church*, 2351–2359. For a sensitive analysis of medieval views about sex, and for what Aquinas says about it, see Jean Porter, *Natural and Divine Law: Reclaiming the Tradition for Christian Ethics* (Grand Rapids, MI: Eerdmans, 1999), chapter 4.

CHAPTER 16. FATHER, SON, AND HOLY SPIRIT (SCG 4,2–26)

1. ND, 1, 63 [4].

2. The origins of what is now referred to as the Apostles' Creed is a matter of debate, but the standard text of it seems to have its origin in a creed of the Roman Church dateable to the second century. The Nicene Creed derives from the First Council of Nicaea (A.D. 325), and the Nicene-Constantinopolitan Creed from the First Council of Constantinople (381). The Council of Chalcedon took place in 451. For editions of the texts coming from Nicaea I, Constantinople I, and Chalcedon, see *Decrees of the Ecumenical Councils*, edited by Norman P. Tanner (Washington, DC: Georgetown University Press, 1990), vol. 1. For the text of the Apostles' Creed, see J. N. D. Kelly, *Early Christian Creeds*, 3rd ed. (London: Longman, 1972). Kelly's book also provides copious historical discussion of the Creed of Nicaea and the Nicene-Constantinopolitan Creed. For a fine account of Christian doctrine during the period from Nicaea I to Chalcedon, see J. N. D. Kelly, *Early Christian Doctrines*, 2nd ed. (New York: Harper and Row, 1960).

3. Aquinas often gives preference to a literal reading of Scripture over other ways of reading it (as discerning, say, its "spiritual sense," which might not have been recognized by this or that biblical author). See Beryl Smalley, *The Study of the Bible in the Middle Ages*, 3rd ed. (Oxford: Blackwell, 1984), 300–306. Also see Beryl Smalley, *The Gospels in the Schools c. 1100–c. 1280* (London: Hambledon Press, 1985), 265 and following.

4. For an introduction to Aquinas's approach to Scripture, and for discussions of some of his specifically biblical commentaries, see Thomas G. Weinandy, Daniel A. Keating, and John P. Yocum (eds.), *Aquinas on Scripture* (London: T&T Clark International, 2005).

5. ND, 4, 37 [5].

6. ND, 4, 39 [9].

7. ND, 4, 39 [10]. I presume that by "passed on to us in a hidden fashion" Aquinas is saying that it is the reality of God that is hidden from us even if we accept Christian revelation, not that the revelation is something handed on secretly. He is saying that if we do not in this life know what God is (see SCG 1,28–36), Christian revelation is not going to enable us to know what God is as God and the blessed do. Rather, it is going to give us true beliefs about God, not an understanding of God's essence (see SCG 3,40).

8. ND, 4, 39–40 [11].

9. For accounts of the history of thinking about the Trinity, see *The Oxford Handbook of the Trinity*, edited by Gilles Emery, O.P., and Matthew Levering (Oxford: Oxford University Press, 2011); William J. Hill, O.P., *The Three Personed God: The Trinity as a Mystery of Salvation* (Washington, DC: Catholic University of America Press, 1982); and *The Cambridge Companion to the Trinity*, edited by

Peter C. Phan (Cambridge: Cambridge University Press, 2011). See also Russell
Friedman, *Medieval Trinitarian Thought from Aquinas to Ockham* (Cambridge:
Cambridge University Press, 2010).

10. As I explained in chapter 8, section 1, Aquinas takes willing and loving to be
seriously related since he takes willing something—as being attracted to it—as
understanding what it is in some way.

11. The natural theology of SCG 1 does not argue that what reason can know of God
entails that there is distinction in God. But it does provide a context for what
Aquinas says about distinction in God while relying on what he takes to be
divine revelation.

12. For a brief account of Aristotle's teaching on relations, and its influence on medieval thinkers, see Jeffrey Brower, "Medieval Theories of Relations," in the
Stanford Encyclopedia of Philosophy online, http://plato.stanford.edu/entries/
relations-medieval/. For a book-length treatment of relations as discussed by
some medieval philosophers, including Aquinas, see Mark G. Henninger,
Relations: Medieval Theories 1250–1325 (Oxford: Clarendon Press, 1989).

13. Trinitarian theology invoking the notion of procession is clearly evident in the
Athanasian Creed (late fifth century). And, as Aquinas was well aware, in John
8:42 Jesus speaks of himself as proceeding or coming forth from God.

14. As I have noted, Aquinas claims that the doctrine of the Trinity cannot be arrived at by reason. His consistently upheld position is that reason can lead us to
know that there is but one God, though it cannot prove that there is distinction
in God as proclaimed by the doctrine of the Trinity. In SCG 1, Aquinas takes
himself to have shown by reason what God essentially is. But he accepts that his
conclusions in SCG 1 do not entail that there might be distinction in God as
proclaimed by revelation.

15. ND, 4, 143 [1].

16. ND, 4, 40 [2].

17. ND, 4, 43 [3].

18. ND, 4, 43 [1].

19. ND, 4, 49 [4].

20. ND, 4, 49 [5]. Compare ND, 4, 51.

21. ND, 4, 55 [1].

22. In SCG 4,9, Aquinas offers a similar biblical rebuttal to what he takes to be the
teaching of Photinus and Sabellius.

23. ND, 4, 62 [1].

24. ND, 4, 75 [1]. For "secret" in this quotation, see note 6 above.

25. These arguments are not ones that Aquinas accepts. Indeed, he goes on to try
to refute them in SCG 4,11. All the same, they are rather skillful philosophical
attacks against his position on God the Father and God the Son.

26. ND, 4, 75 [2].

27. See SCG 1,16.

28. ND, 4, 76 [4].
29. ND, 4, 76 [4].
30. ND, 4, 76–77.
31. ND, 4, 77 [8].
32. ND, 4, 77 [8].
33. ND, 3, 77–78 [9].
34. ND, 4, 78 [9].
35. ND, 4, 78 [10].
36. In this argument, being a relation only in thought is being a relation only in a logical sense, as we might take the "relationship" of a thing to itself to be insofar as it is identical with itself. See Aquinas, *De Potentia* 7,11, ad.3 and *Summa Theologiae* 1a,13,7.
37. ND, 4, 78 [11].
38. ND, 4, 78–79 [12].
39. ND, 4, 79 [13].
40. ND, 4, 79 [14].
41. ND, 4, 81 [5].
42. ND, 4, 82 [8].
43. ND, 4, 83 [9] (with some modifications).
44. Aquinas does not deny that people come to understand insofar as they learn to talk. But he does think that human understanding does not just amount to an understanding of language and the ways in which we use it. His view is that our use of language has to proceed from what is in us apart from its representation linguistically. Aquinas takes language to reflect what precedes it in us, though he also thinks that human understanding can only be expressed in words.
45. ND, 4, 83 [11].
46. ND, 4, 84 [11].
47. ND, 4, 84–85 [12].
48. ND, 4, 89 [18].
49. ND, 4, 92 [2].
50. ND, 4, 93 [3].
51. ND, 4, 103 [15].
52. ND, 4, 104 [1]. In this connection Aquinas cites Matthew 28:19, 1 John 5:7, and John 15:26.
53. ND, 4, 116 [1].
54. ND, 4, 116–117 [2].
55. People nowadays, as always, I suppose, have been cautious in their use of the word "love" since we can love various things and to different degrees. At this point in the SCG, however, Aquinas is thinking of love as a desire in us for something to which we are attracted.
56. ND, 4, 117 [3].
57. ND, 4, 117 [3].

58. ND, 4, 119 [9 and 10].

59. Herbert McCabe, *God Still Matters* (London: Continuum, 2002), 51.

60. For a succinct account of what provoked this division, and of what might be said about it today, see Robert Letham, "The Triune God," which is chapter 6 of *The Oxford Handbook of Evangelical Theology*, edited by Gerald R. McDermott (Oxford: Oxford University Press, 2010).

61. ND, 4, 136 [7].

62. ND, 4, 137–138 [7 and 8]. Here Aquinas is saying what McCabe neatly summarizes in the quote I provided from him above.

63. Boethius, *Liber de Persona et Duabus Naturis* 3.

64. *God Still Matters*, 52.

65. *God Still Matters*, 49.

66. Aquinas, of course, was a biblical commentator in his own right. Yet his biblical commentaries seem to be grounded in doctrinal assumptions in the light of which he reads biblical texts. In his biblical commentaries he does not engage in the kind of historical and linguistic analysis typically found in contemporary biblical scholarship.

67. The *Summa Theologiae* turns directly to the Trinity in 1a,27–43.

68. G. E. M. Anscombe and P. T. Geach, *Three Philosophers* (Oxford: Blackwell, 1961), 118–119. See P. T. Geach, *The Virtues* (Cambridge: Cambridge University Press, 1977), 79: "The common theological doctrine is that—except for the fact that only one [divine] Person became a man, and whatever consequences follow from this—all external works and deeds of God are common to all the three Persons. . . . It is on just this account, Aquinas teaches, that natural reason, proceeding from effects in the world to God as their cause, can tell us nothing about any distinction of the Persons, and so must be silent on the question whether there is only one Divine Person or rather several."

69. I quote, with some emendations, from volume 6 of the Blackfriars edition of the *Summa Theologiae* (London: Eyre and Spottiswoode; New York: McGraw-Hill, 1965), 103.

70. Aquinas takes X to be really related to Y if X stands to Y because of something in X. Thus, for example, he would have said that I am really related to you if I have you in mind. Yet he does not think that my having you in mind entails that there is something real in you constituted by my just having you in mind. Of course, if I have you in mind, it can be said of you that you are being thought of by me. This fact, however, does not mean that my coming to have you in mind entails the coming to be of a new accident in you. So, thinks Aquinas, "Fred is being thought of by John" can be construed as flagging a merely notional relation in Fred, but a real one in John, something in John that relates him to Fred.

71. William Lane Craig, "Toward a Tenable Social Trinitarianism," in *Philosophical and Theological Essays on the Trinity*, edited by Thomas McCall and Michael C. Rea (Oxford: Oxford University Press, 2009), 91.

72. Craig, "Toward a Tenable Social Trinitarianism," 96.

73. For another example of someone endorsing what I take to be Social Trinitarianism, see Richard Swinburne, *The Christian God* (Oxford: Clarendon Press, 1994). For a vigorous and, I think, cogent critique of Swinburne arguing that he is committed to tritheism rather than orthodox teaching concerning the Trinity, see Edward C. Feser, "Swinburne's Tritheism," *International Journal for Philosophy of Religion* 42 (1997). For other criticisms of what might be called "Social Trinitarianism," see Brian Leftow, "Anti-Social Trinitarianism," which is chapter 4 of McCall and Rea, *Philosophical and Theological Essays on the Trinity*.

74. Anscombe and Geach, *Three Philosophers*, 118. For more from Geach on relative identity, see P. T. Geach, "Identity," *Review of Metaphysics* 21 (1967), and P. T. Geach, *Logic Matters* (Oxford: Blackwell, 1972), 7.1 and 7.2. For another defense of the notion of relative identity, see Nicholas Griffin, *Relative Identity* (Oxford: Clarendon Press, 1977). For discussions of the doctrine of the Trinity drawing on the notion of relative identity, see James Cain, "The Doctrine of the Trinity and the Logic of Relative Identity," *Religious Studies* 25 (1989); A. P. Martinich, "Identity and Trinity," *Journal of Religion* 58 (1978); and Peter van Inwagen, "And Yet They Are Not Three Gods but One God" (chapter 12 of McCall and Rea, *Philosophical and Theological Essays on the Trinity*).

75. Geach on relative identity is both applauded and criticized by Harold W. Noonan in "Relative Identity," *Philosophical Investigations* 38 (2015). He is criticized by John Perry in "The Same F," *Philosophical Review* 79 (1970). In "The Plight of the Relative Trinitarian," *Religious Studies* 24 (1988), Timothy W. Bartel castigates the notion of relative identity while arguing for a form of Social Trinitarianism.

76. Appeal to experience of God as something aiding an understanding of the Trinity features quite prominently in David Brown, *The Divine Trinity* (London: Duckworth, 1985).

CHAPTER 17. GOD INCARNATE (SCG 4,27–49)

1. Reference to Jesus as "Christ" historically derives from the fact that "Christ" was applied to Jesus in the belief that Christ was the Messiah promised in the Old Testament.

2. I quote from *Decrees of the Ecumenical Councils*, edited by Norman P. Tanner (Washington, DC: Georgetown University Press, 1990), 1:86.

3. ND, 4, 147 [1].

4. ND, 4, 147 [1].

5. ND, 4, 147–148 [2–4]. In this passage Aquinas is relying on the Vulgate edition of the Bible. Note also that the phrase "in his assumed humanity" is not to be read as implying that Christ's humanity was some kind of lie (as in "Iago as-

sumed the guise of a friend in Shakespeare's *Othello*"). Aquinas is thinking that, in the Incarnation, God the Son assumed humanity by, in the course of time (our time, not God's), taking on (assuming) a genuine human nature.

6. Here I pass over the questions "What are Aquinas's sources for the teachings of the heretics to which he refers in SCG 4?" and "Does Aquinas correctly report what these people taught?" These are difficult historical questions with which I am not competent to engage.

7. ND, 4, 160 [9].

8. ND, 4, 161 [2]. Also see chapter 11 here.

9. ND, 4, 189–190 [1, 2, and 3]. For introductions to Aquinas on the Incarnation, see the following: Richard Cross, "Aquinas on Nature, Hypostasis, and the Metaphysics of the Incarnation," *Thomist* 60 (1966); Michael Gorman, "Incarnation" (chapter 31 of *The Oxford Handbook of Aquinas*, edited by Brian Davies and Eleonore Stump [Oxford: Oxford University Press, 2012]); Eleonore Stump, "Aquinas' Metaphysics of the Incarnation" (chapter 9 of *The Incarnation*, edited by Stephen T. Davis, Daniel Kendall, and Gerald O'Collins [Oxford: Oxford University Press, 2002]); Joseph Wawrykow, "Hypostatic Union" (chapter 10 of *The Theology of Thomas Aquinas*, edited by Rik Van Nieuwenhove and Joseph Wawrykow [Notre Dame, IN: University of Notre Dame Press, 2005]).

10. While happily agreeing that both computers and prime ministers can be said to exist, Aquinas denies that they exist as naturally occurring things with a definite way of being that does not just reflect human concerns or human ways of dividing up things in the world. Those things that primarily exist, says Aquinas, are substances with natures or essences. So, he would say, human beings or horses primarily exist. These he refers to as *entia per se* (beings in and of themselves). He would call computers or prime ministers *entia per accidens* (beings only in a manner of speaking). Why? Because he would take a computer to amount to an assemblage of things brought together by people for a reason, and because he would say that prime ministers are people holding a conventional office, not something that defines them as the human beings that they are essentially and before they even plan on running for office.

11. ND, 4, 189 [2].

12. ND, 4, 190 [2].

13. ND, 4, 147 [1].

14. ND, 4, 191 [4].

15. ND, 4, 191 [6].

16. ND, 4, 192 [12].

17. ND, 4, 193 [13].

18. ND, 4, 194 [3].

19. ND, 4, 194 [3].

20. ND, 4, 194 [3].

21. ND, 4, 195 [7].

22. ND, 4, 196 [9].
23. The analogy recurs in *Summa Theologiae* 3a,6,2,5 and 3a,64,3.
24. ND, 4, 196–197 [11 and 12].
25. ND, 4, 197 [13].
26. ND, 4, 199 [1].
27. See Fabrizio Amerini, *Aquinas on the Beginning and End of Human Life* (Cambridge, MA: Harvard University Press, 2013), chapter 3. For chronological reasons, one can suppose that Aquinas had arrived at this position by the time that he was writing SCG 4.
28. ND, 4, 201 [2].
29. ND, 4, 201–202 [4].
30. Aquinas knew nothing about how conception can now be brought about without male and female human beings having sexual intercourse with each other.
31. ND, 4, 203 [4].
32. ND, 4, 207 [2].
33. ND, 4, 209 [4].
34. ND, 4, 209 [7].
35. ND, 4, 211 [15].
36. Here I find helpful Sara Coakley, "What Does Chalcedon Solve and What Does It Not? Some Reflections on the Status and Meaning of the Chalcedonian 'Definition,'" which is chapter 7 of Davis, Kendall, and O'Collins, *The Incarnation*. See also Aloys Grillmeier, *Christ in Christian Tradition*, vol. 1, 2nd rev. ed. (Atlanta: John Knox Press, 1975), 545. Having briefly summarized the goals of the fathers of Chalcedon, Grillmeier observes: "Even now we find among them no 'theologians,' in the sense of medieval or modern theological techniques. There is no attempt at a philosophical definition or speculative analysis! In theological method Chalcedon is no different from any of the earlier councils. Even if abstract concepts find their way in, the theological method here consists only in 'listening to' the proven witness of the Christian faith. True, the formulas are carefully developed, but only in connection with an already formed tradition. The work of the Fathers of Chalcedon is really 'dogmatic.' Moreover, their grasp of the content of their expressions is more intuitive than speculative. They produce formulas as witnesses to the Word and not as scholars. None of them could even have given a definition of the concepts with which they had now expressed christological dogma."
37. Not all people concerned to defend what they take to be Christian orthodoxy think of God as simple and immutable, as Aquinas does. For two contemporary examples, see Marilyn McCord Adams, *Christ and Horrors: The Coherence of Christology* (Cambridge: Cambridge University Press, 2006), and Richard Swinburne, *The Christian God* (Oxford: Clarendon Press, 1994), chapters 9 and 10.

38. N. T. Wright, "Jesus's Self-Understanding," which is chapter 3 of Davis, Kendall, and O'Collins, *The Incarnation*.

39. John Hick (ed.), *The Myth of God Incarnate*, edited by John Hick (London: SCM Press, 1977), 178. In "Letter to the Editors: Incarnation," *Theology* 80 (1977), 205, Hick says "Incarnation...becomes a matter of degree: God is incarnate in all men insofar as they are Spirit-filled, or Christ-like, or truly saintly."

40. Stump, "Aquinas' Metaphysics of the Incarnation," in Davis, Kendall, and O'Collins, *The Incarnation*, 211.

41. "My cat is a dog" can be thought to be true if it is taken to mean something like "My cat behaves as dogs typically do." Yet, since being feline excludes being canine (cats and dogs being things of different kinds), "My cat is a dog" says something that cannot possibly be literally true.

42. Peter Geach summarizes the two-name theory of predication as follows: "In an affirmative predication the subject is a name and so is the predicate, and the predication is true if and only if the subject-name and the predicate-name stand for the same thing or things." See Geach, *Logic Matters* (Oxford: Blackwell, 1972), 289.

43. Geach, *Logic Matters*, 295.

44. Wiles says this in a response to a review by Herbert McCabe of *The Myth of God Incarnate*. This response originally appeared in *New Blackfriars* 58 (1977). It was republished in Herbert McCabe, *God Matters* (London: Geoffrey Chapman, 1987). My quote from Wiles appears on p. 63 of *God Matters*.

45. McCabe, *God Matters*, 70.

46. McCabe, *God Matters*, 70–71.

47. For someone suspecting Aquinas of Monophysite leanings, see Richard Cross, *The Metaphysics of the Incarnation: Thomas Aquinas to Duns Scotus* (Oxford: Oxford University Press, 2002).

48. Even contemporary Catholic theologians have denied that Christ enjoyed the beatific vision, and many non-Catholic theologians have done so as well. For what I take to be an excellent account and discussion of the thesis that Christ indeed enjoyed the beatific vision, see Simon Francis Gaine, *Did the Saviour See the Father?* (London: Bloomsbury, 2015).

49. McCabe, *God Still Matters* (London: Continuum, 2002), 109.

50. See Jürgen Moltmann, *The Crucified God* (Minneapolis: Fortress Press, 1993). In *The Metaphysics of the Incarnation*, Cross also maintains that the Son of God suffers as God. For a discussion of God and suffering that supports Aquinas's claim that God incarnate can suffer without the divine nature doing so, see Anselm K. Minn, "Why Only an Immutable God Can Love, Relate, and Suffer," which is chapter 9 of *Christian Philosophy of Religion: Essays in Honor of Stephen T. Davis*, edited by C. P. Ruloff (Notre Dame, IN: University of Notre Dame Press, 2015). For an impressive contemporary account of the Incarnation

aiming to follow the teaching of Aquinas, see Thomas Joseph White, *The Incarnate Lord* (Washington, DC: Catholic University of America Press, 2015).

51. For notable examples of these, see Thomas V. Morris, *The Logic of God Incarnate* (Ithaca, NY: Cornell University Press, 1986), and Swinburne, *The Christian God*, chapter 9.

CHAPTER 18. THE FITTINGNESS OF THE INCARNATION, THE
SACRAMENTS, THE RESURRECTION, AND THE FINAL STATE
OF PEOPLE AND OF THE WORLD (SCG 4,50–97)

1. ND, 4, 212 [1].
2. Aquinas's approach to Original Sin owes much to St. Augustine. For an outline of Augustine on Original Sin, see William L. Mann, "Augustine on Evil and Original Sin," which is chapter 3 of *The Cambridge Companion to Augustine*, edited by Eleonore Stump and Norman Kretzmann (Cambridge: Cambridge University Press, 2001).
3. See SCG 4,81, in which Aquinas refers to death as accidental. See ND, 4, 302 [3].
4. ND, 4, 213 [3].
5. ND, 4, 214 [10].
6. ND, 4, 214 [11].
7. ND, 4, 215 [2].
8. ND, 4, 216 [6].
9. ND, 4, 216 [7].
10. ND, 4, 216 [8].
11. ND, 4, 216 [9].
12. ND, 4, 219 [4].
13. ND, 4, 219 [6].
14. ND, 4, 220 [7].
15. ND, 4, 222 [14].
16. In SCG 4,53, Aquinas uses the words "unbecoming" (*indicens*) and "inharmonious" (*incongruum*) as meaning the opposite of *conveniens*. See ND, 4, 53 [1].
17. ND, 4, 224 [6].
18. ND, 4, 224 [7].
19. This objection to the fittingness of the Incarnation presumes that defenders of belief in the Incarnation take the Incarnation to have saved people somehow. This presumption is understandable because many who have believed in the Incarnation have, indeed, taken it to have saved people in some way. Aquinas himself holds that the Incarnation resulted in us being freed from sin and being given grace to be united with God.
20. ND, 4, 225 [12].

21. When Aquinas refers to satisfaction he is thinking of it as a making up for an offense committed. You might wrong me, and I might forgive you. According to Aquinas, however, matters between you and I are not made right just by my forgiving you. He thinks that justice requires that you make some reparation or restitution for the wrong that you have done me, reparation or restitution that balances or matches the wrong done. And he takes Christ to have made reparation or satisfaction for human sin. In doing so, he stands in a long Christian tradition, one most famously, perhaps, expressed by St. Anselm of Canterbury in his *Cur Deus Homo* (*Why God Became Man*). This notion of Christ as satisfying for sin runs throughout Aquinas's SCG treatment of God's saving work for humans, as it does throughout his account of God's saving work as given in other texts that he wrote, such as *Summa Theologiae* 3a,31–59.

22. The reference to satisfaction by death here reflects the Christian tradition, which Aquinas accepted, that Christ's death satisfied for human sin.

23. ND, 4, 227 [28].

24. ND, 4, 228 [2].

25. ND, 4, 229 [3].

26. Here, again, we find Aquinas insisting on a sharp distinction between faith and knowledge while denying that the articles of faith are things we can know to be true in this life given what we are and what we can know by using our natural faculties. As I have shown, he thinks that, by means of causal reasoning, we can demonstrate certain truths about God. But, in the SCG, as elsewhere in his writings, he never wavers when it comes to the idea that the articles of faith have to be revealed to us by one who knows that they are true. One might suppose that God could reveal things to us without becoming one of us and giving us instruction. One might, for example, wonder whether God might not have revealed things to us by presenting us with writing in the sky or something like that. Aquinas, however, does not consider this possibility. Why not? I have no idea. Perhaps he would have said that writing in the sky or the like would leave us unacceptably coerced in some way.

27. ND, 4, 230–231 [5].

28. Here I assume that Aquinas would, for example, say that, much as I love my cat, it is not my equal since it lacks intellect and freedom of choice. Aquinas thinks that people have intellect. He thinks that they can understand what things are and can express their understanding in words the meaning of which anyone can grasp. And he thinks that we can draw on these understandings so as to reason with an eye on what to do in the future. So, he would say, my cat is not my equal or my friend. Friendship, for Aquinas, is a relationship between equals. He does not think that a pet can be a friend of a human being in anything like the way in which two human beings can be friends.

29. ND, 4, 231 [7].

30. ND, 4, 232 [9]. Aquinas's approach to satisfaction has been challenged. For a defense of it, see Eleonore Stump, *Aquinas* (Routledge: London: 2003), chapter 15.
31. ND, 4, 232 [9].
32. ND, 4, 232 [9].
33. ND, 4, 233 [2].
34. ND, 4, 233 [3].
35. ND, 4, 234 [4].
36. ND, 4, 234 [5]. I take it that Aquinas is here suggesting that while angels are wholly immaterial, and while stones are wholly material, the Incarnation fittingly amounts to God becoming something both bodily and immaterial since it amounts to God becoming what he produces as the creator of all things considered as divided into material and immaterial ones.
37. ND, 4, 234 [6].
38. ND, 4, 235 [7]. In the SCG Aquinas does not offer an explanation for how angels came to sin. But he does in the *Summa Theologiae*. See my *Thomas Aquinas's "Summa Theologiae": A Guide and Commentary* (Oxford: Oxford University Press, 2014), 122–124.
39. ND, 4, 234–235 [7].
40. ND, 4, 234–235 [7].
41. ND, 4, 235 [7].
42. ND, 4, 235 [7]. It is not obvious what Aquinas is driving at here. I presume that he is thinking (1) that spatiotemporal things, at one extreme, are purely material, (2) that human beings are closer to God than purely material things since they are not purely material, and (3) that God is wholly immaterial. And I presume that, in the light of (1)–(3) here, Aquinas thinks that it was appropriate for God to assume the spatiotemporal nature closest to him rather than something other than this.
43. ND, 4, 235–236 [8].
44. ND, 4, 236 [9].
45. ND, 4, 236 [10].
46. ND, 4, 236–237 [11].
47. ND, 4, 238–239 [12].
48. ND, 4, 239 [13].
49. ND, 4, 239–240 [14].
50. ND, 4, 246 [30].
51. ND, 4, 246 [31].
52. ND, 4, 246–247 [1].
53. ND, 4, 247 [2].
54. ND, 4, 247 [4].
55. ND, 4, 248 [1].
56. ND, 4, 250 [2].

57. ND, 4, 251 [6]. Donatists were a schismatic group active in Africa from the fourth to eighth centuries. Their most famous opponent was St. Augustine. Donatists were rigorists who held that sacraments celebrated by sinful ministers were invalid. Accordingly, they demanded that converts to Donatism should be rebaptized.

58. ND, 4, 251–252 [1].

59. ND, 4, 252 [1].

60. ND, 4, 253 [3].

61. In SCG 4,69 Aquinas asks whether leavened or unleavened bread can be used in the celebration of the Eucharist. He replies that either will do. What is important for Aquinas is that genuine bread and wine are used when celebrating the Eucharist.

62. ND, 4, 257 [1].

63. For an account of the history of Eucharistic theology, see David N. Power, *The Eucharistic Mystery* (New York: Crossroad, 1992).

64. ND, 4, 268 [1].

65. ND, 4, 257 [4].

66. By "the words of consecration" I mean the words used by a celebrant of the Eucharist repeating Christ's words "This is my body" and "This is my blood."

67. Some would say that his teaching to this effect leaves Aquinas open to the charge that God is a deceiver. For if God brings about what seems to be what it is not, then God is misleading us. I assume, though, that Aquinas takes the Eucharist to be not so much a deception as a revelation, just as he thinks that Jesus was God incarnate without looking like God (whatever that would mean). He thinks that Christ is in the Eucharist because revelation teaches us that this is the case. When it comes to recent discussions of the presence of Christ in the Eucharist, texts that I think worth noting include (1) Michael Dummett, "The Intelligibility of Eucharistic Doctrine," which is chapter 13 of *The Rationality of Religious Belief: Essays in Honour of Basil Mitchell*, edited by William J. Abraham and Steven W. Holtzer (Oxford: Clarendon Press, 1987), and (2) chapters 10–13 of Herbert McCabe, *God Matters* (London: Geoffrey Chapman, 1987), in which McCabe debates P. J. FitzPatrick concerning the Eucharist.

68. ND, 4, 260 [9].

69. ND, 4, 263 [3].

70. ND, 4, 267 [10].

71. ND, 4, 268, [4].

72. Here I am taking "what Aquinas says about the Eucharist" to include not only what he says about it in the SCG but also what he says about it in the *Summa Theologiae*, which I do not take to deviate from what we find in the SCG.

73. I quote from *Luther's Works*, edited by Abdel Ross Wentz (Philadelphia: Muhlenberg, 1959), 6:29.

74. The word "transubstantiation" was widely used in reference to the Eucharist in the twelfth and thirteenth centuries. Attention was drawn to the word by the Council of Trent in chapter 4 of its decree on the Eucharist, where we read: "Since Christ our redeemer said that it was truly his own body which he was offering under the form of bread, therefore there has always been complete conviction in the church of God…that, by the conversion of the bread and wine, there takes place the change of the whole substance of the bread into the substance of the body of Christ our Lord, and of the whole substance of the wine into the substance of his blood. And the holy catholic church has suitably and properly called this change transubstantiation." I quote from *Decrees of the Ecumenical Councils*, edited by Norman P. Tanner (Washington, DC: Georgetown University Press, 1990), 2:695.

75. McCabe, *God Matters*, 146.

76. See Tanner, *Decrees of the Ecumenical Councils*, 1:245.

77. This is the drift of SCG 4,70.

78. ND, 4, 275 [5].

79. This is the drift of SCG 4,71.

80. ND, 4, 277 [1].

81. Aquinas holds that a sinner may be sufficiently repentant and devoted to Christ so as to achieve by contrition not only the grace of forgiveness but also the grace of becoming free from the need to accept some punishment due to sin. But he takes this to be something rare. See ND, 4, 280 [8].

82. See Leviticus 8:10–12.

83. ND, 4, 284 [4]. Aquinas agrees that lots of people can be in danger of death without being sick. But he does not think that people in this state are candidates for extreme unction since he takes that to be offered only to those who seem close to death due to illness or whatever. See ND, 4, 284 [5].

84. When referring to minor orders, Aquinas has in mind that to which people are deputed so as to perform functions distinct from those reserved to priests. He would have recognized four minor orders: those of acolyte, lector, exorcist, and ecclesiastical door keeper.

85. ND, 4, 290 [1].

86. In the SCG, as in other writings, Aquinas is clear that sacraments should not be thought of in magical terms. He always insists that sacraments cannot confer grace on those who receive them while wedded to sin.

87. ND, 4, 285 [1]. Here, Aquinas labors the point that sacraments can be validly celebrated by sinners.

88. ND, 4, 286 [2].

89. ND, 4, 289 [1].

90. ND, 4, 290 [1].

91. ND, 4, 291 [4].

92. ND, 4, 293 [2].

93. ND, 4, 295 [2].

94. ND, 4, 296 [6].

95. ND, 4, 297–298 [1 and 3].
96. Perhaps I should say that Aquinas takes the resurrection of people from the dead to be a future event every bit as predictable as, say, astronomers take eclipses to be. This is obvious from what he says in SCG 4,79–89, though I take its obviousness to be reinforced by the fact that the title of SCG 4,79 is *Quod per Christum resurrectio corporum sit futura* ("That, through Christ, the resurrection of bodies is to come") and by the fact that, also in SCG 4,79, he explicitly denies that what Scripture says about human resurrection should be interpreted as teaching that God has now forgiven us (see ND, 4, 298 [6]).
97. See SCG 4,97.
98. Puzzlement you might have about Aquinas's teaching on resurrection in the SCG might be allayed a bit if you get a sense of patristic and medieval thinking concerning resurrection. For an account of this, see Caroline Walker Bynum, *The Resurrection of the Body in Western Christianity, 200–1336* (New York: Columbia University Press, 1995). For good accounts of Aquinas on resurrection, see Montague Brown, "Aquinas on the Resurrection of the Body," *Thomist* 56 (1991); Silas Langley, "Aquinas, Resurrection, and Material Continuity," *Proceedings of the American Catholic Philosophical Association* 75 (2001). For recent works of biblical scholarship relevant to Aquinas's discussion of resurrection, see Oscar Cullmann, *Immortality of the Soul or Resurrection from the Dead* (London: Epworth Press, 1958); Joel Green, *Body, Soul, and Human Life: The Nature of Humanity in the Bible* (Grand Rapids, MI: Baker Publishing Group, 2008); Robert Gundry, *Sôma in Biblical Theology with Emphasis on Pauline Anthropology* (Cambridge: Cambridge University Press, 1976); Murray Harris, *Raised Immortal: Resurrection and Immortality in the New Testament* (Grand Rapids, MI: Eerdmans, 1983).
99. ND, 4, 297 [1].
100. ND, 4, 299 [10].
101. SCG 4,79 (ND, 4, 299 [11]).
102. SCG 4,79 (ND, 4, 299–230 [11–12]).
103. ND, 4, 300 [1].
104. ND, 4, 300–301 [2].
105. ND, 4, 301 [3].
106. ND, 4, 301 [4].
107. ND, 4, 301 [5].
108. ND, 4, 301 [6].
109. ND, 4, 301 [7].
110. ND, 4, 301 [4].
111. ND, 4, 303 [5].
112. ND, 4, 303 [6].
113. ND, 4, 306 [12].
114. ND, 4, 307 [13].
115. SCG 4,82.
116. SCG 4,82 [5].

117. SCG 4,83.
118. SCG 4,84.
119. SCG 4,85.
120. SCG 4,86.
121. SCG 4,87. Aquinas clearly thinks that there is a physical place "on high" to which the bodies of the blessed can be transported.
122. SCG 4,88.
123. SCG 4,89.
124. SCG 4,90.
125. SCG 4,91.
126. ND, 4, 338–339. In SCG 4,92 Aquinas argues that the will of those to be rewarded with beatitude is unchangeable once they have died. Correspondingly, he argues in SCG 4,93 that the will of those to be damned is unchangeable once they have died. In SCG 4,94 he argues that souls in purgatory also have a will that is fixed in what it is aiming at. In SCG 4,95 he goes on to argue that our wills are fixed at death since death is the end of our bodily (or preresurrection) life in which we make choices as bodily human beings. It has sometimes been suggested that God might give us a series of bodily lives in which we might end up finally conforming ourselves to God. But Aquinas has no time for this notion. He thinks that, at death, we have come to the conclusion of our lives and need to be judged accordingly. For modern defenses of an approach to life after death that counters this view, see John Hick, *Evil and the God of Love*, 2nd ed. with new preface (London: Macmillan, 1985), 341–345, and Marilyn McCord Adams, *Christ and Horrors: The Coherence of Christology* (Cambridge: Cambridge University Press, 2006), chapter 8.
127. The reference here is to Romans 8:21.
128. It should be obvious that SCG 4,79–97 raises many questions that could be considered at length. In what follows I confine myself to a brief discussion of two things that Aquinas concludes in these chapters.
129. For an account of the history of thinking about Original Sin, see Tatha Wiley, *Original Sin: Origins, Developments, Contemporary Meanings* (New York: Paulist Press, 2002).
130. See Yuval Noah Harari, *Sapiens: A Brief History of Humankind* (New York: Harper Collins, 2015), Christopher Seddon, *Humans: From the Beginning: From the First Apes to the First Cities* (London: Glanville, 2015), and Ian Tattersall, *Masters of the Planet: The Search for Our Human Origins* (London: Macmillan, 2013).
131. G. K. Chesterton, *Orthodoxy* (London: Bodley Head, 1908), chapter 2.
132. Kenneth W. Kemp, "Science, Theology, and Monogenesis," *American Catholic Philosophical Quarterly* 85 (2011).
133. See Trent's *Decree on Original Sin*. For the Latin text of this work with English translation, see Tanner, *Decrees of the Ecumenical Councils*, 2:665–667.

134. For what I take to be an interesting and very clear discussion of Roman Catholic views on Original Sin, see Jerry D. Korsmeyer, *Evolution and Eden* (New York: Paulist Press, 1998).

135. I quote from the publication in *L'Osservatore Romano*, English ed., of John Paul II's address to the Pontifical Academy of Sciences, October 22, 1996.

136. See Timothy McDermott, "Original Sin," *New Blackfriars* 49 (January 1968 and February 1968). Also see Herbert McCabe, *God Still Matters* (London: Continuum, 2002), chapter 15.

137. 1 Corinthians 15:42–43.

138. P. T. Geach, *God and the Soul* (London: Routledge and Kegan Paul, 1969), 21.

139. ND, 4, 306 [12].

140. Geach, *God and the Soul*, 26–27. Sir John Cutler (d. 1693) was famous for his parsimony. The anecdote concerning his stockings became well known due to its telling by John Arbuthnot (1667–1735) in a text called *First Lessons in Intellectual Philosophy*. Unfortunately, Geach alludes to the anecdote incorrectly. Arbuthnot speaks of Cutler's stockings as starting off as worsted and ending up as silk.

141. An especially famous philosopher connecting personal identity with memory is John Locke (1632–1704). According to Locke we should distinguish between "same person" and "same human being," and should think that a person continues to exist as long as the person has continuity of "consciousness" of its previous life. See John Locke, *An Essay Concerning Human Understanding*, edited by Peter H. Nidditch (Oxford: Oxford University Press, 1975), bk. 2, chapter 27.

142. Thomas Reid, *Essays on the Intellectual Powers of Man* (Edinburgh, 1785), essay 6, chapter 5.

143. See Peter van Inwagen, "The Possibility of Resurrection," which is chapter 3 of van Inwagen, *The Possibility of Resurrection and Other Essays in Christian Apologetics* (Boulder, CO: Westview Press, 1998). For a lively discussion of resurrection displaying knowledge of Aquinas, see Silas Langley, *Death, Resurrection, and Transporter Beams* (Eugene, OR: Wipf and Stock, 2014). For an intriguing defense of the view that our resurrection can be thought of as occurring right upon death, see James Ross, "Together with the Body I Love," *Proceedings of the American Catholic Philosophical Association* 75 (2001).

144. For a detailed discussion of Aquinas on the time of the resurrection of our bodies, see Bryan Kromholtz, *On the Last Day: The Time of the Resurrection of the Dead According to Thomas Aquinas* (Fribourg: Academic Press, 2010). This book also contains accounts of what Aquinas says about human resurrection throughout his various writings.

145. See Carlo Leget, "Eschatology," which is chapter 15 of Rik Van Nieuwenhove and Joseph Wawrykow (eds.), *The Theology of Thomas Aquinas* (Notre Dame, IN: University of Notre Dame Press), 2005. For discussions of eschatology, see *The Oxford Handbook of Eschatology*, edited by Jerry L. Walls (Oxford: Oxford

University Press, 2008). Aquinas does not feature much in this volume, but it provides copious accounts of eschatological views at odds with those of Aquinas.

146. Stephen T. Davis, "Resurrection," in *The Cambridge Companion to Christian Philosophical Theology*, edited by Charles Taliaferro and Chad Meister (Cambridge: Cambridge University Press, 2010), 123.

147. I say "pretty much" since I do not think that Aquinas takes miracles to involve God intervening in the world. To intervene is to enter into a situation in which one did not exist to start with; for Aquinas, however, God is totally present in all things for as long as they have being.

148. John Morreall, "Perfect Happiness and the Resurrection of the Body," *Religious Studies* 16 (March 1980).

149. Morreall, "Perfect Happiness," 30 and 35.

150. Morreall cites Aquinas only once in his article: as believing that the beatific vision gives happiness to that which enjoys it. By implication, however, he is claiming that Aquinas should either abandon belief in the beatific vision as had by human souls or give up belief in human resurrection.

151. Morreall, "Perfect Happiness," 30.

152. Richard E. Creel, "Happiness and Resurrection: A Reply to Morreall," *Religious Studies* 17 (September 1981).

153. As Creel observes, the notion of unsurpassable human happiness seems incoherent, like the notion of a largest prime number. There is always a larger prime number than any one might care to cite. Similarly, no matter how happy a creature is, it is possible for an omnipotent God to make it still happier.

154. See *Summa Theologiae* 1a2ae,4,7, ad.1.

155. ND, 4, 97 [8].

156. Anthony Kenny, *Christianity in Review* (London: Darton, Longman and Todd, 2015), 36.

Bibliography

Note: Works not listed under the name of the author or title are listed under the name(s) of the editor(s) or translator(s).

Abraham, William J., and Steven W. Holtzer (eds.). *The Rationality of Religious Belief: Essays in Honour of Basil Mitchell*. Oxford: Clarendon Press, 1987.

Adams, Marilyn McCord. *Christ and Horrors: The Coherence of Christology*. Cambridge: Cambridge University Press, 2006.

Ahern, M. B. "The Nature of Evil." *Sophia* 5 (1966).

Alston, William P. *Perceiving God: The Epistemology of Religious Belief*. Ithaca, NY: Cornell University Press, 1991.

Alston, William P. "Why Should There Not Be Experience of God?" In Brian Davies (ed.), *Philosophy of Religion: A Guide and Anthology*. Oxford: Oxford University Press, 2000.

Amerini, Fabrizio. *Aquinas on the Beginning and End of Human Life*. Cambridge, MA: Harvard University Press, 2013.

Anglin, Bill, and Stewart Goetz. "Evil Is Privation." *International Journal of Philosophy of Religion* 13 (1982).

Anscombe, G. E. M. *Collected Philosophical Papers*. Oxford: Blackwell, 1981.

Anscombe, G. E. M., and P. T. Geach. *Three Philosophers*. Oxford: Blackwell, 1961.

Aquinas, Thomas. *Aquinas: Summa Theologiae, Questions on God*. Edited by Brian Davies and Brian Leftow. Cambridge: Cambridge University Press, 2006.

Aquinas, Thomas. *Saint Thomas Aquinas: Summa Contra Gentiles; Book One: God*. Translated by Anton C. Pegis. Notre Dame, IN: University of Notre Dame Press, 1975.

Aquinas, Thomas. *Saint Thomas Aquinas: Summa Contra Gentiles; Book Two: Creation*. Translated by James F. Anderson. Notre Dame, IN: University of Notre Dame Press, 1975.

Aquinas, Thomas. *Saint Thomas Aquinas: Summa Contra Gentiles; Book Three: Providence Part I*. Translated by Vernon J. Bourke. Notre Dame, IN: University of Notre Dame Press, 1975.

Aquinas, Thomas. *Saint Thomas Aquinas: Summa Contra Gentiles; Book Three: Providence Part II*. Translated by Vernon J. Bourke. Notre Dame, IN: University of Notre Dame Press, 1975.

Aquinas, Thomas. *Saint Thomas Aquinas: Summa Contra Gentiles; Book Four: Salvation*. Translated by Charles J. O'Neil. Notre Dame, IN: University of Notre Dame Press, 1975.

Aquinas, Thomas. *Saint Thomas Aquinas: Treatise on Separate Substances*. Translated by Francis J. Lescoe. West Hartford, CT: Saint Joseph College, 1959.

Aquinas, Thomas. *Somme Contre Les Gentils*. Edited by René-Antoine Gauthier. Paris: Editions Universitaires, 1993.

Aquinas, Thomas. *Somme Contre Les Gentils*. Book 1. Edited by Cyrille Michon. Paris: Flammarion, 2000.

Aquinas, Thomas. *Summa Theologiae*. Blackfriars ed. London: Eyre and Spottiswoode; New York: McGraw-Hill, 1964–1981.

Aquinas, Thomas. *Thomas Aquinas: Selected Philosophical Writings*. Translated by Timothy McDermott. Oxford: Oxford University Press, 1993.

Aristotle. *The Complete Works of Aristotle*. Edited by Jonathan Barnes. Princeton, NJ: Princeton University Press, 1984.

Augustine. *The Trinity*. Translated by Edmund Hill. New York: New York City Press, 1991.

Ayer, A. J. *Language, Truth and Logic*. 2nd ed. London: Victor Gollancz, 1946.

Baldner, Steven E., and William E. Carroll (eds.). *Aquinas on Creation*. Toronto: Pontifical Institute of Medieval Studies, 1997.

Barr, James. *Biblical Faith and Natural Theology*. Oxford: Clarendon Press, 1993.

Bartel, Timothy W. "The Plight of the Relative Trinitarian." *Religious Studies* 24 (1988).

Bauerschmidt, Frederick Christian. *Thomas Aquinas: Faith, Reason, and Following Christ*. Oxford: Oxford University Press, 2013.

Brower, Jeffrey E. *Aquinas's Ontology of the Material World: Change, Hylomorphism, and Material Objects*. Oxford: Oxford University Press, 2014.

Brown, David. *The Divine Trinity*. London: Duckworth, 1985.

Brown, Montague. "Aquinas on the Resurrection of the Body." *Thomist* 56 (1991).

Burns, R. M. *The Great Debate on Miracles: From Joseph Glanville to David Hume*. Lewisburg, PA: Bucknell University Press, 1981.

Bynum, Caroline Walker. *The Resurrection of the Body in Western Christianity, 200–1336*. New York: Columbia University Press, 1995.

Cain, James. "The Doctrine of the Trinity and the Logic of Relative Identity." *Religious Studies* 25 (1989).

Caird, G. B. *The Language and Imagery of the Bible*. Philadelphia: Westminster Press, 1980.

Calder, Todd C. "Is the Privation Theory of Evil Dead?" *American Philosophical Quarterly* 44 (October 2007).

Chenu, M.-D. *Toward Understanding Saint Thomas.* Chicago: Henry Regnery, 1964.

Chesterton, G. K. *Orthodoxy.* London: Bodley Head, 1908.

Church, Alonzo. "Review of *Language, Truth and Logic.*" *Journal of Symbolic Logic* 14 (1949).

Coakley, Sara. "What Does Chalcedon Solve and What Does It Not? Some Reflections on the Status and Meaning of the Chalcedonian 'Definition.'" In Stephen T. Davis, Daniel Kendall, and Gerald O'Collins (eds.), *The Incarnation.* Oxford: Oxford University Press, 2002.

Craig, William Lane. *The Kalām Cosmological Argument.* London: Macmillan, 1979.

Craig, William Lane. *The Only Wise God.* Grand Rapids, MI: Baker Book House, 1987.

Craig, William Lane. "Toward a Tenable Social Trinitarianism." In Thomas McCall and Michael C. Rea (eds.), *Philosophical and Theological Essays on the Trinity.* Oxford: Oxford University Press, 2009.

Creel, Richard E. "Happiness and Resurrection: A Reply to Morreall." *Religious Studies* 17 (September 1981).

Crosby, John F. "Doubts about the Privation Theory That Will Not Go Away: Response to Patrick Lee." *American Catholic Philosophical Quarterly* 81 (2007).

Cross, Richard. "Aquinas on Nature, Hypostasis, and the Metaphysics of the Incarnation." *Thomist* 60 (1966).

Cross, Richard. *The Metaphysics of the Incarnation: Thomas Aquinas to Duns Scotus.* Oxford: Oxford University Press, 2002.

Cullmann, Oscar. *Immortality of the Soul or Resurrection from the Dead.* London: Epworth Press, 1958.

Dales, Richard C. *Medieval Discussions of the Eternity of the World.* Leiden: Brill, 1991.

Damascene, John. *Saint John of Damascus, Writings.* Translated by Frederic H. Chase, Jr. The Fathers of the Church, vol. 37. Washington, DC: Catholic University of America Press, 1958.

Davies, Brian. *Aquinas.* London: Continuum, 2002.

Davies, Brian. "D. Z. Phillips on Belief in God." *Philosophical Investigations* 30, no. 3 (2007).

Davies, Brian. *An Introduction to the Philosophy of Religion.* 3rd ed. Oxford: Oxford University Press, 2004.

Davies, Brian. "Is God beyond Reason?" *Philosophical Investigations* 32, no. 4 (October 2009).

Davies, Brian. *The Reality of God and the Problem of Evil.* London: Continuum, 2006.

Davies, Brian. *Thomas Aquinas on God and Evil.* Oxford: Oxford University Press, 2011.

Davies, Brian. *Thomas Aquinas's "Summa Theologiae": A Guide and Commentary.* Oxford: Oxford University Press, 2014.

Davies, Brian. *The Thought of Thomas Aquinas.* Oxford: Clarendon Press, 1992.

Davies, Brian (ed.). *Thomas Aquinas: Contemporary Philosophical Perspectives.* Oxford: Oxford University Press, 2002.

Davies, Brian, and G. R. Evans (eds.). *Anselm of Canterbury: The Major Works.* Oxford: Oxford University Press, 1998.

Davies, Brian, and Brian Leftow (eds.). *The Cambridge Companion to Anselm.* Cambridge: Cambridge University Press, 2004.

Davies, Brian, and Eleonore Stump (eds.). *The Oxford Handbook of Aquinas.* Oxford: Oxford University Press, 2012.

Davis, Stephen T. "Resurrection." In Charles Taliaferro and Chad Meister (eds.), *The Cambridge Companion to Christian Philosophical Theology.* Cambridge: Cambridge University Press, 2010.

Davis, Stephen T., Daniel Kendall, and Gerald O'Collins (eds.). *The Incarnation.* Oxford: Oxford University Press, 2002.

Dixon, Philip. *Nice and Hot Disputes: The Doctrine of the Trinity in the Seventeenth Century.* Edinburgh: T&T Clark, 2003.

Dolezal, James E. *God without Parts: Divine Simplicity and the Metaphysics of God's Absoluteness.* Eugene, OR: Pickwick, 2011.

Dummett, Michael. "The Intelligibility of Eucharistic Doctrine." In William J. Abraham and Steven W. Holtzer (eds.), *The Rationality of Religious Belief: Essays in Honour of Basil Mitchell.* Oxford: Clarendon Press, 1987.

Emery, Gilles, O.P., and Matthew Levering (eds.). *The Oxford Handbook of the Trinity.* Oxford: Oxford University Press, 2011.

Feingold, Lawrence. *The Natural Desire to See God According to St. Thomas Aquinas and His Interpreters.* 2nd ed. Naples, FL: Sapientia Press, 2010.

Ferrua, Angelico (ed.). *Thomae Aquinatis vitae fontes praecipuae.* Alba: Edizione Domenicane, 1968.

Feser, Edward. *Aquinas: A Beginner's Guide.* London: Oneworld, 2009.

Feser, Edward. *Scholastic Metaphysics: A Contemporary Introduction.* Heusenstamm: Editiones Scholasticae, 2014.

Feser, Edward. "Swinburne's Tritheism." *International Journal for Philosophy of Religion* 42 (1997).

Foster, Kenelm (ed.). *The Life of Saint Thomas Aquinas: Biographical Documents.* London: Longmans, Green, 1959.

Freddoso, Alfred J. (ed.). *The Existence and Nature of God.* Notre Dame, IN: University of Notre Dame Press, 1983.

Frege, Gottlob. *The Foundations of Arithmetic.* Translated by J. L. Austin. Oxford: Blackwell, 1980.

Friedman, Russell. *Medieval Trinitarian Thought from Aquinas to Ockham.* Cambridge: Cambridge University Press, 2010.

Gaine, Simon Francis. *Did the Saviour See the Father?* London: Bloomsbury, 2015.

Gauthier, René-Antoine (ed.). *Somme Contre Les Gentils.* Paris: Editions Universitaires, 1993.

Geach, P. T. *God and the Soul*. London: Routledge and Kegan Paul, 1969.

Geach, P. T. "God's Relation to the World." *Sophia* 8 (October 1969).

Geach, P. T. "Good and Evil." *Analysis* 17 (December 1956).

Geach, P. T. "Identity." *Review of Metaphysics* 21 (1967).

Geach, P. T. *Logic Matters*. Oxford: Blackwell, 1972.

Geach, P. T. *The Virtues*. Cambridge: Cambridge University Press, 1977.

Goetz, Stewart, and Charles Taliaferro. *Naturalism*. Grand Rapids, MI: Eerdmans, 2008.

Gorman, Michael. "Incarnation." In Brian Davies and Eleonore Stump (eds.), *The Oxford Handbook of Aquinas*. Oxford: Oxford University Press, 2012.

Grant, Edward. *Planets, Stars, and Orbs: The Medieval Cosmos, 1200–1687*. Cambridge: Cambridge University Press, 1994.

Green, Joel. *Body, Soul, and Human Life: The Nature of Humanity in the Bible*. Grand Rapids, MI: Baker, 2008.

Griffin, Nicholas. *Relative Identity*. Oxford: Clarendon Press, 1977.

Grillmeier, Aloys. *Christ in Christian Tradition*. Vol. 1. 2nd rev. ed. Atlanta: John Knox Press, 1975.

Guagliardo, Vincent A., Charles R. Hess, and Richard C. Taylor. *St. Thomas Aquinas: Commentary on the Book of Causes*. Washington, DC: Catholic University of America Press, 1996.

Gundry, Robert. *Sôma in Biblical Theology with Emphasis on Pauline Anthropology*. Cambridge: Cambridge University Press, 1976.

Harari, Yuval Noah. *Sapiens: A Brief History of Humankind*. New York: Harper Collins, 2015.

Harris, Murray. *Raised Immortal: Resurrection and Immortality in the New Testament*. Grand Rapids, MI: Eerdmans, 1983.

Henninger, Mark G. *Relations: Medieval Theories 1250–1325*. Oxford: Clarendon Press, 1989.

Hibbs, Thomas S. *Dialectic and Narrative in Aquinas: An Interpretation of the "Summa Contra Gentiles."* Notre Dame, IN: University of Notre Dame Press, 1995.

Hick, John. *Evil and the God of Love*. 2nd ed. with new preface. London: Macmillan, 1985.

Hick, John. "Letter to the Editors: Incarnation." *Theology* 80 (1977).

Hick, John (ed.). *The Myth of God Incarnate*. London: SCM Press, 1977.

Hill, William J., O.P. *The Three Personed God: The Trinity as a Mystery of Salvation*. Washington, DC: Catholic University of America Press, 1982.

Hoffmann, Paul. "Does Efficient Causation Presuppose Final Causation? Aquinas vs. Early Modern Mechanism." In Larry Jorgensen and Samuel Newlands (eds.), *Metaphysics and the Good: Themes from the Philosophy of Robert Merrihew Adams*. Oxford: Oxford University Press, 2008.

Hume, David. *An Enquiry Concerning Human Understanding*. Edited by Tom L. Beauchamp. Oxford: Clarendon Press, 2000.

Jaworski, William. *Philosophy of Mind: A Comprehensive Introduction*. Oxford: Wiley-Blackwell, 2011.

Jorgensen, Larry, and Samuel Newlands (eds.). *Metaphysics and the Good: Themes from the Philosophy of Robert Merrihew Adams*. Oxford: Oxford University Press, 2008.

Kant, Immanuel. *Critique of Pure Reason*. Translated by Paul Guyer and Allen W. Wood. Cambridge: Cambridge University Press, 1997.

Kelly, J. N. D. *Early Christian Creeds*. 3rd ed. London: Longman, 1972.

Kelly, J. N. D. *Early Christian Doctrines*. 2nd ed. New York: Harper and Row, 1960.

Kemp, Kenneth W. "Science, Theology, and Monogenesis." *American Catholic Philosophical Quarterly* 85 (2011).

Kenny, Anthony. *Aquinas*. Oxford: Oxford University Press, 1980.

Kenny, Anthony (ed.). *Aquinas: A Collection of Critical Essays*. Notre Dame, IN: University of Notre Dame Press, 1976.

Kenny, Anthony. *Aquinas on Mind*. Routledge: London, 1993.

Kenny, Anthony. *Christianity in Review*. London: Darton, Longman and Todd, 2015.

Kenny, Anthony. *The Five Ways*. London: Routledge and Kegan Paul, 1969.

Klima, Gyula. "Aquinas on the Materiality of the Human Soul and the Immateriality of the Human Intellect." *Philosophical Investigations* 32 (April 2009).

Klima, Gyula. "Man = Body + Soul: Aquinas's Arithmetic of Human Nature." In Brian Davies (ed.), *Thomas Aquinas: Contemporary Philosophical Perspectives*. Oxford: Oxford University Press, 2002.

Korsmeyer, Jerry D. *Evolution and Eden*. New York: Paulist Press, 1998.

Kretzmann, Norman. *The Metaphysics of Creation: Aquinas's Natural Theology in "Summa Contra Gentiles" II*. Oxford: Clarendon Press, 1999.

Kretzmann, Norman. *The Metaphysics of Theism: Aquinas's Natural Theology in "Summa Contra Gentiles" I*. Oxford: Clarendon Press, 1997.

Kretzmann, Norman, and Eleonore Stump (eds.). *The Cambridge Companion to Aquinas*. Cambridge: Cambridge University Press, 1993.

Kromholtz, Bryan. *On the Last Day: The Time of the Resurrection of the Dead According to Thomas Aquinas*. Fribourg: Academic Press, 2010.

Langley, Silas. "Aquinas, Resurrection, and Material Continuity." *Proceedings of the American Catholic Philosophical Association* 75 (2001).

Langley, Silas. *Death, Resurrection, and Transporter Beams*. Eugene, OR: Wipf and Stock, 2014.

Lee, Patrick. "Evil as Such Is Privation: A Reply to John Crosby." *American Catholic Philosophical Quarterly* 81 (2007).

Leftow, Brian. "Anti-Social Trinitarianism." In Thomas McCall and Michael C. Rea (eds.), *Philosophical and Theological Essays on the Trinity*. Oxford: Oxford University Press, 2009.

Leget, Carlo. "Eschatology." In Rik Van Nieuwenhove and Joseph Wawrykow (eds.), *The Theology of Aquinas*. Notre Dame, IN: University of Notre Dame Press, 2005.

Letham, Robert. "The Triune God." In Gerald R. McDermott (ed.), *The Oxford Handbook of Evangelical Theology*. Oxford: Oxford University Press, 2010.

Litt, Thomas. *Les Corps Célestes Dans L'Univers de Saint Thomas D'Aquin*. Louvain: Publications Universitaires, 1963.

Locke, John. *An Essay Concerning Human Understanding*. Edited by Peter H. Nidditch. Oxford: Oxford University Press, 1975.

Luther, Martin. *Luther's Works*. Vol. 6. Edited by Abdel Ross Wentz. Philadelphia: Muhlenberg, 1959.

MacDonald, Scott. "Aquinas's Parasitic Cosmological Argument." *Medieval Philosophy and Theology* 1 (1991).

MacDonald, Scott. "Theory of Knowledge." In Norman Kretzmann and Eleonore Stump (eds.), *The Cambridge Companion to Aquinas*. Cambridge: Cambridge University Press, 1993.

Mackie, J. L. *The Miracle of Theism*. Oxford: Clarendon Press, 1982.

Mann, William L. "Augustine on Evil and Original Sin." In Norman Kretzmann and Eleonore Stump (eds.), *The Cambridge Companion to Augustine*. Cambridge: Cambridge University Press, 2001.

Martinich, A. P. "Identity and Trinity." *Journal of Religion* 58 (1978).

Maurer, A., et al. (eds.). *St Thomas Aquinas, 1274–1974, Commemorative Studies*. Toronto: Pontifical Institute of Medieval Studies, 1974.

McCabe, Herbert. *Faith within Reason*. London: Continuum, 2007.

McCabe, Herbert. *God and Evil in the Theology of St. Thomas Aquinas*. London: Continuum, 2010.

McCabe, Herbert. *God Matters*. London: Geoffrey Chapman, 1987.

McCabe, Herbert. *God Still Matters*. London: Continuum, 2002.

McCabe, Herbert. "The Immortality of the Soul." In Anthony Kenny (ed.), *Aquinas: A Collection of Critical Essays*. Notre Dame, IN: University of Notre Dame Press, 1976.

McCabe, Herbert. *On Aquinas*. London: Continuum, 2008.

McCall, Thomas, and Michael C. Rea (eds.). *Philosophical and Theological Essays on the Trinity*. Oxford: Oxford University Press, 2009.

McCloskey, H. J. "God and Evil." In Nelson Pike (ed.), *God and Evil*. Englewood Cliffs, NJ: Prentice Hall, 1964.

McDermott, Gerald R. (ed.). *The Oxford Handbook of Evangelical Theology*. Oxford: Oxford University Press, 2010.

McDermott, Timothy. "Original Sin." *New Blackfriars* 49 (January 1968 and February 1968).

McGinn, Bernard. *Thomas Aquinas's "Summa Theologiae."* Princeton, NJ: Princeton University Press, 2014.

McGinn, Colin. *Logical Properties*. Oxford: Clarendon Press, 2000.

McGinnis, Jon. *Avicenna*. Oxford: Oxford University Press, 2010.

McGrade, A. S. (ed.). *The Cambridge Companion to Medieval Philosophy*. Cambridge: Cambridge University Press, 2003.

McInerny, Ralph. *Aquinas*. Cambridge: Polity, 2004.

McInerny, Ralph (ed. and trans.). John of St. Thomas, *Introduction to the "Summa Theologiae."* South Bend, IN: St Augustine's Press, 2004.

Michon, Cyrille (ed.). *Somme Contre les Gentils.* Bk. 1. Paris: Flammarion, 2000.

Minn, Anselm K. "Why Only an Immutable God Can Love, Relate, and Suffer." In C. P. Ruloff (ed.), *Christian Philosophy of Religion: Essays in Honor of Stephen T. Davis.* Notre Dame, IN: University of Notre Dame Press, 2015.

Moltmann, Jürgen. *The Crucified God.* Minneapolis: Fortress Press, 1993.

Moore, Gareth. *A Question of Truth.* London: Continuum, 2003.

Morreall, John. "Perfect Happiness and the Resurrection of the Body." *Religious Studies* 16 (March 1980).

Morris, Thomas V. *The Logic of God Incarnate.* Ithaca, NY: Cornell University Press, 1986.

Mulcahey, Michele M. *"First the Bow Is Bent in Study . . .": Dominican Education before 1350.* Toronto: Pontifical Institute of Medieval Studies, 1998.

Noonan, Harold W. "Relative Identity." *Philosophical Investigations* 38 (2015).

Oliva, Adriano. *Les Débuts de l'enseignement de Thomas d'Aquin et sa Conception de la "Sacra Doctrina."* Paris: Vrin, 2006.

Oliva, Adriano. "Philosophy in the Teaching of Theology by Thomas Aquinas." *Thomist* 76 (2012).

Oppy, Graham. *Ontological Arguments and Belief in God.* Cambridge: Cambridge University Press, 1995.

Owens, J. "Aquinas and the Proof from the *Physics*." *Medieval Studies* (1966).

Patfoort, A. *Saint Thomas d'Aquin: Les Clefs d'une Théologie.* Paris: FAC éditions, 1983.

Pegis, Anton. "The Separated Soul and Its Nature in St. Thomas." In A. Maurer et al. (eds.), *St. Thomas Aquinas, 1274–1974, Commemorative Studies.* Vol. 1. Toronto: Pontifical Institute of Medieval Studies, 1974.

Perry, John. "The Same F." *Philosophical Review* 79 (1970).

Persson, Per Erik. *"Sacra Doctrina": Reason and Revelation in Aquinas.* Philadelphia: Fortress Press, 1970.

Phan, Peter C. (ed.). *The Cambridge Companion to the Trinity.* Cambridge: Cambridge University Press, 2011.

Phillips, D. Z. *The Concept of Prayer.* London: Routledge and Kegan Paul, 1965.

Phillips, D. Z. *The Problem of Evil and the Problem of God.* London: SCM Press, 2004.

Phillips, D. Z. *Religion without Explanation.* Oxford: Blackwell, 1976.

Philoponus. *Against Aristotle on the Eternity of the World.* Translated by Christian Wilde. London: Duckworth, 1987.

Pike, Nelson (ed.). *God and Evil.* Englewood Cliffs, NJ: Prentice Hall, 1964.

Plantinga, Alvin. *Does God Have a Nature?* Milwaukee: Marquette University Press, 1980.

Plantinga, Alvin. *God, Freedom and Evil.* London: Allen and Unwin, 1974.

Plantinga, Alvin. *The Nature of Necessity.* Oxford: Clarendon Press, 1974.

Porter, Jean. *Natural and Divine Law: Reclaiming the Tradition for Christian Ethics.* Grand Rapids, MI: Eerdmans, 1999.

Power, David N. *The Eucharistic Mystery*. New York: Crossroad, 1992.

Pseudo-Dionysius. *Pseudo-Dionysius: The Complete Works*. Translated by Colm Luibheid. New York: Paulist Press, 1987.

Quinn, Philip L., and Charles Talliaferro (eds.). *A Companion to the Philosophy of Religion*. Oxford: Blackwell, 1997.

Reid, Thomas. *Essays on the Intellectual Powers of Man*. Edinburgh, 1785.

Re Manning, Russell (ed.). *The Oxford Handbook of Natural Theology*. Oxford: Oxford University Press, 2013.

Rosemann, Philip W. *Peter Lombard*. Oxford: Oxford University Press, 2004.

Rosenberg, Alex. *The Atheist's Guide to Reality: Enjoying Life without Illusions*. New York: Norton, 2011.

Ross, James F. "Creation II." In Alfred J. Freddoso (ed.), *The Existence and Nature of God*. Notre Dame, IN: University of Notre Dame Press, 1983.

Ross, James F. "Together with the Body I Love." *Proceedings of the American Catholic Philosophical Association* 75 (2001).

Roughgarden, Joan. *Evolution's Rainbow: Diversity, Gender and Sexuality in Nature and People*. Berkeley: University of California Press, 2004.

Rowland, Christopher. "Natural Theology and the Christian Bible." In Russell Re Manning (ed.), *The Oxford Handbook of Natural Theology*. Oxford: Oxford University Press, 2013.

Ruloff, C. P. (ed.). *Christian Philosophy of Religion: Essays in Honor of Stephen T. Davis*. Notre Dame, IN: University of Notre Dame Press, 2015.

Rundle, Bede. *Why There Is Something Rather Than Nothing*. Oxford: Clarendon Press, 2004.

Saint John of Damascus, Writings. Translated by Frederic H. Chase, Jr. The Fathers of the Church, vol. 37. Washington, DC: Catholic University of America Press, 1958.

Seddon, Christopher. *Human: From the Beginning: From the First Apes to the First Cities*. London: Glanville, 2015.

Singer, Peter. *Animal Liberation*. New York: Random House, 1975.

Smalley, Beryl. *The Gospels in the Schools c. 1100–c. 1280*. London: Hambledon Press, 1985.

Smalley, Beryl. *The Study of the Bible in the Middle Ages*. 3rd ed. Oxford: Blackwell, 1984.

Sorabji, Richard. *Time, Creation and the Continuum*. Chicago: University of Chicago Press, 1983.

Stump, Eleonore. *Aquinas*. London: Routledge, 2003.

Stump, Eleonore. "Aquinas' Metaphysics of the Incarnation." In Stephen T. Davis, Daniel Kendall, and Gerald O'Collins (eds.), *The Incarnation*. Oxford: Oxford University Press, 2002.

Stump, Eleonore. "Biblical Commentary and Philosophy." In Norman Kretzmann and Eleonore Stump (eds.), *The Cambridge Companion to Aquinas*. Cambridge: Cambridge University Press, 1993.

Stump, Eleonore, and Norman Kretzmann (eds.). *The Cambridge Companion to Augustine*. Cambridge: Cambridge University Press, 2001.

Swinburne, Richard. *The Christian God*. Oxford: Clarendon Press, 1994.

Swinburne, Richard. *The Coherence of Theism*. Rev. ed. Oxford: Clarendon Press, 1993.

Swinburne, Richard. *The Evolution of the Soul*. Oxford: Clarendon Press, 1986.

Swinburne, Richard. *The Existence of God*. 2nd ed. Oxford: Clarendon Press, 2004.

Swinburne, Richard. *Space and Time*. 2nd ed. London: Palgrave Macmillan, 1981.

Tanner, Norman P. (ed.). *Decrees of the Ecumenical Councils*. Washington, DC: Georgetown University Press, 1990.

Tattersall, Ian. *Masters of the Planet: The Search for Our Human Origins*. London: Macmillan, 2013.

Tegmark, Max. *Our Mathematical Universe*. New York: Knopf, 2014.

Torrell, Jean-Pierre. *Saint Thomas Aquinas: Volume 1, The Person and His Work*. Washington, DC: Catholic University of America Press, 1996.

Tugwell, Simon (ed.). *Albert and Thomas: Selected Writings*. New York: Paulist Press, 1988.

Turner, Denys. *Thomas Aquinas: A Portrait*. New Haven, CT: Yale University Press, 2013.

Van Inwagen, Peter. "And Yet They Are Not Three Gods but One God." In Thomas McCall and Michael C. Rea (eds.), *Philosophical and Theological Essays on the Trinity*. Oxford: Oxford University Press, 2009.

Van Inwagen, Peter. *The Possibility of Resurrection and Other Essays in Christian Apologetics*. Boulder, CO: Westview Press, 1998.

Van Nieuwenhove, Rik, and Joseph Wawrykow (eds.). *The Theology of Thomas Aquinas*. Notre Dame, IN: University of Notre Dame Press, 2005.

Walls, Jerry L. (ed.). *The Oxford Handbook of Eschatology*. Oxford: Oxford University Press, 2008.

Warner, Richard, and Tadeusz Szubka (eds.). *The Mind-Body Problem: A Guide to the Current Debate*. Oxford: Blackwell, 1994.

Wawrykow, Joseph. "Hypostatic Union." In Rik Van Nieuwenhove and Joseph Wawrykow (eds.), *The Theology of Thomas Aquinas*. Notre Dame, IN: University of Notre Dame Press, 2005.

Weigel, Peter. *Aquinas on Simplicity*. Bern: Peter Lang, 2008.

Weinandy, Thomas G., Daniel A. Keating, and John P. Yocum (eds.). *Aquinas on Scripture*. London: T&T Clark International, 2005.

Weisheipl, James A. *Friar Thomas D'Aquino*. Oxford: Blackwell, 1974.

Weisheipl, James E. *Nature and Motion in the Middle Ages*. Washington, DC: Catholic University of America Press, 1985.

Welburn, Andrew. *Mani, the Angel and the Column of Glory: An Anthology of Manichean Texts*. Edinburgh: Floris Books, 1998.

White, Thomas Joseph. "Imperfect Happiness and the Final End of Man: Thomas Aquinas and the Paradigm of Nature-Grace Orthodoxy." *Thomist* 78 (2014).

White, Thomas Joseph. *The Incarnate Lord*. Washington, DC: Catholic University of America Press, 2015.

Wiley, Tatha. *Original Sin: Origins, Developments, Contemporary Meanings*. New York: Paulist Press, 2002.

Williams, C. J. F. "Being." In Philip L. Quinn and Charles Talliaferro (eds.), *A Companion to the Philosophy of Religion*. Oxford: Blackwell, 1997.

Williams, C. J. F. *Being, Identity, and Truth*. Oxford: Clarendon Press, 1992.

Williams, C. J. F. "Hic Autem Non Est Procedere in Infinitum." *Mind* 69 (1960).

Williams, C. J. F. *What Is Existence?* Oxford: Clarendon Press, 1981.

Williams, Thomas. "Transmission and Translation." In A. S. McGrade (ed.), *The Cambridge Companion to Medieval Philosophy*. Cambridge: Cambridge University Press, 2003.

Wippel, John F. *Metaphysical Themes in Thomas Aquinas II*. Washington, DC: Catholic University of America Press, 2007.

Wippel, John F. *The Metaphysical Thought of Thomas Aquinas*. Washington, DC: Catholic University of America Press, 2000.

Wippel, John F. "Norman Kretzmann on Aquinas's Attribution of Will and of Freedom to Create to God." *Religious Studies* 39 (2003).

Wittgenstein, Ludwig. *Philosophical Investigations*. Translated by G. E. M. Anscombe, P. M. S. Hacker, and Joachim Schulte. Rev. 4th ed. Oxford: Wiley-Blackwell, 2009.

Wittgenstein, Ludwig. *Philosophical Occasions 1912–1951*. Edited by James Klagge and Alfred Norman. Indianapolis: Hackett, 1993.

Wright, N. T. "Jesus's Self-Understanding." In Stephen T. Davis, Daniel Kendall, and Gerald O'Collins (eds.), *The Incarnation*. Oxford: Oxford University Press, 2002.

Index

CPSIA information can be obtained
at www.ICGtesting.com
Printed in the USA
BVHW031021221218
535919BV00003B/11/P